The Edinburgh History of the Greeks, 20th and Early 21st Centuries
Global Perspectives

Antonis Liakos and Nicholas Doumanis

W0007541

EDINBURGH
University Press

Edinburgh University Press is one of the leading university presses in the UK. We publish academic books and journals in our selected subject areas across the humanities and social sciences, combining cutting-edge scholarship with high editorial and production values to produce academic works of lasting importance. For more information visit our website: edinburghuniversitypress.com

© Antonis Liakos and Nicholas Doumanis 2023

Edinburgh University Press Ltd
The Tun – Holyrood Road
12(2f) Jackson's Entry
Edinburgh EH8 8PJ

Typeset in 11/13pt Adobe Sabon by
Cheshire Typesetting Ltd, Cuddington, Cheshire

A CIP record for this book is available from the British Library

ISBN 978 1 4744 1082 3 (hardback)
ISBN 978 1 4744 1084 7 (paperback)
ISBN 978 1 4744 1083 0 (webready PDF)
ISBN 978 1 4744 1085 4 (epub)

The right of Antonis Liakos and Nicholas Doumanis to be identified as the author of this work has been asserted in accordance with the Copyright, Designs and Patents Act 1988, and the Copyright and Related Rights Regulations 2003 (SI No. 2498).

Contents

Illustrations

Maps

Figures

Note on transliterations

Familiar English spellings have been employed for such well-known regions and islands as the Peloponnese, Attica, Rhodes, Epirus and Corfu, but for less familiar ones more phonetic spellings have been used, like 'Evvia' instead of 'Euboea', and the Greek 'K' has been preferred to the Latin 'C', as seen with 'Kos' rather than 'Cos'. Familiar spellings have been retained for well-known figures such as 'Constantine Karamanlis' and his nephew 'Kostas Karamanlis', and 'Georgios Papandreou' and grandson 'George Papandreou'. While Greek names can appear in a variety of transliterated forms (e.g., Spyros, Spiros, Speros; Georgios, Giorgos, Yorgos; Yiannis, Yannis, Giannis, Yanis), effort has been made to find the English spelling preferred by the person in question, where this can be determined.

Preface and acknowledgements

This volume in the Edinburgh History of the Greeks series deals with the people of Greece and of the broader Greek world, including Cyprus and the diaspora. It covers the last 110 or so years, beginning in 1912, the eve of the First Balkan War, and ending with the onset of the COVID-19 crisis. It focuses on state and society, and how each has negotiated more than a century of dramatic domestic, regional and global change. The book has less to say about party politics than it does about the Greek people. It includes Greece's and Cyprus' cultural minorities, and Greek minorities in other parts of the world. By reading the stories of Greeks within the context of global change and international relations, the book seeks to avoid the trap of 'exceptionalism', which tends to ascribe too much explanatory power to 'the Greek character' and to the Classical and Ottoman historical heritages. By taking a more transnational approach, the book aims for a better sense of what is and what is not distinctive about modern Greek history.

The book is a collaborative work of two historians who share an abiding interest in historiography, in global historical dynamics, historical (especially national) memory and above all, in history as a tool of social inquiry. We worked on and re-drafted every passage and every sentence, even though we never sat together during the writing process: one of us worked in his study in Athens or in his Andros retreat, and the other at his kitchen table in Sydney. The book has also been written with a more global readership in mind: it seeks to explain why Greece, a small country on Europe's periphery, should have been so often in the forefront of global historical developments. After all, a case could be made that the Cold War started in Greece, while during the recent economic crisis pundits around the world were accusing Greece of threatening to bring down the entire world economy. In any case, it is commonly accepted nowadays that national histories ought to be considered from a transnational perspective. Greece and Cyprus are better understood by examining the interplay between the local and the global; between the actions of people on the ground and the great structural changes driven by much more powerful centres of the world.

The authors have many people to thank, and we begin with the most important. Tom Gallant has been an ideal editor: attentive, patient, generous with his time, and was always willing to provide moral support. They also feel extremely fortunate to have had the support of Alfred Vincent, a scholar whose knowledge of Greek culture and history is unsurpassed. He went through the manuscript at short notice, going above and beyond what could be expected from a colleague. We are very much in his debt. The staff at Edinburgh University Press, specifically Carol Macdonald, David Lonergan, Sarah Foyle, Isobel Birks, Fiona Conn and Louise Hutton, were always helpful with clear and prompt advice, as was Jane Burkowski.

Nick was flattered to be invited by Tom to write this volume in his Edinburgh History of the Greeks series, and very grateful that Antonis agreed to co-author it. Working with Tom and Antonis has been a privilege. He acknowledges the support of the Faculty of Arts, Architecture and Design at the University of New South Wales. Nick also feels very fortunate to have friends who were willing to share their insights, including Vasilios Adrahtas, Richard Clogg, David Christian, David Close, Efrosini Deligianni, Yannis Dramitinos, Kostas Katsapis, Eleni Kostakidis, George Kouvaros, Margaret Poulos and Andrekos Varnava. The following non-academics patiently listened to Nick's unsolicited historical monologues: cousin Nick, Stella and the gang, Steve and Liz, his *koumbaro* John and Dimitri the architect. He could also count on the support of his loving wife Helen, daughter Daphne and parents Jack (Ιάκωβος) and Connie (Κοκόνα).

Antonis would like to thank Zeese Papanikolas in Oakland and Rolf Petri in Venice for reading the entire or substantial parts of the book, and Nikos Christodoulakis, Lois Lambrianidis, Alexis Frangkiadis and Georges Stathakis for their comments on the chapter on the Crisis. He wishes to thank the Benaki Museum and ASKI for the photographs provided gratis from their archives, and Yannis Liakos and Tassos Kostopoulos for their permissions to use their excellent photographs. As usual, Myrsini Zorba was a co-traveller in his exploration of contemporary cultural and political history. Finally, he found the co-authorship with Nick, and the team spirit they shared with Tom, to be a grace of Clio (Κλειώ), the Muse of History.

Athens and Sydney, March 2022

Series Editor's preface

The Edinburgh History of the Greeks is a multi-volume, chronological series covering the history of the Greek people from antiquity to the present. Each volume combines political history with social and cultural history in order to tell the story of the Greek people over the course of recorded history in an exciting, novel and innovatory way. Drawing on the rich resources from anthropology, archaeology and history, as well as political science, philology, art, literature and law, the books will be diverse, abundant and vibrant.

The Greeks suffer from too much history, some have said. Indeed, library bookshelves sag under the weight of the massive number of tomes devoted to the history of Greece during the ancient, medieval and modern periods. This series differs from them by focusing on the history of a people, the Greeks, and not a place, Greece. The story will reflect the fluctuating dynamics of change while primary sources and accounts of the lives of individuals and communities will invigorate the text.

The history of the Greeks over the long durée must be told on a vast and at times even global scale, and so the Greek world is taken to include not just the area traditionally associated with ancient Greece or the territory of the modern Greek state, but encompasses all areas where Greeks have settled, including the diaspora of modern times.

Thomas W. Gallant

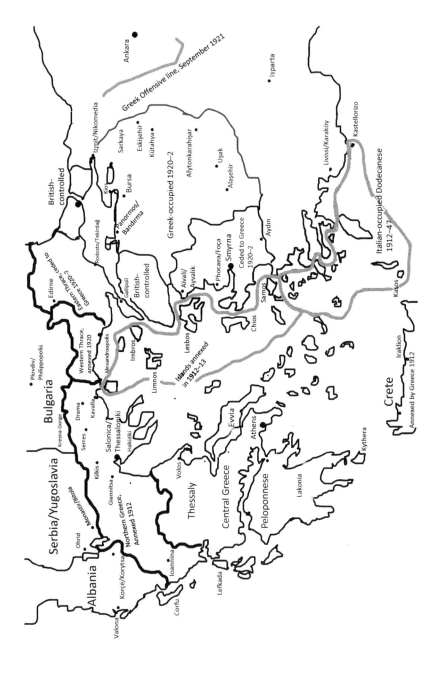

Serbia/Yugoslavia

Albania

Valona

Korçë/Korytsa

Ohrid

Monastir/Bitola

Giannitsa

Kilkis

Bulgaria

Plovdiv/
Philippopolis

Kresna Gorge

Serres

Drama

Kavalla

Edirne

Eastern Thrace, ceded to Greece 1920–2

Western Thrace, annexed 1920

Alexandroupolis

Rodosto/Tekirdağ

Gallipoli

British-controlled

Iznit/Nikomedia

British-controlled

Greek Offensive line, September 1921

Ankara

Isparta

Kastellorizo

Livissi/Karaköy

Italian-occupied Dodecanese 1912–47

Sarkaya

Eskişehir

Kütahya

Kios

Bursa

Panormos/
Bandirma

Greek-occupied 1920–2

Afyonkarahişar

Uşak

Alaşehir

Aydin

Ceded to Greece 1920–2

Smyrna

Phocaea/Foça

Aivali/
Ayvalik

Chios

Samos

Imbros

Limnos

Lesbos

Islands annexed in 1912–13

Kakos

Iraklion

Crete

Annexed by Greece 1912

Salonica/
Thessaloniki

Halkidiki

Ioannina

Corfu

Lefkada

Volos

Thessaly

Central Greece

Evvia

Athens

Peloponnese

Lakonia

Kythera

Northern Greece,
Annexed 1912

Map 1 *The expansion and contraction of Greece, 1912–22*

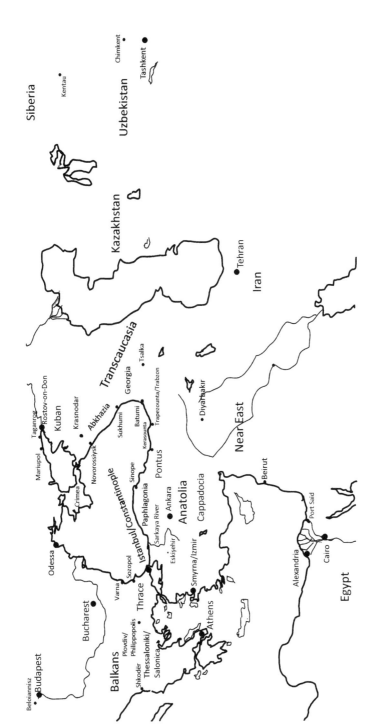

Map 2 *Greek communities in the eastern Mediterranean, Black Sea and Central Asian regions*

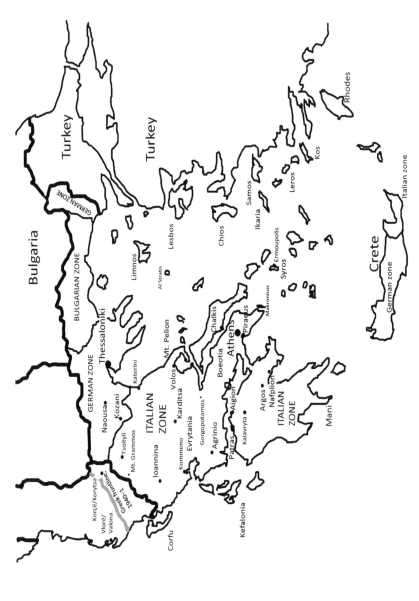

Map 3 *Axis occupation: German, Italian and Bulgarian zones, 1941–3*

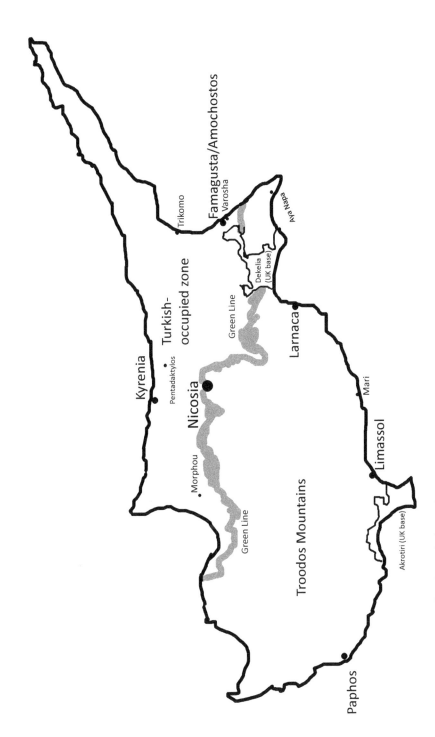

Map 4 Divided Cyprus after the Turkish invasion, 1974

Famagusta/Amochostos

Trikomo

Varosha

Aya Napa

Dekelia (UK base)

Turkish-occupied zone

Green Line

Larnaca

Kyrenia

Pentadaktylos

Nicosia

Mari

Morphou

Limassol

Green Line

Troodos Mountains

Akrotiri (UK base)

Paphos

Map 5 *Greece since 1947*

CHAPTER 1

Introduction: The Greeks at the beginning of the twentieth century

At the beginning of the twentieth century, Greece was in important respects a genuinely modern country. Whereas most Europeans were subjects of empires, two of which, Russia and the Ottoman Empire, had only recently adopted constitutions, generations of Greeks had already been accustomed to regular elections, a parliament and universal male suffrage. Greece's constitutional monarchy was formally dedicated to the interests of a sovereign people or 'nation'. The constitution certainly did accord enormous powers to the crown. King George I (reigned 1863–1913), of the House of Schleswig-Holstein-Sonderburg-Glücksburg, and only Greece's second monarch, controlled the military and could appoint and dismiss governments. But his was also a 'crowned democracy' or 'crowned republic' (*vasilevomeni demokratia*): he was 'King of the Hellenes' (the Greeks), not 'Hellas' (Greece). The political party with the largest number of representatives in the national parliament (*vouli*) could form a government, and all adult males had the right to vote well before they did in France (1874) or Britain (1918). Greece was among the first states to introduce compulsory primary school education (1834), which accounted for the fact that Greek nationals were, on average, more literate than subjects of neighbouring countries. The state had redistributed land to peasants without significant social upheaval or political backlash. Beyond the parliament, one would have found a very lively 'public sphere' of middle-class males who frequented urban cafes, and a dynamic press that did its best to stimulate public interest and excitement in politics. To be sure, this 'public' was exceedingly small, and the social base of the political system was extremely narrow. Most of the population (84 per cent) consisted of illiterate farmers, tradesmen, shepherds and mariners, who in voting followed the lead of local patrons and provincial notables. Women were not granted political rights until the mid-twentieth century. Nevertheless, by the standards of the age Greece could be classed as a progressive polity. It belonged to the world's very exclusive group of liberal democracies.

Figure 1.1 *Athenians celebrate Ash Monday (the first day of Lent) on Philopappou Hill, c.1910.* © ERT

Greece was also a small country in a world dominated by vast empires. It was 63,211 square kilometres, less than half its present-day size (131,957). It included only Attica and Central Greece, the Peloponnese, the Cycladic Islands, Evvia, the Ionian Islands, Thessaly and a tiny part of southern Epirus around the town of Arta. The population was 2,716,595, which was comparable to that of Denmark, Sweden, Finland or Switzerland. Demographic trends indicated that the nation was modernising. In 1907 Athens had 142,754 inhabitants, down from 178,754 in 1896, but this was more than triple its size in 1870. Piraeus was the second largest city, having overtaken Ermoupolis (Syros) as the nation's principal port, and was a centre for modern industrial production (e.g. chemicals and fertilisers). Almost equal in size was Patras, after which there was a handful of regional cities with between 20,000 and 30,000 inhabitants (Ermoupolis 29,088, Corfu 25,808, Volos 23,563, and Trikala 20,992) (Petmezas 1999: 52–85).

Only 16 per cent of the population could be classified as urban, but since the latter decades of the nineteenth century the rate of urban population growth had been exceeding that of the countryside. An important stimulus for this trend were major infrastructure projects like the Corinth Canal and road-building (Synarelli 1989; Gallant 2015: 179–81). Under Charilaos Trikoupis, who was prime minister for much of the 1880s and early 1890s, the state had overseen the construction of almost 3,900 km of new roads and over 1,290 km of railway lines. Inspired by western models of economic development, Trikoupis and his governments created a national environment that was more conducive to commercial enterprise, and which linked local enterprises more effectively with export markets. *Fin de siècle* Athens, the unrivalled heart of the nation, was taking on the appearance of a modern European capital. With its orthogonal urban plan, neoclassical architecture, rows of mansions, and its libraries, stadium, schools, music hall and the National Cathedral, the city was meant to enthral the visitor. Newcomers from the villages and islands would have also been struck by the pace of everyday life, by the crowds of busy commuters, and by the city's seemingly infinite variety of activities, venues and events. Electric trams plied grand thoroughfares such as Panepistimiou, one of the major arteries linking the city's various public spaces. Street lighting had been installed, many roads had been paved, and street advertising sought to catch the eye of an ever-expanding public of consumers. The capital's boisterous press culture featured an extraordinary variety of daily newspapers that fed an expanding readership's appetite for international and domestic news. Although there was a tendency in artistic depictions of *belle époque* Athens to exaggerate its modernity, it is nevertheless true that the great changes experienced in recent decades were in keeping with those of Europe's other national capitals. Its boulevards were teeming with promenading bourgeois families, while shops and outdoor cafes were patronised by women and men dressed in an international, Western style (Bastea 2000: 190; Gallant 2015: 212–19). Athens was mapping out the nation's future.

Nevertheless, it is important not to overstate modernity's power to overhaul and transform. The countryside, where the great majority of Greeks lived, retained its overwhelmingly pre-modern character. Indeed, a visitor from northern Europe or North America would have regarded *belle époque* Greece as an exceedingly backward country in need of a 'civilising mission'. Nearly three quarters of the male population were small landholders who were more focused on subsistence (meeting the family's basic needs) rather than commercial agriculture. Peasants participated only marginally in the market economy and made minimal contributions to the country's economic growth (Gallant 2015: 226). The bulk of the population lived in small villages with fewer than 1,000 inhabitants; settlements of between 200 and 300 or

500 and 600 inhabitants were most common (Gallant 2015: 197). In 1907, the proportion of people on the land was over 67 per cent: the European average in 1910 was 59 per cent, although in other Balkan states the average was over 80 per cent (Boswell 2016: 244–5).

In 1900, the typical Greek lived in a manner that was not much different to that of his or her ancestors. Water was drawn from wells, roads were stone or mud tracks, and the principal mode of transport for most was mule or donkey. Rural families lived in one- or two-roomed dwellings, mostly in nuclear units (married couple and children), but often including members of the extended family (e.g. grandparents, an unmarried aunt or uncle). Homes were simple oblong-shaped structures that were grouped together tightly, quite often on hilltops or steep ridges, and often a lengthy walk from the plots that people worked. A village (*chorio*) worthy of the name was large enough to require its own parish church, with a centrally located open square (*plateia*), where festivities and wedding celebrations were held, and with a council (*koinotis, koinotita*) that oversaw local public affairs. The inhabitants formed a 'moral' community: a primary group that shared an identity and a moral code, and which was a focus of loyalty second only in importance to the family. It was this primary unit that Greeks referred to as their 'fatherland' (*patrida*). The reputation of the *patrida* was a matter of local pride: it was meant to be defended against outsiders or *xenoi*. Villagers also understood their internal boundaries, particularly those relating to gender. Unlike the open-door cafes of central Athens, the traditional village cafe or *kafeneion* was an exclusive male space. The family home was a female space that only male family members could enter freely, while the movements of women outside the home were heavily circumscribed (Gallant 2015: 196–212).

In this village-centred world, Orthodox Christianity permeated nearly every aspect of life. The annual life cycle was structured according to the liturgical calendar (Easter, saints' days, fasting periods etc.), and the local area was also mapped out in the imagination by religious sites such as small chapels (*exoklisia*), smaller shrines and physical sites deemed holy, such as streams believed to offer holy water (*agiasma*). Peasants understood their faith much more through miracle stories or saints' lives than through the Gospels, and through practices (church ritual, fasting, crossing oneself and using incense) than through theology. Their universe included a supernatural order that, on the one hand, included the Virgin Mary, angels and hosts of saints to whom people pleaded for support or miracles, and on the other, the devil and other evil spirits. These entities were believed to intercede constantly in temporal life and to determine life's fortunes. The average Greek (as with the average European peasant) believed in the power of miracles, the danger posed by demons and the evil eye, the healing power of saints, the truth of prophetic traditions and knowledge embedded in dreams (Du Boulay 2009; Doumanis 2013: chs 3 and 4).

As in every other part of Europe, however, the depopulation of the countryside and the decline of village culture had already begun. The young had been setting off for towns and cities, where they learned quickly to adapt to modern ways of living. They encountered bourgeois people who spoke, dressed and behaved in a foreign manner, who had such alien preoccupations as promenading, sports, politics and nationalism. Indeed, throughout the eastern Mediterranean region, in the cities of Egypt and the Ottoman Empire, where large Greek communities were also located, bourgeois men and women were consciously breaking with the Greek village traditions and adapting to more modern ways. The Ottoman periodical press was obsessed by the new (*yeni*), by such things as mechanised transport, modern communications and electrification, which threatened traditions but also augured a more dynamic future (Brummett 2000: 289). Greek émigrés returning from the United States had seen the Statue of Liberty and the rising Manhattan skyline, and they brought back first-hand experiences of living in America, the modern society par excellence. These returnees, who were commonly known as 'Brooklides' (literally 'people from Brooklyn'), had stories that spoke of 'Ameriki' as a solution to life's major challenges. In short stories written by Greek American migrants at the time, 'Ameriki' promised men what Ioanna Laliotou calls a 'magical dissolution of the impossibilities of their lives' (Laliotou 2004: 111).

Who or what was a Greek?

At the beginning of the twentieth century, European states faced the challenge of transforming nationalism into a mass phenomenon and making peasants into flag-waving patriots (Hobsbawm 1992; Hroch 1985; Anderson 2016). Throughout the continent, it was mainly the upwardly mobile and well educated that identified passionately with their nation, its symbols, history and culture, while the bulk of society identified much more closely with their faith, locality, traditions and family (Markwick and Doumanis 2016). The average Greek peasant, whether in the Peloponnese, the Pindus ranges or Asia Minor, identified above all as an Orthodox Christian. Nationalism had certainly made inroads at the popular level in Greece, but among Greeks outside the kingdom, particularly those residing in the Ottoman Empire, it was still a matter of class (see below, pp. 18–21). The campaign to 'nationalise' society and overcome popular indifference to national symbols and ideas in such territories was being waged largely by lower-middle-class activists, very often schoolteachers, but also journalists, military officers, local political officials and public servants (Hroch 1985). The nationalising project was regarded as akin to a civilising mission. In Greece the agents of the nation were state education and the *morphomenoi*: the educated, people with enough schooling to have been imbued with Greek history and literature, and who had developed an acute sense of being a Greek, a *Hellene*. Their mission was to reawaken Hellenic consciousness among the illiterate masses (the *agrammatoi*). In Ottoman territories, middle-class Greek Orthodox Christians adopted Greek nationalism during a period of dramatic political changes that raised important questions about their place in the empire. For them, nationalism also came with upward social mobility (Exertzoglou 1996; Kechriotis 2005). Flag-waving nationalism was as middle class as wearing bourgeois attire, much as an indifference to nationalism was interpreted as a reflection of backwardness. The *morphomenoi* believed that the *agrammatoi* were mired in ignorance and incapable of appreciating their Greek identity and its sublime meaning. Nonetheless, it was the goal of the former to enlighten the latter (Doumanis 1997: 92–6).

Since the 1890s, the frontline of this cause had been Ottoman Macedonia, where the struggle to 'Hellenise' the region's Orthodox peasants was not merely a matter of overcoming local indifference but also a battle against Bulgarian nationalist competition. Indeed, throughout the Balkans and Anatolia (also known as Asia Minor, although that term refers to the western parts of Anatolia), where Western observers noted a bewildering array of cultures, nationalism had not penetrated the masses. Political elites in Belgrade, Sofia and Athens coveted what was left of the Ottoman Empire in Europe, but they also recognised that within these territories 'Serbs', 'Bulgarians' and 'Greeks' were there to be made or lost to rival nationalisms. Efforts to 'make' or 'recover' Greeks were also well under way in Anatolia, where schools, theatre and other educational endeavours were part of a campaign to halt or roll back the spread of the Turkish language among Greek Orthodox communities, particularly in the far eastern regions (Manomi and Istikopoulou 2006). According to the Athenian periodical *Xenophanis*, which was issued intermittently during the 1890s and the following decade, there were many kinds of seemingly exotic Greek communities that had survived centuries of Muslim cultural dominance and oppression, and which were seen as in need of a national reawakening. Of special interest to the writers of *Xenophanis* were the Karamanlides, the Turkish-speaking community of Cappadocia, a region that had been conquered by Muslim Turks three centuries before the fall of Constantinople, and whose Christian population had long since adopted the Turkish language. (Only Pharasa and a handful of other remote villages in central Anatolia continued to speak indigenous Greek dialects (Dawkins 1916). *Xenophanis* did not question their 'Greekness', yet during the national population exchange between Greece and Turkey in 1923, a small number of Karamanlides, who hoped to remain in their homelands, put forward the proposition that they adopt a new identity as Orthodox Christian Turks (Doumanis 2013: 59–60).

But who was a Greek? What did it mean to be Greek at the beginning of the twentieth century? During the struggle over Macedonia, villages that were contested by competing Greek and Bulgarian militias, but which had shown an indifference to such issues, were often forced to declare themselves as 'Greek' or 'Bulgarian', depending on which militia was pointing a rifle at them (Gallant 2015: 168–71; Mazower 2000a: 99). Did the Turkish-speaking Rum of Anatolia's eastern Black Sea coastal areas (Pontus), the Tatar-speaking, Greek Orthodox Urum in Ukraine and Georgia, or the Grecanici, the Greek-speaking (but Catholic) people of Apulia and Calabria in southern Italy, feel Greek? And if so, what did being Greek mean to them?

To begin with, it is essential to note the difference between how people identify themselves and the labels applied to them by authorities and other groups. At the beginning of the twentieth century, people described by diplomats, scholars and social elites as 'Greeks' or 'Hellenes' (Ἕλληνες) did not necessarily refer to themselves by that term. In their analysis of identity, Rogers Brubaker and Frederick Cooper note a difference between identity as a 'concept of analysis', which authorities use to categorise cultural groups, and identity as 'concept of practice': the names that people apply to themselves and which inform their lives (Cooper 2005: 62). What can be said with confidence is that the Orthodox Turcophones of Pontus, the Urum and the Grecanici identified as Greeks because they identified by their Greek Orthodoxy (the first two groups) or by their Greek language (the last group). These respective attributes underpinned their Greekness and distinguished them from other cultural groups. The hard 'Greek' identity ascribed to them by statesmen and academics, but which often puzzled the subjects when approached by visitors from Britain and other parts of northern Europe, should not be confused with the way these subjects viewed themselves.

The mere existence of such groups as the Urum and Grecanici pre-supposed that the Greek world was not only physically dispersed but also culturally fragmented. Within the Ottoman Empire, the Greeks (Rum/Romioi/Romaioi) might have been officially categorised as a distinct nation or *millet*, but they were linguistically and culturally diverse, and certainly not a 'self-enclosed entity' (Greene 2015: 1; Pipyrou 2016; Barkey and Gavrilis 2016). In the eighteenth and nineteenth centuries, however, the Ottoman state strengthened the *millet* system, which in turn encouraged Greek Orthodox elites to regard the *millet-i Rum* (the Greek Orthodox *millet*) as a coherent entity. Meanwhile, with the advent of the Greek state following the 1821 Revolution, a more stand-ardised, canonical Greek identity was being developed. Eventually, that canonical Greek identity would subsume the many other Greek iden-tities. Such nation-led forging of ethnic identity was part of a global trend (Hobsbawm 1992: ch. 3; Hroch 1985; Anderson 2016).

Greeks and Romioi

This volume, which stands in a series dedicated to the history of 'the Greeks', will deal with Greeks as citizens of Greece, including minorities like the Jews, Slav Macedonians and Pomaks, but also Greek Cypriots and Greeks who formed ethnic minorities in such countries as Egypt, West Germany and Kazakhstan. Who were these Greeks? What specifically made this diverse group 'Greek'? From the perspec-tive of identity as a category of analysis, could the Catholic Grecanici be counted as Greeks? It is important not to allow definitions to over-determine the subject. But what cultural attributes included, say, the Greek Orthodox of Pontus or the Urum of the Russian Empire as members of the same cultural group?

Before the 1821 Revolution, the great majority of people we now call Greeks were Ottoman subjects. Western Europeans had persisted in labelling them 'Greeks', as they had done during the Middle Ages, yet these Greeks had also persisted in describing themselves as *Romaioi* (pronounced 'Roméi') or *Romioi* ('Romyi') for a much longer period. The term, of course, derives from 'Roman', which denoted a subject of the Eastern Roman Empire, better known now as Byzantium, in which the Orthodox religion and the Greek language were dominant. By Ottoman times, to be 'Romaios', 'Romios' or 'Rum' meant being

'Greek Orthodox', although it is not altogether clear if all Greek Orthodox Christians did use these terms in every region (Ozil 2013: 9–10, 133 n. 36). The role of the Greek Orthodox Church in determining the group's boundaries was fundamental. In essence, Greeks were people who followed the Byzantine rite and for whom the liturgy was in Koine or New Testament Greek. Thus, in the Russian Empire, the Greek Orthodox were 'Urum' (i.e. Roman/Rum) even through their spoken language was Tatar. In the Ottoman Empire, the Rum (Romioi) formed a distinct legal community. In Anatolia, a Greek Orthodox subject was 'Rum' even if his or her mother tongue happened to be a dialect of Turkish or Armenian. By the same token, the Greek-speaking Muslims of Crete were not Rum, and neither were Greek-speaking Catholics in the Cyclades.

Faith was fundamental in the Ottoman Empire, as it was throughout the early modern world. It structured and bounded the kind of life one could lead. The Church and its rituals regulated the life cycle (baptism, marriage, funerals) and the annual cycle (Easter, saints' days, Christmas) of everyday people. This religion-focused identity was very much a 'concept of practice', but it was reinforced by an Ottoman state that ruled through religious authorities and structures. By the nineteenth century the *millet* system confirmed the Orthodox a legitimate, albeit subordinate, place in the Ottoman order (cf. Ozil 2013: 65–81). Orthodox subjects formed one of the largest and most influential communities within that order. Hence Greek Orthodox subjects could also identify with a larger, trans-local structure or 'imagined' community, with an official leadership composed of high clergy that collected taxes and administered justice. The Ottoman state also reinforced a sense of Rum consciousness when it meted out collective punishment against the community for the transgressions of some of its constituents. During the Greek Revolution, the Archbishop of Cyprus and up to 500 of the local intelligentsia were executed even though the island did not play a serious part. The first stirrings of the Cypriot struggle for unification with Greece can be dated to at least as far back as these executions (Koumoulides 1974).

The struggle for independence waged by 'Romaioi' (Romioi, Rum etc.), however, resulted in the creation of a state called 'Hellas' (Ελλάς) and the insurgents being relabelled 'Hellenes' (Έλληνες). Aside from its immense symbolic significance, the new name was also very useful in distinguishing Greeks inside and outside the new kingdom. Ottoman Greek subjects habitually described Greek nationals as 'Hellenes' and often retained for themselves the name 'Romioi'. Thus, in 1912, when

Greek forces seized the island of Limnos, the distinguished Byzantinist Peter Charanis, then a child, recalled:

> Some of the children ran to see what Greek soldiers looked like.
> 'What are you looking at?' one of them asked.
> 'At Hellenes', the children replied.
> 'Are you not Hellenes yourselves?' a soldier retorted.
> 'No, we are Romans [*Romioi*].' (Kaldellis 2007: 42)

Nationalisation at the beginning of the twentieth century

To what extent did the Ottoman Empire's Romioi identify with the Greek nation in 1900? If popular prophecies were anything to go by, the Romioi would have preferred not to live under Muslim authority. These prophecies, which foretold the restoration of the Byzantine Empire and its Christian emperor, reflected a commonplace desire. As with the Phanariot class in Constantinople, however, the Romioi generally were more interested in stability and prosperity than in national secession or unification with the Greek kingdom. Despite its despotic and 'blood-soaked' reputation, the reign of Sultan Abdülhamid II (1878–1909) had been a golden age for the Romioi, while Greece's *Megali Idea*, the irredentist dream of making Constantinople the capital of Greece, was one that threatened their material interests (Doumanis 2013).

When considering minority communities within the multiethnic empires (Russian, Habsburg, Ottoman), it is crucial to distinguish national secessionism from basic nationalism (Barkey and von Hagen 1997). For middle-class Romioi, Greek nationalism was an expression of the community's self-confidence within the Ottoman domain rather than a secessionist political project. Athens was the critical source of 'Hellenic' influences (flags, symbols and the like), as upwardly mobile Romioi adopted Greek nationalist ideas and traits to reflect their new class status, and to distinguish them from humbler Romioi. Their homes often had portraits of the Greek monarch, George I, and their young boys were photographed dressed as *Evzones*, in the distinctive uniform of the elite Greek infantry battalions. At the time, Constantinople had witnessed the rise of numerous Greek associations, educational institutions and cultural activities (Exertzoglou 1996). Greek nationalism strengthened Ottoman Greek solidarity in the decades approaching the First World War, when the Ottoman order was being reconstituted and when all communities sought to defend their particular interests within the changing political milieu. This was the case after 1908 when the Young Turk Revolution promised the introduction of a new constitution and an inclusive social order, and when Greek nationalism was useful in mobilising the Romioi to promote their position *within* the empire. Although wary of minority nationalisms, the Romanov, Habsburg and Ottoman empires believed that they could accommodate them by offering a stake in the imperial system (Barkey and von Hagen 1997). The Romioi could therefore be nationalists and loyal Ottomans at the same time.

After 1912, however, any thought of incorporating Orthodox Christians into the Ottoman Empire had been abandoned. Over the next ten years, war and ethnic cleansing accelerated the 'nationalisation' of the Balkans and Anatolia. As will be discussed in the next chapter, the complex cultural landscapes of the Ottoman world would be rationalised dramatically, brutally transforming Muslims into Turks and Orthodox Christians into Greeks or Bulgarians. Once resettled, the multiplicity of Muslim cultures corralled into the Republic of Turkey, and the various Orthodox peoples transferred into Greece and Bulgaria, were pressured to forget their pasts and forsake aspects of their culture, especially language. When the Karamanlides were resettled in Greece, they could not speak in public in their Turkish mother tongue, known as *Karamanlidika*. The language did become extinct, but considerable effort went into recording this group's customs and traditions. Fearing that nationalism would obliterate such Anatolian cultures, a cosmopolitan Greek from Istanbul named Melpo Merlier established in 1930 the Centre for Asia Minor Studies in Athens. She employed teams of dedicated fieldworkers to collect thousands of oral testimonies and other kinds of documentation that described life and culture in the 'lost homelands' (*chamenes patrides*) (Papailias 2005: 94). Meanwhile, refugees resisted official pressure to forget their pasts and discard their cultural baggage. Indeed, their new identities as *Mikrasiates* (people from Asia Minor) and *prosfyges* (refugees) reflected a need to remember but also constituted a gesture of defiance against official cultural pressure and host-society hostility. Refugees from the Black Sea–Pontus region rallied together to salvage much of their distinctive culture and claimed a new collective identity as 'Pontians' rather than as Romaioi, which is what they called themselves (Bryer 1991: 320–1; Fann 1991). Much of the culture was salvaged because it was repackaged as a vernacular variation of Greek national identity, in the same way as regional groups could still be (say) Cretan or Corfiot. What is undeniable, however, is the power that a state-sanctioned version of Greek identity would command throughout the Greek world during the twentieth century. It was hegemonic in the sense that it was generally accepted as *the* legitimate bearer of 'Greekness'. Its symbolic power was even dominant in Cyprus, at least from the 1950s through to 1974, during which time most Greek Cypriots privileged their Greekness over their Cypriot-ness.

Migration also had nationalising effects. As industrial capitalism and the global market shifted millions of people worldwide, globally recognisable cultures became ever more important. People crossing the North Atlantic had to conform to an ethnic category that US authorities and the American public could recognise. Hence when the future Hollywood film director Elia Kazan passed through Ellis Island with his Turkish-speaking parents just before the First World War, he would have been recorded by immigration personnel as either Greek or Turk, but not Romios or Karamanlis. In the United States, which received most of Europe's emigrating poor, national categories were also useful in workplaces and everyday life, not only because the host society could not accommodate the multiplicity of identities that settled in their midst, but because the migrants had to form new solidarities with people from their lands of origin. Hence migrants were no longer as indifferent to nationalism as they might have been in their homeland villages. In such conditions, Sicilians and Calabrese finally *became* Italians and were happy to adopt such northern Italians as Christopher Columbus and Guglielmo Marconi as heroes (Gabaccia 2000: 120–8). Host-society xenophobia certainly had similar effects on Greek migrants. As will be discussed in greater detail below, Greek Orthodox immigrants from Greece and the Ottoman Empire, regardless of their regional backgrounds, had little difficulty in forming associations and identifying as Greeks/Hellenes. When the First Balkan War broke out, as many as 45,000 young Greek émigrés rushed home to fight for their country (Saloutos 1964: 114).

The *Oikoumene*: a transnational Greek world

Where were the Greeks? What was their geography? Before the Balkan Wars, Greek communities were commonplace in the Balkans, Anatolia and the eastern Mediterranean. According to a census carried out in 1910–12 by the Ecumenical (Orthodox) Patriarchate in Constantinople, there were 208,478 Greeks in Smyrna, although the real figure was closer to 110,000 (Alexandris 1999: 58; Georgelin 2013: 33). The Patriarchate was much closer to the mark when it came to the imperial capital (199,725) (Alexandris 1999: 68). A census taken in Salonica in 1913 listed 40,000 Greeks, while in Alexandria in 1917 about 25,000 Greeks were recorded (Mazower 2004: 284; Kitroeff 1989: 13–14). Communities could be found around the Black Sea, including the Bulgarian and the Russian Empire's coastlines. There was also a merchant diaspora strewn across Europe, in places like Manchester, Paris and Vienna.

Writing a history of 'the Greeks', as opposed to 'Greece', therefore presents a problem of framing. How can the Greeks in Greece, Cyprus, Russia, the Ottoman Empire and those of the wider diaspora be accommodated into a single historical narrative? This task is made especially difficult because of the diversity of experiences. By the 1930s, many Greeks were living under the Franklin Roosevelt administration, while others were settled in Stalin's USSR. Greek Cypriots, Greek South Africans and Greek Egyptians experienced different kinds of British dominion. What can be said, however, is that in the twentieth century the experience of being a minority, or a specifically Greek minority, did have implications for how one was treated by the state and the broader society. Compared to the empires of the past, the nation states were less accommodating when it came to cultural difference. Greeks in the United States and other Anglophone nations endured xenophobia, while in Transcaucasia (the region of the Caucasus Mountains, including the current republics of Georgia, Armenia and Azerbaijan), Turkey and Egypt they would be expelled en masse.

Diaspora Greeks also had more positive reasons for keeping their Greek identity. In the United States, groups like the Italians and the Greeks found ways of using their cultural capital (ancient legacies, homeland heroes, famous Italian and Greek Americans) to mark out a space in the national imaginary and to project a respectable community image. They would take special pride in one of their own becoming a celebrity (e.g. Frank Sinatra for the Italians, Telly Savalas for the Greeks). There was also the simple but heartfelt desire among émigrés to *stay* Greek. They wished to retain Greek traditions within the family and preserve the language within their communities. Throughout the world, in Greek communities, whether in Africa, Anglophone countries or Istanbul, there was a preoccupation with cultural retention.

Any study of Greeks, whether ancient, medieval or modern, must account for their mobility. Since the Late Bronze Age (1500–1200 BCE) or even earlier, Greek-speaking peoples spread beyond their base's confines in the Aegean. The ecological limitations of Greece, its lack of arable land, the fact that every part of it was close to the sea, and the fact that the region is blessed with numerous sheltered harbours, determined that its peoples would use the sea routinely to make a living and to migrate (Gallant 2015: 221–5). Migration was either seasonal or permanent. It was certainly a way of life. It could be said that Greek migration was a traditional practice that ties together all periods, ancient and modern, and which led to the transference of Greek culture to non-Greek territories. As modern Greek émigrés ventured into various parts of Africa, to the Americas and even to Australia and New Zealand, they carried with them a formula for forming communities that would allow them to 'stay' Greek. This formula included a repertoire of institutions: a church, community council (*koinotis* sing., *koinotites* pl.), language and dance schools, cafes (*kafeneia*), cakeshops (*zacharoplasteia*) and other Greek business. Since these communities were often composed of many different (e.g. regionally diverse) Greeks, over time they also had to develop a shared version of Greek culture, which included a new vernacular culture filled with new practices and renderings of words borrowed from the host society (e.g. in Australia, *frizza* for refrigerator or *taxesia* for taxes).

That determination among expatriates to remain Greek also revealed their sense of living within a transnational 'imagined community': a dispersed Greek 'nation'. The twentieth-century diaspora would be particularly aware of itself as a widely scattered formation, especially as people from a single village or indeed a single family often went in different directions. Siblings were quite often in South Africa *and* Canada, the United States *and* Australia. Although divided by continents, they kept in contact with one another and with their village or town. People from Kalymnos, Kasos and Kythera had not only relocated to different parts of the eastern Mediterranean, but also to Florida, the Caribbean, various parts of the Indian Ocean basin and throughout the vast expanses of the Australian interior. Arid islands like Kastellorizo would spawn much larger populations overseas. At the beginning of the twentieth century, this tiny island, which had deep familial ties with southwestern Anatolian coastline ports, particularly Antifillo/Kaş, also had a diaspora that spanned Odessa, Nantes, Port Said, Alexandria, Sydney and Perth (Australia) (Pappas 1994). The fact that a large proportion of émigrés returned to 'Old' Greece, either temporarily or permanently, also meant Greek villagers were more informed than less mobile Balkan or Anatolian peoples about the wider world and the business and employment opportunities it promised.

Indeed, more so than most peoples of the eastern Mediterranean region, twentieth-century Greeks lived within global networks.

With each wave of émigrés, this global Greek *oikoumene* (literally 'the inhabited world') was renewed and would often expand. After the first significant wave of migrants to the United States in the 1880s, others who followed in their footsteps knew that they could find a 'Greektown'. The handful of pioneers in Chicago in the 1890s (fewer than 250), most of whom arrived in the country without experience in business, managed to create a centrally located 'Greek' business district within a span of twenty years (Demas 2004–5: 108). Every time Greek émigrés in Addis Ababa or Buenos Aires attended Greek churches, Greek language classes, or sat in a *kafeneion*, they were renewing and perpetuating this transnational Greek world.

Cultural retention was easier in communities with substantial numbers. In Ottoman territories and Egypt, Greek cultures did not merely flourish but managed to compete with Greece as rival centres of Greek life. Perhaps the most evocative insights into the kind of 'Greek' life that one could experience within this *oikoumene* could be found in the work of Constantine Cavafy, internationally the best-known Greek poet of modern times. He lived a Greek life and evoked a middle-class Greek sensibility through his writings, yet he hardly set foot in Greece. He lived most of his life in Alexandria, after having lived a few years in Constantinople, Liverpool and London. He could converse in many languages, as was typical of bourgeois Levantine Greeks, while his understanding of being Greek was derived through living in coexistence with other cultures. Like many others, Cavafy moved routinely between cultural worlds, and many of his characters are hybrids: they are Greek, non-Greek and something in between. As with so many Greeks who lived outside the 'centre' of the Greek world, Cavafy live a decentred existence, yet his community cultivated a sense of Greekness that would sometimes influence the centre (Keeley 1976; Clay 1977: 95–7).

The Church and the merchant marine

Before describing the Greek *oikoumene*, it is worth mentioning two transnational structures that played a role in tying it together. Especially significant in this regard was the Greek Orthodox Church (Anastassiadis 2020: 1–2). When the Byzantine Empire fractured after the Fourth Crusade in 1204, the Church replaced the empire and the emperor as the focus of Greek loyalty and identity. Later emperors of the Palaiologos Dynasty (1261–1453) found it difficult to re-establish their authority in places like the Peloponnese, which for decades had been ruled by Latin feudal lords, but where local people had looked to Orthodox bishops for leadership. In this new order, the Orthodox population were bonded together by the Church rather than the state (Angold 2003: 208). The unifying power of the Orthodox Church was reinforced under Ottoman rule, when subject populations were administered as confessional groups, and when authority was invested in the Patriarch of Constantinople. For much of that period, Albanian, Serb, Bulgarian, Romanian, Arabic and Greek-speaking Orthodox Christians were grouped in the same community or *millet*, which acquired more legal substance by the mid-nineteenth century (Stamatopoulos 2006: 259). By then it also began to mean something like 'nation' (Karabıçak 2020: 328–9). The ecclesiastical system and its personnel (bishops, priests, abbots, nuns etc.) formed a corporate entity that enjoyed broad authority throughout the empire. In important ways, therefore, the Church bound every Orthodox person together.

By the late nineteenth century, this large group had fractured into distinct linguistic groups that became the basis for separate nations. From the 1870s on, the Bulgarians and Serbs had their own patriarchates and *millet*. Thus, in 1900, the Greek *millet* consisted mainly of Greek-speaking peoples, but also included were smaller groups of non-Greek-speakers that continued to use Greek in church liturgy. Hence groups like the Vlachs (Aromanian-speakers) and the Albanian-speaking Arvanites in Greece, the Turkish-speaking Karamanlides of central Anatolia and Turkish-speaking Pontian communities of the Samsun region belonged to the same 'imagined' community that included the Greeks of Greece, Constantinople and Alexandria. Even the isolated Greek-speaking villagers of Pharasa, which had survived in the Taurus Mountains of central Anatolia until 1923, and which routinely heard the liturgy in Greek, probably believed they were part of an imagined community that extended well beyond their region.

The Orthodox Church also played an important role in tying the diaspora into the *oikoumene*. As churches were being built or purchased across the United States, émigré communities petitioned the Greek Orthodox patriarchates of Constantinople, Jerusalem and Alexandria for priests. By doing so they acquired a canonically ordained priest who could administer the sacraments and perform weddings, while creating parishes that were incorporated into an ecclesiastical jurisdiction of a globalising Orthodox Church structure. Having lost most of its dioceses following the Asia Minor Catastrophe in 1922, the Patriarchate in Constantinople would nevertheless gain many new parishes in the Greek diaspora during the course of the twentieth century (Kitroeff 2020;

Saloutos 1964; Tsounis 1971). Among the functions of the new global ecclesiastical order was the maintenance of a disciplined clergy that observed Orthodox doctrine and practices. It also served as a trans-continental network that transmitted information, ideas and funds.

The maritime diaspora was another transnational formation. Since the end of the French Revolutionary Wars, Greek shipping interests had dominated seaborne trade in the eastern Mediterranean and the Black Sea. Family companies opened offices throughout Europe, particularly in London, and extended their operations across Eurasia. These operations linked up the merchant communities that had long been established in Europe's capitals and port cities, and which helped Greek shipping interests expand (Harlaftis 1995: 155). Initially led by shipping families from Chios, from the 1870s the industry was headed by Kefalonian and Ithacan family businesses, which dominated the export trade in wheat from the Russian Empire, which at the time was Europe's chief granary. Families used their kinship networks and marriage alliances to consolidate and expand their business networks. The crews of this vast and expanding mercantile marine were mostly Greek, usually men hired from the shipowner's home island.

In the twentieth century, Greek shipping companies expanded their operations worldwide, but particularly in the Atlantic. During the interwar years, the Greek merchant marine was the second largest in the world, and it welcomed new players from Andros and Kasos. New names like Onassis and Niarchos were added to established ones like Kulukundis, Goulandris, Livanos and Embiricos. Many Greeks working for these globally expanding companies, in offices or as crewmen, saw more of the world than did previous generations. The overall number of Greek seamen working on these ships increased from 15,000 before 1914 to around 18,000 during the Depression years (Harlaftis 1995: 225). The great majority of those recruited during the interwar years were still from the home islands of company owners (66 per cent), while about 25 per cent were from Athens and the rest of Greece. Companies preferred to recruit their local compatriots because, as maritime historian Gelina Harlaftis points out, they were a known quantity and were more easily disciplined (Harlaftis 1995: 233). Even so, Greek seamen managed to form strong unions after the First World War and formed a major component of the emergent labour movement. After the Second World War, the merchant marine continued to expand. Collectively, Greek shipping owners came to possess the world's largest merchant fleet. By 1980, islanders had formed 36 per cent of seamen in the merchant marine, with the rest coming from other parts of Greece. By this point, Greek-owned ships were plying sea lanes throughout the world and keeping Greek men at sea for months. Almost 60,000 Greeks were employed as seamen in 1980.

One of the reasons why the Greek merchant marine prospered and dominated global trade was because companies managed to capitalise on kinship and home island networks. Offices and ships were filled with personnel who were familiar and reliable. The company families formed a Greek network that competed but also shared insights and expertise. Together they built a globally connected system that facilitated the movement of Greeks across the world (Harlaftis 1995).

Greeks in the Ottoman Empire

At the turn of the twentieth century the 'Greek world' could be divided into three categories: Greece, the diaspora and Greeks living in ancestral homelands but under non-Greek rule. The last group was located in the Ottoman Empire and Cyprus. This simple picture was complicated by the infusion during the nineteenth century of Greek nationals into the Ottoman Empire, especially Constantinople, Smyrna and Anatolia, and by Romioi who migrated to different parts of the Ottoman Empire. The Karamanlides, for example, had their own expatriate neighbourhoods in the imperial capital (Doumanis 2013: 37–41).

The Ottoman Empire had indigenous Greek populations. They were found in Epirus, Macedonia and Thrace, much of the present-day Bulgarian coast, the imperial capital and its environs, western Anatolia, the Black Sea littoral and some pockets of the central Anatolian plateau. Small communities had also survived in other parts of Anatolia, including near Ankara on the central Anatolian plateau and along the southern Mediterranean coast. In most of these territories the Romioi coexisted with a variety of cultures and were usually in the minority, the exceptions being Epirus and the Ottoman-controlled Aegean islands, including Rhodes and the Dodecanese, which were seized by Italy in May 1912, and which would remain Italian possessions until 1947 (Doumanis 1997).

Important reasons for why Ottoman Greeks chose to remain in their *patrides* (fatherlands), and for why Greek subjects were migrating to the Sultan's domain, were employment and economic opportunity. The decades leading up to the 1900s would be recalled as a *belle époque*, as the Romioi seemed to capitalise disproportionately on international trade growth. It was a boom period for merchants, shipping operators, company owners, lawyers, bankers and the employees of European companies, as well as petty shopkeepers, tradesmen and farmers. Migrants from the Balkans, the Aegean islands and other parts of the empire were drawn to western Anatolia, where land was being reclaimed for commercial agriculture, and where railway tracks were being laid to link Smyrna to markets throughout Anatolia. As a result, the city grew from 100,000 in 1800 to 250,000 in 1900. Migrant farmers moved into the river valleys and settled in villages near Aydın and Alaşehir, where the Muslim population had been declining. These settlers often moved into semi-abandoned villages, which they shared with indigenous Muslims or Muslim migrants from different parts of Anatolia, or Muslim refugees from the Russian Empire (Anagnostopoulou 1997: 191). Towns with near majority Greek Orthodox populations included Aïvali (Ayvalık), Kios (Gemlik), Brylleion (Tirilye) and Mihaliç (Karacabey) (Ozil 2013: 9). One town that was almost wholly Greek was Livissi (Kayaköy) in the southwest corner of Anatolia, but Livissi was a rarity. A large Greek population existed in the Black Sea region between Sinope and Trabzon and the Russian imperial border. These Pontian Greeks were distinguishable by their own Greek dialects and cultural traditions. Their region was the last in Anatolia to be conquered by the Ottoman Turks, and because it capitulated without resistance its Greek population received privileges and was better able to withstand the pressures of Islamicisation (Bryer 1991). At the beginning of the twentieth century, the Orthodox population in the region was still as high as 20 per cent, although the Greek language was no longer spoken in the more western region. Some migrated to different parts of Anatolia, to the mining regions in the central plateau (for example, Gümüşhane/Argyropolis) and the Taurus Mountains, while a major Pontian diaspora was taking shape within the Russian Empire. Meanwhile, Pontian converts to Islam often retained their Greek dialect and Pontian traditions long into the twentieth century.

The most significant Ottoman Greek populations were in two cities: Constantinople and Smyrna. The imperial capital had always had a Greek population, although it had been replenished continuously by immigrants from different regions, who crowded into the neighbourhoods near the city's shores and in Pera (Beyoğlu). At the beginning of the twentieth century, Greek nationals continued to arrive looking for work, and the city became home to Greeks of all classes, including a white-collar class of professionals (lawyers, doctors, clerks), an establishment class known as the Phanariots, and an *haute bourgeoisie* of bankers and financiers (Gallant 2015: 29–30; Philliou 2010). In 1900, when the imperial capital had just under 950,000 inhabitants, the Greeks numbered somewhere between 150,000 and 200,000. Many Greek communities could also be found along the Bosporus and in nearby towns such as Üsküdar and on the Prince's Islands in the Sea of Marmara.

A large concentration of Greeks was found along the western Anatolian seaboard, in towns such as Phocaea (Foça), Alatsata (Alaçatı), Halikarnassos (Bodrum), Makri (Fethiye) and around the Sea of Marmara, like Pandirma (Bandırma) and Rodosto (Tekirdağ). This part of the empire boomed due to international demand for such local raw materials as figs, raisins, cotton and opium. In 1900, 55 per cent of the empire's exports passed through Smyrna, which greeted an ever rising number of ships (1,295 in 1863 to 2,465 in 1900). Between 1900 and 1907 exports increased by one third (Mansel 2010: 160, 173). Although a cosmopolitan city that was home to many European expatriate communities, Smyrna was a magnet for Anatolian Romioi *and* Greek nationals. Most of the city's best schools, its bankers, and half of its lawyers and doctors were Greek. By 1900 Greeks were the largest cultural group in the city (Kontente 2005: 711–13). The prosperity and confidence of the Smyrniot Greek bourgeoisie was reflected in the way it flaunted its enthusiasm for the Greek flag and the Greek monarchy (Mansel 2010: 169–71).

The region around Smyrna also had many Greek communities, as did the farming regions to the northeast and along the Menderes River. Further inland, however, Greek communities were rarer. Small groups could be found in towns such as Eskişehir, Isparta, Konya and Adana. The Karamanlides were a significant presence in the region near Kayseri. Having coexisted peacefully for centuries with their Muslim neighbours, these communities flourished to the extent that they had their own book trade – religious texts and other works were written in Turkish dialect but using a Greek script.

In the Balkans, directly north of the Kingdom of Greece, were a series of Ottoman provinces that Turks regarded as imperial heartland territories: the *vilayet*s of Yanya, Manastir, Selânik and Edirne. The *vilayet* of Yanya included much of present-day Albania and Epirus. While Albania was predominantly Muslim, the region of Epirus, including what Greeks call northern Epirus (the southern end of present-day Albania), was overwhelmingly Orthodox Christian and predominantly Greek-speaking, but it also had sizeable Vlach and Albanian-speaking populations. Between 1788 and 1822, Ioannina

(Yanya) had been the capital of Ali Pasha, the Albanian Muslim potentate. The so-called Lion of Ioannina established a Greek-speaking court, and his city was predominantly Greek-speaking (Fleming 1999). In the *vilayet*s of Manastir and Selânik, the picture was rather more complex. In the countryside, Orthodox Christians mostly spoke Slavic dialects, and seemed as numerous as the local Muslim population. The Orthodox villages of the region were divided between those loyal to the Greek Patriarchate in Constantinople (along with Greek villages in the southern parts of the region) and those aligned with the Bulgarian Exarchate in Sofia. Greek-speakers and Jews were concentrated in towns and cities, although in Salonica, Ladino-speaking Jews formed the single largest community, followed by its Turkish-speaking Muslim community, which included the family of Mustafa Kemal Atatürk. It came as some surprise to the conquering Greek soldiers that the city did not seem very Greek. One Greek officer complained: 'How can one like a city with this cosmopolitan society, nine-tenths of it Jews. It has nothing Greek about it, nor European' (Mazower 2004: 295). The *vilayet* of Edirne, which encompassed Thrace, had a Muslim majority (between 55 and 60 per cent), as well as a large Orthodox Christian minority (as high as 40 per cent), with Bulgarian-speakers concentrated in northern regions and Greeks in southern regions, Edirne and in the larger Black Sea towns.

Cyprus and the diaspora

Formally at least, Cyprus was also Ottoman territory. However, following another of the empire's disastrous wars with the Russians, the Russo-Turkish War of 1877–8, the British assumed control of the island. The third largest in the Mediterranean, it was the only territory east of the Aegean where Greek-speaking Orthodox Christians formed an overwhelming majority: roughly 80 per cent. Thus, Cyprus was as Greek as Crete and Epirus, and any part of the Greek kingdom, yet geographically it was much more part of the Middle East, much closer to Beirut and Alexandria than to Athens. Indeed, far more so than any other Greek territory, Cyprus' fate was tied up with its geographical location and the geopolitical interests of the Great Powers. Britain effectively acquired the territory in exchange for protecting the Ottoman Empire from further Russian territorial encroachment, and in return for a large portion of the island's tax revenues (A. Varnava 2009: 32). Along with Egypt (occupied from 1881), Cyprus was also meant to play a role in Britain's global imperial system by protecting access to its more vital strategic and economic interests in the Mediterranean, the Middle East and Asia generally (Darwin 2009: 1).

A census held in 1901 showed it had 237,002 inhabitants, which was more than 25 per cent higher than it had been two decades earlier (186,173) (Katsiaounis 1996: 175). As with Sardinia and Corsica, Cyprus lacked natural deep-water harbours, hence it had never been a centre of maritime activity. Its economic life was overwhelmingly focused on agriculture: under Ottoman rule six out of seven Cypriots worked the land. The colonisers made some attempt to modernise the territory. By 1900 the British had dismantled its Ottoman system of governance, law, land-holding regimes, taxation and economic relations. Whereas the clergy and especially the higher clergy had enjoyed enormous powers and privileges under the *millet* system, British administration ruled mainly through intermediaries from the rising middle class of commercial operators and professionals. Earlier, most of the arable land belonged to the Sultan under the *miri* system, which gave the smallholders significant state protections. The British characteristically introduced private ownership and security of tenure, which provided valuable freedoms for some but also exposed all landholders to market fluctuations. Consequently, indebtedness and pauperisation became a serious social problem. A major drought in 1886, which saw to a catastrophic 56 per cent slump in wheat production, exacerbated the problem and led to thousands of peasant holdings being sold off by the state and moneylenders (Katsiaounis 1996: 104).

The First World War, which radically increased demands for Cypriot agricultural goods and minerals (see pp. 80–4), provided temporary reprieve to a social problem that became a significant driver of emigration, urbanisation and the rise of a local labour movement. However, as will be discussed in later chapters (Chapters 3 and 8), as elsewhere in the colonial world, social problems were also undermining colonial authority and generating support for anti-colonial movements. As with Greeks in nearby Anatolia, the rising Greek Cypriot bourgeoisie had also taken to Greek nationalism, although their goal was unification with Greece rather than national self-determination. The new elites of Limassol and Larnaca could use Greek nationalist culture to distinguish themselves from the bishops and established landed interests based in Nicosia (Katsiaounis 1996: 182). However, the goal of unification was something shared by both the old and new elites. Indeed, during the first formal meeting with the British governor in 1878, the then Bishop of Kition told him: 'We accept the change of government inasmuch as we trust Great Britain will help Cyprus, as it did the Ionian Islands, to be united with Mother Greece, with which it is naturally connected' (Dodd 2010: 3). The unification issue would eventually produce an irreparable rupture in relations with colonial authorities, and, more fatefully, with the Turkish Cypriot community.

All the while, Greek Cypriot émigrés were joining Greek communities throughout the world. The great expansion of industry and colonial empires from the 1780s also had the effect of making the Greek diaspora more global in scope. Greeks from Greece, the Ottoman Empire and Cyprus were flocking to the industrialising centres of the northeastern United States, laying railway tracks across Africa and the American West, and were present during the mining booms of California, South Africa and Australia. In such places, Greek labourers were often transitioning from labouring to shopkeeping, filling niches in service industries in major cities like Johannesburg and Chicago, but also lonely 'one-horse' towns in far north Queensland, the Congo and the Rocky Mountains region.

Particularly significant was the flow of Greeks between 1890 and 1920 to the United States. The first wave was in the 1880s, led by villagers from the region of Lakonia (2,308 people). A much larger cohort (16,000) from many other parts of the Peloponnese followed in the 1890s. A process of chain migration saw newcomers invite brothers, cousins and villagers with the promise of work and profit. The great majority were males who planned to return home, but an increasing number were intent on establishing roots and raising families. These men returned with brides, organised marriages by proxy, or married American women. By the first decade of the twentieth century, 167,519 had managed to pass health inspections at Ellis Island, from where they spread across the country. A further 100,000 Greeks would also come from Ottoman territories, particularly after 1908, when Romioi often migrated to the United States to avoid conscription in the Ottoman military. Another 184,000 Greek nationals migrated in the following decade (Moskos 1990: 11).

Another important destination for Greek émigrés was British Egypt, which prospered due to high global demand for cotton, and because Egypt was the recipient of significant foreign financial and commercial investment. As many as 120,000 Greeks migrated to Egypt and other parts of Africa between the 1870s and 1930s, although most went no further south than Cairo (Hasiotis 2006: 23). Greek merchants made fortunes and established such great houses as those of Tossizza, Averoff, Ralli, Rodocanachi and Benaki. By the end of the century, the Greek Egyptian elite had expanded, having prospered on the cotton and tobacco trades, but also in finance and newer industries. Greeks also filled niches in various services and manufacturing, including distilleries, chocolate, hotels and river transport (Karanasou 1999: 36). The Greek Egyptian community, however, was socially diverse. It included teachers, bureaucrats and clerks that worked in European firms, as well as shopkeepers, mostly grocers (*bakaal*) and workers. Humble peasants and fishermen from such tiny Aegean islands as Kasos and Kastellorizo found it much easier and cheaper to migrate to Egypt than the United States. In 1866, some 5,000 Greeks worked on the Suez Canal, most (approximately 3,000) being from Kasos (Kitroeff 2019: 45). At the beginning of the twentieth century, Greek Egyptians represented the largest of the foreign communities in Egypt. Between 1897 and 1907, the Greek population rose by 40 per cent, from 38,208 to 62,973 (Tomara-Sideris 2009: 156).

A rather different part of the diaspora was to be found in the Russian Empire. Greek commercial interests had maintained an enduring presence in the Black Sea towns, most notably in Odessa, but from the late eighteenth century a substantial number of rural Greek settlements had been forming in regions to the north and east of the Black Sea that were being incorporated into the Russian Empire. Whereas most urban Greek enclaves were eventually assimilated into the wider Russian community, the relative isolation of these farming communities meant they were able to preserve their distinctive traditions and dialects across generations.

The Russian state welcomed Greek settlers because they were Orthodox and because they helped to dilute or replace the Muslim demographic component of their new Black Sea territories. They included the Urum, who in fact were two distinct Greek Orthodox peoples located respectively in the Crimea and in the region of Kvemo Kartli in Georgia. The provenance of the former group has not been reliably established, but the latter group had arrived from northeastern Anatolia and in several waves. Like the Karamanlides of central Anatolia, the Urum would learn to use Greek script to write in their native tongue (Skopeteas 2015). Another group were Greeks of Mariupol (Marianopolis), who had been settled by Catherine the Great in the town and in local rural settlements, and who were distinguished by their unique Greek dialect (Kaurinkoski 2003). The largest group were Pontian dialect-speakers from Anatolia's Black Sea coast, who had migrated to various parts of Georgia, Abkhazia and Transcaucasia. The earliest arrivals had followed Russian occupation forces when they withdrew from eastern Anatolia in 1828, settling in newly conquered

Russian territories that had been forcibly vacated by Muslim groups. This pattern was repeated in the wake of the Crimean War (1853–6), the Russo-Turkish War of 1877–8 and the First World War period, a process that has been aptly described by a historian of the diaspora, Ioannis Hasiotis, as an informal population exchange (Hasiotis 1993: 87). At the beginning of the twentieth century, there were some 208,000 Greeks living in the Russian Empire, with slightly more than half (106,000) in Transcaucasia, and with most of the rest in Ukraine, Moldavia and other parts of European Russia (102,000) (Giannitsis, Dialla and Hasiotis 2006: 194).

Conclusion

The history of the Greeks in the twentieth century is a global story. Yet there are important reasons why the Greeks of Greece should receive special attention in this book. The first has to do with the fact that significant parts of the wider Greek world effectively disappeared. That was the fate of Greek communities in Turkey and Egypt by the late 1960s. A second has to do with Greece as *the* source of Greek culture: its hegemonic role. For Greeks in the diaspora and Cyprus to some degree, Greece has been the arbiter of things 'Greek'.

Finally, there is the simple matter of numbers. For the first time since the high Middle Ages (the eleventh century), the great majority of Greek-speaking peoples lived within a single political territory. And within that national space, people's lives were shaped indelibly by 'national' experiences. This meant much more in the twentieth century than any previous era because of the expanding role of the nation state in national life, and because of the radical changes in state–society relations. The changes include: the greater state–society intimacy embodied by such concepts as nationalism (love of country), the expanding mutual responsibilities in the state–society relationship (social insurance, welfare, state employment, conscription) and the state's greater interest in the nation's 'bodies', which ranged from guaranteeing health standards to ethnic cleansing and mass killings (Mazower 1998: ch. 3; see also Müller 2011). Government institutions and policies, wars, foreign occupation and economic fluctuations shaped personal experiences and informed collective identities. Whereas diaspora Greeks experienced lives that were shaped by other specific national environments, the great majority of Greeks during the time period covered in this book '*lived*' Greece' (ζήσανε την Ελλάδα/ *zisane tin Ellada*). Being 'Greek' in Greece meant having to deal with the same kinds of daily challenges (workplace, bureaucracy, services) and the same life-changing events (wartime hunger in 1941–2, political repression 1967–74, economic turmoil since 2010) that were shared with other Greek nationals. The book will therefore accord most of its attention to the experiences of Greeks in Greece. For similar reasons, Greek Cypriots, who 'lived' a very different twentieth century, deserve their own, book-length treatment. In this book Cypriot history is covered in the two 'Greek world' chapters (Chapters 3 and 8), and in chapters covering the post-Greek dictatorship period (Chapter 7) and the 2010s (Chapter 11).

CHAPTER 2

The 'long First World War' (1912–1922)

In the late summer of 1914, Europeans committed to a war so violent and traumatic that it fundamentally changed the continent and the world. The First World War transformed cultural identities, systems of government and economies (Müller 2011: 16). It polarised societies along ideological, class and ethnic lines. Europe's Great Powers had entrapped themselves in a desperate struggle that drained national resources and sapped morale, enough so for society to lose faith in the political order and quarrel violently over its replacement (Clark 2012). Although the war formally ended on 11 November 1918, the turmoil and deprivations persisted into the early 1920s. The old multiethnic empires were wracked by horrific civil wars, pogroms and ethnic cleansings, and then disappeared. For Europe it would indeed be a *long* First World War (Gerwarth 2016).

Greece's 'First World War' was even longer. It started with the First Balkan War (1912), which was a dress rehearsal for the larger pan-European conflict, featuring trench warfare, mass armies, the use of machine guns and rapid-fire guns, horrendous casualty rates and mass violence against civilian populations (Hall 2000: 130; Gallant 2015: 316–26). The nation's 'long' war ended in 1922, with the military defeat at the Battle of Sakarya in August, the destruction of Smyrna in early September, and the permanent expulsion of Greeks from Anatolia and Eastern Thrace. By then, Greece and the Greeks had been completely transformed. The country was larger in terms of numbers and territory, its population more culturally and socially complex, but Greek society had been deeply traumatised and its politics hopelessly polarised. The transformative effects of the *long* First World War are the main subject of this chapter.

The Balkan Wars, October 1912–August 1913

The First Balkan War almost sparked a general European conflict. Russian and Austrian forces were mobilised in November 1912, and if war did break out between these two Great Powers, direct French and German involvement was likely. However, cooler heads prevailed in Vienna and St Petersburg that month (Clark 2012: 268). But in at least one important sense, the conflict did serve as a dress rehearsal for the 1914–18 war. It anticipated the kind of civilian-focused warfare that traumatised societies and left deep and enduring political, social and cultural legacies. Indeed, the violence had revolutionary effects, and it would be the hallmark of what many historians have described as Europe's second 'Thirty Years War' (Traverso 2016; Doumanis 2016).

Greece was not alone in its desire to expand at the expense of the Ottoman Empire. Sofia and Belgrade respectively also dreamt of creating a 'greater Bulgaria' and 'greater Serbia'. But each Balkan state had overlapping irredentist ambitions. Greece, Serbia and Bulgaria claimed Macedonia, while Bulgaria and Greece had their eyes on Thrace. These competing interests had made it difficult to broker alliance agreements. Each hoped to steal a march on the rest, but none were confident of taking on the Ottoman Empire alone. Greece's military debacle in 1897 offered a salutary lesson.

Macedonia was their common bone of contention. The region encompassed the present-day Greek province of Macedonia, what is now the Republic of North Macedonia, and the southwestern corner of Bulgaria. Between 1903 and 1908, villagers in the southern regions were caught in the crossfire between rival pro-Greek and pro-Bulgarian paramilitaries, and the Internal Macedonian Revolutionary Organisation (IMRO), proponents of the independence of Slavophone Macedonians. The Balkan states coveted Macedonia because of its agricultural plains, which were extensive by southern Balkan standards, and its port city of Salonica (Selânik, Thessaloniki), a major commercial hub and mercantile gateway to the major routes linking central Europe and the Mediterranean. Greece, Serbia and Bulgaria based their claims on historical grounds. For the Greeks, Macedonia was Alexander the Great's homeland, while Salonica/Thessaloniki had been Byzantium's second city. For Bulgarians and Serbs Macedonia was a significant part of their respective medieval empires, and each claimed its Slavophone inhabitants as their unredeemed brethren. For the Ottomans, the Balkans had been the empire's second heartland. In Macedonia, Muslims accounted for roughly half the population, and they were loyal to the empire, but Orthodox Christians formed a clear majority in the Ottoman Balkans generally (McCarthy 1995: 135). What made Ottoman Macedonia attractive to the neighbouring

Orthodox Christian states is that it could be 'nationalised' through the expulsion of its Muslims and the assimilation of its Orthodox peoples. Local peasants, who had already been convulsed by years of sectarian violence, could be socialised as Greeks, Bulgarians or Serbs, irrespective of their mother tongue (Yosmaoğlu 2014).

Since the national elections of December 1910, which had given him an absolute parliamentary majority, Eleftherios Venizelos and his government focused on restoring the state's finances, modernising the armed forces and bringing Greece out of diplomatic isolation. Yet he shared with politicians of previous generations an obsession with the *Megali Idea*. The Italian invasion of Ottoman Libya in October 1911, and the threatened Italian invasion of Anatolia in 1912, presented the kind of international fluidity that the Balkan states were determined to exploit. Serbia and Bulgaria overlooked their conflicting territorial interests by concluding an alliance in late 1911, ostensibly aimed against Habsburg Austria. In the meantime, Venizelos used his diplomatic skills and formidable drive to reorient Greek diplomacy. His principal predecessor, Georgios Theotokis, had sought to link the kingdom's interests with Wilhelmine Germany, but this failed essentially because Germany had far greater interests in the Ottoman Empire. Mindful of the Serb–Bulgarian pact, Venizelos pushed for a security compact with Bulgaria, which was signed on 30 May. The agreement was for mutual assistance if either nation was attacked by the Ottomans, but like the Serb–Bulgarian pact, its real aim was to dismember the empire's residual European provinces. The Greek–Bulgarian pact also intentionally disregarded, at least for the moment, their rival territorial claims over Macedonia, including Salonica. The unspoken assumption was that each member of the so-called Balkan League, which included Montenegro, would grab as much territory as possible and resolve any disputes at a later point (Hall 2000: 12).

To the surprise of all observers and the Balkan generals, Ottoman defences collapsed very quickly. The war officially began on 8 October, when Montenegro launched an offensive, but it was ten days later, on 18 October, that the Balkan League coordinated a mass attack. Although they had been preparing for an assault, Ottoman armed forces in the region were overwhelmed by well-motivated Balkan armies that struck simultaneously on many fronts. Within a few weeks, the empire had lost all its territories but held on to Edirne, Iskodra/ Scutari/Shkodër in Albania, and Yanya/Ioannina. Serbian troops had captured what is now North Macedonia, and with the Montenegrins had moved into Albania. The Bulgarians had marched in the direction of the Aegean coast and east towards Constantinople, bypassing well-fortified Edirne and coming within 30 km of the capital.

The Ottoman defence strategy assumed that the Greeks would focus on seizing both Ioannina and Salonica. However, the Greeks, led by the heir to the throne, Prince Constantine, concentrated their forces on the latter objective, which meant they could progress quickly through western Macedonia, sometimes in 'blitzkrieg' fashion (Erickson 2003: 219). On 1–2 November, a short but bloody battle ensued at Yenice/Giannitsa, a largely Muslim city some 50 km west of Salonica, and by 8 November the Greeks had encircled Salonica. The Ottoman commander Hasan Tahsin Pasha realised that the situation was hopeless and signalled his willingness to surrender. The Greeks, mindful that the Bulgarians were hurriedly descending on the city from the north, offered the Ottomans generous terms: officers could keep their arms, while gendarmes and police would continue their duties. The Greeks were more worried about the Bulgarians, who, alarmed at the prospect of losing Salonica, diverted an infantry division from Manastir/Bitola, effectively leaving it to the Serbs (Clark 2012: 255). At midday on 9 November, two Greek infantry battalions marched into Salonica, greeted by thousands of flag-waving Greeks, after which there followed an orderly transference of power. Guns were cleaned and handed over, and 25,000 Ottoman soldiers and a further thousand officers were taken prisoner (Erickson 2003: 225). A much smaller force was sent to Ioannina, whose defences had been bolstered recently under German military supervision. Progress was slower on this front, owing to the rugged terrain, but with the support of irregulars and local villagers the Greeks had claimed most of Epirus by December. Ioannina, however, did not fall until 6 March 1913.

Greece's fleet provided the country's most significant contribution to the Balkan League. It successfully blocked Ottoman attempts to transport land reinforcements by sea and assumed control of the entire Aegean. It was also able to claim the remaining Ottoman-held islands, all of which were overwhelmingly inhabited by ethnic Greeks. Taking Limnos was a priority. With its deep-water harbour, it allowed the Greek navy to blockade the Dardanelles and keep Ottoman ships from entering the Aegean. Attempts by Ottoman naval vessels to break into the Aegean and end the blockade on 16 and 18 December were foiled in two very short naval battles (Hall 2000: 65). Limnos was captured within a few days of the conflict (19–22 October). Other strategically important islands like Thasos, Samothrace and Imbros were captured by the end of the month. Tenedos and Ikaria were taken in November, Lesbos in December, Chios in January, and Samos in March.

Ottoman strategy had relied on bringing reinforcements from Anatolia and on the mobilisation of Muslims in the Balkans, but these efforts were poorly coordinated, and the infrastructure needed to move units into position was lacking (Gingeras 2016: 81). As early as 10 November, the situation was perilous enough for the Ottomans to seek an armistice, but the conflict was only ended formally on 30 May 1913. The Treaty of London confirmed most of the Balkan alliance's territorial gains, but it also created an Albanian state (albeit under Ottoman sovereignty), a territory dominated by Muslims who had not sought independence, and who regarded the Sultan as their legitimate ruler. From an Ottoman perspective, the war had been the most disastrous in the empire's long history. It lost 90 per cent of its European territory and 70 per cent of its European population. The swiftness of the Ottoman defeat was unexpected, while surrendering to former subjects was especially humiliating. The defeat, the loss of territory and the massive influx of refugees provoked an existential crisis not only within the Ottoman political class but throughout the Ottoman Muslim public. As one Young Turk newspaper article put it: 'Never have the Ottomans and Muslims been subjected to such disgrace, massacres, and cruelties ... Had our religion permitted it, I would have begged for a law that would oblige all Ottomans to dress in black ... We will carry that blackness in our hearts until the day we get our revenge' (Akın 2018: 18). From a Greek perspective, the war was a spectacular triumph. Greece had acquired southern Macedonia and its capital (hereafter officially 'Thessaloniki'), the bulk of Epirus, Crete and all the islands of the northern Aegean, including Imbros, Lesbos, Limnos, Chios and Samos. The size and population of the Greek kingdom had nearly doubled, from 2.7 to 4.8 million.

Bulgaria and Serbia now shared a border with Greece, and inevitably, there were disputes over the spoils. Each had outstanding, overlapping territorial claims. Bulgaria believed it deserved Thessaloniki. A new war broke out in June 1913, this time between Bulgaria and its former allies, but Bulgaria quickly found itself fighting on more fronts, as the Ottomans and Romania invaded from the east and north, respectively. The Second Balkan War (29 June to 10 August 1913) saw Bulgaria lose most of its territorial gains. The small Bulgarian unit in Thessaloniki was easily defeated by the city's much larger Greek force, while Greek armed forces occupied Kavala and most of the Thracian Aegean coast as far as Alexandroupolis/Dedeağaç. To the north, Constantine, now the king, led the main army as far as Kresna Gorge in southwestern Bulgaria. The Ottomans reclaimed Edirne and Eastern Thrace, but Bulgaria managed to keep Western Thrace under the Treaty of Bucharest (10 August 1913).

In November, Greece and the Ottoman Empire signed the Treaty of Athens, in which the latter conceded Greek sovereignty over Macedonia, Epirus and Crete, but not the islands seized in the northern Aegean. The only islands that were still in foreign hands, the Dodecanese, were retained by Italy, which hoped to trade them for more substantial territorial concessions (Carabott 1993: 285–312).

In Greece, the scale of the victory of the First Balkan War took everyone by surprise: King George I conceded privately that he thought it was all a dream (Kreuter 2015: 761–88). The scale of the conquests suggested divine intervention, and it raised further hopes that the ultimate aim of the *Megali Idea*, Constantinople, was now within reach. Prince Constantine was touted by many as the reincarnation of the last Byzantine emperor, Constantine XI Palaiologos. It was also reported that before the campaign, the prince had been visited in his dreams by St Demetrios, the city's patron saint. Greek nationalism, which had been dominated almost entirely by imagery and stories of 1821, could now draw inspiration from the heroes and deeds of a new heroic era. Having acquired Macedonia and Thessaloniki, the country could make more of the heritage of ancient Macedon, particularly Alexander the Great, and more of the Byzantine legacy. In the squares of towns and villages, memorials were erected to commemorate the war dead. King George and his prime minister, Venizelos, became national heroes. The battleship *Averof* and the Greek infantryman (the *Evzonas*) also became national icons.

Violence and nation-building during the Balkan Wars

The First Balkan War may have been the most significant military triumph in modern Greek history, but it had a darker side that had profound effects on society. In a letter to his wife written just before the onset of the Second Balkan War, a Greek officer reported a world that had been set in flames: 'Everywhere we go, we come across desolation and misery' (Biondich 2011: 81). The same observations could have been made of any war, but the violence of this one was not limited to conventional battles. The new warfare was aided by modern technologies that killed and maimed much larger numbers of people, most especially civilians. The Balkan Wars anticipated a general crisis era that enveloped the whole of Europe not just for the period 1914–18 or 1914–22, but for the ensuing decades, when the tensions arising from rapid social, political and economic change produced horrific bursts of revolutionary and counter-revolutionary violence. Millions were killed and traumatised by social engineering schemes (genocide, ethnic cleansing) to create new political geographies and cultural demographies (Mayer 1981: 3; Doumanis 2016: 1–19; Traverso 2016). Late Ottoman Macedonia had suffered in recent years from protracted struggles between rival nationalist militias, during which peoples who had once lived side by side were encouraged or forced to choose sides. Peoples were pitted against each other in order to generate something known at the time as a 'war of races', which nowadays is called ethnic conflict (Yosmaoğlu 2014: 1). During the Macedonian struggle of the 1890s and 1900s most rival militias were sponsored by rival states, but during the Balkan Wars it was state armies that perpetrated the violence.

The Balkan Wars prefigured a prolonged era that idealised national exclusivity and fostered the persecution of minorities, ethnic cleansing and ultimately genocide. The geographical zone that was most vulnerable to this kind of dystopic engineering contained an intense mixture of populations that had coexisted peaceably for centuries. The zone stretched from the Danube to the Euphrates, and from the Adriatic to the Caucasus. Here, armies and paramilitaries were mobilised to exterminate peoples, and bureaucratic bodies were set up to remove and repatriate populations and to orchestrate forced marches (Delis 2018; Weitz 2013). These schemes required mass support. Majorities were mobilised against minorities. Neighbour was pitted against neighbour. The new warfare could be likened to a civil war in the sense that the standard rules of inter-state military conduct were suspended, and civilians, including women, children and the elderly, became targets of violence. As one historian has put it, the new warfare blurred the distinction between military and political violence: it 'drew civilians into battle, brought colonial methods of warfare to Europe, and polarised collective identities' (Vincent 2016: 390).

The Balkan Wars and the many other struggles of the twentieth century were meant to engineer the political and cultural profile of specific territories: to make Anatolia Turkish, and Macedonia Bulgarian, Serbian or Greek. Modern political violence was the most efficient manner through which the ideal of the nation, territorially grounded and culturally coherent, could be achieved. Thus, Muslim Albanian communities in Kosovo and northern Albania were attacked by Serb and Montenegrin soldiers, who were intent on clearing the area by setting fire to villages, forcing the residents to flee, or conducting massacres (Hall 2000: 137). Serb forces destroyed 80 per cent of the (mainly Albanian) Muslim villages in the Manastir and Skopje regions, and burned each city's Albanian neighbourhoods, killing Muslims indiscriminately. Bulgarian soldiers did much the same to Muslims in their newly conquered Thracian territories. Reports from the ground reveal a pattern of violence. Paramilitary units would arrive first to carry out the worst excesses, followed by regular troops that were ostensibly meant to restore order but who often allowed the crimes to continue. In Serres, Orthodox leaders who had signed a compact with Muslim counterparts to protect each other were unable to stop Bulgarian irregulars from plundering Muslim neighbourhoods and attacking Muslim women. Within hours between 150 and 200 Muslims were killed. In Alexandroupolis/Dedeağaç as many as 3,000 were slaughtered (McCarthy 1995: 147). Much more devastation took place in the countryside, where it was much more difficult to monitor the irregulars' behaviour. A British observer in Western Thrace confirmed that the irregulars were running amok:

> It may be said without exaggeration that there is hardly a Turkish village in the districts of Cavalla and Drama which has not suffered at the hands of Bulgarian Comitadjis and of the local Christian population. In many, scores of males have been massacred; in others, rape and pillage has taken place. (McCarthy 1995: 140)

Ottoman soldiers retaliated in kind when reclaiming Thracian territories during the Second Balkan War, when as many as 50,000 Orthodox Christians fled their homes, including 20,000 Greeks from Edirne (McCarthy 1995: 155). The Greek forces in Thessaloniki were disciplined, but outside the city the story was different. They burned Giannitsa, as they did the Muslim quarters of cities and towns throughout western Macedonia and around Thessaloniki. Prince Constantine personally directed the torching of Muslim villages that lay in his army's path. In retaliation, retreating Ottoman troops burned Christian villages.

During the Second Balkan War, the soldiers and irregulars of the Christian states continued to persecute civilian groups, but the question of which civilians should be persecuted was slightly more complicated. Identities in the contested regions were not stable. Language was not the most critical factor. In Macedonia and Western Thrace, what mattered was loyalty to Athens or Sofia. Slavophone groups could be 'Bulgarisers' (devotees of the autocephalous Bulgarian Orthodox Exarchate), or 'Graecomani' (Greek loyalists and followers of the Patriarchate of Constantinople). When Greek troops moved into Western Thrace in 1913, about 25,000 'Exarchists' fled from Western Thrace to Bulgaria (Gingeras 2016: 88–90). General Leonidas Paraskevopoulos recorded in his diary that the front was beset by 'Fearsome fanaticism: Everywhere Bulgarian villages are burning' (T. Kostopoulos 2007: 52). The city of Kilkis, known in Bulgarian as Kukush, and forty Bulgarian-speaking villages in central Macedonia were wholly destroyed. The Bulgarian bishop in Thessaloniki was murdered while being transferred to southern Greece, as were many of his compatriots. Similar outrages were committed by Bulgarians in their territories, around Serres, Doxato, Nigrita and Melnik/Meleniko. Some 50,000 Greeks were driven from Bulgarian-held territories, where the death toll, including the deaths resulting from the naval blockade and epidemics, totalled between 220,000 and 250,000. The total number of displaced persons ranged between 100,000 and 150,000 (Papaioannou 2012: 185).

States and media did their utmost to generate hatred for enemy peoples. Greek journalists penned racist propaganda that drew on nineteenth-century depictions of Bulgarians as Mongols or sub-humans. Posters depicted Greek soldiers gouging the eyes of Bulgarians, an allusion to the Byzantine Emperor Basil II (976–1025), the Bulgar-Slayer, who, according to legend, blinded nine out of every ten of his Bulgar prisoners (Stephenson 2003: 92). A few years earlier (1911), author Penelope Delta had published a popular children's book entitled *In the Time of the Bulgar-Slayer*, which the great poet Kostis Palamas, who had written a poem about the emperor in 1909, had praised for its fierce patriotism (*patridolatria*) (Stephenson 2003: 108, 121–2). When Prince Constantine succeeded his father, who was assassinated in Thessaloniki on 18 March 1913, he was 'acclaimed', following Byzantine tradition, as 'the Greatest of the Constantines, the Bulgar-Slayer, [Constantine] XII' (Stephenson 2003: 113).

The Greeks were also active in Albania's southern borderlands, another culturally diverse region where identities were unstable, and which Greece claimed as 'northern Epirus'. The Greek army occupied the region in December, and a provisional government was established in February 1914. Its 'army' was composed mainly of deserters and bandits, who were pitted against Albanian militias, thereby subjecting the territory to a vicious cycle of arson, hostage-taking and looting. Towns like Tepelenë/Tepeleni, Frashër/Frasari and Lefkovik/Leskovik, and many villages were burned to their foundations. Meanwhile,

Vlachs who had not declared their loyalties to Greece were also attacked. The Vlach quarter of Korytsa/Korçë, for example, was set in flames. The scale of the violence was enough to draw the attention of the British parliament (T. Kostopoulos 2018a: 80–1). Later that year, local Christian communities suffered retaliation from Muslim Albanian paramilitaries once Greek forces had been compelled to withdraw. The dialectic of violence produced a legacy of enduring enmities between Muslim Albanians and Greeks in the region.

Ethnic cleansing was not altogether new to Europe. In recent decades, Muslims had been driven out of the Russian Empire and parts of the Balkans (Bloxham 2005, 2009). Irregulars were usually involved for the plunder and were willing to drive out the civilians. The overriding aim of the violence, after all, was to support state-directed strategies to erase the Ottoman past and create national territories. The Greeks were quick to Hellenise Thessaloniki by changing street names and removing minarets. The Serbs did much the same in Üsküb/Skopje.

Meanwhile, western governments had been monitoring the horrors committed against civilians. The Carnegie Report on the Balkan Wars (1915) claimed that the conflicts had permanently displaced 890,000 people. Approximately 240,000 Muslim refugees passed through Thessaloniki alone (Carnegie Report 1915: 151; Papaioannou 2012: 132). By 1914 Greece had received some 200,000 refugees from neighbouring Balkan countries, a figure that would double by 1920 (Glavinas 2013: 331). Among the effects of the violence was to transform identities. The experience of ethnic cleansing made many more individual Muslims into Turkish nationalists, and Orthodox Christians into committed Serbs, Bulgarians or Greeks. Cultural prejudices and enmities might have existed before the wars, but the violence was meant to convince each group that they could never coexist. In Anatolia or southern Greece, those who were far away from the violence learned of the horrors from soldiers returning from the front and from propaganda published in newspapers and pamphlets, which typically focused exclusively on the barbarities committed by the enemy. A common trope in these stories was the bayonetting of pregnant women, skewering children before their mothers, gouging out people's eyes, and cutting off women's breasts (Çetinkaya 2014). The aim of publishing such stories was to attract international attention and use alleged war crimes as leverage in territorial settlements, but they were also meant to convince the masses of the barbarity and immorality of other ethnic groups. Each side denied the other's claims and exaggerated the atrocities committed by the other side. What the

Carnegie Report made clear was that all the combatants routinely committed crimes against humanity. All sides were committing rape and mass murder, were burning villages and houses of worship, and were desecrating graveyards. Moreover, the report recognised that the wanton barbarities had a well-formulated political objective: 'The main fact is that war suspended the restraints of civil life, inflamed the passions that slumber in time of peace, destroyed the national kindliness between neighbours, and set in its place the will to injure' (Hall 2000: 138).

Population exchange or war? Greece and the Ottoman Empire, 1913–1914

Violence was not the only option considered by the state. A voluntary population exchange between Greece and the Ottoman Empire was proposed in November 1913, and it remained a serious option for both sides well into 1914. Venizelos proposed an exchange as Greek communities in Eastern Thrace and along the Aegean coast were being expelled, and as war loomed between Greece and the Ottomans over Lesbos, Chios and Limnos. Ottoman government leaders were also very interested in exchanging populations, and on 1 July 1914, an agreement was reached. Muslims from Epirus and Macedonia were to be swapped for Greeks in Eastern Thrace, the Dardanelles region, and from Smyrna and its surrounding region. A mixed commission was set up to consider the details and to oversee the process (Frank 2017: 37).

However, both sides were soon distracted by the crisis that followed the assassination of Archduke Ferdinand in Sarajevo and the possibility of a major European conflict. The mixed commission continued to meet to discuss the population exchange as late as October, but by then both the Greek and Ottoman governments were under sustained pressure to intervene in the general European war. Moreover, Venizelos was convinced of an Entente victory against the Central Powers, which the Ottomans were likely to join, and that this could open the way for Greek expansion into Eastern Thrace and Anatolia, and the ultimate prize, Constantinople (Frank 2017: 37–9).

The 'third' Balkan War begins, 1914–1915

The First World War was in some senses the 'third' Balkan War, given that the first two had destabilised the international order and threatened the future of at least two Great Powers, the Austrian and Ottoman empires. The deeply troubled Great Power alliance system was inextricably tied to the Balkan area and its local issues (Clark 2012: 242). Several factors now made a larger conflict more likely. The Ottoman Empire and Bulgaria were determined to reclaim their losses at the next opportunity, while the victors had further territorial ambitions. The Greeks were aggrieved at having been denied northern Epirus. Serbia had claims on Bosnia-Herzegovina. Austria viewed Serbia's formidable record in the two Balkan wars with such alarm that it was prepared more than ever to resolve its 'Serb' problem militarily. Russia supported Serbia in order to contain Austria; its reputation as a Great Power depended on this, especially since it had recently been humiliated in the Russo-Japanese War of 1904–5. Germany had to ensure that Austria, its closest ally, was not diminished as a Great Power and pledged its support regardless of the consequences. British entanglement in Continental affairs not only threatened the involvement of the world's greatest naval power but also its global empire. For such reasons, the petty conflicts of the Balkans had global implications.

The immediate issue for Greece following the Second Balkan War's conclusion was the fate of Limnos, Lesbos and Chios. The CUP (Committee for Union and Progress), the Young Turk party's formal name, had reclaimed power in early January. Buoyed by the recapture of Edirne and Eastern Thrace, the CUP was determined to press its claims to the islands. The Balkan conflict made clear their strategic significance: the Greek navy had disabled the Ottoman navy by blocking its access to the Aegean from the Dardanelles. The Ottoman foreign minister lobbied hard to secure support, but each of the other Great Powers counselled the need for compromise. The issue nevertheless had the potential of entangling the European powers. A Greek–Turkish war could see the Dardanelles closed, a move that would threaten the Russian economy. In the meantime, the Ottoman government had ordered two dreadnoughts (battleships) to be delivered from Britain in July 1914, which could have ended Greece's domination of the Aegean. Venizelos had secured international recognition for the Greek claim to the islands but no guarantees of military support in the event of a war. All the while, tensions between Greece and the Ottomans worsened with the forced expulsions of tens of thousands of Greek Orthodox Christians from Eastern Thrace and the Aegean coast (see pp. 65–6). As summer arrived in 1914, everyone expected that a 'Third Balkan War' would erupt once the dreadnoughts were delivered (Aksakal 2008: 41–2, 47).

But it was a wholly different Balkan crisis that would precipitate a general war. The assassination of Archduke Ferdinand by a Bosnian

Serb nationalist produced a crisis of baffling complexity, yet which Europe's leaders were aware could easily lead to a catastrophic conflict that none of them wanted (Clark 2012: 555). By August, Britain, France and Russia, with their ally Serbia, were pitted in a war against Germany and Austria. Already weakened by the Balkan Wars, Serbia could not stop the Austrian and German invasion from the north. What remained of the Serbian army was forced to retreat through Montenegro and Albania, after which it found sanctuary on Corfu. Tens of thousands died on this long march. Serbia would eventually lose 1.2 million people, three quarters of its army and a third of its population. The Serb government also fled to Corfu, where it remained from February 1916 to November 1918. The island, which had 100,000 people, gave sanctuary to 160,000 Serbian soldiers and civilian refugees. So horrendous was the Serb death toll that bodies had to be buried at sea. The Ottoman Empire chose to join the Central Powers (Germany and Austria), given that neither partner coveted its Near Eastern territories, and because a Central Power victory would allow an imperial recovery by recouping lost territories. An alliance was signed with Germany on 2 August, only a day after the British had cancelled the delivery of the dreadnoughts. Still, the CUP leadership prevaricated over direct military intervention until the end of October. Bulgaria joined the Central Powers on 11 September 1915, hoping to recover from the debacle of the Second Balkan War. Both alliances courted the Bulgarians, but only the Central Powers could offer them the Serbian part of Macedonia. Once Serbia was defeated, the Central Powers created a war front that stretched from Central Europe through the Middle East, effectively isolating Russia from its Entente partners.

Caught between these two warring camps, Greeks were divided over what to do. King Constantine I insisted that Greece remain neutral. This stance had partly to do with his marriage to Kaiser Wilhelm II's sister, Sophia of Prussia, and was partly because he expected a Central Powers victory. He furthermore believed Germany would respect Greece's neutrality because that would hinder Britain and France in their endeavours to assist the Serbs and threaten the Ottomans. His stance enjoyed general support in a war-weary nation, particularly in its pre-1912 territories, hereafter referred to as 'Old Greece'. Having emerged as a hero from the Balkan Wars, Constantine was eager to further improve his political stocks and increase the monarchy's power and political influence by keeping Greece out of the war. He also hoped to reclaim ground lost to Venizelos' Liberal Party since 1910. Whereas his father had sanctioned Venizelos' rather busy foreign policy agenda,

Constantine had resented his prime minister's interventions in military matters. Venizelos believed that it was essential to join the Entente to protect the country's territorial gains and secure more spoils. His base included the urban classes, the minorities in Greece's newly acquired territories, the diaspora and Greeks living in the Ottoman Empire. If Greece aspired to become a major power in the eastern Mediterranean, it could not abstain from the conflict. The decision, however, had to be justified on security grounds. Thus, Serbia's collapse meant Bulgaria could threaten Greece's northern territories. The Ottomans had made it clear that they were bent on reclaiming lost territories and had been busy expelling Greek Orthodox Christians from the Aegean coast.

The Entente had two objectives in the eastern Mediterranean theatre. The first was to break through the cordon that separated Russia from its allies, which required penetrating the Dardanelles and the Bosporus. Such a move would mean the seizure of Constantinople and possibly knock the Ottomans out of the war. To prosecute the grand scheme, the Entente had to overcome the defences stationed along the Dardanelles. Disregarding Greek neutrality, the Entente simply set up headquarters on Limnos, specifically in Mudros Bay. However, the ensuing Gallipoli Campaign (April 1915–January 1916) would fail to make an impression on Ottoman defences.

The second aim was to open a new front in Macedonia to assist the Serbs. In the autumn of 1915, British and French troops disembarked in Thessaloniki. Venizelos had greenlighted this action while the king was absent and before he resigned as prime minister. The encampment of 300,000 troops, double the city's population, renewed its Babel-like profile: the allied army featured Senegalese, Vietnamese, Indians, Canadians, Australians and New Zealanders, as well as other peoples from Africa and Asia. Camps were set up on the city outskirts, often in marshland. For most of the war, the encamped spent their time digging trenches and on other non-combat activities: they were known disparagingly as the 'gardeners of Salonica'. Although the creation of this front came too late for Serbia, Thessaloniki was where the remnants of the Serbian army regrouped and were stationed for the duration of the war. This new Balkan front stretched from the Adriatic to the Strymon River, but aside from artillery bombardments that produced craters along the border, there was little fighting. Constantine resented the presence of Entente troops in his kingdom and refused permission for the Serb government to relocate from Corfu to Thessaloniki. He even threatened to allow the Bulgarians to occupy eastern Macedonia, which he did in May 1916. Once that happened, the people of Serres,

Drama, Kavala and their surrounding regions were in Bulgarian hands, and were again exposed to the same levels of persecution as in the previous conflict.

The National Schism, 1914–1916

In Greece, the 1914–18 war is not remembered in the same way it is in Britain, France and North America, where memorialisation and historical interest has focused on the devastating impact of the trenches and the ravages of modern warfare. Greek soldiers saw comparatively little military action in these years, but it was a time when Greek politics and society became embroiled in a domestic crisis so deep that conditions seemed akin to a civil war. The core issue was intervention: whether Greece should join the Allies to gain more territories or remain neutral and spare society another war. (Joining the Central Powers was not a serious consideration given the country's geographical vulnerability to British and French sea power, and the fact that the Ottomans were members of the same alliance.) The issue produced a National Schism (*Ethnikos Dichasmos*), a crisis that set the tone for party politics for generations, and which produced a culture of mutual intolerance and hyper-partisanship that abated only with the Axis occupation of 1941–4.

The question is why the intervention issue should have been so polarising. Why were the king and his prime minister prepared to split the country? Why did their partisan supporters persecute, exile and even kill each other? The first and most obvious factor was the deteriorating relationship between Constantine and Venizelos. Each was prepared to violate the constitution to prevail in this heady political duel. Between mid-1914 and early 1917, each played a game of brinksmanship that escalated tensions. A deeper explanation relates to international conditions, the kind of war being fought in Europe and the Middle East, and its reverberations in societies that had already been transformed by mass politics. Since the middle of the previous century there had been growing mass participation and mass interest in national and international politics. But what might be the effects on mass society of a prolonged, demanding and devastating war? Total war involved the mobilisation of all available resources of society, while the high death tolls and tremendous hardships imposed on civilians tested the political and institutional foundations of states, exposing or exacerbating existing tensions and divisions, and creating new ones. By 1917 Russia had succumbed to revolution, and more insurrections were expected in 1918. Although not directly involved for most of the 1914–18 war, Greek society nevertheless experienced acute hardships, including famine, to the extent that it too was politicised.

A third and related factor was general awareness that this war had the unique capacity to destroy and remake states: it held the promise of great glory but also of catastrophe. It was widely expected that the political geography of much of Europe and the Mediterranean would be redrawn, and that the victorious powers would expand at the expense of the vanquished. Greece would be either a winner or a loser in the contest. In this great game, neutrality was not an option. Constantine was subjected to great pressure from his brother-in-law, Kaiser Wilhelm, to declare for the Central Powers. Britain and France were contemptuous of Greek neutrality policy, and ultimately coerced the nation into joining the alliance in 1917. These factors are crucial for understanding the brinksmanship between Constantine and Venizelos. They reflected Greece's acute international vulnerability, but for Venizelos and his followers the war presented unique imperial opportunities. Like many lesser powers, it had grand ambitions but could not achieve them without a powerful patron such as Britain. Since the mid-nineteenth century, there had been a solid consensus within the Greek political class regarding the *Megali Idea* (Skopetea 1988). However, any step towards its fulfilment had to harmonise with the interests of more powerful states, which had their own imperial aspirations vis-à-vis the Ottoman Empire. Britain and France, followed later by Italy, had already dismembered large parts of the empire, while Germany and Austria had secured Balkan territorial concessions. Meanwhile Germany was investing heavily in the Arab provinces. In these fluid international conditions, Greece could gain or lose territories.

Ordinary Greeks were politicised by the National Schism, becoming royalists (*vasilikoi*) or Venizelists (*venizelikoi*). Many had witnessed or knew about the mass killings and expulsions in the Balkans and Anatolia, and peoples in contested territories and borderlands were acutely aware of how easily their fate could be affected by the decisions of statesmen. Communities on Lesbos or Chios, or near the Bulgarian border, knew that their homelands could be handed over to a hostile power. Ordinary Greeks became royalists or Venizelists because they felt insecure, and that anxiety fed into the Schism. Much of Old Greece supported Constantine because they were war-weary and no longer interested in making sacrifices for the sake of a greater Greece. The royalist slogan at the time was for 'a small but honourable Greece'. Much of 'New' Greece (the newly acquired territories) had more direct experience of Ottoman rule, were vulnerable to Ottoman (and Bulgarian) expansion and supported a war that might end it.

A fourth factor that explains the animosities of the National Schism was the broader culture of violence. The conflict was waged by men who had been 'barbarised' during the Balkan Wars, who had dehumanised the enemy, burned their homes, raped their women and looted their belongings. Studies of the Holocaust and more recent conflicts have shown how ordinary men could be made to perform the most ruthless and pitiless violence on innocent people (Browning 2001; Kassimeris 2006). This culture of violence was adjusted for a new war against an internal enemy, and it undoubtedly influenced partisan activists who had no direct war experiences. The dehumanisation of the Other, as reflected in the caricatures of Bulgarians in Balkan War propaganda, and in the writings of the partisan press, used extremist language and imagery to vilify the opposing party. The anti-Venizelist press often referred to their nemesis as Satan (Bohotis 1999: 92). Finally, Greek society was radicalised by the presence of foreign powers, principally France and Britain. They violated the nation's sovereignty and sometimes committed violent acts that caused great hardship and did much to increase popular support for Constantine and the royalists.

In January 1915, the Entente offered eastern Macedonia (the districts of Serres, Drama and Kavala) to Bulgaria and to compensate Greece with territories in Asia Minor. Venizelos was attracted to this bargain, and he also understood his country's vulnerability to British and French naval power. Under the constitution only the king could declare war. With the support of General Ioannis Metaxas and other German-trained General Staff members, Constantine rejected the Entente's offer, and on 25 February Venizelos resigned. He was replaced by Dimitrios Gounaris, but Venizelos was returned in the ensuing June election, which was considered a referendum on the intervention question. By that point, the Entente's campaign on the Gallipoli Peninsula was faltering, the Serbs were in a perilous military position, and there was concern for the plight of Greeks living in the Ottoman Empire. Even though Venizelos had won an emphatic victory, the king insisted Greece should remain neutral. In the meantime, Bulgaria had joined the Central Powers, which placed Thessaloniki and Greece's northern territories under threat. The Venizelist-dominated parliament, which assumed power on 10 August – the delay had to do with the king being ill – voted for war against Bulgaria, but the king dismissed Venizelos and installed a new pro-monarchy government under Alexandros Zaïmis. The Venizelists refused to contest the follow-up election of 25 October, and this allowed the royalists to win in a landslide.

But neither the new prime minister, Stefanos Skouloudis, nor his king could do much to stop the Entente from dragging Greece into the war. On 3 October the Entente had sent a modest force to Thessaloniki that was meant to support the Gallipoli campaign. Publicly, Venizelos protested this national sovereignty violation, but he privately communicated his approval to the Allies. Thessaloniki was now vulnerable to a German, Austrian and Bulgarian push southwards. Christmas 1915 then saw the arrival of troops that had been withdrawn from Gallipoli. Their French commander, General Maurice Sarrail, took control of the city and in June 1916 he proclaimed martial law, putting aside any pretence to respecting Greek sovereignty (Mazower 2004: 308).

Many people in Greece's new borderlands rallied behind the Venizelists because of the king's seeming indifference to their security concerns. Thus, in May 1916, when Germany demanded possession of Greece's Fort Rupel, near the border with Bulgaria, to secure its frontline, Constantine obliged. Loyal officers in the field facilitated its handover to the Bulgarians, while a whole regiment (7,000 men) was also delivered to German authorities and deported to Görlitz, near Dresden. Many officers reacted by rallying behind the Venizelist cause. The king had effectively conceded eastern Macedonia, including Kavala, Serres and Drama, to the Bulgarians, who evicted 42,000 Greeks. Of this group, 12,000 perished after having been squeezed into freight wagons, often between fifty and seventy per wagon, and forced to endure a suffocating week-long journey into exile. Survivors were then worked for twelve hours per day, building roads, laying railway tracks and constructing fortifications (Papaioannou 2012: 747; Koliopoulos and Veremis 2010: 80).

The National Schism II, 1916–1917

In the meantime, Venizelist officers in Thessaloniki formed a secret organisation: the National Defence (*Ethniki Amina*). In September 1916 it staged a revolt and invited Venizelos to form a government. With Greek and Allied naval backing, Venizelos arrived in Thessaloniki for this purpose. In the meantime, the Entente increased pressure on the king and his government in Athens. On 1 December, a French marine force disembarked at Piraeus and demanded the handover of Greek destroyers, but it met stiff resistance from troops and veterans loyal to the monarchy. Following two days of street battles that saw some thirty Greeks and sixty Frenchmen killed, the French were forced to withdraw (Abbott 1922: 160). Anti-Venizelist sentiment was then given full expression in a riot remembered as *ta Noemvriana* ('the November events'), as mobs in Athens went on a rampage against prominent Venizelists. In December the Archbishop of Athens proclaimed the excommunication of Venizelos before a large crowd in the Pedion tou Areos, one of the city's largest parks (Bohotis 1999: 85). The Allies then blockaded those parts of Greece under the king's authority, which led to severe food shortages. Finally, on 14 June, after the Allies had delivered an ultimatum threatening to attack Athens and abolish the monarchy, Constantine left the country.

Venizelos and his government returned to Athens on 25 June 1917 under a French military escort, which then took up strategic positions in the city. The new regime conducted a thoroughgoing purge of the judiciary, government administration and the Church, while it arraigned members of the previous cabinet for high treason for the Fort Rupel affair. Venizelos reinstated the parliament that had been elected in March 1915, the so-called 'Lazarus parliament', and had Constantine replaced by his second son, Alexander, whose older brother, George, had followed his father into exile. The presence of foreign troops in much of the country bred more hostility for Venizelos. Although French forces were eventually replaced in Athens by Cretans, locals continued to feel that they were under occupation. One hostile foreign observer would describe the restored Venizelos administration as a dictatorship (Abbott 1922: 207–9).

However, foreign occupation, like colonialism, could bring some tangible benefits. In the north, where Entente forces had assumed control of the country's infrastructure, improvements were made to the railway system, the ports, postal services, passport offices, and telephone and telegraph systems. The policy of *mission civilisatrice* found expression in a little-known work entitled *L'oeuvre civilisatrice de l'armée française en Macédoine* (*The Civilising Work of the French Army in Macedonia*) (Thomas 1918). After claiming that Macedonia was even more mysterious than Africa, the author reports that French troops built roads, provided clean drinking water, combated malaria and tried to increase agricultural output. Among the outcomes of this 'civilising mission' were numerous archaeological, anthropological and geological studies, as well as accurate modern maps (Mikanowski 2012: 103–21). Yet, as in their colonial dominions, French authorities used coercive methods to carry out their projects and to enforce such unpopular measures as conscription and food requisitioning. Senegalese troops entered storerooms and used their bayonets to prod and poke sacks, looking for anyone avoiding the call to arms. Conscription provoked violence in some regions, such as Halkidiki. These kinds of actions drove many Greeks into the royalist camp.

All the while, Greek political culture had been altered irrevocably. To defeat opponents, political elites on both sides of the aisle ignored well-established conventions and violated the constitution. Royalists and Venizelists forced each other into exile. When in power, royalists either cancelled or radically amended the Venizelist reforms of 1911–14. The Liberals, in turn, adopted illiberal means to reverse the measures of their opponents. A disturbing feature of this new vendetta politics was the violence, which persisted into the post-war years. In revenge for an attempted assassination of Venizelos on 30 July 1920 during a visit to Paris, Ion Dragoumis, one of his political opponents, was executed by Venizelists the following day. Everywhere in Europe, the war had polarised societies and political cultures, with extremists seeking revolutionary social change and vying for power. Millions of men who survived the fighting became politicised by the experience and by the depressed economic conditions on returning home. Armed and embittered, veterans became an energising force in post-war politics. Many joined radical movements on both the right and the left (Gerwarth 2016). If Italy produced the *fascisti* and Germany the *Freikorps*, Greece had the 'Epistratoi', armed groups who imitated the Italians and became 'Greek fascists' (Mavrogordatos 1996). Later, veterans of the Asia Minor campaign would create another organisation known as the 'Palaioi Polemistes' ('Old Warriors'), which would link up with the Greek communist party (Giourgou 2014). The mere existence of these groups reflected a polarised sociopolitical order that had developed through the war years.

Germs: the greatest killer

Humans were not exclusively responsible for the horrendous casualty figures of the 'long First World War'. Indeed, the greatest killers during the Balkan Wars were not machine guns, artillery or bayonets, but epidemics. Of the 100,000–150,000 soldiers killed, about 75 per cent were killed by disease. Cholera, typhoid, smallpox and dysentery wreaked havoc on both sides of the front, as well as among civilians behind the lines. Disease accounted for 60 per cent of all Bulgarian deaths. Soldiers were terrorised more by the enemy they could not see. Cholera had spread along the battlefront in Thrace, affecting Greek and Bulgarian troops, as well as refugees encamped at relocation stations, where they drank water from the contaminated cisterns (Macar 2013: 272–97). Between 1915 and 1918, many more soldiers died on the Macedonian front from epidemics than had been killed by enemy fire. Typhus swept through the Serbian military camp in 1915, while dysentery affected the combatants at Gallipoli, from where it spread to Thessaloniki. Finally, in 1918 American troops brought with them the Spanish Influenza, which swept through camps and civilian populations.

Compared to the primitive conditions endured during the Balkan Wars, frontline soldiers of the 1914–18 war at least had access to modern health facilities nearby (Limnos, Thessaloniki and Corfu). Even so, the absence of roads in the mountains north of Thessaloniki made transporting the wounded to the city's hospitals extremely difficult. Many died on the back of mules or in horse-drawn ambulances. Tent hospitals were overcrowded, with patients often strewn across floors, some on hay and straw, while the diseased and wounded were crowded together. By late 1917, British and French hospitals with 50,000 beds were being built, and the medical services improved with the help of voluntary women's organisations. The best known was the Scottish Women's Hospitals (SWH), which provided female doctors and nurses for military service (Wakefield and Moody 2011).

The chief legacy of the war and the campaign against the invisible enemy was the Greek healthcare system. A ministry of health was established in Greece for the first time in 1917. Whereas health issues had only attracted government attention during a crisis (famine, plague outbreak), or during a refugee influx, health hereafter became a standard issue of state policy. This innovation demonstrated how the war radically reshaped the nature of modern governance.

The problem of victory, 1918–1919

The Salonica Front barely rates a mention in histories of the First World War. Opposing forces were of relatively equal strength, yet both sides were reluctant to waste resources. The Germans did not press the issue, fearing a conflict between Austria and Bulgaria over Thessaloniki. The Entente meanwhile found it challenging to supply its frontline. Thessaloniki's port facilities and the region's transport infrastructure were underdeveloped, while most supplies had to come by sea through submarine-infested waters (Stevenson 2011: 143). By mid-1918, however, the stalemate had ended. By then, Greece had managed to recruit as many as 150,000 men, and Serb forces had been reinforced, while on the other side of the trenches German troops had to be redeployed to other fronts closer to home.

Meanwhile, none of the combatant nations could continue the war without a well-functioning home front. Owing to acute food shortages, morale on the Bulgarian home front plummeted, and by mid-1918 the country seemed ripe for revolution. When the Allies attacked on 15 September, Bulgarian defences collapsed within a few days. Serb and French forces broke through in northern Macedonia, as did Greek and British forces to the south. German and Habsburg reinforcements were despatched on 27 September, but it was all too late. By this point, the die was cast. The Bulgarian army was suffering mass desertions, and the jailed political leader and chief voice against Bulgaria's participation in the war, Aleksandar Stamboliyski, was released from prison to broker a peace deal.

On 30 September, Bulgaria was the first of the Central Powers to capitulate. The Ottoman Empire was now cut off from the other Central Powers. Throughout the war, it had been defending its territories on many fronts (the Dardanelles, the Caucasus, Iraq, the Hejaz and the Levant), fielding 2.6 million men, which was 15 per cent of the empire's population. It had to deal with 32 per cent of Britain's forces (including those of the Dominions), 20 per cent of Russian troops, and sizeable numbers of French and Italian troops. In the meantime, the domestic economy had collapsed, and its finances were shattered. An estimated 1 million men had deserted, 200,000 had been taken prisoner, 325,000 killed, and 400,000 wounded. Only 323,000 men were still at their posts when the empire formally capitulated on the British battleship HMS *Agamemnon* in Mudros Bay, Limnos, on 30 October (Hanioğlu 2008: 180–1). For people in Constantinople, the reality of the Ottoman defeat was made clear by the arrival of Allied ships, among them the *Averof*, which anchored off the Golden Horn on 13 December. Allied troops paraded through the city and were greeted enthusiastically by Christians, particularly Greeks waving the Greek national flag. Feeling anxious about their future, the city's Muslims watched the jubilance of their interconfessional neighbours in dismay (Gingeras 2016: 249).

Greece emerged on the winning side and expected to be rewarded. At the Paris Peace Conference, which began on 18 January 1919, Venizelos focused on attaining territories, specifically northern Epirus and Thrace, and as much of Asia Minor as the conference would allow. He did not press for Constantinople, knowing there would be no support for such a proposition. Asia Minor was tricky. Venizelos had to contend with President Woodrow Wilson's insistence that the peace should promote national self-determination and end imperialism, and that settlements should not set the stage for conflict in the future. Asia Minor had an overwhelming Muslim majority, and none of the areas with ample Greek numbers could be easily defended. When asked for comment, a British General Staff member warned that a Greek occupation in the region 'will create a source of continual unrest possibly culminating in an organised attempt by the Turks to reconquer this territory' (MacMillan 2001: 364). Venizelos countered by providing inflated Greek population figures, and by appealing to a mostly philhellenic and anti-Turkish audience. To them he applied his considerable energy, charm and powers of persuasion. Harold Nicolson was moved to describe him as one of the two 'really great men in Europe' (the other being Lenin), while a US diplomat referred to him as 'the only Balkan statesman who has shown the ability to exercise moderation, farsightedness and sincerity' (Prott 2016: 98–9). President Wilson was moved to say he was the most influential spokesman of the small states (Frank 2017: 191). Venizelos' personal impact mattered, for it compensated for Greece's limited power and modest contribution to the victory. Venizelos also benefited greatly from his friendship with the British prime minister David Lloyd George. Wilson and the French premier Georges Clemenceau were opposed, but they reconsidered when Italian troops occupied Anatolia without authorisation. The settlement of Anatolia suddenly became a colonial matter. Using the excuse of unrest in the region, on 10 May Wilson, Clemenceau and Lloyd George gave Venizelos the green light to despatch Greek troops to occupy Smyrna and the surrounding region. Although sent there ostensibly by the Allies to keep the peace, the Greeks were intent on keeping Smyrna and the wider region: Lloyd George privately promised to Venizelos that the Greeks could annex it. Aware that the decision would destabilise Anatolia, many at the conference tried without success to rescind the decision (Prott 2016: 106–9).

Venizelos' broader strategy to make Greece into a regional power entailed commitments for which the nation was ill equipped and ill prepared. Despite its limited participation in the conflict, Greece emerged from the 1914–18 war with an economy devastated by labour shortages and severe trade disruptions in industries like mining and currant production. Whereas the national finances were sound in 1914, public debt had skyrocketed once Greece entered the war, and prices had risen by 400 per cent (Mazower 1991: 55–63). The First World War proved to be twice as expensive as the two Balkan Wars combined. Moreover, society had been polarised by the Schism and the Venizelos regime's oppressive food requisitioning and conscription policies. Venizelos could take great credit for bringing the nation much closer to realising its *Megali Idea* dream, for which there was bipartisan support, but an increasing proportion of the country, particularly in 'Old Greece', vehemently resented the burdens that came with it. However, the venture's ultimate price would be paid by the civilians of Asia Minor and Eastern Thrace. The fate of Greek Orthodox and Muslim communities in these regions will be detailed in Chapter 3.

Smyrna 1919

On the morning of 15 May 1919, around 7.30 a.m. three regiments of the Greek 1st Division, some 13,000 men, disembarked at the Smyrna Quay. Much of the Greek community, perhaps two thirds of it (Stamatopoulos 2011: 57), lined the Cordon, the quayside thoroughfare, to greet and hail them as liberators. To the crowd's delight, disembarking soldiers danced to mark their arrival. Smyrniots greeted the soldiers with great fanfare, waving Greek flags, throwing flowers and streamers, shouting 'Zito o Venizelos', 'Zito i Ellas' ('Long live Venizelos', 'long live Greece'). The Metropolitan Bishop of Smyrna, Chrysostomos, blessed the Greek regiments.

A day earlier, Allied forces (Greeks included) had arrived to secure the city's fortifications, but an Inter-Allied Commission of Inquiry noted that the preparations for the transfer of power had otherwise proved to be wholly inadequate. The Ottoman governor, Izzet Bey, and the city's large Muslim population, were shocked when told that the Allied occupation force would be Greek. The Ottoman authorities were ill prepared for the transfer of power, and the Greek commanders were also unsure how to occupy a city heaving with inter-communal tension. Ottoman officers were of minor rank and lacked the authority to impose discipline. As the parade of Greek soldiers passed the Ottoman barracks, a shot was fired. Who fired first would become a matter of dispute, but it started a skirmish that incited a riot. Greek soldiers rained bullets on the barracks, and the Ottomans responded in kind until they ran out of ammunition. The Ottoman soldiers who surrendered were then marched off to the Greek ship *Patris*, where they were held, but not before several of them were shot or bayoneted along the way. Meanwhile, local Greeks attacked Turkish residences and looted homes and shops. Greek soldiers were supposed to form a barrier between the Greek and Turkish quarters, but independent

Figure 2.1 *Greek soldiers in Asia Minor.* © ERT

witnesses and a detailed Allied report (*Documents of the Inter-Allied Commission of Inquiry*, 1919)[1] confirmed that Greek troops had participated in the violence and destruction (Prott 2016: 185–6).

As many as three to four hundred Turks were killed following the Greek landing in Smyrna. Outside the city, as Greek forces moved to 'pacify' the zone allotted for occupation, the violence spread (Figure 2.1). Greek soldiers were met by Muslim irregulars and Ottoman troops who had not yet been demobilised. A fierce battle was fought at Aydın, in which Christian and Muslim residents took part, and which destroyed much of the city. Greek troops spread into the Menderes River area and along the coast, from the areas around Kuşadası, opposite Samos, to as far north as Ayvalık/Aïvali, opposite Lesbos. The Inter-Allied Commission of Inquiry found that Greek troops, often with the assistance of Greek irregulars, attacked and robbed Muslim communities. A long list of incidents and casualties was provided in the extensive report and was used by critics to question Greece's suitability for its assigned peacekeeping role (T. Kostopoulos 2007: 99).

These incidents set the tone for the next three years. Etched in Turkish minds and memory was the sight of the city's Orthodox

Christians celebrating the Greek landing and the violence perpetrated against Muslims. In future Turkish commemorations, much would be made of Romioi/Rum betrayal. According to the Turkish nationalist view, they showed their true colours as enemies of the fatherland, who therefore deserved the ill treatment they received (Morack 2017a: 71–89). Yet, as the Romioi of western Anatolia had been subjected to horrific persecution since 1913, they came to see the Greeks as liberators. For Muslims, the persecution of Greeks was in retaliation for the horrors suffered by Balkan Muslims during the First Balkan War. That conflict started a dialectic of intolerance that gave the impression to many observers that the violence was caused by inter-communal or sectarian tensions (Milton 2008: 147). In fact, as many historians have shown, sectarianism had shallow roots in the eastern Mediterranean. The political violence that accompanied nationalism, which polarised communities throughout the region, was a relatively recent phenomenon (Robson 2020: 2; Doumanis 2013a; Yosmaoğlu 2014). Civilian involvement in the violence was extensive throughout the Greek–Turkish War of 1919–22 (Gingeras 2009), but most of it was perpetrated by soldiers, paramilitaries and bandits.

The Greek occupation of Smyrna and the violence that followed did much more to stir Ottoman Muslim passions than the Allied occupation of Constantinople. Protests took place in Anatolian cities, and numerous citizen organisations were formed. After all, Anatolia was the Empire's Muslim and Turkish-speaking heartland, and following the loss of nearly all European and Arab provinces this region and Eastern Thrace was all that was left. Anatolia's partition by the victorious Allies was unthinkable, particularly if much of it was also to be handed to Armenians and Greeks. Muslims feared they would be driven out of Greek- and Armenian-ruled territories. As Mustafa Kemal, the victor at Gallipoli and later founder of the Republic of Turkey, was moved to say, it took the Greek landings at Smyrna to awaken the Turks from their slumber. Having lost the empire, Anatolia's Muslims now saw a need to fight for their homeland.

The other significant legacy of the 1919 Smyrna crisis was that it diminished the general philhellenic spirit that prevailed at the Paris conference. The violence detailed in the Commission of Inquiry report made delegates less amenable to Greek interests and removed any thought of handing over Constantinople (Goldstein 1989: 353). But Greece still had the support of key figures, particularly Lloyd George. His government needed a close ally to support its strategic aims in the region, particularly in the Straits, and to enforce the treaty being drawn up by the Allies. Lloyd George therefore persisted in supporting Greek interests in Anatolia (Goldstein 1989: 339–56).

The war in Asia Minor I, 1919–1920

There was never any doubt as to Greek intentions regarding the Smyrna 'zone'. The plan was to annex the city and as much of Asia Minor as the Allies would permit. Both sides of the National Schism supported the scheme. Venizelos' political adversaries, Gounaris and Metaxas, both living in exile in Sardinia when they first heard of the Greek landing at Smyrna, conceded it was a national triumph. Metaxas mused that it might augur the end of political division (Llewellyn Smith 1998: 153). To make the Smyrna zone 'Greek', however, would require demographic engineering. Muslims within the zone were deserting their homes and farmlands, raising suspicions that 'ethnic cleansing' was afoot (Gingeras 2016: 285). As the Ottoman government in Constantinople waited nervously for the Allies to produce a treaty, which was widely expected to be punitive, officers in the field took matters into their own hands and began organising a response to the Greek invasion. In July and September 1919, Turkish nationalist congresses were held to organise resistance to the Greek occupation and the Allied partition of Anatolia. In defiance of the Ottoman government, which heeded the dictates of the Allies and did nothing to stop the Greek occupation, the congress created a national movement and a national army (Gingeras 2016: 270).

The Greek political elite harboured unrealistic irredentist ambitions in Anatolia, but these were matched by Allied expectations that Anatolia could be partitioned with minimum resources. Expert opinion at the Paris conferences might have predicted the Greek occupation would spark widespread unrest and concerted resistance, yet the brutal peace that the Allies sought to impose had to be somehow enforced. It gradually became apparent to the Turkish nationalist leadership that the Allies were reluctant to commit the military resources needed to impose their will. Allied occupation forces were thinly spread, and much of Anatolia was dominated by local warlords, bandits and demobilised Ottoman soldiers, many of whom were prepared to defend the homeland. The victorious Great Powers were war-weary and suffering economic hardship. The view that Britain and France lacked the will to deal with a Turkish national resistance was put by leading figures of the movement, including Mustafa Kemal, at a congress at Erzurum in July–August 1919, a year before the Allies finally produced a treaty.

It is certainly the case that Britain and France were each more committed to dealing with unrest in places like Ireland and Syria, hence the responsibility for defeating the Nationalists fell largely on Greek and Armenian shoulders (Margaritis 1999: 179). By the end of 1919, British advisers were warning that troop numbers stationed near the imperial capital and the Dardanelles could not enforce a treaty (Llewellyn Smith 1998: 123). The British initially had high hopes in a Venizelos-led Greece serving as its proxy in the region. Lloyd George believed Greece was the 'coming power in the Mediterranean' that would fill the vacuum left by the defeated Ottomans. Venizelos was happy to have Greece play the role assigned to it. To justify the expansion of the Greek occupation zone, he exaggerated the scale of Muslim resistance and proposed that Greek troops should crush it before it was too late. As the Allies' chief enforcer in the region, Greece should expect more territorial compensation. The expansion of the Nationalist movement merely strengthened Venizelos' argument. However, Britain also made it clear that it would not to be drawn into a Greek–Turkish war, for which (as it proved) there was no support domestically and almost none among the otherwise loyal Dominions. Lloyd George and Winston Churchill, then Secretary of State for War, had disabused Venizelos of any idea that the Greeks might be actively supported by British forces (Llewellyn Smith 1998: 124 and 125 n.).

Among the Allies, the urge to punish the Central Powers was much stronger than any aspirations for securing a lasting peace or promoting the principle of national self-determination. France was especially outraged by the Turkish Nationalist attack on French and Armenian forces in Maraş, Cilicia (southern Anatolia) in early 1920 (21 January–10 February). Defeat forced French troops to abandon the city and retreat to Syria. Further attacks forced the French to abandon more cities, such as Urfa, and all the while civilians on both sides, particularly Armenians, were being killed in significant numbers (Gingeras 2016: 280). On the evening of 15 March, the Allies imposed martial law on Constantinople and arrested Ottoman politicians and officers. Plans were drawn up to partition the empire into 'zones of influence'. An independent Armenia was also established. A conference at San Remo in Italy on 19–26 April produced the framework for settling the Ottoman Empire, which would be signed on 10 August 1920 in Sèvres, between Paris and Versailles. The Treaty of Sèvres included Anatolia's partition into Italian, French and Greek occupation zones, and provided for Armenian and Kurdish homelands. All that was conceded to the Ottomans was Anatolia's northern rump, including Ankara.

Although technically under Ottoman sovereignty, the Greek zone, the area already occupied, would be subjected to a plebiscite in five years to determine if it could be ceded to Greece. Plans were already afoot to change the ethnic balance in favour of the Greeks. Meanwhile, most of Eastern Thrace was ceded to Greece, including the once great Ottoman city of Edirne, which was to revert to its original Greek name, Adrianoupolis.

The Allies controlled the capital and the Straits Zone, namely the territories that lined the Dardanelles, the Sea of Marmara and the Bosporus. By the end of spring, the Nationalists were ready to begin operations in this mainly British-held zone. On 14 June 1920, the Nationalists attacked the British at İzmit. By the end of the month, Venizelos was permitted to advance Greek troops beyond the Smyrna zone, occupying much of northwestern Anatolia, including Bursa, the first Ottoman capital, on 8 July. Within two weeks, Greece had occupied a significantly larger zone that covered much of the area south of the Sea of Marmara, which also happened to be home to numerous Greek communities, particularly along the shoreline. Meanwhile, Eastern Thrace was claimed with relatively little resistance in July.

Venizelos expected the rise of local resistance would prompt the Allies to permit the Greeks to venture deeper into Anatolia and destroy the Nationalist movement. British Field Marshal Sir Henry Wilson suggested they could be called on to occupy much more territory, including the Black Sea coast and Constantinople itself (Llewellyn Smith 1998: 127). Venizelos' game was undoubtedly risky but not delusional. The Nationalist movement did not enjoy the wholehearted support of Anatolia's Muslims, many of whom remained loyal to the Sultan. Some ethnic groups, such as the Circassians and Kurds, were more opposed to the Nationalists than to foreign powers, while many peasant communities deeply resented Nationalist requisitioning of scarce food supplies. Meanwhile, the Greeks were relatively well armed and did enjoy some naval and air support. Nationalist forces could not withstand the Greek push into Thrace or prevent the capture of Bursa, and they needed to time to develop the capability for an offensive strategy (Gingeras 2016: 285–7; Gingeras 2009).

The Nationalist triumph was not inevitable, yet it developed into a much more formidable movement than many thought possible at the time. It eventually succeeded in rallying most Muslim ethnic groups and sects. The Greeks underestimated the movement's capacity to build a strong state organisation, to develop a well-trained army, and to rally both men and women, beys, *hojas*, bazaar proprietors, teachers and peasants behind the patriotic cause. The Nationalists set up a government in Ankara which succeeded in challenging the Sultan's legitimacy, particularly after his regime had signed the Treaty of Sèvres. Before they took on the better armed and organised Greek forces in the west of Anatolia, they focused first on less formidable Armenian and French forces in the east. Its leaders also initiated a diplomatic drive to secure military hardware abroad and drive cracks into the enemy alliance.

The war in Asia Minor II, 1920–1922

Sèvres was a dead letter before the enfeebled Ottoman government had signed it. Power and authority had already shifted from Constantinople to Ankara. The treaty, which partitioned most of Anatolia among the victorious powers, was an imperialistic document that reflected power relations in November 1918, not in August 1920 (Helmreich 1974: 332). The Arabic-speaking provinces (Iraq, the Levant, the Hejaz) were lost to the empire, but the remnants of the Ottoman army were prepared to fight on to keep Anatolia. The Allies had not only waited too long to impose peace, but seemed unprepared for the inevitable resistance to its implementation. Lloyd George hoped Venizelos might deal with it, and Venizelos exploited these hopes. Yet none of the Great Powers were prepared to support Greece and commit to another war. Indeed, soon after the signing of the Treaty of Sèvres the Allies were looking for ways to revise it.

Greece itself was weakened by the National Schism, which was reactivated by the prospect of elections scheduled for October 1920, the first since 1915. A reckoning was widely anticipated, but the bizarre death of the reigning monarch raised the stakes. On 2 October 1920, while walking his dog in the grounds of the royal palace, King Alexander was bitten by a monkey and died of septicaemia a few days later. His death triggered a succession crisis, while Venizelos lost the national elections. On 4 November, the Liberals secured about half the popular vote but only won 118 seats in a 369-seat chamber. Even Venizelos lost his seat. A wide-ranging purge ensued, and the leader went into self-imposed exile.

A coalition of royalist parties led by Dimitrios Gounaris formed a government and made two fateful decisions. The first was the restoration of Constantine, who was still a hero to much of the country, but whom the Allies considered a wartime German ally. The move gave the Allies an excuse to renege on commitments to Greece, including promised financial aid. The royalists were nevertheless intent on having their man, and in a rigged plebiscite held in December, the tally showed that just under 1 million voted for the king's return, and approximately 10,000 voted against. The second was the decision to continue the war and hopefully deliver a knockout blow. Sceptical markets had been refusing loans to Greece whilst Venizelos was at the helm, but when faced with the choice of going it alone or withdrawing from Anatolia, the Gounaris government chose the former. It did not want to be saddled with the blame for having abandoned Smyrna and the *Megali Idea*, and it retained at least one powerful supporter. At a conference in London to revise Sèvres in February 1921, Lloyd George encouraged the Greeks to keep fighting, if only to secure Allied possession of the Straits Zone (Llewellyn Smith 1998: 190–1).

Meanwhile, by the spring of 1921 the alliance splintered. On 9 March 1921, the French were unable to defend their Anatolian zone and came to terms with the Nationalists. For the same reasons, the Italians followed suit. Italy was content with Libya and the Dodecanese Islands, while France secured a settled border with its Syrian Mandate. Each also received economic concessions from the Nationalists. Soon after, the latter reached an accord with the Bolsheviks, who along with France and Italy began selling to the Nationalists military hardware and ammunition. The desertion of these allies made Greece's high-risk strategy even riskier. Even a military victory and the capture of Ankara did not guarantee an end to the war: that would depend on the Nationalist movement falling apart. Meanwhile, strategy and operations were affected by the Schism, which saw royalist officers replace Venizelist ones in key positions and in the field, causing deep dissension within the ranks. As historian George Mavrogordatos has emphasised, the Schism should be likened to a civil war that overshadowed the conduct of the military campaign in Anatolia (Mavrogordatos 2015). Retreat would mean humiliation for the royalists, but military victory would trump all the achievements of the Venizelists. The first offensive on 23 March failed. But when another was launched on 10 June, the Greeks broke through and marched on Eskişehir and Afyonkarahisar. The march towards Ankara included a systematic campaign of devastation and ethnic cleansing. A Greek soldier described the destruction:

> We reach a Turkish village and it's burning, and you see Turks inside their homes cooking and others slaughtered, riddled with stab wounds, and who were being set alight and burning. The fire had been set by the 18th Infantry Regiment, which was ahead of us. When we finally caught up with them fear and terror overcame us.

However, the soldier later participated in the destruction of other villages, and by this stage, he was inured to the horrors. Later, his only regret was that he was forced to leave behind the booty he accrued, which amounted to more wealth than he could ever imagine in his home village (Eleftheriou 1986: 42–55).

The Greek army, led by General Anastasios Papoulias, came closer to victory than he thought. The Nationalists had been driven back to within 75 km of Ankara and had suffered 80,000 casualties and desertions. Unbeknownst to the Greek command, the Nationalist leadership gave serious thought to evacuating their capital. Mustafa Kemal believed that the best option was to retreat further inland and fight another day, but the general view was to stay put. According to one historian of the Ottoman Empire: 'The outcome was in doubt until the very end. All summer the Greeks had won victories, taking territory from the Turks – and they continued to do so at Sakarya' (McMeekin 2015: 457). The challenge for Kemal and the Nationalists was to hold out until their own forces were sufficiently armed and prepared to take more offensive action against the Greeks, who had also suffered significant casualties, but who were also running out of money and suffering declining morale. These problems increased over the following year, as Greek and Turkish troops observed an informal ceasefire for much of the time, and governments engaged in fruitless negotiations.

By late August 1922, time had run out for the Greeks. The Nationalists waited through the summer before launching their long-awaited assault. The Soviet Union had supplied them with 37,812 rifles, 324 machine guns and about 45,000 crates of ammunition (McMeekin 2015: 465). Kemal's only risk was possible British intervention, but the latter was hampered by popular unrest in Iraq, which threatened much more vital British interests in the region. Whereas the Nationalists had planned carefully for the assault, the Greek soldiery were at best hopeful that they might be able to hold out. Many were reportedly looking for a miracle (Margaritis 1999: 183). On 26 August the Turkish assault began. During the first day of combat, the Greeks held the line, but on the second the Turks broke through, and a ferocious cavalry attacked ensued. The entire Greek front collapsed. The Greeks retreated in disorder to the Aegean, with the Nationalist army in pursuit. Some 18,000 Greek soldiers were killed or went missing during the Asia Minor conflict, the bulk of them in August 1922 (Margaritis 1999: 186).

Kemal wanted to rid Anatolia of the Greek army and of its entire Greek Orthodox population. His resolve hardened as news was received of the atrocities being committed by the retreating Greeks. Whereas previously the torching of villages and civilian massacres were nation-building exercises, or served tactical purposes, the violence perpetrated against Muslim communities during the retreat was chiefly symbolic: it was retribution for the defeat. Venizelos himself had conceded the Greeks had assumed the role of the barbarian: 'Ours had left no stone unturned, in retreat ... remember ... that terrible retreat, where they left everything destroyed' (Delta 1988: 173). Elsewhere some considered the Greek army's actions during the retreat as a crime against humanity. In the Treaty of Lausanne, the Greek government recognised (Article 59) that it had to pay war reparations to Turkey.

Most of the army managed to escape, but much of the Orthodox civilian population was trapped in Smyrna and other ports. When the Nationalist army entered the city on 9 September, hundreds of thousands of terrified refugees were huddled on the quayside. On 13 September, the Greek and Armenian quarters were set on fire. The conflagration swept through the city, reducing one of the most prosperous and diverse cities in the Near East into ashes. More will be said about the Smyrna events in the next chapter (pp. 75–7); suffice it to say here that the blaze erased almost all traces of Greek life. Although the Nationalists denied responsibility, the destruction of Smyrna would be remembered in popular Turkish lore for having 'cleared the dirt' (*pisliği temizlemek*) (Kırlı 2005: 25–44).

With the Greek army driven out of Anatolia, the British were completely exposed in the Straits Zone. War was averted when France, the Dominions (except New Zealand) and the British public refused Lloyd George's request for a military response. The Chanak Crisis ended Lloyd George's prime ministership, and in subsequent negotiations, the Nationalists attained Constantinople and Eastern Thrace. Edirne was reclaimed by the Turks, while the Greek population of Eastern Thrace was evacuated across the Maritsa River. The Treaty of Lausanne, which replaced the unratified and repudiated Treaty of Sèvres, confirmed the territorial claims of the Nationalists, required Greece to pay war reparations, and mandated a population exchange to rid the empire of its 'seditious' Greek population. Of the Central Powers, only the Turks were able to emerge with a victory.

Conclusion: whose catastrophe?

It is not altogether clear how many Romioi died and managed to make their way to Greece. In 1928, 1,104,217 refugees were registered by

Greek authorities. Given the high mortality rate in the first years following the exodus, and the fact that some 66,000 refugees fled to other countries, it likely that some 1,300,000 Greek Orthodox civilians fled Asia Minor, Pontus and Eastern Thrace. This number is close to the figure produced by the League of Nations, which estimated 1,360,000 refugees. How many perished during the conflict? The number of Greek Orthodox Christians recorded in shelters in Asia Minor was 1,547,952, while those subsequently counted in shelters in Greece was 847,954 (Figure 2.2; Kitromilides and Alexandris 1984–5: 34). The answer, therefore, is approximately 700,000 dead. What of the Muslim population? According to Turkish estimates, 640,000 people died, and 840,000 were displaced (McCarthy 1995: 304). If estimates for Armenians who lost their lives (between 800,000 to 1 million) are added, the war claimed well over 2 million Anatolians.

Greece's military debacle came to be known in Greece as the 'Asia Minor Catastrophe' or simply 'the Great Catastrophe' (*Megali Katastrofi*). Rather oddly, the millions killed and traumatised were not the subject of this national trauma. Historians, politicians and the Greek reading public regarded it as a military tragedy that ended the *Megali Idea*. That the nation was humiliated by its arch nemesis made it

Figure 2.2 *Anatolian refugees in Piraeus.* © ERT

all the more tragic. Books on the subject focused on the campaign, the impact of the National Schism, and the play of international politics. Civilian casualties were discussed, but only in so far as they provided testimony to Turkish barbarity, whilst rarely conceding the barbarities committed by the Greeks.

This 'top-down' perspective, however, was indicative of indifference to the plight of the refugees, and it obscures the real catastrophe. Many refugees recalled the contempt of the Greek officials who withheld news of the military collapse near Ankara, and who encouraged them to stay put despite the approaching Nationalist and irregular forces, depriving them of a chance to escape. The Greek governor of Smyrna conceded that it was better to leave the terrified civilians left behind in Smyrna to their fate than see Greece flooded with refugees. A few days before the catastrophe, Constantine issued a royal decree banning the ferrying of refugees to Greek ports: 'It is forbidden to land persons from abroad if they do not possess regular passports that are legally pre-scribed.' Ship captains, owners, travel agencies and even sailors were threatened with imprisonment (Law 2870. FEK A 119/20 July 1922). The refugees were unwanted.

The Asia Minor Catastrophe was the most traumatic event in modern Greek history because of the way it destroyed thousands of communities and ruined millions of lives. It was a trauma that would define the survivors as social beings for the rest of their lives (Hirschon 1998). As refugees their troubles were augmented by the hostility of the host society and the pressures placed upon them to culturally assimi-late. But they were not the only victims of nation-building schemes. All cultural minorities in Greece (and Turkey and Bulgaria) were subjected to forms of state and host-society oppression, as were Greeks throughout the diaspora. The next chapter, which covers the travails of the Romioi and the Greeks of British Cyprus, also considers the experi-ences of the more substantial Greek communities in the wider world, principally those in Egypt, the Soviet Union, the United States and in other parts of the English-speaking world.

Note

1. https://silo.tips/download/documents-of-the-inter-allied-commission-of-in quiry-into-the-greek-occupation-of# (last accessed 24 August 2022).

CHAPTER 3

The wider Greek world I: The end of the age of empire

The world at the beginning of the twentieth century was dominated overwhelmingly by empires, and about half of the Greek people were dispersed among them, particularly the Ottoman but also the British and Russian empires. The United States had also expanded into First Nations territories and was hence an 'empire' in all but name. However, the multiethnic societies of many of these empires were about to be violently unmixed, and Greek communities would count among the tragic victims of this historical process. A related development was the extension of state controls over resources *within* national spaces, so that executive authorities could control and mobilise people, finance and material assets with increasing efficiency. The historian Charles S. Maier describes this vector of modernity as 'territoriality' (Maier 2016), which also denotes a new tendency of states to discipline 'national communities' and engineer their cultural profile. States were keen to make peasants into nationals through soft power, coercive means or both (Hobsbawm 1992: ch. 2; Markwick and Doumanis 2016).

What was the impact of 'territoriality' on post-imperial societies? How did the state intervene to restabilise and modernise the social order after empire? This chapter considers the fate of Greek minorities that were seen as potentially inimical to the national interest. It examines the destruction of Ottoman Greek communities, the dispersal of the Pontian communities of the Soviet Union and the early portents of minority expulsions in Egypt. Cyprus stands out as an exceptional case, as it remained a British colony throughout the first half of the twentieth century, when the political preoccupations of its population, as with the world's other colonised peoples, were focused on ending colonialism.

In the meantime, Greeks continued to migrate to other countries, principally the United States, northern Europe and Australia, where immigrant communities were free to run language schools and ethnic-language newspapers, form associations and build their own houses of worship. The Greek diaspora that expanded across the world's more advanced industrial economies was more proletarian than commercial, yet in many ways it remained closely tied to the homeland. Hence the National Schism reverberated in North American and Australian communities, and, conversely, the diaspora began to influence life in the centre. Returning Greek émigrés and their experiences of America would also influence their homeland compatriots when it came to negotiating the opportunities and challenges of modernity (Laliotou 2005).

The destruction of the Romioi

How did the Romioi experience the Asia Minor Catastrophe? How did that seminal event change their lives and their sense of themselves? This chapter goes some way towards explaining how everyday Ottomans came to think of themselves as Greeks and Turks rather than Romioi and Muslims, and how their indifference to nationalism was overcome by violence. The previous chapter discussed this transition from a 'top-down' perspective and identified the essential causes of the 'great unmixing' and the genocidal violence that gripped this part of the world during 1912–22, the 'long First World War'. The violence was generated by political elites and perpetrated mainly by soldiers, paramilitaries and bandits. Among the intended effects was fomenting inter-communal hostility, making former neighbours into enemies. Prejudices had always existed, but nationalism sought to instil hard boundaries that would break patterns of cultural intermingling, place people in exclusive cultural silos and, when necessary, pit them against each other. In the mixed villages and urban neighbourhoods of the Ottoman world, Romioi and Muslims had found ways to coexist and cooperate for practical reasons – the same applied to multiethnic societies in other empires (Doumanis 2013; Robson 2020). The violence of 1912–22 went far towards making Greeks and Turks (and Bulgarians) believe they were incompatible. Later, the routine socialisation of the population with nationalist ideals and mythicised history, and with particular emphasis on the villainous 'national enemy', would be common to all post-Ottoman societies.

The beginning of the end, 1912–1914

The Romioi believed that everything changed after the First Balkan War. At the everyday level, relationships with Muslim friends and neighbours were seriously impaired. The usual routines of coexistence

ceased, and communities retreated into exclusive ghettos. The recol-
lections of Anestis Varsitopoulos of Phocaea/Foça, a thriving town
near Smyrna, were typical: 'It was only with the war that we saw each
other as enemies ... Before 1912 they'd come to our weddings and
baptisms ... [Now] we were "at daggers" [*sta macheria*]. The Turks
no longer trusted us' (Doumanis 2013: 152). In the oral testimonies
collected at the Centre for Asia Minor Studies in Athens, in which
Asia Minor, Pontian and Thracian refugees recalled their lives in the
Ottoman Empire and as refugees, subjects claimed that stories of atrocities against Muslims during the Balkan Wars, together with the mass
influx of refugees, influenced a change in their Muslim neighbours.
The common Muslim view was that Christians had forfeited their right
to remain within the empire. The phrase most often recorded in the
refugee interviews was 'the Turks became hostile' (*agriepsan oi Tourkoi*)
(*I Exodos*, vols 1–3). This hostility was fed by a government- and press-
driven propaganda campaign and manifested in popular participation
in anti-Greek boycotts. Rumours abounded that rich Romioi had
been funding the Greek war effort, and that Greek Orthodox railway
staff had conspired to hinder the movement of Ottoman troops to the
Balkan front. Rumours that enjoyed popular currency were that as soldiers the Romioi were cowardly and that most refused the call for conscription – there was more than a grain of truth to the latter rumour
(Erol 2016: 117). A popular myth had it that a rich Romios had purchased the *Averof* for the Greek navy, the cruiser that did most to neu-
tralise Ottoman naval power during the war. Actually, the cruiser had
been purchased by a charitable foundation created by Georgios Averof,
a Metsovo-born Greek Egyptian who died back in 1899 (Çetinkaya
2014: 168–9). The complaint against the Romioi and the ultimate jus-
tification for their expulsion was couched in moral terms: the Romioi
as a collective had betrayed their imperial fatherland, having repaid
Muslim generosity with treachery. In an interview on Greek national
television in 1976, a former prisoner of war who had been assigned to
work as a carpenter on Mustafa Kemal Atatürk's home in 1923, recalled
being berated by the president for his community's treachery. Atatürk
reminded him that his people had been free to wave their Greek flags,
learn their Greek history and perform their Greek plays, but they knew
nothing about Turkish history and culture. Since the Balkan Wars,
however, the Romioi had shown their true colours. 'All of you should
have been put to the sword. None should have been spared.'[1]

The boycotting of Rum businesses had a significant impact. The
practice had been employed in many parts of the world (China, Mexico,

Iran) against colonial commercial interests, and had been used by the Ottomans to protest the Austrian annexation of Bosnia in 1908, and against Greece for its role in the Cretan crises of 1908–9, which spawned a wave of Muslim expulsions to Anatolia. Recent research has proven that the campaigns in 1913 and 1914 were orchestrated and locally directed by CUP officials, governors and bureaucrats (Morack 2017a: 75), and that they precipitated random violence against ordinary Romioi. Foreign consuls reported numerous cases of vandalism, assaults and looting by local ruffians and Muslim refugees. Boycotters picketed outside Ottoman Greek establishments, attacked vehicles and animals carrying goods, and physically prevented Muslims from shopping or doing business with Romioi, often by issuing severe beatings (Çetinkaya 2014: 176–8).

Unlike previous boycott movements, this round had clear nation-building objectives. The aim was to reduce the preponderance of Armenians, Jews and especially Romioi in the empire's commercial sector. The campaign was meant to induce Greek proprietors to emigrate and to see the vacuum filled by Muslims. Much more effective in forcing an exodus was the government's violent terror campaigns to evict the Romioi from Eastern Thrace and the Aegean coast in 1913 and 1914. It hoped to resolve two problems: the presence of an unwanted minority and housing for refugees. The expulsion of Romioi would allow distribution of their abandoned properties to Muslim refugees or *muhacir*. The CUP, and Talaat Pasha in particular, were receptive to Venizelos' proposal for a population exchange in 1913–14 precisely because it dealt with the first problem. But an exchange required time to organise, and in the meantime the *muhacir* had to be fed and housed. It was widely feared that the presence of destitute and unemployed *muhacir* would also increase the crime rate. The solution was to evict Greek communities using what one historian has labelled 'organised chaos' (Erol 2016). According to Halil Menteşe, Talaat's colleague:

> The Rûm [Romioi] living on Izmir's coasts work day and night to implement their Megali Idea. For political reasons, it is necessary to evacuate the Rûm villages and to resettle the Rûm living on Anatolia's coasts ... If they resist, methods of sorts are needed to make them leave by their own will. (Kieser 2018: 176)

Under Talaat's direction, the Teşkilât-ı Mahsûsa ('Special Organisation'), a collection of militias composed of criminals and *muhacir*, were responsible for the spree of attacks on Ottoman Greek villagers and townspeople. Local government officials and gendarmes were ordered not to intervene, while the CUP claimed publicly that the disturbances had to do with local sectarian unrest. As the abandoned properties were to be sequestered by the state and redistributed among *muhacir* families, the militias could kill, rape and loot, but they were required to leave dwellings intact. French archaeologist Félix Sartiaux witnessed 'organised chaos' in the prosperous seaside town of Phocaea/Foça, some 60 km northwest of Smyrna. On 11 June 1914 a rumour had it that shepherds and villagers were being killed by the Teşkilât-ı Mahsûsa in nearby mountains. The following day, as terrified Romioi gathered on the crowded waterfront, hoping to be ferried to nearby islands, news came that the paramilitaries were converging on Phocaea itself. On 13 June the paramilitaries began looting Ottoman Greek houses and killed anyone in their way. Sartiaux reported that local gendarmes simply looked on as some 1,250 Ottoman Greek homes were looted, and he was able to take rare photographs of the town during the crisis (Yiakoumis et al. 2008). Within a matter of days, the entire county of Foçateyn had been effectively emptied of its Ottoman Greek population (Erol 2016: 171–4).

Publicly, CUP leaders denied any involvement in the expulsion operations so as not to invite international intervention, but they were thrilled by its effectiveness. Halil reported that the project was a major success because it had cleared the Aegean region of some 200,000 Greeks by June (Kieser 2018: 176). According to Fuat Dündar, a Turkish scholar who has worked on the pre-war expulsions, the figure is more likely to have been 160,000. Especially affected were Greek Orthodox villages near the towns of Bursa, Çeşme, Seyrek, Edremit, Burhaniye, Kemer, Kınık, Balıkesir, Bergama, Karaburun, Menemen, Ödemiş, Uluabat, Eskice, Mudanya, Bandırma, Çanakkale and along the Kasaba–Aydın rail line (Erol 2016: 196). The CUP were in essence hastening the process of transforming the empire into a nation. As historian Sia Anagnostopoulou has pointed out, the Ottoman Empire had effectively ceased to be 'Ottoman' (1997: 527). However, the ethnic cleansing scheme ran out of time, and many Romioi were still living in the Aegean and Marmara regions when the Ottomans entered the war on 29 October 1914.

Deportations, 1914–1918

In contrast to other major powers that engaged in the First World War, historians know very little about conditions on the Ottoman home front: about social welfare, class relations, labour, economic conditions and life in general in the cities and towns. Until relatively recently, historians of the empire have avoided the topic because it meant confronting the Armenian Genocide, but it is also true that the period did not figure strongly in the memories of the Anatolian refugees, probably because these terrible years were overshadowed by the much more traumatic phase that followed. However, it was during that 1914–18 phase that, except for the Karamanlides, Greek Orthodox elites came to believe they could no longer live securely under Ottoman rule.

Soon after the Ottomans intervened in the war in late October 1914, Allied vessels began bombarding Ottoman towns along the Aegean coast and imposed an effective naval blockade that cut off access to coal and such vital staples as rice and wheat (Akın 2018: 122–3). A major Allied invasion was expected, which indeed occurred on the Gallipoli Peninsula in March 1915. In the meantime, the Romioi still living in Eastern Thrace and along the Aegean coast were, more than ever before, regarded as a national security threat. Romioi living within a kilometre of the coast were therefore deported into the hinterlands of Anatolia, starting with the Thracian Romioi from November 1914. Meanwhile, the Russians had opened a front in the Caucasus and launched incursions into eastern Anatolia and along the Black Sea littoral. Christian groups in these eastern regions, Armenian and Greek Orthodox, supported the incursion. As Russians moved along the Black Sea coast, Pontian communities welcomed their fellow Orthodox invaders as 'liberators'. Meanwhile, Christians behind Ottoman lines were liable for deportation or vulnerable to attacks from Muslim bandit groups or bands of irregulars (*çete*). Many Pontian communities took their guns and hid in the mountains, where they evaded Ottoman troops and the *çete*, and from where they engaged in brutal struggle throughout the course of the war.

The First World War and its international distractions provided the CUP with an ideal cover for mass expulsions and killings. Given that the war threatened the empire's very existence, these radical measures also reflected a sense of anxiety (Akın 2018: 165; Bloxham 2005). Aside from their principal victims, the Armenians, other non-Turkish civilians were targeted for persecution, including Assyrians and Kurds. Deportation was the CUP's principal method. The process of deportation, of marching civilians over long distances, exposing them to the elements whilst denying them adequate food and water, would inevitably kill a significant proportion of the deportees. In the case of the Armenians, deals were also made with bandits and other criminal elements to attack them en route. This method accounted for a sizeable proportion of Armenian lives lost during their genocide (Bloxham 2005). Deportation probably also accounted for most Greek Orthodox deaths during the 1915–18 period. Villagers were called into the square. Able-bodied men were set aside to serve in labour battalions, while their parents, wives and children were marched at gunpoint to various destinations in central Anatolia. Pontian communities were marched across the steep Pontian Alps and south towards Diyarbakır and Kurdistan in general (Stamatopoulos 2011: 87). As many as 100,000 would be removed from Anatolia's Marmara region. Inland communities were spared, as were residents of major centres like Smyrna and Bursa (Gingeras 2009: 45). However, to a British observer in 1918 it appeared as if the entire Greek population of Eastern Thrace had disappeared. In 1917, it was the turn of communities along Anatolia's southern coast to be deported (Morack 2017: 22–3).

The testimonies of survivors give a clear impression that the marches were meant to cull them. Avgerinos Spanopoulos from Paphlagonia (north-central Anatolia) recalled having to walk for ten days, during which time his mother died:

> So did my three-year-old sister. Then cholera swept through, and many more people died. I lost two brothers. We buried them without a priest. News then came from Ankara about my father. He died in the army. Only my brother and I were left. (KMS Paphlagonia 7 Askortasai)

Survivors typically recalled a lack of food and water, having to watch the elderly, children and the sick die by the roadside, to see stragglers being shot, and having to sleep out in the open. Dimitris Thrasyvoulos was nearly 30 when he and his family were marched into the interior towards Afyonkarahisar in 1916. His wife gave birth en route but she, the child and his parents were dead within a month. Melpomeni Papadopoulos was exiled to a place near Sivas, but she lost her two daughters in the snow (KMS Pontus 634 Tripolis). Some groups were marched into villages or towns where local Romioi could provide food and shelter. One woman living in Bursa recalled the arrival of people who had been marched from the coast and who were selling anything they had for bread. 'We opened our doors to them of course, but many had already died given the hardships' (KMS Bithynia 136 Bursa). On reaching their designated terminus, survivors had to eke out an existence, working at any job they could find and living hand to mouth. How many people were displaced? In addition to the pre-war expulsions, another 144,000 were deported from the Aegean coast, whilst the marches accounted for over a quarter of a million (257,019) from the Pontus region. Together with other groups from Thrace and different parts of Anatolia, the general figure for 1914–18 was approximately 620,000 (Stamatopoulos 2011: 65).

Why were the Romioi of Smyrna, Bursa and other major centres spared? Wartime exigencies dictated that cities, being centres of production and commerce, should not be subjected to needless upheaval. Ottoman authorities appeared intent on maintaining 'business-as-usual' conditions in the major cities for mainly economic reasons. Smyrna happened to be under the authority of Mustafa Rahmi Arslan (Rahmi Bey), who, although a friend of Talaat Pasha and involved in the ethnic cleansings in 1914, was intent on maintaining inter-communal peace in his city. By most accounts, all groups felt that life was safer in the cities, although here the poor suffered acute food shortages. That Greek schools continued to function suggests that a 'business-as-usual' approach was not merely tolerated but encouraged. School photographs depicting the entire cohort of students were produced during the war years (e.g. Ozil 2013: 42).

Beyond the cities, however, the state exercised little authority. In a rare study of the Ottoman 'home front', one historian depicts a lawless world infested with *çete* bands: 'Roaming in the mountains and preying on nearby villages, the presence of so many deserters kept the country-side in a perpetual state of insecurity' (Akın 2018: 139). By 1917 there were as many as 300,000 deserters at large, who joined gangs or militias belonging to regional strongmen. Along with local police and other officials, these gangs and militias operated extortion rackets among the villages. By 1917 the banditry had become more brazen, with gangs operating openly and in large numbers, and posing a serious security problem for Ottoman authorities (Gingeras 2009: 65–8). Such was the level of insecurity that villagers reverted to subsistence farming, which severely limited the amount of food reaching town and city markets. The *çete* bands did not spare Muslims, but Christians were mostly victimised given their security was of little concern to state authorities (Doumanis 2013: 156–7).

The First World War effectively destroyed the Ottoman Empire. The CUP leadership believed intervention might have reversed Ottoman fortunes and might even have launched a new age of expansion, but it was a high-risk gamble that hastened the empire's demise. It is worth bearing in mind it had been a catastrophe for all Ottoman civilians. As much as one fifth of the general Ottoman population perished, and millions of people of all faiths had been displaced by military operations, by marauding soldiers and bandits, and by government deportations (Akın 2018: 163–89). People from the Hejaz (western Arabia) had been exiled to Konya, Kurds had been deported to Isparta, Thracian Romioi to Eskişehir, and Armenians were languishing in the deserts of Syria and Iraq (Gingeras 2016: 255, 258). Soldiers and Muslim refugees were fed by supplies sequestered, often brutally, from Anatolian peasants, who harboured a particular animus for the CUP. As one Ottoman officer put it:

> Peasants who constituted 80 per cent of the population bore the brunt of the war. Each household lost several youths. People suffered not only from the enemy's bullets but also from a series of diseases caused by misadministration. This situation provoked the hostility of everyone, especially that of the peasants. (Akın 2008: 194)

By autumn of 1918, when it was clear the war was lost, CUP leaders began seeking peace terms with the United States on 5 October, and then abdicated power on 13 October. In the ensuing months, the surviving Romioi, along with countless Anatolian Turks, Circassians, Bosnians, Zeybeks, Armenians, Jews, Yörüks, Assyrians, Kurds and others, hoped to rebuild their lives. The average Romios yearned for the resumption of normality: work, family life and the peaceful conditions they remembered before the wars. But there were major challenges ahead. Those returning from exile were likely to find Muslim refugees in their homes or find their houses in ruins. During the winter months of 1918–19, many Romioi began to rebuild, prepare their fields and restore their shops and workshops. Sometimes their Muslim friends, as good neighbours, helped them and kept their material goods intact. One woman from north-central Anatolia (Paphlagonia) recalled how her husband returned from a prison camp and found none of the Christians were still living in the village, but he was taken in by 'our Turkish compatriots (*patriotes*)' (KMS Paphlagonia 7 Askortasai). Restoration of church buildings, schools and communal institutions or *koinotites* began. British reports from the spring of 1919 tell of towns along the southwestern coast of Anatolia, from Kuşadası to Bodrum and Kaş, being in various states of disrepair. Kuşadası and Bodrum had been heavily bombed by French naval artillery (PRO, FO286/703, 10 May 1919/23 May 1919).

In 1918, most Ottoman subjects simply wanted to turn back the clock, as did most Europeans. But the old multiethnic order was in ruins. The question that preoccupied every Ottoman subject was: what kind of order would replace it? Before stepping down the CUP sought out US assistance to arrange a peace based on Woodrow Wilson's

Fourteen Points. His principle of national self-determination raised hopes among all the Central Powers of generous peace terms. The Ottomans hoped that they might be able to secure possession of their predominantly Turkish Anatolian homeland. To appease Wilson, a different approach was needed vis-à-vis the Armenians and the Romioi. Before stepping down, the CUP had this in mind when it revoked existing laws to allow surviving Armenians to return to their homelands. Rahmi Bey in Smyrna even mooted the possibility of some communal autonomy to Armenian and Greek leaders (Gingeras 2016: 240, 247, 258). With the CUP gone, Greek Orthodox and Armenian deputies were again able to speak on behalf of their communities in the Ottoman parliament. Following international pressure, a formal inquiry was opened on the deportations of Armenian and Greek Orthodox communities (Aktar 2007: 251–2; Gingeras 2016: 252–3).

Hostilities in the Aegean and the Pontus regions, 1919–1921

When the war ended, deportees were permitted to make their way back to their villages, but those who had escaped abroad preferred to stay put. General conditions in Anatolia remained unsafe. *Çete* and warlords were still at large. Of the 25,000 Ottoman Greeks that lived in Ayvalık before the war, only 8,000 came back. The vast majority of the 5,500 who evacuated Bodrum in 1914 never returned. Housing was a major problem during the six or so months following the signing of the armistice in October. Romioi often found their homes had been allocated by the state to *muhacir* families that were determined not to be displaced again. Many returnees therefore returned with weapons. Foreign consuls reported a spate of violence in the affected areas, particularly during the early months of 1919, as more and more exiled Romioi built up the courage to return. In February 1919, about fifty armed Romioi came back to their native Akköy and drove out the Ottoman authorities, killing a soldier and a gendarme. The British were forced to intervene and sent the Romioi back to Samos, where they had taken refuge during the war years (PRO, FO286/714, 1 May 1919). Sometimes the violence was also about vengeance. Among the Greek troops that occupied Eastern Thrace were men who had been expelled earlier with their families, and who took the opportunity to settle old scores (PRO, FO286/714 L.L. R. Samson, 4 May 1919).

Property claims and the resolution of other inter-communal disputes, however, would depend on the peace treaty and in particular on which territories would remain under Ottoman sovereignty, and which would be divided up among the victors. As the victors negotiated the terms in Paris, Muslims and non-Muslims waited anxiously. Christian communities feared more persecutions if they remained under Muslim rule or indeed another Turkish nationalist regime. Many community leaders in the Pontus and Aegean regions lobbied Venizelos for inclusion in a 'greater' Greece, in the hope that he might be able to sway Allied leaders. The flag-waving Ottoman Greek middle classes clamoured for Greek rule, particularly in Aegean coastal areas, where visiting Greek naval vessels were greeted with great fanfare as liberators. Such displays of imperial disloyalty rankled deeply with local Muslims, who feared the prospect of living under Greek or Armenian rule (Doumanis 2013: 158–9). British, Italian or French colonial rule was barely tolerable, but there was some sympathy for the idea of an American mandate, given Wilson's principled approach to peacemaking and his stand on national self-determination, and given that the United States had no colonial aspirations in the region (Prott 2016: 106).

Therefore, in regions where the Romioi had been campaigning for unification with Greece, or for political partition, Muslims began to organise armed resistance. Thus, in March 1919, many Muslims in the Trabzon area reacted to the Pontian nationalist agitation by forming nationalist militias (*kuva-yi milliye*). These militias were led by warlords like Topal Osman or the Circassian band leader Ethem, who also saw an opportunity for self-enrichment (Levene 2013: 223). During the next four years, the Greek Orthodox communities of Pontus were subjected to violence that was often genocidal. The nationalist militias began to trawl through Pontian village communities, or towns like Bafra (near Samsun), where they massacred the Pontian men, women and children. Communities in the region of Giresun/Kerasounta were subjected to a concerted terror campaign by Topal Osman and his forces (Gingeras 2016: 265; Clark 2007: 113). One woman recalled the day when his men raped and killed the women of the village of Atta. She survived by hiding in nearby bushes (KMS Pontus 235 Atta). The deportation of Pontian communities also resumed once the Nationalist government was established in Ankara in mid-1920. Paraskevi Mavrovounioti recalled having to walk at gunpoint for two months towards Kurdistan, where the survivors of the march worked among villages near Bitlis. Of her village, she knew of only two other families that survived the ordeal (KMS Pontus 948 Eskiören). The deportations increased during the Greek military offensives of 1921, which came close to Ankara itself, and with the appearance of Greek naval vessels off the Black Sea coast.

Many Pontian communities had sufficient warning to avoid deportation and escaped to Russian territory or took refuge in the mountains again. A new guerrilla struggle broke out along the Pontic Alps, placing village communities in the crossfire. Between 1920 and 1922, the Muslim struggle against the Pontian Greeks was brought under the direction of the Nationalist government of Mustafa Kemal, which encouraged warlords and *çete* bands to continue their work. Pontian Greeks like Savvas Vasiliadis of Samsun recalled spending most of those years on the run, surviving in caves or huts, and always hungry. He fought against *çete* bands and Turkish troops, but his band also robbed many Muslim villages (KMS Pontus 328 Omaroglu). It would be an oversimplification, however, to read the struggle as a simple Christian–Muslim conflict. As with other Pontian interviewees, Vasiliadis recalled banding together with Muslim groups that opposed Kemal's Nationalists, and others talked of protection received from Muslim warlords. Their testimonies support a significant point raised in recent studies of this period (e.g. Gingeras 2009): that there were other power struggles at play, and that it took time for Mustafa Kemal to command the support of all Muslim groups (see p. 55). Some of his opponents were open to alliances with the Greek military. Some Pontian communities were protected by warlords opposed to Topal Osman. Minas Karatasidis' band included Armenians and Circassians, who fought mainly against the warlord Atilla Aga and his *çete* band (KMS Pontus 314 Kouzloukioï). When the Nationalists won the war, some Pontian groups were given amnesty provided they left the country (KMS Pontus 755 Funtuklu), but Muslim bands opposed to the Nationalists often fought on for several years.

Western Anatolia, 1919–1922

Since November 1918 the Venizelos government had been encouraging Anatolian and Thracian refugees in Greece to return to their homes. Many had overcome their initial reluctance once Greek troops had occupied the region around Smyrna in May 1919, and especially once government repatriation programmes were implemented after October 1919. Within the Smyrna zone, *muhacir* were often removed from their allocated properties by their former owners. A typical case was that of the *muhacir* families in the village of Gerenköy (near Phocaea/Foça), who were forced out by locals returning from Thessaloniki (Erol 2016: 219). Conditions for Muslims under Greek rule varied. In areas where Muslim armed resistance had been subdued, Greek authority was oppressive but tolerable. In the Phocaea/Foça region, Muslims complained about arbitrary arrests, intrusive inspections and unfair treatment (Erol 2016: 221–3). In Smyrna itself, the Greek governor Aristides Stergiadis was determined to show the world that Greek authority was civilised and set special store on maintaining good relations with the Muslim community. In less secure zones, however, conditions for all groups were much worse. In the large territory that came under Greek occupation in mid-1920, comprising much of northwest Anatolia (including Balıkesir, Panormos/Bandırma, Bursa, Nicaea/İznik, Nikomedia/İzmit and Adapazarı, and stretching south to Kütahya, Philadelphia/Alaşehir and Uşak), Greek occupation forces were too thinly spread to assert effective control. The Nationalists were able to infiltrate and influence much of the region, particularly territory closer to their base in Ankara. As in the Black Sea region, Muslim warlords and *çete*, including bands composed of refugees from the Balkans (Pomaks, Bosnians, Albanians) and the Caucasus (Circassians), were not always in league with the Nationalists. Although the Nationalists tried to rally all Muslims against the Greek 'infidel', and to depict the conflict as a holy struggle or jihad, they faced palpable Muslim opposition. Thus in early 1922 some of the more important Circassian leaders met in Smyrna and decided the interests of their people would be better served by the Greeks (Gingeras 2009: 126).

Within such areas all civilians lived in daily peril and were unable to manage the normal routines of life. Travelling along roads and indeed beyond one's village was unsafe. Robberies and murders were commonplace. Soldiers and officers often behaved as bandits, extorting from families, taking hostages and killing those who resisted. The violence had a sectarian character, but the lawless conditions promoted basic thievery and other criminal activity. Overall, Muslim and Christian militiamen were 'ordinary men' (cf. Browning 2001) – shepherds, shopkeepers, village boys, craftsmen – who had been radicalised by years of war and unrest. As Christian villagers were particularly at risk, they frequently sought the relative safety of larger towns like Bursa and Ankara. According to the *Black Book of the Sufferings of the Greek People from the Armistice to 1920*, a document produced by the Ecumenical Patriarchate of Constantinople, the Romioi were subjected to massacres, random killings and extortionate exactions in every part of Thrace and Anatolia:

> On July 20th [1919], a Turkish-Laz band of 15, murdered Michael Antonoglou and John Vassiloglou on their way from Elmali to Akkeuy.

Five days later another band robbed Nicolas Kleisitou's grocery in Courtkeuy and carried him away. His body was found by chance, at a short distance from the village on August 5th. (*Mavri Vivlos* 1920: 71)

In March Albanian bands murdered the following: John Seraphim Kampakzoglou, Dem. Hadji Kelesis, Ch. Katraftous, Ch. Sivris, Con. Zarifi, Nic. Constandinidi, Au. Drakos, Sot. Drakos, St. Bairambakakis, Dem. Gallios, St. Kouparakis' two sons and Basil Hadji Stoyou. (*Mavri Vivlos* 1920: 73)

On December 3rd Yannakis Papadopoulos from Eukarpion, was shot dead while on his way to Kirk-Kilise. On December 13th, Turks killed the notable and Mouhtar of the village of Koyoun Dere Ap. Mihaloglou. The body bore marks of several knife wounds. In the morning of January 11th, Ath. K. Katchavounis was found dead in the room next to his grocery, bearing marks of 40 axe wounds. (*Mavri Vivlos* 1920: 93)

Matters were somewhat different in Cappadocia, in the general region of Kayseri and Konya, where the Turcophone Karamanlides had always enjoyed a safe distance from all fighting fronts. Their loyalties to the Ottoman Empire were never tested.

The mass exodus, 1922–1925

The retreat of Greek forces following the military rout in late August launched the ugly climax of Greece's 'long First World War' (see pp. 58–9). Most Greek soldiers managed to escape via ports along the Sea of Marmara and the northern Aegean coast, but they had enough time to destroy cities and towns that lay in their path including Uşak, Eskişehir, Alaşehir, Kütahya, Aydın, Nazlı, Manisa and Kasaba. Muslim civilians were subjected to hideous treatment, such as being forced into their mosques which were then set on fire (Stamatopoulos 2011: 95). These actions would inevitably invite retribution against the local Romioi, who tried to flee with the soldiers, but were often trapped or caught behind the advancing Turkish Nationalist line. Their survival was jeopardised by the decision taken by Greek authorities in Athens and Smyrna to withhold news of the military collapse so as not to induce a mass exodus to Greece and create a new political crisis. This calculated and callous decision meant that many more Romioi were caught behind enemy lines and massacred by çete, or were unable to secure passage to nearby islands. In the great panic that ensued, families abandoned their homes and possessions and made their way to any port by any means that they could manage. Families were separated in the confusion, and would often never see each other again, although the more fortunate would reunite in Greece, sometimes decades later. Some succeeded in boarding the few trains in operation, but most went on foot. An unknown number were killed by *çete* bands that now functioned as irregulars for Kemal's Nationalist army. Operating ahead of regular forces, the *çete* butchered Romioi and Armenians in their path. The regular army was more disciplined but not immune from war crimes. In Ayvalık, the Turkish army was greeted by the Christian and Muslim population with cheers of 'Yaşasın' ('Hurrah!'). The Christians were not spared, however. Their bishop was buried alive after he was forced to watch the same done to others (*I Exodos*, vol. 1: 96–7).

Turkish forces entered Smyrna on 9 September, and Mustafa Kemal arrived the following day. Greek authorities, including Stergiadis, had departed a few days earlier, but had left hundreds of thousands of terrified Romioi stranded. Distracted by the political fallout from the military catastrophe, and wishing to avoid a refugee crisis, the Greek political class neglected to produce an evacuation plan for civilians. Romioi from nearby towns and villages had poured into the city and headed for the quayside, where they had hoped to be evacuated to safety. All they found was numerous Allied ships moored offshore, which were under strict orders not to assist Greeks and Armenians, and to keep news from getting out of the violent chaos they could see from their decks. Residents who had not managed an escape locked themselves in their homes or sought sanctuary in European consulates and institutions bearing European flags. For although Mustafa Kemal seemed intent on establishing an orderly transition of authority in city, he seemed unable or unwilling to restrain Turkish irregulars from robbing, raping and killing Greek and Armenian civilians, or to rein in regular soldiers, who were also running amok by the third day. Turkish aggression had initially focused on the Armenian quarter, where massacres took place, and where independent observers witnessed Turkish soldiers setting fires on 13 September. Much of the city was soon affected by a conflagration that only spared the Muslim and Jewish quarters. As the fires approached, civilians abandoned their homes, churches or other buildings and made for the quayside, where panic also spread as the fires approached, and where countless people drowned. By this stage Allied personnel were disobeying orders and assisting in the evacuation of civilians, who were ferried to nearby islands. By 16 September, neither Turkish Nationalist leadership nor the Greek government could resist the pressure to allow an orderly evacuation of women, children and the elderly. Males between 18 and 45 were taken away as prisoners of war and marched off to labour camps.

By 30 September, Smyrna no longer had a Greek population. Aside from the Turkish and Jewish quarters, the city had been sacked. Countless women had been raped. There were plenty of eyewitness accounts of fires being deliberately lit and firefighters being deliberately turned away at gunpoint. The intention was to obliterate the city's cosmopolitan past and make way for its Turkish national future. For decades the city was seen as being the captive of infidels: a reminder of colonial domination. One Frenchman said of his community's losses:

> For us it was a huge loss, nothing exists any longer. The cathedral, the French hospital, the school of the Sisters of Providence, of the Lazarists, of the Brothers, Our Lady of Sion, Sacred-Heart, the church of St. Polycarp, Little Sisters of the Poor, the hospital St. Roch, the Franciscan sisters of Saint-Roch, the Carmelites. All that was consumed by the flames ... (Georgelin 2005: 240)

The horrors of Smyrna were the final, climactic act of the 'long First World War'. Ethnic cleansing had been a signature feature of that war period, but until the Smyrna events of September 1922 these crimes had taken place in rural settings and been sufficiently 'hidden' from the world. Talaat Pasha and the CUP-sponsored militias could terrorise Greek Orthodox communities before 1914 and yet deny government involvement to the international public. Photos taken by archaeologist Felix Sartiaux of Phocea/Foça during the attacks in July 1914 are valuable precisely because they offer a unique photographic glimpse of ethnic cleansing (Dalègre 2012; Yiakoumis et al. 2008). The Smyrna crisis, however, made world headlines through daily reportage. Later, footage of the inferno was seen on cinema newsreels, perhaps the most effective transmitter of news worldwide. It was the weight of Western public opinion that compelled Allied governments to assist in the evacuations. In the contest of perceptions, Greece therefore had at least one victory, as the horrors of Smyrna reinforced Western Orientalist notions of Turkish barbarism.

Thereafter, Greek national memory would only remember the misdeeds of the Turks and forget those committed against Turks, while Turkish national memory would focus on atrocities committed by the retreating Greek soldiers and overlook the Smyrna violence. Beyond this morbid competition over which group was barbaric (e.g. McCarthy 1995), however, lay the more substantive issue of nation-building. The events of Smyrna ought to be seen within the context of the 'long First World War', when Balkan Muslims were driven from their homelands, and after which the Ottomans retaliated in kind. Although not unprecedented, the murderous ethnic cleansings in the Balkans and Anatolia, which intentionally removed whole cultures from a specific territory, were modern in character (Mann 2005: 2; Doumanis 2013b; Yosmaoğlu 2014). They were not generated by ethnic or sectarian differences, but by governments pursuing political projects. Developments in the collapsing Ottoman Empire were harbingers of a much greater conflagration of population engineering in Europe in the coming decades.

After successfully pressuring the British to withdraw from the Straits Zone and Istanbul, the Nationalists were able to set the terms of a new treaty that would recognise their sovereign claims to Anatolia and Eastern Thrace and which would secure the expulsion of Orthodox Christians from these territories. In the population exchange stipulated in the Treaty of Lausanne of 1923, all Romioi, aside from Istanbul residents and the people of Imbros and Tenedos, were to be exchanged for the remaining Muslims in Greece, save for the Muslims of Western Thrace. The Turkish concession on the Istanbul Romioi also had to do with appeasing the US and the attainment of US aid (Yildirim 2006: 72–3). The Romioi of Eastern Thrace had evacuated within a month of the armistice signed on 11 October 1922. The exchange of Muslims stranded in Greece and Romioi left in Anatolia was supervised by the League of Nations, which set up local committees to record the property holdings, and which tried to guarantee an orderly process. Rich Romioi had the means to make their own way to Greece, whereas the poorest were forced to abide by procedures, which often meant waiting for months whilst being forced to share their dwellings with *mucahir* or live in schools and churches for the duration. The Romioi of central and southern Anatolia were herded towards Mersin, Attaleia/Antalya and Makri, those in northwestern regions to Mudania, while Pontians were sent to Samsun and Trebizond. Pontians exiled in Kurdistan were ordered towards the Syrian border. Pavlos Aslanidis was near Diyarbakır when news came of the population exchange. With other Pontians he set out on foot to Syria, was robbed by Kurds along the way, but was received eventually by the American Red Cross (KMS Pontus 752 Zana/Amaseia). Many Pontians ended up in Beirut, from where they were transported to Athens, although some went to Egypt and Cyprus.

The Karamanlides were given time to prepare and allowed a more organised and dignified exit. Accounts of the exodus in oral testimonies sound like biblical stories. Some recalled the appearance of bad omens, such as Halley's Comet in 1910, a locust plague in 1915 and the lunar eclipse that occurred just before the exodus. Rumour had it that Prophet Elijah and St George had returned to protect them from bandits. Each community had time to observe its last liturgy, remove sacred items from each church, including bibles and chalices, and decide which icons to carry and which to bury. Frescoes were covered over with wax; church bells and crosses were removed. One community buried bottles sealed with manuscripts about the history of the village (*I Exodos*, vol. 2: 180). Tellingly, Karamanlides interviewed by the Centre for Asia Minor Studies usually provided lengthy accounts, with many relating fond stories of Muslim friends and neighbours offering assistance and gifts. Anna Giorgiadis of Nevşehir, who was interviewed years later in Kokkinia (Piraeus), recalled: 'During the last days the Turks of the village brought us baskets of grapes, pears, figs: "Please take them to remember us. We will never forget the good we saw in you" … A Turk shows respect and never forgets a good deed, however small' (*I Exodos*, vol. 2: 143). Such nostalgia for homeland and former neighbours could also be read in the testimonies from Romioi throughout Anatolia and Thrace. Whilst presenting pasts that seemed implausibly idyllic, the nostalgic accounts were intended to serve as testimonies to a manner of living that existed *before* the nation, when religious differences and prejudices did not inhibit orderly coexistence, but which nationalists on both sides seemed determined to erase from memory (Doumanis 2013).

The Karamanlides did not wish to leave and were not originally designated for removal, as they were not deemed to have betrayed the 'fatherland' (Yildirim 2006: 62). Some had lobbied Mustafa Kemal for an exemption because they had been loyal to the empire, but only a few 'righteous' Rum were given exemptions. They included a handful of families in Smyrna and Papa Eftim, a renegade priest who had thrown in his lot with the Nationalists and had set up a schismatic church following a feud with the Patriarchate. For the Karamanlides and the Romioi that survived the war and the exodus, Anatolia and Eastern Thrace were now lost homelands. Millennia of Greek life had been extinguished within a fleeting moment.

Cyprus

Situated a mere 65 km south of Anatolia's Mediterranean coastline was a significant part of the Greek world that had been spared the nation-building violence of the 'long First World War'. Greek Cypriot elites had been campaigning for *Enosis* (unification with Greece), but unlike in Crete, an island of comparable size and with a similar balance of Christians and Muslims, ethnic Greeks in Cyprus did not wage a violent insurgency until the 1950s. The chief difference was British power. Although greatly diminished by the experience of the First World War, Britain was still capable of defending its vast empire against anti-colonial movements. Its role as Greece's chief patron in international affairs also complicated matters. Greek consular staff exercised a restraining influence on *Enosis* advocates, who had little choice but to campaign for it politely. By the mid-century, however, the situation would change dramatically. Britain was in a state of advanced imperial decline and Greek Cypriots were using guns in their fight for *Enosis*. What had changed?

The aim of this section is to outline developments in Cypriot society in the early twentieth century. At the time, the island's social structure was modernising. Its working-class and middle-class formations were expanding. Its villagers were migrating to urban centres or across the seas. The island was also being influenced by another global trend, anti-colonialism, which was partly a function of the modern social changes just mentioned (Bayly 2004). To date, the history of modern Cypriot history has usually been written as the struggle for *Enosis*, as if the island's modern history can be reduced to the unfolding of a political programme. The great social changes, however, which explain why ordinary people shifted from being indifferent to nationalism to being willing to fight for it, were responsible for making the *Enosis* movement into a *mass* movement that would eventually overcome British power.

Wartime, 1914–1918

On 5 November 1914, only a few days after the Ottoman declaration of war, Britain formally annexed Cyprus. However, despite its proximity to the Ottoman heartland, its strategic significance was more apparent than real. It did not figure prominently in the strategic thinking of any of the combatants, and it was not contested militarily at any time in the war. Its lack of natural harbours meant it was of little use to the Royal Navy. At the time, Cyprus was an 'inconsequential possession' (A. Varnava 2009: 3), which the British were willing to cede to Greece in November 1915 as an inducement to enter the war. They also seemed reluctant to defend it in the event of an Ottoman invasion

(A. Varnava 2017: 20a). The Ottomans, in turn, seemed unconcerned about an Allied invasion from Cyprus, given that the Anatolian coast opposite was lined by a steep mountain range. The CUP showed scant interest in reclaiming Cyprus, at least in the immediate term. In the 1920s, Kemal Atatürk would invite Turkish Cypriots to abandon their outpost and *return* to their 'homeland' (Mallinson 2009: 9).

Yet Cyprus proved to be quite useful to Britain and its allies as a food basket. As a protected oasis within a sea of hostilities, the island and its substantial farming sector were a convenient source of provisions for troops stationed in the Middle East and especially on the Salonica Front. Cypriot farmers supplied large quantities of barley, carob, wheat, onions, oats, bran, potatoes and raisins, as well as goats and eggs. The colonial government played an active role in promoting production, distributing grants to growers willing to plant corn, and placing restrictions on non-essential goods (A. Varnava 2017: 47). Mules, which were critical for transportation on all military fronts, were bred locally and exported in large numbers. The island was a good vantage point for intelligence-gathering, as a training ground for French legionnaires (the Légion d'Orient) and Armenian military formations, for hospitalising the wounded, and for hosting refugee and POW camps. There were 10,000 POWs in Cyprus by the end of the war. As many as 25 per cent of the male population would volunteer to serve in non-combatant duties, principally as muleteers on the Salonica Front. A major source of the colony's income came from these men, who remitted most of their savings to families back home. Recruits were attracted by generous salaries, bonuses and a land allotment scheme (A. Varnava 2017). Inevitably, locals were affected by inflation and climbing price levels, but the farming population prospered because of high external demand, which also meant high employment. Indeed, Cyprus found the war to be a stabilising influence. Cypriot government revenues climbed during the conflict, from £290,000 in 1914–15 to £610,449 in 1918–19 (A. Varnava 2017: 48).

Given the fact Britain was at war with 'the Turks', the loyalties of Turkish Cypriots were a matter of government interest. As with Muslims throughout the empire, Turkish Cypriots regarded the Sultan as the legitimate ruler, but for practical reasons communal leaders declared their loyalties to Britain, especially as it provided effective protections against the Greek majority. Turkish Cypriot leaders had long been concerned about the prospect of *Enosis*, hence they were keen to impress the British with affirmations of loyalty. As the High Commissioner reported after a conversation with a Muslim leader in 1914, *Enosis* 'would be a grievous calamity to them, robbing them of the feeling of security which they now enjoy … [and would] deprive them of all those moral and material benefits and the great religious tolerance they now enjoy under British rule' (A. Varnava 2019: 38).

Food and employment guaranteed the loyalty of most Cypriots. The only potential source of dissent came from local Greek elites, specifically anti-Venizelists who might also be expected to be pro-German. Anti-Venizelists continued to toast King Constantine at Greek national events and partisan newspapers persisted in attacking Venizelism and its local supporters, whilst being careful not to express any anti-British sentiments. When the nationalist firebrand Philios Zanettos rebuked the Venizelist Bishop of Kition in February 1917 for commemorating British soldiers that were killed in Athens the previous December, he tried to deny his comments later (A. Varnava 2017: 50). Meanwhile the *Enosis* movement had stalled. As was common among native elites in the colonial empires, Greek Cypriot leaders expected their support for the colonisers' war would lead to power-sharing arrangements. Cypriot Venizelists were also keen to work with the colonisers, given Venizelos' close connections with Britain. As their political stocks rose during the war, those of Cypriot royalists plummeted along with those of the Greek king. All the while, the Cypriot iteration of the National Schism fomented tensions within the Greek Cypriot elite, including the higher clergy. The most pressing task of the new Archbishop of Cyprus, Kyrillos III, elected in November 1916, was to heal the divisions within the clergy and laity by appealing to common interest in *Enosis*.

As soon as the war ended, Kyrillos III, as 'ethnarch' (head of the nation), led the renewal of the *Enosis* campaign (Pophiades 2013: 191–3). Supporters were encouraged by Wilson's Fourteen Points and by the fact that Greece, led by the pro-British Venizelos, was a victorious power. By that stage, however, British resolve to retain the island had hardened markedly. Cyprus proved its uses in the military campaigns in the Middle East, particularly the mule corps, and the Sykes–Picot Agreement signalled intentions of maintaining a strong presence in the region. Therefore, Cyprus was again conceived as part of a larger imperial regional strategy. Indeed, throughout the post-war world the dreams of subject elites were shattered by colonial powers intent on strengthening their hold. In response, the *Enosis* movement, like other anti-colonial movements, had to become more structured and assertive in the coming decades. That structure was readily provided by the Cypriot Church, whose influence reached into every village and neighbourhood on the island (Pophiades 2013: 197).

Social problems, 1918–1931

The First World War had also politicised the general population, but for different reasons. The war years seemed to reverse a long-term trend of rising economic inequality and pauperisation, but all economies that had prospered because of high wartime demand, as did many Latin American nations, also suffered from the dramatic drop in post-war demand. Most of the affected nations would experience serious social turmoil and political upheaval. Cypriots also had to deal with longer-term problems. Peasants continued to fall into debt, usurers continued to charge exorbitant interest rates, sometimes as high as 30 per cent, and properties were again being seized or sold off at bargain prices. Between 1881 and 1931, the population almost doubled (186,173 to 347,959), and while much of that increase was found in the cities, namely Nicosia, Limassol, Larnaca, Famagusta, Kyrenia and Paphos, the number of landless labourers had tripled between 1891 (8,476) and 1929 (31,422) (Katsourides 2014: 21, 23). The worst years were 1923–6, when there were 11,798 forced property sales. A 1930 government report noted that 16 per cent of the peasantry was landless and 50 per cent of small landholders were living in poverty. By 1928, 82 per cent of peasant landholders were in debt, owing an average of £36, which was 36 times average weekly earnings (Katsourides 2014: 25, 27).

By the mid-1920s, however, British authorities began to take an interest in the island's political economy. To that point British rule seemed to have no purpose other than to keep Cyprus until a purpose was found, or to deny it to rival powers because of its strategic location in the eastern Mediterranean. The fruits of Britain's civilising mission were certainly hard to see. A railway link had been opened between Famagusta and Nicosia in 1905, but it did not seem to impress the people in the areas it serviced. Very few roads had been constructed, and plans for a much-needed port at Famagusta had been abandoned. The only significant legacy of British rule was the tax system, which was resented rather than admired, the more so as the proceeds were not reinvested locally. Prior to 1914, most of the revenues collected were meant for the Sultan as tribute, but the sultanate used them to service a loan needed in 1855 to fund its participation in the Crimean War. From 1914 to 1926 the moneys were diverted to British bondholders who had invested in the loan. For this reason, the colonial government in Cyprus had been forced to operate on a shoestring, with a tiny administration and police force. During the interwar years, however, governments throughout the colonial world were heavily engaged in development projects, particularly in modern infrastructure (railway tracks, dams, bridges, urban development), and in introducing technologies such electricity and modern transport machinery (Stanard 2016: 230). The chief aim was to make the colonies much more profitable and thereby restore the diminished standing of international powers like Britain and France. Another aim was to 'sell' the benefits of empire to the natives. In the nearby Dodecanese, the Italian colonial governments invested heavily in local infrastructure to impress the world but also the Greek locals, whose loyalties they hoped to win. The impressive redevelopment of Rhodes in particular, but also Kos and Leros, and the employment opportunities which these works provided during the interwar years, had locals acknowledging the distinct benefits of Italian rule (Doumanis 1997). The British had seemed uninterested in making a similar impression on Cypriots. As one colonial official would later put it: 'the Italians have put a lot of money into Rhodes. We have taken a lot of money out of Cyprus. The time has come to show that we can play the same game as the Italians' (Markidis and Georghallides 1995: 72).

A new approach was signalled in 1925, when Cyprus was declared a Crown Colony. It was now administered by a governor rather than a mere high commissioner, and there was an increase in the number of local representatives in its legislative council. The appointment of Sir Ronald Storrs in November 1926 indicated a new determination to improve relations between the government and the subject population. He had a degree in Classics and a knowledge of Classical Greek, and he was experienced in dealing with Greek bishops in Egypt. By most accounts, Storrs also behaved like a man with a mission. He was determined to revive a failed colony where nothing had been done to promote the empire, but where Greek communities had been teaching the Greek national curriculum and raising the Greek flag. The Union Jack could only be seen at Government House (Storrs 1937: 546, 551). Storrs made a point of visiting nearly all its towns and villages, and by charming his hosts with his knowledge of Greek. He tried to make the colonial administration more professional, and make officials and clerks work harder and longer. He built an extensive library that inevitably featured a vast Classical literature selection (Morgan 2010: 112). Among the changes that Storrs instituted was to recognise the national sentiments of Cypriots as 'Greeks' and 'Turks', if only to demonstrate the British Empire's willingness to accommodate nationalities.

The first challenge to British authority, 1931

Storrs' most significant achievement was to secure the termination of the Tribute in 1928. This action promised to release local revenues for local public investment and give the British a chance to demonstrate the benefits of empire. There was also some discussion of the Cypriot people being compensated for being over-taxed. Unfortunately for Storrs, this all coincided with the Great Depression, which would have a greater impact on colonised peoples than on Europeans or Americans. Indeed, the colonial powers exacerbated its impact by squeezing the colonised more than ever, extracting more resources, and cutting the pay of colonial workers and peasants. As much as they could, the colonial powers foisted the costs of the Depression on the colonies (Stanard 2016: 229–30).

The Cypriot economy was deeply affected by the global slump. About 82 per cent of peasants were already in debt in 1928, but their lot would worsen with the collapse in agricultural prices and a major drought in 1931. The mining industry, which had been the focus of foreign investment and a major employer of local labour, began to lay off workers. Some mining companies went out of business. The colonial government in Nicosia made matters worse by tightening the colonial budget, as seen in April 1931 when Storr decided to balance the budget by increasing taxes. In an extraordinary move, Greek and Turkish members of the Legislative Council voted it down, but Storrs then overruled the Council. Cypriots later learned that London was not prepared to refund the taxes that they had over-paid to the Exchequer.

The Great Depression was a major stimulus, perhaps the greatest, to anti-colonial activism around the world. On Cyprus, the economic crisis and British maladministration affected all social categories, and for the first time Greeks of all classes began to see *Enosis* as the solution. On 21 October a protest was held outside Government House in Nicosia, where the Bishop of Kition, who had recently resigned from the Legislative Council, proclaimed a revolution. A riot ensued, as the protesters attacked the small contingent of baton-wielding police, and Government House was set alight. Rioting also took place in other centres. Although there were no reported casualties, the destruction of the seat of government proved to be a turning point. It was a violent act that marked the beginnings of a much more antagonistic relationship between the coloniser and the colonised.

The British responded with repression. Emergency laws were introduced, municipal elections suspended, and press censorship imposed. Reinforcements were called in from Egypt and Malta, and the leaders of the protests were incarcerated. On 28 October the Legislative Council was suspended. As the Council had given Greek Cypriot leaders a forum to voice their opposition, Storrs and his successors set about drawing up a new constitution that saw it replaced by an advisory body (Markides and Georghallides 1995: 69). In the meantime, the governor ruled the island like an autocrat. Neither Storrs nor his replacements would show an interest in restoring Cypriot representation in government, nor did they give the advisory body much business. Over the next decade and a half, the British managed to contain Greek political activism and the *Enosis* cause, but social grievances did find expression through the phenomenal growth of the communist movement.

The Cypriot Left

Throughout the interwar years, rising private debt and the dislocating effects of modern economic change had ordinary Cypriots, both Christian and Muslim, looking to political movements that addressed their social and material needs. What can be gleaned from political speeches and articles written by the emerging leaders of such movements was a sense that *Enosis* was a distraction from the problems preoccupying most Greek Cypriots. Thus, in April 1924, a peasant congress attended by 150 Greek and 65 Turkish delegates from all over the island assembled to discuss matters such as the abolition of the Tribute and the need for an Agricultural Bank: it specifically rejected calls to discuss *Enosis*. Attempts to create mass parties, such as the Agrarian Party and the Popular Party, each of which had performed well in elections for the Legislative Council in 1925, had failed by 1930 because the leadership lacked conviction on social issues. The political Left, however, grew in strength precisely because it spoke to those issues (Katsourides 2014: 77, 83). By the interwar years, a sufficiently large working class had formed. Labour associations had been organised by stevedores and by workers in construction, tailoring, tobacco processing, baking and carpentry. The Cyprus Labour Party was created in Limassol in 1922, and by August 1926 had been renamed the Cypriot Communist Party. Its primary aim was ameliorating social conditions, it sought to include Turkish Cypriots, and it deemed *Enosis* a secondary matter at best. That much was conveyed by a report sent two years earlier (February 1924) to the British Labour Party:

> Regarding the national question, i.e., Union with Greece, which for a long time has been the demand of the bourgeoisie, it leaves us partially indifferent ... If the British Labour Party were to give Cyprus to Greece as promised, the Cypriot Communists would join hands with the Greek proletariat ... If the Labour Government were to keep Cyprus, we would enjoy the socialist regime and celebrate the liberation of the working and agrarian population of the Island. (Katsourides 2014: 88)

The same report, however, also stated that *Enosis* could not be ignored. For as Cypriot society was slowly modernising, it was also increasingly receptive to political ideas and issues like anti-colonialism, which was also seen as a solution to many of the problems. *Enosis* had been as much a call for political liberty as it was an expression of local Greek national identity, matters for which ordinary Greek Cypriots were increasingly showing an interest. By the same token, any association with the colonial regime was deemed by more and more Greeks as shameful. That was particularly the case after 1931, when any illusions of British benevolence were dispelled, and when it was made clear that the colonisers had limited interest in the welfare and aspirations of the great majority of Cypriots.

In the meantime, the labour movement grew only modestly in the 1930s thanks to government crackdowns on local political associations. In 1937 there were only 6 unions and 67 members, but as official suppression relaxed, the movement expanded dramatically: 46 unions and 2,544 members in 1939, 62 unions and 3,389 members in 1940, and by the end of the war, 90 unions and some 10,000 members (Katsouridis 2014: 182–3; Dodd 2010: 6). Many leftist Cypriots also enlisted in brigades to fight Franco in Spain (Katsourides 2014: 184–5). Led by the communist party AKEL (*Anorthotiko Komma Ergazomenou Laou*), which was founded on 14 April 1941, the Left presented the Church with a serious rival for leadership of Greek Cypriot society.

However, the challenge for AKEL and the Left generally during the 1930s and 1940s was the fact that *Enosis* was also developing into a popular cause at the same time, and that compromised their appeal to Turkish Cypriots. As in the First World War, the matter of *Enosis* was again put aside during the Second World War, in the vain hope that loyalty would come with rewards. It did not, and the issue of national self-determination would arise again very quickly, as will be discussed in Chapter 8 (see below, pp. 267–70). The same held true for the rest of the colonial world. India would lead the dismantling of the empire, and other colonies would follow. In Cyprus and indeed throughout their empire in Asia and Africa, the British were to find it impossible to convince the colonised of the benefits of empire.

Greeks in the early Soviet Union

In October 1917, the Bolshevik movement seized power in Russia. By 1921, as the Russian Communist Party, later the Communist Party of the Soviet Union, it had asserted its authority over most of what was the Russian Empire. From 1928, under the leadership of Joseph Stalin, the party drove the creation of a modern, socialist society at breakneck pace. What is often overlooked is that Soviet society met these challenges as a collective of peoples or nations. The empire was reconstituted as a federation of socialist republics that not only recognised the titular nationalities (e.g. Russians, Kazakhs, Uzbeks and Georgians) but also the minorities within each republic. Although many in the party regarded nationalism was a bourgeois phenomenon, Lenin and Stalin recognised its potency and sought to mobilise it rather than fight against it (Christian 2018: 348; Martin 2001). However, nationality would also be used as a category for scapegoating and determining access to resources.

   Within this context, Greek identity found new meaning. The thirty or so years after the Russian Civil War can be divided into two phases. During the more liberal conditions of the 1920s, the era of NEP (New Economic Policy), all groups benefited from the policy of *korenizatsiia*, which translated roughly as 'indigenisation'. The Greeks and most other cultural groups were encouraged to celebrate their national cultures. Under Stalin, however, some minorities were regarded as a security threat and were subjected to punitive treatment, especially groups that could be linked culturally to neighbouring countries. In these conditions, which held from the Great Purges (1937–8) through to Stalin's death in 1953, being Greek was a serious liability.

   The October Revolution of 1917 had presented various challenges to the Greek communities. During the ensuing Russian Civil War (1918–21), the well-established commercial community in Odessa regarded the Bolsheviks as an existential threat and threw their support behind the counter-revolutionary White Army. They also supported a Greek military expedition despatched by the Venizelos government to Ukraine in 1919 (A. Karpozilos 1999: 139–40). Many rural Greeks, however, including villagers near Mariupol and Sevastopol, sided openly with the Bolsheviks. Some did so because the Tatars supported the Whites, and some others because they had adopted agrarian socialist ideas, as did the Pontian peasants of Southern Caucasus, who supported the Socialist Revolutionary Party. In the same region, Ioannis Passalidis, a surgeon from Sukhumi, became a member of the parliament of the short-lived Georgian Democratic Republic (1917–21). However, before the Red Army prevailed, some 50,000 Greeks had emigrated (A. Karpozilos 1999: 140).

The remaining communities recovered quickly from the devastation of the Civil War. When the dust had settled, Greek peasants were still in their villages and Greek shopkeepers and workers were operating in various Black Sea ports. The Communist Party leadership recognised it could not subject the population to more upheaval and privations after eight years of war, and to the sacrifices required in building a socialist society. It also had to refloat the economy. During the period widely associated with NEP, when the Soviet state operated a mixed economy that included small-scale private enterprise, the Greeks were able to rebuild their lives. One peasant from the Transcaucasia region recalled how the temporary restoration of a market economy was a boon for tobacco producers: 'We in the villages lived very well because in our region we grew tobacco. If you were a tobacco grower and worked hard you earned a lot of money. Tobacco crops were purchased by the state … [The state] paid well' (Agtzidis 1995: 145–6).

It was also a good time because of *korenizatsiia*. The Soviet state encouraged its extraordinary range of nationalities to develop a written form of their languages where these did not exist before, and produce books, newspapers, movies, folk music and museums, each of which was expected to promote communism. Soviet Greek communities debated which form of Greek should be the language of education and newspapers (Agtzidis 1995: 145–6). While the majority spoke Pontian dialect, many community leaders pushed demotic Greek, which they labelled 'Ionic'. Needless to say, *katharevousa*, the language imposed by conservative elites in Greece, was not considered. In Novorossiysk, a musical play written in 1928 by one Damon Eristeas called *Revolution in the Language* ends with the funeral of *katharevousa* (A. Karpozilos 1999: 149). The supporters of 'Ionic' recognised that newspapers had to continue publishing in Pontian because 'the workers and peasants were not schooled in the common language [i.e. demotic]'. On 10 May 1926 a congress of teachers decided, with the permission of the Party, to simplify the Greek alphabet and adopt a phonetic orthography (Agtzidis 1995: 154). The proponents of the Pontian language believed it should also be taught in schools because it was the 'language of the [Greek/Pontian] workers of the USSR' (Agtzidis 1995: 163).

Campaigning for its use in schools was the newspaper *O Koumounistis*, which was published in Batum and was the most widely read in the early 1930s. It had 370 correspondents and serviced 300 cities and villages in Transcaucasia, and was written almost exclusively in Pontian dialect, which was useful during the First Five-Year Plan and Collectivisation (A. Karpozilos 1999: 147). As with the other Greek newspapers – *Spartacus* in Novorossiysk, and *Kokkinos Kapnas* ('Red Tobacco Grower') in Sukhumi – all articles were written by journalists who were committed to the Soviet state's objectives, and who were expected by the state to instruct readers and keep them abreast of developments.

Collectivisation and the Great Terror

In 1929 the state had begun to move peasants off private holdings and on to collective farms, which provoked resistance that the state was prepared to overcome by any means. Greeks were caught up in the ensuing upheavals, which eventually saw tens of millions killed, and which traumatised all survivors. One farmer from Kuban recalled how some Greeks were also categorised as 'kulaks' ('tight fists'), wealthier peasants who ostensibly threatened the people's socialist aims and were treated as enemies of the state:

> In 1929 Collectivisation … expanded. They forced everyone to join in. If anyone resisted, they [the authorities] came and threw all their belongings onto the street and would nail the doors shut. So you took yourself, your wife, your children and went to another village and had to start again. Our fields were seized by the state … In 1929 the jailing started. We had no bread, nothing. We fell into deep poverty. Until 1929 things were fine. Stalin destroyed everything. They divided us into kulaks, middle farmers, and paupers. If you had one cow, they decided you were a kulak. (Agtzidis 1995: 211)

Another survivor, one P. Nikolaidis, recalled the great famine that followed the implementation of the programme:

> The famine started in 1929 but was greatest in 1933. It was greater than the famine of the civil war of 1921. From Bela Rezinska not even a third of the people survived. We carried thousands of the dead bodies in vehicles, and we threw them into mass graves. (Agtzidis 1995: 214)

Such scenes were not unusual in the Soviet countryside. By the mid- to late 1930s, the state leadership was clearing the countryside of 'kulaks' and resettling them beyond the Urals. The Greeks were also among the national groups specifically targeted by the state repression (Kuromiya and Peplonski 2014: 87). From August 1937 the state security arm, the NKVD, specifically targeted 'diaspora' nationalities (i.e. Poles, Latvians, Estonians, Finns, Iranians, Chinese, Bulgarians, Slav Macedonians, Koreans and Romanians). Each nationality was the subject of a specific 'Operation' (for example, the 'German' or the 'Polish Operation'). Over 1.5 million people were arrested in these diaspora group operations between 1937 and 1938, and the execution rate of Greeks arrested was over 80 per cent, among the highest (Martin 2001: 337–9). The reason why these groups were selected cannot be determined by their behaviour. Stalin and his government had decided that 'enemies of the people' had to be purged. It was never clear whether the police officials who carried out the violence knew the people they were arresting, beating up and executing (Rittersporn 2013: 184). What is plain is that Greekness was stigmatised within the Stalinist regime, hence Greek (and other foreign) toponyms in the Crimea were Russified during the latter stages of the war (Polian 2004: 152). Especially vulnerable were those who had only recently migrated from Anatolia. Whereas the established populations were Soviet citizens, the more recent arrivals had Greek passports that had been abundantly distributed by Greek emissaries (Ascherson 1995: 190).

Survivors of the first round of deportations testified to what it was like to live at the sharp end of Soviet state political violence. Christos Sidiropoulos recalled:

> We would see them coming in the night in their motorcars. We called it 'the black raven' (*to mavro koraki*). They took people and would leave with them. There were no courts … no lawyers and the like. After a hasty process they sentenced people on false charges. They'd say 'You sabotaged a factory. Sign your confession here.' If you did not sign you were beaten. You were forced to sign. Of those who were deported in 1937, very few returned. You could not even approach the places where they were held … After these deportations many families vanished. (Agtzidis 1995: 232)

Kostas Peridis recalled:

> The deportations started in 1937 and happened mainly in Ukraine and Russia … I know a family from Kuban of six brothers. One happened to be in Sukhumi [Abkhazia, Georgia], the rest were in Kuban. Only the one in Sukhumi lived. Of the five deported, none returned. (Agtzidis 1995: 230)

The most destructive aspect of the so-called Great Terror for national groups were the mass deportations. The relocation of diaspora nationalities was essentially an exercise in ethnic cleansing border regions, where the regime feared local national groups might develop networks with nearby 'motherlands'. As they were concentrated on or near the Black Sea, Soviet Greeks were seen as too close to Greece. An unknown number of Greeks were deported to Central Asia during this period, and in the meantime Greek schools and the Greek-language press were shut down. By August 1938, the last of the Greek schools were teaching in the language of the titular nationalities (Russian, Georgian and so on) (Pohl 1996: 199–201).

When Nazi Germany invaded the Soviet Union in June 1941, minorities either supported the invaders or kept to themselves. Before the advancing Axis forces, the Stalin regime had indigenous Germans, Romanians, Bulgarians, Armenians, Crimean Tatars, Greeks and many other 'suspect' elements removed further east. The first wartime deportations of Black Sea Greeks occurred in April 1942, as Axis forces made their way towards Stalingrad. For the next decade or so, these populations would remain scattered across the Urals, Siberia, Kazakhstan and other parts of Central Asia, forced to live on collective farms and labour camps with meagre rations. The deportations continued after Axis forces were driven from Soviet territory. Partisan sources claimed that most Greeks, like most minority groups, neither resisted nor collaborated, but the official position was conveyed by Lavrentiy Beria, the head of the state security apparatus (NKVD), who claimed that 'German authorities received assistance from the Greeks in trade, transportation of goods, etc' (Pohl 1996: 103–4). An order was issued in June by Stalin himself to remove all the Greeks, as well as all the local Bulgarians and Armenians – 39,000 people in total – to various parts of Kazakhstan and Uzbekistan. By July 15,040 Crimean Greeks had been deported on trains in appalling conditions, while another 8,300 Greeks without Soviet passports were also deported from the Rostov and Krasnodar areas (Polian 2004: 153).

The Soviet Greeks were therefore as much the victims of nation-building as were their Ottoman counterparts. Like so many millions of Soviet citizens they were casualties of Stalin's mobilisational drive to transform Soviet society and economy, and his regime's punitive responses to groups believed to be frustrating that drive (Christian 2018: 367). Soviet scholars long debated the question of 'Stalinism' and especially whether its proclivity for violence and terror was something innate to Bolshevism or whether it should be attributed to the man himself: could there have been Stalinism without Stalin? It is certainly true, however, that the persecution of Greeks (and so many other groups) would only cease once Stalin was dead.

White nationalism in the Anglophone world

All the while, Greeks continued to migrate voluntarily across oceans and continents, albeit in smaller numbers than had been the case before 1914. The First World War and the contraction of the world economy in the interwar years, which greatly reduced the global demand for labour, profoundly affected transnational migration movement. So too did the discriminatory immigration policies of most of the host countries. US Government Acts in 1921 and 1924 greatly reduced the Greek intake. Between 1925 and 1929, 10,883 were permitted entry under a family reunion provision, but only 737 were accepted without it (Kaloudis 2018: 81). These restrictive policies often reflected popular domestic attitudes towards foreigners, as the First World War and the economic turbulence that followed intensified inter-ethnic prejudices not just in Europe but also in places like the United States.

Before the First World War, Anglophone settler societies like the United States, Canada and Australia had expanded by expelling, decimating and marginalising Indigenous or 'First Nations' peoples (Bayly 2004: 432–50). At the same time, these societies also depended on regular infusions of immigrants, which in turn fostered forms of settler nationalism that placed considerable weight on the importance of race. Established groups, mostly Anglophone Protestants, wished to defend their dominant political, social and economic position, and often did so by seeking to keep their nation 'white'. Much more than in Europe itself, the 'white man' in the new worlds believed his 'race' was under threat. By the First World War, each of the settler societies had developed national identities based on 'whiteness' (Anagnostou 2004; Anagnostou 2009). This imperative found expression in forms of racial apartheid, employment exclusion, and immigration policies that barred border entry on ethnic and racial grounds. Thus, as soon as Australia achieved effective independence from Britain in 1901, its parliament legislated the 'White Australia' policy to stop further entry of Asian immigrants, which was used to prevent the entry of 'insufficiently' white peoples like the Greeks (Piperoglou 2018).

At the everyday level, Greeks in every part of the Anglosphere were never allowed to forget their social marginality, as they were often abused for their 'Mediterranean' appearance and poor English. Anti-Greek hostility could be particularly pronounced in the United States, where one could find businesses producing signage or press advertisements such as 'No Sailors, dogs or Greeks allowed' or 'John's Restaurant. Pure Americans. No Rats, No Greeks' (Anagnostou 2004: 35). Many communities were persecuted by the Ku Klux Klan. In July 1922, Greeks in Atlanta, Georgia, created the association known by the acronym AHEPA (American Hellenic Educational Progressive Association; Figure 3.1) principally to combat this violent organisation, which boycotted Greek businesses and physically threatened outspoken community leaders. Even in the new worlds, therefore, Greeks were oppressed by exclusivist nationalism. Greek Americans also struggled as communities and as families over the issue of assimilation, and how 'American' they should become to be considered socially acceptable to the host society.

Similarly, in parts of the British Empire, during the First World War anti-Greek sentiment led on some occasions to open violence. In early 1917 in Johannesburg, youths and war veterans rioted and destroyed Greek small businesses (Mantzaris 1999: 123–4; Hendrickx et al. 2006: 252). Earlier, on 9 December 1916, in the Western Australian mining town

Figure 3.1 *Greek Americans visiting Athens, 1930. Delegates of the fraternal organisation American Hellenic Educational Progressive Associations (AHEPA). © ERT*

of Kalgoorlie, some 2,000 soldiers and local youths went on a rampage, destroying cafes, confectionery shops and other Greek-owned businesses. A police inspector reported that

> A 2,000 strong crowd 'smashed windows of shops occupied by Greeks. Plain-clothed and uniformed police were unable to prevent the destruction of property and looting of premises. Twenty-two arrests were made, mainly youths and also two soldiers. A variety of charges were laid including wilfully damaging property, unlawful possession of goods and disorderly conduct.' (Yiannakis 1996: 205)

Fifteen business properties were destroyed, as well as another six premises in the nearby town of Boulder. Australia had been devastated by the large number of young men killed and wounded both in the Gallipoli campaign and more recently on the Western Front, but the catalyst was a newspaper article that referred to an incident in December 1916, when Allied troops suffered casualties whilst trying to seize control of Piraeus. The article made much of King Constantine's sympathies for Germany and his brother-in-law Kaiser Wilhelm II. Some leading figures in this mainly Kastellorizian Greek community tried to explain that they were Venizelists, but the rioters were not interested in the abstruse details of Greek politics (Yiannakis 1996: 205–6).

A much larger riot took place in the summer of 1918 in Toronto. On 2 August, demobilised soldiers, including amputees and others with serious injuries, had gathered for a veterans' convention. Many had come to believe that foreign immigrants like the Chinese and the Italians had profited greatly while 'white' folk had been sacrificing their lives for Canada. The convention was held near Toronto's 'Greektown' with its many cafes and restaurants. Although there were only some 3,000 Greeks living in Toronto at the time, they operated a third of its cafes and restaurants. These establishments also employed many young Greek males, most of whom were recent arrivals. Although recent immigrants were ineligible for service in Canada's armed forces, Greek Canadian males who were eligible were not keen to enlist. In either case, the veterans resented all so-called 'slackers'. The violence started when a disabled veteran was rumoured to have been assaulted by a 'slacker', a Greek waiter at an establishment ironically named 'The White City Café'. At 6 p.m., hundreds of veterans went on a rampage, ransacking restaurants, destroying Greek properties throughout the night. Some boasted that they were 'hunting Greeks' to give them a beating. Calm was restored by 2 a.m., but by then Toronto's Greektown had been destroyed (Gallant et al. 2005).

'White' racism in the Anglosphere gained strength in the interwar years, and particularly in times like the Great Depression, when jobs were scarce. The hardening of attitudes towards 'non-whites' was reflected in the racially discriminatory immigration policies of Canada (1919) and the United States (1921). Established Greek immigrants felt pressure from authorities and the host society to assimilate. Families were caught in the invidious position of trying to retain their culture while also trying to keep it largely hidden. It was important not to look 'foreign'. The Greek American writer Helen Papanikolas captured this dilemma in one of her fictional characters, who could not find employment until he realised that his foreign-ness was the obstacle:

> One night I couldn't get to sleep and it came to my mind, 'I'm in America and I must be like Americans.' ... First, I went to a Greek barbershop and for 10¢ I got a shave and a haircut. I told the barber to shave my mustache and comb my hair in the middle. The next store was a Jewish second-hand shop selling clothes and hats and shoes, so I got a blue suit, derby hat, American shoes, American shirts, a bow tie, and dressed up like a million dollars. Next morning at the Edison Phonograph Company, I was the first one in the space at that door where the man was. And, as soon as he came out, I took my hat and said, 'Good morning.' I knew how to speak a few words then. I got the job. He called me first. (Karampetsos 1998: 90–1)

To avoid discrimination altogether, many took the decision to assimilate fully. They did so by speaking English exclusively and by not teaching Greek to their children. Those who believed that they could manage both identities, being both Greek and American, had to negotiate the modern or 'American' values that challenged old world patriarchal norms, parental authority and sexual restraint. The Greek American historian Theodore Saloutos, possibly drawing on personal experience, referred to an inter-generational struggle over such matters as 'dating', arranged marriages and exogamy (Saloutos 1964: ch. 15). Growing up in Nebraska during the 1930s, the future Secretary of Commerce under the Nixon Administration Peter G. Peterson recalled how his parents' efforts to raise him as a Greek embarrassed him in countless ways: 'My biggest challenge as a boy was trying to fit in. But fitting in was really tough, because I wanted to be 100 per cent American. They [his parents] pulled furiously in one way, I the other' (Peterson 2009: 2). Being forced to dress like an *Evzonas* at Easter was the cause of acute embarrassment which teasing locals likened to cross-dressing (Peterson 2009: 21). Females had to endure the additional problem of parents who insisted on maintaining strict patriarchal norms, denying the kinds of freedoms that were enjoyed by their brothers and by American girls. It sometimes affected their prospects of getting married: 'Every Greek community in the U.S. has stories of second-generation spinsters, the "good" daughters of parents who followed the customs of their homeland and destroyed the lives of their children' (Karampetsos 1998: 75).

Greek émigrés had to learn to live with the bigotry of bosses, foremen, neighbours and customers, never feeling completely welcomed by the broader community. During the interwar years, the children of Greek Canadians recalled taunts as an everyday reality. A Canadian-born man remembered how 'Toronto was so Anglo-Saxon, and [that] they resented anyone speaking a foreign language'. Greek children confronted racism in the schoolyard, where they were called 'dirty Greek', 'freaks' and 'greasers' (Mina 2015: 88). To avoid discrimination, many adopted English surnames (e.g. Milliotis to Miller, Petropoulos to Peterson), or more easily pronounceable but Greek-sounding names such as Kazan instead of Kazantzoglou, Agnew instead of Anagnostopoulos, Aniston instead of Anastassakis, and Sampras instead of Vroutsouris. The names 'Pappas' and 'Poulos', the most common Greek names in English-speaking countries, were distinctively diasporic creations. They replaced embarrassingly long multisyllabic surnames that began with 'Papa-' (e.g. Papanastasiou) or ending with '-opoulos' (e.g. Paleologopoulos), which other Americans, Canadians and Australians mocked and found difficult to pronounce. On an everyday level, Greeks tended to be discreet, for members of the public often took offence at the mere sound of their language, or at the music emanating from Greek weddings, festivals or picnics. In the Australian town of Warwick, the proprietors of the Belle Vue Café instructed staff to 'Speak quietly so as not to attract the attention … Always speak English and never Greek when customers are present'. Restaurateurs were sensitive to the fact that even the smell of Greek food could alienate customers. Menus only featured 'American' or 'Australian' food, such as steak, fries, and bacon and eggs (Figure 3.2; Alexakis and Janiszewski 2016: 151).

However, the bigotries that Greek immigrants suffered in the Anglosphere were not enough to deter them from establishing roots. A significant factor was the role of the state, which did not persecute migrants or sponsor violence against them. Indeed, Greek settlers found it was possible to live and thrive with a hyphenated identity: to be Greek-Americans, Greek-Canadians, Greek-Australians and South

Figure 3.2 *Greek-Americanisation: Hollywood Café and Milk Bar, central Sydney, 1940s. Photo courtesy D. Vanos, from the 'In Their Own Image: Greek-Australians' National Project Archives, Macquarie University, Sydney*

African Greeks. The great Hollywood mogul from the Peloponnese Spyros Skouras did not need to Americanise his name. Indeed, mainstream xenophobia abated gradually, partly because the host society became increasingly accustomed to certain groups – Greek diners and cafes became a familiar feature of North American and Australian life respectively – and partly because immigrants, particularly the children of immigrants, conformed culturally by speaking with American- or Australian-English accents, by adopting local cultural mores such baseball or surfing, and by embracing local rituals such as Thanksgiving or the King's Birthday (in Canada, Australia, South Africa and New Zealand). The United States had the additional attraction of giving Greek immigrants access to 'America', which was globally acknowledged as the most advanced culture and powerful symbol of modernity (Figure 3.1). Movements like AHEPA signified an intention to integrate into, if not assimilate with, American life, whilst middle-class and upwardly mobile Greek Americans, who were negotiating their identities as Greeks and Americans, could present to folks back home a prime model of how to be modern (Laliotou 2004).

From peasants to proprietors, 1920–1940

To be sure, the typical Greek in the diaspora was an 'economic' migrant, whose motive for leaving the homeland was material rather than cultural. It remained the case that most Greeks in the United States had no intention of settling permanently, but to make money, support their families and pay for dowries, and return to Greece in a better financial position. Whilst more than half a million Greeks had been admitted into the United States by 1931, roughly 40 per cent, or 197,000, had returned (Saloutos 1956: 29). Unlike immigrants from northern or eastern Europe they did not become commercial farmers or, like the Portuguese, engage in commercial fishing. The colony of sponge fishermen in Tarpon Springs, Florida, was an exception to the rule (Kaloudis 2018: 80). What they wanted was cash, and when they got it they tended to purchase small shops and restaurants.

Greek Americans were also engaged in the labour movement and participated in many bloody strikes. Some 40,000 were miners, and many of them played a significant role in 1912 in the Western Federation of Miners strike at the copper mine at Bingham, Utah, and in 1913–14 in the Colorado Coal Strike (Z. Papanikolas 1991). In New York, Greeks played a significant role in the radical Furrier's Union, in Chicago they were important in the textiles mills, and in Lowell, Massachusetts, most were members of the IWW (International Workers of the World). Greeks were also active in the anti-fascist movements of the 1930s, while 200 participated as volunteers in the Spanish Civil War. The New York-based Greek Maritime Union was active during the Second World War in supporting maritime connections with occupied Europe, while the Greek Workers' Federation (1935–7) was renamed the Greek American Union for Democracy (Georgakas 1996; K. Karpozilos 2017).

Social networks continued to influence migration patterns. Nearly every village had a pioneer who found his footing in an obscure place such as Coonabarabran in north-central New South Wales in Australia, or Saskatoon, capital of the Canadian province of Saskatchewan, and sparked a chain migration process. In the 'new worlds', the son of a humble peasant could aspire to becoming a businessman and a community leader. Panayiotis Katsehamos presents a typical case. Born on the island of Kythera in 1890, he passed through Ellis Island at the age of 17 (he claimed to be 19) with the intention of returning, which he did in 1912 to fight in the Balkan Wars. In 1921 he left his new wife and two children in Kythera and set forth to Australia, eventually settling in the northern New South Wales town of Bingara, where he established a cafe in partnership with a cousin. The intention was to bring his family once established. In 1936 he and his partners had built a state-of-the-art movie theatre, and Panayiotis, now Peter Feros, had become a proud town elder and business leader (Prineas 2006). Many émigrés like Katsehamos not only supported their families back home with dowries and schooling costs, but either individually or with the support of expatriate associates, they endowed their village with a school or church. But many business ventures failed, as did Katsehamos' cinema in Bingara. He was not able to bring his family to Australia until 1947. Migration had kept them apart for the most part of three decades (Prineas 2006).

From the 1920s, the Greek diaspora featured more families. The restrictive immigration quotas introduced by the United States government after 1921 often forced émigrés to commit to living permanently in the new country. In 1920 only a quarter of Greek Americans were American born, but within twenty years the locally born were the majority (Moskos 1990: 32–3). This group inevitably felt more rooted in the new world: they became less an extension of Greece and more committed to America. The interwar Greek communities would be composed of families rather than young males; the latter were either returning to Greece to bring back a bride or marrying non-Greek women. Many of the 30,000 that were permitted entry into the United States between 1925 and 1945 were young brides (Moskos 2000: 105).

During the economic boom of the 1920s, many more diaspora Greeks managed to make the transition from labouring to small business. The ready availability of finance was a contributing factor. In Australia the rapid growth of Greek-owned cafes throughout urban and country Australia was financed mainly by successful Greek businessmen. Rather than sending most of their money to Greece, prosperous Greek Americans invested locally: in the property market, the service industries (hotels, restaurants, restaurant supplies, catering), food processing, and in the entertainment industries (Saloutos 1964: 273). In all parts of the diaspora, including Africa, Greeks continued to fill niches in the services sector, largely because they acquired working experience in established Greek businesses, and because they could access information and finance via established Greek social networks, as well as from the burgeoning Greek-language press. Historian Charles Moskos also notes that in the United States those who began in menial occupations ventured into businesses that were closely related to those jobs. Thus shoe-shiners opened their own shoe repair shops, while:

> Fruit peddlers and flower vendors became owners of groceries and florist shops. Confectioners opened up their own stores to such an extent that sweet shops became virtually a Greek monopoly in this country. Pool halls were another venture with heavy Greek concentration ... Many Greeks became wealthy in real estate and stock market speculation. The affinity between Greeks and food service became an American social phenomenon ... the Greek entry into American capitalism was notable in the restaurant business. (Moskos 1990: 44–5)

In Canada and Australia, the number of restaurants and cafes owned by Greeks also proliferated because wives and children provided proprietors with free labour, but also because they could exploit new immigrants who otherwise found it very difficult to enter the labour market, particularly during the Great Depression. Australian unions opposed 'non-white' immigration because migrants competed for scarce jobs and undercut local workers. As James Ploudias said in 1928: 'Australians wouldn't give us jobs, we had to rely on the Greek cafe' (Alexakis and Janiszewski 1995: 21). British authorities were struck by the fact that almost all young Cypriot males in London in the 1930s were working as waiters and kitchen hands in establishments owned by other Greek Cypriots (Oakley 1987: 31). The trade-off, however, was that waiters and kitchen hands could study the business whilst acquiring English. Later they were able to operate their own business in the next suburb or town, often with a loan from their boss, who was often a relative. In Australia, Greek-owned cafes expanded across the country through a chain process, as new cafe owners sponsored more relatives from Kythera, Ithaca and Kastellorizo, who would then start their own cafe in another town and employ family members arriving from Greece.

Building communities

Those wishing to establish roots in the United States, Canada and Australia wanted to live in a Greek community. To create a community required a conscious effort from energetic émigrés who were prepared to put in the time to create and manage the associations that would organise social engagements and support Greek cultural practices. Earlier generations of émigrés in North America had learned to form community councils or *koinotites*, which took on the role of performing the necessary fundraising and legal work required to build churches or buy disused churches of other denominations. With the expansion of Greek communities in interwar America came a proliferation of *koinotites* and therefore parish churches. There were 60 Greek Orthodox churches across the country in 1916, 140 in 1923, and about 200 by 1930 (Moskos 1990: 34, 36). In Canada, Australia and other parts of the diaspora, where numbers were much smaller and dispersed, there were still only a handful of churches.

The parish church was the most important community institution because of its role in annual and life-cycle rituals, and because most émigrés had come from traditional village communities, in which religion informed nearly every aspect of social life. Being Greek still meant being Greek Orthodox. In the meantime, as with many other nationalisms (e.g. Polish, Serbian, Croatian) Greek nationalism was tightly entwined with the national faith. The parish church in the diaspora would play a role in National Independence Day celebrations, while the parish priest would frequently give sermons on patriotism and patriotic themes. Hence the church was a 'national' institution whose importance was recognised even by the non-devout and non-believing émigré (Kitroeff 2020).

Such was the importance of the parish church that diaspora leaders competed fervently and sometimes violently over questions of church administration, finances and ecclesiastical authority. Communities often became hopelessly divided over such matters because they reflected social and ideological fissures. A typical situation presented itself in Sydney, a community with a strong Kytherian presence. During the 1920s, management of a local parish was contested between the Kytherian-dominated *koinotita* and supporters of a bishop who had been appointed by the Ecumenical Patriarchate, but who enjoyed the support of non-Kytherians. In Melbourne the bishop's opponents were Ithacans, the city's largest regional group (Tsounis 1971: 142–5). These disputes usually intersected with ecclesiastical conflicts between patriarchates, the Church of Greece, and independent or autocephalous Greek Orthodox churches. Thus, Sydney's Kytherian-dominated *koinotita* sought the services of defrocked priests and support from another patriarchate (Doumanis 1993; Tsounis 1971: 165). Throughout North America, where *koinotita* board positions were hotly contested by Venizelists and royalists, church life was dominated during the interwar years by the Ecumenical Patriarchate's attempts to assert its authority over the North American archdiocese. Supporters of the archdiocese were usually Venizelists and the more assimilated Greek Americans (Moskos 1990: 36; Saloutos 1964: ch. 14).

These schisms were often bitter and long-running, the more so because Greek symbols and culture attained a greater resonance for Greeks living in *xenitia* (foreign lands). Émigrés also remained even more attached to their local origins. They preferred to mix and intermarry with people from their particular *patrides* (father-lands): their home village, region or island. They seemed particu-larly eager to participate in their own regional associations (*syllogoi*), and as suggested in some Church conflicts, they could often develop deep animosities for Greeks of other regions. It was not uncommon for (say) Peloponnesians, Cretans and Cypriots to refer to other Greeks as 'foreigners' (*xenoi*). Thus, in the larger Greek centres like New York and Chicago, Arcadians, Messenians and Cretans pre-ferred to attend their own regional dances. So too did Kastellorizians in Perth, who formed their first association in 1912, as did the Melbourne Ithacans in 1916, and the Sydney Kytherians in 1922. Sydney also had *syllogoi* for Peloponnesians from Akrata (established in 1924), Mytilineans (1927), Cypriots (1928) and Ithacans (1935) (Tsounis 1971).

Meanwhile, 'Pan-Hellenic' organisations like the *koinotites* were more vital when it came to education (Greek language classes) and religion (creating parishes). During the interwar years, such organisa-tions could also serve political functions. After its establishment in Atlanta in 1922, AHEPA spread across the United States and Canada. The first Canadian AHEPA branch was established in Toronto in 1928, after which chapters were founded in every other major Greek-Canadian centre. AHEPA deserves special mention as a trans-diaspora organisation, and as an organisation that tried to represent Greek inter-ests while trying to stay above ideological divisions. Its promotion of Americanisation drew criticism from sections of the Greek press and the wider community that believed its agenda was too assimilation-ist. The Greek American Progressive Association (GAPA) emerged as a rival organisation that, unlike AHEPA, conducted its meetings in Greek and held functions with Greek music and dancing (Moskos 1990: 42).

Wartime and respectability

Given that Greece fought with Britain during the Second World War, the diaspora in the Anglosphere had altogether different experiences to those of the previous war. Throughout the world, newspapers praised the 1940 Greek campaign against Italian forces in Epirus, while British, Australian and New Zealand troops fought side by side with the Greeks during the German invasion in 1941. Greeks fondly recited words attributed to Churchill during the Epirus invasion: 'Hence we will not say that Greeks fight like heroes, but that heroes fight like Greeks!' In the meantime, the diaspora rallied quickly to support their homeland, using associations like AHEPA to raise funds, lobby governments and play such supportive roles as selling war bonds for the US government. They were especially important in hastening a US response to the Greek famine of 1941–2. Greek Americans formed the Greek War Relief Association, under the chairmanship of Spyros Skouras, who at the time was president of Twentieth Century Fox. It would play a critical role in organising food supplies that were later distributed by the Swedish Red Cross. Community leaders, bishops and marooned Greek diplomats each played a part in bringing the plight of the homeland to the attention of governments (Saloutos 1964: ch. 17). In Australia such a role was played by the consul general Emilianos Vrisakis, who led local famine relief efforts.

Overall, Greek communities within Allied territories were treated respectfully by the state. Unlike their Italian counterparts, Greek Australian businesses were not scrutinised by authorities for profiteering this time: to avoid social harassment and internment, some Italian business operators pretended to be Greek (Tsounis 1971: 294). Diaspora Greeks enjoyed the respect of the wider community by sharing in the sacrifices of their adopted nation. Most young Greek males did serve in British Dominion or US armed forces; among them were Leo A. Loumbas, the first Greek American killed in action in the South Pacific (*Hellenic News*, 22 July 2017), and Andrew Mousalimas, who in 2018 was awarded a Congressional Gold Medal in recognition of his wartime service (*National Herald*, 23 March 2018). Whereas most Greek Canadians and South Africans served in the European war theatre, Australians like the war artist Tony Rafty (Raftopoulos), who later became his country's leading caricaturist, served mainly in the Pacific theatre.

Theodore Saloutos claims that by the end of the war, when *Evzones* (traditionally dressed Greek soldiers) took their place in victory parades in major cities in North America and Australia, the Greek American community was able to enter an 'era of respectability' (Saloutos 1964: ch. 18). However, the wider community was not yet ready to abandon its desire for a 'white' and monocultural society. Few Americans would have been impressed by the fact that the Andrews Sisters, the world's most famous female singing group, were the daughters of a Greek grocer from Minnesota. Decades would pass before Greeks ceased to sense the heat of white nationalism and xenophobia, and before someone like Telly Savalas could invent a character that was openly Greek and yet widely beloved.

Note

1. http://www.youtube.com/watch?v=Vo9KNdDI8ts.

CHAPTER 4

State and society during the interwar period (1922–1940)

Greece had changed dramatically by the end of the 'long First World War' (1912–22). As one politician put it: 'those of us that survived the last war ask ourselves is this the same planet, or have we moved to another, having abandoned the earth' (Merkouris 1933: 3). The Greek state had come into possession of vast new territories and now had a much larger and more diverse population. The lands and peoples also presented challenges that pre-war Greece was not equipped to manage, and which therefore required a new kind of state focused on societal need rather than 'high' politics (diplomacy, irredentism). What kind of political economy was required to manage and stabilise this bigger and culturally diverse 'Hellas'? How were the many new peoples to be transformed into good citizens and committed patriots? How might Salonican Jews, Pomaks, Slav Macedonians, Karamanlides and Pontians be integrated with the host society?

Governmentality rather than governance

Throughout interwar Europe, governance was an object of experimentation (Moses 2016: 329–31). The old political order had vanished by 1918, but there was bitter division over what might replace it. Any ideological movement with a following had its hostile countermovement. Leninism was pitted against Wilsonian liberalism. The utopian dreams of some were the dystopic nightmares of others. But the one concept for which there was a consensus was *étatisme*: the radical extension of the power and purpose of the state in society. This reality was recognised in Greece as much as anywhere else, particularly given the challenges presented by the refugee influx. According to economics professor and future prime minister Xenophon Zolotas, the keynote feature of twentieth-century Greek economic and political thought was that 'only through state intervention and guidance can the orderly economic progress of Greece be guaranteed' (Zolotas 1936: 21).

Figure 4.1 *Greek café in Patras, c.1930. The* kafeneion *as a male domain, with cigarette advertising depicting women in modern bathing costumes. Photographer Maynard Owen Williams*

In the wake of the Asia Minor Catastrophe and the ensuing chaos, an officer movement known simply as 'Revolution' (*Epanastasi*) had seized power. It then made three decisions that would have lasting consequences. Firstly, it committed the then prime minister Dimitrios Gounaris and other leading government and military figures to trial for the debacle in Asia Minor. Each was sentenced to death and executed the same day. This rough justice, which made headlines around the world, was meant to defuse popular anger for the defeat. Secondly, the regime removed the constitutional impediment to the appropriation of large estates. These properties were to be redistributed to refugees, who between late 1922 and 1923 were arriving daily by the thousands. Finally, on 25 March 1924, it abolished the monarchy. There were only three republics in Europe before the war, but by the end there were thirteen. Like Turkey, Greece entered the 'long' 1912–22 war a monarchy and emerged from it as a republic.

Militarism was also a feature of the new political reality. It applied to Greece as much as it did to Turkey, where Mustafa Kemal ruled the new republic with his former generals. Officers were not content to return to their barracks or retire to write memoirs. Many of them had much bigger ambitions and believed they had a better understanding of everyday people than politicians because of their daily contact with soldiers. War taught the importance of corporate discipline and solidarity. Hence the military espoused a form of radical autarchy, which was shared by many politicians as well, including Alexandros Papanastasiou, who was to play a leading role in reforming interwar Greek agriculture. The rise of interwar *caudillos* like Kemal in Turkey, Salazar in Portugal, Franco in Spain and Antonescu in Romania would also have an impact on the Greek political class, particularly those connected with the military. The trend found its expression in Nikolaos Plastiras and Ioannis Metaxas, in Theodoros Pangalos and Georgios Kondylis, and in Stylianos Gonatas and Alexandros Hatzikiriakos (Hering 2006: 1194–1245). The brutalising effects of the war years and the deep acrimony of the National Schism, which had protagonists accusing each other of treason, left its mark on such men. Indeed, the brutalisation of politics found its most far-reaching effects among the officer class.

In the immediate aftermath of the war, however, governments were meant to abide by liberal democratic norms that were monitored by international bodies. The League of Nations had laid the groundwork for progressive governance by introducing policies and international standards for protecting minorities, refugees and labour, and for the provision of social welfare and public hygiene. It brought together social reformers with experience as government advisers, who helped to frame policies and to advise new states like Czechoslovakia and older ones like Greece. It was an age when there was much experimentation with forms of governance, and when governments across Europe exchanged ideas and borrowed institutional models and practices in order to adjust to new domestic political realities. Of great importance, too, were the movements opposed to liberalism. Communists read the First World War as the collapse of the old order, and they aimed to replace it with a new order inspired by the Bolshevik Revolution of October 1917. Fascists believed the war augured the death of liberalism, and sought to create a new Europe based on race, discipline, hierarchy, national values and the end of modernism. During the interwar years, these competing visions were fought out in an undeclared European civil war that found expression in a series of inter-state conflicts, uprisings, *coups d'état* and dictatorships (Traverso 2016).

In Greece, the challenge presented by the new populations (minorities and refugees) was primarily one of economic need: nutrition, land redistribution, housing, public transport and public infrastructure in general. As governments were not accustomed to dealing with complex problems of political economy, national development and social security, they had to rely on a new kind of civil servant produced in German or French schools and trained as a committed *étatiste*. Thus, while the new elite civil service was shaped by society's social problems, at the same time, it also defined the social problems through its technocratic perspective. The approach was therefore paternalistic. The new civil service saw its role as leading an immature and backward society to maturity and progress. During the interwar years, an engine room of senior civil servants and academics from the University of Athens would map out reforms relating to the economy, welfare, education and the constitution. Most of them shared the political views of another circle known as the *koinoniologoi* (sociologists), who were academics and professionals linked to Alexandros Papanastasiou and the left of the Venizelist party. Reforms were championed by former students of German or French universities who were inspired by interwar German socialism and French solidarism (Liakos 2016: 215–17). Most civil servants shared the political views of liberal governments, which showed them favour but which also frequently frustrated their efforts. They nevertheless served all governments, including the Metaxas dictatorship of 1936. In the interwar years, the Greek civil service was the bedrock of *éstatisme*.

Every government department was expected to conduct its work with scientific rigour. At the same time, reform policies had to be informed by original research, as confirmed by the panels of experts that were recruited abroad to introduce changes to education, health, agricultural and other public policies. The experiences of the First World War, the general mobilisation and the provisioning of troops, and the execution of major infrastructure projects by the military also meant there was consensus that all developments at every stage should be orchestrated centrally. This approach was shared by the army, which had excavated harbours, redirected rivers, drained swamps (as happened in Macedonia), restored train and telegraph networks, and updated infrastructure. The army built many of the bridges found in Greece's mountainous regions which are still in use today. The civil service worked with the University of Athens to organise workshops on botany and pharmacology. Planning, programming and auditing were the hallmarks of modernity in the interwar years.

However, there were significant impediments to progressive reforms. While the new civil service responded dynamically to the era's massive challenges and represented a fresh new approach to governance, it did not have a free hand. It remained subjected to the authority of the traditional bureaucracy, military fiefs and local party leaders.

Settling the refugees

By far the most significant challenge was the refugee crisis that struck in the autumn of 1922. Greek authorities were not adequately prepared for an influx – in February, the Ministry of Foreign Affairs had to decline a request from the consulate in Beirut to receive a mere 180 Greek refugees because it could not guarantee them housing and employment (Katsapis 2011: 133). In September alone, as many as 40,000 refugees arrived in Piraeus. Severely overcrowded ships brought passengers carrying typhus and tuberculosis, which meant people had to be quarantined in the harbour's open spaces. Many died each day, their bodies scattered around camp perimeters and threatening further contagion. The initial wave of refugees had escaped from Anatolia in any way they could. With the support of the Red Cross and such US organisations as Near East Relief (later known as the Near East Relief Foundation), the government provided tents and then shelter in schools, churches and theatres. Families also offered asylum, bringing many into their private homes. That was the case in rural Macedonia, where the government requisitioned barns, fields and food from local families to provide it to the refugees. The resentment of host communities, which ran very deep, was partly attributable to the shock of being inundated by foreigners, but also to the higher taxes and the requirement to share resources (Kontogiorgi 2006: 74, 169).

It is difficult to underestimate the scale of the refugee crisis and the plight of its victims. Once released from quarantine, many would roam from place to place in search of lost relatives or somewhere to settle. In the general panic that followed the military debacle in late August, family members were frequently separated, only to learn later that their relatives had either been killed or had ended up in different parts of Greece. As late as the 1960s, people listened to a midday radio programme called *I anazitiseis tou Ellinikou Erithrou Stavrou* ('The searches of the Greek Red Cross'), which invited anyone that recognised the names of the missing to make contact. Many had long since perished in refugee camps or along roadsides. Others had been rescued by foreign vessels and ended up in other countries, where young children and orphans were given new identities and then lost their mother tongue. There were also some 450,000 people left stranded in Anatolia. Under the auspices of the League of Nations, a population exchange was carried out between Greece and Turkey in a more orderly and supervised manner.

The challenges presented by refugees, especially their resettlement, would preoccupy every Greek government until the outbreak of the next war. Temporary emergency camps were initially set up in the ports where the refugees were received, especially in Piraeus, Thessaloniki, Kavala and Iraklion (Figure 2.2). Some of these makeshift camps, usually located on the city outskirts, became permanent shanty towns or slums known as *prosfygika* (refugee quarters) (Hirschon 1998; Kiramargiou 2019). To meet the challenges of settling this vast displaced population, the government had spent the equivalent of £4 million, but also had to secure an extraordinarily large loan of £12.3 million, at a relatively high interest rate of 8.71 per cent – the standard rate for government loans at the time was 4 to 5 per cent. A supplementary loan was needed by 1927 (£9 million, at 7.05 per cent interest), of which one third was dedicated to the needs of the refugees (Kontogiorgi 2006: 77, 81–2). Yet another was secured in 1931. The cost of servicing these loans together with interest amounted to 40 per cent of the annual state budget (Tounta-Fergadi 1986).

The refugees were to be distributed into rural and urban areas. Most had come from rural Anatolia; hence about 53 per cent were resettled in the Macedonian countryside. There were two principal reasons why the state paid special attention to the rural colonisation of Macedonia. First, vast tracts of farmland in Macedonia had been vacated by displaced Muslim and Slav Macedonian peasants, causing a collapse in agricultural output. Second, the newcomers were meant to dramatically alter the region's ethnic profile and give it an overwhelming Greek majority. Six hundred thousand people were settled in Macedonia. Greece was seen at the time as a laboratory for resettling displaced peoples, and the Refugee Settlement Commission, set up by the League and chaired by the American Henry Morgenthau, was regarded as a 'monument of rationality' (Kontogiorgi 2006: 330; see also Greek Refugee Settlement Commission 1926).

Slav Macedonian peasants, known simply as *dopioi* (locals), particularly resented the fact that refugees were resettled on former Ottoman estates known as *çiflik* (Greek *tsiflikia*), which were usually prime arable properties (Karakasidou 1997: 154). Newspapers routinely reported disputes that frequently led to violence. Communities that arrived more or less intact from a particular town or locality, with its priest or mayor, were best able to work together and defend their claims from locals. The normal pattern was to resettle families that shared the same culture or regional origin, for example Thracians, Pontians and Karamanlides. The typical family was allocated a vacated Muslim house, a plot and some farm animals. All new settler communities were in dire need of building materials, farm animals, seed and tools, and had to contend with roads and general infrastructure in disrepair. The most significant problem, which statistics also fail to relate, was that the average plot was too small to support a family, forcing them diversify their economic activities.

Overall, resettlement was carried out efficiently, making it a model for other programmes such as that taking place contemporaneously in Bulgaria. The League of Nations did not allow the Greek government to manage the financial aid because it deemed it too inefficient and corrupt. That role was played by the Refugee Settlement Commission, which carried out its responsibilities until 1930.

Far less official attention was paid to urban refugee settlement. The Refugee Settlement Commission and state bodies provided housing, some of which survives in Athens today, but the housing units were generally too small and ill equipped to meet the average family's basic needs. Refugees frequently took the initiative to build their own homes on the very land where they had set up tents; the properties were later ceded to them by the state. Using whatever materials they could find, the refugees constructed homes in overcrowded slums or 'shanty towns' that survived into the 1950s, or they built 'settlements' consisting of tightly bunched dwellings, as seen in Kaisariani, Toumba and other refugee suburbs, often adopting old Ottoman toponyms with the addition of the word for 'new' (such as Neo Kordelio, Nea Mudania and Nea Ionia). The poorest slums were unsanitary and vulnerable to disease outbreaks, as happened at the 'Teneke Mahala' (literally 'tin neighbourhood') near Thessaloniki's railway station, where families were crammed into basic one- or two-room hovels made of flattened sheet metal (Mazower 2004: 366). In the beginning, houses were forced to share water and bathrooms, which inevitably led to disputes between neighbours. A consequence of the lack of state services was the formation of local associations that dealt with drainage, water, electricity, roads and transport, and which also became hubs of radical politics. Indeed, the refugee slums also became the 'red' centres of Athens, Piraeus and Thessaloniki. Meanwhile, the paltry assistance received by urban refugees exceeded anything available to the local poor, which led to violence in places like Kilkis, Kavala and Serres (Katsapis 2011: 125–69). Refugee neighbourhoods also produced memorials to the lost homelands, including churches dedicated to the patron saint of the region or locality back home, housing the few icons and relics that they managed to salvage.

The social and cultural divisions among the refugee population were also reflected in settlement patterns. Wealthy Smyrniots were reunited in Nea Smyrni (New Smyrna), a new town located between Athens and the coast, whereas the poor of coastal Asia Minor, Pontus and Cappadocia were crammed in with poor Peloponnesians in suburbs to the west of Piraeus, where the land was dry and arid. About 300,000 were settled in greater Athens (including Piraeus), where refugees would account for a third of the urban population. Another third consisted of recent migrants from rural Greece. About 100,000 refugees were settled in Thessaloniki (Macherá 2002: 118), thus making what had recently been an intensely multiethnic city overwhelmingly Greek.

An even more significant challenge facing the refugees in urban centres was employment. To be sure, the interwar years did see unprecedented growth in the industrial sector and especially in small-scale manufacturing. Textile and carpet factories employed much of the refugee labour, particularly women, from the settlements that lined the railway tracks. A few Asia Minor businessmen managed to escape with some capital, and they were able to use their social networks to re-establish their enterprises and find a toehold in local markets. Industrial expansion benefited from the lending policies of the National Bank of Greece and from duties on imports. The combination of an expanding domestic market, reconstruction, ready finance, low wage costs and protection from foreign competition produced a minor industrial revolution. Within six years of the refugees' arrival industrial production doubled, but the structure of the industrial sector did not change. Greece's industrial landscape resembled an archipelago of small workshops and small-scale enterprises, among which there were also a few medium- to large-scale operations employing a few hundred people. A large percentage of refugee labourers, especially in the north, were employed in tobacco processing. However, this interwar industrial spurt was not dynamic enough to have an impact on foreign markets or absorb the available labour pool. The labour market was still characterised by underemployment and seasonal jobs. Too many workers were forced to scramble to find bits of work to attain a living wage. A side effect of urban underemployment was rural underemployment, as peasants often depended on supplementary work in towns, while Peloponnesian peasants, who previously would head off across the Atlantic, were obstructed by restrictive US immigration laws.

The refugees found that attaining citizenship was a relatively simple matter of registering at an official office. Social acceptance, however, was another matter. Refugees were typically treated with indifference and often with overt hostility. Many of them changed the ending of their names to sound more Greek – many with surnames ending with the Turkish suffix '-oglou' (literally 'son of') substituted the more Greek sounding '-idis', '-iadis' or '-opoulos', but the sights, sounds, smells and tastes of the refugee settlements evoked a foreign world that was exotic and too 'Turkish' for local liking. Rallies were held against these 'Turks', who were commonly referred to as *tourkosporoi* ('Turkish seed') and *yiaourtovaftismenoi* (literally 'baptised in yoghurt'), and against *oglou-kratia* (meaning Turkish dominance) (Mavrogordatos 1983: 194). Such slurs corresponded to the kinds used in Turkey against refugees from the Balkans: *yarı gâvur* ('half-infidel') and *gâvur tohum* ('infidel seed') (Glavinas 2013: 351). Aside from cultural bigotry and preferential treatment in state resource allocation, much of the host population resented the refugees for political reasons. At least initially, the newcomers were staunch Venizelists, largely because they blamed the royalists for the military debacle in August 1922 and for abandoning Anatolians to their fate. In turn, the royalists and their allies resented the refugee vote, which kept them out of power, and which, according to historian George Mavrogodatos, 'truly dominated the politics of the era': without it, the monarchy would not have been abolished, and the anti-Venizelists would have won every election after 1926 (Mavrogordatos 1983: 182–5; see also Hering 2006: 1175).

Although an extremely diverse group, as indeed was the host population, the newcomers embraced their new collective identity ascription, 'refugees' (*prosfyges*). Aside from the shared trauma of displacement and their xenophobic reception in Greece, the term *prosfyges* was retained as an official category. Some had been classified by the state as *antallaximoi* ('exchangeables') before departing their homelands, and for many years after 1923 they expected to be compensated for the loss of properties in Anatolia and Eastern Thrace. Within a short space of time, communities produced 'refugee-fathers' (*prosfygopateres*) who lobbied on their behalf in government and within the Venizelist party.

In due course, the refugee communities would have their own intellectual and cultural leaders. They also had their own newspapers and magazines, in which they recorded their histories, fiction, poetry, customs and folklore. A continuous stream of publications was produced on Anatolian and Thracian folklore and traditions, especially as many feared these would be forgotten within a generation. Accordingly, they also wished to establish their traditions as legitimate vernacular cultures of the Greek nation, in much the same way as regional traditions such as Cretan or Epirote had been recast as varieties of Greek culture. However, there was little room for manoeuvre when it came to language. Spoken Pontian was forbidden in schools: children were punished if they uttered Pontian terms. Spoken Turkish, which was the mother tongue of much of the refugee population, was restricted to the family home, much as 'Kritika' was among Muslim Cretans in Turkey. Refugee communities saw no reason, however, to part with their other traditions. They sought acceptance as Greeks but insisted on retaining a deep affection for their *chamenes patrides* ('lost homelands'). Refugee identity would be predicated on deep nostalgia for these *chamenes patrides*, and on the miseries of expulsion and resettlement. That bitter experience, or as it was called at the time, *o kaïmos tis prosfygias* ('the sadness of refugee-hood'), was expressed in the literature of Elias Venezis and Stratis Myrivilis, and in the lyrics of the underground musical genre 'Rembetika', which had been popular on both sides of the Aegean before 1922 (Salvanou 2018).

Of course, Turkish society also has a complicated relationship with its refugee history. Millions of Turks today are the progeny of refugees from the Russian Empire and the northern Balkans, but the 1912–22 period brought new waves from Greece, while much of the Republic's early leadership came from homelands now in Christian hands. The fathers of modern Turkey were refugees in a sense. Mustafa Kemal was born and educated in Thessaloniki (Selânik). The Muslims removed from Greece by 1923 numbered between 388,146 and 463,534 (Tsetlaka and Athanasiou-Marina 2011: 171–90; Yildirim 2006: 91). Their removal was organised and supervised by a committee of Greek and Turkish officers. Some were Greek-speaking Bektashis, including the Valaades from central Macedonia, who ended up in Eastern Thrace. Another expelled community was the Dönme, Jews who converted to Islam but practised Judaism in secret, and developed a syncretic faith combining Sufi and Jewish mystical traditions. Many became ethnic Turks and Sunnis but retained memories of their origins. The Greek-speaking Muslims compulsorily settled in Turkey found their new homeland alienating (Tsetlaka and Athanasiou-Marina 2011: 173). Cretan Muslims were never fully embraced by the host society, and they would continue to regard Crete as their homeland. As one Turkish Cretan wrote to his Greek Cretan friend: 'I don't recognise the place or the language, I am not considered Greek by the Greeks, Turk by the Turks, Arab by the Arabs, I am finding things very difficult' (Glavinas 2013: 351).

Minorities, foreigners and refugees

There were two views on how to build the nation after 'long First World War'. One approach was inclusive: anyone could acquire Greek national consciousness, regardless of language, religion or place of origin. This view, which considered citizenship an inalienable right, *jus soli*, was supported by Venizelos. But it was a minority view. The alternative majority view was that ethnic origins were essential, which was more akin to *jus sanguinis*. Citizens had to be *ethnic* Greeks, *Ellines to genos*, meaning that their mother tongue had to be Greek and their religion Greek Orthodox. The rest were *allogeneis* ('foreigners'), potentially *esoterikoi ekthroi* ('internal enemies'). For them, citizenship was negotiable. Citizenship could be withdrawn from non-Greeks arbitrarily for breaking the law or for security reasons (Christopoulos 2012: 75–84). Such discrimination was precisely what the League of Nations wished to counter by seeking legal protections for minorities, but it had difficulty enforcing them. Throughout the interwar years, the League was flooded with petitions from minority groups whose rights were being violated (Prott 2016: 226).

Government policy on minorities was also influenced by national security concerns and particularly neighbouring states that might target the loyalties of minorities. The most important decision in this regard was the resettlement of most refugees in Macedonia, where 'minorities' had been the majority. The fact that the Slavophones of the region spoke varieties of standard Bulgarian meant their loyalties might be with Bulgaria. As the government distrusted such groups as well as the refugees, southerners from 'Old Greece' and Crete staffed the civil service and other positions of provincial authority, while young minority and refugee males were mixed in with autochthonous Greeks on compulsory military service. To contain the impact of minority votes, which Venizelists believed had cost them the 1920 election, Jews, Slav Macedonians and Muslims were placed into separate voting blocks.

The most significant linguistic minority were the Arvanites, whose ancestors had migrated to Greece during the Middle Ages and had formed communities that dotted the highlands and some coastal areas. Many could be found close to Athens and the Saronic Gulf islands. The Arvanites had long since acquired Greek through public education, and for working purposes, but continued to use their Albanian dialect (Arvanitika) at home. Patriarchal and insular, this group was not receptive to rival national influences, least of all from Muslim-dominated Albania, which did not attempt to claim the Greek Orthodox Arvanites as its 'lost children'. On the contrary, many families, especially from the islands, counted among the nation's elite. Venizelos cited the examples of his Deputy President, Emmanuel Repoulis, General Panagiotis Danglis and Admiral Pavlos Koundouriotis, each of whom came from Arvanitika-speaking regions, to show that linguistic diversity did not threaten national identity (Embirikos and Baltsiotis 2019: 100–5).

Greeks had a different attitude to the other significant Albanian-speaking minority, the Chams. This Muslim group was essentially stranded in Greece when the border with Albania was drawn in 1913. Since then, Chams had been embroiled in land rights disputes with Christian Epirotes and refugees. During the Greek–Italian war of 1940, Cham men were removed from the border region with Albania and were only allowed to return when Greece was under Axis occupation. As was often the case among persecuted minorities, the Chams collaborated with the Axis by forming armed militias that persecuted the Greek population. After liberation, they suffered punitive retaliation, and all trace of Chaim life and culture was obliterated. Community archives and schools were torched. The mosque of the town of Paramythia was blown up and its foundations ploughed into the ground (Manta 2004). Those who survived the massacres fled across the border.

The Vlachs were another linguistic minority who, like the Arvanites, were ascribed a legitimate place in the nation because they had coexisted with Greek-speaking communities for centuries, and because they were Greek Orthodox. Because theirs was a Romance language (also known as Aromanian) indigenous to the Balkans and closely related to Romanian, the Vlachs were deemed by Romania as 'Romanians', and Bucharest funded some Vlach schools. However, the relationship was of limited interest to both the minority and its 'motherland': Romania had no territorial claims on Greece. Like the Arvanites, the Vlachs did not occupy a contiguous space that might encourage calls for autonomy, let alone nationhood. Furthermore, it was widely recognised that

Arvanites and Vlachs contributed to the Greek War of Independence as fighters, donors, intellectuals and merchants, as well as politicians. Ioannis Kolettis, Greece's first prime minister (1844), for example, was from a Vlach-speaking Epirote community. Italian attempts during the Second World War to create armed militias in the Pindus Mountains failed miserably (Kahl 2009).

The population group that presented the most significant challenge to national security and state assimilationist objectives were the Slav-speakers of the northern provinces, especially Macedonia. This group lived in rural areas, where they worked as pastoralists and farmers, as well as construction workers and pedlars. Before 1912 large numbers of Slav-speakers had been employed on large Muslim estates (*çiflik*). The group had distinctive cultural traditions and social features that it shared with other South Slavs, such as the *zadruga*, a commune unit composed of an extensive kin group dominated by a male elder or patriarch.

Before 1912, the national loyalties of Slavophones had been contested by rival nationalists and militias because they occupied a territory deemed vital by both Greece and Bulgaria on economic, strategic and historical grounds, and because most members of the group were indifferent to national and ethnic categorisation. That much was suggested by the fact of their self-designation as 'locals' (*dopioi*). Therefore, rival nationalist movements believed that this 'proto-national' group was ripe for nationalisation. One of these movements was the Internal Macedonian Revolutionary Organisation (IMRO), which campaigned for an independent Macedonian nation state. It had supported the Ilinden Uprising in 1903, when Slavophone villages revolted against Ottoman authority, seeking autonomy, land redistribution and other social goals. The insurrection was brutally suppressed. A hundred and ten villages were torched, and many fled to North America, where they formed vibrant communities and cultivated a distinct national identity that was described as distinctly 'Macedonian' (Danforth 1995). After the Balkan Wars, the more significant competition for the loyalties of the Slavophones behind Greek borders were neighbouring states Bulgaria and Serbia's successor state Yugoslavia. Therefore, they were treated by Greek police and state authorities as a security threat and were subjected to conditions that resembled a foreign occupation. Authorities also associated the group (unfairly) with the Left. Their oppressed circumstances drew the attention of the Communist International, while the Greek Communist Party (KKE) decided it would support Slav Macedonian autonomy, even though support for KKE was tepid at best. That changed, however, when the Metaxas dictatorship (1936–41) began implementing policies of forced assimilation (Mavrogordatos 1983: 251). The regime made the language illegal. Those arrested were fined, beaten and sometimes forced to consume castor oil. Families were pressured to Hellenise their surnames, to display Greek flags outside their homes and businesses, and to paint their homes in blue and white. Although many Slav Macedonians identified strongly with Greece, many, sometimes even the siblings of Greek loyalists, reacted to state coercion by declaring an undying enmity for Greece (Danforth 1995). However, another significant factor was the distribution of former Muslim properties and the bias shown by the Greek state for Anatolian and Thracian refugees. This made for lasting enmities between Slavophones and refugees that were expressed more openly during the Second World War, when they often took up with opposing sides.

What were their numbers? Estimates are subject to rival nationalist manipulation. According to the censuses that included a question about mother tongue, there were 81,844 Slavophones in Greece in 1928, 94,509 in 1940, and 41,017 in 1951. The largest concentration was in the northern territories near Edessa, Florina and Kastoria. Half the communities near Florina were exclusively Slav Macedonian, and another quarter were mixed with refugees, Vlachs or Arvanites (Karakasidou 2002: 132–3). In the diaspora, Slav Macedonian families continued to speak their mother tongue at home, although they were often divided on the question of which nationality to declare. In Australia, as in Greece, both before and after the Second World War, families would often split over the matter (Danforth 2000).

The terms of the population exchange left a significant number of Muslims in Western Thrace, which had already been an oppressed minority under Bulgarian rule (1913–20). The region's Pomaks, a Muslim Bulgarian-speaking population based in the Rhodope Mountains, astride the current Greek–Bulgarian border, had been subjected to forced assimilation policies by Sofia. When a new border was drawn in 1920, those on the Greek side of the border were pressured by Muslim elites in the region to see themselves as Turkish. As opponents of Kemalist secularisation, however, they also demanded of Pomaks a stricter observance of Sharia law, and more traditional dress for women.

By the time Greek administration was introduced in 1920, Western Thrace had 74,730 ethnic Turks, 11,848 Pomaks, 54,092 Bulgarians, 56,114 Greeks, and 7,906 Jews, as well as a small number of Armenians.

The region was then swamped by 303,879 refugees from Pontus, Asia Minor and Eastern Thrace, and quite suddenly, the Greek Orthodox population went from a sizeable minority to become the overwhelming majority. During the 1920s, Western Thrace was a refuge for anti-Kemalists like the last Grand Mufti of Constantinople. Under Turkish state pressure, however, the Greek government was forced to evict anti-Kemalist religious elites, after which the vacuum was filled by pro-Kemal secularists (Meinardus 2002: 87). During the Second World War, the Bulgarians reoccupied all but the territory bordering with Turkey and resumed their policy of forcibly assimilating the Pomaks. In 1944 the region was briefly administered by the Greek resistance movement, EAM, and then in 1945 by the Greek army. Throughout the war, the Muslims of Western Thrace, partly because of Turkish neutrality, did not collaborate and abstained from involvement in wartime politics. Nevertheless, the region was placed under martial law in the immediate post-war years, which led to restrictions on movements and random house and checkpoint inspections by authorities (Kalantzis 2016).

Every new city acquired during the Balkan Wars and following the incorporation of Western Thrace had a significant Jewish community. Ioannina was home to about 2,000 Romaniotes, Greek-speakers who could trace their history back to Byzantine times. Elsewhere, however, the predominant group were Ladino- or Spanish-speakers, who had until recently formed the largest single ethnic group in Thessaloniki and had dominated the city's economy and culture. Thessaloniki had been one of the world's great Jewish centres, with fine synagogues, schools, libraries, hospitals, philanthropic institutions, a press, sports teams and political organisations. When the Greek armies arrived, the community was 61,439 strong, and it featured all classes, from wealthy merchants and bankers to middle-class professionals and bureaucrats, to poor *hamals* (stevedores) and the fisherman who eked a living in the Thermaikos Gulf (Mazower 2004: 303).

The community did not welcome the end of Ottoman rule, as the empire had guaranteed Jews conditions in which they could live under their own laws and traditions. Many aspects of the new national order would inevitably hurt Jewish life. Thus in 1924 Saturday was replaced by Sunday as the official day of rest, and then, in 1934, all 'foreign' schools were closed, including Jewish schools. Many locals had chosen to emigrate since 1912, although not always because of Greek rule. Many departed because of wartime deprivations and the city's destruction by the Great Fire of 1917, which devastated the Jewish quarter

(Molho 2001). However, the vastly expanded Greek Jewry had diverse interests. Jews did not vote as a bloc, although many in the community bristled at the anti-Semitic rhetoric of the Venizelist press, and after 1913 tended to vote against parties that were seen to be promoting militarism. Whereas some were concerned with the preservation of traditions, an unusually high number of Greek Jews were linked to the country's incipient socialist movement. Indeed, interwar Thessaloniki produced the nation's most significant socialist organisation, the *Federasión* (Liakos 1985; Naar 2016: 22). Unlike their elders, a new generation of Thessaloniki Jews came to embrace Greece as their homeland, and despite the rise of rabid anti-Semitism in their city during the 1930s, regarded themselves as Greek Jews (Fleming 2008: 108; Naar 2016: 285–6; Naar 2020).

After 1922, the city's Jewish community would be outnumbered by the settlers from Thrace, Pontus and Asia Minor by two to one. By 1928 Thessaloniki was 80 per cent Greek Orthodox. Having been evicted from their homelands because of their religion, many refugees demanded the eviction of Jews from their new homeland. Newspapers like *Makedonía* played an important role in fanning anti-Semitism, as did the publication of anti-Semitic books, including a Greek translation of *The Protocols of the Elders of Zion* (Fleming 2008: 94–5). In 1927 an anti-Semitic fascist organisation was founded, the National Union of Greece (EEU or EE) or *Chalyvdokranoi* (because they wore helmets). Its leadership was composed of refugees and was widely supported by the authorities, war veterans, the Venizelist party and the Church. Jews were attacked in the markets and in poor neighbourhoods in pogrom-like outbursts. The climax came in the summer of 1931, when hundreds of *Chalyvdokranoi* set fire to the Jewish community of Campbell, which had provided temporary housing for victims of the Great Fire of 1917.

This upsurge in anti-Semitism explained the rise in Jewish emigration to France and the United States. Poorer Thessalonikan Jews made for Palestine. They found a new identity as *Oley Yavan* (Greek migrants), cultivating an identity as Greeks, as did Romaniote migrants in New York. One of the paradoxes of this period is how those who were designated as 'foreigners' (*allogeneis*) in Greece adopted a Greek identity abroad, where it served as a point of differentiation from other Jews.

Strangely (and finally), the minority that figured most prominently in Greek literature was also the most obscure. These were the Gypsies or Roma. The best-known references appear in Alexandros

Papadiamantis' *I Gyftopoula* (*Gypsy Girl*) (1884), in Georgios Drosinis' *To Votáni tis Agápis* (*Garden of Love*) (1901) and above all in Kostis Palamas' *Dodekalogos tou Gyftou* (*Gypsy's Dodecalogue*) (1907). These works presented an exotic image of a group that was otherwise ghettoised and despised. Religion is relevant here. Christian Gypsies had existed in southern Greece, but more came with the population exchange, while Muslim Roma had lived in northern Greece and especially in Western Thrace and had been exempted from the population exchange. Paradoxically, Muslim Roma were the only members of this group that acquired Greek citizenship: new Christian Roma only attained it by the late 1970s. In the 1928 census the Roma population was 4,998, and by 1940 there were 8,141 (Trubeta 2001).

Greece's expansion during the 'long First World War' made it a more culturally diverse country. Territorial enlargement had diluted the Greek majority, a 'problem' that was only partially remedied by the population exchange. Nevertheless, while assimilating refugees and newcomers to a national type was a major preoccupation, the state had even more pressing issues to resolve. How was the nation to manage economic reconstruction in the wake of ten years of war and social dislocation? How would it manage the rehabilitation of the rural sector, given there were far more mouths to feed?

Rural reform

The acquisition of the northern territories and the exchange of populations made Greece more rural than it was before 1912. The national economy was still overwhelmingly dominated by agriculture, which continued to engage the highest percentage of the population (approximately 60 per cent), and to account for the largest percentage of GDP (Gross Domestic Production).

The reconstruction of the rural sector was therefore of vital importance. The new lands were deserted and underdeveloped, and in dire need of irrigation and drainage systems, and of a modern transport infrastructure. The most immediate problem was the collapse of the indigenous rural population because of ethnic cleansing and wartime dislocation. The refugees were the obvious remedy, but the population exchange brought many more people than needed. Accommodating them required one of the most radical rural reform programmes ever seen in Europe, which included the sequestration of large estates and ecclesiastical properties. Eventually, the state was able to acquire 12 million *stremmata* of private and ecclesiastical land, of which two thirds were earmarked for the refugees and the rest for local farmers. The reform was enacted hesitantly by Venizelos' Thessaloniki-based government in 1917 but was seen through by the Papanastasiou government of 1923–4 (Marketos 2000: 261–86).

In the interwar years, tobacco assumed the role that was once played by currants. Tobacco exports made it possible to service national debts and purchase not just food imports but also industrial wares. Tobacco production had started in Thrace and Macedonia before the Balkan Wars, but in the 1920s it became the staple export commodity that refugee farmers found profitable even with their small plot allocations (Mazower 1991: 87). Tobacco processing and merchandising also became a significant source of employment in the new territories. In the 1920s, tobacco employed one in seven Greeks, while cities in eastern Macedonia and Western Thrace, which thrived on cigarette production, also became centres of the Greek labour movement (Petmezas 2002: 219).

Among the state's ambitions was to create a class of independent smallholders and to overcome low rural productivity. Even though 70 per cent of farmland was dedicated to cereal production, Greece depended on cereal imports (Mazower 1991: 88–9). The lead was taken by the Ministry of Agriculture, which had been established in 1917, and which featured departmental units dedicated to specific commodities: wheat, tobacco, cotton, olive oil and currants. The Ministry required farmers to join cooperatives and sell basic commodities through these to improve price competitiveness, and made cheap loans accessible by establishing the Agricultural Bank (1929). It also oversaw major land reclamation programmes that included draining marshes and lakes, redirecting rivers and building dams. These works changed the Macedonian landscape and virtually doubled the available arable land.

State policies did lead to substantial productivity improvements even in the southern provinces, which also managed to surpass pre-war production levels by the mid-1930s. Productivity increases were achieved without significant new technologies, although greater use of fertilisers played an important role (Petmezas 2002: 244–6). Even more important, indeed critical, was the emergence of a new group of qualified functionaries, some two thousand young agronomists, veterinarians, engineers, geologists, sociologists and agricultural economists. These were graduates from Greek and foreign universities who applied their scientific expertise to drive the modernisation of the agricultural sector. Teams of experts toured the villages and the fields to advise farmers on new seeds, on modern methods for cropping, fertilising and harvesting, and on preserving produce. Cooperatives also played a vital supportive role by establishing schools, providing credit, machinery and information regarding goods distribution, by guaranteeing commodity prices and by storing surplus produce. Cooperatives complemented the services of the Agricultural Bank, whose agronomists inspected villages and conducted research on produce and land use.

Each commodity presented challenges, and each was subject to state regulation through a special government department (*Kentriki Ypiresia Diachiriiseos Eghorion Proïonton*). Wheat and tobacco received special attention; the former because it was the staple of the Greek diet, and the latter because of its foreign exchange value. Regarding wheat, the state was involved at all stages of production and marketing. Before the First World War, wheat producers could meet only 50 per cent of domestic demand, but by the eve of the Second World War, they satisfied 75 per cent of it, and by 1960 the country was self-sufficient. Modernisation and state intervention had significant gender and political implications, as skilled labourers were replaced by a larger, unskilled and lower-paid workforce that consisted mainly of women. This challenge ignited violent but well-organised protests. The new regulatory environment also made the average peasant less vulnerable to the authority of local notables. During the nineteenth century, villagers lived under the thumb of local notables, often merchants *and* usurers, who bought at low prices and lent money at high interest. The same figure was usually the local politician; hence a system of exploitation and patronage was built into the state order. However, during the interwar years, the cooperatives and the new regulatory order were driven by liberal and left parties, while conservative politicians were also supportive of a more regulated economic environment. One of the first measures of the dictatorship of 1936, for example, was to impose controls on rural debts. Under Metaxas, rural cooperatives were part of a corporatist programme that included state-controlled unions, youth movements and civil associations.

Not all rural producers were caught in this wave of modernisation. In remote mountainous regions, where the market could only play a limited role, traditional subsistence modes endured. But government policy on agriculture did have revolutionary effects. From mountainous regions to the semi-arid islands, peasants engaged much more with the market and certainly much more with the international market. The transformation was evident in the rapid disappearance of the traditional dress (Figure 4.1). Among the islands, trousers were replacing the traditional baggy pants or *vrakes*, and western hats and caps were being preferred to traditional headgear. Some observers were stunned by the transformation:

> If one comes out today [1931] to the countryside, he will see in many farming areas the preoccupations of the cities. This is readily seen in women's clothing, which is unlike what is seen in the villages. In all rural areas the people of the countryside are wearing clothes, mostly of their own making, men are not wearing skirts, nor are women. (Mavrogordatos and Chamoudopoulos 1931: 47)

Western European photographers often overlooked these sartorial changes because they were drawn to the exotic and locally distinctive subject matter.

The agrarian sector's dependence on the state was a significant legacy of the interwar period. Small-scale farming was supported by state subsidies, cheap credit, the reduction of rural taxes and the occasional wiping out of debt, as Venizelos did in 1931 and Metaxas in 1937. At that point, the rural sector's debt burden amounted to 50 per cent of its income (Ploumidis 2011: 106). Agrarian reforms also had the effect of inflating public and foreign debt and of increasing the tax burden on the urban population (Petmezas 2012: 241). Yet the overall impact of the state on the rural sector was positive. It addressed challenges of epic proportions and largely succeeded in its aims. It modernised rural production and vastly improved the provisioning of the nation's food needs, despite rising birth rates, a colossal influx of refugees, and international restrictions on emigration.

Agricultural policy was motivated to a large extent by ideological considerations as well. It held a central position in the political platforms of all governments, whether Venizelist or anti-Venizelist, in both parliamentary regimes and dictatorships. Every interwar government believed a society composed mainly of contented farmers would be less susceptible to political radicalism, particularly communism. The mainstream parties wanted a class of conservative peasant smallholders. Such ideas were commonplace in interwar Europe, when 'urbanism' and 'professional parasitism' were held responsible for severing people from their cultural and communal roots. Agrarianism was a popular ideology that promoted the moral and cultural fibre of the peasantry, who were celebrated by all kinds of political regimes as the embodiment of the nation (Boswell 2016: 254). Agrarian parties were prominent in other Balkan countries, where rural people formed the great majority of the population (75–80 per cent), while agrarianism also continued to resonate strongly in Fascist Italy and Nazi Germany, where farmers were 44 per cent and 20 per cent of the population, respectively. In Greece, agronomists were valued for more than just their scientific expertise. They were treated as the 'high priests of nature': as generals leading armies of farmers (Ploumidis 2011; Zabala 2018).

The politics of agriculture was similar across Eastern Europe, where governments had to address the rise of rural radicalism and were determined to keep rural communities and urban labour movements apart. In Greece, and generally in southeastern Europe, the added attention accorded to agrarian issues was also a consequence of the declining value of agricultural commodities and the increased dependence on global markets.

The politics of assimilation

Among the tectonic adjustments to be made was the incorporation of new regions whose economies were only recently part of an Ottoman order. Suddenly, Macedonia, Epirus, Western Thrace, Crete and the islands of the eastern Aegean were sealed off from neighbouring territories by hard borders. Cities like Thessaloniki, Ioannina, Alexandroupolis, Florina and Serres were now cut off from centres like Manastir, Edirne and Istanbul. Lesbos could not continue its intimate relationship with Ayvalık and the Gulf of Edremit. Chios' close links with Izmir and Çeşme were severed. Now all roads and sea lanes led to Athens. The exception was the Italian-occupied Dodecanese, which were cut off from both Anatolia *and* Greece. The creation of new transport and communications networks tying the new regions to the national centre was an urgent matter. The most crucial piece of infrastructure was the railway. Before the war, there were two separate interregional train lines in operation: Athens to the Peloponnese and Athens to Larissa. In 1920 these lines were integrated into a national network that incorporated Macedonia and Thrace's Ottoman railway lines. By 1935 a national transport network by rail and bus services was in operation throughout continental Greece.

Former Ottoman cities had to be Europeanised and Hellenised. Transforming 'Salonica' into 'Thessaloniki' required the evisceration of much of the Ottoman built environment. Its minarets, mosques, hammams and bazaars disappeared or were converted for other uses. The city's de-'Orientalisation' also involved the introduction of neoclassical public buildings, boulevards and war memorials (Trasokopoulou-Tzimou 2020: 364–7). Perhaps the most explicit assertion of re-Hellenisation was the restoration of the medieval churches that had been converted into mosques after the Ottoman conquests. Thus, Thessaloniki's Hagia Sophia was restored as a functioning church, Kazancılar Camii once again became Panagia Chalkeon, and Kasımiye Camii was again St Demetrios'. Destruction caused during the Balkan Wars and, to a lesser extent, the First World War also cleared some traces of Ottoman legacy, as was the case in Serres. In Thessaloniki much of that legacy was lost during the Great Fire that raged through the central districts in August 1917. Similar developments could be gleaned in Old Greece as well. Even the centre of Athens was redesigned to appear more like a national capital. The royal palace became the national parliament, and a memorial to the unknown soldier that acknowledged all the nation's famous battles was erected in front of it. Syntagma Square was renovated and was used to enact national rituals, including military and school parades.

Hellenisation required name changes to villages and towns, rural toponyms, streets and squares. Most Slavic, Turkish, Albanian, Italian and Vlach names were replaced by older Greek names that had long since disappeared from maps. A committee composed of archaeologists, university professors and high civil servants was formed to either revive ancient Greek names or make up new ones. For example, in western Macedonia, the Ottoman town of Kayılar became Ptolemaïda, referring to the Egyptian Hellenistic dynasty. Anaselitsa or Nasliç, which was home to Vallahades (Greek-speaking Muslims), became Neapoli. Two municipalities close to Volos, Nea Ionia and Nea Anchialos, referred to very distant places: the former to the Asia Minor coastline directly opposite and the latter to Anchialos/Pomorie on Bulgaria's Black Sea coast. The new topography memorialised a larger eastern Mediterranean Greek world that had vanished. Meanwhile, a de-Hellenisation process was in train in the Italian-occupied Dodecanese Islands, where aside from name substitutions and significant changes to the built environment, archaeologists were charged with a mission to celebrate Roman and medieval Italian (Venetian and Genoese) legacies to link the region's history more firmly to Italy (Doumanis 1997; Peri et al. 2009).

To celebrate the centenary of 1821, which was held in 1930 rather than 1921, Venizelos delivered a speech in Tripolis (Peloponnese) saying that the first century of Greek history was dedicated to national independence and territorial expansion. Now, he said, with the Treaty of Lausanne (1923) and the start of the second century of independence,

Greece should strive to integrate with Europe's advanced nations. His slogan was 'From Kolokotronis to Pasteur', suggesting the new heroes should be scientists.[1]

In 1929–30, Venizelos' education minister, Georgios Papandreou, completed a major national reform programme focused on cultural integration. Its chief weapon was the primary school. Some 4,000 schools were built across the country in a massive programme that had to be subsidised by a substantial Swedish loan. As primary schooling was now compulsory, all the nation's children were exposed to Greek national culture (flags, costumes, symbols, maps) and schooled in the national language. The school building was also a symbol of the nation. Many of the country's best architects were employed to produce buildings that expressed the new identity of Greece and conformed to a national aesthetic. Schools became sites of national belonging. Every town and village had one or more schools and war monuments that served as focal points of national celebrations. Communities gathered at least twice a year in school grounds to commemorate wars. Children held parades and recited poems before memorials and school buildings, which were decorated with wreaths (Raptis 1997: 378, 410–13; Giakoumakatos 1987).

The language question remained a source of conflict. The political elite argued bitterly over which version of the Greek language should be used in public discourse and taught in classrooms. Demotic was taught in primary schools without interruption between 1928 and 1932, which also happened to be years when Venizelos was prime minister (Mackridge 2009: 294). But to anti-Venizelists, demotic was as abhorrent as communism, and they continued to insist on *katharevousa*. Given the need to integrate minorities and refugee groups that often spoke different dialects and languages, the need to resolve the problem was particularly pressing. A modernising economy also needed a literate population. At the time, literacy rates were extremely low: half the population over the age of 8 was illiterate. In this period, the chief proponents of demotic Greek were younger intellectuals who had graduated from German universities, trained in modern education theories and were influenced by social democratic ideas. However, their advocacy of radical educational reform merely stiffened the resolve of the establishment, especially the Church hierarchy and professors at the University of Athens. Both sides of this polarising issue agreed that the nation should be culturally homogeneous and that challenges presented by the new populations required a resolution, but governors of the new territories feared that if *katharevousa* was imposed in schools, the minorities would never learn to speak Greek (Raptis 1997: 227–8). The same concern had compelled the Venizelos government in 1917 to give proponents of demotic the responsibility of implementing the necessary reforms and oversee the production of primary school text-books. In 1924, by which time the Venizelists had returned to power, new colleges had also been established to train teachers. In the mean-time, a significant role was ascribed to the new university established in Thessaloniki. The university planned for Smyrna, which was to pay special attention to eastern cultures and languages, served as the blue-print for the University of Thessaloniki, which became the progressive counterpoint to the conservative university in Athens. The former taught subject matter that had been anathematised by the old establish-ment, such as Slavonic languages and Jewish studies. Accordingly, it championed the demotic cause.

The sweeping educational reforms of 1929 imposed a single cur-riculum on all schools, whether public, private or ecclesiastical, and on schools catering to minorities. Demotic was established as the lan-guage of primary schools and technical colleges. Adult education for 'non-Greek-speakers' (*xenofonous*) provided for the teaching of basic modern Greek language, history and geography. Meanwhile, restric-tions had been placed on the operations of foreign-owned schools, which were no longer permitted to teach Greek children between the ages of 6 and 12, and which were now required to teach the national curriculum. The universities were also under the firm control of the Ministry of Education, which appointed government representatives to each of them to monitor their operations and activities, and to draw up new ordinances covering the next fifty years (Raptis 1997: 414–18).

Inevitably, radical education reform unleashed extreme reactions and moral panic. Opposition came not just from the royalist camp but also from within the Liberal Party, with Venizelos often caught in the middle. Reforms were overturned with every change in govern-ment. The most formidable opponent of reform was the Church and such religious organisations as *Zoi*, which used a modern conserva-tive discourse to address the issues facing families and communities. They were prepared to combat anything seen to be challenging Greek national religious traditions and family values. Such organisations did not, as their detractors claimed, reflect Greek backwardness and parochialism. Rather, they appeared to be modelled on conservative religious movements in Germany and France (Gazi 2011).

Much less contentious was the use of antiquities to define Greece and its place in the world. In the interwar years, Greeks were encouraged to see their country through European eyes, meaning through the optics of travel writers, and more broadly through the imaginary *Hellas* found in European literature (Leontis 1995). Monuments, archaeological sites and museums provided a mental map of the country, creating a picture of Greece that was far removed from the refugee slums, peasant hovels and 'Oriental' realities deemed a source of embarrassment. Foreigners were presented an idealised Greece that was both national *and* cosmopolitan. Classical archaeology had played a central role in the making of national identity in 1821, but in the interwar period early Christian and Byzantine sites and museums would also be used. The linking of tourism and archaeology can also be gleaned from an emerging infrastructure of hotels, roads and transport facilities designed to take visitors to and from historical sites. The National Tourism Organisation used photography and posters to advertise abroad, thus developing Greece as a 'brand' (Vlahos 2016). Major theatre events, such as the *Delfikes Eortes* initiated by the poet Angelos Sikelianos and his dancer wife Eva Palmer, and the festivals of the ancient theatres at Epidaurus and Athens, promoted an idealistic vision of Greece to visitors that also had an impact domestically. In a sense, a cultural 'superego' had been created: an exemplary Greekness that anyone worthy of the name 'Greek' was expected to observe (Damaskos and Plantzos 2008). The keyword of the era was *Ellinikotita* ('Greekness'), a trait or property unique to Greeks from the Minoans to the present. *Ellinikotita* was what the Greek landscape, Cycladic statuettes, mythology, Classical statues, Byzantine icons and more recent folk music held in common. The concept usefully bridged the traditional and the modern, ancient, medieval and contemporary, Greece and Europe, folk traditions and high culture, the old and the new (Tziovas 1989).

Modernism provided a national ideology with a twentieth-century aesthetic, yet it never managed to appease a reactionary establishment (Matthiopoulos 2003). The civil service, the police, bishops, heads of education, politicians and party leaders were opposed to anything that appeared to threaten tradition and to expose society to corrupting foreign influences. Even under the Metaxas regime, artistic freedom was tolerated so long as it had limited public exposure, but since it could now be seen beyond urban salons, galleries and Athenian lecture halls, modernism was deemed to be dangerous. Thus, when it came to cinema, the most powerful cultural medium of that era, the Metaxas regime imposed asphyxiating levels of censorship (Karalis 2012: 21).

The incorporation of early Christian and Byzantine history into the national canon, together with the folk traditions evolved during the centuries of Ottoman and western domination, gave the Greeks from Asia Minor, the Black Sea and other parts of the Balkans considerable scope to situate their pasts within this new revised national framework. The refugees themselves, through their brotherhood organisations and community publications, began to integrate their particular histories into a more inclusive national narrative (Salvanou 2018). This attempt at a smooth process of incorporation of the different Greek pasts did not go unchallenged. Marxist historians introduced the concept of class division and the role of class consciousness into Greek history (Skliros 1908; Kordatos 1924). Both were greeted by the academic establishment with shrill hostility. Indeed, the strength of reactionary political culture in Greece was such that it inhibited the development of the social sciences, for anything that might problematise the national narrative in any conceivable way was automatically proscribed. It was also conveyed through attitudes to gender. When Roza Imvrioti tried in 1926 to teach history in a teaching college, the public fallout extended to parliament. For many, women were not fit to teach history, let alone Greek history (Repousi 2012).

Seeds of the welfare state

The 1912–22 war period had sharpened social disparities. By the end, average per capita income had fallen, prices had doubled, and inflation increased sixfold. The conscription of a huge percentage of the male population had a devastating effect on small farms, as did internal migration, with peasants taking advantage of war-related employment opportunities. Furthermore, demobilised soldiers often preferred to settle in urban centres, where they crammed into overcrowded working-class slums. Early public inspection reports on living and working conditions describe a world of Dickensian misery and squalor. Meanwhile, shipping and commercial interests had profited exorbitantly in wartime. British observers noted that Greece was forced to secure loans to pay for its war effort, but it also relied heavily on private Greek sources. The state lacked the political will to pay its war debts through taxation, preferring instead to borrow (Mazower 1991).

Greek labour unrest increased from the end of the First World War. Throughout Europe, the labour movement had been emboldened by the Russian Revolution. The ensuing years saw a rise in the number of Greek labour unions and growth in membership. In 1918, socialist and labour organisations established the General Confederation of Greek Workers (GSEE). Despite his suspicions of the labour move-ment, Venizelos lent his support for the GSEE as he did to the crea-tion of a socialist party, in part because he hoped to bring it under his influence, and because through it he hoped to secure influence in the European socialist movement, which he expected would have a role in peace negotiations. But he underestimated the extent to which the war had radicalised the Greek labour movement, and the extent to which the movement was drawn to communism (Leontaritis 1979). It had also been radicalised by state violence. Before the war, strikes were viewed almost sympathetically by the press and the public as an understandable response to the challenges of modern life. But as society became politically polarised so too did extreme attitudes to labour activity. Thus, the first general strike in 1923 was suppressed by truncheons and guns, and many protesters were killed. Such punitive retaliation from authorities had to do with official paranoia about the Greek Communist Party. Despite its small size, the party was treated by authorities as a ubiquitous mortal threat, which meant all social protests and radical ideas were repressed savagely. Authorities came to interpret most forms of social dissent as the vanguard of a communist takeover plot.

However, to mitigate the radicalising effects of the 'long First World War', the refugee deluge, the impact of industrial technology and the economic crisis, the state successfully implemented a series of noteworthy stabilising measures. The first dealt with rental housing. The refugee influx and other demographic developments exposed a severe housing shortage in Athens, Piraeus and many other cities. In 1916 laws were passed that imposed strict controls on rent and tenant evictions. These measures, supported by workers and the union movement, did not merely benefit the poor but also the many lower-middle-class shopkeepers and businessmen who depended on rented premises. The laws also acted as a disincentive on investment in real estate, effectively restricting transactions and freezing the housing market and commercial property in central Athens (Potamianos 2016: 485). The freeze on rents was just one social protection afforded by the state. Another was to turn a blind eye to illegal housing construction outside the urban residential zones, which violated the 1923 building code. These makeshift settlements, which addressed the immense pres-sure for new housing, were later legalised *ex post facto* and became an established part of the modern Greek city. Between 1922 and 1940, the authorised zone for housing construction in the Athens-Piraeus area increased from 3,264 to 11,600 hectares (Leontidou 1990: 77).

Another important stabilising measure was price controls. Measures imposed in 1916 remained in place, particularly on food prices and especially on bread. Given that revolutions are driven by hunger, all governments ensured that the public had daily access to bread. The state supervised wheat and flour production, the distribution of flour to bakeries, and the allocation of bread rations to consumers in times of need. Severe penalties were imposed on profiteers who tried to manipulate bread prices.

Labour market regulation was one of the chief sources of social conflict in the interwar years. Professional associations sought to restrict access to trades by pressuring authorities to strengthen restrictions on licences. Pressure to relax restrictions came from skilled refugees and war veterans. Shopkeepers sought the imposition of quality controls and pricing on street vendors. The dominant concern was 'oversupply', as the surplus of vendors had intensified competition. The strategic responses to the phenomenon included either the typical liberal solution of letting the market decide, or end access to certain professions and establish closed workshops. Professional associations often prevailed on politicians to secure market protections through their capacity to mobilise votes.

Governments around the world used tariffs to protect local manufacturers and producers, but in Greece, much as elsewhere, such measures brought mixed results. Prior to the Great Depression, industries that received heavy protection were soap (215 per cent), bricks (50–90 per cent), cement (60–5 per cent), beer (62 per cent) and paints (35–50 per cent) (Mazower 1991: 96). Whilst tariffs gave protections to large Greek industries, they penalised the small-scale operators who relied on imported materials, such as carpenters who needed timber. Finally, governments tried to compensate trades that were made redundant by modern technologies and mass production. For example, makers of handcrafted cigarettes wanted large manufacturers to be taxed. Buggy drivers demanded compensation because motor transport services had destroyed their profession. Even musicians sought recompense because records and record players had seriously reduced demand for live music at many venues. Some groups were able to get politicians to intercede on their behalf. As late as the 1970s, part of the price for ferry tickets was dedicated to compensating ferrymen who had become redundant when port renovations made it possible for larger vessels to dock and allow passengers to walk on board (Liakos 2016: 130–1, 398–401).

Such demands reflected the degree to which identities were tied to professions, and by making concessions the state found a way to mitigate the social effects of modernity. Elsewhere in Europe, governments used taxation to ameliorate the social impact of liberal capitalism, but large-scale tax evasion made it an ineffective approach in Greece. Tax reform was attempted in 1919, but interwar governments generally lacked the will to root out tax evasion and extract revenues from the private sector or indeed from peasant smallholders. Hence the fiscal system depended on indirect taxes and assessable incomes, namely salaries and wages, which meant the tax burden fell more on the urban middle and working classes (Dertilis 1993).

Meanwhile, through the International Labour Organisation (ILO), the League of Nations recommended a series of reforms that were meant to improve living and workplace standards. In 1914, the first Venizelos government had already legislated several progressive measures, including the legalisation of unions, an age limit on child labour (12 years old), the abolition of evening shifts for women and children, limits on working hours, and making Sunday a weekly holiday. An inspection body was set up to monitor workplace compliance with national laws and to record complaints. Employers were critical of many of these recommendations, arguing that European labour standards could not be applied to Greece until its economy had developed to a European level. From 1920 the ILO set out to establish international standards that would prevent market competition from driving down labour costs. The positions of Greek governments and employers were therefore antithetical, as the latter believed that the adoption of international standards would undermine competitiveness. The introduction of the eight-hour day, and health and safety standards, were particularly contentious. In such tussles, Europe's social democratic unions could invoke the determinations of the Peace Conferences and the ILO, which stated reform was necessary to lessen the attractions of communism, and which in the Greek case made requests for loans contingent on compliance with international labour norms (Liakos 2016: 253–67).

The development of Greek social policy was too slow, hesitant and piecemeal to be fully effective, but the idea that the state should provide citizens with essential services was set in motion. The most significant innovation was the creation of the Social Insurance Institute (IKA) in 1934. Created with the active support of the ILO, IKA was designed to promote links between workers, employers and the state, and to address such social concerns as maternity leave, regular healthcare, children's health services and aged care. It paid particular attention to refugees and those who had migrated recently from the countryside, and in a broader sense, to the promotion of civic values (Liakos 2016: 339–552).

The state was most effective when it came to public health. At the beginning of the interwar period, malaria and tuberculosis were still endemic, while the refugee crisis exposed the inadequacies of state and local government health services. Poor water provisioning in urban areas added to the nightmarish conditions in the slums, with their prefabricated structures and the absence of street lighting, sewerage, garbage collection and transport services. Most streets were unpaved; hence city dwellers were plagued by dust in summer and mud in winter. Primary care services did not exist, and hospitals were still regarded as charity institutions (Gardikas 2018). In 1927 a dengue fever epidemic affected between 80 and 90 per cent of the population. In response to these health crises, the state introduced services for garbage collection, clean water and sewerage, and a League of Nations committee recommended a general health programme that included a public health inspection service for schools, and for rural and urban homes. It also recommended a school of public health to organise campaigns, particularly against malaria, and to train teams of hygienists (Kyriopoulos and Karela 2011; Liakos 2016: 314–35). The state consulted with the public and showed interest in preventative medicine and in creating hygienic environments. Families were required to notify health authorities when a family member was ill, while those suffering tuberculosis and other infectious diseases were quarantined. In the villages, which rarely ever saw a doctor, a battle was waged against 'practical' or traditional healers, and with the initiative of the Greek Refugee Settlement Commission (RSC), farmers' associations recruited retired doctors and organised surgeries (Kyriopoulos 2008; Katsapis 2011: 125–69). Special attention was paid to children and mothers, 'the nation's biological capital'. In cooperation with Minister of Health Dr Apostolos Doxiadis, the 'Patriotic Foundation' would be the principal body for the establishment of local clinics, kindergartens, school canteens, vaccination programmes and the distribution of health pamphlets with basic information on personal hygiene. Red Cross volunteers staffed the movement. The new initiatives came in response to an unprecedented urban population explosion, and new interest in eugenics and fears of 'national degeneration' (Theodorou and Karakatsani 2010; Trubeta 2013). Throughout Europe, motherhood, natalism and the health of children were matters that attracted government attention. The welfare of families became a critical measure of a nation's strength, and national health standards were recognised as vital to national security interests (Moses 2016: 333–5).

Crime and public order in some of the new conurbations were placed under the supervision of an urban police force (*Astynomia Poleon*), which Venizelos established in 1918. This force was modelled on the British Metropolitan Police and was managed initially by a team of senior British officers led by Sir Frederick Loch Halliday, former police commissioner in Calcutta. His colonial experiences were relevant. The *Astynomia Poleon* was meant to be a police force that did not carry firearms, and which tried to cultivate positive relationships with the public. It employed modern methods such as regular patrols, keeping records on criminals, regulating public noise levels, overseeing public cleanliness standards and vendors' use of public spaces, and monitoring traffic violations and the activities of foreign dissidents. Crime management response was supported by statistical research, select units that dealt with prostitution and managed permits, and networks of informants providing intelligence on criminal activity. Finally, it provided a state security service (*Ypiresia Asfaleias tou Kathestotos*) that monitored and recorded the activities of communists, including their publications and movements (Fotakis 2016).

The labour inspector who visited the factories, the policeman who patrolled and monitored the city streets, the female nurse who visited homes and schools to monitor hygiene standards, and the agronomist who advised the villagers all presented an image of a new liberal order. But this coexisted with older characteristics of governance, such as bureaucratic indifference and arbitrariness, and police coercion, as seen in the rough manner in which police officers from southern Greece treated refugee communities in the north (Katsapis 2003: 108). During the 1930s, strikers were killed and injured by armed soldiers in Thessaloniki, Kalamata and Volos. In 1933, the assassination attempt on Venizelos was a conspiracy hatched within the security service that the government had created.

Until 1936, Greece was a liberal democracy, yet the citizenry was sometimes subjected to violent and spasmodic outbursts of state violence, which was more reminiscent of the behaviour of Europe's authoritarian regimes (Linz and Stepan 1996). Such oscillations between extremes were typical of the way Greece was governed in the twentieth century.

The economic crisis

The Great Depression dominates the interwar years. Historians of most nations consider it the period's constitutive event: all earlier developments led to it, everything afterwards flowed from it. This general rule did not apply to every country, however. For Greece, the whole of the interwar period was beset by rolling political and economic crises. The country did not need the Wall Street Crash to experience long dole queues, as seen in 1922–3. The 'Depression' as a specific crisis would hardly figure in Greek social memory.

It was certainly a global crisis, a 'highly pathological period', to quote John Maynard Keynes (Middleton 2016: 179), that had many causes and was experienced differently. In every country, the course of the crisis was also influenced by the way governments managed it. Its impact on Greece was complicated. Here, it accelerated economic expansion and restructuring, but it hindered technological progress and kept the economy in a protectionist cocoon. The crisis struck during Venizelos' last period in office (1928–1933), when it undermined reforms that had been enacted since the early 1920s. Moreover, it forged new political alignments and aggravated social tensions. The shifting of the political centre of gravity to the right prepared the way for the dissolution of parliamentary democracy and the establishment of a dictatorship.

Like other Balkan countries, Greece experienced quite impressive rates of industrial growth in the 1930s, with an average growth rate of 8 per cent between 1932 and 1937. This trend, which seems counterintuitive given the global economic environment, is partly explained by very low costs in labour and raw materials. However, profits were not invested into upgrading technologies: in 1936 a report found that most industrial machinery was between thirty and forty years old (Mazower 1991: 250–53). Evidently, state interventions in industry had not been as efficacious as had been the case in agriculture. Policy was based on two pillars. The first was credit support for family and small-scale cooperative enterprises, which was part of a scheme that extended to rural smallholders. Politically, the aim was to promote the formation of a conservative political constituency. The second was foreign investment. Greece seemed an attractive site, particularly after receiving a massive loan for refugee resettlement. Investors flocked to Athens for government contracts in programmes that seemed less risky than local industries. Contracts for public works, such as the drainage projects in Macedonia, the

Athens waterworks and the tram and telephone networks, were won by British and US firms (Dritsa 1990).

To play its new role, the state needed a central bank to regulate commercial banks and stabilise the currency. Before the Great Depression, central banks had become a commonplace feature of the world economy, as seen with the establishment of the Bank of Greece in 1928. Three other institutions created in this period were the Senate, which evoked the spirit of corporatism and conveyed the interests of the professions; the Council of State to oversee the legality of administrative reforms; and the Supreme Economic Council, a body of businessmen, senior government officials, bankers and academics, which provided economic advice to government.

Between 1924 and 1930, Greece battled to stabilise its currency and public finances despite the expenses that came with integrating millions of new citizens. It tried the usual methods of making cuts to the civil service, which had doubled in size during the war, although since then the population had also doubled. Cuts were also made to civil service salaries, while indirect taxes were increased. By 1928 Greece was able to join the gold standard, and for a moment the drachma was considered one of the world's strong currencies. During the early stages of the crisis, there was reason to hope that Greece might fare relatively well, but that all changed when Britain abandoned the gold standard in September 1931. Believing now that currency value was a measure of the nation's reputation, the Venizelos government waged a 'battle of the drachma'. Indeed, all parties agreed on this matter, as there were widespread concerns about creditworthiness and the need to complete still unfinished development projects. Moreover, if the drachma were depreciated Greece's foreign debt would increase in inverse proportion. However, investors instead converted their drachmas to other currencies and sent their money abroad. With the drachma under tremendous pressure, the foreign exchange rate fell dramatically. For the first time, the real economy began to feel the effects. The number of unemployed grew from 75,000 in 1928 to 237,000 in 1932 (Liakos 2016: 413). Crop failures compounded the problem, with reports of people beginning to starve. New loans were stalled by the International Financial Commission and the League of Nations' Financial Committee, which demanded austerities (closure of schools, wage cuts and the like). Having exhausted all possibilities and drained the nation's entire foreign exchange reserves, the Venizelos government surrendered in April 1932. Gold was abandoned, the drachma was devalued

50 per cent against the British pound, and Greece defaulted on its loan repayments. The nation was bankrupt.

The effects of bankruptcy were felt immediately. Without having to service debts, which had reached as high as 10 per cent of government spending, the government could now focus more on programmes that promoted economic growth. Devaluation also reduced imports and thereby stimulated local production, particularly of textiles and building materials. Consequently, during the 1930s, Greece's growth rate was surpassed only by Japan and the USSR. The reduction of imports, however, particularly in machinery, along with high tariffs, made the sector uncompetitive. All Greek governments, but particularly the conservative governments that were in power between 1932 and 1935, did not believe industry would play a major part in the nation's economic future. Rather than being reinvested in industry, profits were directed towards land, which in turn created a real estate bubble but also helped to improve housing in the refugee quarters and outer suburbs of Athens (Kostis 2019: 180–216).

The Depression had particularly adverse effects on peasant families in Old Greece that had benefited from regular remittances, but which now found that source of money had been diminished by migration restrictions and economic difficulties in the diaspora. Relatives in the United States were further discouraged by the exchange rate and many of them had lost savings deposited in Greek banks. Such developments diminished their confidence in the Greek economy, and many Greek Americans would thereafter commit wholeheartedly to their new homeland, feeling they no longer had a stake in the old. Meanwhile, the difficulties of their remittance-dependent relatives in Greece were compounded by government austerities (K. Karpozilos 2017: 181–90).

From National Schism to dictatorship

Despite significant policy achievements since 1922, some of which were Herculean in scale, the Greek state, or rather its parliamentary system, appeared to most observers to be unstable and corrupt (see Gallant 2016: 210–20). The prime cause was the ongoing National Schism. Politicians and the military remained hopelessly divided along royalist and Venizelist lines. The involvement of the military in politics raised the stakes. The 1920s had witnessed several coups and attempted coups (1922, 1923, 1925 and 1926) by rival factions. Tensions if anything increased during the Depression years, when the burning political issue was whether Greece should remain a republic. The battle lines of *to Politeiako*, literally 'the polity question', were between those defending the parliamentary system and those who sought its abolition and restoration of the monarchy. Plastiras led two attempted coups against conservative governments, one in 1933 and one in 1935 with Venizelos' backing. The monarchy/republic battlefront was crossed by another front that divided those wishing to retain the parliament and those calling for dictatorship, although both sides admired Mussolini and other European dictators (Marketos 2006). Clearly, the deep social cleavages created during the long First World War had not had enough time to heal (Hering 2006: 1009). Tensions persisted between indigenous groups and refugees, and between conservatives and communists. These divisions were expressed in voting patterns and were fuelled by the economic crisis.

Some intellectual, artistic and social movements were not implicated in the Venizelist–royalist conflict and did reflect the new world that had been in the making since the war period. Although a small movement in the interwar years, feminism expanded and found expression through many causes. Women activists called for equality and voting rights, improvements to family law and an end to workplace discrimination. Although feminist organisations differed on specific issues and strategies, they all linked women's rights to democracy, which was regarded as the necessary foundation for guaranteeing the rights of both women and men. Feminism represented the most innovative intervention in interwar political theory and democratic politics. It set a stark contrast to the authoritarian politics that dominated the public sphere during the 1930s, and it was inevitable that feminist organisations, including women's business organisations, would be demonised by right-wing political parties. Greek women did not have voting rights, except during the municipal elections of 1934. Before Metaxas had them disbanded, Greek feminist organisations managed to communicate and develop links with anti-fascist organisations throughout Europe (Avdela and Psara 1985).

What united the political elite was fear of social upheaval and communism. Even though the Left had no representation in the parliament before the previous war, and despite the fact that the Communist Party could only muster between 3 and 10 per cent of the vote in interwar elections, the state nevertheless treated it as an existential threat. One such measure was the 'Special Law' (*Idionymo*) passed by the Venizelos government in 1929, against 'whoever seeks the implementation of ideas whose manifest purpose is the overthrow of the established order by violent means' (Mazower 1991: 35). The law was used to break up labour organisations and strikes and to imprison and exile left-wing leaders. It was an effective tool for counteracting the growth of the labour movement and the cause of Greek social democracy. The state preferred to deal with so-called 'labour fathers', usually corrupt and double-dealing unionists, and introduced compulsory state arbitration in disputes between labour and capital. However, none of these measures managed to avert strike actions, which were dealt with violently by police and the military. Bloodshed in Thessaloniki, Kalamata and Volos between 1935 and 1936 paved the way for martial law and dictatorship on 4 August 1936 (Fountanopoulos 2005: 231–76).

While fascism would have a negligible following in Greece, many intellectuals and supporters of both sides of the National Schism were fascinated by Mussolini, Hitler and their respective regimes in power. Dictatorship per se, moreover, was an attractive idea to many in Greece, including Plastiras and even Venizelos. More broadly, the attractions of authoritarian governance reflected the shallow roots of liberal democracy in Greece and indeed throughout much of Europe, but it was also a function of the extraordinary social and economic upheavals since the First World War. However inept and corrupt in some instances and situations, liberal democracy was not given a chance to establish its roots, as right-wing and conservative elements railed histrionically and campaigned ceaselessly through the press against effete and crooked parliaments. Newspapers, intellectuals and politicians were determined to impress the idea that parliamentary rule in Greece was irrevocably corrupt and morally bankrupt, despite its formidable feats in settling refugees, incorporating underdeveloped northern territories and making tangible improvements in agriculture. The intellectual Georgios Theotokas was typical of the critics of the interwar republic when he claimed 'There is something rotten in Greece.' He meant everything was rotten: its institutions, political order, economy, education and society itself (Theotokas 1996: 249).

To Politeiako was more than simply a question of republic or dictatorship. For many liberals, dictatorship could provide temporary respite from the turmoil and a chance to reconstitute a properly functioning liberal order. Venizelos himself favoured a short-term dictatorship to strengthen the executive's hand over the parliament and produce a more stable democracy. General Plastiras, who led the 1922 removal of the monarchy and oversaw its replacement by a republic, was an admirer of Mussolini. Urban educated elites were torn between their fear of social upheaval on the one hand, and abhorrence for the hopelessly divided politicians and the officer class on the other. Others called for an end to parliamentarianism, and the imposition of a national dictatorship led by one of the nation's best and brightest.

Indeed, few believed that the parliamentary system could manage the nation's crises. In this Greece was not unlike much of Europe, although in many cases democracy was not easily defeated and had to be violently dismantled (Vlahopoulos 2012; Orzoff 2016: 269–71). Therefore, the factors that contributed to the making of the Metaxas dictatorship were many (Hering 2006: 1255–87; Alivizatos 1995: 267–84). Those who had previously contemplated dictatorship were influenced by the role of the state as a social engineer. Those who believed the economy needed top-down direction also held that society had to be disciplined by a strong executive. The idea that economy and society ought to operate as a single, well-oiled machine was a common-place. As Metaxas put it:

> From the moment that the Greek state followed the same path as the other contemporary states and began regulating even the minor aspects economic life, our parliamentary system not only became redundant but it became a hindrance to the proper workings of society and to efforts to deal with the problems of today. (Boyiatzis 2012: 230)

The country slid inexorably towards dictatorship in March 1935, when a foiled *coup d'état* by pro-Venizelist officers (Figure 4.2) became a precedent for further attempts. On 10 October Prime Minister Panagiotis Tsaldaris was removed from office by another *coup d'état* by the royalist general Georgios Kondylis. The republic was abolished by a vote of the parliament and King George II was recalled from his exile in Britain. The restoration was ratified by a plebiscite scrutinised by the British and US ambassadors, although some royalists were allowed to vote as many as twenty times (Vlahopoulos 2012: 355). Weary of politi-cal conflict, both Venizelists and anti-Venizelists alike, as well as the middle classes that had benefited from the recent spurt of economic growth, rallied behind the constitutional monarchy. The trigger for the dissolution of the parliamentary system was the election result in April 1936, when the rival parties received the same number of votes. The Communists won 10 per cent of the vote, but more importantly held the balance of power and therefore could determine which party would form a government. The opponents of parliamentary democracy cited this extraordinary situation as proof that the system was hopelessly flawed and dangerous. The major parties agreed to install Ioannis Metaxas as prime minister, despite his well-publicised

Figure 4.2 Coup d'état, March 1935. *Armed soldiers take up positions in the streets of Athens.* © *ERT*

views on dictatorship. On 4 August, a dictatorship was established in consultation with the monarchy (Hering 2006: 1194–1254).

The 4 August Dictatorship abolished not only the parliament but also political parties and the free press. As was typical in Europe, the dictatorship was established through the issuance of emergency laws, purges of the military and civil service, the dissolution of elected local government councils, sackings of academics from university posts, the closure of radical newspapers and the imposition of censorship on newspapers, magazines, books, songs, plays and films. Even Classical works, including ancient Greek tragedies, were not spared. Schools and the public services were purged of people deemed to be harbouring dangerous ideas, while the political opposition, especially Communists, were exiled to small, desolate Aegean islands or jailed without trial. The regime created a secret police and surveillance system that monitored all social gatherings, including family gatherings. Among the methods used against dissidents, whether real or suspected, was torture, which included forcing men to sit on a block of ice or drink castor oil. Victims' confessions were made public in the press.

The ideology of the Metaxas dictatorship was a mixture of nationalist ideas and patriarchal notions embedded in traditional society. Metaxas was presented as the father of the nation, while the people were all 'his children'. Men and women were meant of course to conform to their traditional roles. The dictator himself made clear his abhorrence of modern art, but unlike other conservatives he did not reject demotic Greek and in fact recognised its utility. He commissioned Manolis Triantafyllidis, a major proponent of demotic associated with the University of Thessaloniki, to produce a demotic grammar, for which he wrote the preface (Mackridge 2009: 301). Another leading demoticist, Alexandros Delmouzos, who had earlier been dismissed from his academic post, was restored to his position by Metaxas.

The dictatorship mimicked features of fascism in Italy and Germany. It copied Italy's youth movement, the *Opera Nazionale Ballila*, when it established the *Ethniki Organosi Neolaias* (National Union of Youth). It copied fascism's propaganda methods, using the radio, the cinema, the megaphone, posters and spectacular stage shows (Kallis 2021: 197, 210). Like the other strong men of his era, Greece's dictator was the focus of a state propaganda goal that made him the personification of the nation's values. Thus, Metaxas was presented as the nation's First Labourer, its First Farmer and the Father of the Country. Seemingly inspired by the Third Reich, he made grandiloquent claims to having established the Third Hellenic Civilisation (Classical and Byzantine being the first two). Yet he disregarded many aspects of fascism, and like Spain's Francisco Franco, with whom he had much more in common, Metaxas recoiled at its more revolutionary features. Like Franco, Metaxas was more interested in countering modernity than in promoting revolutionary change, while Greece did not even have an equivalent to Spain's home-grown fascist movement, the Falange. However, the monarchy in Greece was to play a more prominent role in national affairs than in most European dictatorships. King George, who spent much of his exile in Britain, played a significant role in making Greek foreign policy more pro-British as the general international crisis deepened.

Tellingly, Metaxas' Greece continued to follow Britain's lead in international affairs and was not aligned with either Germany or Italy. In any case, Mussolini's aggressive expansionist policy in the eastern Mediterranean, his regime's determination to retain the Dodecanese Islands and its intention to dominate the Balkans precluded any Greek–Italian alliance. The king regarded the dictatorship as an interim regime without a clear sequel. He aimed to entrench the monarchy by securing the loyalties of the state machinery and the armed forces. Metaxas, on the other hand, regarded dictatorship as a permanent solution to the *Politeiako*.

Metaxas could be described as a product of *étatisme*. He believed an all-powerful state was best suited to meeting the challenges of the modern world, and that such a state made parliamentary democracy redundant. Well before the dictatorship, Metaxas had claimed the question was not whether Greece *would* abandon parliamentary democracy but *when*. A strong state would emerge either through a communist revolution or a right-wing dictatorship. If the cult of the state was a general characteristic of modern dictatorships, Metaxas embodied the cult better than most. He was not a product of paramilitary organisations, as were Mussolini and Hitler. He had commanded an army, enjoyed the support of King Constantine and the respect of Venizelos, and was the leader of a small right-wing party that was not associated with the hopelessly divided parties of the National Schism.

However, his new order had to focus on the looming international crisis in Europe and Mussolini's increasingly belligerent attitude towards Greece. As the regime watched the gathering clouds of war, it planned for the nation's defence. Ironically the weapons it acquired were German, which it secured by trading tobacco and other raw materials. Then, for a brief moment, the nation united as never before. When, on 28 October 1940, Metaxas famously said 'NO' to Mussolini's insistence that Italian troops occupy Greek sovereign territory, he knowingly committed the nation to war. His stance drew unanimous public support. For a moment, Greek society, including its political class, were as one. The National Schism, which had crippled Greek politics throughout the interwar years, had finally ended. Another schism, however, was waiting around the corner.

Note

1. The *Neologos* newspaper of Patras, 13 October 1930.

CHAPTER 5

The Occupation: Greece under the Axis (1941–1944)

On 28 October 1940, at 3 a.m., the Italian ambassador delivered his government's ultimatum to Metaxas. Greece stood accused of committing hostile acts along its border with Albania, which the Italians had invaded and occupied since April. It was also accused of allowing the British Royal Navy to operate in Greek waters. Metaxas was given three hours to respond (Gooch 2020: 134). Mussolini needed a war. Britain and France had stood in the way of Italy's ambitions to expand its 'Roman Empire' in the Mediterranean, which to that point consisted merely of Libya and the Dodecanese. Germany's stunning victories across northern Europe in the spring provided a unique opportunity, but a sudden deal with the French and the British might have seen that window shut quickly. The Italian dictator also wanted a victorious 'parallel war' to put Italy on a more equal footing with its Axis partner. Greece, an even weaker power than Italy, seemed easy prey. Aside from its islands, Greece had never been a target of Italian expansionist dreams, but Mussolini had convinced himself and many around him that Greece would fall easily and give him the kudos he desperately lacked. He told foreign minister Galeazzo Ciano that he would send in his 'resignation as an Italian' if there were objections within his government to his decision (Gooch 2020: 126).

In recent months, Metaxas had been trying to avoid reacting to Italian provocations. In August 1940, he claimed he had been counselled by Hitler not to retaliate after the Greek battleship *Elli* was torpedoed off the island of Tinos (Clogg 2002: 36). In the end, it was the Führer who gave Mussolini the provocation he needed. Infuriated by Hitler's recent political interventions in Romania, which he claimed fell within Italy's sphere of influence, Mussolini made his decision in a fit of anger. He complained to Ciano: 'This time I'll pay him back in his own coin. He'll learn from the newspapers that I have occupied Greece and so restored the balance between us' (Bosworth 2002: 376). Unlike the First World War, Europe did not sleepwalk into the second. Hitler and Mussolini had deliberately set out to destroy an international order based on legal principles and designed to end imperialism. The fascists wanted to restore the principle of right of conquest. Greece was one of many European countries that were dragged into a war for which they bore no responsibility.

This purely externally driven crisis had radical domestic consequences. It would dismantle the state and turn the Greek nation upside down. The war fully exposed the country and its people to unprecedented violence. Such was its scale that it tested the legitimacy and meaning of everything: state authority, basic human rights, relations between state and society, and relations between cultural communities and social classes. It drove divisions within communities and families. This chapter focuses on a very short period: a forty-two-month phase that began with the Axis invasions in April 1941 and ended with the evacuation of German forces in October 1944. Such was its impact, however, that it reconstituted the nation in nearly every respect.

Defeated victors

The war began well. The threat of invasion was greeted by a nation-wide explosion of patriotism. Young men rushed to enlist. Panagiotis Kanellopoulos, then a young statesman and academic, recalled a rare moment when the country had unity of purpose: 'Returning to Athens on 2 November 1940 I felt, both as an ordinary citizen and as part of a nation, the great national pride and ethical joy felt by all the Greeks' (Petrakis 2006: 194). The Metaxas dictatorship had polarised the nation, but his handling of the ultimatum proved to be an effective rallying cry. Although poorly equipped, Greek units composed mainly of men from Epirus, who had an intimate understanding of the terrain and conditions, halted the advance and then pushed Italian forces deep into Albania, capturing villages and towns such as Korytsa. For Italy it was a military disaster. When the Greeks came close to seizing the port of Valona, a panicked Mussolini was talked out of asking Hitler to organise a truce (Hondros 1983: 42).

For Mussolini this Greek invasion was a disaster of his own making. Italian forces were ill prepared and were despatched at the wrong time of the year. The Epirote border region was shrouded in fog and deluged by heavy rains. Run-off and mud impeded movement. Italian forces were unable to exploit their superiority in arms and numbers, and their humiliating retreat inevitably impacted on morale. So too did the heavy snows and freezing conditions that set in by 9 January, by which time heavy reinforcement had been despatched from Italy.

A counterattack in early March against depleted and resource-starved Greek positions came to nothing. Meanwhile, soldiers on both sides wrote home about hunger, frostbite, lice and diseases, and about frozen limbs that had to be amputated because of gangrene.

Italy's defeat had serious ramifications for the Axis powers. It prompted the British to send reinforcements to Greece, which was seen as threatening German access to Romania's oilfields and made Franco even more hesitant about joining the Axis. The defeat also affected pro-German sentiment in Belgrade and negotiations with the recently defeated French. Above all, plans for the projected invasion of the Soviet Union were compromised and had to be postponed until the Balkans were secured. Hitler had treated Mussolini as a mentor, but his Greek disaster was the greatest of a series of Italian debacles that changed the relationship between the Axis powers completely. Once Germany had assumed full control over military operations against Greece, Italy was effectively downgraded from ally to minion (Santarelli 2005: 59–66).

On 6 April 1941, the German invasion of Greece began, initially through Bulgaria and then Yugoslavia. The German 12th Army of 250,000 men faced a Greek force of some 90,000. Three days later, German troops marched into Thessaloniki. Despite the support of some 57,000 British, Australian and New Zealand troops, Greek defences in Macedonia could not hold out against German blitz-krieg tactics and superior arms and numbers. Dominion forces were essentially sent to encourage local resistance, and to withdraw if that failed: the commander of New Zealand troops Major General B. C. Freyberg thought it 'clear to everybody that intervention in Greece must end eventually in evacuation … [W]e were and had always been in a hopeless position' (Stockings and Hancock 2013: 514). As defences crumbled, the Greek government panicked. On 16 April the Minister of War, Georgios Papadimas, ordered Greek troops to demobilise. On 18 April the prime minister, Alexandros Koryzis, committed suicide. Attempts to form a new government were thwarted by the usual squabbling between royalist and Venizelist generals (Hondros 1983: 52). On 23 April the king fled the capital, and General Georgios Tsolakoglou signed an armistice without the approval of his commander in chief, Alexandros Papagos. On 27 April, the Wehrmacht entered Athens and raised the swastika over the Acropolis. An airborne invasion of Crete in May completed the German victory, but not before savage fighting that featured bayonet charges. Meanwhile, Germany's ally Bulgaria was busy reoccupying eastern Macedonia and Western Thrace. On 23 April,

Tsolakoglou made it clear that he was ready to form a government that would stand with Germany. For Tsolakoglou and other 'quislings' that stepped forward in 1940, Axis victories presented a chance to roll back the progressive reforms and modern cultural trends of recent years, and to rebuild the nation along more authoritarian lines. Inspired by Marshal Philippe Pétain's *L'état française*, and by the name used by Kapodistrias during the War of Independence, Tsolakoglou labelled his regime 'Greek State' (*Elliniki Politeia*).

The common soldiery felt wounded pride rather than humiliation. Having defeated the Italians, but overwhelmed by the German onslaught, the Greeks insisted on capitulating formally to the latter and not to the former. Unlike in occupied France, however, where society continued to be governed and heavily policed (Jackson 2001: ch. 11), the defeat in Greece produced a crisis of authority. The state had effectively disintegrated as the Wehrmacht descended on Athens. As in Anatolia in August 1922, common soldiers were again abandoned by the military elite. Tens of thousands took to the road and walked back to their towns and villages without provisions. Most kept their weapons. Most people felt betrayed when the news reached them that their king and his government had fled the country. Their departure severely compromised the legitimacy of the state (Margaritis 2009: 34–40).

This crisis of legitimacy, which would reverberate in Greek political life for decades, would be compounded by a quisling government that could do very little to protect Greek society from Axis oppression and malign neglect. Whilst espousing the values of nationalism, it could not persuade Germany against delivering eastern Macedonia and Western Thrace to Bulgaria, or against handing most of the country to the defeated Italians (Petrov 2007: 151–73). Worst of all, it could not address the most basic needs of society during its darkest years. Unlike Pétain, Tsolakoglou had no personal standing in society and did not have a well-functioning state apparatus at his disposal. Neither he nor his successors were able to develop a mass support base for their puppet regimes.

Axis occupation: general features

Over the next three and half years, Greece was occupied by three Axis powers: Germany, Italy and Bulgaria. The Italian occupation ended in September 1943, when Italy withdrew from the Axis, after which its Greek territories were seized by Germany. Many Greeks had lived under foreign occupations before, but the Second World War would be remembered as *the* Occupation (*i Katochi*). This experience stood out because of the scale of the terror and violence, the depth of deprivations suffered, and the civil conflict it generated. If the Venizelist–royalist conflict had exercised the passions of the upper and middle classes, the Occupation cut deeply into every community, every village and countless families. It politicised the mass of the population and set the tone for Greek political life for much of the rest of the century.

Compared to occupied peoples in Western Europe, those in Greece and in other parts of Southern and Eastern Europe were subjected to a more colonial approach to social discipline, meaning authorities were prepared to use the brutal methods reserved for peoples deemed to be less civilised. The ready recourse to violence was certainly in keeping with fascism's approach to political opposition, but in wartime rank-and-file soldiers were expected to set aside their humanity and act without pity. Mario Roatta, one of Italy's most brutal generals, demanded that his troops desist from being 'good Italians' and demand not 'an eye for an eye, tooth for a tooth', but 'a head for a tooth' (Rodogno 2006: 452). This heavy reliance on violence was also meant to compensate for limited manpower. After all, German troops would be concentrated on the Soviet Front, leaving a small minority to man other fronts and occupation zones. But territories like Yugoslavia and Greece, where rugged physical geography was ideal for guerrilla warfare, exposed Axis vulnerability. The occupiers met the Resistance with utterly ruthless forms of reprisal, but only succeeded in fostering bolder resistance and convincing most peasant communities to support the guerrillas.

Indeed, Axis occupation forces were never able to occupy Greece fully: they were unable to monitor and control most of the mainland and the hinterlands of such large islands as Crete and Evvia. Italian and German troops launched raids from their strongholds, using overwhelming firepower when required, but would then have to withdraw to their strongholds. Each withdrawal left a power vacuum. The occupiers could police urban centres and main roads, but not at all hours, especially not at night.

As Axis forces and Greek resistance groups engaged mainly in guerrilla warfare, the human costs of this occupation were borne mainly by civilians. Their support was vital to the success of either side; hence men and women of all ages became military targets. Countless Greek village communities suffered massacres or discovered after having returned from hiding that their homes had been torched, and food and livestock stolen. People were often forced to watch family and neighbours being executed or to see their corpses dangling at the end of a rope. Such atrocities were typical of guerrilla warfare. Writing sometime after the war, legal scholar Carl Schmitt stated that the protagonists in the occupied territories behaved like 'modern guerrillas', who had 'moved away from the conventional enmity of controlled and bracketed war, and into the realm of another [war] which intensifies through terror and of counter-terror until it ends in extermination' (Schmitt 2007: 11). As a former Nazi, Schmitt's reasoning gives some idea of how the suspension of the legal conventions of war was justified in German minds: how 'civilised' nations sanctioned barbarity. The barbarisation of warfare was deemed necessary, and it could also be seen in the behaviour of Germany's Axis partners and the Resistance. Italian units tasked with clearing rebels in mountainous Central Greece had been ordered to shoot them on sight, imprison their families and torch their homes. Such brutalities were meant to be routine. One commander had issued his authorisation in advance: 'I need not be asked to authorize the application of these orders. Such authorization I have already given. It will be necessary to inform me after the event' (Rodogno 2006: 344 n. 30). Guerrillas developed a similar mindset. Following a battle with a collaborationist unit in the Peloponnese, the communist resistance fighter Aris Velouchiotis said 'Don't talk to me about prisoners when we have our own dead' (Priovolos 2018: 218). During the second half of the war, when German authorities were recruiting locals as paramilitaries, Greeks were committing atrocities mainly against other Greeks. Paramilitaries traumatised large swathes of the population, meting out their own forms of justice and leaving long trails of destruction. Such lawlessness tore at the fabric of Greek society.

The three Axis powers had different reasons for occupying Greece. At the beginning of 1941, the main concern of the Bulgarian government was to somehow avoid a war on its own soil, into which Turkey might also be drawn (Crampton 2007: 253). If forced to choose sides, Bulgaria was inclined to support Germany because of strong trading ties, because Germany seemed likely to win the war, and because an alliance might see a 'Greater Bulgaria' restored. Hitler had already revised the map of central Europe and was likely to be amenable to the territorial aspirations of a valued ally. Having been notified of Germany's intentions to invade Greece, and believing, as one general put it, that it was 'better they pass through as friends rather than as enemies', the Bulgarians signed a pact in Berlin a day before German troops arrived on their soil (Crampton 2007: 255–6). As it happened, Bulgaria did regain many territories lost in the Second Balkan War, while also receiving Thasos and Samothrace. However, none of these spoils were formally ceded to Bulgaria, at least not yet. To maintain its leverage with its junior Axis partner, Germany assigned them to be occupied and administered. With some haste, the Bulgarians subjected these territories to intensive cultural assimilation policies to make the case for annexation when the time came. At least initially, such measures drew few objections from Slav Macedonians, since their spoken language bore a close resemblance to Bulgarian, and because they had been subjected to 'Serbianisation' in Yugoslavia and 'Hellenisation' in Greece (Crampton 2007: 258–9).

Italy's intentions for Greece were typically vague. Its political class believed strongly that Italy should have a Mediterranean empire, but its scope was never clear. In June, an official document stating Italy's war aims included the Italian annexation or control of Nice, Corsica, Tunis, Malta, southern Switzerland, Cyprus, Egypt, Iraq, Djibouti, the Gulf coast of Arabia and Aden (Knox 2000: 78). Greece was missing from the list, but it became the focus of Italian ambitions in 1939, and particularly once other options had been removed by Germany. Certainly, the Greek islands and the west coast of the Greek mainland were targeted for annexation. From a strategic perspective, Greece was deemed a 'Mediterranean Norway' that had to be kept out of British hands. Although Italy's imperial dreams came crashing down in Epirus in the winter of 1940–1, Hitler entrusted most of Greece to Italian administration to shore up Mussolini's greatly diminished standing at home, and because German manpower and resources had to be deployed against the Soviet Union (Knox 2000: 103–4).

Once Greece had been occupied, it became an important base for supporting Germany's Afrika Korps, which was meant to contain the British in North Africa and possible Allied incursions into Mediterranean Europe. Germany also conceived its occupation of Greece as a form of cultural annexation, given the ancient Greeks were deemed members of the Indo-Germanic race. The conquest was therefore read as a 'return' to a hallowed land that had suffered centuries of racial decay (Chapoutot 2016: 15). German propaganda claimed its own troops were the true successors of Leonidas and his 300 Spartans. The Nazi Party newspaper celebrated the Wehrmacht's success at Thermopylae on 25 April as part of 'The Victorious Advance to Athens' ('Der Siegeslauf nach Athen') (Chapoutot 2016: 91–2). Although not technically *Untermenschen* (sub-humans), the Greeks were treated as tainted stock and no different to Levantines. Regular soldiers were told to avoid the local women on racial grounds (Mazower 1993: 207). Racial conditioning also ensured that the process of entrapping, robbing and despatching Greek Jews to the death camps would be conducted with brutal efficiency.

Wartime governance

Aside from the German, Bulgarian and Italian occupation administrations, there were three Greek governments: the government in exile, the puppet regime in Athens and, towards the end of the war, the PEEA (Political Committee of National Liberation) or 'the Mountain Government', which was formed by the largest armed resistance movement. Much of Greece, particularly the highlands, was dominated by EAM (the National Liberation Front) and its military arm ELAS, but Epirus belonged mainly to its rival EDES (the National Republican Greek League), while local partisan groups retained considerable authority in places like Crete and parts of Macedonia.

German rule began with a frenzy of looting. Official requisitioning of food stocks and other resources proceeded with aggressive efficiency. Right of conquest appeared to drive an orgy of pillaging by soldiers and officers. 'The Germans are looting for all they are worth', claimed one startled American observer (Mazower 1993: 24). The frenzy had to do with the imminent handover of most Greek territory to the Italians, but the looting never stopped. Between 1941 and 1944, the Axis powers would strip the Greek economy of half of its GDP (Manousakis and Chronakis 2019: 43–5). The nation's division into three occupation zones, each with their separate administrations and interests, contributed to the general economic chaos and to the collapse of the production and distribution systems. Three facts sufficiently convey the magnitude of the disaster. First, the country's GDP declined to about half of the pre-war level (1942: 55 per cent, 1944: 53 per cent). Second, revenues, which covered 96.1 per cent of expenses in 1938, declined to 22 per cent in the second year of occupation, 18 per cent in the third year and just 6.3 per cent in 1944. Third, occupation spending rose to 250 per cent of total government spending in the first year. It reached 500 per cent in the final year (Manousakis 2014: 505–40). All the while, the Germans maintained a *c'est la guerre* attitude. In response to the extreme food shortages of early 1942, Hermann Goering uttered: 'We cannot worry unduly about the Greeks ... It is a misfortune that will strike many other people besides them' (Mazower 2008: 280).

The Germans did put considerable thought into how Greece might serve the Reich's strategic objectives in North Africa. That meant investing in infrastructure, especially airports and ports, and war industries. More than 40,000 workers were employed in Athens in the munitions industry (e.g. the Bodosakis company), in the aircraft industry and in the shipyards, where ships were either stripped down or repaired. Shipwrecking and scrap metal production flourished with the destruction of naval and other sea vessels. Industries that served the needs of the occupation forces certainly thrived. Axis authorities also showed particular interest in mining and metallurgical industries (Manousakis 2014: 403–29). Indeed, during the first two years of occupation, Axis authorities were the largest employers in Greece, providing work for 10 per cent of the nation's labour force. Compulsory labour was also deployed in defence and maintenance projects, while some 18,000 Greek labourers were sent to Germany to help make up for severe labour shortages.

Italy's imperial aims involved making the territories it planned to annex profitable and turn them into living space for Italians (*spazio vitale*). However, what Italy could do in practice was another matter altogether. In the interwar period, the governors of the Dodecanese had the resources to drive large-scale economic programmes and a forced-assimilation policy (Doumanis 1997: 52–7). In wartime, however, Italian authorities had no resources. In the Cyclades, Greek schools stayed open and Italian classes were still extracurricular (Lecoeur 2009: 129). Attempts to promote economic autonomy among Italy's Aegean islands failed because they could not survive without external subsidies. By the middle of 1943 an official report from the Italian Foreign Office considered the search for *spazio vitale* a dead issue (Lecoeur 2009: 61). The Bulgarians had no interest in assimilating ethnic Greeks in their occupied zone. Rather, their objective of integrating eastern Macedonia and Western Thrace into the Bulgarian nation involved the removal of somewhere between 100,000 and 150,000 ethnic Greeks. It also required the installation of an entirely new civil administration filled with Bulgarian personnel. Bulgarian became the language of schools, and Church Slavonic replaced Greek in churches, which were placed under the ecclesiastical jurisdiction of the Holy Synod of Sofia. Cities and streets were renamed, and signage was replaced. Authorities considered it an imperative to 're-educate' Slavophones, fearing two decades of Greek rule had turned them into Greeks. The aim was to make amends for previous failures to assimilate a group which Bulgarian authorities continued to believe were ethnically

Bulgarian. By the same token, the authorities were deeply suspicious of ethnic Greeks who had chosen to assume a Bulgarian identity. This group included native Bulgarian-speakers from cities which once had large Greek communities, particularly Plovdiv/Philippopolis and the cities of Bulgaria's Black Sea coast. Many of these suspected 'crypto' Greeks had already suffered ethnic cleansing following the Balkan Wars. They understood switching identities could mean the difference between keeping one's home and being ethnically cleansed. As one ethnic Greek said to another: 'learn Bulgarian because Greece is dead' (Dragostinova 2011: 252–4).

What of the Greek government in Athens? The character of state administration in occupied territories varied, but it was always clear that its role was to respond to German needs rather than to those of the occupied population. Greece's first quisling government was by all accounts a colourless and inert collection of senior officers, which suited the Reich. All that was required of them, claimed German Foreign Minister Joachim von Ribbentrop, was to be compliant and keep the machinery of government running (Hondros 1983: 78). Tsolakoglou was at the helm for twenty months (30 April 1941 to 2 December 1942), and like the other quislings he would later claim that he buttressed the Greek people from the worst effects of German domination (Tsoutsoumpis 2016: 20). By the end of 1942, as Axis fortunes began to turn, greater demands were made on quisling governments. In Greece, the Germans expected a more active response against the partisans. Tsolakoglou was replaced on 2 December 1942 by the German-speaking gynaecologist and academic Kostantinos Logothetopoulos, but he failed to impress and was soon replaced (7 April 1943) by the seasoned politician and ardent anti-communist Ioannis Rallis. Like many conservatives in Greek society, Rallis came to regard the Resistance as a greater threat to the nation than the occupiers, and he had some success in mobilising mass opposition (Hondros 1983: 81).

In the meantime, government and state bureaucracy continued to function, but government personnel did little more than collect their pay and pilfer public resources. Civil service pay remained attractive despite hyperinflation; hence collaborationist governments used their control of the public service to reward loyalists with jobs. For example, the number of National Bank of Greece employees rose by 50 per cent, while the number of people appointed to jobs in IKA quadrupled (Manousakis 2014: 418). Public regard for what counted as the state was also affected by manifest corruption. Public assets, food and other confiscated materials were treated as spoils and routinely divided up between government officers, judges, bureaucrats and the police (Manousakis 2014: 378). Police working with Italian forces, or supporting German counterinsurgency operations, usually expected a share of the loot acquired during operations. A former police commissioner criticised the police at the time for mixing enforcement duties with criminal activity, and for effectively operating like common gangs (Charalambidis 2012: 220–1). All the while, the Athens government seemed indifferent to the needs of a society that had suffered mass dislocation and economic collapse. It barely responded to what turned out to be the greatest famine in the nation's history.

Food and famine

For most Greeks the Second World War was a time of hunger (*pina*). Everyday life in the cities featured a daily struggle to find food. Children grew up thinking that being perpetually hungry was normal (Figure 5.1). Many of them remembered long periods of eating nothing but boiled wild greens (*horta*) without oil, and their mother having to hang bread from a rope to keep it safe from rats. Emaciated children walked the streets. Marin Rigoutsos, the honorary French consul based on the island of Syros, described conditions when hunger was compounded by the bitter winter cold of January 1942:

> Haggard faces, swollen eyelids and the heavy tread of the victim who senses that the cruellest of deaths awaits him; this is the ghastly sight you come across if you have the courage to go for a walk round the centre of a town which is itself, close to death. (Lecoeur 2009: 91)

The impact of the war-induced famine was compounded by the effects of a food crisis the previous year, when the domestic harvest was much too small to meet national subsistence requirements. The German invasion itself predictably disrupted harvesting whilst also causing mass dislocation. Dejected soldiers crossed paths with villagers and townspeople fleeing air raids. As they descended on cities, soldiers and civilian refugees competed for scarce food stocks, but there was no state authority to organise food relief and shelter. A Swiss doctor working with the Red Cross later reported: 'If all the Greeks based their hopes of being fed solely on the efforts of the Government, no one would remain alive' (Mazower 1993: 53).

Famine struck in the winter of 1941–2, killing upwards of 200,000 people, mainly in the Athens and Piraeus area and the islands

Figure 5.1 *Children waiting in a bread line during the Occupation, 1941. © Benaki FA_6_2045*

Figure 5.2 *Bodies collected during the famine of 1941–2. © Alamy GG29Y4*

(Figure 5.2). German plundering was the primary cause. Neither German nor Italian authorities appeared to give much thought to how the subject population might be fed. Other factors included the breakdown in inter-regional transport and communications, which meant heavy reliance on local food sources, along with inflation, panic buying, hoarding and the British naval blockade (Hionidou 2006: 33–4). A large shipment of Australian wheat that had been ordered just before the war was confiscated by the British and sold elsewhere in the Middle East (Hionidou 2006: 17). Whilst Axis and Allied authorities did not intend to starve the Greek people, relief was delayed by a dispute over who should provide it. British public opinion and pressure from the United States forced Churchill's government to lift the blockade: the latter feared that making exceptions would encourage further requests from other occupied countries (Fleischer 1988: 193–216; Clogg 2008: 39–53, 58–84). The Red Cross supervised food supplies from Turkey, although the initial shipments, which arrived between October 1941 and January 1942, were too small to have much impact (Hionidou 2006: 15–17).

Needless to say, the costs of occupation, which amounted to one third of pre-war GDP, were paid by the Greek people. The prices of goods traded between Germany and Greece were determined unilaterally by the former. German authorities also paid for Greek products and services with a special currency (Reichskreditkassenscheine) that was used only in the occupation zones, and which was not exchangeable with the Reichsmark (Klemann and Kudryashov 2012: 193–201). These factors destabilised the drachma, as did rampant inflation. To curb inflation and stabilise the economy, German authorities decided to defray some of their expenses, as well as the costs of Rommel's campaign in North Africa, as a loan from the National Bank of Greece. The first instalment of the loan was paid just before the German withdrawal from Greece in 1944. This was never repaid or recognised by West German or post-unification German governments (Fleischer 2010: 73–6; Christodoulakis 2014).

The price of food and food substitutes rose astronomically. The price of 1,200 grams of bread rose from 10 drachmas in 1941 to 153,000,000 drachmas in 1943. By the end of the occupation, a gold sovereign was worth 111 billion drachmas (Manousakis 2014: 505–40). Hyperinflation had rendered paper money worthless. The cost of living rose exorbitantly, as prices changed by the day and sometimes by the hour. People had no choice but to rely on bartering. The real currency now was bread rations and other food items. In these desperate conditions, urban dwellers sold off their assets, trading gold sovereigns or anything they could in exchange for food. City dwellers walked to nearby villages, spending hours searching for something to eat. They carried with them embroideries, silver cutlery or any item they could carry, even furniture, hoping to exchange them for cereals or oil. Urban Greeks, particularly more recent immigrants from the villages, relied heavily on food from kinfolk in the countryside. An important reason why the refugee neighbourhoods (*ta prosfygika*) suffered disproportionately was that they had no family ties in the countryside.

The famine's first casualties were the urban poor, those displaced by the aerial bombardments, and soldiers from the islands who were trapped on the mainland. Within a short space of time, however, famine struck all cities, towns and island communities. By early winter, the city streets were littered with corpses. Wheelbarrows carried the dead to mass graves while emaciated children and older adults begged for food. The length and impact of the famine varied according to region. Ermoupolis on the island of Syros was one of the worst affected towns because of overcrowding, but more so because it had lacked a hinterland where people might forage for food. The prohibition on boat fishing also denied access to marine resources. The Italian governor commented in January 1942:

> I observed with my own eyes the haggard, anguished and yellowish faces of the majority of the population; a state that was not yet obvious before I left and which now affected not just the poorer people, but was common among the rich. (Lecoeur 2009: 68)

There were two famines during the occupation. If the first, that of 1941–2, mainly affected cities, the second impacted the countryside in the winter–spring period of 1944. These conditions also fostered the spread of malaria, dysentery, typhus and tuberculosis. The death rate for the first winter was possibly as high as 200,000, while the total wartime figure was anywhere between 250,000 and 400,000 (Hionidou 2006: 32–48). Some families concealed the death of a loved one to keep their food stamps. Parents threw dead children over cemetery walls at night for the same reason. There were reported cases of cannibalism. Death by starvation was a harrowing experience, while the typical famine-related diseases such as tuberculosis, especially in children, as well as tumours and nerve and eye diseases had long-term effects among survivors, who also had to contend with mental trauma (Skouras and Chatzidimos 1947, 1991).

Conditions improved when the Red Cross was permitted to import food and when the occupation authorities stopped exporting Greek food stocks to Germany. Between 1942 and 1943 the economy was stabilised, but from the spring of 1943 it was affected by German preparations for a possible Allied invasion from Africa, by a counterinsurgency campaign and by Italy's withdrawal from the Axis. Thousands more German troops were deployed to Greece, which dramatically increased the costs of the occupation. The counterinsurgency campaigns affected food production, particularly in the affected regions, while the tens of thousands of villagers who sought refuge in the cities had to be housed and fed. Meanwhile, communities in the Aegean archipelago, especially among the more arid islands that subsisted on maritime activities, which were now banned by the Axis, suffered acute food shortages throughout the war. Many escaped to the Turkish coast in small boats in the dead of night. Turkish authorities moved them along to Aleppo, from where they were distributed by Allied authorities to refugee camps in Palestine, the Sinai, Egypt, Ethiopia, the Congo and various British African colonies. Between 20,000 and 23,000 Greeks would find refuge in these camps (Michailidis 2017).

The Tsolakoglou government did implement a relief plan, but its efforts favoured political supporters and certain categories of workers, leaving the rest with rations too meagre to meet minimal nutritional needs (Hionidou 2006: 117–19). Far more effective responses came from parish and neighbourhood committees, and various other voluntary organisations. These bodies distributed food in the factories, civil service buildings and schools, and operated soup kitchens. Once it became available, international humanitarian aid proved to be most effective in alleviating the immediate crisis and in meeting the nutritional needs of urban dwellers for the duration of the war. Both the Swedish and the Swiss Red Cross managed relief during the famine of 1941–2, drawing on funds raised mostly by Greek Americans. The ships brought mainly cereals, but also milk powder, medicines and other essentials. Soon, most families came to rely on food stamps. Assistance was provided by a network of some 3,000 committees that were frequently obliged to negotiate with occupation authorities and local armed groups (Valden 2017: 34–9). Inevitably, aid was used as a political tool. Greek government authorities found ways of channelling aid to their own families and supporters, whilst denying it to villages controlled by or suspected of supporting the Resistance. As one Italian general put it, 'Remember that hunger is the rebels' worst enemy and therefore it is necessary to deprive them of every source of sustenance' (Santarelli 2004: 292). The availability of aid in the cities had the effect of drawing villagers and their families away from rebel-dominated areas as the counterinsurgency expanded in 1943 and 1944.

Before the counterinsurgency, Greek village families not only managed to subsist on their own resources but had enough to feed relatives in the cities. Nevertheless, the war would exacerbate the problems of a rural sector that was already beset by low productivity, declining incomes and underemployment. The famine exacerbated the problem of rural overpopulation, as many of those who had managed to relocate to cities were forced to return. As numbers swelled, peasants resorted to tilling land that was unsuited for cultivation. An extraordinary proportion of the Greek population tried to subsist on agriculture. Inevitably, incomes plunged below the poverty line, and with emigration routes completely blocked, the rural sector became a social powder keg. The tensions that flowed from this deepening rural crisis undoubtedly influenced the extraordinary levels of violence that Greeks inflicted upon each other during the later years of the war and during the ensuing Civil War.

There was considerable scope, however, for peasants to profit from desperate urban dwellers, or to supply those who bought produce in the provinces and sold it on the black market in the cities. Hundreds of black marketeers travelled each day from Athens to Boeotia, Thessaly and even Macedonia to source produce, as the amount of food being sold on the black market each day could be as much as 350 tons (Voglis 2006: 29). Black markets sprouted on the edges of town, often under the protection of armed gangs. In time these markets came under the control of a small number of operators who had developed extensive networks and had expanded their operations. Hyperinflation, lawlessness and the circulation of gold sovereigns contributed to the expansion of a black market that met a wide array of basic needs, and trafficked in people, gold and guns. The black market featured an extensive network of thousands of people. Profiteers thrived and amassed great fortunes because they were able to move commodities from distant production sites to consumers. Such operators usually enjoyed protection and support from the authorities, who took a cut of the profits. Black marketeers also supplied raw materials and agricultural products to the military, and received contracts for major works with German companies (Manousakis 2014: 372–91).

Real estate transactions revealed the extent to which the new economy was concentrating wealth in fewer hands. During the war, 43,000 properties were sold in Athens, and somewhere in the vicinity of 350,000 properties were sold in Greece as a whole. There were approximately 60,000 buyers, some of whom developed huge portfolios, especially the hundred or so individuals at the top who accumulated more than fifty properties each (Manousakis 2014: 497–503). Aside from real estate, the same period saw an increase in luxury imports and a flourishing art trade. Class disparities and callous indifference were never more on show, for while people starved in the streets, some were living the high life. Clubs and casinos did a roaring trade in wartime Athens and Thessaloniki (Manousakis 2014: 484–504).

The Resistance and the search for a new identity

The German victory in April 1941 shattered but did not vanquish the patriotic spirit that had united the nation against Mussolini a few months earlier. Many demobilised officers, politicians and other public figures neither resisted nor collaborated, but took a 'wait and see' approach. The extraordinary depravations inflicted by Axis rule, however, roused many other Greeks, particularly young men and women, into taking action despite the threat of brutal repression. Patriotism was the chief galvanising force through which Greeks of all classes and political persuasions could express their dissent to foreign violation of national sovereignty. It also informed the humanitarian support that ordinary Greeks provided their fellow citizens through grass-roots movements. All Resistance movements regardless of ideological leanings likened their struggle to the Greek War of Independence: all who engaged in anti-Axis activities imagined that they were upholding an honoured tradition of popular struggle for liberty and national independence.

Everywhere in Europe, patriotism offered the best hope for rallying popular opposition against Axis imperialism and occupation. The European Left, which led resistance movements in Axis-occupied territories, would not have had much impact had it not appealed to the patriotic sensibilities of everyday people (Markwick and Doumanis 2016; Hobsbawm 1992: 145).

Yet the Second World War also developed into an ideological struggle and a quest to create a new world. The previous war had destroyed the old European order, but the question of what should replace it remained unresolved. Aside from seeking to assert German domination of Europe, Hitler also sought to abolish liberal democracy and to crush Bolshevism, and for that he earned the admiration of Europe's other right-wing regimes, including that of Metaxas. However, the sheer brutality of Hitler's new order, the fact that it subordinated all other nations to the interests of one national community (i.e. Germany) and that its authority was enforced by unremitting violence, had the effect of fostering a revival of Enlightenment values. The war reinvigorated interest in progressive causes that had fallen into abeyance in the interwar years, such as democracy, social equity and human rights (Mazower 1998: 140, 182). In most cases, patriotic resistance movements also hoped to recast state–society relations along progressive lines. National liberation was seen as a struggle to create a new country, and to reset the terms of what it meant to be Greek.

Within a year of the invasion, hundreds of thousands of activists had transformed Greece into a hostile environment that refused to allow Axis troops a moment's rest. Occupation troops felt safer in the city centres and in their bases. They rarely mingled with crowds and avoided straying into suburban streets and villages. From the summer of 1941, at least ten resistance organisations were in contact with the Allies in the Middle East, passing on information about Axis movements and receiving instructions for sabotage activities. From the end of 1942, the Greek Resistance was able to stage battles against Italian troops in the Macedonian hinterlands and seized control of such major towns as Naousa and Karditsa. From 1943, large parts of the country, including the central mountainous region and adjoining lowlands, were effectively liberated territories. The largest cities were also contested grounds.

The Resistance emerged 'from below'. It started with the food crisis, which prompted the formation of urban voluntary associations. These bodies were organised by civic-minded employees within factories and offices, sometimes led by business proprietors, and by groups of telephone operators, railway and bank employees, and various civil service branches. These spontaneous movements formed the seedbed from which emerged larger ones that would perform broader civic duties, particularly 'National Solidarity' and the 'National Workers Liberation Front' (EEAM), which were forerunners of the chief resistance organisation, the National Liberation Front (EAM).

EAM

Aside from leading the struggle against the Axis occupiers, EAM provided the Greek people with leadership after the king and his government had absconded abroad. It earned mass support and quickly acquired national prominence by being much more effective than the collaborationist government in providing food relief where needed, which it did through a subsidiary arm called 'National Solidarity' (*Ethniki Allilengyi*) (Hionidou 2006: 238). During the course of the war, it distributed about 20 million kilos of food. It punished hoarders and levied taxes to support Resistance fighters and welfare services, which included 73 hospitals, 671 surgeries and 1,245 pharmacies (Close 1995: 72). It also set up popular courts in the countryside, organised strikes in the cities and took measures to counter the activities of the black market (Charalambidis 2012). Even in traditional royalist regions like the Argolid, EAM earned respect for putting an end to cattle rustling (Kalyvas 2006: 258–60). Although its practice of levying taxes, sequestering food stocks and punishing collaborators, whether alleged or real, was deeply resented by many, even its detractors recognised that it provided a semblance of governance. The historian William H. McNeill, who was present in Greece in late 1944, described EAM as an underground movement that operated as if it were a state (McNeill 1947: 20, 22–6). By engaging the support of everyday Greeks, giving them a stake in the national cause and attending to their basic needs, EAM consciously showcased a form of inclusive and purposeful governance.

EAM was launched on 9 September 1941. Its core members also belonged to the Communist Party (KKE), but the participation of other socialists, followers of agrarian parties, liberals and even conservatives, including former Metaxas youth members, made it more of a popular front. In many ways, EAM represented a decisive break from the past, in that the old patronage networks were irrelevant, whilst the membership was roused by the concept of 'people power' (*laokratia*), and the very idea that the state could genuinely represent the interests of the people. It was generally agreed that such a movement was needed to oversee collective action and mutual assistance in the desperate early phases of the occupation. Even conservative groups, at least during the first two years, sympathised with EAM's aims.

EAM's progressive spirit was exemplified by its promotion of local self-government. Village-level initiatives to address such pressing matters as water management or primary education emerged spontaneously in the immediate aftermath of the German invasion, but by the end of 1942 EAM was implementing a comprehensive plan to empower all village and town communities with local democratic bodies that allowed for wide social participation, and which included women. Through such bodies, in which all men and women over the age of seventeen enjoyed voting rights, communities could address long-standing problems of inequity and corruption. In the village of Argalasti on Mount Pelion, to take one example, severe food shortages were addressed by rationing programmes (Mazower 1993: 274). The most striking and popular feature of this movement was in the administration of justice. Normally, legal redress was beyond the means of most citizens, but under EAM each village hosted a weekly tribunal that operated free of charge, hearing cases in demotic Greek rather than unintelligible *katharevousa*. Although punishments were often determined by local traditions or the general will, rather than by law, this popular dispute resolution mechanism gave ordinary Greeks ready access to justice (Skalidakis 2014: 211–12).

Through EAM, the Greek Communist Party was suddenly able to play a more significant role in national life. It was still a small party when the war broke out, but its tight organisation and internal discipline helped to make EAM an effective national movement. Leading communists knew not to promote their ideology within the organisation as they were keen to retain the involvement of non-communists. Cadres used patriotic language rather than 'communist speak', avoiding references to terms like 'socialism' and such stock phrases as 'the dictatorship of the proletariat'. A typical example was the colloquial tone of EAM's manifesto, 'What Is EAM and What Does It Want?', written by Dimitris Glinos, the long-time campaigner for demotic Greek. Many progressive intellectuals rallied to EAM, such as education reformer Roza Imvrioti, academics like Alexandros Svolos (constitutional law) and Petros Kokkalis (medicine), lawyers such as Georgios Simitis, father of future PASOK prime minister Kostas Simitis, and economists like Angelos Angelopoulos, a member of a powerful financier family. The participation of such luminaries showed EAM was a broad-based progressive front. It attracted the most liberal-minded members of the educated class, especially teachers, lawyers, agronomists and doctors, who were especially useful as they already played a leadership role within their local communities. Women could thrive in this new environment. Even village women, who were usually hidden from public view, became involved in political demonstrations, and often spoke in village meetings for the first time. When EAM was launched it only had a few hundred members, but within three years that number swelled to somewhere between 1.5 and 2 million.

Initially, the structure of EAM could be likened to a series of islands. Cells emerged quickly in towns with unionised working-class communities and refugee neighbourhoods. In the countryside, its expansion depended on local factors. In the Thessalian plain, for example, EAM grew rapidly because of a strong radical tradition that opposed the power of the landed estates (*tsiflikia*). In his parts of Central Greece, the communist leader Aris Velouchiotis had enough personal appeal to attract a considerable popular following to the cause. EAM gained the support of staunchly anti-royalist islands of the Eastern Sporades (Lesbos, Chios, Samos, Ikaria), who found it easy to transfer their allegiances, and the support of minorities like the Vlachs and Slavophones in western Macedonia, who felt they had been cheated in the redistribution of lands vacated by Muslims. By the same token, EAM had less success with refugee groups in western Macedonia who had received the vacated lands. It found it hard to penetrate traditional royalist regions in the Peloponnese, and in regions like Epirus and Crete, which had their own, home-grown resistance movements (Close 1995: 96–8). These early geographical patterns signalled the kinds of challenges that EAM faced as it sought to build a national consensus, yet the speed by which it spread proved that much of the country was receptive to its calls for inclusive politics.

A significant factor in its success was the use of patriotic language and imagery. EAM propaganda was saturated with familiar patriotic ideas, words and imagery of the Greek Revolution of 1821, which it disseminated through the schools, through literature, posters, songs, leaflets and the church pulpit. Ordinary Greeks responded by participating in EAM-organised national commemoration days, which were widely celebrated despite the official ban. An upsurge of patriotic fervour was shown on 28 October 1942, the first anniversary of Metaxas' famous 'No!' (*Ochi!*) response to Mussolini's ultimatum, when between 25,000 and 30,000 protesters clashed with the Italian *carabinieri* in Athens. That spirit was exemplified by such organisations as the Pan-Hellenic Union of Militant Youth (PEAN), a courageous movement that carried out assassinations and bombings, and among other things destroyed the offices of an anti-Semitic organisation in Athens (Varon-Vassar 2009: 159–63).

Movements like PEAN had difficulty attracting recruits, however, because their aims were exclusively political and because their activities were too dangerous for most people. What made EAM so much more successful as a mass movement was its preoccupation with the needs of ordinary people and their daily challenges. It connected with the masses and was able to mobilise them when necessary. Thus, in February–March 1943 EAM organised protests that succeeded in forcing the cancellation of a compulsory labour recruitment drive for building Axis defences and security installations. EAM also foiled attempts at recruiting labourers to work in Germany and volunteers for duties on the Eastern Front. It supported striking workers and organised demonstrations over social grievances. It was also behind countless minor acts of dissent, which it promoted through the press and graffiti. Furthermore, it provided improvised loudspeakers so that political speeches could be projected from rooftops. The ideological aims of EAM were particularly appealing to young men and women, who numbered about 600,000, many of whom joined its youth movement EPON (United Pan-Helladic Youth Organisation) (Varon-Vassar 2009: 380, 390–1, 399, 418–33). The young were typically more willing to participate in street demonstrations before nervous policemen and trigger-happy occupation forces, and more likely to take up arms and head for the mountains. Quite often, they did so against their parents' wishes. Many of these parents were politically conservative, but they were often influenced by their children to support EAM. The young were also typically the most idealistic activists; their patriotism was informed by such concepts as liberty and social emancipation. Such idealism found expression in the literature and poetry that flourished within the Resistance movement. The most famous case was a stirring poem delivered at the funeral of the great poet Kostis Palamas on 28 February 1943, by another poet, Angelos Sikelianos, which called for a national reawakening. The event sparked the largest protest against the occupation. Overall, the war period witnessed a proliferation of small reading groups, literary events, poetry recitals and other literary forums, which had no precedent in peacetime. The Resistance became a laboratory that produced a new generation of Greek writers and artists, whose works often reflected the violence and despair that pervaded everyday life during the occupation (Papatheodorou 2010: 181–97).

However, not all Greeks found a unity of purpose under EAM's lead. The least significant anti-EAM groups were the collaborators. Local anti-Semitic and fascist movements hoped that they would be invited to share state power, but German authorities found they were too small and socially marginal to be of much use. Much more important were the royalists and Venizelists who had vacated the political sphere, who could not accept that EAM was anything but a communist front, and who preferred to remain inactive until the departure of Axis forces. However, as EAM grew in strength and expanded its influence, many royalists and Venizelists began to take on more politically active roles. It was the popular protests of early 1943 that sparked fears of an EAM political takeover, and which triggered the rise of anti-EAM movements.

EAM's history, therefore, falls into two phases. The first seemed like more 'innocent' times, as most of the nation rallied in support of the movement's struggle against a brutal occupation. From early 1943, however, the patriotic struggle gradually slipped into an undeclared civil war. Societal fissures had been opening up in Greece, as they had done in other occupied territories. France had its *guerre franco-française*, much as Italy would suffer a *guerra civile*. But in Greece and in Yugoslavia the civil wars were on a much more massive and destructive scale.

'All the Hellenes used to carry arms'

> It should be explained that in early times both the Hellenes and the Barbarians who dwell on the mainland near the sea, as well as those on the islands ... turned to piracy, under the lead of their most powerful men, whose motive was their own private gain and the support of their weaker followers, and falling upon cities that were unprovided with walls and consisted of groups of villages, they pillaged them and got most of their living from that source ... On the mainland also men plundered one another ... Indeed, all the Hellenes used to carry arms because the places where they dwelt were unprotected, and intercourse with each other was unsafe; and in their everyday life they regularly went armed just as the Barbarians did. (Thucydides 1.5–6)

In his classic history of the Peloponnesian War in the late fifth century BCE, Thucydides prefaces his account with reflections on life before the *polis* and before the rule of law. The words 'all the Hellenes used to carry arms' (1.6.1) could have described the Greek mainland during the Second World War, and earlier during Ottoman times and for much of the nineteenth century, when bandit groups (*kleftes*) dominated many rural areas. Some of their members had been employed by the Ottoman state as Christian militias (*armatoloi*) to curb banditry. The *kleftes* also played a critical role in the Greek Revolution and in later irredentist campaigns (Koliopoulos 1987). From a European perspective, the preponderance of such groups in the Balkan uplands added to the region's image as the continent's barbaric doorstep (Todorova 2009: 122). Yet throughout the interwar years armed bands had also become a feature of political life in many European countries and were often aligned with specific parties and sometimes served the needs of the state. Right-wing bands like the *fascisti* and *Freikorps*, led by 'chiefs' like Mussolini and Hitler, did battle with other armed groups in major cities and towns. Armed bands constituted a response to the expansion of state power throughout the first half of the twentieth century, but also reflected the crisis of legitimacy that many states faced due to the dislocating effects of war and the Depression. As one historian has put it, the 'paramilitarisation' of politics was stimulated by both the expansion and the retrenchment of state power. This phenomenon reached its climax during the Second World War, when militias in occupied territories exploited the vacuum of state power and took up the fight against the Axis powers, while other groups were employed to enforce Axis authority (Pritchard 2016: 596).

Many armed formations dominated the territories that Axis and Greek government authorities were unable to control. In Greece, as in much of occupied Europe, they were also responsible for many of the war's crimes against humanity. For the battle line did not simply run between regular and irregular military formations, but directly through the home front, as opposing forces split societies, violently pulling civilians into their respective orbits. The war also produced bands that reflected ethnic divisions (Vlachs, Slav Macedonians, Turkish-speaking Pontians) (Marantzidis 2006). The larger anti-Axis formations like ELAS (the Greek Popular Liberation Army), the military arm of EAM, and the Security Battalions created by the puppet regime in 1943 to crush the Resistance, basically fought along two fronts: that between the Axis and the Resistance, and that which divided the Left and the Right. The latter would eventually include the Greek middle classes and those who sought the restoration of the pre-war political order. The Left always considered the Axis front to be the most important, while the Right came to see the war against the Left as more vital. Fighting along these fronts was hard and bloody, but there would be considerable side-swapping as the war progressed and as the Left grew in power.

How did these armed groups come into being and what were they fighting for? The first kind, the largest in terms of size and territorial range, were the Resistance armies, namely ELAS and EDES. While ELAS was created for EAM, the rival partisan army EDES was led by Napoleon Zervas, a retired Venizelist officer who had participated in the pro-Venizelist coup of 1926. EDES was much smaller than ELAS and regionally focused. It began as a republican movement, but by the end of the war Zervas would throw his weight behind the monarchy. More will be said of these two movements in the next section; suffice it to say here that they posed the main challenge to Axis authority. Greek partisans, mainly those of ELAS, were also known as *andartes* (rebels).

The second kind consisted of the traditional bands led by local chiefs, which were generally autonomous, self-reliant and particularly useful given their guerrilla warfare skills. Since they were motivated by parochial need, they forged alliances with a variety of Resistance groups, such as the National Cretan Organisation, the Panhellenic Freedom movement in Macedonia (PAO), and EDES in Epirus. A third kind consisted of demobilised soldiers who re-formed into small armed bands to fight the *andartes*. The most significant were 'X' (the Greek letter 'chi') in Athens and the Defenders of Northern Greece in Thessaloniki, along with various officer associations in the southern Peloponnese. Whilst small in number, these groups played key roles in the eventual formation of an anti-EAM front, and in facilitating the return of a government that had been formed in exile in 1941 mainly by former politicians.

The fourth category were the collaborationists, who not only fought against the Resistance movements but also took part in the Holocaust. The EEE (*Ethniki Enosis Ellados*/National Union of Greece), also called 'the Three Es' because of its acronym, but nicknamed 'Greek Eliminators of Jews', had formed in 1927 and was responsible for setting fires in Thessaloniki's Jewish district in 1931. During the occupation, EEE emerged as the chief Greek national socialist party. It daringly criticised German authorities for failing to move quickly enough against the Jews in Thessaloniki and later provided eager assistance in arresting Jews and stripping them of their assets (Kavala 2018: 183–207; Dordanas 2018: 208–27). The group also fought the partisans and perpetrated atrocities against civilians accused of aiding and abetting them (Dordanas 2006: 117–54, 356–61). Similar organisations in Athens proved to be less effective, where the local Jewry had stronger social bonds with the wider community. The largest was ESPO (the Greek Socialist Patriotic Organisation), but it was effectively destroyed by PEAN.

The fifth kind, the Security Battalions, were the main achievement of the prime minister Rallis, whose government to that point lacked an army. The idea of creating anti-Resistance units was first proposed to the Germans by Republican officers, including the former dictator and virulent anti-communist Theodoros Pangalos. He harboured hopes of preventing the king's return in the event of a German defeat, but the Germans entrusted recruitment instead to Rallis, who initially tried to make it a royalist outfit. However, the old politics gave way to the more urgent task of combating the Left, and Pangalos was to play a significant role in the recruitment of Venizelists. Many demobilised officers did join for ideological reasons, but many also bristled at the idea of joining a collaborationist force. The government threatened to withdraw their pensions and food stamps, which worked in some cases, but it also forced many to escape to the Middle East or join the partisans. Overall, the Security Battalions, which were under German command and which accompanied German units in anti-insurgent operations, were motley collections of anti-communists and paupers who needed work. By the summer of 1944, 16,625 men had joined (Hondros 1983: 82). The government provided food, equipment, ammunition, vehicles, fuel and other materials that the partisans lacked. To claim the patriotic high ground, recruits were dressed in uniforms that resembled the traditional national military costume of the *Evzones*, which included a kilt (*fustanella*) and shoes with pom-poms. Yet, as with all collaborationist formations in occupied Europe, the Security Battalions pledged loyalty to the Führer. As one German officer put it cynically, their essential role was to save 'precious German blood' (Fleischer 1994: 388–9). Even so, Battalionists claimed to be a patriotic force that was fighting a greater evil. According to their leaders, 'only their weapons were foreign. The defenders, their hearts, their souls … all were Greek' (Galanis 2018: 123).

The sixth and final category among the armed groups were the officers and regular soldiers that had escaped to the Middle East and joined the army of the government in exile. Known as the Royal Greek Middle East Force, they participated in operations against the Axis in North Africa, including the Battle of El Alamein (October–November 1942), and later in the Battle of Rimini in Italy in September 1944. This force was dominated by royalist officers of various ranks, but it also accepted Venizelist officers who often hated EAM much more than they did royalists (Close 1995: 93). The royalist cause was strengthened in April 1944, however, when the officers who did acknowledge EAM, and demanded it be recognised, staged mutinies that led to dismissals and incarcerations in British detainment camps in the Sahara. The mutinies effectively accelerated the rapprochement of royalists and the more politically conservative Venizelists, purged the government in exile's army of its more progressive elements, and confirmed it as a conservative and anti-communist political force. This political shift was confirmed by the formation of an exclusively royalist crack unit known as the 'Mountain Brigade', which would fight in Allied operations in Italy, and which would later serve as a 'Praetorian Guard' to the government in exile following its return to Athens in late 1944 (Katsikostas 2010).

Why did Greeks join these armed groups? Phaidon Maidonis, to take one example, abandoned the comforts of his bourgeois home in Athens and joined EDES in the rugged mountains of Epirus (Fleischer 1984). Meanwhile, Nikos Mitsis had left Epirus to find work in the capital, where he was radicalised by young leftists, but returned to Epirus because of the famine in Athens. Once home he joined his local ELAS unit. In each case, Maidonis and Mitsis became Resistance fighters to pursue certain ideals, but many who fought with (and against) these idealists were motivated by very different reasons or had been forced to join. The war politicised everyday Greeks in complex ways, but people joined for many reasons. Patriotism came first, but many followed the lead of powerful patrons or regional strongmen. Some recruits followed their siblings. Some were selected to serve by the village elders. Others did so because they were hungry and unemployed (Tsoutsoumpis 2012: 51–61). These were important considerations for assessing the effectiveness of each group and the ways it operated, and these were the kinds of factors that influenced the civil wars that broke out throughout much of occupied Europe (Roshwald 2016). It was a war of ideology that fed on many other economic, cultural and social tensions. The stresses of war brought into stark relief the other factors that divided Greeks, such as ethnic antagonisms, as seen when Turkish-speaking Greek bands in Macedonia collaborated with the Axis because rival Slavophone bands fought with the Resistance. There were also the countless interpersonal grievances that saw people inform on neighbours and kin to pursue vendettas. Such non-ideological strains nevertheless tended to feed into the larger ideological struggle, bringing the war into every village square and every household. In other words, a war that began as a Greek–Axis struggle became a pandemic of violence that affected every social being. From a bottom-up perspective, it gave the manifold strains in social life a left- and right-wing hue that would shape interpersonal relations and life in Greece for decades.

Both the Resistance and collaboration units were also commanded by middle-aged men, and included officers who had been decommissioned after the 1935 coup, or who had simply become inactive after the German victory in April 1941. Whether on the Left or the Right, ELAS or EDES, or in other competing movements like the Security Battalions, these seasoned officers had similar career paths. Many of them began their careers in the Balkan Wars, had experienced the First World War and the Asia Minor campaign, had declared their political loyalties for either the monarchy or Venizelos, and were involved in the interwar coups. Stefanos Sarafis (leading general of ELAS), Napoleon Zervas (head of EDES), Dimitrios Psarros (head of the 5/42 Evzone Regiment, armed wing of resistance movement National and Social Liberation), Euripides Bakirtzis (first president of the 'Mountain Government', 1944), Ioannis Tsigantes (Envoy of the Allied Command), Komninos Piromaglou (co-founder of EDES) and Neokosmos Grigoriadis (President of the Council of the Mountain, 1944), were just some who fought in various previous conflicts. Once comrades, many were now mortal enemies. Those who joined ELAS were entrusted with additional political responsibilities (Shepherd and Pattinson 2010). Recruits were now expected to assist farmers with their crops, fix wartime property damage, promote EAM's political programmes and defend civilians against anti-EAM operations. Most recruits were very young and hence more responsive to political indoctrination. Three quarters were between 17 and 30 years of age (Mitsopoulos 1987: 629).

While playing host to the government in exile, the British also developed relations with Greece's Resistance, including ELAS. Numerous British officers under the Special Operations Executive (SOE) in London ventured into occupied territory to assist in coordinating Greek Resistance activities with Allied strategy. Among the British agents embedded in Greece were archaeologists, classicists and historians, who were able to use their expertise on Greece to navigate its terrain and liaise with its peoples. They included N. G. L. Hammond, C. M. Woodhouse, J. M. Cook and P. M. Fraser, who would later become distinguished academics (Clogg 2000: 33). ELAS's misgivings about the British were appeased by the flow of gold, arms and medical supplies (Skalidakis 2014: 139). During the North African campaign, Britain's priority in Greece was to sabotage German bases, cut supplies to the Afrika Korps and pin down German troops that would otherwise be deployed elsewhere. The most significant act of sabotage organised by the British, ELAS and EDES was the bombing of the viaduct of the Gorgopotamos River in Central Greece on 25–6 November 1942 (Operation Harling), cutting the only rail line from central Europe to the ports of southern Greece, where ships to North Africa were refuelled. Once the Afrika Korps was forced to surrender in early 1943, the aim was to persuade Germany, through false intelligence, into thinking the Allies were preparing to re-enter Europe through Greece. The alliance with ELAS, however, was always one of convenience for the British. By 1943 Churchill's government was already reducing its support for EAM and seeking to strengthen its opponents.

Social profiles of ELAS and EDES

In his *Theory of a Partisan*, originally published in German in 1962, Carl Schmitt claimed that guerrilla fighters were either hapless apolitical folk who were simply defending their homelands, or ardent political revolutionaries. ELAS included both. It was committed to national liberation, but a significant part of it also saw liberation as a step towards world communism. In that sense the ELAS fighter was also a partisan: a highly mobile irregular that was valued 'not only in his military-technical capacity but also philosophically' (Schmitt 2007: 32). He or she could fight for liberty as well as wage class struggle. Of all the armed formations that featured during the war, only ELAS fought for a new Greece and a new world. In combination with EAM, it sought a complete break with the past, particularly the old political order and the patron–client politics at the ground level, and to reconstruct Greece both politically and socially.

Established in January 1942 by KKE, ELAS came to be the armed wing of EAM. Through ELAS and its operatives, EAM was able to extend its influence across most of mainland Greece, while ELAS was able to build on EAM networks and organisations. It was the summer of 1942 when the first armed bands began appearing in the mountain villages of Central Greece, carrying the national flag, showing due respect to the church and local traditions, and promising to protect the local people and their lands. Over the coming months, the many bands merged into ELAS. By the summer of 1943 ELAS had somewhere between 20,000 and 30,000 permanent soldiers and reserves. Whenever operatives infiltrated villages and towns, they punished collaborators, expected the local gendarmes to join or disband, and introduced self-government and popular courts. They replaced established government institutions with those of EAM, quite often with local support. They collaborated with community elites, usually the local priests, teachers, doctors and merchants, whilst also winning favour by burning tax, banking and court documents that recorded peasant debts.

In effect, ELAS was driving a revolution in the countryside without having declared one. To be sure, there were limits to what such a revolution could do in rural Greece in 1943. Agrarian revolutions normally involve the redistribution of land and debt cancellations, yet most estates had already been broken up by previous regimes, and Metaxas had already dealt with most debts. The most pressing issues, overpopulation and underemployment, were hard to address even in peacetime. The collapse of government services, which were amply provided in the interwar years, was an additional source of hardship, as was the severe lack of fertilisers, seed stocks and draught animals. Where ELAS could have a revolutionary impact was in empowering those who always lacked power, and in subverting traditional social roles and relations (Vermeulen 1993: 113–33). Thus, the popular courts made illiterate peasant folk less vulnerable to lawyered local elites. Young women could now move about the village or town without male supervision, especially as the needs of the Resistance required them to play roles that made them publicly visible. Women also had to take the floor in assemblies, take up arms with guerrilla units and even ride horses – a female cavalry unit would operate in Thessaly. Most ELAS women worked with logistics and in medical services, while some women assumed political executive roles. This kind of mass participation by women constituted a grass-roots challenge to the traditional Greek gender divisions of labour, rights and duties (Poulos 2009: 77). In such ways ELAS/EAM was forcing rapid modernisation.

Fighting units were also objects of modern experimentation. As units were composed of volunteers and conscripts from very different social backgrounds, maintaining discipline required a deft combination of persuasion, ideological training and coercion. Regular meetings were held to discuss pressing issues. It was the experience of fighting as a unit that forged a spirit of solidarity, which was needed given the harsh conditions that guerrillas were forced to endure on a daily basis. Discipline was maintained by a captain, a popular figure who not only led the unit but also liaised with villagers, and who knew how to persuade or coerce them when necessary. Military matters were in the hands of veteran officers or officers trained in ELAS's military academy. Finally, each unit had a political leader who was in charge of political education and implementing the political line. This tripartite form of leadership featured at all levels of the ELAS structure.

Whilst ELAS was based in Central Greece and Macedonia, it had a strong presence in other mountainous regions like the central Peloponnese and Evvia, and in towns like Patras and Aigion (Tsoutsoumpis 2016: 17). In the greater Athens-Piraeus area, units had been established to control suburbs and the city outskirts, while the Organisation for the Protection of People's Combatants (OPLA) served as ELAS's killing unit (Chandrinos 2012). The streets of the capital witnessed countless bloody encounters. Neither ELAS nor the other Resistance organisations ever managed to defeat Axis forces, but they did succeed in denying them full control of occupied territories and in forcing the diversion of Axis manpower and other resources away from the major fronts. ELAS's activities made it difficult for the Germans to use Greece as an effective bridgehead to North Africa, particularly after the Gorgopotamos operation, which involved the cooperation of ELAS, EDES and the British. In the last year of the occupation, 8,200 Germans were killed in battles with ELAS (Tsoutsoumpis 2012: 240).

ELAS units were overwhelmingly composed of Greeks (including Jews and Slavophones), but from 1943 these would be complemented by demobilised Italians, as well as anti-fascist Germans and other recruits from the occupied countries that had deserted the Wehrmacht (Chandrinos 2020). But while ELAS set out to win hearts and minds, it also managed to alienate communities and create popular opposition. As with most Resistance movements in occupied territories, its greatest challenge was procuring weapons and food supplies, and as British support diminished in the later period, ELAS relied more heavily on an increasingly resentful peasantry. Rising disaffection was also a response to the counterinsurgency campaigns from mid-1943, as people often blamed the Resistance for drawing the Axis and the violence to their localities. It was in this period that ELAS began to use coercive methods against villagers and took more punitive actions against rival Resistance groups and collaborators. Any assessment of civilian responses to the Axis and the partisans must also account for the fact that many leveraged their power to protect their communities or themselves, or for personal profit. Thus, those with a grievance against EAM/ELAS sometimes sought the support of their rivals or even the German authorities, and sometimes channelled that power against neighbours or estranged family members. Axis authorities throughout Europe relied on denunciations as a form of community self-policing (Fitzpatrick and Gellately 1997), but it had the effect of dividing communities as well as drawing the partisans into intra-community affairs. Indeed, EAM/ELAS alternated between using persuasive and coercive means to secure support.

EDES was ELAS's only serious rival Resistance force. Founded in Athens in February 1941 but based in Epirus, EDES pledged its loyalties to the government in exile. Its leader, Zervas, a native Epirote, knew how to exploit traditional kin and patron–client networks to generate support and active recruits. The British favoured EDES because it was not communist and hence supplied it with ample amounts of gold and arms, hoping it would become a counterweight to ELAS. The successes and growth of ELAS, however, pushed EDES to the right and behind the royalist cause. Zervas enrolled many idealistic youths from the Athenian middle classes like Phaidon Maidonis, but he relied much more on traditional Epirote chiefs. EDES therefore featured a curious combination of kleftic bands and urban bourgeois liberals, whose members struggled with mutually incomprehensible social and cultural codes. The cultural gap was the sources of many problems: Zervas was often forced to mediate between parties over slights and traded insults.

There were moments when EDES and ELAS worked together, as happened at Gorgopotamos, and there were genuine attempts to create a joint headquarters under British supervision. The relationship was hampered, however, by deep mutual mistrust. Open hostility broke out in the mountains of western Greece in October 1943, and the ensuing conflict inevitably affected their respective struggles against the Germans. Later, EDES had secured a ceasefire with the Germans in order to retrieve territory from ELAS, but it was forced to accept a ceasefire with ELAS in February 1944, following international intervention that included British and Soviet governments (Smith 1993: 66–7; Fleischer 1984; Mazower 1993: 329–30). After that, EDES operated only within Epirus, but the defeat of ELAS had become its priority. Although EDES had denounced the Security Battalions, it sometimes cooperated with them, particularly in Athens, where many EDES members had joined the Battalions. It also worked with militia chiefs in Macedonia that had collaborated with the Axis. The relationship between EDES and ELAS was therefore indicative of the way ideology came to trump patriotism.

The politics of German violence, 1943–1944

On 10 July 1943 the Allies landed in Sicily, and within a few days Allied aircraft were bombing Rome. Mussolini was sacked on 24 July and arrested the following day, after which the king's new government, led by Marshal Pietro Badoglio, hoped to somehow come to terms with the Allies without alerting the Germans. During the so-called Forty-Five Days between Mussolini's arrest and Badoglio's formal announcement of an armistice (8 September), Italian troops in Greece were in limbo. Many hoped that their war had come to an end and they would be returning home, but there had been minimal preparation for the inevitable German reactions. In Kefalonia in late September 1943, the Wehrmacht massacred some 5,200 Italian soldiers of the Acqui Division. This is considered one of the Wehrmacht's greatest war crimes in southern Europe. Many Italian soldiers managed to find refuge in the Greek mountains, but many of those captured were sent to the Eastern Front (Rossi 2016). A collateral result of the Italian surrender was that the partisans were able to seize Italian arms and munitions.

Once the Italians surrendered in September 1943, Lieutenant General Alexander Löhre's Wehrmacht and Waffen SS units launched a brutal counterinsurgency campaign to wipe out the partisans.

Physical geography and its effective use by the Greek Resistance would make this a costly exercise. Comparisons with Western Europe are illuminating. In 1943, France and the Low Countries, which had a combined population of approximately 57 million and covered 623,000 sq. km, required a German occupation force of 790,000. Greece had only 7 million inhabitants and 132,000 sq. km (including the Dodecanese), yet it soaked up some 300,000 German troops. One German soldier was required for every twenty-five locals, or nine soldiers for every 4 sq. km. Thus, four times as many soldiers were needed to control Greece, and two times as many (1.8 to be exact) per square kilometre.[1] Conditions in Yugoslavia, which Nazi Germany also hoped to control through Axis partners and with minimum German deployment, were even more exacting. There were never enough Axis troops to suppress well-organised Resistance movements in the steep mountain ranges of the Balkans, yet particularly in Yugoslavia, excess Axis brutality was instrumental in boosting the power of the Resistance (Calic 2019: ch. 8).

Initially, Axis forces approached the insurgency problem by sending small detachments into the Greek mountains to weed out the partisans, but that tactic bore little fruit. By early 1943, as EAM/ELAS stocks rose, the Germans committed more fully to a counterinsurgency campaign (*Säuberungen*) that would, as much as possible, be made to coincide with a locally led and generated counter-revolution. The main target of the counterinsurgency was ELAS, and it involved the destruction of villages that supported it. The broader aim was to terrorise the whole of rural Greece but also drive a wedge between the villages and the Resistance. This programme did bear fruit, but the results were mixed. Its greatly intensified the violence and deprivation in rural Greece, and as a consequence many villages focused their resentments on the partisans, particularly in regions that had been traditional conservative strongholds. In such cases, resentment had to do with locals being terrorised and brutalised by the partisans. At the same time, the violent excesses of counterinsurgency forces further expanded ELAS's social support base. The overall effect of the counterinsurgency campaigns of 1943 and 1944 was to extend the war into the Greek countryside, and bring mass dislocation, destruction and famine.

As many more Germans were being killed, the violence perpetrated against civilians escalated. Officers expected soldiers to discard notions of European civility and to deal with locals without pity. After having destroyed and extinguished four villages near the Cretan capital Iraklion between 1 and 4 May 1944, a German notice warned that 'in future [we] will smite each and every person who is guilty of links with the bandits and their English instigators' (Beevor 2005: 160). Everyone knew the rule that fifty Greeks would be culled for every slain German soldier, and that a German officer was worth 200 Greek civilians. Such threats were always carried out in order to dispel any doubts of German convictions. The price was sometimes paid by political prisoners. On 1 May 1944, 200 inmates in the notorious Haidari concentration camp in Athens, many of them communists, were executed in retaliation for the assassination of a German general near Sparta.

Other methods used to terrorise civilians included the macabre practice of publicly exhibiting corpses. Bodies were sometimes piled up in streets, or left dangling in the town squares and off bridges. Towns and city neighbourhoods linked to the Resistance were subjected to sudden blockades and mass arrests. Home searches were often conducted in the dead of night. Public beatings and summary street executions were held for minor infringements. Such acts were aimed at removing any sense of security and, as psychologists noted at the time, to establish an 'agonising apprehension for the unknown' (Skouras and Chatzidimos 1947, 1991: 115).

It is difficult to underestimate the scale and ferocity of the terror that swept the Greek countryside. Aiding and abetting the partisans was deemed a betrayal to be paid for in blood. From 1943 onwards, 1,170 villages were torched for harbouring partisans. German units killed men, women, children and the elderly indiscriminately, burning homes, warehouses and stables. Kommeno in southern Epirus, for example, was a village quietly hidden among orange groves near a lake. On 16 August 1943, the day after a major religious festival, the village was attacked by a death squad that killed indiscriminately. A monument was later erected in the village square to the unbaptised babies, children, mothers, fathers, grandfathers and grandmothers who were massacred (Meyer 1999). Seven hundred people were massacred in the region of Kalavryta in the northern Peloponnese, where fifty villages and towns were torched (Meyer 2002). Similar attacks were reported in Distomo in Boeotia, Pyrgos near Kozani, Lingiades in Epirus, Drakeia near Volos and in Chortiatis near Thessaloniki. Greek collaborators had also participated in the carnage (Dordanas 2007).

A wave of terror also swept through the cities. People went missing as they ventured out of their homes, usually without leaving a trace. Whole neighbourhoods were attacked. An operation would begin by German and Security Battalion troops surrounding a suspect neighbourhood, in order to seal off escape routes. People were then forced to gather in an open setting or square, and suspected activists were signalled out and tortured or executed in front of family and neighbours. These reprisals were called *bloka* (blockades) and cost thousands of lives, and they were common in 1943 and 1944. The case best remembered is depicted in the 1965 film *To Bloko* ('The Blockade'), on the massacre at Kokkinia in Piraeus in August 1944, where over 200 civilians were killed. Much of the dirty work was done by Battalionists, who sometimes conducted *bloka* on their own initiative. ELAS retaliated in kind against villages associated with known collaborators, and by targeting the relatives of Battalionists. In 1944, as Germany began reallocating troops to the collapsing Eastern Front, ELAS committed mass reprisals against Security Battalions in the Peloponnese and against other collaborationist groups in central Macedonia. Numerous executions were carried out in western Peloponnese (e.g. Meligala) and in central Macedonia (e.g. Kilkis).

By this stage, the occupation was clearly transitioning into a civil war. The dividing lines were hardening. Athens, Piraeus and Thessaloniki were divided cities, with 'red' refugee suburbs like Kaisariani and Vyronas pitted against anti-communist fortresses like Kolonaki and Thiseion. When the Special Security police unit, which targeted communists, murdered KKE leader Elektra Apostolou, OPLA retaliated by killing fifty political opponents (Chandrinos 2012: 226–7). OPLA had been created initially to protect demonstrators from snipers, but it became a hit squad that assassinated black marketeers and Security Battalion personnel and their relatives.

The first years of the war, when most Greeks found common cause against foreign adversaries, now seemed a distant memory. Greece once again became polarised. As both sides expanded and gained in strength, the scene was set for a bloody showdown. However, for one group at least, the only enemy that counted was Nazi Germany.

The extermination of Greek Jews

The story of the Greek Jewry during the war is usually told separately from that of the rest of the Greek population. While the Jewish communities certainly present a special case, their fate was nevertheless entwined with that of the rest of the country (Benveniste 2001). From the outset, the puppet regime in Athens signalled its intention to cooperate with German demands regarding the treatment of Jews. Whereas the Metaxas dictatorship had extended protections against anti-Semitic activism in Thessaloniki, the Tsolakoglou government immediately withdrew them, proclaiming that Greece too had a

'Jewish Problem', which had to be 'definitively solved within the framework of the whole New Order of Europe' (Apostolou 2018: 94). Meanwhile, in Thessaloniki, local officials and anti-Semitic activists were anxious to expel the city's Jews, and to expropriate their belongings and properties well before German authorities were ready to make their move. In other words, Greece was not just a setting for the Holocaust: some Greek authorities, local elites, anti-Semites and collaborators played active roles in perpetrating the destruction of the local Jewry (Antoniou and Moses 2018). Moreover, by the Second World War Greek Jews were more than just 'Greeks' on paper. Being Greek meant a great deal to those who grew up in the 1920s and 1930s, who managed to escape to the mountains and fight as partisans, and for those who were able to survive Auschwitz. The survivors were often made to feel very unwelcome by Greek authorities, and often by old neighbours on returning to their homes. Many were compelled to remake their lives in Israel, the United States or Argentina. Yet many also retained, and indeed further developed, an interest in their Greekness (Fleming 2008).

Before the persecutions began in 1942, the Jewish population in Greece, according to the Central Israelite Council, was 77,377. By war's end, only 10,226 had survived. Eighty-six per cent of the community perished: almost one in nine. The proportion of those killed was one of the highest in Europe, comparable to the Netherlands (86 per cent) and much higher than France (30 per cent) (Chandrinos and Droumpouki 2018: 31–2). In Thessaloniki, where the bulk of the Jewish population resided, the death toll was 96 per cent, yet in other communities, three out of four managed to survive. Survival rates depended on the occupation authorities that happened to be in charge in a particular area, on relations between Jewish and non-Jewish community elites, relations with the Resistance, and the different ways in which Jewish leaders responded to the crisis. In Thessaloniki much of the community, particularly older generations that had come of age under the Ottomans, had been reluctant to integrate and had developed few ties beyond the Jewish community. Some community leaders also led their people unwittingly into Nazi traps. In contrast, most of the Jews of Athens, Volos and Chalkis had much stronger ties beyond the community, and had astute leaders who encouraged members to flee. Therefore, many more managed to survive (Benveniste 1998; Kavala 2009).

Comparing experiences in Thessaloniki and Athens is quite revealing. In the former, German authorities received a great deal of assistance from local Greek institutions, including the Church and the press. Many journalists did their best to foment anti-Semitism. When Jewish entrepreneurs, merchants, professionals and workers were expelled from their unions and associations, they received very little support from their Gentile colleagues. In such ways the community was progressively isolated from the rest of Thessaloniki. In 1943 the city council seemed particularly amenable to German demands, partly because it feared the eventual handover of the city to the Bulgarians, but also because its members shared an interest in the removal of the local Jewry and the erasure of its legacies (Saltiel 2020: 113–34). Local interests often initiated the persecutions and appropriated Jewish buildings and spaces, as happened with the site of the Jewish cemetery after its destruction in 1942–3. Properties in the Jewish quarter were auctioned as soon as the inhabitants had been expelled. Jewish street names were changed, and synagogues and other community buildings were destroyed (Saltiel 2020: 28–31; Antoniou and Moses 2018). Thessaloniki also had an active anti-Semitic movement that included armed pro-Nazi gangs that apprehended Jews and delivered them to authorities.

In Athens, the community was much smaller, only 3,000 in total, but numbers had swelled during the war, as some 10,000 arrived as refugees from Thessaloniki. Greek elites and the Church responded energetically to their needs, supplying them with fake identities, creating support networks, moving them to safe places and helping them escape abroad. The chief of police, Angelos Evert, had organised a clandestine network that issued Jews with Christian identity cards. Among many individuals who hid Jews in their homes was the future mother-in-law of Queen Elizabeth II of England, Princess Alice of Battenberg, who spent the war working in soup kitchens and nursing orphans. Also involved in helping Jews were Spanish, Argentinian, Hungarian and Turkish diplomats.

Some 2,500 Jews from Thessaly and Central Greece took shelter in remote mountain villages, where they were given pseudonyms and enjoyed the protection of EAM. An EAM proclamation of Autumn 1943 stated the following:

> The Jews are Greeks as much as we are. They fought at our side. They live and think in the same way as we do … The condemnation of their race is absurd. A more capable or clever race does not exist … For these reasons, we shall fight with every possible means against the persecution of the Jews … We shall help the Jews and hide their children. (Chandrinos and Droumpouki 2018: 27)

With money provided by Jewish organisations in Palestine, EAM also ferried about 2,000 Jews from Evvia to Turkey. Over a thousand young Jewish men and women had also joined ELAS and other EAM organisations, serving as physicians, teachers and nurses. Of the four ELAS division leaders who liberated Thebes in October 1944, two were Jewish (Louis Koen and David Brudo). Many Jews from Chalkis, Agrinio and Katerini managed to survive because they joined the partisans (Benveniste 2014: 27–133; Bowman 2012; Chandrinos 2020).

Thessaloniki's Jewry presents a far more depressing story. Many of its more affluent members had managed to escape before the round-ups, but most of the poor remained. The process of dissolving the community started as soon as the Germans marched into the city. Units known as *Rosenberg Sonderkommandos*, under the direction of Hitler's chief ideologue Alfred Rosenberg, immediately confiscated the community's manuscripts, books and heirlooms (Mazower 1993: 237). Traditional councils were abolished, and a new one was set up with appointees such as Zwi Koretz, a conservative rabbi who tried to maintain calm in the community but who unwittingly assisted in the regime's schemes, including the deportations to Auschwitz. Jewish archives were requisitioned, a register of properties was compiled, the community was confined to three ghettos, and its members were forced to wear a Star of David. The Germans then requisitioned all Jewish real estate and bank deposits and seized all assets found in shops and warehouses. Those who escaped the Jewish ghettos were treated mercilessly if caught. Three young men between 18 and 19 years of age were caught in Thessaloniki as they tried to escape to join the Resistance. They were executed in front of 2,000 people in the Baron Hirsch ghetto on 8 April 1943. Two other men, Alberto Benveniste and Nissim Kamchi, aged 50, were executed because members of their families had escaped the deportation (Hantzaroula 2021: 80).

German personnel and Greek anti-Semites tried to steal Jewish assets before they were confiscated by the German state. Even senior figures in the Axis administration, such as the notorious military governor of Thessaloniki, Max Merten, busily extorted Jewish families and amassed vast fortunes (Moysis 2011: 68–85). When orders were issued to assemble for deportation to Auschwitz, Jews were required to bring jewellery and other valuables, which were immediately confiscated. Officers and soldiers took furniture, rugs, crockery and chandeliers from Jewish homes and sent them to Germany. Meanwhile, local gangs robbed Jews as they were being pushed on to trains. Then there was the official looting. German authorities created the Department of Jewish

Property Management, which confiscated Jewish property for 'safe-keeping' and had composed a list of beneficiaries that included collaborators. Jewish commercial and industrial properties, workshops, houses and vacant lots, gold and other valuable commodities became currency during the occupation and post-occupation periods. The local diocese and the city administration received all kinds of requests for housing and even household items that had been officially expropriated. On 19 October 1943, a Greek volunteer in the German army requested that Jewish property be given to his wife because he felt obliged to fight somewhere far away 'against the enemies of European Civilisation, that is, against the Bolsheviks and the British, [and where he] may be killed' (Dordanas 2006: 409). The confiscation and administration of Jewish Greek property was organised by the puppet government of Ioannis Rallis, which founded the Central Service for the Custody of Jewish Property (KYDIP) in July 1944 (Hantzaroula 2021: 81).

The deportations from Thessaloniki began in March 1943, when families from the ghettos were first relocated to a transit camp next to the train station. Twenty-four train loads, each carrying 2,300 to 2,800, departed every three to five days. (Curiously enough, the large anti-Axis demonstrations by students and workers that were held at the time appeared to ignore the mass deportations (Saltiel 2020: 140–3). Train carriages were sealed and had no facilities, and after days of travel many died from lack of food and water. Passengers were told they were going to Krakow and even exchanged their drachmas for złoty. All the while, 'lawful' procedures were followed. Train tickets were sent to the Jewish community from the ministry responsible for railways, although there was no indication that passengers would be forced into cattle wagons. Prices were discounted because the excursion tariffs were covered by funds raised from the requisitioned properties. Of the 52,185 Jews who arrived in the camps, 37,386 were sent immediately to the gas chambers (Hantzaroula 2021: 80)

Things worked out differently in Athens. Rabbi Elias Barzilai destroyed community documents that listed Jewish addresses and, with EAM support, helped many to escape to the mountains. To stop members of the community from gathering at the synagogue, where they were likely to be apprehended, he arranged to have it bombed. Many families left their homes and adopted false identities, but just before Easter in 1944 many were caught whilst collecting their rations. In Thessaly many Jewish families were saved by the fact that they were close to areas under partisan control, and by the fact that many of them had close connections with the families of EAM members

Figure 5.3 *The deportation of the Jews of Ioannina, March 1944. © Kehila Kedosha Janina 2021. All Rights Reserved*

(Hantzaroula 2021: 114). Most of the other Jewish communities in Greece fell into German hands. In Ioannina (Figure 5.3), the culturally conservative, Greek-speaking Romaniote community did learn of the fate of the Thessaloniki Jews but failed to escape in time (Schminck-Gustavus 2008). The 2,000-strong community of Corfu was sent to Piraeus and then loaded on trains. Those on Zakynthos were saved due to the bravery of the local mayor and the bishop. When told to provide the names of all Jews, they returned only two: their own. Allied torpedoes tragically killed the Jews of Chania as they were being shipped to Piraeus. The 1,700 Jews of Rhodes and Kos were among the last in Europe to be sent to Auschwitz. Finally, just over 4,000 Jews in Bulgarian-occupied Greece were delivered to the Germans for extermination. Bulgaria was the one Axis power that succeeded in protecting its own citizens but handed over Jews in newly annexed territories (Danova and Avramov 2013, vol. 2: 859).

At Auschwitz, Greek Jews had acquired a reputation for being physically robust and good for labour duties. About 1,000 were sent to the Warsaw Ghetto after the uprising there to remove corpses and debris (Benveniste 2014: 160–1). Many had been mobilised into the *Sonderkommandos*, the teams that took corpses from the gas chambers to the crematorium, removed gold fillings from teeth, and crushed bones under SS supervision. Most were executed later so that they could not give evidence. Greek Jewish women participated in the *Sonderkommando* uprising of October 1944 at Auschwitz–Birkenau, where they blew up a crematorium. Some left testimonies in rolled-up pieces of paper inserted in bottles or tins, which they hoped might be discovered later (Natzari 2018; Greif 2005: 40–50, 286–309, 375). It was also a Greek Jew who attempted to inform the outside world what was happening in the camps. With the help of the Polish Resistance, a camera was smuggled into Auschwitz, which a *Sonderkommando* named 'Alexis' used to take four photographs from Crematorium 4. The evidence was smuggled in a toothpaste tube to London, providing exceedingly rare photographic footage of activity in Auschwitz (Didi-Huberman 2008). Alexis was quite possibly the Greek naval officer Alberto Errera, who had joined ELAS but was arrested in March 1944 in Larissa. In Auschwitz, he continued to work in Resistance networks. He killed two SS officers during an escape in August 1944, but he was recaptured, tortured and executed not long after. His corpse was placed at the camp entrance as a warning to others, but he inspired a *Sonderkommando* revolt two weeks later (Fleming 2008: 160). In these camps, the Jews of Greece, whether Romaniote or Sephardi, two groups who had little to do with each other in the past, all became 'Greeks'. Here, Ladino, the Judeo-Spanish language, was known as 'Greek' (Fleming 2008: 151). These and other Jews from southern Europe had little in common with the Yiddish-speaking Ashkenazi majority, which added to their vulnerability as inmates. Many memoirs, however, attest to the solidary and resourcefulness of the Greek Jews. Primo Levi refers to them 'as carriers of solid, grounded and conscious wisdom in which all the traditions of the Mediterranean are matched', and they were considered 'as the most compact national core in the camp, in this respect the most civilized' (Fleming 2008: 149).

But few of them were living when the Russians liberated Auschwitz on 27 January 1945: a mere 2,000. Typically, the survivors faced more difficulties on their return. Having lost most (if not all) family members and friends, they returned to their homes to find them occupied by strangers, and then discovered that it was nearly impossible to reclaim them in the courts. Despite very long and strenuous legal struggles, only 300 properties and 50 shops would later be returned to their owners (Dordanas 2006: 398–437). Between 8 and 9 per cent of Jewish properties in Thessaloniki were recouped by former proprietors, while the 170 survivors who returned to Ioannina could not access their homes (Fleming 2008: 177).

Anti-Semitism was palpable in the wider Greek community at the end of the war. In Thessaloniki, for example, camp survivors were insensitively described as 'unused soap' (Lehrman 1946: 50). More seriously, the Greek state made it patently clear that it did not consider the surviving Jews to be Greek. It offered incentives to returnees, whether they came from the camps or the mountains, to emigrate to Palestine. Survivors from the Dodecanese Islands, which were to be annexed to Greece in 1947, were sent to Italy because they had been granted Italian nationality before the war. Jewish men were given the option to enlist in the government's army, during the civil war, or to emigrate and relinquish their citizenship (Beze 2019). Jewish *andartes* languishing in government prison camps were given the emigration option as a condition of their release. Overall, most survivors found the experience of returning home so alienating that they emigrated to Palestine or the United States (Benveniste 2014: 135–235). And yet, as noted earlier, many of them found new meaning in being Greek. In Israel, where émigrés from Greece again found themselves among an Ashkenazi-dominated Jewry, they were known as 'Greeks', with all the stereotypical attributes that came with the name (Fleming 2008: ch. 9).

Laokratia: the people's state

From 1942 onwards EAM/ELAS came to dominate the bulk of the Greek mainland to the north of the Gulf of Corinth. One could travel from the outskirts of Athens to the Yugoslav border without having to leave 'Free Greece'. The partisans had emasculated the puppet regime by cutting its lines of communication with the provinces. One of Tsolakoglou's ministers admitted that beyond Attica no one took the government seriously (Tsoutsoumpis 2016: 19–20). ELAS had also broken up many independent Resistance groups or had forced them to join. EAM was, therefore, the only serious alternative to Axis authority in Greece. Having overseen the formation of local governments by the autumn of 1943, the next step was to create a national government.

The Political Committee of National Liberation (PEEA), which was established in March 1944, had the rudiments of a state system, with ministries and departments. It was initially headed by the academic

lawyer Alexandros Svolos, and its executive branch included representatives from institutions operating under the auspices of EAM. The
participation of communists, socialists, agrarians and left liberals gave
it a 'popular front' profile. In May 1944, a national council or constituent assembly (*Ethniko Symvoulio*) was convened in Korischades in
the mountainous Evrytania area in Central Greece. Between 1.5 and
1.8 million voters in both EAM- and Axis-dominated territories elected
200 representatives to sit in the assembly (Nikolakopoulos 2005:
233–4). The first meeting codified legislation and sorted out matters
relating to the government apparatus and the justice and taxation
systems. While ELAS was confirmed as the national army, the *Ethniki
Politofilaki* (National Militia) was established to replace the existing
police force, along with a new department of finance that combined
taxation and agricultural policy. Plans were drawn up to introduce
an education system based on interwar demotic educational reforms.
Governors were appointed to regions, including areas with a heavy
Axis presence, thereby creating an entirely new civil structure to serve
the nation. The franchise extended to women, who also enjoyed the
right to participate in government administration and take leadership
roles (Skalidakis 2014: 185–240).

Formally, therefore, PEEA claimed to be a national government dedicated to democratic principles and to be the genuine expression of the
Greek people. It tried to address matters of public interest, such as the
administration of justice, food rationing, tax collection, forestry, salt
farming, surgeries and health services, wartime property damage and
public education. The broader aim was to demonstrate a commitment
to governance that was lacking in the old political order. The head of
the British Military Mission at the time, Christopher Woodhouse,
acknowledged that EAM brought communication systems, schools,
institutions, legal facilities, theatre and many other benefits of civilisation and culture, and essentially 'set the pace in the creation of something that the Government of Greece had neglected: an organised state
in the Greek mountains' (Fleischer 1995: 66).

That the state should be the expression of the popular will was
reflected in the concept of *laokratia*. It meant 'people's state' or 'people's democracy': *laos* translates as 'folk' or 'the people', hence *laokratia*
referred to a state that was a function of the popular will. Although
there was confusion about what that meant in practice, the term resonated widely, as did allusions to the Greek Revolution of 1821, which
was also a popular movement, thereby placing the *laokratia* within a
revered national tradition. Its meaning was evoked by its most popular

institutions: the village courts, local administration, welfare organisations and the youth movements. It was expressed clearly in Article 5 of the PEEA constitution: 'All Greeks, men and women, have equal political and civil rights' (Poulos 2009: 82). For numerous men and women, *laokratia* meant a great deal because it spoke to a progressive future. For some observers, this was readily apparent among women. One US intelligence officer reported: 'We first laid eyes on the women soldiers of Karpenisi … Dressed like male warriors, with serious faces, these girls shared the hardship of partisan life equally. The men respected them because they had already shown by their capabilities in war.' These fighting women were often frustrated by the ELAS leadership's attempts to limit their involvement in battles. Recruits in Thessaly claimed, 'we might be illiterate, and uneducated, but we know how to fight' (Poulos 2009: 88; see also Gekas 2020).

In wartime, however, PEEA could not function as a conventional state. It obviously had to contend with the Axis occupation forces, the puppet regime and the collaborators, but it also faced serious challenges at the ground level, where PEEA directives often conflicted with those of EAM's local self-governing institutions. PEEA's economic policies reflected a mixture of free-market and *étatiste* ideas, but without banks and currency with exchange value, its policies had very limited effect. Moreover, as the counterinsurgency escalated and brought much greater social dislocation to the countryside in 1943, EAM/ELAS found more and more people were less willing to follow its lead. The unity of the early years evaporated, as opposition to EAM's authority expanded and crystallised.

Mounting opposition to EAM

The question of how much support EAM continued to enjoy by 1944 remains a matter of contention. According to data collected by historian Ilias Nikolakopoulos, EAM was dominant in Thessaly, Macedonia and the suburbs of Athens, and commanded the loyalties of younger Greeks, but it did not have majority support (Nikolakopoulos 2005: 233–4; Fleischer 1995: 69). Aside from those who believed adamantly that EAM was a communist front organisation there were many who held to conservative political values, and who were horrified by such progressive political reforms as democratic local governance and the popular courts. People of an older generation, especially males, were shocked by EAM's promotion of women's rights. Joining the movement violated every rule of female conduct, every cherished patriarchal value (Hart 1996: 152). Even girls from middle-class families found it difficult to overcome parental disapproval and often joined secretly. As one woman recalled:

> My parents didn't know. And naturally, not all parents approved of all this. First of all, because of the physical danger … and often because their ideologies were conservative, they thought you should just sit there, put your head down, and wait for the liberation. (Hart 1996: 165–6)

Many traditionally conservative Greeks became more active opponents of EAM as the liberation approached and they contemplated the implications of an unfettered imposition of *laokratia*.

Many more came to oppose EAM as victims of its violence and policies, including villagers in regions that were traditionally royalist and hence politically conservative. One region where *laokratia* did not seem to mean 'freedom' was in the Argolid Plain in the northeastern Peloponnese, an area mainly of small landholders and royalist voters (Kalyvas 2006: 254). During the first two years of the occupation locals did their best to avoid attracting the attention of the occupiers or the quisling government. Neither resisting nor collaborating in any definitive sense, most were content to subsist until the unwelcome foreign oppressors went away. Italian occupation troops and the local gendarmerie had been able to limit ELAS activity in the Argolid. When Italy surrendered in September 1943, however, ELAS moved in quickly and perpetrated atrocities against communities that refused to comply with goods requisitioning and other demands (Kalyvas 2006: 257–60). Conditions were different in the main cities, Argos and Nafplion, where the local elites tried to secure a pact between rival forces in order to achieve a peaceful transition.[2] From April 1944, the Germans and the Security Battalions launched operations to weed out EAM/ELAS, initially attacking cells in Nafplion and Argos, and then following through in the plains and eastern hills in May. Hundreds of villagers were brutally and indiscriminately killed in these operations, but once it was widely believed that the Germans were in full control of the wider region, some villages decided to throw their lot in with the enemy, or were coerced to do so by Germans and collaborators, who also demanded EAM sympathisers be handed over for execution. As Germany began evacuating Greece, ELAS was able to reclaim lost ground, overcoming local armed groups and burning villages accused of colluding with the Germans (Kalyvas 2006: 264).

The political choices made by ordinary people in the Argolid said more about the extremely adverse conditions to which ordinary men, women and children were subjected than it did about their patriotism or moral character. Historians of the Second World War have in recent times abandoned the simplistic idea that occupied peoples were either 'resisters' or 'collaborators', and instead recommend more nuanced examination of how classes, cultural groups, genders, generations and city–country relations were affected by wartime violence, hunger and dislocation (Drapac and Pritchard 2017: 132–8). In such situations, some profited greatly by collaborating with those who exercised the violence, but most people were forced to choose sides to improve their chances of survival. Ordinary folk in the Argolid, and indeed in much of occupied Europe, were caught up in a vicious struggle between rival armed forces, and were presented with difficult, often impossible, moral choices (Gildea et al. 2006: 206–9). These experiences would have long-term consequences. People who were once indifferent to politics and political ideology, or who wore their politics lightly, were transformed into committed communists or anti-communists.

EAM/ELAS did not plan a seizure of power. Rather, its principal political objective was to play a significant role in a post-war government. Whilst it could seize power in the event of a German evacuation, the EAM leadership, including most of the communists, did not believe that they could then challenge the Allies. In Yugoslavia, Marshal Tito and his People's Liberation Army had also bowed to Allied pressure and agreed to a coalition government (Calic 2019: 161–3). To strengthen its position vis-à-vis the Allies, however, EAM/ELAS kept expanding its power throughout mainland Greece so that at liberation it could negotiate from a position of strength. It wanted Greek politicians returning from exile to find a very different country: one that had been reborn as a *laokratia*, with a well-functioning government (PEEA) and a heroic army (ELAS) that had stood its ground against the national enemy (Figure 5.4).

What they would find, however, was a society deeply divided along social, political, regional and ethnic lines. Athenian society was polarised by turf wars conducted by ELAS against right-wing groups (Close 1993: 114–15). The middle-class-dominated centre was surrounded by a ring of 'red' refugee suburbs controlled by ELAS militias. In the Aegean islands, the presence of British commandos had imposed control by political moderates. The Peloponnese was divided into pro- and anti-EAM regions, while in western Macedonia, as many as fifty-two villages, many of them Turkish-speaking refugee communities

Figure 5.4 *ELAS supporters rally in Ioannina following the end of Axis rule, late 1944.*
© *Benaki FA. 14_1707*

that had been armed by the Germans, were now under siege by ELAS forces. Although ELAS continued to extend its authority by alternating between persuasion and violence, increasing reliance on the latter greatly expanded the social support base of its opponents (Papastratis et al. 2018: 25–124). Liberals were alienated by ELAS's more egregious actions, such as the destruction of the Resistance group National and Social Liberation (EKKA), which had operated in Central Greece near Delphi. In February 1944 its leader, Colonel Dimitrios Psarros, had been pressured to disband EKKA. Although Psarros had submitted to ELAS authority he refused to disband the group. In response, he and 350 of his men were attacked in the early hours of 17 April by ELAS forces led by Aris Velouchiotis, who was acting without orders. Most were killed, and many of the rest were subjected to torture (Close 1995: 113). The incident sent shock waves across the country and generated a groundswell of support for the government in exile and even the collaborationists (Close 1995: 123–4).

EAM's claims to national leadership were also undermined by other factors. First, there was the fact that country's food needs were met largely by foreign aid: the International Red Cross for much of the duration of the occupation, the British-headed Military Liaison (ML) during the period of German withdrawal, and the United Nations Relief and Rehabilitation Administration (UNRRA) once the war had ended. Consequently, people were aware that their basic needs were being supplied by the Allies rather than the *laokratia*. Second, EAM did not have reserves to support its own currency, without which it had to rely on other forms of currency to pay for basic services, including the salaries of its civil servants. Third, EAM's greatest problem was its vulnerability at the international level. The communist-led Yugoslav Resistance movement was able to secure increasing Allied support as it achieved military predominance, yet over the same period, support for the Greek Resistance decreased. Nor was any assistance forthcoming from the Soviet Union, which continued to withhold military aid to the Greek communists. Yet unlike the Yugoslav communists, who could operate without British assistance, their Greek counterparts could not. Whereas the Soviet Union would give Tito the green light to liquidate opponents, it would continue to require KKE to cooperate with British leadership (Close 1995: 120–1).

Countdown to liberation, May–November 1944

As Britain's wartime prime minister, Winston Churchill developed an obsession with Greece. His primary objective, and that of most of Britain's political class, was the preservation of the empire. It was the Italian invasion in 1940 that forced Churchill to recognise Greece's strategic role as a buffer to Britain's vital interests in the Middle East. Turkey was more important in this regard, but by committing to Greece's defence he could reassure the Turks that Britain would come to their assistance in the event of an Axis attack (Lawlor 1994: 121, 124). All the while, the Americans had always suspected that Britain's preoccupation with the Mediterranean strategy had more to do with its imperial interests. Tellingly, Churchill's Greek fixation increased as Germany's defeat became inevitable. For now, Britain's task was to re-emerge from the war as a first-rank power, and that meant retaining the empire and upholding its broader strategic and commercial interests (Darwin 2009: 516–17, 524). Such was the importance of Greece in Churchill's mind that he was prepared to haggle secretly with Stalin over spheres of influence in the Balkans. On 9 October 1944, on his own initiative and without American consent, he secured for Britain 90 per cent influence over Greece, 50 per cent over Yugoslavia, 25 per cent over Bulgaria and 10 per cent over Romania. Meanwhile, much as it sympathised with Greek comrades and their struggle, the Soviet leadership had been considering a division of Europe into spheres of influence since the middle of 1943. To secure Eastern Europe, Britain's Mediterranean interests had to be conciliated.

The 'Percentages Agreement' was a happy meeting of minds. In effect, Churchill had ring-fenced Greece but traded away the rest of Eastern Europe in the bargain (Reynolds and Petchatnov 2018: 483; Stavrakis 1989: 34–5). The agreement confirmed EAM's isolation and Britain's primary role in shaping Greece's post-war future.

Britain's Greek policy also dictated that it should have a staunchly pro-British regime, which not only meant installing the government in exile, but also restoring the king. One British official revealed a colonial mindset when he wrote: 'There is no question of imposing the King on the Greek people by British bayonets' (Clogg 1979: 391). Whilst Greek communists were divided over whether EAM should seize power when the chance presented itself, the dominant EAM view was firmly against it (Fleischer 1995: 73). For all its power, EAM had to contend with the fact that the Greek people saw Britain as an ally, and that they were generally pro-British. More to the point, it would be difficult to convince a war-weary and traumatised population to commit to another war against a powerful ally, should the British respond militarily to an EAM/ELAS seizure of power. KKE members were also mindful that Stalin, keen to maintain his compact with Churchill, ruled against such a move.

Early signs of division within EAM nevertheless became obvious during a meeting of all Greek parties in Lebanon on 17–20 May 1944 – missing were the royalists, who refused share a room with communists. The aim was to establish the formation of a government of national unity. Given its predominance in Greece, EAM assumed its delegates could bargain from a position of strength, while KKE insisted that they demand a majority of cabinet seats. However, Georgios Papandreou, former Venizelist minister and the government in exile's prime minster, was determined to take the 'wind out of EAM's sails'. He accused EAM of monopolising the Resistance and threatened that, should it provoke a civil war, his government would call on the support of the Allies. Fearing that they might become completely isolated, EAM delegates buckled and accepted a junior role in a future government of national unity (Vlavianos 1992: 41).

The Lebanon conference affirmed Papandreou's position within the government in exile and brought various non-EAM parties together. In combination with the royalists, who dominated the army of the government in exile, these disparate groups would begin to mount a formidable challenge to EAM in the struggle for the nation's future. For EAM the conference marked the beginning of its demise. KKE lambasted the delegates on their return and repudiated the agreement. The issue brought into sharp relief the differences between KKE and non-communists within EAM, who were more desperate to maintain relations with the Allies. The latter also harboured growing concerns about KKE's more assertive behaviour within the movement. But just as it appeared EAM was set to splinter, on 29 July KKE reconsidered and backed the agreement. The reasons for the volte face are not clear, but it probably had to do with the looming liberation, and the prospect of being completely isolated both domestically and internationally (cf. Hondros 1983: 227–30; Vlavianos 1992: 42; Fleischer 1995: 73). EAM's junior status was further confirmed in an agreement signed on 26 September in Caserta, Italy, to which the government in exile had relocated. It concluded that Germany's evacuation must be followed by a peaceful transfer of power to Papandreou's government of national unity. It was agreed that all Resistance movements should desist from taking the law into their own hands, that none should try to claim Athens, and that all must accept the new government's authority (Hondros 1983: 232).

Meanwhile, on 8 September Soviet troops crossed the Danube into Bulgaria. The Germans had to evacuate some 300,000 troops from Greece and deploy them along fronts further north. The bulk of the army was withdrawn in a carefully orchestrated plan that was marred only by Hitler's reluctance to permit retreat. As a result, 11,800 German troops were left stranded on Crete, and 11,200 on Rhodes, Kos and Leros (Frieser 2017: 1090–2). As mainland strongholds were being abandoned, ELAS forces moved in swiftly, dissolving local police units and prosecuting collaborators. In some regions the people accused of collaboration were lynched by angry mobs, but for the most part EAM ensured that proper procedures were followed in the popular courts (Dordanas 2011: 51–65). The staggered nature of the German withdrawal presented an opportunity for EAM to expand its presence in mainland Greece in an orderly fashion, introducing people's courts and welfare services, and thereby promoting the *laokratia*. When German troops finally evacuated Athens on 12 October, ELAS abided by the Caserta agreement and made no attempt to take the city, although its troops did amass on the city outskirts and were already in control of many outer suburbs. The rank and file were shocked to be told they would not be marching triumphantly through the capital, although many would later mingle with the revellers in the city (Chandrinos 2012: 321–7).

The people of Athens celebrated the liberation as the Germans drove away, but relief was accompanied by apprehension. The city's EAM supporters used the opportunity to celebrate but also to proclaim *their* victory. Thousands held demonstrations in Syntagma Square and the main thoroughfares of central Athens, waving Allied flags and carrying placards with *laokratia* slogans. The scale of the demonstrations certainly had the intended effect of intimidating the Athenian 'bourgeoisie', who became ever more convinced that the communists would at some point seize power. Novelist Georgios Theotokas feared the coming of a new kind of war:

> Who knows what this mobs wants, even its most self-conscious members? ... We are dealing with an irrational force here. The Russian Revolution is in the air, as is the French Revolution, the Paris Commune, and the national independence war, and who knows what other vague notions we have yet to ascertain. The people have found and constantly suckle on the term 'Laokratia' ... It's the first time during these tumultuous days that I felt in Greece so strongly, so clearly, the deep societal divide, the atmosphere of class war. (Theotokas 2005: 509–13)

It soon became obvious, however, that the anti-EAM camp had also acquired a mass following. On 18 October other Athenians came out in force to welcome the return of the government from exile and its British military escort. The streets of the capital therefore presented both revolutionary fervour and bourgeois anxiety.

Over the coming weeks, as Greece was meant to be preparing for political reconciliation and building mutual trust, the parties were instead engaged in a tactical war of position. EAM/ELAS continued to strengthen its control of the Greek countryside and its programme of liquidating rival groups. The Papandreou government, which relied on British armed support, tried to claim strategic posts in Athens with the support of the X organisation, RAN (Romilia-Aulon-Nisoi) and other anti-EAM or collaborationist bands. The government also smuggled in large caches of arms that it secretly distributed among the police and the Security Battalions (Charalambidis 2014: 34–5). Although most Greeks wanted a peaceful transition to a new order, such positioning manoeuvres merely fuelled mutual suspicion: EAM supporters were increasingly convinced the returned government was determined to crush the *laokratia* and restore a conservative right-wing order, while EAM's opponents grew more certain that it was plotting a communist takeover. In most liberated nations, the Allies used their military superiority to restore the power of the state, but not in Yugoslavia, Greece and Albania. In Greece, the British were simply unable and unwilling to commit the military resources to compel ELAS to disarm, but they did try to make up for this by arming its opponents. Such conditions made the reconstruction of state structures and political stabilisation exceedingly difficult.

The Papandreou government's chief challenges were the demobilisation of all armed groups and the creation of a national army. Every liberated nation in Europe had to deal with the problems of restoring state power, disarming militias and curbing the activities of armed gangs. In Belgium, for example, 8,000 state gendarmes had to contend with 70,000 Resistance fighters. Everywhere in Eastern and Western Europe, disarming the armed was a major challenge (Pritchard 2016: 599). In France, where the Resistance had earned enormous prestige, General Charles de Gaulle oversaw the absorption of much of it into the national army. A similar solution was considered but quickly abandoned in Greece. On 9 November, the government in exile's 'Mountain Brigade', which had fought at the Battle of Rimini in September in Italy, marched into Athens to strengthen the government's control of the capital. It paraded through the centre of Athens before crowds of celebrating supporters. As a stoutly royalist outfit, its mere presence raised suspicions of a planned return of the king. Merging it with ELAS to form the new national army was an impossible task.

The mere presence in Athens of ELAS soldiers and the Mountain Brigade meant there was always a risk of clashes, particularly as neither the government nor the leaders of EAM were able to maintain discipline within their own ranks (Farakos 2000: 267–8). Neither the government nor the British could monitor the machinations of collaborationist groups, who had an interest in fomenting discord. Nor was the EAM/ELAS leadership in complete charge of its captains and KKE cadres. While British troops and ground-level operatives were distributing food, and by their presence giving ordinary Greeks some hope for a peaceful national reconstruction, British leaders were contributing to the growth of discord by treating EAM as the enemy. General Ronald Scobie made it difficult for Papandreou to moderate relations with EAM by allowing right-wing staff within the Greek War Ministry to rearm and effectively rehabilitate armed collaborationists. Those seeking to uphold the alliance were thwarted by elements within their camp, as exemplified when Scobie vetoed Papandreou's proposal to disband the Mountain Brigade, and when ELAS operatives assassinated an officer in Athens on 25 November (Close 1995: 132–3).

In these conditions, it was nearly impossible to hold a consistent line and build trust across the political divide. Athens was a powder keg. It was only a matter of time before someone provided a spark.

The 'Battle of Athens' and the defeat of EAM

Matters came to a head on 1 December, when Scobie ordered the partisans to disarm and undersigned a decision to have George II return to Athens. On 3 December EAM held a peaceful mass protest in Syntagma Square. Without warning, police and snipers opened fire and killed eleven unarmed civilians (Figure 5.5), wounding a further sixty. Believing the incident had been incited and organised by the Greek right, EAM/ELAS attacked police stations and government buildings, whilst trying to avoid engagement with British forces. Violence quickly spread across the city, and British troops were inevitably drawn into what Churchill misleadingly described as a communist putsch. ELAS kept its units out of Athens, but over the next few weeks partisans in the city and EAM supporters fought street battles against some 30,000 British troops and Greek forces aligned with the government. The British had seized and fortified the Acropolis, as well as maintaining control of the city's ports and the airport. Heavy artillery

Figure 5.5 Dekemvriana. *Dead protester in Syntagma Square, December 1944.* © *Alamy EG6N3M*

and tanks were deployed, while sixty planes strafed and bombed ELAS positions in the suburbs. Many civilians were killed, and as happened only two years earlier, mass graves were again being filled with corpses. This violent upheaval, the greatest in the capital's recent history, was described in British and American dailies as 'the Battle of Athens', but in Greek collective memory it is remembered as *Ta Dekemvriana* ('the December events') (Charalambidis 2014). Developments were closely monitored in London. In a telegram to Scobie, Churchill told him to 'act as if you were in a conquered city where there was a rebellion in progress' (Close 1995: 138). The British took some 7,500 civilian hostages and removed them to camps in the Sahara. EAM retaliated by seizing a similar number of civilian hostages and marched them into the countryside. Meanwhile, conflicts erupted within the Left, as KKE loyalists attacked Trotskyites and other KKE dissidents.

At the time, and throughout much of the post-war era, many would mistakenly regard the *Dekemvriana* crisis as a failed communist takeover. The fact is that ELAS did not attempt to seize Athens in October when it could have done so virtually unopposed, and it did not deploy its main forces in December, when it continued to enjoy superiority in numbers. Rather, ELAS fighters sought vengeance against their Greek opponents but had no clear orders as to how to deal with British troops, who gradually attained the upper hand. Even so, by mid-December the British were prepared to hold talks. On Christmas Day 1944, following an international outcry, Churchill and his Foreign Secretary Anthony Eden visited Athens and held a meeting of the heads of all movements, including EAM. The widely respected Metropolitan of Athens, Archbishop Damaskinos, was made vice regent, and plans to restore the monarch were postponed. Papandreou's removal and his replacement by the popular veteran and anti-royalist General Nikolaos Plastiras signalled another concession to EAM. But no agreement was reached, and the violence continued. Meanwhile, the British had time to prepare and apply a more concerted military solution. On New Year's Day, a major offensive was launched with massive reinforcements – by mid-January, there were 75,000 British troops in Greece. By 6 January, ELAS had been driven out of Athens.

The battle claimed 5,500 military and civilian lives. ELAS entered negotiations with the Plastiras government, and an agreement was reached a month later (12 February) at Varkiza near Athens. It was arranged that ELAS and their Greek opponents would lay down their arms. Thousands of ELAS fighters heeded the orders of their leaders. Often in tears, they left their guns in piles before armed British and government soldiers. In return, they were promised a referendum on the monarchy, limited amnesty for the monarchy's political loyalists and the removal of collaborators from government positions. In fact, Varkiza marked ELAS's defeat. Once disarmed, it could not enforce the agreement or stop the British-backed government from unscrupulously imposing its unilateral authority.

A great deal of ink has been spilled to explain the strange demise of EAM/ELAS: why the dominant military power in Greece did not seize power when it could have, and why both sides of the conflict at the end of 1944 seemed unprepared for a showdown that was widely anticipated. None of the leaders planned and sought an encounter, and when it erupted, the conflict revealed a confusion of purpose. Even the British were not prepared to wage a military struggle at the time (Baerentzen and Close 1993: 89–90). What can be said is that the Battle of Athens, which ended on 6 January, had effectively destroyed EAM/ELAS as a political force. The struggle revealed the weakness of EAM's support base. Between 1941 and 1943 the movement had shown moral leadership at the head of a popular patriotic front, but its support base narrowed as the German-led counterinsurgency generated deep ruptures in Greek society. Towards the end of the occupation period, it was clear that the Greek people were not united, and were certainly not willing to support an EAM/ELAS seizure of power if it meant warring against the Allies (Baerentzen and Close 1993: 90). Moderate EAM members also began distancing themselves from the more radical elements in the party and the ruthless treatment of civilians (Fleischer 1995: 75). The movement's moral authority was shaken during the crisis by the seizure and brutal treatment of hostages. The most shocking case was ELAS's round-up of 8,000 hostages, many of whom were arrested because of their bourgeois appearance or because they came from well-to-do Athenian homes.

By this stage of the war, most Greeks, like most Europeans, longed desperately for peace and had no stomach for further conflict. In letters sent home from Greece, British soldiers conceded they did not understand the purpose of the fighting; they were troubled by the fact that they were having to break into apartments and shoot at civilians, and by the fact they could barely distinguish friend and enemy. They also noted that in both warring camps, the desire for peace was much stronger than the desire to keep fighting (Chasiotis 2019: 178–99). And yet, the Greek people would be dragged inexorably into another war. EAM might have been destroyed by the December crisis, but the British-backed government was unable to follow up and impose its authority across the country. In the months that ensued, the Right persecuted former EAM/ELAS operatives and forced many of them to retreat to the mountains and to regroup. Men in Greece were again carrying arms. As it happened, Greece was the only part of liberated Europe where the full restoration of state power failed, and where the war led to civil war.

Notes

1. http://www.eie.gr/nhrf/institutes/ihr/projects/GermanOccupationDatabas e/GermanOccupationDatabase_en.html# (last accessed 22 June 2021).
2. https://enthemata.wordpress.com/2014/12/14/dorovinis-2/.

CHAPTER 6

The Civil War (1945–1949)

One could argue that the Cold War began in Greece and China. Their civil wars served as the first frontlines of a new global conflict, where communist guerrillas who had cut their teeth fighting the Axis occupiers were now pitted against 'nationalist' armies. Each received virtually no support from Moscow, and both wars ended in 1949. But the Chinese communists won their war, and so their insurrection became the Chinese 'Revolution'. In Greece the communists were defeated, and the victors insisted on describing the struggle as a mere 'anti-gang operation' (*symmoritopolemos*). Korea, which became the next frontline, was famously described by the Truman administration as the 'Greece of the Far East'. Here, the US and its allies, including Greece, set out to stop the domino effect in East Asia.

The international setting is crucial for an understanding of the origins and the course of the Greek Civil War. The country's future was determined partly by the changing global strategies of Britain and the United States during the 1940s. Britain was able to keep the Left out of power, but it was unable to stabilise the country, halt the recrudescence of paramilitary violence and reverse the slide to civil war. Right-wing movements were ideally positioned to exploit Britain's weaknesses. In contrast to what happened elsewhere in post-war Europe, the far Right was able to infiltrate the Greek state and the armed forces, and to eventually claim power. The looming Cold War gave it leverage with the British and the US and licence to operate in broad daylight. The Right also used its leverage to ignore British and US disapproval of its violent excesses and its drive to create a reactionary political order. The story of Greece during the second half of the 1940s was therefore about how a tail managed to wag a dog.

This chapter discusses the horrific ordeals of Greek society and how the Right came to dominate the Greek state. It also considers why persecuted leftists were able to regroup and conduct a well-orchestrated insurgency. Yet it was also a war that was intimately tied to a global crisis. The following pages therefore emphasise the extent to which

Greece's civil war was a chapter of the Cold War. It should be read as part of a global conflict that included China, Korea and Vietnam, and whose course and outcomes were influenced by a combination of greater power and local-level interests and exigencies.

Britain, the empire and the eastern Mediterranean

Britain had hoped to re-emerge from the war as a global power of the first rank. It was desperate to retain the empire and its limitless resources and, above all, to maintain privileged access to energy sources in the Middle East. Given its strategic location in the eastern Mediterranean, Greece had to be kept within its sphere of influence – hence Churchill's willingness to concede Bulgaria and Romania to Stalin in the secret 'Percentages Agreement'. Never before had Britain maintained such a strong military presence in the eastern Mediterranean as it did during the Second World War. The United States suspected that this fixation explained British reluctance to reopen a front in Western Europe. Tellingly, Churchill insisted on being the senior partner in the Mediterranean theatre of operations (Darwin 2009: 523–5). When Clement Attlee's Labour Party succeeded Churchill's Conservatives in the 1945 election, it seemed just as determined to protect Britain's vital interests in the eastern Mediterranean, only now the chief threat was the Soviet Union. Of particular concern was Stalin's pressure on Turkey to share control of the Straits, which he reiterated in a note to Ankara in August 1946 (Athanassopoulou 1999: 50). By this stage, the United States had also come around to the view that its wartime ally was a global threat that had to be contained.

In early 1945, having brought EAM/ELAS to heel, British authorities and the new government in Athens set out to restore central state authority over Greece. First, British troops established their presence throughout the country, signalling to people in the towns and the countryside that the new government enjoyed the support of the Western Allies and the international community. Second, these troops were supported by the (ostensibly) politically neutral National Guard, which was meant to replace ELAS and all the other armed groups; the Guard was meant to serve as the Greek state's military arm until a new national army and police force could be formed. Third, governance structures set up by EAM were dismantled, making way for institutions that represented the authority of the 'legal' state in Athens. State-appointed officials were despatched to every regional and prefectural centre to replace EAM authorities.

These three steps were completed by the end of March 1945, but the British were aware that the Right were also using the National Guard to persecute leftists. The Guard had been created back in November 1944 with the agreement of all parties, including KKE, to serve the new state's interim army. During the *Dekemvriana* emergency, however, it was joined by men who had served in the Security Battalions, X (Chi) and EDES. In reality, the National Guard was an anti-communist force that the British tolerated because it proved to be a useful ally. After Varkiza it was meant to enforce the terms of the treaty, but it saw its mission as the annihilation of the Left. It conducted random house searches, beat up opponents, raped women and carried out targeted assassinations. It attacked leftist organisation offices and smashed left-wing printing presses. This white terror, of which more will be said below, was devastating. The communist newspaper *Rizospastis* claimed that within a year of the signing of Varkiza, 70,000 people were arrested, 1,192 people were killed and 6,413 people were injured (Margaritis 2001: 176). Although British authorities and successive Greek governments were concerned about the behaviour of the National Guard, neither seemed able or willing to rein it in (Kousoulidis 2016; Lazou 2016; Margaritis 2001: 93).

In the meantime, like the rest of Europe, Greece was engaged in reconstruction. Most states recognised the need for central planning and state control to manage inflation and ensure modest wealth redistribution. In Greece, economic reconstruction was hampered by the white terror and left-wing reaction, but also by the ability of powerful economic interests, many of them wartime profiteers, to stymie government policies and secure their own interests.

In 1945 governments were concerned mainly with the threat of hyperinflation and the need to promote confidence in the newly restored drachma. The first serious attempt to address these colossal problems was the 'Varvaressos Experiment', named after its author Kyriakos Varvaressos, an economics professor who was deputy prime minister between June and September. Varvaressos had spent the war years in Britain, observing closely how Churchill's government managed inflation, and he was present at the Bretton Woods Conference in July 1944, which established the international monetary system. Varvaressos was therefore familiar with the dominant state-managed approach to currency stabilisation and economic recovery. Under his stewardship, the restored Greek state made its first attempts to organise national economic affairs. He was mindful that profiteering and other distortions caused by the Axis occupation had concentrated wealth in even fewer hands. He was also aware that many of the wealthy in question were, as one economic historian has put it, 'undermining the drachma and fueling inflation by speculating in gold, while others were contributing to inflation by restricting production or hoarding goods and raw materials' (Lykogiannis 2001: 122). Varvaressos' broad aim was to stabilise prices and salaries by using state controls to suppress the former and increase the latter. He proposed rationing, firing civil servants hired during the occupation, halting the external flight of capital and gold, and stopping transactions in gold. His policy was a mixture of Keynesianism and protectionism, and initially, at least, he enjoyed British support. But stiff opposition arose from many quarters, particularly once he attempted to tax the wealthy through a nine-month 'Special Contribution' scheme. Despite assurances from his government that he would receive its full backing, his attempts to enforce rationing, price controls and other measures failed in the face of resistance from shopkeepers, tradespeople and importers, as well as from public servants. Rising inflation damaged the programme's credibility, and by 1 September Varvaressos had resigned. The 'experiment' ended, and the chaos resumed. A lifeline then came with the London Agreement in January 1946, which foresaw the cancellation of the previous debt and issuance of a new loan. More important was the establishment of the Monetary Committee (*Nomismatiki Epitropi*), in which British and US representatives participated and made all significant decisions relating to the economy. So in the immediate aftermath of the war the Greek economy was placed under external supervision.

Britain's failure

Between October 1944 and February 1947, Greece experienced what could be described as a British occupation. Aside from the armed presence of British troops, the Greek government had to answer to the ambassador, Sir Reginald Leeper, whose powers were likened by one of his staff to those of a colonial governor (Sfikas 1991: 323). Indeed, London expected Leeper to manage Greece as one would a colony. To quote Parliamentary Under-Secretary Hector McNeil: 'I ... think that Colonial treatment ... is the only method which offers any hope of nursing Greece towards solvency and political stability' (Louis 1984: 85). In despatches between London and British authorities in Athens, Greece was frequently described as 'backward', 'extravagant' and 'irresponsible', and therefore in need of a firm hand (Louis 1984: 85–6). London also exerted its influence through the British Financial Mission, the British Military Mission and the British Police and Prisons Mission, and by inserting advisers in all the chief ministries. The Greek army and police received equipment and training, while 31,000 British troops were stationed throughout the country. Until the March 1946 elections, Greek prime ministers were appointed by London (Sfikas 1997). The choice of politically moderate prime ministers reflected Britain's initial determination to avoid civil war: Papandreou (26 April 1944–3 January 1945), Plastiras (3 January–8 April 1945), Petros Voulgaris (8 April–17 October 1945), Archbishop Damaskinos (17 October–1 November 1945), Panagiotis Kanellopoulos (1–22 November 1945), Themistoklis Sofoulis (22 November 1945–4 April 1946), Panagiotis Poulitsas (4–18 April 1946), Konstantinos Tsaldaris (18 April 1946–24 January 1947) and Dimitrios Maximos (24 January–29 August 1947). At the time, the typical senior government politician was an elderly gentleman who belonged to an old interwar party and who sometimes barely understood contemporary issues. The differences between the two leading parties, the Liberals and the Populists, were minimal. Each of these prime ministers worked respectfully with Leeper and other British officials. No significant government or military decision was carried out without British assent.

One area in which Britain had a significant impact was food relief. The whole of liberated Europe had a food crisis: in the immediate post-war years, there was food-shortage-related rioting in Italy and the threat of famine in the Netherlands. In Greece, the British army was favourably received in most parts of the country because of a general yearning for peace and order, but also because it was responsible for distributing food aid. From a British and government perspective, aid was also meant to draw popular support away from the Left. The government in exile had used its formidable international connections to ensure that food relief work was in train within days of its return to Athens in October 1944. The British had no scruples distributing the aid strategically, ensuring it reached conservative and right-wing families and neighbourhoods, while denying it to hostile ones. The latter were forced to choose between the Left and relief from hunger (Tsilaga 2007).

Yet the failure of the Varvaressos Experiment also indicated the limits to British influence, especially as compliance was not tied to any long-term aid. Leeper was fully aware of the growing infiltration and influence of right-wing reactionaries and former collaborators within the government and other institutions, but he could do little to stop it. In fact, as the Cold War deepened during 1945 and 1946, the British grew increasingly indifferent to complaints against right-wing terror and police brutality. As Christopher Woodhouse, then Second Secretary to the British Embassy, pointed out at the time, 'the Right take our approval for granted' (Close 1995: 165).

The simple fact was that Britain did not have the power to secure the kind of liberal–conservative political order it preferred. It installed what was essentially a royalist government that was defined by anti-communism and tacitly approved of the white terror. The onerous international commitments required for the retention of the empire and keeping the Soviet Union at bay were too great, and they tested the tolerance of the war-weary British public. Managing these challenges was financially crippling: at the time Britain was not just hopelessly in debt to the United States, but also owed money to its Dominions and colonies. On 20 January 1947, Chancellor Hugh Dalton stated he was 'very doubtful indeed about this policy of propping up weak states in the Eastern Mediterranean against Russia' and urged an end to the 'endless dribble of British taxpayer's money to the Greeks' (Steil 2018: 21). In February, Britain reluctantly 'quit' India, referred the Palestinian problem to the United Nations, and was grateful that the United States was willing to assume its role in Greece. In March, 40,000 British troops were pulled out, and about half a billion dollars in aid was withdrawn from Greece and Turkey (Steil 2018: 22).

The Americans

Whereas Britain's dealings with Greece had been motivated by national self-interest, those of the US were couched within a more idealistic global vision: one that involved transforming the world in accordance with core American values. As was the case in the previous war, the United States believed it essential that the Second World War should also produce a world order based on international law, human rights and the peaceful resolution of inter-state disputes. But it also believed in 'aided self-help', which promoted individual participation rather than state regulation. It wanted a world consisting of liberal democracies engaged in free trade, and which was therefore incompatible with fascism, colonialism and communism. Having helped to destroy fascism, the US needed the support of the colonial empires to contain the much more insidious threat now posed by communism. Throughout 1946, as the spirit of cooperation between the Soviet Union and its wartime allies dissipated, the Truman administration articulated a policy of Soviet containment. The chief concern was the fate of Europe, partly because it was the world's other industrial heartland, and partly because it was by far the largest consumer of US goods (De Grazia 2005; Ellwood 2012). Almost as important was the Middle East and its oilfields. Greece was significant because the communist insurgency directly threatened both regions: the US Secretary of State Dean Acheson famously likened Greece to a rotten apple in a barrel:

> In the past eighteen months, I said, Soviet pressure on the Straits, on Iran, and on northern Greece had brought the Balkans to the point where a highly possible Soviet breakthrough might open three continents to Soviet penetration. Like apples in a barrel infected by one rotten one, the corruption of Greece would infect Iran and all to the east. It would also carry infection to Africa through Asia Minor and Egypt, and to Europe through Italy and France, already threatened by the strongest domestic Communist parties in Western Europe. The Soviet Union was playing one of the greatest gambles in history at minimal cost. It did not need to will all the possibilities. Even one or two offered immense gains. We and we alone were in a position to break up the play. These were the stakes that British withdrawal from the eastern Mediterranean offered to an eager and ruthless opponent.[1]

Hence, when Britain signalled its intentions to withdraw its military and financial backing, the United States was compelled to fill its role in Greece and commit to a global anti-communist strategy. On 12 March 1947, President Truman announced that Greece would be given $250 million in economic and military assistance (Turkey would receive $150 million) and told Congress that the US would use its resources to support 'free nations' under Soviet threat. The Greek crisis was the catalyst for the 'Truman Doctrine', an extraordinary policy that signalled an ongoing commitment to the fight against global communism, which was justified as a struggle for liberty and freedom. As the president noted in his memoir:

> The ideals and the traditions of our nation demanded that we come to the aid of Greece and Turkey and that we put the world on notice that it would be our policy to support the cause of freedom wherever it was threatened. (Edwards and Spalding 2016: 34)

US determination to contain the Soviet Union had profound implications for domestic politics and inter-state relations in the eastern Mediterranean. Greece was reconceived as part of a vital geopolitical frontier known as the 'Northern Tier', which stretched from the Adriatic to the Balkans, the Black Sea, the Caucasus and Caspian Sea region, and through to Central Asia (Kuniholm 1980). In 1947 Greece was regarded as a frontline state in the global struggle against communism. Greek communists were now considered a threat to the 'free world', while they saw themselves as frontline soldiers in a global revolution (Iliou 2002: 30). In the meantime, Turkish foreign policy had also shifted. Soviet pressure had forced Ankara to relinquish its neutrality and join the Western camp. It was also compelled to give up its claims to the Dodecanese Islands and the Eastern Sporades (including Lesbos, Chios and Samos). Turkey's standing was weakened by its wartime neutrality and by evidence that it had been seeking an agreement with Nazi Germany to attain these islands. This early phase of the Cold War was a time of enforced cooperation between the two traditional enemies. It also had an impact on ecclesiastical matters. In 1947, the United States played a role in the election to the Ecumenical Patriarchate of the North American Archbishop Athenagoras, who was even flown to Istanbul in the 'Sacred Cow', Truman's presidential plane. The aim was to install a powerful prelate who would counter the influence of the Russian Patriarch, and who enjoyed considerable influence over Orthodox Churches under Soviet authority (Furat 2010: 346–8; Leustean 2010: 3–6; Kitroeff 2020 ebook: 219).

The Greek Civil War was a conflict that the US believed it could manage. In July 1949, Acheson wrote to President Truman: 'The civil war in China was beyond the control of the government of the United States ... It was the product of internal Chinese forces, forces which this country [US] tried to influence but could not' (Nachmani 1993: 93). But the US could guarantee the defeat of the communists in Greece, and in the process learn more about how to be a global superpower. As the head of the aid mission to Greece, John Nuveen, made clear in February 1949:

> We have already found cause to regret our inexperience by what has happened in China. Greece is a long way from China, but it has most of the problems that we faced in China, which are problems that exist in other critical situations in this troubled world ... Greece is a God-given opportunity for us to learn the facts of international life (Nachmani 1993: 92)

Yet there were limits to what the United States, the world's greatest power, could achieve even in Greece. US society was also war-weary and had been demanding a swift return to peacetime conditions. Accordingly, US troop numbers around the globe were scaled back from 12 million during the war to 1.4 million by 1947. No troops were sent to fight against Mao's communists or their counterparts in Greece. Nor could the United States install in Greece the kind of liberal democracy that was meant to flower under its global hegemony. Like Britain, it also needed allies in Greece to defeat the communist insurgency. The US needed the old political class but also the radical Right, which could be relied on to actively combat the Greek Left. Its Greek allies, in turn, used their leverage to secure the restoration of the monarchy and to construct a political order that was formally democratic, but which was reactionary in practice.

Purging the legacies of EAM

Among the most urgent tasks of the Right in power was the removal of what its members described as *miasmata* (miasma) from all public institutions, especially EAM members but also those known to have sympathised with the movement. This purge was carried out in three ways. The first was a simple but ruthless round of sackings in all government departments and services, from head civil servants to humble street cleaners. *Miasmata* were also dismissed from school and university teaching positions, from the upper clergy, the justice system and the banks. Another method was to convict people for acts committed during the Axis occupation that impartial observers would recognise as Resistance activities. Those who participated in *Laokratia* institutions were often charged with 'abuse of authority'. By September 1945, the government had already arrested 16,225 on political charges (Sakkas 2000: 196). Thousands of men and women were being crowded together in prisons. In the meantime, government employees still under suspicion had to prove their innocence or convince authorities that they had been ideologically reformed. From 1948, governments required that anyone seeking public sector employment, access to higher education, licences or passports had to obtain a 'Certificate of Social Health' (*Pistopoiitikon Koinonikon Fronimaton*). These were issued by the police and verified the soundness of one's political and social values (Papastratis 2000).

Perhaps the biggest challenge facing the post-war order was the suppression of progressive ideals that had been expressed in the *laokratia*, particularly those related to popular participation and gender rights. Terror seemed the most effective weapon, for it removed the temptation to commit acts of dissent and it conditioned citizens to comply with the authorities. Denied political options, citizens could be expected to accept their fate but also come to appreciate the stability and prosperity that the regime could provide. In the meantime, however, terror was also used to wreak vengeance. Members of the National Guard or armed irregulars were determined to settle scores with former partisans, particularly any who had attacked their villages and family members. Ordinary criminals were also involved. In the environs of Evrytania, for example, the hunt for leftists was orchestrated by a convicted bandit leader named Grigoris Sourlas from Thessaly. By the end of 1945, some 600 paramilitaries were operating in the region. Particularly notorious was a group known as the *Ethnikophrones* (National Loyalists), who committed a spree of murders, and inflicted torture and various other humiliations on their victims. They were known to break into homes and kidnap women (Sakkas 2000: 196–9). These irregulars often coordinated their activities with authorities. Leftists were also attacked in the prisons (Lazou 2016: 115–17).

Former partisans who took to the mountains were pursued by government forces and private militias, who then claimed to be conducting a campaign against leftist bandits (*listes*) and gangs (*symmorites*). These campaigns had the effect of extending the terror to leftist villages that might be tempted to give them aid. The anti-communists earned notoriety for beheading captured guerrillas and removing the heads of dead ones, and then parading these through villages to the beat of traditional drums known as *daoulia* (Figure 6.1). During these macabre ceremonies, the militias forced mortified onlookers to donate money. In larger towns, leftist bodies were left for days exposed in the main square or hanging on lampposts. This particular phase of the terror began in the summer of 1945, when the heads of Aris Velouchiotis and his comrades were exhibited in the central square of Trikala – Velouchiotis had committed suicide on 16 June following an ambush (Voglis 2007: 54–8; Lazou 2016: 356–7).

The third way was to institute a permanent state of emergency, which provided a legal framework for the terror. Military courts condemned scores of former ELAS fighters to death, including women. By the summer of 1946, legislation and emergency decrees had been generated to criminalise political opposition and dissent, allowing state functionaries to act arbitrarily and punitively against known and suspected political enemies. These functionaries formed a power network that successive governments found difficult to control, and

Figure 6.1 *Parading the severed head of an executed Communist soldier during the Civil War. © ASKI*

which in the coming years would operate as a 'deep state' or *parakratos* (Alivizatos 1995). The human rights violations and other excesses committed under the auspice of this regime were a frequent source of embarrassment to their British and US patrons.

In this new order, Greece's recent past and its inconvenient truths had to be forgotten. The state had to reframe how the war and the Resistance could be remembered, producing a new narrative that demonised the Left and which overlooked the collaboration of the Right. EAM and ELAS were labelled as criminal and seditious organisations. The wartime partisans were dismissed as 'Slav-Communists', 'EAM-Slavs' or 'foreign-supported gangsters'. The Left replied with their own insults (e.g. 'royalist fascists'), but it lacked the means to compete in this propaganda war. The state set out to re-educate Greek society with the support of the established press, including the nation's largest and oldest newspapers, and by using public radio, the Church pulpit, the schools and university lecture theatres. At the local level, the campaign was led by educated notables who already exercised influence in the towns and villages, especially lawyers, clerics, doctors and large landholders.

The slide to civil war, 1946

Greece reverted to a state of war because the Right refused to coun-
tenance a future that included the Left. The Treaty of Varkiza was
supposed to begin the orderly transition to liberal democracy, with
free elections earmarked for 31 March. However, officers who led the
National Guard believed Greece could only be saved from communism with a strong dictatorship. In their view the politicians in Athens
were too feeble to protect the nation. That was the thinking that drove
the ensuing white terror (Close 1995: 152–3). Those who were targeted but escaped arrest formed armed bands that eventually became
a movement dedicated to the overthrow of the British-backed government and the establishment of a communist state. The British and the
government in Athens were then forced to develop more concerted
counterinsurgency responses. In this fashion, Greece slid into civil war.

Political events also played a role. The Right set out deliberately to
undermine preparations for the 31 March elections by intimidating
leftist families and communities. In protest, the Left and many centrists boycotted the vote, the effect of which was to allow the Right to
win an overwhelming majority of seats in the new parliament and to
form a government under Konstantinos Tsaldaris. The Left was now
confronted by a right-wing government that effectively approved of
the white terror and was even set on removing centrists from positions
of authority and the public service (Close 1993: 166). Tsaldaris stepped
up the executions of leftists, and revived aspects of the Metaxas repression system, such as incarcerating political prisoners on remote islands,
expanding police powers to search and jail suspects, and the humiliating practice of forcing leftists to sign public retractions. His government
also gave the police carte blanche against suspected leftists in the lead-up
to the 1 September referendum on the monarchy – under British pressure, it had been brought forward from March 1948 (Close 1993: 167).
According to official statistics, 68.4 per cent had voted for restoration,
but British and US observers reported that 'undue' influence had been
exerted on leftist and centrist voters. (Although George II did return to
Greece, he died on 1 April from arteriosclerosis and was succeeded by
his brother, Paul.) A British parliamentary delegation also concluded
the Right had secured its vote by arresting and deporting local EAM
and trade union leaders, by the 'intimidation of Left-wing supporters
who had been driven from their villages and dared not return to vote'
and by ensuring that 'all local officials were supporters of the government, and all the machinery of provincial administration was in their

hands' (Vlavianos 1992: 232). Greek Palace archival sources confirm that methodical vote-rigging that implicated high-ranking officers, politicians and newspaper owners would continue after the restoration (Lazou 2016: 180–1). According to Christos Zalokostas, a politician with close ties to the palace:

> The money will be used to form gangs of twenty men each, consist-ing of reliable patriotic citizens, led by an officer in civilian clothing, with the aim of eliminating communist leaders, which will paralyse the whole anarchistic organisation by cutting heads … During the elections it was proved that wherever there was a nationalist group … people voted massively for the Populist Party, but wherever commu-nist gangs dominated … no one dares to vote, and abstinence was at its highest. With regard to the plebiscite, the need to have our own gangs operating in elections is obvious. (Lazou 2016: 149)

As the Right hardened, so too did the Left. KKE was still the best organised party of the Left, but mass arrests and the white terror had taken their toll. Communist intellectuals and periodicals continued to engage in public debates on national affairs and economic policy, but too many party members were languishing in prison, awaiting execu-tion or had gone into hiding. Fear of persecution also forced many to desert the party and its local-level organisations. Until February 1946, KKE policy had been to seek participation in a government coalition. But as the white terror expanded, it became patently clear that the Right and the state were bent on its destruction. An armed revolt was discussed during a meeting of the central committee in mid-February 1946, but that option was rejected owing to the government's military preponderance and the fact that it enjoyed British support. Led by General Secretary Nikos Zachariadis, who had spent the war years in a concentration camp in Germany, the party resolved to keep seeking a political solution, and to use its growing strength in the mountains to force the government into negotiations:

> In the first place the unfolding of the armed resistance to the armed terrorism of the reaction constitutes an additional dynamic device directed against the enemy for the purpose of a peaceful, normal development and only if such development becomes in the meantime entirely difficult and impossible, shall the armed struggle change its nature from *defensive* to *offensive*. (Vlavianos 1992: 183)

The Left was not in a good position to mount a concerted armed offensive in early 1946. It lacked the most basic supplies, includ-ing munitions and food. Scarcity of food and other amenities made village communities dependent on British aid, hence their support could not be guaranteed for another guerrilla war (Close 1995: 181). Consequently, KKE opted for an urban political campaign that would harness the kind of popular support EAM enjoyed in wartime, augmented by the unions and other mass organisations. However, the post-war state was much better equipped than its quisling counterpart to deal with urban dissent. The reality was that armed conflict was inevitable, but Zachariadis' hesitation had to do with the fact that such a struggle required Soviet or Eastern Bloc support, which was not forthcoming. At least not yet. In the lead-up to the March elections, he had been busy drumming up support from communist governments in Eastern Europe. Zachariadis and KKE had faith that communist states would eventually provide the military aid needed to wage a revolutionary struggle.

Therefore, the March 1945 elections made inevitable a war that no one had planned for or wanted. The white terror gave the Left no choice but to start an insurrection, and the British allowed their clients to take that risk. As historian David Close has put it, all parties were 'trapped in a situation which precluded the exercise of statesmanship, or even of realism, if realism be defined simply as a recognition of one's self interests' (Close 1995: 183).

Fighting the Civil War, 1946–1948

Something like 500,000 men and women took part in the fighting between 1946 and 1949. At one stage there were 200,000 men on the government side. Estimates for the opposing side are far more difficult. Between 70,000 and 100,000 either volunteered or were conscripted, although at any given time it had a core active force of somewhere between 20,000 and 26,000 men and women (Margaritis 2001: 236).

Left- and right-wing bands had been skirmishing in the mountains of the Peloponnese, Central Greece and southern Thessaly prior to the March 1946 elections, but the fighting expanded through the spring and summer, when the police and army were drawn in. In accordance with kleftic tradition, left-wing bands were initially known by the names of their captains, but in August KKE had charged Markos Vafiadis, a politburo member who had active experience in guerrilla warfare during the Axis occupation, with the task of bringing these bands under a single command. The result was the 'Democratic Army of Greece' (DSE/*Demokratikos Stratos Elladas*). Under 'Markos', as he was commonly known, the DSE avoided pitched battles against a larger and better-armed enemy, employing classic guerrilla tactics instead. Bands would ambush the enemy and elude capture by withdrawing to hideouts, many of which lay across the northern border. The fact that the DSE could access neighbouring countries for sanctuary proved very useful, while further south bands were able to outmanoeuvre government forces with the support of well-functioning logistical and intelligence-gathering systems (Gerolymatos 2016: 241).

On paper, the National Army enjoyed overwhelming superiority. Aside from numbers, it was better armed and well fed. It also had an air force at its disposal that could bomb communist hideouts, observe movements and ambush convoys. But it also had significant weaknesses. The initial problem was the quality of recruits. Most experienced soldiers had been demobilised and were reluctant to leave their jobs or homes to fight a new war. Many were also personally conflicted about having to fight a civil war. Meanwhile, the British were not prepared for training a new conscript army for the particular challenges of guerrilla warfare, nor were there enough Greek officers and sergeants available to play that role. Indeed, the National Army was not ready to take on the DSE until the end of 1947, thereby forcing the government to rely more on the police (Close 1995: 200).

Morale was also a problem. Many recruits harboured some sympathy for the 'enemy', especially those who had once belonged to EAM and its youth movement EPON, and those who had benefited from their services in times of need. Some knew that friends and relatives, even siblings, were fighting on the other side. During the early phases of the conflict, some recruits switched sides, sometimes even during battle (Voglis 2014: 169–71). The government's response to men in this category was to despatch them to re-education camps on Makronisos, a deserted island off the coast of Attica that became infamous as the 'island of martyrdom' (*nisi tou martyriou*). Eleven hundred officers and about 27,000 soldiers were kept there during the course of the conflict (Gerolymatos 2016: 230). Inmates were required to renounce communism and their past leftist activities or those of their parents. They were subjected to a so-called 'national baptism', which included brutalising rituals and torture that sometimes led to fatalities. The victims sometimes fought back. One riot resulted in 17 deaths, 60 being injured and 250 death sentences. Before those who were re-educated were sent off to fight, they were required to compose statements in which they abjured their leftist pasts. These statements were read out from the pulpit in their family parish (Voglis 2004; Alvanos 1998).

Reluctance to fight extended to youths from liberal and conservative backgrounds, who were not moved by the call to fight the 'Slav-
Communists' and 'EAM-Bulgarians'. The formation of a wholly new
national army, however, did present a unique opportunity to create a
force that was virulently anti-communist and ideologically uniform.
For decades the military had been politically divided, but the officers
who built the new army, men who had been trained under Metaxas,
who defeated the pro-EAM mutineers in the Middle East and fought
the Left during the *Dekemvriana*, were well positioned to create
a solidly right-wing constituency. Greece's new post-war military
supported Tsaldaris' Populist Party, but it also claimed for itself a
political role as the true custodian of the nation. Most officers at
the time regarded the military as independent from civilian authority, and believed it had the right to circumvent the government to
save the nation from communism. They would have launched a
coup in 1946 had the Greek army not been so dependent on British
resources (Close 1995a: 131). The most ardent exponents of this
view were IDEA (*Ieros Desmos Ellinon Axiomatikon*/Sacred Union of
Greek Officers), a shadowy organisation of right-wing officers formed
back in 1944 (Gerolymatos 2016: 229). In these early post-war years,
its members had already infiltrated the government to undermine
political moderates, and even managed to pressure King Paul to
reappoint Tsaldaris to office during a political crisis in August 1947
(Close 1995a: 148). Its hopes were effectively realised in January 1949,
when the king, who appeared to be of the same view about the role
of the army in Greek society, appointed General Alexandros Papagos
as commander in chief. Papagos was given emergency powers until
the end of the Civil War (Voglis 2014: 347–50). When Papagos was
forced to resign in May 1951 under controversial circumstances, the
general, who was held in the highest esteem by the armed forces, had
to order outraged leaders of IDEA to cancel a planned *coup d'état*
(Close 1995a: 154).

The preoccupation with politics compromised the National Army
as a military force. Its leadership had given insufficient attention to
preparing recruits for the challenges of guerrilla warfare, which meant
they were often outfought by their more experienced adversaries. It
suffered from a shortage of seasoned officers, most of whom had either
been killed in battle or discredited by their association with the quisling regimes or their links to EAM. Poor discipline affected the chain
of command and disrupted the planning and execution of operations.
The National Army did manage major offensives against the DSE

between April and October 1947, clearing some areas and inflicting significant casualties, but by the end of each campaign the enemy was able to reclaim lost ground. In contrast, the DSE had developed quickly as a formidable force, not simply because of the experience and expertise provided by former ELAS fighters but also because it managed to train impressionable peasant youths into ideologically committed and battle-hardened guerrillas. It was also able to exploit the country's mountainous terrain as effectively as had ELAS during the war. In October 1948 the US commander General James van Fleet claimed that at the battalion level and below the DSE was superior (Close and Veremis 1993: 119). By the winter of 1947–48, some senior Greek commanders and British observers feared that the DSE might win if they could hold out (Close and Veremis 1993: 109). In due course, however, the National Army had time to correct its deficiencies. It enjoyed British and then US support, and by the end of 1948 it was able to exploit its overwhelming superiority in numbers and weaponry. By then, it also had talented officers like Papagos at the helm, who assumed supreme command on 21 January 1949. A better-functioning chain of command had been introduced, and effective strategies to fight a guerrilla force had finally been adopted. General Thrasyvoulos Tsakalotos, a gifted field commander, managed to eliminate the DSE in the Peloponnese in late 1948 by breaking its intelligence network (Gerolymatos 2016: 271).

All the while, the DSE was starved of military hardware and supplies. Although it was given basic resources from neighbouring communist countries, it had to tax the areas it controlled and often used violent methods to extract what it needed. It established people's courts and operated schools as EAM/ELAS had during the war, but it also conscripted local youths, including boys and girls in their teens. Six out of ten were recruited from mountain villages, of which one in three were young women (Voglis 2014: 237). Forced recruitment was perhaps the most significant source of popular opposition to the DSE, and it explained the high desertion rates. The Civil War was harder to sell as a 'people's war'. Villagers resented the violence and deprivations that the DSE struggle brought to their doorsteps. Most Greeks resented the war, regardless of which side of politics was at fault.

Yet despite its many problems and disadvantages, the DSE performed remarkably well in operational terms, eluding government forces, striking unexpectedly and capturing some major towns. But it could not consolidate its gains and never managed to improve its position in any significant sense. In October 1946, its numbers were significantly increased, possibly by one third, when the President of Yugoslavia, Josip Broz Tito, ordered Slav Macedonian units to fight with the DSE. However, the merger also meant that KKE had to accommodate Slav Macedonian nationalist aspirations, thereby seriously alienating mainstream Greek public opinion (Close 1995: 211). More serious still were the everyday problems of fighting a guerrilla campaign that was lacking in popular support. Its units were always forced to operate in hostile territory and in extreme conditions that tested each individual's mettle. Hunger was a constant problem, and during the winter months many foot soldiers died of frostbite. If ELAS could claim much of the country as 'Liberated Greece', DSE was restricted to remote villages, mountain hideouts and cross-border camps. While operating in Greece, guerrillas were hounded, usually hungry and thirsty, and often dressed in rags.

Civilians in the war zones

In his international bestseller *Eleni* (1983), the Greek American journalist-writer Nicholas Gage tells of his mother's execution by communist guerrillas in 1948. Before her death, however, she secured the escape of her children from their DSE-held village, who were then able to join their father in the United States. She was then tried and convicted in a 'people's court', based on a neighbour's testimony. Although criticised for presenting an anti-communist depiction of the Civil War – the film adaptation (1985) was the subject of widespread protests in Greece – his mother's story was very plausible in the many regions that were contested by the DSE and National Army. A similar story was told in Dimitra Petroula's *Pou'nai i mana sou mori* (*Where Is Your Mother, Girl?*) (2011), in which she recalls having witnessed her mother's execution by right-wing paramilitaries in Mani in the southern Peloponnese. For much of the war, DSE operatives took villages by surprise, summarily executed government officials (mayors, gendarmes etc.), seized food stockpiles, recruited villagers, often at gunpoint, and then withdrew to their mountain hideouts (Gerolymatos 2016: 245). These actions usually cost lives, destabilised local economies and inflicted enduring traumas. A typical case is that of George Iassonidis of Vrondi, a village near Kozani in western Macedonia. He later emigrated to Australia, but the violence he witnessed as a child affected him for the rest of his life. He recalled that in 1947 Vrondi had already become a refuge for other villagers until it, too, was raided by the DSE:

And the rebels struck – I don't remember what date it was – they fought in our village and they killed one of our villagers, they killed him at a distance of ten metres from our house, I recall, they killed that fellow. They also killed a third cousin of mine, a young man at the time, who had no involvement, they killed him too. Hey, they looted the village, they burned the village, they stole the animals, sheep, the lambs, the big animals, they stole them and they destroyed the whole village in general, and they took them and fled back to the mountain. (Damousi 2015: 90)

Villagers then moved 4 km away to the relative safety of nearby Tsotyli, a larger centre, where Iassonidis and his family spent much of the rest of the war, living in an uncle's basement while others resided in huts erected by the National Army. He recalled that people subsisted at the time by eating boiled weeds (*horta*), while some who tried to return to their village for provisions simply never returned: 'many went secretly, there were many that the rebels killed, we suffered very, very much'. He also recalls his family having to retrieve his uncle's tortured body, which was so disfigured that the guerrillas were too embarrassed to hand it over (Damousi 2015: 91).

Kim Kalyvas, who also emigrated to Australia, was in Tsotyli during the war years. His father was a local shoemaker and a communist, which meant that he had suffered at the hands of the government:

Well, but because ... my father was a communist, as soon as the Civil War started, exile! Beatings, jail, one thing and another, they sent my father to jail. Later, we were still there, they even took me too to ... the police, and the military police, they beat me up badly, not just once or twice, my legs [or feet] are defective, I've got broken ribs here ... Because I was the son of a left-winger ... And they also sent me to a military court. It was in those days, that's the way it was. (Damousi 2015: 96)

More so than Iassonidis, however, Kalyvas understood that in this conflict, he, like all regular Greeks, was a mere subaltern. He was fodder in a power struggle between much larger political interests. 'During the Civil War, it didn't matter. If you were left, if you were right, that was it. It was the war. And so a lot of people suffered. A lot of people got killed, which they shouldn't have' (Damousi 2015: 96).

Every civilian in the war zones lived in peril. Villages suffered raids from both sides, with each attack claiming different victims. People gambled by declaring their loyalties for one side, hoping it would turn out to be the winning one. Political identities crystallised when people saw their loved ones butchered by the communists or government forces. In the municipality of Ktimenion, which is situated immediately north of Evrytania in Central Greece, numerous civilians were executed as their village changed hands. In Agia Triada, for example, which had 773 people in 1940, 50 were killed during the Civil War, of whom 7 were executed by the DSE and then 17 more were killed by the other side. Petralona, which had 297 people in 1940, suffered 26 deaths, 9 of which were identified with the Right and 17 with the Left. Similar patterns of violence obtained in the municipality's other villages (Sakkas 2000: 201–2). According to historian John Sakkas, the killings destroyed the fabric of these communities, 'poisoning or breaking down traditional relationships of solidarity'. As one of his informants from Agia Triada told him, 'Villagers who previously were kind, generous, and politically indifferent or neutral were fanaticised and began to persecute relatives and friends with unprecedented ferocity. Whole families were split or uprooted, or perished altogether'(Sakkas 2000: 203):

> My village was split into two. The civil war divided people, it ruined families, kinships, friendships. On one side there were the real patriots, 'the saviors of the nation', and on the other there were the 'Commies', the traitors. At the local [*kafeneion*] we were always on our guard, we always looked round before we said anything; after all, it only took one word out of place and you were in trouble.

Because the guerrillas depended on village communities for food, the government ordered the relocation of communities to areas beyond the DSE's reach. Many were temporarily resettled in shanty towns in Athens and Thessaloniki. Children were placed in so-called 'children's cities' (sing. *paidopolis*), where they slept in barracks and were schooled during the day. By February 1948, 485,000 people in total had been relocated, and by war's end, the number was 666,374, making it roughly 10 per cent of the nation's entire population. Many were simply dumped on the outskirts of government-controlled towns (Laiou 1987: 64–75; Voglis 2014: 85–92). The policy proved costly in terms of livestock and crop production. The government had to organise breadlines and rations for the displaced. In the end, only a small proportion of this new refugee population would return to their villages. Most would remain in the big cities or would join relatives and village compatriots in the United States, Canada and Australia.

The Civil War saw 40,000 combatants die and an indeterminate number of civilian casualties. Around 3,500 political prisoners were executed, while between 50,000 and 80,000 were imprisoned or exiled for lengthy periods, sometimes for decades (Voglis 2014: 383).

Children's experiences

Since the First World War, international humanitarian agencies had shown concern for children and their exposure to wartime violence, the effects of family separation and nutritional standards. Such issues were of particular concern at the end of the Second World War, when tens of millions of children in the liberated territories and Germany were left homeless (Zahra 2011: 4). Greece was among the liberated territories that was teeming with children who had lost parents and siblings or had been separated from them. When German troops withdrew in late 1944, Greece had between 340,000 and 375,000 orphaned children. The Civil War prolonged this crisis. By the end of the conflict, one in every eight children had lost one parent, while approximately 36,000 had lost both (Van Steen 2019: 4).

Although the treatment of children by both sides of the political conflict was driven in part by humanitarian motives, policy was also influenced by political considerations. Thus, in the DSE-controlled areas of northwestern Greece, children under 14 years of age were removed and relocated to Eastern Bloc countries, partly for their safety and partly to free parents for military duties. Some families willingly handed their children over to ensure their safety. Others were coerced. About 20,000 children were taken to places as far away as Romania, Hungary and Poland. During the latter stages of the war, as the DSE became ever more desperate for recruits, some were brought back when they had reached the age of 14, as they were deemed old enough for combat duties (Danforth and Van Boeschoten 2012: 67).

The relocation of children by the communists was denounced as child abduction by the government, which referred the practice to the newly formed United Nations as a human rights violation. Critics also called it a *paidomazoma*, a highly charged term that was used to describe the infamous Ottoman child levy (Danforth and Van Boeschoten and 2012: 37). To be sure, the government was also removing the children of leftists from the war zones. Some 18,000 children whose parents were languishing in jail or were killed in the fighting were placed in orphanages supported by funds raised by Queen Frederica, an unusually activist royal consort. Orphanages and children's camps were established to 'save' (*paidososimo*) and 'safeguard' (*paidofilagma*) the children of leftists (Van Steen 2019: 49). The queen took a high-profile role during the Civil War by rallying upper-class women to perform charity work, erect memorials and perform other practical and ceremonial duties as called for by their nation. Unlike the Left, which gave women new identities as warriors, the Right deployed women in traditional roles. Queen Frederica was presented as the 'mother of the nation for ever' (Danforth and Van Boeschoten 2012: 85).

Families were fractured by the Civil War, sometimes irreparably. Some children remembered watching their mothers being forced to give them up at gunpoint, while others saw them pleading with the authorities to take them away from their war-affected region for their health and safety. Some of the girls and boys who had been sent by the communists to places as far away as Budapest or Prague had siblings in the queen's orphanages. Many children were born in prisons or in the women's camp in Trikeri (Daliani-Karampatzaki 2009). The largest number of dislocated children were found languishing in refugee camps or shanty towns. In 1949, Nikos Kiaos, who would later become a distinguished journalist, was only six when he was to be sent from Naousa to somewhere in Eastern Europe. With both parents in prison, he was living with his grandmother. It was decided, however, that the boy was too sick to travel and was left in his grandmother's care. He was later taken by relatives to see his mother in the Averoff Prison in Athens, and three years later, when his mother was released, to see his father on the island of Aï Stratis (interviewed by Liakos, 15 July 2018). Tens of thousands of people who had been children at the time could tell similar stories (Figure 6.2). After the war, children often had to search for their parents or other surviving family members. Those in Eastern Europe only managed to reunite with loved ones much later, sometimes in places like Australia. When reunited after many years, children found their parents had sometimes remarried and had children who spoke a different language (Danforth and Van Boeschoten and 2012: ch. 6).

International adoption was a focus of humanitarian interest in the wake of the Second World War, given the sheer number of orphans produced by the conflict, and because it was deemed preferable to place children in families rather than have them institutionalised (Zahra 2011: 237). Americans led the movement, with the US being the major recipient of orphans from Germany, Greece and elsewhere. Although driven by humanitarian concerns and considered an aspect of Europe's reconstruction, international adoption also aligned with US foreign policy objectives. The Displaced Persons Act of 1948 allowed wartime orphans to be adopted by families in the US, while the Emergency Migration Act of 1953 permitted the entry of migrants from South

Figure 6.2 *Elderly peasant women from Macedonia exiled on the tiny island of Aï Stratis.*
© *ASKI (Βασίλης Μανικάκης/Αρχεία Σύγχρονης Κοινωνικής Ιστορίας)*

Europe, including 17,000 from Greece. In the United States, a major role was played by the philanthropic organisation AHEPA, which had lobbied the US Congress and Senate in 1949 to take as many as 50,000 orphans and other victims of the 'Communist war' (Van Steen 2019: 95). For AHEPA and for Greek authorities, the adoption of the children of leftists was especially important as it would weaken the Left and reduce its influence on the country. Of particular interest were children in northern Greece and the infants of parents facing execution or lengthy prison sentences.

However, state officials and various interest groups saw opportunities to profit in trafficking the children of leftists. Authorities were known to pronounce parents and close relatives as unsuitable for parenting, or to classify living parents as dead, in order to have children eligible for adoption. For a fee, forged certificates could be provided by Greek authorities that affirmed that the child had no parents or responsible relatives (Van Steen 2019: 73). A conspiracy in orphan trafficking extended to the other side of the Atlantic, and it involved high-level figures in the Greek American community, including leading AHEPA figures Leo J. Lamberson and Stephen Scopas, who had lobbied hard to facilitate adoptions in the early 1950s, but were later accused of 'selling babies' to American families (Van Steen 2019: 140). In 1962, another scandal broke out, this time in Greece, where operators of the Public Nursery School of Thessaloniki were tried and convicted of trafficking children (Brouskou 2015: 108–10, 157–65). One estimate has it that 3,500 children were victims of this affair, but the real number was probably much higher (Van Steen 2019: 168).

Military developments, 1948–1949

The communists' military aim was to claim control of Macedonia and Thrace, make Thessaloniki their capital and, with material support from Stalin and Eastern Bloc countries, pursue the 'liberation' of the rest of the country. That foreign support would be crucial for defeating the US-backed National Army (Gerolymatos 2016: 246). In April and May, Zachariadis personally met with Tito and then Stalin to try to secure their backing, and then, on 16 July, he declared on Radio 'Free Greece':

> the welfare of Greece and the high treason of the fascists has forced us to take urgent and radical decisions. The task must be completed. All the necessary preconditions exist. Completion means the creation of a Temporary Democratic Government in the area of Free Greece, ruled by the Democratic Army. (Vlavianos 1992: 241)

However, that support from Stalin and the Eastern European regimes never materialised. As noted above, the DSE performed impressively throughout the conflict, and even managed to capture such significant towns as Karditsa, Karpenisi, Florina and Naousa (Margaritis 2001: 153–212). In the summer of 1948, it defended a stronghold in the Grammos mountain area on the Albanian border against aerial attacks. But the material support that did come from Yugoslavia and Albania was very limited and hardly compared to that which the National Army received from the US. The DSE could not operate like a conventional army and claim and hold cities and provinces. It had no choice but to be a guerrilla force that sheltered in mountain hideouts.

To the very end the DSE, or at least its core units, fought on and persisted in taking on increasingly daring missions. But when the DSE's supply lines from Yugoslavia were severed in July 1949, the war was effectively over. Tito's falling out with Stalin the previous year, and the economic blockade imposed on Yugoslavia by the

Communist Bloc, forced Tito to seek US aid. The price was to seal the border with Greece. The last military encounter took place in August along the steep, wooded mountains along the Albanian border, after which the remnants of the DSE were forced to cross the border under heavy air bombardment. On 16 October 1949 the DSE effectively admitted defeat when it announced on Radio 'Free Greece' that it had ceased hostilities (Vlavianos 1992: 245). Units stranded within Greece remained at large, but they were eventually extinguished the following year. The DSE wounded who were left behind in makeshift hospitals in mountain caves were later found to have died of starvation, infections or neglect.

The Soviet refusal to be drawn into the Greek communist insurgency is vital in explaining its defeat. Stalin's encouragement of Zachariadis' plans in 1948 proved to be a momentary lapse from that line. Even before the 'Percentages Agreement' and certainly during the Civil War, Stalin was unwilling to risk direct military engagement with the Western Allies, especially as he was made to understand that Britain and the US were prepared to fight for Greece (Rajak 2010: 206). Privately, Soviet officials tried to warn their Yugoslav counterparts of the consequences should the DSE win (Kramer 2014: 296). Meanwhile, the Truman Doctrine was passed into law in May 1947. In June, an American Mission for Aid to Greece, headed by Nebraska's former governor Dwight Griswold, gave the US unprecedented authority over Greek military and economic policies. A year later, its responsibilities were divided between the Joint United States Military Aid Group, Greece and the Economic Cooperation Administration (Iatrides 1997: 242–3). At the time, William H. McNeill observed the country was full of American officials imposing their 'advice' (McNeill 1957: 35). Although its forces did not see combat, the US provided an abundance of new weaponry, transportation and communications technologies, a fleet of fighter planes, military uniforms and canned food. US officers helped plan and advise on the overall strategy and specific military operations.

Under US pressure, the National Army was forced to improve its strategic and operational approaches to the insurgency. More effective approaches were devised for securing areas taken from the enemy. Localised units were installed to relieve the National Army from guard duties, which had soaked up half the military's resources. Finally, the National Army functioned more effectively once competent rather than politically reliable officers were appointed to positions of authority. Papagos was able to reduce political interference in promotions and strategic operations, and he managed to impose much greater discipline. By 1949 the National Army had talented officers like Tsakalotos, who, after having eliminated the DSE in the Peloponnese, managed to claim control of much of Epirus and central Greece. Theodoros Grigoropoulos was able to do the same in Thrace and eastern Macedonia. By that time, US money was beginning to drive growth in the Greek economy, which enhanced the government's capacity to manage military operations (Close and Veremis 1993: 114–15).

In the end, Greece did not become a battleground between the superpowers, as many had feared. The Soviet Union did not want to risk a hot war in the Balkans, while US power determined that only one side could win in the Greek Civil War. The communists were doomed. Their tenacity, however, ensured that a movement that was essentially fighting a rearguard action in 1946 nevertheless managed to mount a formidable military struggle until the summer of 1949. But the scale of the conflict was enough to again turn the Greek nation upside down. Although its causes could be traced to 1943 and the Axis occupation, the conflict stands as a discrete story. And because it was a civil war, it had enduring social and cultural ramifications in Greek society. It indelibly shaped the politics of the rest of the twentieth century.

Note

1. https://www.marshallfoundation.org/library/digital-archive/6-029-stateme nt-congressional-leaders-february-27-1947/.

CHAPTER 7

The post-war era (1950–1974)

Post-war Europe enjoyed a prolonged economic boom that brought with it unprecedented social mobility and rising living standards. It was a veritable 'golden age', as society began to enjoy living conditions that previously had been available only to the privileged few (Hobsbawm 1994: 256–68). Greece was a participant in this revolution, albeit belatedly. When the Civil War ended in August 1949, the path lay open for the most extraordinary social and cultural transformation in Greek society. By the 1970s, the traditional village communities in which Greeks had lived since the earliest times had all but disappeared. Most now lived in cities and towns, and it was increasingly common for families to own an automobile, appliances (especially refrigerators), cassette recorders and television sets. Consumer practices and youth cultures were being imported from Western Europe and even more from the United States. Young women had discarded headscarves and other traditional social restrictions. Greece had in other words become a modern country.

By another vital measure, however, Greece was stuck in the 1930s. Almost uniquely among countries that had fought the Second World War, the country's reactionary right-wing politicians continued to wield considerable power and influence. They abhorred many aspects of modernity, particularly such cultural manifestations as miniskirts and rock 'n' roll. And yet all the while, as in authoritarian Portugal and Spain, Greek society was changing. In April 1967 a *coup d'état* made Greece the only European nation in the Western camp to dissolve its liberal democratic institutions. It took another economic crisis (1973) and a reckless irredentist venture (Cyprus 1974) to annihilate the power of the Greek far Right.

People moving

The story of Greece's great social transformation began amidst the wreckage and debris of war. In 1947, the urban planner Konstantinos

Doxiades released a thorough survey of the damage inflicted by the Axis occupation in Greece to estimate the cost of reparations. His study showed that as many as half a million Greeks had been killed, a figure equivalent to 7 per cent of the population. Many thousands more had also been disabled and displaced. The destruction of countless villages left an acute housing shortage. Roads, buildings, bridges, ports, the Corinth Canal, mines, water supply, communications and transport facilities desperately needed repair. Agricultural exports had ceased. Three quarters of Greek shipping had been lost, and one in four sailors had drowned. The nation had lost as much as 70 per cent of its wealth. The general economy was in disarray. Inflation was out of control, forcing people to barter. The value of real wages had plummeted. Large transactions were made using gold. Domestic trade was at one fifth of pre-war levels. Rationing was the only way to get food to hungry families. The average calorific intake was half of the pre-war level. One in five families were homeless, after 11,788 houses had been destroyed. The Greek population was utterly dependent on food relief provided through the Red Cross and UNRRA (Frangiadis 2007: 157). The Civil War delayed recovery by hampering reconstruction and adding further destruction. It proved impossible to repair most roads, and these remained in a terrible state even in the Peloponnese, traditionally the most generously funded region by state expenditure. The insurgents had, moreover, placed landmines on many more roads. The Athens–Thessaloniki railway line was not restored until the end of the Civil War; the fighting destroyed 100 railway stations and 798 bridges (Close 1993: 11).

Among the effects of the violent traumas, destitution and political persecutions were forced and voluntary mass movements. Nearly half the population had either fled or abandoned their birthplace. By 1977 as many as 1.3 million youths would have left the country (Emke-Poulopoulou 1986: 59). One in six people between the ages of 25 and 33 departed. The emigration flow was much larger than that of the pre-1914 period. Although initially the exodus focused on Australia and North America, in the 1960s it was channelled mainly towards Western Europe and especially West Germany. To be sure, Greece was following a broader European trend. Between the 1920s and 1970s, 9.4 million people had abandoned Europe, and 2.6 million southern Europeans had emigrated during the same period, many to northern Europe. More detail on emigration will be outlined in Chapter 8; suffice it to say here that while thousands continued to emigrate abroad from southern Greece and the islands, most Greek émigrés were from northern provinces that had suffered more directly from the ravages of the Civil War.

Greece's fast-growing economy could not meet the vastly expanding population's demands for full-time employment. By 1961 Greece still had an unemployment rate of 6.1 per cent, the highest in Europe, where the average was a modest 2.4 per cent. A dynamic sector of society, these émigrés also became a vital source of fresh ideas regarding human rights, modern social norms and gender equality, and they paved the way towards adopting new technologies and new mental outlooks. By the economic crisis of the mid-1970s, about 300,000 émigrés had returned, bringing with them the experiences of living and working in places such as West Germany and Australia. Some returned to their farms and contributed to the renewal of the agricultural sector, but most resettled in cities (Venturas 1999: 79–94; Fifis 2015: 209).

Domestic migration was just as impressive in scale. Most of it headed for Athens. The capital received an annual intake of 30,000–40,000 people. In 1928 the city's population was 800,000. In 1951 it was 1,378,000, and by 1971 it was 2,540,000. One third of the nation's population lived in the greater Athens metropolitan area (Kapoli 2014: 262). The greatest demographic expansion in Greek history was achieved in the post-war decades, as the number of people in cities began to outnumber those living in the countryside. Although the rural reforms of the 1930s had begun to pay dividends by the 1960s, the political violence and suffocating surveillance of the intervening years, along with the rural sector's inability to absorb rural labour, added to the mass exodus. Many villages, especially in the more remote mountainous regions, were rapidly deserted. With the demise of the countryside, many of the old customs and ways of life disappeared.

Migration patterns were uneven. During the 1950s, most of the internal migration consisted of islanders and southern Greeks. Movement from northern provinces was mainly channelled abroad, and the exodus might have been on an even larger scale had there not been politically motivated restrictions placed on them. During these years of mass exodus, the entity that kept society together was the family. It is undoubtedly clear that the traditional family networks continued to provide a bridge between periods and between places. Families continued to facilitate movement between villages and cities and between countries. During wartime, villagers had fed their relatives in the towns and cities with food baskets, while remittances flowed as usual between sons and daughters in the diaspora and parents and siblings back home. Much as Kytherian husbands in Australia lived for long periods apart from wives and children, sometimes for decades, so did many *Gastarbeiter* in West Germany leave children to be raised in rural Macedonia by their grandparents. Leftists released from prison were forced to rely on family for finance and other means to become self-employed and launch small businesses. Both external and internal migrants relied on their social networks to find employment and satisfy their social (friendships, marriages) and political needs. Villagers not blacklisted politically could retain their voting rights when they migrated, as village political networks also extended to urban centres (McNeill 1977). Somehow villagers managed to integrate into the fabric of urban life. Families transposed gender roles and honour codes to their new settings, thereby explaining the persistence of honour crimes in the cities (Avdela 2002). Many traditional values such as male privilege persisted. Regardless, the family was critical for managing the challenges of this era, much as it had done in the catastrophic years of the early twentieth century. In his analysis of the family's social and economic role, sociologist Constantine Tsoucalas described it as 'multifaceted', for it could resolve problems by drawing on a range of skills and resources (Tsoucalas 1987).

The migrations of the post-war era altered the country's social and economic framework much more radically than earlier waves. The life-changing decisions of young village women and men to remake their lives in towns and cities were fundamental in driving the other changes that transformed life in Greece and the foreign lands that received them. What historian Peter Gatrell says for Europe applies to Greece: 'Without putting migration and migrants at its heart, the history of Europe since the end of the Second World War is incomplete' (Gatrell 2019: 2–3).

Economic reconstruction and US dollars

The reconstruction of Europe meant more than just repairing infrastructure and restarting economies. People also wanted changes that addressed the economic insecurities of the interwar years and the kinds of educational and medical services that could guarantee each citizen the chance of a better future. In Greece, reconstruction also meant having to industrialise the economy, for interwar economic policies had focused on the rural sector in order to increase its capacity to absorb labour and to squeeze out of it more income. At best, rural policies minimised the problems caused by stresses of population growth and global restrictions on emigration. Paradoxically, the war provided a solution in that it applied what the Austrian political economist Joseph Schumpeter once described as 'creative destruction' (Schumpeter 1943: 82–5). Wartime devastation hastened the transfer of human and material capital from the country to the city, thereby completing Greece's transition into an urban society. Its impact on the currant industry provided another example. The crisis of over-production during the interwar years was finally resolved when wartime food scarcity forced farmers to dig up currant vineyards to plant cereals. One could argue that creative destruction, combined with the constructive Marshall Plan, was chiefly responsible for Greece's spectacular post-war recovery.

Reconstruction had to be financed, and it fell on American governments to fill that need. Financing European reconstruction met two interrelated US interests: the rehabilitation of the most important US export markets and the need to contain Soviet expansion. Flooding the region with dollars would enable Europeans to continue buying 'American' and dreaming of having an American standard of living, which together proved more effective in combating communism than GIs and military hardware. The Harry Truman (1945–53) and Dwight D. Eisenhower (1953–61) administrations also expected their money to shore up liberal democratic institutions, help allies achieve financial self-sufficiency and adhere to the principle of global free trade. Because of the desperate economic conditions faced by US aid recipients, the last point could not be enforced, but the US did make most Western Europeans choose consumerism over political activism. Regarding Greece, it was hoped that, as William H. McNeill put it at the time, 'the excessive concern and fanaticism which the people now manifest for political parties and programmes would diminish' (McNeill 1947: 223–4; Ellwood 2012: 310). But Greece, like the rest of Europe, became part of a US global strategy that involved a radical reordering of international affairs and unprecedented intrusion in domestic politics, which would inevitably make the Americans and their influence in Greek life subjects of political contention.

Given its backwardness, Greece was considered a unique challenge: a laboratory for political, economic and cultural 'Americanisation'. US advisers were involved in all areas of governance and political economy. Greece had already received two injections of aid: the first under the auspices of UNRRA, which provided $454 million in 1945 and 1946 to meet such basic needs as food relief, reviving agricultural production and fighting malaria; the second under the British, who in 1946–7 also set up the Monetary Committee, which continued to operate into the 1990s. The Marshall Plan brought $700 million in aid, which was 5.5 per cent of the total aid budget for Europe, making Greece the sixth-largest recipient. US aid reached as high as 10.8 per cent of the Greek GDP in 1948–9, 16.7 per cent in 1949–50 and then 14.5 per cent in 1951–2 (Steil 2018: 343; Machado 2007: 58–9, 142). In total, it received $2 billion in economic aid and $1.2 billion in military aid over a ten-year period (1944–55), of which 85 per cent came from the United States. The bulk of the aid was received between 1947 and 1953 (Kakridis 2021).

Every aid recipient was expected to manage their funds and programmes to wean themselves off aid dependence. France provided a model through the Monet Plan. In many cases, the US winced at the levels of state intervention and the insistence of some governments on nationalising key industries; on the other hand, the US encouraged the Italian government to be more interventionist than it was prepared to be (Steil 2018). More so than in other allied nations, US administrators had misgivings about the competence of the Greek state and public sector. That view was encouraged by many in Greece: Queen Frederica herself told George Marshall that the Greek political elite was 'hopeless' (Machado 2007: 60). The mere fact that government departments and programmes were inundated by US advisers partly reflected a lack of confidence in Greek officials to spend the aid wisely. A small committee called the Economic Cooperation Administration (ECA) was set up within AMAG (American Aid for Greece), a body that was established earlier. US presidential envoy Peter Porter proposed that the aid be tied to major political and economic reforms in order to encourage structural changes. This American mission, which at one point was staffed by 240 Americans and 500 Greeks, was described by politician Spyros Markezinis, then Minister of Coordination and Planning, as 'an American supreme government'. The first chief of the mission, John Nuveen, later described it more tersely as 'an American Junta' (Machado 2007: 71). Once the Civil War ended, the mission used its influence to drive infrastructure projects through joint committees. Thus, the US Army Corps of Engineers and private US companies were employed to repair or rebuild 3,500 km of roads, 250 bridges and most of the highways. The mission oversaw the creation of a much-needed national electricity grid and the introduction of agricultural innovations, including transforming salt marshes into rice paddies (Machado 2007: 65–7). The mission driving these developments also intervened in all aspects of economic life, down to the most minor details. It had far less success in imposing its will on administration, taxation and anything that threatened the interests of Greek elites, although many of its failures were due to the staff's ignorance of Greek issues and culture. The mission often behaved like a colonial overlord and seemed impervious to local sensitivities: as one member of the mission put it, 'we were guilty of a little hubris' (Machado 2007: 73). That arrogance had much to do with the sheer scale of the US largess, which was equivalent to one quarter of Greece's GDP (including military aid) and financed 67 per cent of imports. To be sure, half of US aid was spent on military equipment and other military-related expenses, which continued after the war because of Greece's participation in the Korean conflict (1950–3).

The more profound and enduring influence of the United States came in the form of soft power, which presented Europeans with the most compelling vision of the future (Ellwood 2012: 1). Since the beginning of the century that vision was refracted through music, symbols, stories and charismatic persons, especially movie stars, but also through consumer capitalism, and business and work practices (e.g. Fordism, Taylorism). 'Americanisation' had been affecting Greek society since the 1890s in subtle ways, principally via the influence of émigrés who sent back remittances and materials (letters, photos, technologies like cameras), and via those who repatriated. After the Second World War, however, for Greeks and most Europeans, 'America' symbolised the promise of affluence more than ever. American films, which continued to dominate globally, depicted a country where much of society was prosperous and where even the average working-class family could aspire to own a home and an automobile.

The pillars of economic growth, 1953–1971

In the immediate post-war years, Greece experienced economic growth rates not seen before in its history. The starting point was the introduction of the new drachma (equalling 1,000 old drachmas), which was devalued by 50 per cent and introduced price stability at the exchange rate of US\$1 to 30 new drachmas. By then, the average growth rate was 7 per cent, which accorded with a global trend over the same period, and which was impressive when set against the European average of 4.8 per cent. Among the milestones achieved in that period was the European Economic Community (EEC) membership application in 1961, which also signalled Greece's orientation towards Europe.

The three pillars of this expansion were infrastructure, foreign investment and domestic financing. The last was the most important, as it financed as much as 90 per cent of national economic growth over that period (Psalidopoulos 2014: 212). Growth was also secured by policy continuity despite changes in government, which included exchange rate restrictions, fiscal discipline, budget surpluses, restraints on consumer spending, suppression of wages and agricultural commodity prices, and maintenance of tariff protections.

Newfound confidence in the drachma encouraged Greeks to bank their money and contribute substantially to national savings, while remittances flooded in from the diaspora, from recent émigrés and the merchant marine. The remittances alone amounted to about 10 per cent of national income. The National Bank of Greece played a significant role in the economy over the next half-century, financing public, semi-public and private ventures. Smaller banks, like the Hellenic Industrial Development Bank (ETBA), provided additional financial resources. The state also executed major infrastructural projects such as the expansion of the national electricity grid. Before the war, electricity was supplied by 340 local companies, the largest of which was the Athens-Piraeus Electrical Company, established by a British firm (Power and Traction Finance Company) in 1925. Hitherto, supply was unreliable, expensive and provided through limited networks. The Marshall Plan funded the repair of the existing electricity grid and the creation of the Public Electricity Company (*Dimosia Epicheirisis Ilektrismou*/DEI), which was organised and initially managed by the US company EBASCO. DEI was a public utility that oversaw lignite mining, thermal and hydroelectric plants, and a national electricity grid that eventually serviced the entire country. Despite some resistance, it absorbed all smaller companies and imposed a single national price (Pantelakis 1991). Electricity was the most effective tool for driving economic growth and nation-wide modernisation, although it finally reached the remotest mountainous regions and islands only in the 1980s. Once introduced, electricity revolutionised everyday life, even affecting relations between generations. As a dependable and seemingly infinite energy source, it introduced efficiencies into daily chores, making them easier and simpler, shortening the work hours needed for cooking, washing, cleaning and keeping the household warm. It reduced inter-generational dependence, promoting the dominance of the nuclear family and liberation from the traditional patriarchal authority. It was also the prerequisite for participation in the consumer economy.

Another innovation that changed life and required massive national investment was the telecommunications provider OTE (*Organismos Tilepikoinonion Ellados*).

Foreign investments in mining, chemical and fertiliser plants, shipyards and refineries were facilitated by legislation that offered guarantees and favourable incentives and privileges. Most of that investment poured in during the early to mid-1960s, a period of global economic expansion and stabilisation in the Greek economy. This period witnessed the arrival of the French company Pechiney, which invested heavily in bauxite processing and aluminium production. At the same time, Esso Pappas built an industrial complex in northern Greece that included a refinery, a steel plant and a petrochemical plant. Other major companies that established a presence included the Italian company Pirelli, which built a car tyre factory in Patras, and Philips and Dow Chemicals. In 1967 the dictatorship made it possible to set up offshore companies. Foreign investment was mainly in large-scale industrial enterprises, new products and export commodities: it accounted for 42 per cent of total exports in the 1960s (Giannitsis 2011: 525–97; Kazakos 2001: 172–3).

Investment also came from the merchant marine. This industry, which paid no taxes, enjoyed a privileged place in the Greek economy and society. Shipowners like Aristotle Onassis and Stavros Niarchos were treated like national royalty and were featured constantly in the press. Between 1952 and 1962, the shipping fleet under the Greek flag tripled in size and increased fivefold in terms of tonnage. However, the part of the Greek shipping fleet that flew foreign flags for tax purposes was five times larger. To service the growing tourist industry, Onassis bought the government-owned airline company TAE in 1956, relaunched it the following year as Olympic Airways, and upgraded the fleet and service quality during the 1960s to international standards (Harlaftis 2001: 402, 590–1).

Greek economic development was, above all, financed by domestic savings. By 1966 these accounted for 86 per cent of national economic growth compared to 13 per cent by foreign investment (Psalidopoulos 2014: 212). Households were acquiring new, durable consumer items. By the 1960s, local goods competed with European imports and captured a large share of the domestic market. Countless smaller trading and construction companies would also emerge in this period. Operating outside of the major construction sites were numerous contractors and small building firms that created the built environment of Athens and other cities.

Agriculture and industry

By 1950, food production had been restored to pre-war levels, imports and deficits were being financed by US dollars, and much of the nation's damaged infrastructure had been repaired. Of great significance was the elimination of malaria. Greece was one of the world's first nations to have that scourge removed through the use of DDT (Gardikas 2008), which in turn opened up wetlands and saw an almost thirteenfold increase in the production of rice, which now contributed to the nation's export income (Evelpidis 1953: 153). Wheat production also expanded markedly because of mechanisation, fertilisers and land reclamation. By the early 1950s, Greece met three quarters of its grain needs, and by 1957 it was self-sufficient (Evelpidis 1953: 153–4; McNeill 1957: 55, 101).

Agriculture remained a key focus of government policy in the post-war years. Major fertiliser factories were established in northern Greece, and tractor numbers quadrupled. Thessaly and Macedonia's extensive plains focused on cotton and sugar beets, which replaced currants and tobacco as the chief export agricultural commodities. As in the interwar years, the state continued to monitor all aspects of the trade in primary products, from harvesting to marketing. Indeed, aside from rural depopulation, endemic rural poverty was resolved by state guarantees to rural commodity prices, which kept rural incomes low but kept families well above the poverty line. Such measures were also designed to counter radicalism and tie rural voters to the new political order. It therefore served the latter's political interests to minimise the rural exodus, but that impeded the restructuring of the rural sector along commercial lines (Petmezas 2012).

However, the consensus from all sides of politics was that Greece should focus on expanding its industrial sector. Former finance minister Kyriakos Varvaressos recommended exploiting mineral resources to meet high international demand and help small industries and producers of consumer goods (Varvaressos 1952, 2002: 257–68). As it happened, an expanding industrial sector managed to absorb much of the surplus rural labour. Between 1951 and 1971, there were significant increases in mining and manufacturing production and construction, utilities and transportation. The construction industry was particularly important because it depended on domestic raw materials and stimulated the growth of related industries. Chemical industries expanded significantly in the 1960s, while the mining and metallurgical industries contributed significantly to Greek exports: from 1 per cent of total exports in 1961 to over 8 per cent by the second half of the decade (Kostis 2018: 350). Manufacturing, which expanded but not as much as was hoped, was nevertheless able to meet the growing demand for consumer items such as textiles, clothing and processed foods (Close 2002: 51–3).

The rise of the middle classes

Greek families faced social challenges and economic opportunities as never before. Family-run farms dominated the countryside, while towns and cities consisted mainly of small family-owned and -operated businesses and workshops. There were as many self-employed as there were wage earners. New sectors like tourism consisted mainly of family-run businesses. Tax evasion and cheap loans supported this vital, family-driven economic expansion.

Athens' emergence as a megacity contributed significantly to the transformation of Greek society. The neighbourhoods that had lined the edges of the old city to house refugees and newcomers during the interwar years were now complemented by new ones that covered much of the plain of Athens. 'Do it by yourself' was the motto of the American advisers in the early 1950s, which encouraged homeless families with construction material and tools to build their own dwellings (Kalfa 2019). The newcomers came to greatly outnumber indigenous Athenians. The rail line between Kifissia in the northwest and Piraeus to the southeast cut across the city, with the industrial zones, commercial houses and poorer residential districts on the eastern side of the tracks, and the middle and upper social strata concentrated on the other side. The scale and social geography of post-war Athens reflected the changes in Greek society, as did the new realities that came with living in apartments and in neighbourhoods filled with strangers.

Reconstruction changed the urban landscape, as the *polykatoikia* (multi-storey apartment building; Figure 7.1) became the commonplace form of habitation in Athens and in every other city. The extraordinary post-war demand for housing was resolved by a practice known as *antiparochi* (apartments for land), which referred to an agreement between apartment-block builders and owners of urban plots: the latter gave land to the developer in return for one or more apartments, while the developer sold the rest. This method of producing *polykatoikies* was fast and cheap. It gave families even with the most modest means central heating and basic modern amenities, and it facilitated private ownership. The system also ensured that new neighbourhoods would

Figure 7.1 *Athens old and new. Modern apartment building in Patission Avenue, Athens, 1960. © Benaki Museum (Αρχείο Φατούρου) ANA_061*

feature greater social complexity, with people of different occupations, classes and regional backgrounds residing in the same building. Families renovated their existing homes as their finances improved, which contributed to the upgrading of the whole neighbourhood. In such ways social segregation was avoided or minimised during Greece's post-war economic boom.[1]

Housing construction absorbed half of private investment and one third of total investment, which was the highest in Europe. Whereas most expenditure on housing construction in Europe went on public housing, in Greece 99 per cent of it was for private dwellings. However, the housing market lacked planning and oversight. A grey concrete landscape proliferated across the plain of Athens and came to characterise most cities and towns in Greece. During the early stages, housing quality was of a low standard, as were amenities. New suburbs emerged on the outskirts, which often lacked electricity, where families were sometimes forced to share water from tanks, and where the streets were often reduced to mud in winter and dust in summer. Many new neighbourhoods initially lacked schools, medical services and public transport facilities. Nevertheless, housing construction was one of the locomotives that drove the nation's economic boom and shaped urban Greece's current modes of sociability, everyday life and aesthetic profile. American and European anthropologists working on Greece in the post-war years and into the 1980s persisted in studying village communities that had held to the traditional ideas and customs of their ancestors, yet the great bulk of the Greek population, who had either moved to urban centres or were bringing urban culture to the villages, were fast becoming very different social beings (Hirschon 1998; Lambropoulou 2009; Kalfa 2019).

Athens' rapid expansion necessitated urgent reform of its transport infrastructure, but instead of complementing existing systems, the city authorities decided in 1953 to rip out the tram system and construct massive boulevards to accommodate that great symbol of the consumer economy and private prosperity, the automobile. There were 3,000 privately owned cars in 1950, and 90,000 by 1965, after which the figure would double every five years. Owning a private car (*yotachi*) was prestigious, and it symbolised such modern values as privacy and individualism. The city was flooded with cars, which took up every available parking (and non-parking) space and routinely caused spectacular traffic jams. Traffic brought a new source of tension into everyday life, while pedestrians spent much of their time avoiding moving vehicles and negotiating their way between them. Meanwhile, Athenian skies acquired a haze of car exhaust fumes. Pollution soon became a major problem for the capital and other cities as well.

In the meantime, modernisation slowly found its way to the villages. New housing gradually replaced traditional dwellings, and would include plumbing, heating and electrical appliances. At the time of the Marshall Plan, movies were occasionally screened publicly before crowds in the village centre, but by the late 1960s and early 1970s television sets were finding their way into every household. Men were no longer spending most of the evening hours at the *kafeneion* among other men but in their homes with the family. Patriarchal norms meant that women were left with household duties, but their lives were made easier by electrical appliances that made cleaning and cooking less arduous and time-consuming. The time saved was devoted either to part-time paid work or social life. Such dramatic changes in everyday life were especially pronounced in working-class families, which enjoyed increasing access to affordable electrical appliances manufactured in Greece. Gradually, over the course of the post-war period, the benefits of modern living were extended to the lower social orders and outwardly to urban peripheries and the villages.

The 'affluent society' had arrived, as had expectations of further progress and prosperity. The days when Greece was beset by wars and its people subjected to deprivations seemed to have faded into the past.

Tourism

The new age also brought an unprecedented number of visitors. Numbers would grow exponentially over the ensuing decades, as would their contribution to national income. The steady stream of visitors coming to see ancient ruins was complemented in the post-war years by a much larger number who were coming for sun and sea. For Western Europeans, North Americans and Australians, Greece was an idyllic setting that attracted high-society leisure seekers, as well as writers and artists. By the 1950s and 1960s, jet-setting celebrities, royals and tycoons were luxuriating on yachts and private islands, and were sometimes spotted by paparazzi at performances in the ancient theatre at Epidaurus or the Herodes Atticus Theatre in Athens, wearing the latest fashions. During the summer of 1951, the famous French haute couture designer Christian Dior chose the Acropolis to photo-shoot his latest fashion collection.

Another category consisted of bohemians who took their inspira-tion from the country's antiquities and dramatic landscapes, or found solace in traditional villages that had yet to be modernised. Small bohe-mian colonies were established in places like Hydra, where movies were often shot because it seemed to represent an unspoiled Greece. For many years Hydra was home to the Canadian singer-poet Leonard Cohen and the Australian writers George Johnson and Charmian Clift (Genoni and Dalzeill 2018; Samson 2020).

Mass tourism had a far more profound impact on Greek domestic life, and it provides a more telling example of how global changes impacted Greek society, and how that society adapted to and exploited the challenges. Tourism promoted new services and stimulated a com-prehensive range of domestic economic activities. It was driven essen-tially by the post-war boom and rising incomes that made vacationing in the Mediterranean increasingly accessible to British and German workers, who were also receiving paid holidays. Moreover, tourists exploited the drop in transport costs and the increase in the number of school holidays to go abroad. Many were also taking advantage of mass holiday packages provided by tourism companies. More broadly,

northern Europeans of all classes preferred vacationing on sunny
Greek beaches rather than at their local resorts in the Baltic and North
Atlantic. Pop youth culture, along with the impact of popular film and
massive marketing campaigns, increased interest in sunbathing, body
exhibitionism and health. The very attractions that once drew the jet
set were opening up to the masses.

Greek tourism took off towards the end of the 1950s. A stimulus was provided by three international films (Figure 7.2): *The Boy
and the Dolphin* (1957), with Sophia Loren and Alan Ladd; Jules
Dassen's *Never on a Sunday* (1961), with Melina Mercouri; and
Michael Cacoyannis' *Zorba the Greek* (1964), which starred Anthony

Figure 7.2 *Projecting Greece through international film.* Boy on a Dolphin *(1957) with
Sophia Loren;* Zorba the Greek *(1964) with Antony Quinn and Alan Bates; and* Never
on Sunday *with Melina Mercouri (1960).* © *Alamy Images FFAK3R, RWEMDN and
E0X3E4*

Quinn. Travel magazines began promoting Greece as an internationally recognisable brand. Once poverty-stricken islands like Mykonos
and Santorini attracted VIPs and celebrities from around the world.
Domestic tourism also developed apace, as the expanding middle
class took to the seaside and rented rooms from local families. The
post-war construction boom was partly associated with the creation of
tourism infrastructure. At the beginning of the 1950s, the only islands
that could accommodate a substantial tourist intake were Rhodes
and Corfu, but the ensuing years saw a proliferation of luxury hotels
modelled on those found in California and the French Riviera, which
would include golf courses and tennis courts.

Typically, the tourist industry expanded with minimal state
regulation. Large companies scrambled to buy up the best seaside
properties, building facilities without regard for local environmental impacts. Smaller operators constructed shoddy facilities that
encroached on the beaches. The boom's environmental impacts did
raise concerns. Architect Solon Kydoniatis declared that Greece's
environment had suffered more damage in two decades of mass
tourism than it had done in the previous 5,000 years (Nikolakakis
2017: 146). The tourism boom was nevertheless welcomed by all
post-war governments, although there was a marked preference for
the high-end kind. The military dictatorship of 1967–74 was the
most enthusiastic, for it linked tourism to foreign investment, and
hoped it would contribute to international acceptance of its regime.
International tourism developed rapidly, reaching 1 million visitors
annually in 1966 and increasing to 3 million by 1973. The number
continued to climb to 5 million in 1981, 10 million in 1995, and
20 million in 2015. The trend was of course reversed in 2020–1 by the
COVID-19 pandemic.

One of the most critical effects of tourism was to open the Greek
economy to international competition. Thus, the influx of foreign
airline carriers had implications for the protections enjoyed by Olympic
Airways. Regulations regarding Sunday shop closures, fixed shopping
hours and the eight-hour day for employees were abolished. Airports
multiplied and sea routes expanded. Only some poor habits were maintained: tax avoidance was, if anything, enhanced by the tourism trade.

Structural weaknesses

Throughout the 1950s and 1960s, the damage that decades of war
had wrought was repaired. However, these impressive feats did not

mean that the economy had been sufficiently stabilised or that the private sector grew fast enough to absorb the unemployed and the under-employed. Despite achieving historically high growth rates, Greece also maintained one of the highest unemployment rates in Europe. Per capita income increased while agricultural exports and industrial production lagged. Agricultural commodity prices were dropping while Greeks were becoming increasingly reliant on imported industrial and manufactured goods. The trade imbalance was corrected by tourism and remittances from the diaspora and the merchant marine. Between 1955 and 1982, remittances accounted for 4 to 5 per cent of gross national income and one third of undeclared income.

There were also new burdens on the national budget. In the early 1950s, as many as 2.5 million people, one third of the population, remained dependent on the state. Somewhere between 160,000 and 200,000 were employed in the armed forces, giving Greece one of the largest standing armies in Europe and among the largest per capita in the world. Moreover, many disabled and displaced families lived on government welfare, and a large proportion of them were employed in the public sector.

State intervention affected every aspect of the post-war economy. Tariffs shielded the market from foreign competition, and there was extensive regulation on foreign trade. The state banking system supervised state regulations, although it was subjected to unofficial political and economic pressure. Friends of the government in business had special access to contracts and information. State support could come through favourable bank loans and subsidies. It was via the banks that the politicians dispensed favours, controlled interest rates and directed investment into areas of policy priority. Private stock and capital markets played no role.

These structural problems lay hidden during the period covered in this chapter, but they would surface during the global oil crisis of 1973, when the US abandoned the gold standard and fixed exchange rates ended. A year before, Greece could boast record employment and economic growth. The economic crisis that followed the Arab–Israeli conflict and the embargo imposed on Israel's supporters by the Organisation of Arab Petroleum Exporting Countries (OAPEC) ended the global boom and would spark political crises everywhere. It not only hastened the end of military dictatorship in Greece but brought down the whole power structure that had dominated political life since the Civil War.

Illiberal democracy

Throughout the post-war years, Greece seemed on the surface a liberal democracy. During the 1950s, parties of all shades, with the significant exception of KKE, were able to contest national elections – there were eight over the next seventeen years. The first three governments were formed by centrist parties and led by moderates like the liberal Sofoklis Venizelos (August 1950–October 1951) and Plastiras (November 1951–October 1952). The ensuing decade (1952–63) featured a conservative ascendancy led at first by Alexandros Papagos (1952–5) and then Constantine Karamanlis (1956–63). Karamanlis' Greek Rally and its successor, the National Radical Union (*Ethniki Rizospastiki Enosis*), won four consecutive elections (1952, 1956, 1958, 1961), after which the centrist Georgios Papandreou was able to lead the Centre Union (*Enosis Kentrou*) to two wins (1963 and 1964). However, with his election the stability that had characterised political life since the early 1950s appeared to unravel. The mere fact that a centrist was in power rankled with the Right, but there was also the fact that his ascendancy appeared to give licence to political progressives to express their aspirations more openly. Despite Papandreou's strong performance in the 1964 election, he soon became embroiled in a political crisis that led to a clash with the monarchy in 1965. The point at issue was who controlled the military: the monarchy or the parliament? This confrontation split his government and led to his resignation. By this stage, centrists and leftists were prepared to participate in protests and demonstrations, which they did when Papandreou was unseated. King Constantine II (1963–7) then appointed a series of caretaker prime ministers, all moderate conservatives (Stefanos Stefanopoulos, Ioannis Paraskevopoulos, Panagiotis Kanellopoulos), none of whom were able to restore stability to political life.

If Greece seemed to function like a liberal democracy, when it came to the mechanics of governance it retained practices that all Greeks recognised as corrupt. Thus, politics continued to operate on a clientelist model. Constituents supported political patrons who dispensed favours, and when in power, they were able to allocate public resources to supporters while denying them to political opponents. Such practices led to a bloated and highly inefficient public service filled with poorly trained and under-motivated personnel (Close 2002: 88–9). The post-war years witnessed an expansion in patron–client systems, as many more people needed licences and business loans or retirement and veterans' pensions. As in Italy, the Greek welfare budget was significantly smaller than the European average. In 1960 it accounted for 5.3 per cent of GDP, whereas the European average was 10 per cent. In northern and northwestern Europe, welfare was a civic right; in Greece, it was considered a form of charity dispensed for political purposes. The state allocated Queen Frederica a significant budget to distribute to worthy charities, including the dowries of poor girls: in the mid-1960s, her budget was comparable to that of the Ministry of Health and Welfare (Meynaud 1974: 339–42).

What was different about the post-war era was how the Civil War affected the distribution of power. Post-war governments, even conservative ones, had to contend with a coalition of powerful interest groups that wielded considerable influence and sometimes played a determining political role, acting as a 'shadow state' (in Greek political jargon, *parakratos*). This informal coalition could change governments, topple prime ministers, order executions and, as in 1967, form a dictatorship. Aside from the monarchy, this power network included the military, the secret services, the American Embassy and other influential organisations and individuals. Its self-appointed role was to guarantee that parliamentary democracy did not diminish the gains made in the Civil War and to counteract any sign of a Left resurgence. Some of the network's elements, particularly the military and the security services, including the police, operated with a very broad interpretation of 'the Left', which included centrists like Papandreou and many modern cultural influences like rock 'n' roll (Katsapis 2007). This mission explains why the network incessantly undermined Papandreou's Centre Union and finally imposed a dictatorship just before the elections set for May 1967, which Papandreou was widely expected to win.

The post-Civil War state featured both a formal state apparatus and the shadow state: a combination of parallel structures and roles, formal and informal, visible and invisible. The wartime promise that all parties would participate in post-war politics was soon forgotten. Instead, the winners punished and then marginalised the losers, perpetuating the deep animus that began with the National Schism of the First World War and extended through to the Civil War. The post-war state silenced those who once supported EAM and the communist insurgency, and more ominously, it pressured them to renounce their past and switch loyalties. Therefore, as happened in Francoist Spain after 1939, there was no attempt at national reconciliation. Those who continued to attract the suspicion of authorities were denied access to resources (public service jobs, licences and the like), while dissidents and suspected malcontents continued to be incarcerated, tortured and exiled. The post-war state was able to establish its domination over Greek society. However, it was not able to secure what the Italian Marxist Antonio Gramsci called 'hegemony', meaning popular legitimacy (Gramsci 1977).

The post-Civil War ruling order was not a coherent entity, however. During the latter stages of the Civil War, Papagos held the factions together because they respected him for overseeing government restoration through the parliament. Papagos relinquished his position as commander in chief of the army, donned civilian clothing and founded the most prominent conservative party, the Greek Rally (*Ellinikos Synagermos*) in 1951. After winning national elections the following year, Papagos held the monarchy and the military together. Meanwhile, the military maintained close relations with the United States, whose supplies and money helped it win the Civil War while maintaining considerable autonomy vis-à-vis the government and the monarchy. It also monitored its secret organisations, including IDEA, which featured many high-ranking members of the officer corps, and the Union of Young Greek Officers (EENA) (Papachelas 1998; Karamanolakis 2010).

Relations between the constituent parts of the post-war ruling order were never stable. Papagos kept the military in tow, but when he died, the monarchy sought to reassert its authority in military matters, although the machinations of Queen Frederica, in particular, had the effect of alienating many leading military figures. Not all officers were royalists: the Junta would formally abolish the monarchy again in 1973. It was never clear where the centre of power resided. The question of who made decisions was raised publicly at least twice: first in 1952 when communist Nikos Beloyannis and his comrades were executed despite an international outcry, including a petition signed by Pablo Picasso, Charlie Chaplin and Jean-Paul Sartre; and secondly, following the assassination in 1963 of parliamentarian and United Democratic Left leader Grigoris Lambrakis.

US influence also shifted, mainly when Greek foreign policy interests conflicted with other NATO members. The Right never gave up on the dream of a 'greater Greece', including northern Epirus (southern Albania) and Cyprus. Although Papagos was a staunch supporter of US policy and the North Atlantic alliance, his relationship with the US was compromised when his government supported Cyprus' unification with Greece (*Enosis*). US influence waned as it became increasingly unable to balance Greece's conflicting interests with Britain and Turkey. The Right also found it challenging to maintain good relations with the US as the Cyprus issue became increasingly intractable (see pp. 267–81). Overwhelmingly, Greeks supported *Enosis*, which therefore allowed the Left to play the patriotism card against their US-backed opponents (Kazamias 2014; Stefanidis 1999).

Surveillance and punishment

Since the Civil War, the Right had claimed a monopoly on patriotism. It identified itself strongly with the country's folk traditions, Greek Orthodoxy and Hellenism, which considered Greece as the birthplace of Western Civilisation. During the Cold War, educated Greeks regarded Hellenism as inimical to communism, which they deemed to be more suited to the Slavic races. The Right was also determined to erase memories of the wartime Resistance and deny it any credit. Rather, the post-war state bombarded the public with anti-communist propaganda, and made extensive use of state radio and cinemas. Before every movie, audiences were treated to ten minutes of the latest government-controlled news.

Meanwhile, the incarcerations continued. Suspected dissidents were kept in check by a grossly inflated security apparatus consisting primarily of the National Guard Battalions (TEA) and the National Guard Units (MEA), and by paramilitary organisations. As had been the case since the Balkan Wars, dissidents were sent to camps on remote Aegean islands, where prisoners sometimes outnumbered the local inhabitants. In 1951 Aï Stratis, for example, was home to some 500 islanders but 3,350 prisoners (Sarantakos 2004: 19–20). Makronisos functioned as the major rehabilitation camp for political detainees until 1957. On the island of Leros, former Italian colonial buildings were used during the latter years of the Civil War to house the children of guerrillas and as an asylum, taking in many who had been driven insane by torture. The military Junta would later establish two more camps on the island, housing somewhere between 40,000 and 100,000 people. Many of these camps and prisons were closed in 1963 when centrists formed a government, but were promptly reopened in 1967 by the military dictatorship.

Citizens, in general, were subjected to systematic and intensive surveillance by the state security apparatus, which recorded movements, social meetings, and what people were saying and reading. Political gatherings and offices were under constant watch. Authorities wanted to know what citizens were doing and thinking. Like all modern authoritarian regimes, this one was concerned with its popularity and all forms of dissent. The government recorded and filed detailed information on millions of individuals, with particular emphasis placed on 'social attitudes' (*koinonika fronimata*). These files could determine people's fate, such as their chances of attaining a job, a licence or the necessary paperwork to emigrate. The state decided if one was an internal enemy, a term that was usually a synonym for 'communist', although it was also automatically ascribed to ethnic minorities (Muslims, Slav Macedonians). People of interest were further classified as 'dangerous', 'accomplices', 'sympathisers' or suspects of unknown orientation. Alternatively, there were those who were considered true patriots, and earned that honour by their 'healthy attitudes' (*igii fronimata*). They were subdivided into those who made their views clear through their overt political actions, those who were inactive but above suspicion, and those who were merely law-abiding and not considered suspicious. Family links mattered. Citizens were automatically categorised as 'suspicious' (*ypoptos*) because of a family member's activities.

Personal profiles were assembled after extensive research, and the information was used for issuing 'certificates of social attitudes' (*pistopiitikon koinonikon fronimaton*). These were necessary for anyone applying for a public service job, for getting a licence for (say) a motor vehicle, for teachers wishing to attain a school posting, and for anyone seeking to emigrate or join the merchant marine. Large companies required such certificates from prospective employees. The number of files far exceeded the national population – there were some 15 million individual records because different security services units operated in different areas; hence people crossing zones for work or social purposes had two or more files (Karamanolakis 2019: 68). This surveillance system also supplied confessions and other kinds of political declarations. To gain their release those imprisoned or in internal exile had to renounce communism, their former comrades and their past actions, and claim that they had been misled into betraying the fatherland. They were further expected to swear to be law-abiding citizens and true patriots. In the early 1950s, confessions were published in newspapers. Later, authorities merely required subjects to get police certificates regarding their 'social attitudes' or adherence to the law. The production of files, the procedures to attain confessions and declarations, and the tribunals set up to judge cases required yet another vast bureaucracy to be added to the already bloated civil service.

Such heavy surveillance had much of Greek society living in fear. Citizens were forced to practise self-censorship, compelled to speak evasively and behave in such a way as to avoid scrutiny. Ordinary Greeks lived under the threat of being denounced by estranged relatives or neighbours. The loss of a trading licence, for example, could mean ruin. The surveillance regime was intense during the Civil War and the 1950s, relaxing somewhat in the early and middle 1960s but then resuming with greater force under the military dictatorship. It captured the essence of the post-war political order: anti-communism. The state needed a coercive apparatus to uphold the Civil War outcome and regulate the relationship between state and society.

Politics in the shadow of the Civil War

The first two governments of the early 1950s were shaky centrist coalitions, with a state apparatus that had been extensively purged of its centrist public servants. The Right assumed dominance under Papagos and his Greek Rally party. Although a scion of both the Right and the military, Papagos was able to build a broad electoral base by forging links with the liberal centre, as De Gaulle had done in 1947 in France with *Rassemblement du Peuple Français*. In November 1951 Papagos won 114 seats out of 258, but he waited until the November 1952 elections to attain a much larger share of votes and seats. Despite a difficult relationship with the monarchy, which actively campaigned against him, Papagos was able to form a government: an electoral reform had given his party 80 per cent of seats in Parliament with just under 50 per cent of the popular vote. Papagos remained an immensely reassuring figure for the political elite. He secured more aid from the US for its leases on bases in Greece, and he challenged NATO over Cyprus. Papagos was able to make these changes because he enjoyed unchallenged personal authority within his party. Whereas previous conservative parties had operated like nineteenth-century gentleman's clubs, Greek Rally and its successor, National Radical Union (ERE 1956–67), were more like well-drilled military units under a domineering leader. Early in 1955, however, Papagos became seriously ill and subsequently died in October.

During Papagos' long illness, the monarchy promoted the 48-year-old Constantine Karamanlis, one of his most talented ministers, with a view to restoring its influence over the government. But Karamanlis proved to be his own man. More decisive and competent than his predecessor, he not only put his own stamp on the party but was determined to chart a new political direction. This was reflected by the fact that he changed the party's name, and by the fact that he sought to attract more votes from the political centre while not excluding members of the far Right. Although not a 'new man' in national politics, given that he first entered Parliament in 1936 and had held ministries in the late 1940s, Karamanlis nevertheless seemed less obsessed with the Civil War and showed genuine interest in leaving its politics behind. Some of the more extreme forms of repression were relaxed, and some political prisoners and exiles were released. He supported the vote for women, and established closer trading ties and migration agreements with Europe. In 1959 his government applied to join the EEC. The quest for closer ties with West Germany, however, meant waiving reparations and the return of 'loans' extracted by the Nazi regime, and stopping actions against Nazi war criminals (Spilioti 2000). Handsome and well spoken, Karamanlis cut a modern political figure on the political stage, but while he might have been a politician of the new era, much of his party was still preoccupied with the politics of the Civil War. Moreover, to the average Greek, his was still the party of the Right, which remained at the helm of a highly repressive security apparatus (Meynaud 2002; Nikolakopoulos 2001; Rizas 2016).

What of the political opposition? Despite the bloody destruction of the Left only a few years earlier, and the Papagos–Karamanlis ascendancy, there was always a potential support base for centrist and left-leaning parties in the burgeoning urban centres and in the traditional leftist neighbourhoods. From 1954 on, such parties won a series of mayoral elections, usually in coalitions that included centrists, giving them a presence in the public domain. Founded in 1951, the United Democratic Left (*Eniaia Demokratiki Aristera*/EDA) served as a rallying point not just for those who had lost the Civil War but for those who also wanted to move beyond its politics. It was undoubtedly linked to the Communist Party. It pushed similar policies; much of its support base had been tied to KKE and EAM. Political opponents regularly accused EDA of being a communist front, although Papagos himself would claim that 'on the basis of objective data' they were different entities (Gkotzaridis 2016: 115). Moreover, unlike KKE, EDA sought power through the electoral process and was committed to social democracy. The challenge for EDA was to address the shifting needs and interests of Greek labour in an era of rapid economic transition, and to harness the mood for political change. In 1958, EDA had made progress, and its share of the popular vote rose to 25 per cent, which was less than Karamanlis' ERE with 41 per cent but greater than Sofoklis Venizelos' Liberals' 20 per cent.

These elections signalled the coming of Greece's 1960s, as a new generation looked for a more progressive and open political system, demanding reforms that reflected the needs of a rapidly modernising society. The decade witnessed the meteoric emergence of young people as a worldwide political force for change, as they began to agitate for such progressive international causes as the anti-war and peace movements. In Greece they found expression in organisations like the Lambrakis Youth, named after murdered progressive politician Grigoris Lambrakis (see below, p. 255). Its activities reflected the spirit of a generation weighed down by state-directed conformity, conservatism and repression. That mood for progressive political and social change was mirrored in the music of Mikis Theodorakis and other composers, as well as writers and other artists who were actively pushing for radical change in line with the demands of comparable movements in Western Europe (St. Martin 1984; Gkotzaridis 2016; Lambrinou 2017).

However, the first signs of a revival of progressive politics appeared to tap the anxieties of the more extreme elements of the Right. Initially, the first serious challenge to the Right's domination came from the old Venizelist liberals, when the 'Democratic Union', a coalition of centrist parties, won more of the popular vote in the 1956 elections than did Karamanlis' ERE. But by the 1958 elections, EDA emerged as the chief opposition party, raising alarm bells even within the political centre. These elections appeared to cause great unease within the military, which had always wanted a dictatorship and feared that Greece's liberal political system could reverse the outcome of the Civil War. The mere fact that a Left party had become electorally competitive was enough to incite conspiracies that involved members of the military hierarchy, the police and former members of the Security Battalions. These networks stood in readiness to seize power (Dordanas 2011), and their existence was revealed to Karamanlis by the chief of the General Staff and a political moderate, Petros Nikolopoulos. Although shocked at first, Karamanlis seemed willing to live with it, as suggested when Nikolopoulos was forced to retire in September under right-wing pressure (Gkotzaridis 2017: 650–1). Indeed, it appeared that the government was prepared to use its reserve powers to defend its interests. With rare candour, a leading intellectual of the Right, Konstantinos Tsatsos, admitted to Ilias Iliou, a member of the EDA, that 'Western states have Catholicism and social democratic parties to keep the communists at bay. We have neither. We will not fold our arms and surrender. We will deal with you with the security forces and other state mechanisms' (Nikolakopoulos 2017: 146).

The Greek 1960s

The fortress mindset that characterised the Greek ruling elite could be seen on 17 April 1967 during a Rolling Stones concert in Athens. The British rock 'n' roll group symbolised much that conservatives hated about cultural modernity, particularly the rebelliousness and sexual ambiguity evoked by the performances of its lead singer, Mick Jagger. Newspapers mocked the youths who filled Panathinaikos Stadium that evening as silly *yieyiedes* ('yeah-yeah-ists', inspired by the Beatles song 'She Loves You'), but state authorities regarded them as a serious political threat. The concert lasted only twenty minutes. The police arrested the band's manager for trying to distribute red flowers to the crowds; what upset them was the colour. When roadies tried to intervene they were also detained, prompting the band to bring the show to an abrupt close. In the ensuing riot, students were beaten. The city's chief of police, who was present at the concert, dispersed the *yieyiedes* after switching the lights off and plunging the stadium into darkness (Katsapis 2007: 366).

The youth rebellion of the 1960s was a global phenomenon. Socially conservative generations, raised during the austerities of the 1930s and 1940s, clashed with 'baby boomers' who wanted a world that was more politically, socially and sexually liberated. The rise of youth culture in Greece, symbolised by rock 'n' roll, blue jeans and miniskirts, together with pinball machines (*flipe-rakia*), billiards and jukeboxes, and inspired by popular films and massive marketing campaigns that promoted libertarian behaviour, activated a wave of moral panic that was whipped up by state authorities, bishops and the conservative press (Katsapis 2013; Avdela 2013). In places like Spain and Greece, however, tertiary students were at the vanguard of progressive politics, and as a consequence the young attracted much closer attention from state authorities than elsewhere (cf. Sánchez 2010: 191). To be sure, the relationship between student activism and youth culture was complicated. Many on the Left also considered *yieyiedes*, hippies and pop music to be culturally noxious (Katsapis 2007: 249). But for the Right youth culture was one of those degenerative influences that threatened such traditional institutions as patriarchy and the family, and in the febrile imagination of the Greek Right it was easily linked to communism. The 'Sixties' is a distinct period of interrelated cultural and political trends, and the middle years of the decade bore witness to a global crisis in which society was running ahead of politics. It was symbolised by the challenge to establishments led by the young (Marwick 1998; Chaplin and Pieper Mooney 2018).

In 1950s Greece, the Left could still express itself through the arts and supporting EDA, but the party's impressive electoral performances also reflected a modernising society with new aspirations and which yearned for progressive reforms. Moreover, by the end of the decade, the pall of fear had abated, and ordinary Greeks seemed more willing to express their disquiet about living standards, services and public infrastructure. In this regard they were no different to societies throughout Western Europe, where criticism of government had been constrained by a post-war desire for national healing and reconstruction, and by fear of Soviet expansion, both of which had subsided by the 1960s. Greeks and other Europeans were more willing to criticise governments and political elites, and to seek more in terms of political rights, social equity and justice (Conway 2020: 255; Close 2002: 103).

Wishing to capitalise on the mounting mood for change, in September 1961 Papandreou formed the Centre Union (*Enosis Kentrou*), just in time to contest the national elections in October. In response, military officers organised a conspiracy to influence the outcome, but their overzealous and ham-fisted methods backfired, as the police and armed gangs intimidated tens of thousands of people into casting their vote for the government (Close 2002: 104). The conspiracy, dubbed 'the Pericles Plan', was meant to claw back the losses incurred in the last election, and it appeared to deliver Karamanlis the vote numbers he needed. But the ballot-rigging and fraud were so blatant that it gave rise to a new culture of mass political activism. Papandreou capitalised on the public's outrage by leading a campaign that questioned both the election results and the government's legitimacy. Dubbed 'Relentless Struggle' (*Anendotos Agon*), it attracted mass support and held demonstrations that often turned violent. It was during one such protest in Thessaloniki in May 1963 that Lambrakis, the pacifist and independent parliament member, was assassinated in broad daylight. The brazen nature of this killing was meant to intimidate government opposition, but it only increased public anger and raised suspicions of state complicity. The fact that the murderers would be treated with extraordinary leniency suggested to most observers that the order came from above (Gkotzaridis 2016; Gkotzaridis 2017: 646–73).

The Right was obsessed with keeping the Left at bay. The lesson it took from the 1940s was that the Greeks were susceptible to left-wing ideology, and that any concessions to it would simply hasten the return of communism. Papandreou's *Anendotos Agon* therefore seemed particularly dangerous. Although a liberal, his populist oratory and ability to rally large crowds seemed to reawaken radical sentiments and the courage to challenge authority. In the meantime, tensions had also developed *within* the Right. Karamanlis, who at the time was facing significant challenges regarding the constitutional settlement in Cyprus (discussed in Chapter 8), not only had to contend with an increasingly anxious Right but also a monarchy that was as keen as ever to use its political prerogatives. Karamanlis stepped down in June 1963 after he had failed to secure constitutional changes that would have increased the powers of his office. The trigger was a planned royal visit to London in July, which Karamanlis feared might expose King Paul and Queen Frederica to demonstrations prompted by the Cyprus crisis. When the couple disregarded his advice, Karamanlis resigned. Rather than call fresh elections or appoint Papandreou, the king appointed his former adviser and now ERE leader Pangiotis Pipinelis as interim prime minister.

The period from 1963 to 1967 was a time of relentless political upheaval and crisis. Papandreou's Centre Union won in November 1963 and was able to extend its majority substantially in fresh elections in February 1964. During his short, two-year tenure, Papandreou's Centre Union passed a spate of welfare and educational reforms, including raising pensions and workers' wages. He released most political prisoners from jails and internment camps and curbed the activities of the security services. He introduced free university education and mandated the use of demotic Greek in education, which prompted histrionic reactions from the Right (Mackridge 2009: 315–16).

What made it a crisis-ridden period, however, was the obvious fact that the Right never accepted the legitimacy of Papandreou, and that he regularly came into conflict with the monarchy. Matters came to a head when Papandreou tried to impose his authority on the military. The new king, the 24-year-old Constantine II – Paul had died in March 1964 – refused to let the Prime Minister take the portfolio of the Ministry of Defence because Papandreou's son Andreas was alleged to have been involved in a non-right-wing military conspiracy known as *Aspida* (Shield). The so-called *Iouliana* (July Crisis) pitted the prime minister against the monarchy. The king had been plotting a change of government by encouraging members of the Centre Union to desert Papandreou and join in a new government. On 15 July 1965 Papandreou resigned. Hoping to avoid the return of a Papandreou-led government, the king appointed a series of prime ministers and 'apostate' governments – there would be three before the end of the

year and five in all. At the time, Papandreou held rallies and campaigned on the slogan 'Who governs Greece? The King or the People?'
(Christidis 2016). The crisis lasted until 3 April 1967, when the moderate Panagiotis Kanellopoulos, the then leader of ERE, formed an
interim government, having earlier agreed with Papandreou to contest
fresh elections in May. Each was keen to end the instability and ward
off a widely rumoured *coup d'état*. The *Iouliana* did not just refer to the
crisis of July 1965, but to the whole period of popular protests, strikes,
rallies and riots that had rocked Greece since 1961. The movement
expressed the spirit of Greece's 1960s, of a society trying to escape from
a prison erected by the Greek Civil War (Papanikolopoulos 2013).

A coup did take place within a few weeks. It was led by officers determined to roll back the progressive changes and influences of recent
years, and to preserve the Civil War settlement. The political elite had
failed to adapt to a nation experiencing a rapid social and economic
transformation. In 1966 Kanellopoulos could see that:

> If we continue to speak as we did twenty years ago, we will lose, that
> is Greece will lose, that great part of the youth that gained awareness
> in an age of space and astronauts. We are not separated from 1946 by
> twenty years. We are divided by a century. (Lambrinou 2017: 193)

Indeed, those in power in Greece and the United States were still speaking as if the 1960s were the 1940s. It was this tyranny of anachronism
that, according to US documents, prompted around thirty to forty
officers to seize power. They did so because the elections scheduled
in May 'might see cooperation between the political Center and the
extreme Left, with the extreme Left holding the political balance as it
had in 1936 and again in 1944' (Schmitz 2006: 64).

The Junta, 1967–1974

During the spring of 1967, the Greek public was nervous about the
possibility of a military coup. There were discussions about that prospect in the left-wing newspaper *Avgi*, although on 20 April it gave a
number of reasons why it would *not* happen (Kornetis 2013: 43). The
prospect of a Papandreou victory in elections set for 27 May raised
questions about whether the shadow state would step in and rule
through a dictatorship. At the time, the men who had the king's ear
were undoubtedly in an anxious state and were recommending a
'deviation' (*ektropi*). They were convinced that Papandreou, despite
being an anti-communist, was the thin edge of a communist wedge: a

Centre Union victory threatened to accelerate the nation's movements along a dangerously radical path. Of particular concern was the influence that Andreas Papandreou and the radical wing of the party would have on a Centre Union government. Andreas had spent many years in the United States, where he espoused a form of Kennedy-era liberalism, but the Right feared he, more so than his father, would infect Greek society with his radical politics. Viewing the situation through its Civil War lenses, the Right genuinely believed that a Centre Union victory would beckon destruction (Nikolakopoulos 2001: 45). Deviation from the constitution and suspension of political life were also suggested by Karamanlis, but he called for a 'controlled democracy' rather than a dictatorship (Kouroundis 2018: 71–133).

The coup took place on the morning of 21 April. It not only took the Greek people by surprise, but also most of the shadow state: the US embassy, the monarchy (except some of its staff) and the military chiefs (Karakatsanis and Swarts 2007: 43). Tanks rolled into the centre of Athens. Politicians were arrested and removed to secure locations. The coup leaders suspended the constitution of 1952, abolished political parties, banned demonstrations and imposed press censorship. Predictably, thousands of leftists were interned in prisons or exiled to island camps.

The train of events on the first day also made it clear that the shadow state was deeply divided by the coup. Later that morning, a startled Constantine II received its leaders, Colonel Georgios Papadopoulos, Brigadier General Stylianos Pattakos and Colonel Nikolaos Makarezos, who delivered a document stating that they had the blessing of their commander in chief, General Grigorios Spandidakis. The conspirators sought the legitimacy that only the king could bestow upon them, but they were also prepared to move forward without his blessing. This was clearly not the dictatorship that much of the political elite wanted, partly because they could not control it, and partly because its leaders were considered vulgar upstarts. Class was an important factor here. The leading fifteen officers came from humble backgrounds; many had a traditional village upbringing and resented the social elites that dominated the upper echelons of the military and the state (Close 2002: 117). Aside from believing they were grounded in the 'real' Greece, the conspirators also believed that only they, as salt-of-the-earth patriots, possessed the will and fortitude to save Greece from communism and from modernity's corrupting influences.

To the wider world, the regime was referred to as 'the Colonels', but Greeks described it as 'the Junta' (*i Chounta*). International condemnation came quickly, including from the United States, albeit temporarily

(Karakatsanis and Swarts 2007). By this stage, Washington had developed a more cynical assessment of Greece as more 'Third World' than European: as a country unable to grasp the nettle of political modernisation. The apparent lack of political maturity displayed since 1963 required, according to State Department papers, 'a deviation in Greek constitutional development'. It was not a case of 'whether *force majeure* would be applied to the political situation but rather who would apply it' (Schmitz 2006: 61–2). The Colonels were not seen as an ideal solution, but they were preferable to another Papandreou government. That attitude was also expressed more tersely with gendered language. When US ambassador Phillips Talbot decried the 'rape of democracy', the CIA operative in Athens, John Maury, quipped, 'how can you rape a whore?' (Ganser 2005: 221). The respected *New York Times* columnist Cyrus Sulzberger responded to the 'rape of democracy' cry by claiming Greece was not a 'virgin'. He reasoned that there had already been eight coups since the First World War (Sulzberger 1970).

The Junta seized power without a coherent theory or programme. The events of 21 April were celebrated as a 'revolution' and the regime claimed initially to operate through a 'revolutionary council', but it did not promise innovation or a new order as Metaxas did in 1936. On the contrary, coup leaders considered their role was that of a praetorian guard. Papadopoulos stated that the regime would oversee a transition to a directed or managed democracy, one in which hierarchy had to be respected and citizens had to exercise self-discipline. His fears were typical of those who believed modernity had to be contained by authoritarian rule. Papadopoulos tried to convey that progressive ideas and the influences of more advanced societies had generated unreasonably high aspirations in Greek society, even in the remotest villages. Such expectations, he claimed, bred anarchism, which had to be suppressed by a strong paternalistic state (Papadopoulos 1968: 140–1). The '21 April Revolution' was therefore presented as a temporary, moderating measure: a parenthesis. The dictatorship's self-proclaimed purpose was to guarantee modernisation by suppressing the social instability and political unrest that arose from it. Aside from applying controls to modernisation, the Junta saw its mission as reinstituting the values espoused by the Right, which were a combination of virulent anti-communism and ultra-nationalism. Its slogan, *Ellas Ellinon Christianon*, literally 'Greece of Christian Greeks', linked the dictatorship to the nationalism of the Civil War.

Over time, however, Papadopoulos, backed by Pattakos and Makarezos, put his stamp on the regime. Formally, Greece still had a government and a prime minister (Konstantinos Kollias) appointed by the king, but real power was exercised by the Junta, which had taken the precaution of removing from the armed forces officers who might be more loyal to Constantine than the Junta. A purge eventually saw one in six officers forced into retirement (Veremis 1997: 161). Nor did they trust the king himself, who, they learned, had been plotting a countercoup with his loyal generals. That attempted coup took place on 13 December, but it was poorly organised and unravelled quickly. On hearing news of its failure, the king and his family fled to Rome. In keeping with its praetorian role, the regime quickly appointed a regent, mindful that the monarchy was still venerated in the armed forces and in regions like the Peloponnese. However, the botched countercoup strengthened the power of the Junta leaders, who were now confident enough to claim the most senior government positions.

For most of the dictatorship, Papadopoulos was prime minister (December 1967–October 1973). Pattakos served as his deputy, although he shared the job towards the end with Makarezos, who oversaw economic affairs. Each member of the troika also held other ministries. Papadopoulos also acted as regent (1972–3). A dubious plebiscite in September 1968 ratified the new constitution, which ignored civil rights, made the military independent from civilian oversight and ratified the Junta's power. As one French commentator put it: 'La Grèce n'est, pour l'instant, qu'une royaume sans roi, un régime libérale sans libertés, une parlementarisme sans Parlement' ('Greece for now is a monarchy without a monarch, has a liberal regime but no liberties, a parliamentary system but no parliament') (Woodhouse 1985: 56).

Inevitably, the state apparatus was purged of those who did not possess the 'right' mindset. Government positions were also filled with appointees. Very few of them were experienced politicians. Inevitably, corruption increased as friends of the dictatorship were given access to jobs, licences and cheap loans. While in power, the Junta imposed martial law, filled the jails with political prisoners, restored the surveillance systems and resurrected the use of loyalty certificates (Figure 7.3). It overhauled school curricula and restored *katharevousa* as the compulsory medium. Children were subjected to state propaganda, and to much more parading and patriotic rituals. Every textbook had the regime's insignia, which featured a silhouette of a soldier superimposed on the Phoenix rising from the ashes. The regime curbed what it regarded as foreign intrusions, like long hair and miniskirts, both of which they banned. It drove protest music and the Ottoman and drug-associated genre rebetika underground.

Figure 7.3 *Students brought before a military court in Thessaloniki, 1970.* © *Antonis Liakos*

Yet the Junta endured for seven years, largely because it could rely on the army, which shared the regime's cultural preoccupations and had remained loyal during the countercoup. It also benefited from the fact that the Greek economy continued to grow, which meant the Junta reaped the political benefits of relatively high employment and growing state revenue. Economic boom conditions partly explain why the Junta did not encounter much resistance during its early years, as did the fact that there was no bloodletting as often happened after a coup in Latin America. But internationally the response to the coup was hostile, and it generated a new wave of philhellenism that was inspired by the legacy of Classical Greece and was committed to the restoration of democracy. Greek exiles and émigrés, including celebrities such as Mikis Theodorakis and Melina Mercouri, organised anti-Junta campaigns. Such movements ensured that the Junta was treated as a pariah. Greece was expelled from the Council of Europe in 1969 for human rights violations, and it was the subject of international sanctions. Yet it had at least one crucial friend. It retained the support of the United States, which at worst imposed token sanctions such as temporary reductions in military aid.

Domestically, the regime lacked a mass constituency, and it was generally regarded as a parvenu in politics. The first significant protests took place at the funerals of Georgios Papandreou in November 1968 and the Nobel Prize-winning poet Giorgos Seferis in September 1971. The most important attacks against the regime were Alexandros Panagoulis' failed assassination attempt on Papadopoulos on 13 August 1968, and the mutiny by royalist naval officers on the destroyer *Velos* on 23 May 1973. Until that year, however, the regime had not encountered significant domestic challenges. The political opposition was split into several organisations, including PAM (Panhellenic Anti-dictatorship Front) and PAK (Patriotic Liberation Movement), which included Theodorakis and was led by Andreas Papandreou. The communist Left splintered following the Soviet invasion of Czechoslovakia in 1968 into pro-Soviet and Eurocommunist factions, but the period saw the emergence of a more diverse Greek Left that included Papandreou's PAK, which was a populist movement that served as a precursor to PASOK. The leaders of the two largest parliamentary parties (illegal during the years 1967–74) reacted cautiously to the regime. Some of them, like Karamanlis and his former colleague Evangelos Averoff, left open communication channels with the military. But even they came out publicly against the dictatorship in April 1973, when the first cracks in the regime appeared.

The fall of the Colonels

The regime did try to build a popular support base. Such populist measures as clamping down on tax evasion by the rich (at least in its first year), promoting sport and spending heavily on public amenities, did have some traction even among those who hated the Junta. But it failed to develop a a significant social constituency as Europe's interwar fascists had done. A possible exception was the ever-shrinking agrarian population, whose members benefited from generous loans, debt cancellation and other assistance measures, giving many of them the sense that their own people were in power (Bika 2012: 245–48). Critically, the Colonels failed to rally the Right. They were hampered by the fact that they did not enjoy the approval of either the monarchy or conservative politicians. Nor did Papadopoulos seem capable of growing into his role. He lacked the charisma and political judgement needed to overcome his low social standing and lack of refinement. He was no Metaxas or Papagos. The Colonels did appeal to people who shared their social profile and Cold War mentality: the ardent anti-communists, ultra-nationalists and those who believed in a strong authoritarian state. However, they could not rely on the wholehearted support of this constituency either. Such hard men as Brigadier Dimitrios Ioannidis, the head of the military police and one of the original conspirators of April 1967, was wary of Papadopoulos' attempts to liberalise the system and appease international criticism. The regime's relaxation of censorship laws, for example, was the type of measure that such reactionaries believed would permit the return of anarchy.

The Junta began to unravel during the global economic crisis of 1973. Like its predecessors it had promised deregulation, reduced taxation and the expansion of credit. In 1972 Greece had both high growth rates and (near) full employment, but a sudden fivefold increase in oil prices, from $3 to $15 per barrel, led to a hike in industrial costs and skyrocketing inflation, which reached as high as 30 per cent. The Junta's anti-inflation policies had the effect of reducing corporate lending and cutting back on construction, which was still the largest sector in the economy, leading inevitably to higher unemployment. Suddenly, the ruling regime faced an economic crisis and a huge political problem (Iordanoglou 2020: xl–xliii).

Devastated by high inflation and unemployment, the citizenry was more willing to express its discontents openly. That was especially true of university students, who spearheaded social protests, and who, inspired by student movements around the world, particularly in Thailand and Chile, increasingly made their voices heard. Students were incensed by state repression and brutal treatment by the police. The violent suppression and the mass arrest of students at the occupation of the University of Athens law school in February 1973 marked the beginning of a period of intense student unrest. Their protests persisted for ten months, which again placed the dictatorship under the international spotlight (Kornetis 2013: 228–9, 246–8). Meanwhile, the monarchy's alleged role in the *Velos* mutiny gave Papadopoulos the excuse to establish a republic. He made himself president and promised elections for a 'managed parliament'. He appointed Spyros Markezinis as his prime minister. Markezinis had been one of the few experienced politicians who took up Papadopoulos' invitation to cooperate in the military regime's new political plans. These promises, followed by an amnesty that released thousands of political prisoners from exile, did not convince the students that the government was sincere. So, the unrest continued. Matters came to a head in the wake of the global oil crisis. On 4 November violence broke out during a memorial service marking the fifth anniversary of Georgios

Papandreou's passing. The climactic event was the student occupation of the Athens Polytechnic (*Politechnio*) between 14 and 17 November 1973. This spontaneous protest evolved into a general mass protest. The students even set up a radio station that broadcast calls for action against the Junta.

The occupation of the Polytechnic transformed the city centre into a sea of mass street demonstrations. Students took over universities and schools in Thessaloniki, Ioannina and Patras. These actions created an anti-Junta mood across Greece. The movement provided a unique opportunity for the Greeks, especially the young, to express openly and to the world their opposition to the dictatorship (Kornetis 2013: 257–70). But in the early hours of 17 November, the tanks rolled in, and the protests were brutally crushed. Thousands were arrested and eighty were killed.

The event, which made headlines worldwide and brought the dictatorship into further disrepute, gave the extremists within the regime an opportunity to replace 'the Colonels' and impose a regime that was even more restrictive and oppressive. On 25 November, Brigadier Ioannidis and the military police deposed Papadopoulos and his colleagues, claiming that they had been corrupted by the spoils of office and had betrayed the goals and ideals of the 21 April Revolution. Ioannidis replaced the president and the prime minister with his own men. Months of intense repression ensued, as restrictions that had been relaxed in recent years, such as press censorship and curfews, were restored.

However, the new regime was staffed by officers and security personnel with even less political experience than their predecessors, and with no political programme. Facing an impasse, the Ioannidis regime revived irredentism. In Cyprus, where long-running negotiations between Greek and Turkish Cypriot leaders seemed close to collapse, Ioannidis instigated a *coup d'état*. On 15 July 1974, Archbishop Makarios, the island's president and no friend of the Junta, was overthrown, and Nikos Sampson, an ex-EOKA (National Organisation of Cypriot Militants) executioner, declared himself president with the aim to annex Cyprus to Greece. Ioannidis was convinced that Ankara would not respond to this major treaty violation, but it did. On 20 July, Turkish forces invaded Cyprus, bringing Greece and Turkey to the brink of war. A general mobilisation followed, but it soon became apparent that the Greek armed forces were ill prepared for a major war (Kızılyürek 2019: 727–60).

Unable to face the consequences of its actions, the Ioannidis regime simply evaporated. On 23 July the president, General Phaidon Gizikis, having agreed with other senior military staff that the state had to be returned to civilian stewardship, called a meeting with former senior politicians, including ex-prime ministers, who agreed to recall Karamanlis to oversee the transition. Ioannidis attended the meeting but was told to leave. As he left the room, he effectively 'left' politics. He continued in his role as head of the military police for the next seven weeks (Woodhouse 1985: 163), but was eventually arrested, tried and sent to prison, along with the other Junta leaders. Papadopoulos and Ioannidis were convicted of numerous crimes but spared the death penalty. Each died in prison, in 1999 and 2010, respectively. Makarezos and Pattakos were also given long prison sentences.

It took a catastrophe to end the dictatorship and the shadow state. To borrow the words of Lampedusa in *Il Gatopardo*, a phrase that has been frequently applied to modern Italian politics, Greek conservative politicians did not fully comprehend that 'everything must change so that everything can stay the same'. They refused to adjust to the rapidly transforming society that was more urban, better educated and seeking a greater share of power. Crucially, they failed to attain the support of the urban middle classes, which joined the left-wing push against the dictatorship (Valden 2018). The crisis of 1974 also changed US–Greek relations fundamentally. The United States lost credibility among Greek elites for its inability to restrain the military and prevent the catastrophe on Cyprus, but especially because of its unwillingness to restrain Turkey from expanding its occupation of Cyprus in August. After that, all annual protest marches in Athens would end at the US Embassy. Greece withdrew from NATO, gradually downgraded relations with the US and simultaneously upgraded it links with Europe.

On 24 July, Karamanlis, aboard the French president's plane, landed in Athens at 3 a.m. A few hours later, he was sworn in as prime minister to form a government. The nation had turned a new page in its political history.

Note

1. https://www.bloomberg.com/news/features/2020-07-15/the-design-history-of-athens-iconic-apartments.

CHAPTER 8

The wider Greek world II: From nationalism to multiculturalism

The decades following the Second World War saw the return of the 'minorities question'. The last of the colonial empires were being dissolved and replaced by nation states, where the principle of nationality was usually interpreted in terms of state boundaries having to coincide with cultural and linguistic ones. Around the world, Greek minorities experienced the corollaries of the 'question' very differently. The most extreme examples were Egypt and Turkey, each of which expelled them. In West Germany, Greek and other southern Europeans were invited to work, but not to settle. The fact that they were dubbed *Fremdarbeiter* ('alien workers') and then with the milder term *Gastarbeiter* ('guest workers') suggested their presence raised concerns about their 'acceptability' on cultural grounds (Gatrell 2019: 143). In Britain, the United States, Canada and Australia, Greeks and Greek Cypriot immigrants were able to settle permanently, but here too governments and host societies expected newcomers to assimilate and leave their cultural baggage behind. By the later decades of the century, however, Greek Americans, Greek Canadians, Cypriot Greeks in Britain, Greek Australians and Greeks in Germany had become prosperous communities in the world's most prosperous countries. By then, most of the nations in question practised forms of multiculturalism, had outlawed ethnic discrimination and were celebrating cultural difference rather than merely tolerating it.

This chapter takes up where Chapter 3 left off, but begins with Cyprus, with its most unusual post-colonial history and its equally unusual 'minorities question'. This former British colonial territory had seen imposed upon it a 'neutered' post-colonial existence and an unworkable political system to suit the strategic interests of much greater powers (Anderson 2008). In 1974, in response to a political crisis engineered by another foreign power (Greece), Turkey violently partitioned Cyprus so that its Turkish minority did not have to live under Greek majority rule.

The 'Cyprus Problem' in international affairs, 1950–1955

Cyprus was spared the devastation of the Second World War. If anything, the island benefited from high wartime demand for its commodities, bringing high employment and giving greater bargaining power to unions, which saw a rise in membership. The colonial government also responded with a series of positive labour reforms, including a minimum wage rate. In 1941 leaders of the defunct Communist Party regrouped and, with the blessing of Moscow, established a new party: AKEL. Like Greece's EAM, AKEL was a popular movement with a progressive agenda that included state-funded welfare and fairer tax policies. It was also committed to unification (*Enosis*) with Greece. While it recognised Turkish nationalism in a bid to appeal to the Turkish Cypriot community, AKEL nevertheless regarded *Enosis* as the key to emancipation from colonialism. The term carried many meanings. All Greek Cypriot groups believed it would bring freedom from foreign oppression and foreign-imposed backwardness (Alecou 2016: 13). And certainly, all Greek Cypriot parties had to be pro-*Enosis* to be viable in electoral terms. For AKEL, the fight for *Enosis* was a fight against the British, which therefore made it a genuine anti-colonial movement (Alecou 2016: 16).

AKEL quickly became the leading political force on the island. Membership rose from 3,224 in 1942 to 5,000 by the end of the war. On 21 March, during the first municipal elections since the early 1930s, it won Limassol and Famagusta. In the 1946 elections, AKEL won all the cities and towns, and six of the nine rural municipalities. When the British convened a meeting to establish a Consultative Assembly in 1947, it was a communist party that spoke for most Greek Cypriots.

Its ascendancy proved to be short-lived, however. Conditions seemed propitious for the Left in 1945, given the fascist defeat in Europe and the Labour victory in Britain. But the Cold War soon blanketed the world, and the hostility of British authorities and all other parties towards AKEL hardened. The Church of Cyprus was the chief alternative centre of authority. Under Archbishop Makarios II (1947–50), the Church made clear its opposition to colonialism *and* to communism: it sent a message through the press that no communist could be a Christian and a Greek. AKEL's decision to participate in the Consultative Assembly, which was seen as an opportunity to influence constitutional change (Alecou 2016: 169), nevertheless exposed it to accusations that it was not committed to *Enosis*. The Consultative Assembly was organised by the British in response to local pressure for better governance through constitutional reform, but it was also seen by many as a means of pre-serving British sovereignty, hence the Church and parties of the Right refused to participate. By participating, AKEL suffered electoral defeat in the following elections, after which it reverted to an uncompromis-ing pro-*Enosis* position to regain lost ground.

Much had changed in Cypriot society since the burning of Government House in 1931. While still keen to address social issues, the vast majority of Greek Cypriots were now focused on *Enosis*. The shift reflected a global anti-colonial mood inside the world's colonial terri-tories, especially as the colonial masters had used the resources of their empires to defeat Germany, Italy and Japan, and were now seeking to exploit them further for the purposes of reconstruction. When the war ended, anti-colonial leaders like Jawaharlal Nehru in India, Kwame Nkrumah in Ghana and Sultan Mohammed V of Morocco made it clear in the international press and in public forums that colonialism 'had to go', and that a new world based on progressive principles had to replace the old (Gildea 2019: 69). In most European empires, the colonised had seen their masters humiliated by the Axis powers, had (again) demonstrated loyalty and (again) contributed blood, sweat and tears for the colonial master's war against fascist tyranny, and were now impatient for self-determination. In 1950, the Cypriot Church organ-ised a plebiscite that proved that earlier indifference to *Enosis* had been overcome. The vote in favour among Greek Cypriots was 95.7 per cent (French 2015: 94). Inevitably, these developments frightened the Turkish community, which had also been troubled by AKEL and fears of a communist takeover. From its perspective, British rule provided protection from the Greek majority, and now it was also prepared to seek it from Ankara. Its leaders advocated the island's partition, a view that was anathema to Greek Cypriots. The issue drove a deepening wedge between the two communities.

By 1950 the future of the island had become an issue known inter-nationally as 'the Cyprus Question'. In the past, Cypriots made their political claims through representations to the colonial governor and London, but in the 1950s Cypriot leaders were making approaches to Athens, Ankara and the United Nations. Equally relevant was the impact of the Cold War and the new role of the Middle East in world affairs. Cyprus' close proximity to the oil-rich Middle East and the great Cold War frontline states, Greece, Turkey and Iran, that stood between the USSR and the oilfields, made the island a vital strate-gic interest. Britain, in particular, was concerned about its access to petroleum and its loosening grip on Egypt and Palestine. There was also Britain's dream of somehow reversing its shrinking status as a world power. Indeed, the Middle East was probably Britain's most vital strategic theatre of interest. In 1956, Prime Minister Anthony Eden claimed that the retention of the island was essential to Britain's welfare: 'No Cyprus, no certain facilities to protect the supply of oil. No oil, unemployment, and hunger in Britain. It's as simple as that' (Brown 2004: 39).

Greece and Turkey were also drawn more deeply into 'the Cyprus Question'. In the past, Greece had been reluctant to alienate Britain, but after having fought against the Axis and won the first struggle in the international fight against the red menace, Greek governments began to press in international forums for unification. The British, in turn, were prepared to allow its relations with Greece to deteriorate if need be. The United States was also of the view that, given the island's strategic value, the democratic aspirations of the Greek Cypriot people took second place. Perhaps more importantly, the US also wished to appease Turkey because of its primary role in containing Soviet expansion. Turkey's concerns were twofold: to protect ethnic Turks on Cyprus and prevent it from being ceded to Greece. Turkey had relinquished its claim to the island in the Lausanne Treaty of 1923, and during the interwar years, like Greece, it tried to keep out of Cypriot affairs so as not to jeopardise relations with Britain. Ethnic Turks were even encouraged by Ankara to migrate to Anatolia. The rise of the *Enosis* movement, however, along with more active Greek state lobbying internationally, fostered a more strident Turkish position regarding the island's fate. It is important, however, to note that there were limits to how far Greek and Turkish governments were prepared to be drawn into the Cyprus imbroglio. Both were much more concerned about defence issues and the threat posed by the Soviet Union. They were, in fact, keener to sign a defence pact with Yugoslavia (the Balkan Pact of 1953). In each case, governments had to be goaded into action on Cyprus by the press and public opinion. Thus, following the Greek Cypriot plebiscite in 1950, the Turkish nationalist press transformed Cyprus into a critical public issue, yet it was as late as the end of 1953 that Ankara began to meet regularly with Turkish Cypriot representatives.

The momentum for *Enosis* was provided by Cypriot bishops, who used the 1950 plebiscite to steal a march on AKEL, and who in October elected the 39-year-old Michael Mouskos as Archbishop under the name Makarios III. He had the energy, charisma and political savvy needed to rally Cypriot society and draw mass support away from AKEL. Critically, he brought the *Enosis* cause on to the international stage. As Britain refused even to discuss the matter, Makarios set out to mobilise public opinion in Greece, which compelled the government of Sofoklis Venizelos in February 1951 to proclaim its official support for *Enosis*. In November, Greece reluctantly brought the matter to the United Nations' attention and raised it again in September 1953, although it preferred to deal directly with Britain and reach a bilateral solution. British intransigence eventually forced Papagos' government to go yet again before the United Nations in August 1954. But in the ensuing debate in December, the British minister responsible for the colonies stated that Cyprus would never be granted full independence. Britain also did its best to draw Turkey into the Cyprus imbroglio, because Ankara supported British sovereignty and would block any chance of *Enosis* in the future. Indeed, 'Turkish objections' to *Enosis* and to independence became Britain's chief argument at the UN (Holland 1999: 43–4).

The EOKA insurgency and the short road to Independence

His diplomatic offensive having failed, Makarios authorised on 11 January 1955 a new terror offensive against the British. A few months earlier, an armed movement had been formed by Georgios Grivas, a Cypriot-born colonel in the Greek army, who a decade earlier had led the right-wing security force, 'X', an organisation that was mentioned above (see p. 171). After a meeting with Makarios in Athens in July 1952, Grivas formed EOKA (*Ethniki Organosis Kyprion Agoniston/* National Organisation of Cypriot Militants), and on 1 April 1955 it carried out a series of bombings against British installations across the island. The second wave of attacks on 19 June targeted the police, military personnel and government officials.

Between April 1955 and March 1957, EOKA and its supporters tested the British forces' mettle with numerous acts of sabotage, assassinations, bombings and rioting, which in turn forced Britain to send more troops and material. The appointment in October 1955 of the empire's most senior military officer, Field Marshal Sir John Harding, reflected the gravity of the situation (French 2015: 91). Initially, Harding aimed to stabilise the situation by eliminating what he believed was a small group of insurgents, and only to allow negotiations for a political solution. He hoped to find a solution with Makarios that would set the conditions under which the Cypriot people could be won over and convinced of the benefits of British rule. He also wished to present Cypriots with a show of strength. Soon after arriving, he declared a state of emergency, submitting Cypriot society to unfamiliar restrictive conditions. By doing so, Harding played into Grivas' hands. EOKA drew the British into a conflict that would unsettle Cypriot society, make the island ungovernable, and mobilise it against colonial rule. Excessive colonial retaliation, including executions, incarcerations, increasingly brutal treatment of unruly civilians and mass protests (Figure 8.1), all of which were well publicised internationally, discredited Britain on the world stage. The ultimate aim was to induce Britain to take flight rather than fight (French 2015: 48).

Although it never had more than a few hundred fighters, EOKA appeared to have some 25,000 people serving in various auxiliary roles, and it had cells throughout the island (French 2015: 64). However, the guerrilla campaign in the Troodos Mountains failed because the British were better trained and armed. EOKA could never hope to win through conventional warfare, but was very effective with its terror campaign, especially as it enjoyed popular support. Using an elaborate intelligence network, it penetrated the police and the colonial government. Its operatives provided information on when and where to attack, and they forewarned EOKA of impending security

Figure 8.1 *Greek Cypriot schoolboy protesters arrested by British soldiers in 1955 during the Cyprus Emergency.* © Alamy E0MM21

operations. Greek Cypriot fighters assassinated British personnel not just at checkpoints or other military posts but also while shopping or resting in their homes. Recruits were mainly poor young men between 16 and 25, whom EOKA trained to be merciless killers. The organisation's effectiveness had much to do with Grivas himself, who enjoyed absolute authority, and whose experience leading 'X' during the Greek Civil War prepared him well for orchestrating a terror campaign. Grivas made all the significant decisions from his secret hideout on the outskirts of Limassol, from where orders were issued through couriers to every part of the island. The intention of Grivas' 'hit-and-run' tactics was to induce a heavy-handed British response, which in turn would alienate the Cypriot people and encourage them to join the rebellion. As Grivas put it, the British were like 'tanks' searching for 'field mice', although that also meant that civilians bore the brunt of the counterinsurgency operations (Lim 2018: 18). Ordinary Cypriots were subjected to constant searches of their homes and businesses, and they had to endure punishments and pay fines collectively.

EOKA's popularity grew, but its tactics also divided Cypriots. Collaboration with the resistance was often motivated by fear, for EOKA dealt ruthlessly with people who were linked in any way with the British, including women married to British personnel. The police force lost most of its Greek officers for fear of reprisals. Neighbours often beat up neighbours employed by the colonial government. In the later stages of the insurgency, when Grivas successfully orchestrated a policy of boycotts and non-cooperation designed to make the colonial administration and economy unworkable, many Greek Cypriots complied because they feared reprisal. The turn to intimidation and violence alienated much of Greek Cypriot society, including many middle-class *Enosis* advocates. Many were incensed by the fact that the new politics set Cypriot against Cypriot, or because EOKA was led by a right-wing coterie who brought the politics of the Greek Civil War to Cyprus. As a virulent anti-communist, Grivas also orchestrated actions against AKEL, which still had a large support base. Overall, 187 'traitors' were executed during the conflict, many of them leftists.

A more significant cleavage, however, was opening between the Greek and Turkish communities. Grivas deliberately avoided targeting the Turkish community, but the great majority of police officers were Turkish, and hence most of the attacks on police resulted in Turkish casualties. Turkish police officers, in turn, were implicated in the heavy-handed treatment of Greek protesters. In Trikomo, for example, Turkish police attacked the protesters with batons, and a British officer witnessed a policeman throwing a 2-year-old child from a window (French 2015: 226). A factor explaining the proliferation of the violence was the British banning of AKEL in December 1956. This move created a sizeable political void because AKEL was the only mass movement prepared to negotiate with colonial authorities.

Most importantly, the British had arrested Makarios a month earlier and exiled him to the Seychelles. AKEL was proscribed because the British were especially worried that the communists might capitalise on the emergency. However, with Makarios unable to influence Cyprus' affairs, the British were left with Grivas, who remained hidden in the shadows and was not interested in negotiations. In March 1957, however, Grivas was forced to declare a unilateral truce because of the effectiveness of British counterinsurgency actions in recent months. EOKA ceased its activities for much of 1957, but Grivas used the interim to reorganise and rebuild EOKA, launching a new round of terror attacks at the end of the year and an effective non-cooperation campaign in 1958 (Lim 2018: 18).

The insurgency now took a more dangerous turn. EOKA and then the Turkish government began to incite inter-communal violence for strategic purposes. It was around this time that the British effectively transformed the capital into a divided city, which it has remained ever since. On 30 May 1956, a month after the eruption of violence, colonial authorities installed barbed-wire barricades that separated the Turkish and the Greek zones (Kızılyürek 2019: 192). Initially, EOKA's strategy was to draw security forces away from beleaguered guerrilla units in the mountains. Ankara encouraged rioting on 25–6 January 1958 to disrupt the plans proposed by the then governor, Sir Hugh Foot, for Cypriot self-determination (French 2015: 258–9). The riots, which saw four Turks killed by security forces, opened a front between the Turkish Cypriot community and the colonial government, which alarmed the British, as they relied on Turkish police. To appease the community and Ankara, Britain granted Turkey a veto in all future negotiations. In the meantime, Turkish Cypriots had formed an equally ruthless equivalent to EOKA, the Turkish Resistance Movement or TMT (*Türk Mukavemet Teşkilatı*). It was established in July 1957 and was just as capable as EOKA in rallying and terrorising its community. It, too, hunted down its own collaborators and leftists (Kızılyürek 2019: 229–83). Their aim, and that of Ankara, was to incite disorder to secure the island's partitioning. In June 1958, leaders of the Greek and Turkish communities began to mobilise for a sectarian struggle. Following the massacre of Greek Cypriots in Kioneli/Gönyeli on 12 June 1958, TMT and EOKA ramped up the inter-communal killings. It was an exceptionally violent summer, as the perpetrators did not spare children, women or the aged (Kızılyürek 2019: 345). It was at this point that Turkish Cypriots began seeking security in specifically Turkish enclaves, much as Greeks fled to regions under firmer Greek control. There were 252 mixed villages in 1931, but by 1960 there were only 114, and even in the remaining mixed villages, Turkish and Greek neighborhoods and markets functioned separately. It proved to be the first stage of the island's partition (Ioannou 2020: 46). The colonial government now faced the prospect of an all-out sectarian civil war; consequently, its security forces faced the prospect of fighting on two fronts. On 5 August the two sides agreed to a truce, but the British were now resigned to the fact that finding a political solution acceptable to both Greek and Turkish Cypriots was almost impossible. With the threat of a sectarian civil war that might also start a war between Greece and Turkey, the British released Makarios from his exile in the Seychelles. Once the British government under Harold Macmillan (1957–63) allowed Turkey to participate in talks about the island's future, Makarios effectively abandoned *Enosis* and accepted independence as the only way forward.

In the meantime, the British government had been trying to broker a political solution. Simply exiting would open the prospect of a war between Greece and Turkey, which had serious Cold War security implications. Macmillan saw that Britain's interests in the Middle East could be served by just having military bases on Cyprus, 'two Gibraltars' at the more critical end of the Mediterranean. That left the door open for Cypriot independence. This proposal fitted well with Macmillan's vision of an empire transitioning into a 'commonwealth' from which Britain could still benefit, and he would attain Mediterranean bases much larger than Gibraltar (French 2015: 289). However, Macmillan's solution also involved establishing separate Greek and Turkish administrations, which was acceptable to Turkish Cypriots because it was seen as setting the stage for partition, but unacceptable to Greek Cypriots (French 2015: 271). In December 1958, the Turkish and Greek governments, each of which needed a solution in order to focus on more pressing issues vis-à-vis the Soviet Union, stepped in and took the lead in finding a resolution with the contending parties (French 2015: 287–8). An agreement was signed in Zurich in February 1959. The Republic of Cyprus came into being in August 1960. EOKA and TMT ceased fighting and declared an armistice (Kızılyürek 2019: 374).

The first Cypriot Republic, 1960–1974

The Greek Cypriot people succeeded in forcing an end to colonial rule, but they attained neither genuine political independence nor a workable constitution. Neither the Greek nor the Turkish community had cause to celebrate, as each had been explicitly denied their principal desires: *Enosis* and *Taksim* (meaning 'partition') respectively. The Treaty of Guarantee, signed on 16 August 1960, determined that Cyprus could not join any other state or be partitioned. The new republic's sovereignty was compromised by the fact that Britain, Turkey and Greece were designated as guarantor powers; any could intervene in its affairs if the settlement was breached by the parties. In essence, the arrangement protected the Turkish Cypriot community, since only the Greek Cypriots would want to breach it, in which case they would incur reprisals from Turkey. The only satisfied party was Britain, which received its two large bases in the Akrotiri and Dekelia areas respectively, amounting to 252 sq. km.

Another source of Greek Cypriot disaffection was that the Turkish minority, which formed less than 20 per cent of the population, had been granted more powers than were warranted by their numbers. According to the constitution agreed to at Zurich, the president had to be a Greek and the vice president a Turk, and each could veto legislation. The composition of the legislature and public service was divided 70/30, and the army 60/40. The latter was a major problem, especially as the Turkish Cypriots insisted on distinct Turkish and Greek units: the Greek side feared a sizeable Turkish force would eventually be deployed to achieve partition. At the municipal government level, the two communities had separate voting blocks, which gave the Turkish minority great powers even where their numbers were very small. In the state's legislature a majority of Turkish delegates was needed to pass acts relating to defence, taxation and electoral matters.

Stable and effective governance would also be hampered by deep mutual mistrust. The Greek community had been handed a humiliating solution that merely fuelled the desire for *Enosis*. The first government, led by Archbishop Makarios, contained a large number of EOKA men who were especially keen to resume the struggle. The Turkish community, led by TMT men, expected their Greek neighbours would never accept the Zurich agreement, and therefore continued to believe that partition was the only realistic solution. Neither party regarded the bicommunal government as legitimate or permanent. Greek- and Turkish-Cypriot paramilitary organisations had been busy importing arms and men from Greece and Turkey respectively, each preparing for an anticipated breakdown in communal relations (M. Varnava 2020: 54). The new Greek clandestine organisation was named 'Akritas', and was led by Nikos Sampson and Polykarpos Yorkadjis, both of whom also happened to be ministers in the Makarios government. In fact, Akritas, whose mission was to prepare for a final confrontation with the Turkish Cypriots, was known to Makarios and the Greek military leadership (Kızılyürek 2019: 442–61).

Dysfunction affected all areas of government that required inter-communal agreement. The parties could not agree on such crucial issues as how to organise the military, government education funding and taxation policy. In the five major urban centres, where Greek and Turkish communities ran separate municipal governments, there were intractable territorial demarcation disputes. Any proposal to develop more workable arrangements at all levels of government was usually thwarted on suspicion that it might enhance Greek or Turkish powers, or further the *Enosis* or *Taksim* causes. In November 1963, without notifying his Turkish vice president (Dodd 2010: 48), Makarios proposed amendments to the constitution and presented them to London, Ankara and Athens. These included the removal of the president's and vice president's veto powers, and that municipal administration, the justice system and the armed forces no longer be organised along Greek–Turkish lines. He also requested that the proportion of Greeks and Turks in the civil service should reflect Greek and Turkish population numbers.

The flat rejection of Makarios' proposals by Ankara and the Turkish Cypriot leadership triggered communal violence, which began on 21 December in Nicosia and then spread throughout the island. As the violence unfolded over the ensuing months, with mass attacks, hostage-taking, assassinations and executions, the burning of villages and revenge attacks, all Turkish Cypriots fled from towns and areas where they were in the minority, and found safety in the enclaves. On 30 December 1963, the dividing line separating Nicosia's Greek and Turkish communities was enforced, and a buffer or 'dead' zone, later renamed 'the Green Line', was established. By August, 25,000 Turkish Cypriots had abandoned or been forced out of their homes, deserting seventy-two mixed villages and twenty-four exclusively Turkish ones (M. Varnava 2020: 139). Politicians and public servants had also withdrawn from, or were prevented from participating in, their roles. For all intents and purposes, the island was now partitioned: the enclaves were small but would eventually expand to account for about 10 per cent of the island (M. Varnava 2020: 141; Kızılyürek 2019: 493–524).

Britain sent its peacekeepers in January and began negotiations, but these efforts failed. The matter was put before the United Nations, which passed a resolution on 4 March 1964 to despatch a peacekeeping force. In the meantime, in Ankara, the troubled government of İsmet İnönü had hoped for a joint British and Greek intervention, but public pressure at home forced it to take unilateral action. By June, it was ready to despatch military forces, but was stopped from doing so by the United States: President Lyndon Johnson wrote a famously forthright letter to İnönü that essentially demanded Turkey desist from taking any action (*Middle East Journal* 1966: 386–7).

The violence abated by autumn, and a stalemate ensued. For the next few years, a series of proposals were put by the UN, Britain, Turkey, Greece and the US, none of which were likely to win a consensus. For the moment, the Greek Cypriot side had made significant gains, having claimed control over the island's administration and services. To the chagrin of the Turkish Cypriot leadership, the Makarios government was also being treated by the international community as *the* government of Cyprus. Britain's decision to deliver on promises of financial aid in March 1965 (£1.5 million) to the Makarios government drew protests from the Turkish Cypriot camp, whose efforts to attract international sympathy for their plight seemed to have little effect (Dodd 2010: 71).

Makarios nevertheless faced a series of significant problems. He was firmly convinced that *Enosis* was not feasible, but he had to contend with hardliners in his own ranks who wished to resume the dream of unification with Greece. The leading proponent for *Enosis* was Grivas, who had strengthened his hand in the Greek Cypriot military forces during the recent crisis and had the ear of the monarchy and politicians in Athens. Grivas had been lobbying them to support a fresh struggle against the Makarios government (M. Varnava 2020: 187–9). Both communities since 1955 had been terrorised by their own paramilitary organisations, which enforced a regime of censorship and control, and eliminated dissidents and independent voices. Journalists and trade unionists from both communities, as well as members of AKEL, were tortured or executed (Kızılyürek 2019: 649–715, 852–3). The other problem was the Turkish Cypriot community, which was much more resilient than the archbishop's government had anticipated. Makarios understood that a permanent political solution required an accommodation, and expected his opponents would be more amenable, given that uprooted Turkish Cypriots would wish to return to their homes and jobs. Despite the community's straitened circumstances, whether in a spirit of communal solidarity or because they were coerced by TMT to stay put, Turkish Cypriots stood their ground and refused to bargain away any of their constitutional rights (Dodd 2010: 53–4). Indeed, over time, the enclaves were being developed as the basis for a Turkish Cypriot homeland. Led initially by TMT leader Kenan Çoygun, Turkish Cypriot politicians, bureaucrats and judges eventually created a government authority that encompassed all the enclaves (M. Varnava 2020: 142–5).

Communal violence resumed in November 1967 following a violent clash over the control of a road between Nicosia and Limassol. The incident, in which twenty-eight Turkish Cypriots were killed, brought renewed threats of Turkish military intervention, which in turn raised the prospect of war between Turkey and Greece. To avert a destructive struggle between two NATO allies, US Foreign Secretary Cyrus Vance was despatched to Athens and Ankara. The Greek government, which by this stage was in the hands of the military Junta, whose leaders were aware of Turkey's overwhelming military strength and strategic advantages, was forced to make concessions that would appease Ankara, such as the withdrawal of some 7,000 Greek military personnel that were present on the island. In fact, the Junta wanted the Cyprus issue to be resolved to stabilise relations with Turkey; Makarios was constantly pressured to make concessions (M. Varnava 2020: 350).

In the meantime, Greek and Turkish community leaders agreed to resume direct talks. A series of difficult meetings took place over the ensuing years, led, for the most part, by former TMT leader Rauf Denktaş, the most formidable Turkish Cypriot political figure of his generation, and the leading Greek Cypriot politician after Makarios, Glafcos Clerides. The issue of how to organise the municipal councils remained the most significant stumbling block, essentially because the Turks placed a premium on controlling their communal affairs. Their leaders insisted on pressing collective, as opposed to individual, rights and their resolve was strengthened by the knowledge that their plight was considered a significant policy priority in Ankara. Each year there were new rounds of talks, but each time discussions would grind to a halt. One British diplomat referred to the process as being in a 'benign stalemate', yet both sides needed a breakthrough (M. Varnava 2020: 441). The Turkish community did not wish to be confined to the enclaves forever: many Turks were in fact working in Greek-controlled territories. Nor did the Greek community wish to live with the permanent threat of Turkish military intervention. The 1967 crisis had demonstrated how easily and quickly that could happen. Between June 1972 and July 1974, a new negotiation formula was organised under the auspices of the United Nations, and involving a representative of the then General Secretary Kurt Waldheim, as well as constitutional experts from Greece and Turkey, appeared to give the negotiations a 'kiss of life' (M. Varnava 2020: 537–8). By July 1974 constitutional arrangements had been devised to give Turkish Cypriots enough control over their communal affairs. At the same time, there was agreement on proportional representation in government, judicial administration and the civil service, and the removal of the vice president's veto powers. A breakthrough seemed more promising than ever, but political conditions within Cyprus itself, and indeed in Athens and Ankara, also made it seem as if a breakthrough was *less* likely than ever.

Turkish invasion and the refugee crisis, 1974

In both camps there were powerful elements opposed to any agreement. This was especially true of the Greek camp and its staunchest *Enosis* proponents. Elections held in 1970 also suggested that this opposition to a negotiated settlement had considerable support in the community: a pro-*Enosis* party led by Grivas' former lieutenant Nikos Sampson polled strongly. Sampson was dubbed 'the butcher of Omorphita' by Turkish Cypriots for his role in violent clashes in Küçük Kaymaklı in December 1963. In recent years, a rift had opened between Makarios, Clerides' moderate United Party and AKEL on the one hand, and on the other, right-wing movements such as Akritas, the Phoenix *Enosis* Youth movement and the National Front, who wanted *Enosis* at any cost. Although Makarios never formally renounced *Enosis*, these right-wing parties regarded him as a traitor because he was prepared to negotiate with the Turkish community. In 1970 the National Front had been responsible for many violent political attacks and probably an attempted assassination on Makarios: the archbishop would survive several attempts on his life. In 1971 he had to contend with a new nationalist movement, EOKA-B, which Grivas had founded with the Greek military Junta's assent, which played a major supportive role. The Papadopoulos-led regime in Athens asserted the right to determine Cyprus' fate and dictate its policy, but Makarios was not a compliant supplicant. Nor did the archbishop want his homeland ruled by the Junta. A supporter of Greek pro-democracy activists, Makarios was regarded by the Junta as an enemy.

By 1973 Cypriot security forces had all but defeated EOKA-B, and on 27 January 1974, Grivas died of a heart attack. Although the chief threat to negotiations appeared to have been removed, EOKA-B retained a strong presence in the Cypriot National Guard. To this point, the Papadopoulos-led Junta had been careful to avoid provoking Turkey and heeded warnings from Washington to desist conspiring against Makarios. The succeeding Ioannidis-led Junta, which had assumed power on 25 November 1973, was much less cautious. Ioannidis had personally participated in vicious attacks on Turkish Cypriots when he was an intelligence officer a decade earlier. He was committed to *Enosis* and seemed confident that the US would restrain Turkey from responding militarily. After secret consultations with the CIA, which informed the White House, Ioannidis ordered officers of the National Guard under the command of Greek officers to overthrow Makarios. The White House, in turn, did not do enough to restrain the reckless Ioannidis; nor did it do enough to restrain the inevitable Turkish retaliation. There has been endless speculation as to whether the key US figure, Secretary of State Henry Kissinger, demonstrated either malign or purposeful neglect. The notorious Sampson took over as the interim president, which, given his well-known hostility to Turkish Cypriots, set alarm bells off in Ankara.

The coup gave the Ankara government an opportunity to invoke the Treaty of Guarantee and force a favourable solution to the Cyprus Question. On 20 July Turkish troops invaded the far northern province of Kyrenia. Paratroopers landed and cleared a corridor linking Kyrenia to Nicosia and the Turkish Cypriot enclave to the south. After playing with fire and having no effective response to the crisis, Ioannidis and the Junta fell from power on the 23rd. Sampson was removed a few days later. Turkish troops occupied about 300 sq. km by the agreed ceasefire on 22 July, although that had increased to 430 sq. km by 8 August, when high-level talks began in Geneva. By the morning of 13 August, Ankara demanded the creation of autonomous Turkish regions and set a 10 p.m. deadline for a response. Ankara's haste had to do with pressing an advantage that might be lost if the UN Security Council, set to meet in two days, issued a resolution calling for a halt to the military campaign. It also found it difficult to keep its armed forces in check. After refusing a Greek Cypriot request for a ceasefire, Ankara ordered a resumption of the offensive in the early hours of 14 August. By this time, Turkish troop numbers had increased, tanks were brought in, and the Turks enjoyed complete air domination. Within three days, Turkish forces seized over a third of the island (37 per cent).

Mass killings of Greek Cypriots in the North and Turkish Cypriots in the South, the execution of hostages during the battles, along with rape, displacement and looting, were witnessed by ordinary people of both communities (Kızılyürek 2019: 790–823). The second phase of the invasion was catastrophic for the Greek community. Families abandoned their homes and fled south before the advancing Turkish army. To encourage the flight of Greek Cypriots, the Turkish air force bombed towns and villages, and rumours of Turkish atrocities quickly spread while troops and tanks advanced slowly to ensure that territory was 'cleansed'. The Turkish president Bülent Ecevit told Kissinger that no refugees would be allowed to return to their homes (Asmussen 2008: 257). By September, there were 225,000 refugees at large: 154,000 Greeks had fled to the Greek zone, 800 Turks fled north to the Turkish zone, while about 50,000 Greeks and almost 8,000 Turks took refuge at the British bases. Some 35,000 Turks were stranded behind Greek lines, and 20,000 Greeks behind Turkish lines. By mid-1975, there were still 10,187 Turks and 10,294 Greeks behind enemy lines. Denktaş and Clerides agreed to a voluntary population exchange. Whereas most Turks moved north as soon as they could manage, most Greeks tried to stay put, but all except a few hundred Greeks in the north were coaxed by various forms of official and unofficial harassment (Asmussen 2008: 272). The consensus estimate has it that 160,000 Greek Cypriots were displaced by the invasion, and that 50,000 Turkish Cypriots were relocated to the North. The chief concern of the Greek population was that the partitioning of the island might be permanent. In the North, Greek homes were distributed among Turkish refugees, but of much greater concern was the introduction of settlers from Turkey, whose presence was intended to alter the demographic balance.

Living in Istanbul after the population exchange

The fate of the Rum of Istanbul had been closely tied to the Cyprus Question. The fact that the Treaty of Lausanne (1923) had excluded them from the Greek–Turkish population exchange had been a source of resentment in Turkish political circles, but the crises in Cyprus between 1950 and 1964 would present the conditions that Ankara could exploit to resolve its Rum problem.

Most Ottoman Christians had already either fled or perished before the formal population exchange: only 192,000 were removed from Turkey after the Treaty of Lausanne came into force. The Constantinopolitan Greeks and the people of Imbros (Gökçeada) and Tenedos (Bozcaada) were excluded, as were Muslims in Western Thrace. Fearing a repeat of the events in Smyrna, thousands of Constantinopolitan Greeks had fled before the Allies departed Istanbul. The exodus began so abruptly that the second-hand furniture market was flooded by goods from people in desperate need of cash.

Istanbul's Greeks once constituted a sizeable percentage of the city's population and were dominant in numerous professions and trades. Many of the city's grandest buildings bore the names of Greek families whose business networks traversed continents. These included the bankers who, until recently, had dominated the empire's finances. In 1922, however, in the wake of the Turkish Nationalist victory, the new nation and its government regarded their presence as an affront to that achievement and as an impediment to the new nation's economic sovereignty. The state, therefore, barely concealed its intentions to evict them. A series of discriminatory laws were issued to sequester Greeks' properties, bar them and other non-Muslims from certain professions, and make it difficult to operate businesses and community schools. Foreign companies were required to replace non-Muslim employees with Muslims. Two thirds of the Constantinopolitan Greeks operating as barristers were disbarred. The properties of absent Rum or any properties outside the city limits were confiscated, and their businesses suffered relentless inspections and punitive fines. Another measure required Greek schools to hire Turkish teachers: in 1926, this measure amounted to 40 per cent of the community school budget. These steps alone contributed significantly to the flight of Constantinopolitan Greeks to Greece: school attendance dropped from 24,296 in 1920–1 to 5,923 by 1926 (Alexandris 1983: 134). Between 1924 and 1927, Turkish statistics showed that the community as a whole had plummeted from 279,788 to 100,214 (Alexandris 1983: 142).

The rapprochement between Greece and Turkey in 1930 appeared to remove the pressure on the community, especially as Venizelos agreed to abandon the property rights and compensations claims of the exchanged populations. Greeks could again travel freely throughout the Republic, and wives and children living in exile were permitted to return. Venizelos even met with the Ecumenical Patriarch, Photios II, who was no longer referred to by the Turkish state as a mere bishop (Alexandris 1983: 195). Although numerous discriminatory and oppressive measures remained in place, the rapid decline of community numbers was halted. By 1935, Turkish statistics showed a modest increase to 103,839, with the community still running six lycées, thirty-eight other schools and forty-eight parishes (Alexandris 1983: 324–7).

A significant number of ethnic Greeks therefore chose to remain in Istanbul, despite the Kemalist Republic's desire to erase its Ottoman legacies and create an ethnically homogeneous nation. The punitive measures applied to meet these ends conveyed the apprehensions of a regime that had only recently won a desperate war against the perceived annihilation of their country, and which believed survival into the future required a loyal, solidly Turkish nation. 'Turkification' not only entailed the exclusive use of the Turkish language in public, but the adoption of a national culture and of fixed Turkish surnames, given surnames often betrayed one's non-Turkish origins (Türköz 2018). The Kemalist state also applied its heavy hand to the nation's economic policies, particularly during the presidency of İsmet İnönü (1938–50); this was a potential problem for the Istabul Greeks because of the common perception that they were exceedingly wealthy and privileged. During the Second World War, the state issued a punitive wealth tax (*Varlık Vergisi*) to offset inflation and counter profiteering, and it found the non-Muslims a soft target. To administer an emergency wealth tax introduced on 11 November 1942, boards of assessors greatly exaggerated the value and income of non-Muslim firms, and proprietors who failed to pay were incarcerated or exiled to inland Anatolia. The effects were devastating. Non-Muslim businesses were ruined overnight, and their properties were seized and auctioned. Of the 315 million Turkish lira collected before the tax was repealed on 15 March 1944, 280 million were squeezed out of the non-Muslims (Alexandris 1983: 232).

Conditions would again improve for non-Muslims after the war, but from 1954 Istanbul's Rum found that their fate was now linked to the *Enosis* campaign on Cyprus. The entire community, including Ecumenical Patriarch Athenagoras, was pressured to declare support for Turkey's position on the matter, and their reluctance fuelled a press campaign against them. The popular perception that the Rum remained disloyal appeared to be vindicated. On the evening of 6 September 1955 mobs attacked Rum homes and businesses throughout the city. This was the beginning of 'the September events' (*Ta Septemvriana*). According to historian Alexis Alexandris, the mobs spread across the city, destroying '1004 homes, 4,348 shops, 27 pharmacies and laboratories, 21 factories, 110 restaurants, cafes and hotels … 73 churches, 26 schools, five athletic clubs' and desecrated the two main Greek cemeteries (Alexandris 1983: 259). Shops all along İstiklal Caddesi, the famous promenade in Beyoğlu that runs through to Takism Square, were ransacked. Some women were raped in their homes, and one monk at Balıklı was burned alive, but on the whole, the assailants focused on the destruction of property. The police knew of the impending attack and forewarned some of their Rum friends, but they stood by as the violence ran its course. Although the tanks eventually arrived, it is generally accepted that the attacks enjoyed the national government's assent and that the secret services had orchestrated them. The event shook the community to its core.

In fact, the *Septemvriana* frightened and repulsed most of Istanbul's citizens, who believed that the rioters were bussed in from outside. Traumatised Greeks began to desert the city, with most heading for Greece. A larger number, however, left in 1964, again following further troubles on Cyprus. In March that year, the Turkish government abrogated the treaty signed in 1930 that had allowed Greek passport holders to remain in the city. The measure affected at least 10,000 Istanbul Greeks, who were expelled from the country immediately, including many who were married to Turkish citizens. They were not permitted to liquidate their assets, and they could leave with only one piece of luggage and 22 liras (Vryonis 2005). The rest of the community and the remaining Greek inhabitants of Imbros and Tenedos also began to emigrate. The population plummeted from about 76,000 in 1965 to just 7,000 by 1978, and by the new century the approximate figure that is usually cited is 2,000. Neighbourhoods like Tatavla, Tarlabaşı and Fener, where the *Politiko* accent was commonly heard in shops and from street balconies, were deserted or were becoming slums housing poor migrants from eastern Anatolia. The great majority of Turkey's Rum population relocated to Greece, although some of their progeny would return in the wake of the Greek economic crisis of 2008.

Greek Egyptians and the end of empire

Formally at least, Egypt gained national independence in 1922. However, Britain granted independence on its own terms, and retained enormous influence over its foreign policy and economy, maintaining a strong military presence and control of the Suez Canal. In effect, Egypt was subjected to a barely concealed form of crypto-colonialism, in that it continued to play its crucial role in imperial strategy and communications, while its economy remained hostage to colonial interests (Herzfeld 2002: 900–1). Greek commercial interests, which retained a strong stake in cotton production, and those of other minorities, continued to flourish in a 'nation' whose government was not permitted to protect its own industries with tariffs and promote other domestic interests. Although the Greeks were a diverse group that included workers, Egyptians nevertheless believed that they and other foreign communities were 'middleman' minorities that were prospering in a captive economy.

The 1920s would be remembered as the high-water mark of Greek life in Egypt. While 'Infidel' Smyrna had been reduced to a smouldering ruin, the Greek community of cosmopolitan Alexandria was still in its halcyon days. Greek culture had reached a peak in theatre and literature. Schools and sporting activities expanded. Constantine Cavafy, the world's best-known Greek poet, finally left his clerical job and was able to focus on his writing. He gave expression to his own times in poems that drew insights from the many layers of Mediterranean history, evoking moments of beauty, tenderness and erotic pleasure. His poetry also evoked life in imperial worlds in their twilight. He spoke for a Greek Egyptian presence that stretched back to the days of Alexander the Great, but which was about to be extinguished.

For the moment, Greek numbers in Egypt expanded because of the influx of refugees from Anatolia: between 1917 and 1927, the population had increased from 82,658 to 97,793. Over the same period, the community in Alexandria grew from 25,393 to 37,106, and that in Cairo from 15,250 to 20,115 (Kitroeff 1989: 13–14). Greek Egyptians (*Ellinoegyptioi*, *Yunani*) ranged from the wealthy grandees of the cotton trade to working-class men and women who played a prominent role in the union movement and the political Left. Greek Egyptians could be found in white-collar jobs: in the professions, shopkeeping and, above all, in office work. The European firms that dominated the Egyptian economy preferred Greeks because of their fluency in the major European languages. The social profile of the community was reflected in its sporting interests. Football was popular among all groups, but the middle classes were enthusiasts of athletics, tennis and rowing. In 1924, as the last Greeks were being herded out of Anatolia, a Greek athletics organisation was established in Cairo (*Ellinikos Athlitikos Omilos Kaïrou*) (Adamantidou 2005: 43).

Like the other European communities, Greek Egyptians tended to live apart from the Egyptian population. However, following independence and because of the growing agitation for an end to colonial controls, more and more Greek Egyptians recognised the importance of engaging with the nation's institutions and people. Greek leftists were among those at the forefront of the labour movement (Gorman 2005, 2009, 2009a, 2013). Greek Egyptians could not, however, remove the taint of colonialism. Egyptians generally resented Britain's military and economic controls, especially when the Depression led to a collapse in the price of cotton, which depressed wages as much as 50 per cent, while food prices skyrocketed (Marsot 2007: 104).

General unrest and a renewed campaign for full sovereignty led to the Anglo-Egyptian Treaty of August 1936. The withdrawal of most British troops from Egypt soon followed, as did the abolition of the capitulations on 8 May 1937. However, British forces returned in full force during the Second World War, but when it ended the Egyptian state continued using its powers to engineer the 'Egyptianisation' of the national economy, passing discriminatory legislation that saw foreign business leaders, bankers, clerks, tradesmen and workers replaced by local men. In July 1947, for example, the state passed a law that required that employees of every joint-stock company had to be at least 75 per cent native Egyptian. Given the limited prospects for re-employment, Greek clerks and workers who were made redundant began to emigrate.

Tensions between Egyptians and Europeans continued after the war, culminating in the Cairo riot of January 1952. Mobs attacked the properties of foreign companies and nationals, and in July, Gamal Abdul Nasser launched a successful *coup d'état*. His mission was the Egyptianisation of Egypt. In October 1956, the seizure of the Suez Canal, which was still under British control, started a short war with Britain, France and Israel, but under international pressure the latter were forced to withdraw. Following the crisis, Nasser's government nationalised foreign-owned properties, starting with those held by British, French and Jewish companies and private individuals. Greek Egyptians were initially spared, since many had opposed the invasion and since Greeks generally made common cause with the locals. Greeks employed at the canal were retained, as their expertise helped the locals manage the canal. However, laws passed in 1961–2 to nationalise large and non-Egyptian-owned enterprises dealt a fatal blow to the community. Owners of factories and larger stores would arrive at their premises one morning to find that they had to hand over the keys to new management. In some cases, former proprietors were employed as advisers to keep the business afloat.

Unlike the Greeks in Anatolia and Istanbul, those in Egypt had time to plan their exit. As one historian has put it, it was a 'silent migration' that received considerable assistance from community organisations, such as the Greek Chamber of Commerce in Alexandria, which used their extensive business and social networks across the world to guide people (Kitroeff 2019). Greek Egyptian associations also sprang up quickly in the diaspora to assist with the passage of others leaving Egypt (Dalachanis 2015: 326–36). By the 1970s, the Greek community was as small and as insignificant as that in Istanbul.

Greeks in the Soviet Union and Eastern Bloc

Axis troops swept through those parts of the Soviet Union that happened to contain most of its Greek population. Those who survived the horrific occupation conditions then faced further persecution from Soviet authorities. In July 1944, 15,040 Greeks were deported from Crimea, Kuban and Georgia (see Map 2). The last major round of deportations came in May 1949, when the Communist Party Central Committee decided to clear the Black Sea area of 'political unreliable elements' like the Greeks (Polian 2004: 169, 182).

The deported communities travelled for many days, locked up in carriages normally used for transporting goods or livestock. Under armed guard, the victims were not told where they were going or what was in store. One Sotiria Pavlidou recalled that one day the 'train stopped in a barren place. There were no houses, or water. They told us this was our permanent home now. We then clashed [with the authorities]. We started to yell and react. A clash happened. Fifteen men, Greeks, were killed' (Agtzidis 1995: 266). Deportees were then placed in special settlements or camps in Kazakhstan and Uzbekistan, where they were required to remain, and from where they would not be released until 1956 (Pohl 1996: 104–7). The last deportations from Transcaucasia and Black Sea areas were carried out in August 1950.

The deported were allocated to work camps in Kazakhstan and Uzbekistan, where they were used for construction, mining and other industries. Christos Sidiropoulos recalled the prison-like conditions: 'They put us into barracks that once held Japanese POWs. When they left, we replaced them … There were five families per barrack. It was freezing in winter' (Agtzidis 1995: 267). Families were required to remain within the bounds of their settlement. Escape and capture would lead to imprisonment and twenty years' hard labour. The deportations also had the effect of breaking the Greek language 'nation'. Families were dispersed over a vast land mass. Greek classes were forbidden, as was reading books in Greek. During the time of exile, language retention collapsed from just under 73 per cent to 41.5 per cent (Pohl 1996: 109; Pohl 2000: 288).

The death of Stalin in 1953 permitted the state leadership team and the dictator's ultimate successor, Nikita Khrushchev, to grant more freedom of cultural expression. In this new atmosphere of greater openness, Greek language teaching, newspapers and theatre productions enjoyed a limited revival among the exiled groups in central Asia and those still living in the Black Sea region. A lively community of Greek communist refugees had also formed in Tashkent. Soviet Greeks and indeed all Soviet citizens benefited from a general improvement in living standards. On the whole, however, being Greek was still a liability. From 1967 into the 1970s, some restrictions on movement and cultural expression were reimposed by the Brezhnev regime. Meanwhile, the titular nationalities or dominant ethnic groups of the Soviet republics (e.g. Latvians, Uzbeks, Armenians) continued to monopolise party and bureaucratic positions in their republics. Minorities like the Greeks found it difficult to secure the patronage needed for such jobs (Pratsinakis 2013: 57–8).

On the whole, much of the Soviet Greek population had been fragmented by the expulsions and state terror under Stalin. It was also increasingly susceptible to Soviet soft power. Soviet society was urbanising at a rapid rate, enjoying better living standards, including rising consumption levels (Gatrell 2006: 403). These changes consolidated the legitimacy of the regime and the Soviet Union, as did the leading role it played in world affairs. Like the United States, it was presenting itself as a great society of the future. It showed, among other things, the capability of building nuclear weapons and sending humans into space. Therefore, as with other nationalities, Greeks, particularly the younger generations, were identifying more with the Soviet Union. Greek culture no longer influenced their way of life as much as it had among earlier generations, and there was a significant rise in out-marriages. By 1970, less than 40 per cent declared Greek as their first language (Pratsinakis 2013: 57–9). If anything, Greekness was acquiring a new 'symbolic' significance as something linked to Classical Greek culture learned in schools, rather than with Pontian and other folk traditions (Pratsinakis 2013: 60). Only those living in compact rural communities, as in Ukraine and Georgia, continued to identify primarily as ethnic Greeks. Outside of these communities, Greek language still survived within the family unit. For the most part the spoken form was Pontian Greek, which was persevered as a living language in the Soviet Union at the same time as it was disappearing among Pontian communities in Greece.

Civil War refugees

All the while, another Greek community had formed in the Soviet Union since the end of the war. The Greek Civil War saw as many as 100,000 people being evacuated or driven to Eastern Bloc countries. KKE had reallocated over 27,000 children for their safety (Danforth and Van Boeschoten 2012: 47). About 45,000 Greeks crossed the Bulgarian border because of the Civil War, where, as elsewhere in the Eastern Bloc, the state provided housing, education facilities and employment. The preferential treatment given to the refugees grated with indigenous Bulgarian Greeks, who often despised them on political grounds, and some even boycotted fundraising efforts to assist them (Dragostinova 2011: 256). Families were often split up during this dispersion. For children, the experience would often be remembered as an adventure, but for adults it was traumatic. Moreover, being forced to live in exile was an intensely bitter pill to swallow. Many would only be permitted to return to their homelands in the 1980s.

In 1949, as the last Soviet Greeks were being deported to central Asia, a new wave of Civil War refugees arrived. When the last of the defeated communists crossed the border into Albania and Yugoslavia, Stalin had them moved further north for two basic reasons. One was that the Albanian government was nervous about the Greek state using the large Greek guerrilla presence on its side of the border as a pretext to invade and claim southern parts of Albania. Indeed, Stalin did not wish to have problems with the US and its allies at any point along Greece's long northern borders (K. Karpozilos 2014: 67). The other reason had to do with the huge labour shortages in Eastern Europe and Central Asia. The new communist governments in Poland, Czechoslovakia and Hungary regarded the Greek refugees, the bulk of whom were young men and women, as a godsend. Of the 58,300 refugees, 15,000 were sent to the Soviet Union, 13,000 to Czechoslovakia, 9,000 to Poland, and 7,000 to Hungary. The rest were in Bulgaria and Romania (Tsekou 2013: 56, 169). Those destined for the Soviet Union, many of whom were Slav Macedonians, were sent to Uzbekistan, where they were distributed into fourteen settlements near Tashkent. This mission was to help make Tashkent a model socialist city, particularly as local Uzbeks were reluctant to leave their farms. It was hoped that this group, which contained half of the KKE membership, would channel its ideological energies into this new project, which they were told was preparation for the socialist projects that would later be introduced in Greece (K. Karpozilos 2014: 76–8).

Whilst deprived of their Greek citizenship, the refugees were not made citizens of the communist countries. Rather, all the refugees, from Hungary to Tashkent, were placed under the authority of the Greek Communist Party, which operated as a 'refugee land' or state without territory, and which maintained close control over its citizenry. The capital was in Bucharest, where the Party had a radio station, printed newspapers and periodicals, and ran a book publishing house. Between 1947 and 1968, it published 1,488 books, as well as newspapers and journals (Matthaiou and Polemi 2003). The Greek newspaper *Popular Struggle* (*Laikos Agonas*) was an important Greek-language resource for communities throughout the Eastern Bloc (Tsaroucha-Szabo 2006: 178). While most young men and women were sent to industrial zones, Greek intellectuals, artists and KKE cadres were relocated to Moscow and other Eastern Bloc capitals. In Hungary the refugees founded a new town just south of Budapest. The construction of Beloiannisz, named after the Greek communist hero Nikos Beloyannis, began in May 1950, and the town became the centre of the political and cultural life of refugees in east central Europe. It had a nursery, a kindergarten, a doctor's surgery, offices of both the community and the Greek Communist Party, various stores and a cultural centre (Tsaroucha-Szabo 2006: 177).

The Greek refugee state was thrown into turmoil, however, following the death of Stalin and the emergence of a new party line on Stalin and his legacy. Fissures developed within every refugee community between Stalin's stalwarts and supporters of the new line. On 11 September 1955 rival factions came to blows in Tashkent, leaving 118 people wounded (K. Karpozilos 2014: 83). The crisis deepened in 1956. A month after Khrushchev's denunciation of Stalin in February, the Central Committee of KKE voted to remove Nikos Zachariadis, who was closely identified with Stalin and had dominated the party since 1945, from his position of General Secretary of KKE. Another split would occur in 1968, after the Soviet invasion of Czechoslovakia. By that point, the party had fragmented further, and the refugee government was no longer functioning. Greek refugees had become more attached to their host countries, and their children were entering their educational systems and becoming assimilated.

The 20,000 or so children that had been relocated to communist states during the Greek Civil War – statistics vary from 12,659 to 27,200 – were aged between 3 and 14, and most were living in Hungary, Czechoslovakia, Poland and Romania. Between 1948 and 1952 the Greek state lodged a series of protests with the United

Nations, which had to consider which of the children had been removed against the will of their families. With additional involvement from the Red Cross and communist states, about 5,600 of these children were returned to their families in Greece by 1958 (Danforth and Van Boeschoten 2012: 81). The rest grew up in children's homes, under a unique programme run throughout the 'refugee land' by the Greek Committee for Child Support until 1956. The children were then placed in the educational system of the host countries (Danforth and Van Boeschoten 2012: 71–3; Tsekou 2013: 160–77).

All the while, Greek political refugees had no contact with the indigenous Greeks of the Soviet Union and what remained of the old Greek diaspora in Eastern Europe. The refugees did not see themselves as part of the same diaspora. Rather, they identified as exiles who made it their mission to return home. They left Greece as illiterate peasants, and eventually returned as skilled workers, while some (10 per cent) returned with university degrees. Many carried the guilt of having lost the struggle, and of having survived when so many of their comrades had been killed or imprisoned. They were also scarred by the acrimonious party schism. These experiences are captured in a large body of literature written by exiles, which gives a sense of the travails that exiles faced in post-war Soviet or Central European societies. Among the best-known works is the novel *Achilles' Fiancée* by Alki Zei, which is about a middle-class left-wing Athenian named Eleni who follows Achilles to Tashkent, a disappointingly arid place where the Greeks seem more divided than at home. Eleni returns to Greece in the early 1960s, but most of the exiles were to return only after the Junta fell and especially when PASOK came to power in 1981. The difficulties of their *nostos* ('homecoming') are sensitively portrayed in Theo Angelopoulos' 1984 film classic *Voyage to Cythera*. The protagonist returns after twenty-five years, only to find his house in ruins and his wife unable to recognise him. He has been permanently uprooted by history (Karalis 2012: 210).

Greeks in the former Soviet Union

During the years of exile in the steppes of central Asia, the Black Sea Greeks did manage to retain fragments of their language, culture and distinct identity. Under the liberalised conditions of Perestroika (early 1980s through to 1989), Greek culture enjoyed a period of rediscovery and revival. Numerous Greek associations emerged from Moscow to Almaty, which organised Greek festivals and Greek language classes. By the late 1980s Pontian organisations from Greece linked up with

Pontian communities in the Soviet Union, which had the effect of stimulating interest in Pontian culture within a group that had simply assumed they were 'Greek'. One social scientist recalled delegates saying such things as: 'We didn't know we were Pontian Greeks before we came to Greece or before the Greeks came to the FSU [former Soviet Union]' (Voutira 2006: 390).

By 1989, the demographic profile of the Soviet Greeks had changed dramatically. According to official statistics, there were 358,000 Greeks, the largest numbers being in Ukraine (104,000) and Georgia (100,324), Russia (80,500) and Kazakhstan (almost 50,000) (Giannitsis et al. 2006: 201; Pratsinakis 2013: 66). With the dissolution of the Soviet Union, however, came a resurgence of nationalisms and yet another 'minorities' crisis, as each newly independent republic took a less tolerant view of its minorities. The problem was exacerbated by depressed economic conditions that had new governments more focused on the interests of their national majorities. Many Greeks in Georgia were made to feel not only marginalised but unwelcome. An ethnic Greek who grew up in Tsalka, Georgia, recalled the moment when he was told he no longer belonged: 'Tsalka is not our land, because the Georgians have come and told us that it is not our land ...' (Popov 2010: 72). It was the civil war in Abkhazia and Georgia (1991–3) that forced a sudden exodus of ethnic Greeks. In Abkhazia the Greek population declined from 15,000 to 3,000.

During the tumultuous 1990s, Greece assumed greater importance as the 'homeland'. For Greeks in the Russian Federation, where they were well integrated into the broader society, migrating to Greece was more an economic consideration (Popov 2010: 72–3). The same held for the well-established communities in Ukraine. For most, however, the chief issue was security. During a congress of Greek associations in April 1991, where some delegates even proposed the idea of Greek territorial autonomy around two Greek enclaves in Transcaucasia, most delegates from central Asia and Transcaucasia expressed their wish to emigrate to either Russia or Greece (Voutira 2006: 394). Most Greeks from the former Soviet republics who migrated in these early years chose to move to the Russian Federation because of their facility with Russian and because it was a familiar environment (Voutira 2006: 386). But after much lobbying by Pontian organisations at home, Greek governments encouraged 'repatriation' to Greece, which prompted the deluge of the early 1990s. Between 1990 and 1995 about 140,000 arrived. By 2002, six out of seven Greeks in Georgia and Armenia, countries that had been ravaged by ethnic conflict, had fled (Pratsinakis 2013: 65).

Most settled in northern Greece, including Thrace, where they served to counterbalance the Muslim minority. Some had linked up with kin in Greece and other parts of Europe (Voutira 2006).

By 2000, the Greek population still living in the former Soviet Republics was now concentrated overwhelmingly in Ukraine and in the Russian Federation, where economic conditions had markedly improved. Those who had migrated to Greece had done so freely and could always return. In fact, émigrés in Greece soon began referring to 'Russia' as their homeland, especially once they began to encounter bigotry and discrimination. In Greece they were called *Rossopontioi* (Russo-Pontians) and in the short term were treated like a foreign minority (Popov 2010: 80). Many would move back and forth, between the old homeland and the new, or return permanently because the Russian Federation in particular afforded them better opportunities. In that sense, Russia came to play the same kind of role that the United States, Australia and other diaspora destinations performed: as a solution to Greece's limitations.

The overseas diaspora, 1950s and 1960s

The end of the Second World War marked a new chapter in the history of human mobility. The war was responsible for the greatest forced migrations in European history: 30 million people were displaced during the war, but another 12 million between 1945 and 1950. As noted in the previous section, the Greek Civil War contributed its share of refugees to Eastern Europe. A smaller wave fleeing to Western Europe consisted mainly of middle-class, educated youths, many of whom had taken part in the *Dekemvriana* during the winter of 1944–5, and who faced persecution, imprisonment and even execution. Thanks mainly to French government scholarship schemes and the work of the French Institute at Athens, most of them were sent to study in France. In December 1945, the ship *Mataroa* carried 123 award-winning students, 40 of whom happened to be communists selected by the French Institute to secure their safety, including the young philosopher Cornelius Castoriadis. This was the first of a series of national 'brain drains' (Manitakis and Jollivet 2018).

In the 1950s and 1960s, record numbers of Europeans migrated voluntarily across the seas and between European countries (Fauri 2015: 104). Between 1955 and 1977, the number of Greeks that moved abroad was 1.23 million, but discounting the returnees, the estimated figure of permanent émigrés was about 1 million (Venturas 1999: 79). In the

1950s, most went to Australia, Canada and the United States, while in the 1960s, more émigrés favoured northwestern Europe. This area accounted for 61 per cent of all émigrés in the post-war years: 29 per cent in 1959, but 68 per cent in 1961 and 75 percent in 1965. West Germany received the bulk of them. The next largest group was in Belgium, followed by Italy (Venturas 1999: 80–1).

The great majority of people who left Greece in the post-war years were economic migrants. In the 1950s, two thirds left for Australia, the United States and Canada. A smaller number also made their way to South America: 7,740 between 1955 and 1977, mainly to Argentina and Brazil, where they initially found labouring work in industry (Damilakou 2006: 294). Of the transoceanic destinations, the United States was the most familiar and the one that most preferred. Between 1945 and 1965, 75,000 Greeks entered the country. By 1970, there were 177,275 Greek-born Americans and a further 257,296 American-born claiming Greek descent (Moskos 1990: 63). The intake would have been much larger but for the continuation of official restrictions that were relaxed only slightly. Numbers increased following the 1965 Immigration Act, which gave special treatment to those with close relatives in the United States; these would then account for four out of five new Greek arrivals (Moskos 1990: 54). That explains why the newcomers settled in cities with pre-existing Greek communities, joining relatives in established Greek enclaves like Astoria in Queens or Chicago's Greektown (*Neos Kosmos*, 7 February 2017). Newcomers took on jobs in 'traditional' Greek American businesses such as diners, where relatives made up most of the workforce. This wave also branched out into pizza parlours and restaurants serving Greek food (Moskos 1990: 55). However, as with the previous wave, the newcomers did not want their children entrapped in a life of hard menial labour. They emphasised the value of education with a view to entering the professions. As social prejudice towards southern Europeans decreased, Greek Americans faced fewer obstacles to socio-economic advancement, with some reaching the highest positions in business, government and the entertainment industry. By the 1970s and 1980s, countless Greek Americans had achieved national prominence, including Spiro Agnew, vice president under Richard Nixon, and Michael Dukakis, the longest-serving governor in Massachusetts history and the Democratic presidential candidate in 1988.

Because of official US restrictions, the chief destination for Greeks during the 1950s was Australia. The country had only 7 million inhabitants in 1945, with an economy largely dependent on wool and wheat exports. Japan's recent expansion into the South Pacific compelled the state to orchestrate the expansion of its industrial sectors, for which it needed a large injection of labour. To this end, a government department was created for the exclusive purpose of importing and processing immigrants. With the assistance of the Intergovernmental Committee of European Migration, some 46,000 Greeks arrived in Australia between 1954 and 1960 (Limnios-Sekeris 2015). A larger number followed in the 1960s, most of them ferried by ocean liners belonging to the Chandris shipping company. By 1966 the Greeks numbered 146,000, and by 1971 the number reached 160,200, with the majority in Melbourne, Australia's manufacturing centre, and almost one third in Sydney (Doumanis 1999: 65). Another major destination was Canada, where the Greek community received 107,780 newcomers between 1945 and 1971. Canada's Greeks followed the same patterns as those who migrated to Australia and the United States. They settled in cities, worked in menial occupations, often ventured into small business and pushed their children through the education system (Chimbos 1999: 91).

Greek diaspora associations, including the *koinotites*, provided some assistance to the post-war wave, but more often these émigrés found jobs and housing through family and neighbourhood information networks. Greek-owned cafes and restaurants provided many with their first job, but most quickly found work in factories, as any trade union restrictions on foreign labour had been removed. Greek émigrés frequently moved between jobs in search of better pay, and often held more than one job at a time. The work was usually hard and dispiritingly monotonous. Women often laboured as seamstresses and dressmakers, assembly-line workers in factories, or cleaners. Such work affected their physical and mental well-being in the long term, but they were also mindful of their material goals, which were to accumulate capital and either return to Greece or remain and promote the upward mobility of their children. Most typically, post-war immigrants improved their material circumstances by taking advantage of cheap housing markets. Families pooled their savings to place a deposit on a cheap house in a working-class neighbourhood, and most were able to relocate to leafy suburbs within a decade or two of arrival. It was also common for émigrés to start small businesses that required limited English, particularly in food retail. If Greek Americans continued to operate diners and moved into pizza parlours, in Australia the preference was for fish-and-chips shops, hamburger shops and so-called 'milk bars', which served milkshakes and sodas (flavoured milk drinks and carbonated beverages). The milk bar, which was particularly popular with the young, was a concept imported to Australia by Greeks transiting through the United States before the war (Janiszewski and Alexakis 2003: 177–97). The most common retail outlet by the 1960s, however, was the humble grocery store, which thrived before the expansion of supermarket chains in the mid-1970s.

Having achieved a level of material success that seemed less attainable back home, and having become accustomed to life in the diaspora, the majority of Greek migrant families did not return to Greece. Repatriation plans often changed when they returned to Greece to visit or with the intention of resettling. They often found that America, Canada and Australia had changed the way they worked and conducted their lives, and therefore Greece seemed foreign to them.

The pattern of social mobility was similar to that of Britain's expanding Greek Cypriot community. According to the 1961 census, Britain received over 42,000 Cypriots, of whom three quarters were Greek. The movement continued after independence. Between 1961 and 1981, the estimated size of the Greek Cypriot population increased from 33,518 to 67,461 (Oakley 1987: 5). New male immigrants initially worked as labourers, while the bulk of the women were seamstresses and dressmakers, for which there was great demand in the 1960s. Approximately half of the men worked in restaurants owned by established Cypriot immigrants. Within a few years, much of the staff had moved on and started their own establishments, opening restaurants, cafes, tailor and dress shops, and hair salons (George and Millerson 1967: 285). By 1967, almost 20 per cent of Cypriots were running small businesses, which was twice the national average. The food they prepared was usually 'English': Costas Eleftheriou served his customers 'chops, lamb chops, pork chops, mixed grills'. As was the case in North America and Australia, the host society had an aversion to sharper Mediterranean flavours, including olives and fetta, and often recoiled in disgust at the sight of grilled octopus or fried calamari. Typically, proprietors found that 'the shops' (*ta magazia*) consumed all their waking hours, and rarely closed their doors. Family members, including children, were expected to help to save on labour costs (Panayi 2008: 159–60).

The flood of new Greek migrants to Britain, Australia and Canada in the post-war years increased demand for associations and regional brotherhoods (e.g. *koinotites*, *syllogoi*), cultural spaces (e.g. traditional *kafeneia*) and specific services (e.g. baptismal and wedding catering, suppliers of olive oil and other Greek goods). Many more Greek soccer clubs and political associations were created. The regional fraternities (*syllogoi*) were especially important, as new migrants preferred to mix and intermarry with their own *patriotes*, by which they meant people from the same region or island rather than other Greeks. The *syllogoi* held regular dances (*chorous*) and raised funds for their villages, towns and islands back home. More important still were the churches, which expanded dramatically in number. With the Greek government's endorsement and despite the opposition of most *koinotites*, the archbishoprics of North America and Australia oversaw the creation of numerous parishes and church buildings that were funded by communities at the local level (Kitroeff 2020; Doumanis 1993).

The unusually high number of Greek associations in English-speaking countries reflected a remarkably strong desire for cultural retention. Greek migrants wished to stay Greek. Newcomers to the United States were less seduced by the symbolic projections of 'America'. Nor did the others seem much interested in becoming British, Canadian or Australian. They preferred soccer to cricket or gridiron football, ate only Greek food, celebrated name days rather than birthdays, and always spoke Greek amongst themselves. However, Greeks were concerned about the Greekness of their children, who often regarded their cultural background as an embarrassment and found it difficult to transition between a Greek-speaking private domain and an Anglophone public one. Parents tried with varying degrees of success to limit assimilation, usually by insisting on Greek in the home, requiring attendance in Greek language classes, and enrolling them, especially daughters, in Greek dance classes.

And yet Greek migrants were transformed as people in less obvious ways. The concept *xenitia*, which translates roughly as 'living in a foreign milieu', meant something quite specific in advanced industrial economies. The average migrant had come from a peasant background and was immersed into a working-class urban environment that operated by very different rules and in a different language. Adapting to this new life required a change to what social scientists describe as the *habitus*: the outlooks, attitudes, deportment and practices that one develops in a particular society. Aside from learning to negotiate US, Australian, Canadian and British bureaucracy, tax regimes, retail and medical systems, they adapted to the kinds of social rules applied in the workplace, everyday business dealings and social interactions in public. Greek migrants adopted a lifestyle that was completely different from that of the village in which they were born, but also from that which their siblings and cousins had adopted in Athens, Thessaloniki and other major towns.

The experience of emigration was challenging and heart-breaking. Parents who waved their children goodbye understood that they might never meet again. As the years and decades went by, the emigrants became estranged from family members in the homeland, particularly siblings, because they had lived apart for decades, but also because they lived different lives. Mistrust and discord often arose over the management and inheritance of family properties, especially once it was clear that the émigrés were not returning, or if they had become sufficiently affluent. For a variety of reasons, therefore, returnees did not just feel that Greece was foreign but that it was also alienating.

Europe's guest workers, 1960–1990

While many post-war Greek émigrés crossed the Atlantic and Indian oceans, the majority moved elsewhere in Europe and, more specifically, to the German Federal Republic. Indeed, West Germany received more Greeks than any other country in the twentieth century. The reasons were simple. German industries had been the most powerful in Europe before the war, while the damage inflicted by the war was less than expected. The sector was also able to re-emerge in conditions highly favourable to rapid regeneration, including the stable system of monetary and trade relations established at Bretton Woods, favourable tax concessions to large firms, and a corporatist system that regulated relations between capital and labour (Herbert 2019: 503–5). West German industry also had ready access to vast pools of labour at home and in the East, but after the erection of the Berlin Wall in 1961 it had to invite labourers from southern Europe.

Greek émigrés preferred West Germany because it was relatively close. Bavaria, the Rhineland, Westphalia and Baden-Württemberg could be reached by train, possibly within a day. Migrating to Belgium, Switzerland or West Germany was a far less fateful decision for Greek labourers than crossing an ocean. It was also impressed upon them by the authorities that their presence was meant to be temporary. Indeed, one survey showed that only 7 per cent of Greeks who had been in West Germany intended to stay. Even though many émigrés would stay for more than a decade, their ties to Greece remained intimate. One could quickly return home to attend to pressing family matters, such as a funeral. It was not uncommon for people to undertake two or more working stints in Germany. Much later, when travelling to Greece by plane or car became more affordable, Greek German families vacationed every summer in their home village. These migrants came mostly from the northern provinces of Macedonia, Thrace and Epirus, as well as from Crete and the Ionian Islands, and were less likely to have relatives in the United States and other parts of the diaspora.

West German governments were keen to regulate the labour intake. Agreements were signed with southern European states, including Greece (30 March 1960), where the German Labour Office maintained offices in Athens and Thessaloniki to vet candidates and prepare them for employment in German industry. In just over a decade, foreign labour in West Germany skyrocketed from 1.1 per cent of the work-force in 1960 to 10 per cent in 1973. Between 1960 and 1976, the number of Greeks in Germany rose from a mere 5,000 to 623,320 (Venturas 2002: 135). The Greek government also signed agreements with Belgium, which needed workers for its mines. Between 1953 and 1964, Belgium received only 20,069, essentially because of an aversion to mining. One migrant recalled: 'Before I came to Belgium, if you said that I would be descending 1,000 metres into a shaft, I would not have believed you.' Another admitted: 'Of the many that came, about half returned immediately. Once they entered the elevator and were dropped down into the shaft ... many could not stay, many left immediately' (Venturas 1999: 191–2). Most Greek Belgian miners jumped at the first opportunity to switch to cleaner and safer jobs (Venturas 2002: 34).

Generally speaking, Greek guest workers found living in Northwest European industrial cities dispiriting, particularly before the arrival of spouses. They were forced to adapt quickly to rather arduous, highly disciplined 'Germanic' work regimes, and, given that much of their income was sent home, there was little disposable income to spend on leisure activities, and few outlets catered to such activities. At first, their living conditions were spartan and sometimes so bad that they became the subject of newspaper exposés. In Düsseldorf in 1967, for example, one article described *Gastarbeiter* living quarters in this way:

> There are six Turkish and Greek guest workers living in a space no larger than 15 square meters. The beds are stacked one on top of the other and crowded together. All the men are lying in bed, though its only 8:30 in the evening. But what else should they do in this hole? There aren't even enough chairs ... The floor is bare and filthy, the walls no different. You search in vain for a picture, a curtain ... (Herbert 2019: 218)

Greek community formation in northwestern Europe was different from the pattern found in the English-speaking world. Given high occupational mobility, guest workers often showed little interest in creating parish churches and regional associations. In turn, the Greek Orthodox hierarchy seemed less motivated to develop an ecclesiastical structure. Émigrés to West Germany and Belgium were also linked more closely to the Left and with the union movement, which addressed some of their early social needs.

For the first few years, the lives of guest workers were centred on the factory floor and the apartments they shared with other Greeks. The typical Greek migrant worker was a man between the ages of 25 and 32. By the end of the 1960s, their social lives improved once Greek women began arriving in larger numbers. It was not uncommon for couples to leave their children with relatives back home so that they could both work full time, but many more German Greeks were now raising families with children whose first language was fast becoming German. Many were also choosing to stay at least until retirement. The decision to remain was often easier for women, who sometimes cherished their new-found freedoms in German cities (Kontos 2009).

The global economic crisis of 1973 brought a halt to further labour recruitment. From this point on, the only option for emigration was through the official family reunion programme. Between 1973 and 1987, the Greek German population almost halved, from 407,614 to 256,396 (Kontos 2009: 32). Returning home had always been the objective of the typical Greek migrant in Europe. Up to 40 per cent of the first wave of Greek *Gastarbeiter* had returned by 1964. Approximately 1,200,000 Greeks migrated to West Germany between 1960 and 1999, and an estimated 894,000 of them returned home. However, the longer many of them stayed, the more they were prepared to form community structures as seen in North America and Australia. By 2000, there were some 600 Greek associations, including 140 *koinotites*, in operation in Germany.

Inevitably, however, living and working in West Germany and a united Germany socialised Greek migrants as much as those living in the United States. Returnees and especially their children found acclimatisation to comparative urban disorder, bureaucratic dysfunction and poor services profoundly alienating, as they did their initial treatment as 'foreigners'. One survey of second-generation returnees notes that:

> Virtually all our second-generation 'returnees' told similar stories of
> the objective difficulties of living in Greece, where chaos, corruption,

rudeness and clientelism frustrate so many aspects of life (not least finding a decent job), and are contrasted with the order, efficiency, politeness and meritocracy of society in Germany. (Christou and King 2010: 643)

Conclusion

In their coverage of the Greek world since the beginning of the twentieth century, Chapter 3 and this chapter have emphasised the significance of state formation, or to be more specific, the great shift from multiethnic empires to culturally defined nation states. Greek communities that once thrived across various empires became minorities in nations that, for various reasons (symbolic, security, economic), regarded their mere presence as problematic. They were exiled by Stalin's regime and expelled by Egypt and Turkey. But while Greeks were being marginalised and ejected in some regions of the world, they were flocking to other regions that promised prosperity, and which became increasingly accepting of cultural difference. In North America, Western Europe and Australia, émigrés were able to thrive in advanced post-war economies in desperate need of labour, and where governments had relaxed discriminatory immigration policies. Canadian and Australian governments eventually embraced multiculturalism, which made migrants like the Greeks even more loyal to their new country.

CHAPTER 9

Springtime for democracy: Metapolitefsi (1974–1985)

July 1974 was the watershed of Greece's twentieth century. It marked the sudden end of the post-Civil War political order and the return of parliamentary democracy. Hereafter, all Greeks could exercise their political rights freely. Dissidents no longer feared persecution, the Left operated in daylight, and elections were held without fear of intimidation. A new era had dawned. It was later dubbed 'the *Metapolitefsi*', which denoted regime change and political transformation, implying a general acceptance of the legitimacy of democratic institutions. This had to do with the catastrophic failures of the Junta and with the consolidation of democracy internationally. By the mid-1970s, when Spain, Portugal and Greece emerged from authoritarian rule, the pathway to a democratic future had already been marked out by other Western European countries. That political transformation was to be complemented by changes in society that were just as significant. The next ten years for Greece witnessed extraordinary cultural and social ferment, as citizens used their freedoms to remake their lives and develop new identities. The *Metapolitefsi* began with an explosion of mostly peaceful but energetic grass-roots activism. It was dominated by a spirit of collectivism and featured progressive changes to family, gender, sexual and religious authority. In a sense, the Greek '1960s' were in full swing in the mid-1970s.

By 1985, however, Greeks were following other Europeans along a different path. They were now more focused on consumerism and private interests. By then, most governments were seeking to shrink the state and promote market deregulation. This was the new world that was increasingly dominated by neoliberalism, and by accelerating globalisation driven by new technologies such as the personal computer and the World Wide Web (Berend 2010: 167–8).

In such ways, the 1980s gave birth to the present. By the end of the decade, Greece was fast becoming the society that we recognise today. It was also the decade in which the seeds of the political and economic crises of the early twenty-first century were planted.

Southern Europe in context

The Greek dictatorship ended at roughly the same time as its much older Spanish and Portuguese counterparts. The Iberian states had followed similar political, social and cultural pathways since the Second World War (e.g. Shubert 1990: ch. 5). Societies in each case had laboured under stultifying right-wing authoritarian rule, under regimes that seemed determined to freeze time and prevent the kinds of cultural and social changes that were already in train in northern Europe and North America. Unprecedented economic change, however, tore up the fabric of traditional society, presenting enormous challenges that neither regime could contain. That the three dictatorships ended at roughly the same time was no coincidence.

Despite record emigration rates, Greece's population had grown from 7.7 million in 1950 to 8.3 million in 1960, and to 8.8 million in 1970. Over the same period, Portugal and Spain grew from 8.8 and 30.3 million to 9.6 and 33.8 million respectively. Births in Greece outnumbered deaths by two to one. Greek society became predominantly urban. Athens doubled in size between 1960 and 1970. Between 1960 and 1973, Greece, Spain and Portugal's urban populations grew from 55.9 to 66 per cent, 56.6 to 68.2 per cent, and 29 to 40 per cent respectively (Tomka 2013: 11).

By the 1970s, the great majority of Greeks had already deserted the villages. Consumer practices and social life were changing even more rapidly than before, given the influence of mass tourism and growing access to Western consumables, films and ideas. Popular music and foreign films, which accorded special attention to the young and relationships, generated interest in lifestyles and behaviour that grated with authorities and older Greeks, who were anxious about the spread of permissive values among the young (Accornero 2016: xii–xvi; Avdela 2013: 472–3; Katsapis 2013). Once exceptional and taboo, many more came to perceive premarital sex as normal. Contraceptives had been in common use from the early 1970s. The young also had changed in appearance. Boys now preferred hair that was longer and unkempt, while girls dressed in ways that flaunted their sexuality. Headscarves had completely disappeared except among older women. The young moved about more freely in cheap automobiles, motorbikes or scooters, and met in their own 'hangouts', such as cafes that catered to both sexes. The 'boîte', or nightclub, disco and tavern had become popular venues, where people could listen to all kinds of musical genres, especially Western music. The period also witnessed the emergence of gay communities. Society was generally becoming more accustomed to nudity and partial nudity in the theatre, on the big screen and at the beach (Kafaoglou 2018). Led by the young, Greek social mores were changing.

There was intense interest in all aspects of modern culture and its challenges. Small publishing houses, theatre groups, music bands and record stores acted as cultural intermediaries, giving the young access to an ever expanding market in cultural products. Greece's delayed '1960s' came into full swing once the pall of political repression and censorship was lifted. From the summer of 1974 youth were freer to drive the transformation of cultural norms by questioning and flouting established rules of social behaviour (cf. Kornetis 2015). The old generation lamented the loss of manners, polite behaviour and reverence for tradition and authority, but these impressions also reflected the waning of patriarchal power and privilege. As Eric Hobsbawm put it, youth culture was a matrix for a broader cultural revolution 'in the wider sense of a wider revolution in manners and customs' (Hobsbawm 1994: 330).

Social change had anticipated the fall of the dictatorships, but the catalyst for more dramatic change was a global economic crisis. The southern European dictatorships had benefited greatly from the long post-war boom that kept a lid on social discontents, but the oil crisis of 1973 brought them quickly to the surface (see Chapter 8; Graham and Quiroga 2012: 502–3, 511–12). Governments around the world, even the most competent among them, were baffled by the concurrence of rampant inflation and unemployment. Democratically elected governments were generally voted out of power, while the dictatorships of Spain, Portugal and Greece were each confronted by a crisis of legitimacy. Three months before democracy was restored in Greece, Portugal's forty-two-year dictatorship fell during a bloodless coup known as the 'Carnation Revolution' (*Revolução dos Cravos*). In Spain, the Franco regime recognised that it could not survive in its post-war form and tried to engineer a five-year transition to a 'guided' democracy (Vincent 2008: 199–224). The manner in which each dictatorship unravelled would influence their particular transitions to democracy. In Spain the process was drawn out because of the enduring power of the military: when Franco died in November 1975 the proponents of democracy had to tread warily and slowly. By contrast, Portugal experienced a coup led by progressive officers that set off a series of crises, including a countercoup and the formation of six provisional governments. As with Franco's regime, the Colonels also planned for a 'guided democracy' under the stewardship of Markezinis, and had they succeeded the military might have retained its place in Greek political life (Tzortzis 2020: 154). As it happened, the Colonels were replaced by a more reactionary dictator, whose regime was humiliated by the Cyprus debacle and disintegrated overnight. Civilians with recent political experience filled the power vacuum immediately. Karamanlis' provisional government was unbeholden to the military and free to prepare for the establishment of a genuine democracy.

As fledgling democracies, the obvious next step for Spain, Portugal and Greece was to forge closer ties with 'Europe'. Franco and Salazar had used the Iberian Peninsula's relative isolation to limit the influence of 'advanced' Western societies, but by the 1970s physical distance was easily overcome by modern mass communications and cheap travel. Geography also mattered less to Greece in another sense. In the past, the country's location had determined its geopolitical fate, being on the margins of empires and then on the frontline of the Cold War. After 1974, it could begin to function as if it were in the centre of Europe. The Ministry of Foreign Affairs managed relations with Turkey and the Balkans quietly and largely behind closed doors. Instead, politics in Greece, much as in Spain and Portugal, focused much more on domestic political and economic matters, and each also saw a need to join the European Economic Community. Joining 'Europe' was about creating and consolidating political institutions and civil societies. And as seemed to be the case among EEC member states (particularly West Germany), Spain, Portugal and Greece hoped to leave the rancorous divisions of the past behind them. By taking a European route to the future, each of the post-junta regimes were promising the citizenry a future free of political oppression (Kornetis and Cavallaro 2019: 2).

A new political landscape

The shift from dictatorship to democracy in Greece was sudden and peaceful, and it enjoyed overwhelming popular approval. This 'velvet revolution' can be partly explained by the fact that the 1967 regime had very shallow social roots, but mostly by its disastrous role in the Cyprus crisis. The regime had engineered a coup that risked direct military confrontation with Turkey, for which it was unprepared. It then bungled the general mobilisation. Worse still, the public was made aware that the regime and the military were unprepared for war. The crisis fatally undermined the military's moral authority as the nation's guardian. The Junta's humiliation therefore extended to the military as a whole, which had to accept it had no place in Greek political life.

Even so, the new conservative government under Karamanlis trod warily. It retained (albeit briefly) the Junta's appointee, General Phaidon Gizikis, as transitional president of the republic. Anti-democracy forces were still at large, and in the ensuing months his new government had to deal with at least four conspiracies. It opted against a wholesale purge to avoid provoking another coup, but it quickly removed pro-Junta officers from leadership roles. Five hundred were forced to retire, and a further 800 were reassigned to posts that made it harder for potential conspirators to meet and plot (Veremis 1997: 173). Rumours of officers plotting continued to circulate into the 1980s, but there was only one conspiracy that drew significant media attention. On 24 February 1975 at least thirty-seven officers were arrested by the police. Some were hauled off by police in their nightwear, hence their conspiracy was dubbed the 'pyjama coup' (*praxikopima tis pitzamas*). The affair brought the cause of the military in politics into further disrepute, and it provided an excuse for a thoroughgoing purge of the army (Kremmydas 1984: 54–5; Veremis 1997: 173).

A more serious matter was the fate of the Junta leaders. The trial (Figure 9.1) was held in July 1975 and was broadcast live on television

Figure 9.1 *The two Junta leaders Ioannidis and Papadopoulos on trial, 1975 (second row, second and third from the right).* © *ERT*

and radio, thereby allowing the Greek public to sit in judgement. Throughout the proceedings, Papadopoulos, Pattakos, Makarezos and Ioannidis said very little and showed no contrition. The political objective of the trial was to draw a line under the past. All four were issued the death penalty, but each sentence was later commuted to life imprisonment. Eight other leading figures were handed life sentences. Overall, about 100 were convicted for their roles in the regime and for crimes committed during the *Polytechnio* uprising. A select number of torturers were also brought to justice (Kallivretakis 2017: 223–79). Fewer still were tried for similar crimes in Portugal, while in Spain the parties agreed to a 'Pact of Forgetting' (*Pacto del ovlido*), which left most of the regime's crimes unpunished.

The sudden collapse of the Greek dictatorship meant that some measures could be taken very quickly. Thus, political prisoners were released en masse. Thousands were allowed to return to their homes, where they were welcomed as heroes. Exiles that had been living abroad, including such artists, writers and actors as Melina Mercouri and Mikis Theodorakis, immediately boarded planes bound for Athens, as did intellectuals who had fled much earlier, such as philosopher Cornelius Castoriadis, Marxist scholar Nikos Poulantzas and sociologist Constantine Tsoucalas: each would have a significant influence on *Metapolitefsi* youth. Banned newspapers started to recirculate. Proscribed political parties were suddenly free to operate in public. In some quarters, red flags with communist symbols were unfurled over balconies along with Greek flags.

As in 1944, politicians who had taken refuge in their private domains or exile quickly resurfaced and re-entered the public sphere: men like Karamanlis, Georgios Mavros, Evangelos Averoff, Andreas Papandreou, Charilaos Florakis, Konstantinos Mitsotakis and Leonidas Kirkos. However, this 'old guard' had to adapt to a new politics and the fact that Greek society demanded an unfettered democracy. The public expected the kinds of civil liberties and political rights that Western Europeans took for granted. Critically, Karamanlis set the example. Although a deeply conservative man who had not criticised the Junta openly, except in its early days, he understood that the kind of 'guided' democracy that Papadopoulos had mooted was not an option. Nor could the fully fledged democracy that he himself now favoured coexist with a shadow state. The Left also appreciated the need for moderation and cooperation. Communist leaders accepted the rule of law and that they had to function within a liberal democratic framework. Talk of revolution was henceforth reserved for memorial speeches.

The new parliamentary democracy had four challenges before it. The most immediate was the military standoff with Turkey. Given the parlous condition of Greece's military forces, Karamanlis had very little room to manoeuvre. It was up to the United States and NATO allies to pull the two member states back from the brink of war and to stabilise conditions on Cyprus, but Washington was embroiled in Watergate and the resignation of President Richard M. Nixon. Turkey used the distraction as an opportunity to seize a third of the island. The new government in Greece could do little in response, except withdraw from NATO. The Greek Cypriot population in Turkish-occupied territory had been driven south, while in February 1975 Turkish Cypriot leaders had declared the occupied north an independent republic. Other contentious issues were maritime territorial claims and oil drilling rights in the Aegean, which dated back to the beginning of the 1973 oil crisis period, and Muslim rights in Western Thrace (Heraclides 2010; Tsitselikis 2012). The three issues would remain enduring sources of tension between these neighbouring states, and explain why they remain to this day among the world's most heavily armed states (Dertilis 2018: 777).

The Karamanlis government had mixed success when it came to Junta loyalists from institutions of authority. The Church seemed off limits. Hierarchs who owed their promotions to their support for the Junta kept their positions, whereas all mayors, provincial prefects and other significant civil authorities were replaced. Karamanlis did not extend the purge to lower-level positions to limit the social impact of regime change, yet it was also true that he did not wish to alienate former Junta supporters, who were expected to rally to his new party. There was a limited purge of the judiciary, but student pressure ensured a much more extensive one in the universities. The bureaucracy was also cleaned up to some degree, but this did not mean it became more meritocratic and apolitical. After every election, the winning party continued to fill vacancies and new positions with their party supporters.

The third challenge was the fate of the monarchy. The newly restored parliament had determined that the dictatorship was responsible for an illegal suspension of the constitution. In theory, therefore, there was a case for the monarchy's restoration. Yet whereas the accession of King Juan Carlos was widely regarded in Spain as a stabilising measure, in Greece the monarchy had been a politically partisan body and a fundamental component of the post-Civil War order. Its role in undermining both the Karamanlis and Papandreou governments, and in legitimising the Junta in April 1967, had not been forgotten.

Karamanlis himself was no friend of the monarchy and opposed its return, but had to tread warily to avoid splitting his own conservative constituency, which explains why he held the first free national elections on 17 November and a separate vote on the monarchy on 8 December.

In October, Karamanlis founded a new conservative party, New Democracy (*Nea Demokratia*/ND), which won the November 1974 elections with a convincing popular vote, gaining 220 seats in the 300-seat parliament. It defeated the coalition led by the revived Centre Union and a newly formed socialist party led by Andreas Papandreou, the Panhellenic Socialist Movement (PASOK). Karamanlis promised that his party could guarantee a smooth transition to democracy and capitalised on widespread fears that the military might take advantage of social instability. The rally cry was 'either Karamanlis or tanks' (Diamandouros 1984: 59). The monarchy was rejected in the December referendum by 70 per cent of voters. Constantine Glücksburg, the former king, accepted the verdict, and since then there has been no serious interest in the monarchy and its restoration.

The 1974 election unveiled a new political terrain. New Democracy, which secured 54.37 per cent of the popular vote, presented itself as a centre-right party that espoused free-market liberalism yet which also attended to the basic needs of a modern society (*koinonikos fileleftherismos*). Its main goals were the consolidation of democracy, stabilising the state system and joining the EEC. The party remained in power until 1981, during which time it succeeded in consolidating a liberal democratic order without exclusions (Chatzivasiliou 2010). The main opposition party was initially the Centre Union led by liberal Georgios Mavros, which had been the party of Georgios Papandreou, but lost support because its policy platform was too similar to that of ND. Much of the old Centre Union leadership was absorbed into ND, while much of its following would switch to PASOK, which had performed disappointingly in the 1974 elections – the enormous crowds that protested in the streets and took up strike actions during the early months of the *Metapolitefsi* gave the impression that the Left would perform much better. Papandreou had launched his party with his 'Declaration of 4 September 1974', which laid out a radically progressive vision for Greece, but which did little to attract support in a time when society prioritised stability over radical change. Hence three quarters of the electorate voted for the centre-right parties (ND and Centre Union). PASOK only managed just over 13 per cent of the popular vote and gained only 22 seats. The other Leftist parties that contested the 1974 elections were the two factions of KKE (pro-Soviet and Eurocommunist) and the old EDA party, but together they only managed 10 per cent of the popular vote. The National Democratic Union (*Ethniki Demokratiki Enosis*), a royalist party that appealed directly to the dictatorship's supporters, only managed to attract 1.1 per cent of the vote.

The country's political terrain had begun to shift by the November 1977 elections. While ND retained its majority, it lost 49 seats (retaining 171 seats, with 2.1 million votes), while PASOK won 93 seats (1.3 million votes) and became the main opposition party. It was the 1981 elections, however, that set the pattern of politics for the next twenty years. PASOK won and had a significant mandate to rule. It claimed almost half of the popular vote (48.7 per cent or 2.72 million votes), while the ND vote fell to 36 per cent (2.03 million votes). KKE claimed 11 per cent or 620,000 votes (Nikolakopoulos 1990: 203–37). The results proved to be significant in political, ideological and symbolic terms, particularly for Greek communists – the combined vote of the left parties was over 60 per cent, which to that point was unparalleled in the history of Western Europe (Sassoon 1996: 638). The communists, who had been anathematised and excluded from political life since the Civil War, were now treated on equal terms and enjoyed access to public sector jobs. Some former ELAS captains, including Markos Vafiadis, who headed the rebel government in 1948–9, sat in the parliament as members of PASOK. Some described their return as the 'revenge of the losers' (*revans ton ittimenon*), i.e. those defeated in the Civil War. Former Resistance fighters and guerrillas were returning from exile and claiming their right to a pension. The history of the Second World War and the Civil War were now topics that could be debated openly. PASOK ensured that the history of the patriotic wartime Resistance was integrated into the official national historical narrative (Asimakopoulos and Tassis 2018).

The 1975 constitution affirmed Greece as a presidential-parliamentary democracy, with a president as the head of state, elected by the parliament. The government was led by a prime minister whose party (or coalition) commanded most of the parliament. Parties enjoyed statutory recognition, but it was the prime minister's privilege to appoint ministers, and his party selected the head of the National Bank and made leading judicial appointments. In the meantime, Greek politics settled into a two-party system. Between 1974 and 2002, the government alternated between ND and PASOK, with each party commanding mass support across the country, to the extent that party affiliation became a significant identity marker. Greeks by and large were divided into followers of PASOK, or *pasoktsides*, and supporters of New Democracy, or *neodemokrates*. Affiliation influenced the company one chose and the cafe one patronised, but as in other Western democracies families, siblings and friends could maintain intimate ties despite conflicting political loyalties. Party membership remained strong throughout the last quarter of the twentieth century, even in the diaspora, where PASOK and ND associations were formed.

The new radicals

PASOK was the dominant party of the last quarter of the twentieth century and the period before 2008. It was a new radical party that revived familiar slogans, such as 'national independence' (*ethniki anexartisia*), 'popular sovereignty' (*laïki kiriarchia*), social liberation (*koinoniki apeleftherosi*) and democratic process (*demokratiki diadikasia*). Its success was partly attributable to its leader, Andreas Papandreou, a charismatic personality who indelibly shaped its purpose and led the party until his death in 1996. 'Andreas', as he was known to the broader public, was a gifted orator and campaigner who articulated the common people's problems and fanned their prejudices. But while his charismatic personality certainly played a role in enhancing and solidifying PASOK's strong social base, its left-populist agenda was driven by its grass-roots membership. The party's success rested on its organisation, on how it set out to appeal to different interest groups, and how it developed and maintained a highly committed mass membership. The latter was strongly encouraged to be active at the grass-roots level. In contrast, Karamanlis, who was never called by his first name, did not see the need to develop ND as a mass party. But as ND's electoral fortunes faltered in the 1980s, his successors were forced to copy the PASOK model.

PASOK was the radical expression of the *Metapolitefsi*. The 'Declaration of 4 September 1974' echoed the spirit of EAM by calling for a complete break with the past and for a future defined by popular sovereignty, liberalisation and democracy. It also presented itself as the 'anti-party': anti-establishment, anti-American, anti-big business and anti-political elites. In the more free-market and deregulatory 1980s, however, it made a series of adjustments in policy and in language to keep its middle-class and youth support base. Hence it remained in power for three decades, aside from two intervals (1989–93, 2004–9).

PASOK's success was attributable partly to its ability to adapt to the country's changing social fabric (Close 2002: 153–4).

The ideology of PASOK and that of its leader had their roots in 1960s American progressive liberalism. Papandreou was also influenced by theories regarding global inequality, including dependency theory and world-systems theory, which considers certain regions of the world as structurally dependent on the most advanced economies. He believed that Greece was an American dependency and that it had to break with the past so it could build a socialist economy. He was equally hostile to the Soviet centralised model of socialism, supporting instead a coalition of grass-roots movements that sought local autonomy. PASOK absorbed a range of conflicting ideological currents and created a platform on which different grievances and aspirations could be expressed. For two decades, the party served as a middle ground of Greek society, where different interest groups could come together and influence the remaking of their society.

Like Eleftherios Venizelos, however, Andreas Papandreou became a polarising national figure who attracted ardent loyalists and fierce enemies. Andreas was denounced by his critics as a demagogue who fanned the flames of populist resentment, even though he was born into the Greek establishment and political elite. Despite his social background, Papandreou could speak to all groups and penetrate the factional barriers, but he was also difficult to read. He introduced a form of doublespeak or political spin through which he could change the meanings of terms and introduce new ones so that even the most radical policy change could be made to seem moderate (Zorba 2019).

But PASOK was not just the rubber stamp of its leader. It was a major European socialist party with a core following of diverse groups. It appealed to farmers, workers and students, but also to a dynamic middle class that included engineers, technical professionals and liberal intellectuals. It was also supported by Civil War exiles and long-time communist activists who had been disappointed by their own leadership and who now placed their hopes in the party that held the levers of power. A younger generation of politicians whom the Cold War's fratricidal politics had not contaminated followed Papandreou into national and local government. PASOK considered itself a 'people's party', and its rhetoric was populist, contrasting the 'underprivileged' with the '200 establishment families' that many believed controlled the country (Elefantis 1991). In other words, PASOK was more than just Andreas. Millions supported it. Thousands belonged to it. And a dedicated group of mid- and high-level politicians staffed it.

Promising *allaghi!* ('change!'), PASOK won an emphatic mandate in 1981. It was the first time in Greek history that a left-wing party had formed a government by winning a legal national ballot. The triumph of such a party in Greece was a wholly new phenomenon. The mere fact that PASOK and the other left-wing parties managed less than a quarter of the popular vote only seven years earlier suggests that it was already a very different country. The next section considers the transformation of Greek society that began under Karamanlis' New Democracy and continued under the party committed to *allaghi!*

Reforms, 1975–1985

During the first years of the *Metapolitefsi*, Greeks walked cautiously into the sunlight. But as in Spain and Portugal, as fears of reaction from the military receded, society used its newfound freedoms to make radical changes to its social and cultural fabric. The state would play a critical role in these changes. Both ND and PASOK recognised that reform was essential to keep abreast of rapid social change but also for shaping it.

One area that received very early attention from policymakers was education. The need for reform was evident during the dictatorship: it motivated students to organise protests against the Junta in 1973. ND education minister Georgios Rallis introduced the first reforms, which included the extension of compulsory education from 6 to 9 years, the reintroduction of demotic Greek as the language of teaching instruction at all levels, the separation of junior and senior high schools, and the introduction of vocational education. Rallis essentially implemented Georgios Papandreou's 1964 education reforms, which conservatives had virulently opposed at the time. More taboos were broken after 1981. A new set of rules were introduced that made it easier to learn to write the modern language correctly. The complex and largely redundant set of symbols introduced into Ancient Greek in the post-Classical age, which children were required to memorise, was replaced by a simple mark over the accented vowels. To give working-class children better access to higher education, the exams required for entry to senior high school were abolished, Greek Classics (e.g. Homer, Euripides, Plato) were taught in modern translation, and students of social and political studies could enter university without being required first to have mastered Classical languages.

The role of school inspector was abolished, and the powers of headmasters and headmistresses were diminished. Although still subject to the state's overriding authority, each school was run by a teachers committee. Other reforms that evoked the spirit of democratisation were the abolition of school uniforms, the formation of student committees, which gave young people exposure to democratic political processes, and annual commemorations of the *Polytechnio* uprising. New social science subjects and new history programmes were introduced. The reforms enjoyed the general support of teachers, many of whom had come out of the student protest movement and who were inspired by spirit of the *Metapolitefsi*. Finally, university administration was democratised. Governance was now provided by committees made up of academic staff and student representatives, although critics claimed this led to a dramatic drop in discipline and academic standards (Therianos 2018: 600–17).

Above all, it was the reforms to family law and gender equity that marked the most radical departure from the past and which captured the spirit of the new age. The *Metapolitefsi* heralded a new kind of household that was less patriarchal and more considerate to the rights of women and children. Reforms that reduced the power of the state and the Church in private life included civil marriage, the decriminalisation of adultery, consensual divorce and a woman's right to retain her birth surname. Other reforms that followed Western European patterns included reducing the age of consent from 21 to 18 and the sharing of equal responsibility between men and women regarding parental obligations, children's education and work. A council for gender equality was set up in 1982, while the period saw a spate of feminist literature dealing with workplace issues and sexual liberation. Progressive social reform also extended to women in the remotest villages, whose entitlement to a pension gave them some independence and further undermined traditional male authority. There were also significant changes to children's rights, including legislation that abolished illegitimacy as a legal category. Similar reforms were enacted in Spain and Portugal (Vaiou and Psarra 2017).

However, the welfare state came late to Greece, as it did to Spain and Portugal, and the delay had adverse implications. Economic conditions in the 1970s were not conducive to enacting expansive economic agendas. In northwestern and central Europe, especially Austria and West Germany, record economic growth, powerful unions and an acceptance even among conservatives of the necessity of strong state intervention had enabled welfare-state capitalism to flourish and transform society. In contrast, post-dictatorship southern Europe had severely fragmented labour markets and outmoded welfare schemes. Moreover, reforms were introduced when industrial sectors were stagnating, and at a time when the US, Britain and other parts of Western Europe were moving toward labour market deregulation, limited state intervention in the economy and weakening the welfare state (Ferrera 1996: 17–37). Moving against the current, PASOK increased public spending to protect employment and push through welfare reform measures. It extended social security coverage (IKA) to all citizens, including comprehensive medical insurance. Every citizen had a right to a pension, and the amount allocated was increased significantly. For the first time, the elderly could count on a social security safety net. Numerous international conventions were ratified, such as the International Labour Organisation and the UN's conventions to protect mothers and children. The reforms, however, had significant flaws. The benefits were uneven, being overly generous in some cases and inadequate in others. The social allowance insurance system lacked equity, transparency and sustainability. To be sure, according to some international rankings, income inequality dropped markedly during the 1980s and 1990s, but the trend would go into reverse in the ensuing decade (Förster and d'Ercole 2005).

Every Greek enjoyed much greater access to healthcare. Until the 1980s, services for rural people and the self-employed were extremely limited, and access often depended on personal connections. There were also great disparities in the quality of treatment. The chief aims of healthcare reform included universal access, strengthening the public health sector and shifting the emphasis from intervention to prevention. Both major political parties shared these aims. In preparation for these reforms, the ND government commissioned studies and formulated plans influenced by the distinguished paediatrician Dr Spyros Doxiadis. A priority of PASOK's first term was the establishment of a national healthcare system (*Ethniko Systima Ygeias*/ESY). Led by Paraskevas Avgerinos and Georgios Gennimatas, the system was modelled on Britain's National Health Service, which was the flagship of the British welfare state, and was influenced by the World Health Organisation's declaration at Alma Ata, which mandated healthcare as a human right. The statement emphasised the need for preventative medicine and access to public health services. The reforms led to the construction of medical centres and new hospitals throughout the country, increasing the number of available beds by 50 per cent. However, PASOK was unable to roll out a comprehensive healthcare system because of budgetary constraints and obstruction from professional unions and other powerful occupational groups, such as the bank employees, who refused to give up their particular private health insurance benefits. The most noteworthy reform dealt with mental health. Greece incurred notoriety for the hellish conditions of its asylums in Dafni (Athens), Thessaloniki, Corfu and especially Leros, which became the subject of several international exposés (Maynard 1989: 1213; Merritt 1989; Bloch 1990: 129–33). Embarrassed by these revelations, the authorities overhauled the system, which involved the release of many patients and the introduction of upgraded facilities.

There was urgent need for legal reform after seven years of dictatorship. Much work focused on repealing or changing legislation to allow the repatriation of political exiles, although that did not extend to Slav Macedonians, who formed 50 per cent of that group (Tsekou 2013: 11). Those who fought in the National Resistance were finally recognised as patriots. Confiscated properties were returned and veteran fighters were given pensions. Laws targeting youth culture were abrogated, such as the 1958 law (no. 4000) on *tediboismos* – the term referred to the so-called 'teddy boys' youth subculture of the 1950s, which authorities associated with delinquency. A truncated version of the post-war security system persisted under ND, which kept a more discreet eye on leftist activities. The fate of the enormous body of files that had been collected over the decades remained an open question until 1989, when they were destroyed. Their loss was only lamented by historians, who regarded them as important historical source materials (Karamanolakis 2019: 143).

Legal reform focused on citizens' rights. The *Metapolitefsi* put a premium on popular sovereignty, leading PASOK to introduce legislation creating checks and balances in the legislative process and mandating a judicial review of the constitutionality of new laws. PASOK's reforms for local-level government went a step further by introducing participatory democracy and the decentralisation of decision-making. Hence, the provinces ceased to be subject to the dictates of the centre, which had the additional benefit of undermining the old patronage networks. The change breathed new life into provincial politics and the political parties, generating much greater grass-roots interest in local issues and fostering more organic connections between Athens and the provinces.

However, very little was done to address the nation's most intractable problem: the public sector. If anything, it became more bloated and inefficient, making it an even greater burden on the economy. Party loyalty remained the essential criterion in recruitment and promotion of the majority of the public service, as in the previous era. Throughout the post-war years recruitment had been the exclusive preserve of the

Right. In 1981, PASOK rewarded its loyalists with jobs that had been denied to them for decades, but it did the same in ensuing elections. And as it was also committed to creating a welfare state, which required an expanded bureaucratic apparatus, PASOK bloated the sector to an unprecedented degree. Personal connections (*mesa*) also continued to take precedence over merit. A system mired in excessive red tape continued to subject people to the rigid application of rules, which some could avoid if they were lucky enough to have *mesa*. Employee indifference and *efthinophobia* ('fear of responsibility') diminished public sector productivity and service quality (Close 2002: 179; Herzfeld 1996). Politicians were quite aware that there was a problem. Thus, in 1994 PASOK appointed an independent authority (*Anotato Symvoulio Epilogis Prosopikou*/ASEP) to promote merit-based hiring. It is worth noting, however, that there was nothing exceptional about the Greek public service. The complaints of the average Greek would have resonated in Italy and in other southern European countries (cf. Ginsborg 2001: 10–11).

The culture of the *Metapolitefsi*

In North America and Western Europe, the 1960s was a time when everyday people, particularly minorities, pushed back against authorities. That 'pushback' found expression in various cultural forms. Critical roles were played by youth movements and modern media, and by theatre, cinema, music and literature (Chaplin and Pieper Mooney 2018: 2, 4). It was a time when poetry was delivered in song, as shown in the works of Georges Brassens, Léo Ferré and Jacques Brel in France, and Joan Baez and Bob Dylan in the US. A notable feature of the decade was the blending of high and low culture, and the synthesis of folk, popular and Euroepan music. Greece was part of this global phenomenon, where the 1960s were associated with particular soundtracks. For many, it was the music of Mikis Theodorakis, Manos Hatzidakis or Stavros Xarchakos, and songs based on the poetry of Giorgos Seferis, Odysseas Elytis, Yiannis Ritsos and Nikos Gatsos that characterised the sound of the period. Musicians like Dionysis Savvopoulos brought the influences of rock music and French and American ballads into their own work. Others, like Yannis Markopoulos, added the Cretan and Pontian lyra. In Greece much as elsewhere, music was a metonym for the times.

Despite its diversity, much popular music during the 1960s and the dictatorship era shared a consistent political message. It was directed against consumerism, political apathy and Americanisation. It inevitably attracted the attention of the police, who made a point of monitoring and recording what was being sung even at family parties and in taverns. The cultural realm was therefore a political space, replete with utopian imagery. A theatrical performance might provoke state intervention and debate in the parliament and the popular press, as happened following a performance of Aristophanes' *The Birds* by the *Theatro Technis* (Art Theater) of Karolos Koun at the Herodes Atticus Theatre in Athens on 29 August 1959 (Koun 2008: 217–29). Music had influenced the making of new political identities, as was evident in the Lambrakis Youth movement, and it invested politics with emotion and ideals (Papanikolaou 2007). The dictatorship's efforts to eradicate cultural resistance of this kind only served to give it greater political poignancy.

The spirit of the Greek 1960s was at its strongest after 1974 and found its most potent expression in stadium concerts (Figure 9.2). Artists like Theodorakis, Markopoulos, Christos Leontis, Thanos

Figure 9.2 *Open-air concert featuring Maria Farantouri and Mikis Theodorakis, September 1974.* © *Alamy E10YM9*

Mikroutsikos and Manos Loizos filled stadiums with tens of thousands of fans, who during performances chanted political slogans and defiantly raised their fists in the air. Concerts assumed the character of religious ritual. The music frequently sounded like a stirring heroic march and was meant to elicit powerful emotions. Crowds were often led in song by such cultural icons as Mercouri and Theodorakis, and singers such as Maria Farantouri, Nikos Xilouris, George Dalaras and Maria Dimitriadou. The lyrics described the sufferings under the dictatorship, the exploitation of workers and peasants, and the wartime Resistance. The concerts crafted a new national narrative that focused on the people's history, and one that evoked a new spirit of optimism and freedom. Songs that featured explicitly political lyrics included 'Epitafios', a Ritsos poem put to music by Theodorakis, 'Ta Logia kai ta Chamena Chronia' (lyrics Manos Eleftheriou, music Yannis Markopoulos), Dionysis Savvopoulos' 'Vromiko Psomi' and Thanos Mikroutsikos' 'Politika Tragoudia'. Political slogans that were often heard included 'Deliver the Junta to the People' (*Dose ti Chounta sto Lao*), 'National independence' (*Ethniki anexartisia*), 'Power to the people' (*Laiki kyriarchia*) and 'Americans out' (*Exo oi Americani*). In these concerts the crowds expressed their sentiments about contemporary injustices, such as the Turkish occupation of northern Cyprus and solidarity with peoples labouring under dictatorships or imperialism. When Theodorakis set to music Pablo Neruda's *Canto General*, audiences of 30,000 to 50,000 sang along in Greek and Spanish, in solidarity with Chileans suffering under Augusto Pinochet's dictatorship.[1]

The *Metapolitefsi* was greeted by an explosion in publishing. Numerous small publishing houses appeared, specialising in radical political works and in foreign translations of seminal texts of the American and European New Left. Publishing itself was democratised, as the new era featured the production of countless 'home-made' political pamphlets and short-lived magazines. Conferences on politically charged topics were held frequently on university campuses, in schools and in workplaces. In other words, the end of the dictatorship released a torrent of expression that took many forms and politicised many aspects of Greek cultural life (Papadogiannis 2015).

Under the dictatorship, watching films or going to the theatre was a political act. Theatre in particular served as a medium for directing criticism at the regime, and it thrived despite threats of imprisonment to anyone involved in productions. Numerous new experimental theatre groups and small venues had emerged, some so small that actors performed within arm's reach of the audience. Companies staged Classical and foreign plays that could easily be read as critiques of the regime. Never before or since were so many of Bertolt Brecht's works performed. Especially important had been *Eleythero Theatro* (Free Theatre), a highly innovative company founded in 1970 by students, which had been especially effective at making Brecht speak to its audiences (Van Steen 2015: 287–8). The most overt challenge to the regime, however, came in the summer of 1973 with the production of *To Megalo Mas Tsirko* ('Our Grand Circus'), a play offering an alternative perspective on the nation's history, which riled the censors and forced the producers to cut the play by half (Van Steen 2015: 216). Its inspiration was Ariane Mnouchkine's *1789*, which similarly gave French audiences a 'people's view' of the nation's past. Tens of thousands came to see *To Megalo Mas Tsirko* for that reason. According to one observer, 'The performances became massive political demonstrations, the biggest ones of the seven-year dictatorship – even before the events at the Polytechnic' (Van Steen 2015: 194).

Theatre became more overtly political during the *Metapolitefsi*. Plays were now performed before mass audiences and made frequent and explicit references to recent politics and history. They often criticised social groups that had supported the Right, particularly the 'petty bourgeoisie', which was accused of indifference to the common good and to human rights. Cinema had an even bigger impact because of its wider social reach. Despite its inordinate length, Theo Angelopoulos' *The Travelling Players* (1975) was seen by 200,000 viewers. Based on Aeschylus' *Oresteia*, a trilogy about family violence, 'The Travelling Players' follows a theatrical group as it tours the countryside during the period from the Metaxas regime through to the aftermath of the Civil War. The military and the police assisted in the production, thinking the film was simply about the *Oresteia*, but the movie effectively inverted the official historical line about the 1930s and 1940s. Despite its success in Greece, Karamanlis' government thought it too left-wing and blocked its entry to the Cannes Film Festival. Greeks also finally got to see Costa Gavras' award-winning 1969 film *Z*, which was based on the Lambrakis assassination (see pp. 248, 553–5). Another landmark was Pantelis Voulgaris' *The Stone Age* (1985), which directly addressed the persecution of the Left during the 1950s, conveying the post-war period's character from the perspective of its victims (Karalis 2012: 170–80).

Naturally, these victims were eager to address the past. The *Metapolitefsi* was a period of historical debate and revision, which took place in newspapers, magazines, popular conferences and political youth festivals rather than in the universities. The most sensitive topic was the Axis occupation and the official version that had cast the collaborators as patriots and the Resistance as traitors. That version was retained in school textbooks through to 1981, while ND was in government. The Left, including PASOK, had been demanding revision. The latter had been busy developing its version of history, constructing a radical narrative that incorporated the liberal Venizelos and the communist Aris Velouchiotis, thereby claiming to be the party of progress and social justice. Such counternarratives offered much-needed correctives to the dominant line, but they presented an uncritical depiction of the Left, overlooking, among other things, the violence perpetrated against civilians by the partisans and the DSE. Among the bestselling books in 1975 was the Greek translation of Dominique Eudes' *Les Kapetanios* (1970), which over-romanticised the captains (*kapetanioi*) of the resistance.

A noteworthy feature of popular history in this period, which was expressed through cinema, theatre, musical concerts and popular literature, was how 'the people' (*laos*) replaced the state as the subject of the national narrative. Tellingly, the term *ethnos* was avoided because it had been overused and abused by the post-war Right and the dictatorship. Rather, historical writing deployed such key concepts as *Romiosyni* ('Romios-ness'), which was read as 'the people' as distinct from the state. It worked well with the established view of Greece's '3,000 years of continuity', as formulated by Constantine Paparrigopoulos in the mid-nineteenth century, given that there had not been a continuous history of statehood, whereas the people could be deemed timeless. *Romiosyni* was associated with traditional Greek heritage, which was thought to persist in contemporary popular culture and in the Greek soul. As such *Romiosyni* became a concept that was more grounded in the lived experiences of everyday Greeks, who had suffered at the hands of the Greek state and foreign powers. There was, however, another Greek identity, Hellenism, which was associated with a Classics-inspired high culture that was remote to that experience of common people (Herzfeld 1982; Herzfeld 1987). The emotional power invested in the term *Romiosyni* is evident in Ritsos' landmark poem of the same name, written during the Civil War (published 1954), and set to stirring music by Mikis Theodorakis in 1966. The lyrics 'under his arm he holds his Romiosyne tightly like a worker holds his cap in church' convey both its intimate informality and sacredness. The following verses of Ritsos captured the spirit of the *Metapolitefsi*, particularly when sung by one of its most famous singers of protest songs, the contralto and future PASOK MP Maria Farantouri. The lyrics speak of a people and a beast, a fall and resurrection, humiliation and vengeance:

> *Ti Romiosyne mi tin kles*/Don't cry for Romiosyne
> *Eki pou pai na skipsi*/There where it bends down
> *Me to sougio sto kokalo*/With a knife in her bone
> *Me to louri sto sverko*/With a leash around her neck
> *Na ti, petiete apaxarchis ki anatrivete ki therievei*/Here she is! Lunging
>   suddenly with strength and fury
> *Ki kamakoni to therio me to kamaki tou iliou*/And skewers the beast
>   with the sun's trident. (Ritsos 2001)

Another key concept was *ithageneia*, which translates roughly as 'indigenousness', linking Greeks to their deep history (Markopoulos et al. 1972). The term helped to mediate between 'Western' and 'civilised' on the one hand, and between 'popular' and 'modern' on the other, as *ithagenis* Greeks rediscovered their authentic selves (*afthentikotitas*) that had never been distorted (*nothefti*) by Western culture, the state and urban life. *Ithageneia* was also a call for a new appreciation of Greek folk culture and tradition. Finally, the term *antistasi* ('resistance') was another that figured prominently in the language of the period: it was deemed an innate component or unchanging feature of the Greek character. The new national narrative focused on a people forced to wage relentless struggles against foreigners who wished to suppress their freedoms and exploit their resources. In this drama, foreign oppressors and their local collaborators were pitted against the people, who were always being betrayed and exploited. This essential 'us versus them' historical schema provided the basic elements of a new populist identity (Svoronos 1975).

History was robustly contested during the *Metapolitefsi*, and that was especially true of academic history. Studying history was popular among intellectuals, many of whom had returned from exile and had imbibed the progressive developments in French, British and German historiography, such as the focus on social history and the experiences of subordinated groups (the working class, cultural minorities). They questioned Greece's established historical profession's focus on nations, high politics and great men, claiming instead that they should be examining society, especially inequalities and injustices. When exiles like Nikos Svoronos, Philippos Iliou, Spiros Asdrachas and Angelos Elefantis returned they challenged untenable orthodoxies with critical history. They confronted the conservative nationalist

approach to the past championed by the Right, but also the new populist line being developed by the Left and PASOK. This 'new' history
movement called for social history or studies that made people and
society rather than elites and the nation state the focus of analysis.
They called for scientific history in the sense that it should be based on
archival research and driven by open questions. They also called for a
thoroughgoing revision of contentious periods of Greek history, especially the 1940s. Under their influence, the newspapers and magazines
were flooded by historical essays. In 1976 the magazine *Anti* produced
a major study on popular culture and tradition, capturing the key ideas
that were in the air at the time, and foreshadowing the development
of two dominant approaches to history (Karavidas 2015). The first
approach was to treat folk culture as an artefact of that past that no
longer existed. That approach also focused on the drivers of change in
Greece, such as the Enlightenment, commerce and populism, and the
barriers to change, such as the Church and the peasantry. Opposed to it
was a nativist view that extolled Orthodox popular culture, and which
regarded Western power as a destructive influence. It directed its anti-
imperialism at Western cultural imperialism. The questions raised at
the time concerned not just recent history but also how to reconstitute
'the new face of Hellenism' (Apostolidou 2003).

In July 1977 the newspaper *Ta Nea* published a major study entitled
'Should We Rewrite Our History?' (4–26 July 1977), to which historians
like Svoronos and Kostis Moskof responded in various ways. Historical
revision had become a national preoccupation. State-owned banks
founded research institutes to promote historical studies. PASOK
funded historical research. The University of Crete invited Svoronos to
produce a new historical curriculum based on social history. The teaching of history was revised in the universities to make it a means for
social inquiry rather than an affirmation of nationalism and its values.
The *Ethniko Idrima Erevnon* (Hellenic Research Foundation), together
with the journal *Mnemon*, became the heart of a new historical profession that was now in step with the profession globally. All the while, a
yawning gap emerged between the kind of history that was being produced by academics, who, like their colleagues around the world, were
deconstructing national and popular myths, and sections of society
that identified closely with these myths. Critical history undermined
the cherished beliefs of both the Right and the Left, although in Greece
and in most other liberal democracies, these changes to the study of
history had limited impact beyond the academy, and particularly in the
media and at the popular level (Liakos 2004).

The rise of feminism became one of the more salient lineaments of the *Metapolitefsi*. In 1974 the Women's Rights Association (*Dikeomata tis Gynaikas*) and the Democratic Women's Movement (*Kinisi Demokratikon Gynaikon*) were founded or refounded. These organisations focused on family law reform, workplace and education rights for women, and greater representation for women in government. They affiliated with political parties that quickly developed women's sections. At the same time, women's sections of different parties often co-operated when it came to key reforms and the drafting of legislation. They provided the necessary pressure to force change in a male-dominated system. Meanwhile, another significant women's sphere opened up in 1975 with the emergence of feminist magazines and other publications dedicated to 'women's liberation'. Greek feminism's motto was: 'I do not belong to my father. I do not belong to my husband. I want my self' (*Den ime tou patros mou, den ime tou andros mou, thelo ton eafto mou*). Those who participated in women's initiatives focused on patriarchy, violence against women, on sexual and reproductive freedom, and on abortion and other rights relating to women's bodies. The movement argued that gender difference and gender roles were socially constructed and not biologically determined. Activists often preferred the term 'gender' (*koinoniko fylo*) rather than 'women' (*gynaikes*) in their studies of politics, work and history. Most feminist intellectuals were young and cosmopolitan, and were keen to develop ties with transnational and national women's movements. They translated seminal books and articles, and applied feminist theories and ideas to their work. The journals *Skoupa* (1979), *Dini* (1986) and *Katina* (1989) played significant roles in addressing stereotypes and changing public discourses on gender relations. As with Spanish feminism, Greek feminism caught up with the global movement's second wave, which had flourished in the 1960s and had focused on women's political rights. The third wave of feminism emphasised individual rights regarding male violence, sexuality, reproduction and other matters overlooked by the first wave (Repousi and Psara 2017).

The rise of feminism in this period, as with the emergence of queer communities and queer rights activism, reflected broader changes in attitudes to sexuality and gender. By now, women's participation in higher education was growing, as was their presence in social services. Such changes signified greater financial independence and personal autonomy. The use of the term *sexualikotita* ('sexuality') in public discourse also pointed to changing ideas concerning male sexuality. Whereas male homosexuality was once defined by the kind of homoeroticism found in the poetry of Dinos Christianopoulos and the paintings of Yannis Tsarouchis, it was now replaced by same-sex communities and couples that focused on affective relationships. The same applied to lesbians. Both same-sex communities were seeking recognition and a place in the public domain. In 1977 the *Apeleftherotiko Kinima Omofylofilon Elladas* (the Greek Gay Liberation Movement/ AKOE) emerged and published the periodical *Amfi* (1978–90). The following year saw the establishment of *Aftonomi Omada Omofylofilon Gynaikon* (the Independent Gay Women's Group) and its publication *Lavris*. Their aim was to combat stigmatisation and to seek decriminalisation of same-sex relations between consenting adults. The group gained public support following the public controversy over the wrongful incarceration of a young gay man named Christos Roussos, whose ordeals are the subject of the Giorgos Katakouzinos' 1982 film *Angelos*. Roussos was given a life sentence after killing his abusive lover, who had forced him into prostitution. After ten years of humiliating treatment in prison and psychiatric hospitals, he was refused a pardon by President Christos Sartzetakis but granted one by Karamanlis in 1990. Indeed, the year 1990 proved to be an important one in the history of human rights in Greece. It coincided with the publication of the Greek translation of Michel Foucault's *Discipline and Punish*, and the first articles of Gilles Deleuze, Félix Guattari and other theorists that were published in *Amfi*, which linked biopolitics to sexuality and repression in psychiatric hospitals and prisons. It was also the year when the scandal over the conditions of Leros' psychiatric hospitals made international headlines. These developments helped to influence a general consensus for the promotion of human rights in Greece (Yannakopoulos 2016: 173–89; Vamvakas and Panagiotopoulos 2010).

A public consensus eventually emerged on a date for commemorating the *Metapolitefsi*'s foundation. The 24th of July 1974, which marked the fall of the Junta, was overlooked because it was engineered by military and political elites. Rather, the chosen date was 17 November 1973, the bloody climax of the *Polytechnio*, given it was a popular uprising in pursuit of progressive social and political values. The students' sacrifices were then commemorated annually in a ritual that looked like a Greek Orthodox Good Friday epitaph procession. Red carnation wreaths were laid at the *Polytechnio* itself, followed by a parade headed by a bearer of the Greek flag with red stains that symbolised the protesters' blood. The procession marched past the parliament and along Leoforos Vassilisis Sofias, a wide avenue that led directly to the US Embassy. The *Polytechnio* itself has remained a site of memory that relates to democratic values and the structures of power and influence. Each year, the commemoration raised questions about social justice, and whether the students' sacrifices had been in vain. The *Polytechnio* myth in that sense functioned as the *Metapolitefsi*'s conscience.

However, 'the culture of the *Metapolitefsi*' was also fleeting. It did not become the nation's dominant ideology. It had emerged out of the 1960s from under the shadow of authoritarianism and as a culture of resistance. In the 1980s it was embodied by the former international film star and now politician Melina Mercouri, a feminist who played roles that subverted patriarchal norms and challenged Greek masculinity. As PASOK's long-serving Minister of Culture (1981–9, 1993–4) she embodied the spirit of *Metapolitefsi*. However, even she had to balance that resistance spirit with being a member of a government in power. The great star performed the role of national hero when she led calls for Greece's long-standing claims for the return of the Parthenon sculptures from the British Museum. Yet she also anticipated what is nowadays known as the decolonisation of museums, which requires that they recognise cultural diversity in society. While exploiting national symbols such as the Parthenon in international forums, she was also pushing the decentralisation of culture at home through the formation of localised theatrical companies (*Demotika Periferiaka Theatra*) and cultural centres (Zorba 2014: 303–48).

'The culture of the *Metapolitefsi*', which has been criticised as the underlying cause of Greece's present-day malaise (e.g. Kalyvas 2008), in fact had many facets. In the years that followed 1974, a considerable minority of youth continued to see the *Metapolitefsi* as the starting point of a revolution. Various social circles and counterculture movements emerged, some of which were part of the underground punk rock scene, and which had formed a vague political and cultural space named *o choros* ('the space'). They frequented specific bookshops, record shops and cafes in central Athens and Thessaloniki, and specific districts like Exarchia. They participated in violent demonstrations and squatted in buildings in the city centre, creating a culture of fury, social protest, unrest and solidarity with the destitute and other dissidents (Kassimeris 2005; Kassimeris 2013; Kitis 2015: 1–36; Apoifis 2017). Wholly separate to that experience were the clandestine terrorist groups. The most enduring was the 17 November Revolutionary Organisation (*Epanastatiki Organosi 17 Noemvri*/17N), which killed twenty-two people between 1975 and 2002. For them, *Metapolitefsi* and Junta was the Janus face of imperialism and lumpen-bourgeoisie power. When 17N members gunned down CIA chief Richard Welch in Athens in December 1975, the US Congress ceased investigations into the CIA's illegal activities behind Watergate and focused on combating terrorist organisations. Greek police were given better training and equipment for anti-terrorist operations. Parliament also passed strict anti-terrorist laws that gave the authorities the tools needed to combat terrorism (Kiesling 2014: 9). Even so, Greek terrorism proved to be much more difficult to crack than the Red Army Faction (Baader–Meinhof gang) in Germany, the Red Brigade in Italy or Dev-Yol in Turkey.

Balancing on two boats

The *Metapolitefsi* occurred when the world was facing its most serious economic crisis since the Great Depression. Its effects were particularly felt in southern Europe, where it triggered double-digit inflation: in Greece it peaked at 32 per cent. The crisis called into question the viability of certain industries, the purpose of union movements and the cost of the welfare state. West Germany, which had been the locomotive of growth in Europe, shed much of its large southern European guest worker population, and hence many of its Greek workers. Greece's social and economic challenges found public expression through strikes: one newspaper claimed that 'strikes had become the normal way of expressing the interest of community groups' (*To Vima*, 12 June 1977). In such conditions, could the post-Junta Greek state fulfil its social contract with the people?

Unions were very active following the fall of the dictatorship. Wage levels had been stagnant throughout the post-war years and lagged behind those in other southern European states. Armed with the slogan 'Let's bring the *Metapolitefsi* to the factories', unions were quick to secure such significant reforms as the five-day, forty-hour week, and significant pay raises that increased faster than GDP, all of which lifted living standards. The period also witnessed the rise of autonomous and militant trade unions that operated outside the authority of the General Confederation of Greek Workers (GSEE). This development could also be observed in Spain and Portugal, where the dictatorships had controlled unions under a corporatist system, and where many unionists after the dictatorships remained committed to 'workerism' (*operaismo*), which held that the working class should be the central driving force of economic life (Tronti 2010: 186–9). This trend led to the formation in 1979 of the Federation of Industrial Workers' Unions (*Omospondia Biomichanikon Ergatoupallilikon Somateion*/OBES)

(Ioannidis 2019). This form of labour radicalism was common throughout Western Europe during the 1970s, but it was particularly strong in
Italy, Spain and Greece, where strikes could be violent and where factories were sometimes occupied by the workers. Labour unrest under
the Karamanlis government, which extended to the rural sector, helped
sweep PASOK into power in 1981. Once in power, PASOK increased
the minimum wage, raised pensions and increased the number of
people who could receive one. At the same time, people in the countryside gained much greater access to social welfare and other benefits.
Thus, despite the difficult economic conditions, private consumption
and living standards continued to improve into the 1980s.

All *Metapolitefsi* governments had to manage the often contradictory
demands of an expanding welfare state on the one hand, and the need
to drive economic growth on the other. The Karamanlis government,
which introduced some of the most far-reaching changes in the Greek
economy, had an eclectic policy approach that was reflected in the three
men it chose to run economic affairs. The governor of the National
Bank of Greece, Angelos Angelopoulos, was a Keynesian. He had been
a professor and finance minister for the EAM government (PEEA) in
1944 (see pp. 188–90), and he had been the publisher of the progressive
magazine *Nea Oikonomia* (*New Economy*) (1946–67). The governor of
the Bank of Greece, Xenophon Zolotas, who was in charge of monetary
policy, was a neoclassical economist. The minister in charge of coordinating economic affairs was Panagiotis Papaligouras, who had previously served in the Papagos and Karamanlis post-war governments,
but who was often criticised for 'socialmania', which referred to the
practice of nationalising failing enterprises. The first private enterprise
nationalised by ND was Aristotle Onassis' Olympic Airways, which
had been unprofitable since the 1973 oil price hike. Next were Stavros
Niarchos' refineries. The government then turned to companies owned
by Stratis Andreadis, which included banks, shipyards, a refinery, the
railway network of Athens, insurance companies, chemical plants and
the Athens Hilton. ND nationalised the urban transportation system,
and the aviation and munition industries. Its 'socialmania' was in line
with government practice across Western Europe, where intervention
was deemed necessary to save key industries and to secure the functioning of essential infrastructure and services.

ND economic policy was also focused on joining the European
Economic Community. The Treaty of Accession, signed on 28 May 1979,
made Greece the first of the post-dictatorship states to join. Spain and
Portugal signed accession agreements in June 1985. Joining, however,

posed significant challenges, as it meant that protections to key sectors of the economy would be reduced. Highly uncompetitive local industries were exposed to European competition. Greece's treaty made some provision to give industry and agriculture time to adjust to open and competitive markets. In the meantime, a second global energy crisis, brought on by the Iranian Revolution in 1979, saw prices skyrocket by 150 per cent. Thus, when Greece joined the EEC it was in the midst of a perfect storm: costs had spiked just as sales and competitiveness had slumped. Nor could ND or PASOK follow the Bank of Greece's advice and freeze wages – the population could not make more sacrifices after seven years of income stagnation. To cushion the economy, PASOK implemented a mixture of protectionist measures, extensive state-guaranteed lending, and the abridgement of government contracts. After 1982, employment protection became a priority for state economic policy, as the return of thousands of Greek nationals and the arrival of immigrants from Eastern Europe produced a sharp rise in labour force numbers. Another reason for the crisis in Greek industry had to do with falling investment since the 1973 oil crisis. Many of the most prominent multinationals pulled out of the country, including Esso Pappas, Ethyl, Pirelli and Goodyear. Many of Greece's largest industries went bankrupt or were operating at a loss to keep staff employed (Giannitsis 2011: 525–97).

Industrial policy between 1975 and 1990 centred on what was described at the time as 'problematic or excessively indebted companies' (Psalidopoulos 2014: 309). The problem of too much debt forced the National Bank of Greece to buy shares in the affected companies, most of which then became bank property. Among the leading businesses in trouble were munitions company Pyrkal, the cement giant AGET Iraklis and the corporation Piraiki-Patraiki. There were also entire industries that were affected, such as textiles, consumer goods (e.g. Izola), paper, metallurgy and mining. A restructuring business agency (*Organosis Anasynkrotisis Epichiriseon*/OAE) was established in 1983 to rescue or liquidate companies with more than 30,000 workers. The problems of the industrial sector, along with the majority of commercial enterprises financed by commercial banks, brought the Bank of Greece to the brink of collapse (Psalidopoulos 2014: 309–11).

Another contributing factor to Greece's economic problems was the merchant marine and its diminishing returns. Once a pillar of the Greek economy, the industry had been hard hit by the 1973 oil crisis, which greatly affected owners and employees, and which substantially affected the flow of remittances. The crisis also affected Greek banks that had financed and insured shipping companies. Shipyards that employed thousands of workers shuttered, as did many related industries. Throughout Greece companies encouraged early retirement, placing incredible burdens on insurance funds, which then had to be subsidised by the state. These developments contributed to expanding budget deficits, which grew ever larger with increasing trade imbalances. Meanwhile, governments continued to support small and medium-sized businesses and continued to subsidise agriculture (Pagoulatos 2006: 379–84).

Could the state do otherwise? Neither Karamanlis nor Bank of Greece governor Zolotas could be described as socialists. But in Europe's most advanced post-war economies, even conservative parties had embraced Keynesian economic policies and saw the need for significant state intervention in economic life. The challenges of the two World Wars and the search for stability following these catastrophes gave governments no option other than to manage economies and reduce social inequalities (Piketty 2014: ch. 8; Scheidel 2017: ch. 5). These experiences influenced policy-making in all governments well into the 1970s. In a memo sent to Karamanlis in 1975, Zolotas warned of an emerging urban real estate bubble and widespread tax evasion among higher-income earners. He recommended that instead of issuing loans which exacerbated the problem of national debt, the government should increase taxes on large landholdings, enact a state monopoly on fuel and imported luxury items, and suppress consumption on imports. Zolotas complained that he could not continue printing money and risk further inflation just to support ND's expansionist economic policies (Psalidopoulos 2014: 279–81).

By 1985, however, a wholly new kind of economic order was in the making. The crisis-ridden 1970s produced many losers but also some winners. Opportunities were presented by Middle Eastern oil-producing countries which were flush with 'petrodollars' following the oil price hikes that they were keen to invest in construction or in refinery companies. Many Greek companies flourished as recipients of such investment, the more so because Greece had maintained good relations with the Arab world after the 1956 and 1967 Middle East crises, and because they had started trading with the Persian Gulf states, Libya and Saudi Arabia. Greek shipping companies began shifting their focus more on transporting and refining petroleum. The scale of economic activity prompted *Metapolitefsi* governments to take a far greater interest in the Arab world and its politics. The glut in petrodollars was also a boon for the financial sector, which was the greatest beneficiary of the 1970s economic crises. The world was awash with money that was managed neither by states nor international organisations, but by private corporations. Foreign exchange was also pouring into Greece because of tourism. *Metapolitefsi* governments were pressured to relax state monetary policy and reform regulations on credit that had been in place since the 1930s. As a consequence, interest rates were being decided by the needs and interests of borrowers. In Greece, as in the rest of the world, the relaxation of credit and interest rate controls greatly enhanced the power of bankers. The critical year was 1985. Over the next two years, government policy focused on stabilising and combating inflation, which improved economic indices and brought higher returns on capital investments. Even though PASOK soon abandoned these practices, pressure for deregulation and liberalisation continued to shape government economic policies.

Throughout the *Metapolitefsi*, economic growth stagnated while inflation and unemployment rose. The rate of GDP growth during the 1960s was 7.5 per cent. It fell to 3 per cent in the 1970s and 1.5 per cent in the 1980s. Investment followed a similar downward trajectory: from 10.2 per cent to 1 per cent. Meanwhile, inflation jumped from 3.4 per cent under the dictatorship to double that number during the *Metapolitefsi*, and it continued at high rates for over two decades. From Papadopoulos to Papandreou and through to the end of the century, unemployment climbed from zero to just under 8 per cent. National debt doubled with each decade: 19.3 per cent in 1961–73, 33.6 per cent in 1974–81, 60.0 per cent in 1982–93 (Psalidopoulos 2014: 45–50, 259–338). These trends were not a consequence of the restoration of democracy, given the fact that the other twelve Western European states also experienced comparable economic downturns. Their annual growth rates fell from 5.2 per cent in the period 1961–73, to 2.2 per cent for the years 1974–85. The Greek experience conformed more closely to those of other southern European states, where the economic crises cut deeper. Here, growth rates plummeted: Italy saw annual growth rates reduce from 5.4 to 2.8 per cent, Spain from 7.2 to 1.8, Portugal from 6.9 to 2.2, Greece from 8.5 to 1.7 (European Commission 2006: 184–96). In each case, progressive social change happened in a global economic environment experiencing a structural transition that persisted into the 1980s, which included stagflation, which combined high inflation and high unemployment. The most significant consequence of these crisis years was the shift in economic thinking from Keynesianism to the free-market ideology espoused by Margaret Thatcher in Great Britain and Ronald Reagan in the United

States. By 1985, PASOK and ND leaders had come around to the new way of thinking.

The end of the *Metapolitefsi*

In 1985 the PASOK government applied for a loan from the EEC to address the ballooning foreign trade deficit, which had reached 8.7 per cent of GDP.[2] The EEC required the implementation of a stabilisation programme as a precondition of the loan. Finance Minister Kostas Simitis responded by introducing policies to combat inflation and reduce the deficit by cutting public spending. The drachma was devalued by 15 per cent, wages were no longer indexed to inflation, some tax exemptions were abolished and incomes returned to pre-1980 levels. Then, in February 1986, Greece signed the Single European Act, which was meant to prepare member states for the creation of a single market by 1992. All were required to deregulate. By signing, each member accepted EEC controls and reduced state intervention in economic life (Tsarapatsanis 2018: 369–88). Along with the other four southern European states, the Greek government implemented policies designed to attack inflation, reduce deficits and control wages. Simitis' economic reforms were having the intended effect in the short term, but PASOK was shaken by a popular backlash. Simitis was forced to resign from his ministerial position in 1987, and the reforms were abandoned. Greece then descended to the bottom of economic rankings, falling behind the rest of the member states, including Portugal and Ireland. By the end of the decade, the Greek economy ranked last in terms of convergence with EEC goals, but also in terms of economic competitiveness, dependence on EEC and state subsidies, investment, inflation and growth (Close 2002: 169).

Deregulation of the Greek economy was bound to be a difficult transition. After all, in 1984 there were still eighty different legislated business interest rates, for which borrowing criteria had nothing to do with the cost of money or loan security. At the time, the public sector still enjoyed preferential treatment, which meant private borrowers suffered higher costs and often needed social connections in government and the banking sector to secure loans. This highly regulated economic environment had been in place since the 1930s, when the state sought to shield the economy from the worst effects of the Depression. But since then, the regulations had facilitated the making of a thickening web of privilege and interests. It was a web that would require a great deal of time and political will to unravel.

In the meantime, deregulation and liberalisation were having a profound impact on Greek social life and consumption practices. A special role was played by imported goods that were now much more readily available. A striking example was Scotch whisky, which became the *Metapolitefsi*'s drink of preference. Sales increased tenfold in the 1970s, with consumption increasing by 279 per cent between 1981 and 1991 (Bampilis 2013: 2). Whisky-drinking became a prominent feature of new kinds of leisure activities, particularly at night club venues known as *ellinadika*, where patrons sat at tables and sang along with stage performers and bands. The same was true at the lower-grade and more raucous *skyladika*, where such rituals as plate-smashing and dancing on tables developed. Meanwhile, interest in traditional Greek drinks like ouzo and *tsipouro*, which once symbolised Greek masculinity and male sociability, had declined. Thus, whisky consumption marked a break from the past, but it also symbolised the tightening relationship between Greek consumerism, individual prosperity and globalisation. Buying bottles of Scotch at nightclubs was a heroic act precisely because it was expensive, but also because intoxication gave, as one anthropologist has argued, a new rising middle class a few moments to negate its social and economic responsibilities, or indeed to defy, through excess consumption of whisky, EEC and government economic planning (Bampilis 2013: xv).

By the mid-1980s Greece had become a consumerist society. The purchasing power of the working class had increased, but it was the middle classes that embodied the culture of consumerism, and set the example for others to follow. Indeed, the middle classes were the real winners of the *Metapolitefsi*, as suggested by changing demographic patterns. During this period, the population of central Athens fell by 15 per cent, as wealthy and upper-middle-class households relocated to the northern and coastal suburbs, where housing and facilities could better support their new lifestyles. Between 1970 and 1990 the suburbs more than doubled in population. Retail services changed accordingly. The small shops in the downtown market were replaced by supermarkets, which changed consumer habits and relations between vendors and shoppers (Maloutas et al. 2006: 10). Living in the suburbs and daily commuting dramatically increased the need for private automobiles. Consequently, the volume of traffic shot up, leading to air pollution and the formation of a massive smog cloud that permanently blanketed the city.

Consumption influenced new social habits and outlooks, and the way Greeks managed their leisure time. All classes and both sexes frequented cafes and bars, exercised in gymnasiums, took up sports, watched television, and developed hobbies and new reading interests, most of which required routine engagement with the market for consumables. The extension of the electrical grid brought consumables and appliances to the remotest rural villages, which raised living standards and promoted more private lifestyle pursuits. Towards the end of the *Metapolitefsi*, these kinds of changes had eroded the collectivist spirit described earlier in this chapter (see pp. 317–26). Indeed, it was consumption rather than politics that constituted the main field of social competition. Modern lifestyles, consumer practices and changing mentalities went hand in hand with undermining the ideological grip of the state, the Church and the political parties. Spain and Portugal went through identical processes: from authoritarian paternalism to collectivism and mass democracy, and then to mass consumerism. In Spain, the latter was reflected in the term *pasotismo*, or 'dropping out', which referred to indifference to social issues and politics (Kornetis et al. 2016: 13).

The link between democratisation, the revival of mass politics and mass culture, and the advent of mass consumerism in southern Europe was drawn by Pier Paolo Pasolini in the Italian newspaper *Il Mondo* (11 July 1974), just after the outbreak of the Portuguese Revolution:

> The mass culture cannot be an ecclesiastic, moralistic and patriotic culture: rather it is directly linked to consumption, which has its internal laws and its ideological self-sufficiency, such as automatically creating a power which no longer knows what to make of the Church, the Fatherland, the Family … Thus, Portugal should no longer be a severe, tight-fisted, archaic nation: it should be immersed in the great universe of consumerism. (Accornero 2016: xiii)

That observation could certainly be applied to Greece. By the mid-1980s there were clear signals that the *Metapolitefsi* was petering out. On a warm, moonlit night in July 1983, more than 50,000 Athenians watched a concert on the beach in the ritzy resort suburb of Vouliagmeni. With drinks in hand, they swayed to the music of Loukianos Kilaidonis. But this concert was very different from the concerts of several years earlier. This time there was no political messaging. The concert had a style that was more uplifting than inspiring. It offered a line-up of rock music classics mixed with rebetika, soundtracks from Hollywood movies and current commercial hits. The shift away from collectivist ideals intensified over the ensuing years. In 1987, the new magazine *CLICK* advertised expensive clothing and nightclubs and made a virtue of luxury and leisure. Similar magazines followed, with such foreign-language names as *Elle* (1987) and *Marie Claire* (1988). Advertising pushing prestige brands became ubiquitous. The wealthy were seeking new ways to show their social status, but these magazines did not merely target the wealthy. They also celebrated a new identity that was modern, cosmopolitan and optimistic, and to which the lower classes could aspire. Changing tastes, new modes of public expression and expectations of a more sumptuous life represented a distinct departure from the culture of the *Metapolitefsi*.[3]

By the mid-1980s, there was also a noticeable shift within PASOK in public discourse, from the language of democratisation and social justice to nationalism. In 1985 the newly elected president, Christos Sartzetakis, a conscientious judge who had presided over the investigations in the Lambrakis case, became better known for describing Greece as a 'brotherless nation' (*ethnos anadelfo*).[4] Meanwhile, singer Dionysis Savvopoulos defined the Greek personality as follows: 'And whether with antiquity or with Orthodoxy, the Greeks live in their own galaxy.'[5] In 1986, the Minister of Education, Antonis Tritsis, reinstated the teaching of Classical Greek in primary and junior high school. The intent was to teach the language through its 'diachronic evolution' to better connect children with the nation (Mackridge 2009: 326). It constituted a symbolic act given the ideological significance that the *Metapolitefsi* had earlier accorded to demotic Greek as an accessible and socially equalising medium.

No political party had a monopoly on nationalism now. Indeed, as would be the case in many European states, the chasm that once divided the Right and the non-right, social democratic and centre-right parties, had been effectively bridged. PASOK, the party of change that was able to mobilise the masses and respond to its calls, like its sister social democratic parties in Italy, France and the Iberian Peninsula, had become a mainstream party led by men in suits, and who were open to cross-party deals and alliances. Meanwhile, in the late 1980s numerous scandals involving prominent politicians, including Andreas Papandreou himself, increased public cynicism towards the political class.

The *Metapolitefsi* was the formative period of contemporary Greece, which is why it remains an obsession of present-day public discourse. 'The culture of the *Metapolitefsi*' bespoke collectivism. It was the culture of the masses and of resistance, and it was built on the concept of 'progressive ideas', most of which were quietly abandoned in the ensuing era. *Metapolitefsi* could be considered the Greek contribution to the global 1960s.

Cyprus, 1974–1980s

Before leaving the *Metapolitefsi*, it is important to consider developments in Cyprus, on which the dictatorship left its most lasting and catastrophic legacy, but which would experience its own kind of *metapolitefsi*. For while Greeks were celebrating democracy in July–August 1974, Cyprus had just suffered its greatest catastrophe. Tens of thousands of Greek Cypriots had fled their ancestral homes, many of whom were forced to live in refugee camps while agonising over the fate of relatives. Most Cypriots, Greeks and Turkish, were mourning their dead. The most familiar image of Cyprus that was seen throughout the Greek world was a map that showed the north bleeding, and the words 'I don't forget' (*den xechno*). The Republic of Cyprus lost over three quarters of its agricultural resources (76 per cent), just under half of its manufacturing, 56 per cent of its mining, 87 per cent of its tourism facilities, its leading resort (Famagusta) and export harbour, and its international airport (Christodoulou 1992). The provisional government was headed by Glafcos Clerides, and then by Makarios, who returned in December to deal with a shattered country struggling with a massive refugee crisis, which was only partially resolved by the distribution of abandoned Turkish Cypriot properties in the south. Inevitably mass displacement increased the unemployment rate to 30 per cent (Zetter 1992: 10).

By far the dominant issue, however, was reunification. The so-called Green Line that ran from south of Famagusta through to the western end of Morphou Bay, cutting through the capital Nicosia, had been patrolled by UN Peacekeeping forces, and presented an impenetrable barrier. Like Berlin, the island's capital was divided by a wall. While the Greek Cypriot government sought justice at the international level, the Turkish Cypriot leader Rauf Denktaş insisted any resolution would require a federal solution that guaranteed the security and full autonomy of the Turkish community. Negotiations began in 1977 only after Makarios had signed an agreement that would consider 'bizonality', indicating a willingness to accommodate Turkish Cypriot autonomy. The chief sticking point was, how much autonomy? Denktaş sought to push the advantage provided by the heavy Turkish military presence to secure full autonomy and make Cyprus a confederation. Makarios' successor, Spyros Kyprianou, argued that this was untenable as it allowed the Turkish community to secede or conduct its own policies. Underlying all negotiations was Greek Cypriot resentment in having to accede to the demands of a small minority, and the Turkish Cypriot refusal to accept its status as a minority. Although the Turkish military presence gave the Turkish community an overwhelming advantage, Greek Cypriots tried to redress the power imbalance by attaining the moral support of the international community. It tried to use its seat at the United Nations and its tightening relationship with the European Union to put pressure on Ankara. Greece's accession into the EEC in 1981 not only strengthened its hand vis-à-vis Turkey but also the hand of Cyprus. Denktaş proclaimed the north an independent state in 1983, but the move merely hardened international opposition.

All further talks (1986, 1988, 1989 and 1992) failed, as neither side was prepared to concede on the federation/confederation question. Positions were hardened when the Republic of Cyprus formally applied to join the European Community in 1990, which threatened Turkey's own chances of joining, given Cyprus could use its veto powers as leverage in reunification talks. In 1996 Greece and Cyprus agreed to a unified defence doctrine (*Eniaio Amyntiko Dogma Ellados Kyprou*) (Ioannou 2020: 90), which was another sign that high-level political talks were going nowhere. In fact, alternative avenues were being explored by ordinary civilians. Several years earlier a Greek Cypriot woman named Titina Loizidou had filed a case against Turkey in the European Court of Human Rights for denying her access to her legally owned properties. The court ruled in her favour, ordering Turkey to pay compensation. The Loizidou case, however, demonstrated the strengths and the ultimate weakness of the Greek Cypriot case. Turkey found the Cyprus problem affected its international relationships and interests, yet international pressure was never compelling enough to force Turkey's hand. Ankara's stance on Cyprus enjoyed popular support in Turkey, and Denktaş's hard-line position was backed by most Turkish Cypriots. Loizidou's spirited attempt to seek personal justice through an international court reflected Greek Cypriot frustration with the stalemate that had obtained since 1974. In August 1996, Greek demonstrators broke through the Green Line, which led to two males (cousins Tassos Isaac and Solomos Solomou) being killed: one was caught on camera being clubbed to death within the Green Zone by far Right nationalists.[6]

Both communities were deeply traumatised by recent history: Turkish Cypriots by the communal violence in 1964, and Greek Cypriots by the 1974 Turkish invasion. These events hardened ethnic identities and inter-communal relations, and they served as a significant impediment to reunification talks. Each community was fed with the myths and versions of history that cast Greece and Turkey as perennial enemies. The conflict would remain in a state of suspension: it would be described as a 'frozen war' (Bryant and Papadakis 2012: 2). The 1974 crisis had also changed how Greek Cypriots saw Greece. Given the Greek dictatorship's role, *Enosis* was a dead cause. Once a defining political goal of the Greek community and core element of Greek Cypriot nationalism, many Greek Cypriots, particularly on the Left, rejected the ascription of being 'Greek' (Papadakis 1998).

Greek Cypriot refugees carried a wound and always spoke of having to endure *anchos* ('anguish'). Many refugees would later claim to have suffered related illnesses in later years, although a study led by British anthropologist Peter Loizos showed the refugees did at least have ready access to medical care, and that facilities had improved markedly after the invasion. The government also provided housing assistance and free education (Loizos and Constantinou 2007: 88–9). In fact, the catastrophe also marked a new beginning for Greek Cypriot society, for while reunification relations remained the chief political issue, the citizenry was also able to exploit the peace and stability that followed to expand and flourish.

Indeed, the irony of the 1974 invasion was that the Republic of Cyprus became far more prosperous than the occupied north. The north had marked advantages in terms of natural resources and facilities. Turkish Cypriots now held the island's largest agricultural zone and the coastlines with the best-developed tourist facilities. Yet the region's economy remained depressed, largely because earnings from agriculture continued to decline in all Mediterranean economies, and because of sanctions imposed upon it by the international community. The fact that the north was heavily militarised also meant that it no longer appealed to holidaymakers. The south recovered within a short space of time, as indicated by unemployment statistics, which were at depression levels in late 1974, but which had fallen to a mere 1.7 per cent by 1979. The recovery was led by services and tourism, but the south was also able to attract significant investment and take advantage of the petrodollar glut in nearby oil-producing countries. In some ways the Cypriot economic miracle was merely the resumption of trends that had begun in the 1960s. Post-colonial economic indices present a clear pattern of growth leading up to 1974, and a resumption of those trends after 1976. GDP in 1962 was 116.2 million CY Lira, had doubled by 1970 (227 million), and grew dramatically again by 1973 (335.8 million). The loss of much of the nation's agricultural and mining resources in 1974 saw GDP drop to 257 million in 1975, but two years later GDP exceeded pre-war levels (419 million in 1977), after which the rate rose exponentially: from 1,024 million CY Lira in 1982 to 2,519 million in 1989. The statistics for per capita income reveal even more dramatic change. Thus in 1962 per capita income was 203.2 CY Lira, and by 1975 it was 453 CY Lira. But by 1980 it was 1,547 CY Lira and by 1985 it was 2,784 CY Lira (Kammas 1992: 71–2).

The boom was led by the private sector, but a significant role was also played by the Kyprianou governments of the 1970s and 1980s, which produced a series of 'Emergency Action' plans that were carried through into the 1990s. The state focused on how a small but well-positioned economy could exploit the opportunities of the wider region. Initially it had to solve a massive refugee resettlement problem, but then it responded quickly to the needs of the tourism sector, which required accommodation facilities and new infrastructure, including a new airport near Larnaca, and transport networks to link the island's resorts and tourist sites. It also built a dual carriage highway between the capital and its new principal port in Limassol, where facilities were radically upgraded. The island's chief resort had been Varosha (near Famagusta), which the war had reduced to a dead zone, but within a short space of time another resort emerged further south in the once sleepy town of Aya Napa. In 1972 it had only 126 beds, but by 1994 it had almost 16,000 (Warner et al. 1997: 84). The contribution of tourism to GDP increased from 3.5 per cent in 1970 to 9.4 per cent in 1980, and from 15.7 per cent in 1985 to 23 per cent in 1990. Cyprus also capitalised on opportunities presented by conflicts in the Middle East, which increased the demand for Cypriot produce, while the troubles in nearby Beirut made Cyprus an alternative haven for offshore enterprises, thereby adding to the government's tax receipts. There were only 83 foreign companies based on the island in 1976, but the number climbed to 3,598 by 1985 and 8,087 by 1991 (Kammas 1992: 73–4). An important role in the republic's economic recovery and dramatic growth was also played by the labour movement, which maintained discipline when it came to wage claims, but which worked with business to channel more money into social insurance (Neocleous 2019: 177).

Economic modernisation went hand in hand with political modernisation. Since its independence the nation had been led by a cleric, whose leadership of Greek Cypriots was based on his charisma as an 'ethnarch' and as head of his community in accordance with Ottoman tradition, rather than as the head of a modern political party (Anagnostopoulou 2013). His death in 1977 removed the last vestiges of the Ottoman system. Leadership thereafter would be contested by the heads of modern political parties that held competing ideological platforms. A year earlier, political veteran and conservative-liberal Clerides had founded the Democratic Union (DISY), a party of the centre Right that became a rallying point for nationalists, liberals and others opposed to the other major party, AKEL. DISY and AKEL each enjoyed the support of roughly one third of the Cypriot electorate, yet each managed to cancel the other out until the 1990s. It was the more centrist Democratic Party (DIKO), founded by another political veteran, Spyros Kyprianou, which was able to form governments with the support of the Socialist Party (EDEK) and AKEL. DIKO was in power until 1993, led by Kyprianou (1977–88) and then by George Vassiliou (1988–1993). Clerides then held the presidency for exactly ten years (28 February 1993–28 February 2003). Political modernisation also came with the introduction of municipal elections in 1986 and the vast expansion of local authority posts, which signalled greater interest in local politics and participation.

Much as Greek politics after 1974 constituted a rejection of the politics of the past, the Cypriot version of *metapolitefsi* involved a reinterpretation of the purpose of politics, which had been preoccupied by *Enosis* and inter-communal constitutional arrangements. The motive for joining the EU was to give Greek Cypriots more leverage in their negotiations with Turkey, and even if that failed, membership would at least give Greek Cypriots greater international security. Clerides put it plainly in a newspaper interview in 1994:

> If Cyprus becomes an EU member, the intervention of Turkey in an EU country will become an imponderable action. We will thus remove the unilateral intervention right of Turkey under the Treaty of Guarantee, and in constitutional matters, and in many issues raised by the Turks, we will have the trump cards. (Karatas 2011: 20)

The idea of linking the EU to the Cyprus Question had its genesis in the 1980s, when it was first put forward by some of Andreas Papandreou's key advisers, namely Pericles Nearchou and Andreas Christodoulou, and later by Yiannos Kranidiotis, all of whom happened to be Cypriots (Stavrou 2009: 151). The Vassiliou government signed a Customs Union Agreement with the EU in 1987, and then lodged an application for formal membership in 1990. In 1994 the EU announced it would include Cyprus in a new round of enlargement.

Turkey reacted by threatening to annex northern Cyprus, to which Greece and the Republic of Cyprus responded by strengthening the defences on the island and in the Aegean. By 1997 relations between the two Greek states and Turkey had reached a low point, when the Clerides government ordered a Russian S-300PMU-1 air-defence missile system, which Ankara threatened to destroy before installation. When it became clear that EU membership would proceed, Turkey's stance began to alter, especially as its own membership ambitions were brought into play – its eligibility to join was confirmed by the EU at a summit in Helsinki in December 1999. Other factors that forced a resumption of talks included pressure from the US and Britain, each of which was promoting Turkey's EU membership for regional strategic reasons. The lead, however, was taken by the UN, which organised a series of talks between December 1999 and March 2004, and which produced a series of resolution plans. The election in 2002 of Recep Tayyip Erdoğan, who made it his primary goal to see Turkey join the EU, generated more optimism. All these initiatives created hopes for a future free from the old enmities. On April 2003, five points along the barricades that had divided the island since the late 1950s were opened, allowing Greek Cypriots to move between north and south, to see their old homes and visit old friends not seen in decades. Intellectuals from both sides founded the Association for Historical Dialogue and Research and took several initiatives to promote inter-communal communication (Ioannou 2020: 56, 65).

After much negotiation, the fifth iteration of the so-called Annan Plan, named after UN General Secretary Kofi Annan, was put to Greek and Turkish Cypriot voters on 24 April 2004, only a few days before an EU meeting that confirmed Cyprus' accession to the EU. Sixty-five per cent of Turkish Cypriots accepted the plan, and despite immense international pressure 77 per cent of Greek Cypriots voted against it. Their opposition can be attributed mainly to the concerns about Turkey's role as a guarantor power, the very limited provisions for property restitution, the ongoing presence in the north of mainland Turkish settlers and the complex governance arrangements (Ker-Lindsay 2011: 68–9). After decades of separation and disparate economic development, Greek Cypriots simply also did not wish to put at risk what had been achieved since 1974. Ironically, the Greek Cypriot vote effectively consolidated the island's partition and put an end to hopes of reunification (Heraclides 2011; Heraclides and Çakmak 2019; Ioannou 2020).

Notes

1. https://www.youtube.com/watch?v=g8kiKAxBIF4 (last accessed 19 December 2018).
2. https://www.theglobaleconomy.com/Greece/Trade_balance/.
3. *Ta Nea*, 25 July 2020. https://www.tanea.gr/2020/07/25/lifearts/loukiano s-kilaidonis-37-xronia-apo-to-parti-tis-vouliagmenis/.
4. https://www.sartzetakis.gr/points/thema1.html.
5. https://www.youtube.com/watch?v=uPccdW23PvU.
6. https://www.refworld.org/docid/3ae6a9fe50.html.

CHAPTER 10

European integration and globalisation (1985–2008)

The period since 1990 is difficult to label. Was it an 'age'? Were the 1990s and 2000s a continuation of the twentieth century, or did they mark the beginning of something new? It seems too early to tell. Of course, there are some ways in which these decades undoubtedly represent a departure. Recent global histories have highlighted dramatic environmental degradation and climate change and have considered the impact of digitisation and the global economy's financialisaton as critical developments of the new millennium (e.g. Iriye 2014). Many of these changes are associated with accelerated globalisation. Although worldwide interactions and interdependencies have shaped political and cultural life throughout the world since the eighteenth century (Conrad and Osterhammel 2018), what was different about this period was the scale and intensity of transnational and global connectivity.

What is more, the benefits and drawbacks of international entanglements were experienced more acutely than ever at the everyday level. Ordinary Greeks felt the extremes of globalisation. They basked in the global spotlight during the 2004 Olympics, but they also found themselves at the sharp end of the worldwide economic crisis that began in October 2008. This chapter considers what on balance was modern Greece's golden age, but which was also the period in which the causes of the economic crisis of the 2010s took root.

Greece's '1989'

The year 1989 marked a significant moment in world history. The Berlin Wall fell unexpectedly, and soon after, communism in Europe collapsed, the Soviet Union was dissolved, and new states emerged in its place. For Greece, the Cold War had already ended sometime during the 1980s. In the June 1989 elections *Synaspismos*, a far-Left coalition that included KKE, held the balance of power, and it briefly formed a coalition government with ND. The very idea of the Communists in power would have been unthinkable to the generation that fought the Civil War. Moreover, both in Greece and elsewhere, the dominant economic system had also changed with the opening up of national markets, the internationalisation of financial systems, and the privatisation of public assets and services, all of which heralded the rise of neoliberal free-market capitalism. By 1989, victory was at hand, and the Soviet-led system was no longer viable (Zeiler 2014: 326). A parallel development was the revolution in communication technologies, which increased the speed of information transmission and reduced Internet connectivity costs, thereby making the world more intensely integrated. The infrastructure came together through a series of developments, including the launching of communications satellites and the laying of fibre optic cables across seabeds. The inauguration of the Internet in 1983 and the World Wide Web in 1989 was followed by the plummeting costs of technologies and information networks, leading to the democratisation of the Web (Dickinson 2018: 313–14). Cultural transmission moved very freely and was no longer simply a matter of shipping American products to the rest of the world. An example is reality television. Originally a Dutch invention in 1997, the reality show *Big Brother* was quickly copied in many countries: in Greece, it was adopted by the private television channel ANT1 (Antenna 1) in 2001. Email and PDFs replaced old technologies like telexes and fax machines. Yesterday's 'must-have' computer was replaced by a newer improved model. Soon, computers more than three years old were being dumped in landfills, abandoned factories and warehouses.

Much about this transition period was not widely predicted, particularly the partitioning of the Soviet Union, the violent dissolution of Yugoslavia and the wars in the Caucasus. The political map of Europe and Eurasia changed dramatically. Four countries, the Soviet Union, Yugoslavia, Czechoslovakia and East Germany, disappeared, and twenty-one new ones took their place. The birth of some was accompanied by war and ethnic cleansing, as had been the case in the post-imperial national configurations of the early twentieth century. The shocking violence in Yugoslavia and the Caucasus in the 1990s, and more recently in Ukraine, were not, however, the inevitable consequences of 1989, but were the consequence of numerous factors, some local, some not. Their results were widely felt. Greece received a large influx of ethnic Greeks from some of these regions.

The year 1989 was also a dramatic one in Greek politics. Like most other social democratic parties in Europe, PASOK had lost its radical character and looked to the market to resolve social inequality and to raise living standards. But as with its Italian counterpart, Bettino Craxi's

Partito Socialista Italiano, it was now entangled in several corruption scandals that involved senior ministers. Andreas Papandreou himself was alleged to have taken bribes from rogue banker George Koskotas. New Democracy, now led by political veteran Konstantinos Mitsotakis, won the most seats in July 1989, but it was not enough for him to form a government. ND's Tzanis Tzannetakis led the first coalition government, which lasted until October, after which there were two caretaker prime ministers: Ioannis Grivas (12 October–23 November) and the octogenarian banker Xenophon Zolotas (23 November–11 April). It took three elections within a space of ten months (July and November 1989 and April 1990) for ND to form a government in its own right, albeit with a slender one-seat majority.

A veteran of the old Centre Union and grandnephew of Eleftherios Venizelos, Mitsotakis held power from April 1990 to October 1993. Karamanlis assumed the presidency, which he held until March 1995. Like Karamanlis, Mitsotakis was an extremely experienced politician: he first entered politics in 1946. He had been ND leader since 1984, during which time he modernised the party, but he commanded neither the authority nor the respect that Karamanlis once did. Governing with a majority of one proved difficult, especially when some of his own senior ministers opposed his policy positions. There were many high-level resignations, particularly over his attempts to rein in public spending and raise revenues by selling off inefficient public enterprises. Attempts to impose some fiscal discipline required political capital that Mitsotakis lacked. Together with strong trade union opposition, and considerable public disenchantment over the increase in duties on petrol, increases in VAT, and cuts to agricultural cooperatives and pension funds, Mitsotakis faced a difficult re-election. An avowed free-market liberal, many saw him as an agent of Thatcherism or Reaganism. In November 1993, he was defeated by a frail Papandreou, who campaigned against Mitsotakis' economic austerities. When PASOK was returned to government, however, it had to meet the goals needed for entry into the European Monetary Union (EMU), which required deregulation and liberalisation. PASOK found a way by negotiating a corporatist solution between capital and labour, working with the General Confederation of Greek Workers and the Federation of Greek Industries. In essence, PASOK continued along an economic path it had set before Mitsotakis, and which Mitsotakis had pushed along.

Though in failing health, Andreas Papandreou held the premiership from November 1993 to January 1996. For much of it, he was incapable of working more than a few hours a day. He was also dogged by a scandal centred on third wife, Dimitra Liani, who ran his private office and controlled access to him. Papandreou depended increasingly on her and other close associates. They often made decisions when he was too ill to do so, alienating his senior ministers and the government generally. He passed controversial measures, such as the embargo against FYROM and the refusal to devalue the drachma to meet EMU qualification targets (Featherstone and Papadimitriou 2015: 98–100, 108). Meanwhile, from mid-1995, Papandreou's support within the party was crumbling. He was bedridden for most of his final days in office, and yet, though obviously incapable of fulfilling his duties, he seemed unwilling to resign. 'Andreas' eventually stepped down on 17 January 1996 and died in June.

Kostas Simitis took up the reins and led the party for the next eight years. He was unusual in having no 'dynastic' pedigree, being neither a Venizelos, a Rallis, a Karamanlis nor a Papandreou. He had studied in West Germany and Britain, was involved in early anti-Junta resistance activities, and then returned to West Germany, where he spent most of the Junta years as an academic. As a politician, he held senior economic ministries under Papandreou in the 1980s and 1990s, but he was a critic of his leader's management style. In the September 1996 elections, PASOK under his leadership won with a comfortable fifty-four-seat majority, empowering him to move the country towards Europe. Unlike his predecessor, Simitis was more policy-driven and managerial. He preferred collective decision-making through his ministers, and regular meetings of his ministerial council (Featherstone and Papadimitriou 2015: 154).

By 2000, Simitis had earned a reputation as a moderniser and a reformer. He removed religion from state identity cards while toning down the nationalist rhetoric when discussing relations with Greece's neighbours (Close 2002: 246). Under his stewardship, Greece joined the EMU and adopted the euro as its currency, and the country seemed to have the financial and logistical know-how to stage the 2004 Olympic Games. That year was the high point of the post-*Metapolitefsi* period. Greece had experienced several years of economic growth, and its GDP ranked twenty-eighth in the world. While the country anticipated the Olympics, an even greater source of excitement was the national football team's unexpected victory over Portugal in the European Championship final in Lisbon, Greece's greatest footballing achievement. With each victory during the competition, Greeks poured into the streets of every town and city in celebration.

The year 2004 was therefore a good year for Greece. The games went off without a hitch, while the country won international acclaim for the opening and closing ceremonies. The national squad won a respect-able tally of sixteen medals, including six gold. Simitis had resigned before the March 2004 elections, making way for a new generation of leaders with very familiar names: George Papandreou (b. 1952) and Kostas (Konstantinos) Karamanlis (b. 1956), the nephew of his name-sake. Relatively young (47) and with no prior ministerial experience, the younger Karamanlis had almost defeated Simitis in the 2000 elec-tions and then triumphed twice over Papandreou (2004 and 2007).

It was during Karamanlis' tenure that the dire consequences of Greece structural problems began to bite and Greek society became more visibly restive. As many had predicted, the Olympic Games were crushingly expensive, and the fact that they were debt financed merely exacerbated the nation's underlying economic problems. The modern-ising reformer Simitis had failed to address them. Karamanlis – who wanted to be known by the more informal 'Kostas' as he cultivated a 'common man' image that set a contrast to his aloof uncle – seemed a typical centre-right politician. The path forward was to deregulate, cut taxes and run a better economy than his centre-left opponents. In reality, Karamanlis seemed to be steering along a familiar path to the one charted by his PASOK predecessors. According to OECD reports, the public sector expanded under his watch (OECD 2012).

Kostas Karamanlis was much more successful than his predecessor Mitsotakis in keeping his party united (March 2004–October 2009), though he did not dominate it as his uncle once did. It was during his tenure that the state faced its most serious challenges since the 1970s. The record-breaking fires in August–September 2007 exposed its lack of disaster preparedness, including its failure to follow EU guidelines and use special EU funds to combat what was a pro-nounced effect of climate change. The spontaneous youth riots that engulfed the country in December 2008, following the police shoot-ing of a teenager (see pp. 380–2), were directly related to the labour market's incapacity to absorb the young. By far the most serious chal-lenge, however, would be presented by the Global Financial Crisis (GFC) (see Chapter 11).

What is the historian of Greece to make of the period between the end of the Cold War and the Greek crisis? It is tempting to read the history of that period as a prelude to the economic crisis, especially as the prime cause was a structural debt problem that had been left untreated by successive PASOK and ND governments. However, the

GFC was not inevitable, nor indeed were the EU's decisions to apply harsh austerities. Nor is any nation merely an 'economy'. The rest of the chapter does seek to explain the origins of the crisis, but it also addresses the period in its own terms, considering both its twentieth-century continuities and developments that suggest that Greece was entering a new era.

The road to Europe

Since the end of the *Metapolitefsi*, Greek society has faced the challenges of globalisation and European economic integration simultaneously. If Greece was guided along its modernising path by 'America' in the post-war years, in the *Metapolitefsi* and post-*Metapolitefsi* periods, it was beating a path towards 'Europe'. Existing member states had reservations about inviting such a relatively backward economy into its club, but these concerns were outweighed by the symbolic benefits. The EEC henceforth included in its ranks the birthplace not just of democracy but of 'Europe' itself. Culture trumped economics (Karamouzi 2014).

Three stages marked Greece's entry into Europe: the Single European Act (SEA) signed in 1986 in order to create a single market by 1993; the Maastricht Treaty of 1992, which formally established the European Union, European citizenship, and common European foreign and security policies; and finally, monetary union in 2001. In the meantime, there were parallel developments that included a 'cohesion policy' assisting Greece and other backward economies in meeting membership requirements regarding deregulation and tariffs. Another was fiscal stabilisation and preparation for the economy to meet the criteria for European integration. Finally, changes had to be made at the institutional level to reduce state intervention and accommodate economic liberalisation. EU legislation went hand in hand with globalisation, promoting trade liberalisation and deregulation, the internationalisation of capital markets and banking, and the movement of capital in search of profits. Thus, the Greek economy was simultaneously being globalised and integrated into the EU (Pagoulatos 2006: 440).

In the meantime, Greece was experiencing social changes similar to those taking place in other Western countries. Industry and manufacturing were being overtaken by the services sector, a shift that had profound political, social and cultural ramifications. The decline of industry and agriculture, which EU integration intensified, inevitably impacted on rural and working-class solidarities and identities. The change was also being driven by technology, principally information technology (IT), digitisation and the Internet. In Greece, adaption to the new technologies was funded mainly by the EU, which demanded wholesale structural changes that affected Greek society at every level. These demands affected institutional cultures and the rules that both Greek employers and employees had to follow, promoting greater integration of administrative and financial systems. Nevertheless, some things did not change enough, such as widespread tax avoidance, political corruption, and public inefficiencies and waste. European pressure was not strong enough to force all the changes needed.

In the late 1970s, PASOK had opposed entry into the EEC for political and economic reasons. It identified the EEC with NATO – the rhyming slogan was *EOK kai NATO, to idio syndikato* ('EEC and NATO, the same syndicate') – whilst it was also mindful that membership would require the removal of tariff protections for Greek industries. Once in power, however, PASOK toned down the rhetoric, finding a greater appreciation for the financial benefits of membership, and for the boost to Greece's security vis-à-vis Turkey. After all, the nation's borders were now the EEC's borders. Papandreou was able also to negotiate better terms. In 1982 his government issued a memorandum requesting financial assistance to compensate for losses incurred by tariff reductions and other convergence requirements. He even threatened to veto the EEC's enlargement if these concerns were not addressed (*Bulletin of the European Communities* 1982: 90–3). The response was the establishment of the Single European Act (SEA) in 1986. It not only improved existing economic conditions but helped to create structures to implement decisions. It calibrated domestic policy with European priorities. The success or failure of national priorities and domestic politics were measured by the extent to which they met EU standards. A clear indication of the EEC and EU's impact was the new kind of vocabulary that entered political discourse, and the way 'Europe' framed political outlooks.

However, incorporating the continent's underdeveloped south led to the commonplace criticism that the nations in question became dependent on the EEC/EU, receiving more resources than they contributed. Critics accused Greece of using the EEC as its milch cow and, worse still, of seeing no reason to change. There is little doubt that the political elites and their clients misappropriated funds. Nevertheless, it is also the case that there were sufficient resources to enact far-reaching structural changes, including reforms to infrastructure and the Greek market, and the policy adjustments needed to converge with EEC standards. Because of these policies, Greece was better able to deal with globalisation's impacts and opportunities (e.g. mass tourism), and manage the general shift from agriculture and industry to services. The most significant change, both politically and symbolically, was the abandonment of the drachma, the currency created soon after the nation's inception. The adoption of the euro marked a new beginning, as Greece immersed itself in a new transnational economic and moral environment.

The three lifebuoys

Financial support for Greece was delivered in three successive programmes addressed to poorer member countries. The first was under the Integrated Mediterranean Programmes (IMPs), which included Greece, parts of France and Italy, and Ireland (1986–92). The second was the Community Support Framework (CSF) (1989–2006), which extended the same kind of assistance to the new members in Eastern Europe, and the third was the National Strategic Reference Frameworks (NSRF) (2007–20). All three programmes served as temporary lifebuoys for member states until they could float freely after making the necessary adjustments to the single market. The amount of financial aid received by Greece rose from 0.84 per cent of national GDP in 1981 to 5 per cent in 1993, but by the time the crisis hit, it had fallen back to 3 per cent. Measured in euros, it started with 124 million in 1981 and reached 4 billion in 1993, and between 1994 and 2007 it ranged between 3 and 5 billion. It peaked at 5.8 billion euros in 2008 (Oikonomou and Kalantzis 2018).

This massive flow of money could be likened to the Marshall Plan. And as happened with the Marshall Plan, European money was not channelled through the Greek state budget. The processes by which the funds were distributed reflected certain essential changes in civic life, contributing to greater civic consciousness at ground level (including in the regions). For whereas the Americans operated through US-run bodies and personnel, in this instance, the EU collaborated with elected bodies at the local level. As more citizens were involved in planning and decision-making, the EEC contributed to the energisation of local politics that had started under PASOK in the 1980s (see p. 316). In the meantime, new investment groups emerged that included local-level, grass-roots enterprises, and public–private partnerships, while communications with European authorities were managed by, or were mediated through, technocrats and consultants. Money was managed through five-year programmes, which required forecasting, planning,

coordination, accounting, observation of standards and effective management methods, and these processes also required close cooperation
between Europe and the local Greek authorities. The introduction of
computers and a new environment defined by the 'knowledge society'
and 'e-government' facilitated these collaborations, which prompted
stronger civic cultures and practices.

Another meaningful EEC policy led to the creation of the
'Independent Administrative Authorities' (*Anexartites Dioikitikes
Arches*). These were statutory bodies independent of the state, created
to monitor standards and push for changes in government administration cultures. The Supreme Council of Personnel Selection (*Anotato
Symvoulio Epilogis Prosopikou*/ASEP) was set up to oversee the filling of
civil service positions and teaching posts. Another, similar reform was
the appointment of an ombudsman to protect individual rights and
deal with discrimination based on gender, religion or ethnicity. The
state recognised minority rights, which was a necessary move given
that there were many discriminatory laws still in place. For example,
Catholics had not been permitted to teach in public schools. Muslims
of Western Thrace had had to endure a variety of restrictions and
were therefore promised 'legal equality – equal citizenship' (*isonomia-
isopoliteia*) (Anagnostou and Triandafyllidou 2006). Such changes were
driven to a large extent by awareness of European ethical sensibilities
regarding discrimination and gave a sense of how EEC membership
would affect Greek political culture and practice.

The European funds that Greece received were aimed mainly at
upgrading economic infrastructures, promoting the development of
new products and production methods, facilitating the transition to
modern information technologies and upgrading worker training.
The focus was on agriculture, industry, tourism, transportation and
communications. Included were funds for retraining civil servants.
The Integrated Mediterranean Programmes (IMPs) featured many
projects, mainly at the provincial level, some of which assisted farmers,
small businesses and tourism operators. There were also major infrastructure projects, like the new Athens international airport (at Spata),
a modern highway network, the Rio–Antirio Bridge connecting the
north Peloponnese to Central Greece, and new hospitals, schools and
universities. Most of these projects were in the provinces and did much
to decentralise power in Greece.

Half of the funds were invested in the ailing agricultural sector,
which found it extremely difficult to survive increasing international
competition, particularly after the GATT talks in Uruguay in 1986,

where the EEC agreed to reduce protections for farmers. Agricultural productivity had increased between 1920 and 1980, and farmer incomes had tripled in real terms through government assistance, cheap credit, mechanisation and improved methods. But by the 1970s the sector had reached its productivity ceiling. The chief problem was the size of Greek farms, which were roughly one third the size of the average European farm holdings. Consequently, successive governments continued to provide farm subsidies. Thus, in the period 1981–2001, rural incomes increased as agricultural competitiveness decreased. In the meantime, the farming population continued to shrink.

European resources were meant to supplement those provided by Greece, but the latter often failed to provide its full share. Consequently, when the flow of European resources ended, so too did many programmes and projects. Many infrastructure projects were left unfinished, and others were completed but were operating with obsolete or out-of-date technologies. Huge amounts of money were squandered. European funds also gave the old patron–client system a new lease of life. Many of the projects involved partnerships between the public and private sectors, particularly in construction and telecommunications, and saw the development of exclusive relationships between politicians and business interests. The latter lobbied for government contracts and procurements. The traditional clientelist system, whereby politicians distributed favours to clients in exchange for votes, was updated and now more centralised. Business interests that had access to the political parties had many more chances to exploit public programmes.

During the 1990s and 2000s, European financial aid and low-interest loans contributed to increased consumerism and rising living standards, but to achieve the EU's cohesion policy goals, the pace of reform had to move much faster. Greece lagged, and the gap was widening. More serious still was the local economy's declining competitiveness. The domestic economy had no chance of competing against the more advanced member state economies, and as a consequence, Greece was flooded with imports. The trade balance for agricultural products began with a surplus and slid into deficit, while European industrial and manufacturing goods replaced Greek ones. The more prosperous that Greeks became, the more the country sank into debt. The national trade deficit with Europe was 4.7 per cent before accession, but doubled during the first decade and continued to grow every year thereafter. The current account deficit grew to exorbitant levels: From 3 per cent of GDP in 1994–9, it exceeded 10 per cent in the seven years following the adoption of the euro, reaching 15 per cent in 2008 (Giannitsis 1994; Psalidopoulos 2014: 315).

Meanwhile, government expenditure increased. Although a surplus was achieved in the 1990s, it quickly dissipated and turned into a deficit (Andreou and Maravegias 2018: 59–60; Triantopoulos 2018). Greece was not the only member negatively impacted by the EU cohesion policy. Many studies have questioned whether it reduced disparities among member states, and have criticised its implementation as overly bureaucratic and lacking clear objectives. The European Union was designed for prosperity and not for a crisis, for boosting consumption but not production (Sapir et al. 2004). That said, twenty years of EU political intervention could not be expected to address two hundred years of uneven economic development on the continent. Furthermore, while cohesion policy might not have reduced disparities, it appears to have stopped them from widening further.

Rolling back the state

Greek political elites regarded participation in the EMU as an opportunity to roll back the state. The new consensus in the 1990s was that the state should abandon expansionary fiscal policy, focus on reducing inflation, establish a stable exchange rate for the drachma, which was entered into the European Monetary System (EMS) in 1998, and focus on supply-side economics. In other words, the dominant discourse in Greece and indeed around the world was that the market knew best. Governments were openly committed to drastically reducing the public deficit, inflation and interest rates. As happened in the US during the 1980s and Europe in the 1990s, Greek banks welcomed radical deregulation. In 1997 the Bank of Greece became independent and was linked up with the European Central Bank. The new economic policy took away the government's flexibility to adjust the Greek economy through currency devaluation. Relations between the state and the unions changed. ND had confronted the unions during the period 1990–3, but, as was typical of the period, it was centre-left governments, such as SDP in Germany, that managed to introduce market reforms and effectively reduce the power of unions by trading workers' rights for pay increases (Psalidopoulos 2014: 313–89).

The first stabilisation programme had been implemented in 1985 in conjunction with a large EEC loan repayable in two years. During the governmental crises of 1989 and the early 1990s, when inflation spiked to 20 per cent and the national debt rose to 15 per cent of GDP,

Greece was forced to request another loan. The second stabilisation programme was implemented in 1990–3 by the Mitsotakis government. The third started in 1994 under Papandreou and Simitis, and it covered the period to the monetary union in 2001. The targets were included in the 'Revised Convergence Programme for the Greek Economy 1994–1999', which was prepared by economist and government adviser Yannis Stournaras. It planned for inflation reduction and restrictions on general government borrowing that would lead to debt reduction from 15 per cent of GDP in 1990 to 1 per cent by 1999.[1] It predicted the state budget's primary surplus would rise from 2 per cent to 6 per cent of GDP within that same period, and, finally, it expected a revenue increase through the horizontal broadening of the tax base and by clamping down on tax evasion. It also predicted the privatisation and modernisation of the banking system and that the country would meet the budgetary and fiscal prerequisites for entrance into the eurozone. A large part of the Greek economy made the necessary adjustments to function in a more deregulated system. Employer–employee relations changed accordingly, as seen with the introduction of more flexible working arrangements, the reduction of employer contributions to social insurance plans, the use of employment agencies, the proliferation of contracting and subcontracting, and the rise of outsourcing. All the above changed daily life and the workplace, especially as experienced by younger people entering the workforce for the first time. Employment was now much less secure, uninsured and subject to more flexible working-hour arrangements (Bithimitris 2018: 134–61).

The decline of industry and rise of finance

The Greek economy's most profound problem was declining productivity, which was primarily a function of deindustrialisation. The collapse of Greek industry came in two waves. The first, in the 1980s, swept away enterprises that could not compete after the first tariff reductions. The second wave hit in the early 1990s, when 130 firms employing 6,000 people went bankrupt. The two waves had effectively destroyed an industrial sector that had been created in the interwar years, relying heavily on government subsidies (up to 50 per cent), on imported technologies that were now outdated, and on very low labour costs. As energy-intensive industries, they also found it hard to overcome rising energy costs. Industrialists took their capital and invested their money abroad, forcing the state to rescue many of their companies. The state, however, did not have a renewal strategy. On the contrary, it made these enterprises even more inefficient by hiring more staff than was needed and handing them to state-run unions. By the second wave, however, governments realised that the vulnerable industries could not be rescued. Both state-owned enterprises and newly bankrupted ones were liquidated, and their assets sold. The banks, which had been burdened with salvaging industry in the 1970s and 1980s, became more profitable and focused more on profit-making ventures, particularly public sector projects. However, the liquidations were not enough to unburden the state of the debts it had accrued, as there were many unpaid bank loans and early retirements that had to be funded (Pagoulatos 2006: 445–51).

The rapid decline of industry was offset by foreign investment, which brought short-lived prosperity as it was channelled towards acquisitions and mergers rather than industry, as had been the case in the 1960s. Investment then had come from the US. Now it came from Europe, particularly Germany, and investors had been interested in acquiring the most dynamic enterprises. Most acquisitions occurred in the retail sector, particularly in state industries that had been privatised, such as transportation, telecommunications and energy. With the global recovery of 1993, Greece's economy also picked up, with GDP rising by 3.5 to 4.2 per cent, followed by a GDP growth rate of about 3 per cent. However, the growth spurt did not last, because it was based on large construction projects of finite duration, such as the new Athens ring road (Attiki Odos) and the metro systems of Athens and Thessaloniki, and facilities for the 2004 Olympics. International finance had flowed into construction companies such as Aktor, Terna and Rodon, energy industries such as Motor Oil, technology giants like Intracom and food companies such as Delta and EEE (Giannitsis 2011: 586–97). Once the Olympics were over, however, there was a vertical drop in activity. The growth spurt did have positive effects on Greek productivity, but the benefits were not shared widely, and unemployment remained high, hovering between 10 and 12 per cent between 1995 and 2004 compared to the EU average of around 9 per cent.

In the 1990s and 2000s, the line dividing public and private, the state and the market, shifted more radically than at any time since the war. The period witnessed the dismantling of most state regulatory systems, including the Currency Commission established in 1945. The special interest rates for industrial exports were abolished. Meanwhile, the power of the banks was affirmed, given they handled 90 per cent of Greece's resources. As the Greek financial system transitioned from drachmas to euros, it attracted closer scrutiny from international bodies and operated now within an international market. The new regulations aimed to integrate the Greek banking system into the mechanism that would guarantee the euro's stability (Psalidopoulos 2014: 324).

The main objective of economic modernisation was for companies to attract investments from the financial markets. Indeed, the improving economic outlook from 1997 onward and the prospect of joining the Monetary Union generated high expectations of ever-increasing profit-making. The banks encouraged engagement with the stock market to reduce corporate lending. This move would free up capital that could be lent to small businesses and private individuals. In these conditions, the Greek financial market expanded rapidly. People from all walks of life began betting on the stock market, about which they often understood very little. However, the changes also produced serious imbalances in the nation's economic life. Greek industries were unable to absorb the capital generated, which resulted in turning the stock market into an immense bubble. The stock market's de-escalation led to a demolition. Millions of Greeks lost their savings. The collapse of the stock market was a clear sign that the new economy of the 1990s was built on weak foundations, because rising incomes in Greece during the 1990s were not supported by rising productivity (Pagoulatos 2006: 457).

From drachma to euro

Greece adopted the euro on 1 January 2001, with banknotes and coins issued on 1 January 2002. When Greece joined, its economy was on an upswing. The year before (2000), per capita GDP was 50 per cent of the European average, but it grew with the euro and reached 66.9 per cent in 2008. More impressive still was consumption. Easy credit, low interest rates and access to financial opportunities contributed to a spending spree on things like new or second houses, motor vehicles and expensive durable goods. Private lending, fuelled by the interest rates, reached 48 per cent of GDP (European Commission 2006: 46, 56).

A key characteristic of consumer culture is the constant growth of expectations. The new consumerism of the 1990s and 2000s was dominated by interest in technologies that were in global demand. Whereas consumers in the 1970s and 1980s bought items that were made in Greece, in the 1990s and 2000s most of their purchases were imported. As consumer demand expanded, the economy's capacity to meet it decreased. Imports, therefore, increased exponentially, and the trade deficit widened. From the middle of the euro's first decade what was coming into the country was double what was leaving it (Chardouvelis 2007: 10).

In the meantime, government spending had been growing, as Greece prepared for the Olympics: greater Athens looked like a vast construction site. During the games and long after they had finished, the state was criticised for its profligacy, but public spending never exceeded the European average as a share of GDP. It is also worth noting that Greece was very late in implementing its welfare state, and government spending had been well below the EU average in the 1990s. In 1960 government expenditure was 20.6 per of GDP, whereas the EU average was 30.4 per cent; in 1980, it was 29 per cent compared to the EU's 45 per cent, but in 1989, the rates were the same (49.9 per cent to 49 per cent). By 2006, there had been a slight shift: 46.1 per cent to 47.5 per cent.

The source of the mounting debt problem lay elsewhere. The state could not finance its projects from tax revenues and other domestic sources. Hence the deficit grew from 3.1 per cent of GDP in 1999 to 7.4 per cent in 2004 (European Commission 2006: 184). The peak year was 2002, following the adoption of the euro. There were visible signs of the problem, but the course was difficult to correct once Greece had joined the Monetary Union. It was the European Central Bank (ECB) that controlled monetary policy, while borrowing costs reflected European, not Greek, conditions. The only solution was to reduce the public deficit and public spending, and reduce expenditure on, among other things, welfare, schools and hospitals.

External borrowing and collapsing productivity

State borrowing from external money sources grew in the 1980s for three fundamental reasons. First, tax revenues lagged behind government expenditure because of widespread tax avoidance. The state still seemed incapable of combating evasion. Large companies continued to find legal loopholes to minimise their taxes, while the rich mastered the art of transferring money to tax havens inhabited only by the world's expanding list of billionaires (Ogle 2017). In Greece, however, tax evasion involved a broad cross-section of society and was estimated to be equivalent to one third of the nation's revenues. The informal economy was one quarter of GDP. The problem was endemic among small and middle-sized businesses and in the white-collar professions.

The solution, to reduce spending or improve tax collecting, was the subject of an interminable and futile debate. Salaried employees and wage earners continued to carry the largest share of the tax burden (Kostis 2019: 528–33).

The second factor relates to matters already discussed: the decline of agriculture and industry, which had to do with the flood of cheaper or more desired imports, compounding the balance of payments problem. The third factor was the liberalisation of government lending rates and their adjustment to market forces. The state no longer received preferential rates from the banks, which meant the cost of money increased and government debt ballooned, leading to more borrowing. Most of the country's borrowing needs were met from external sources. For these three reasons, the ratio of public debt to GDP jumped from 28 per cent in 1978–80 to 116 per cent in 1993. It fell in the mid-1990s, only to jump back up by 1997 because the government adjusted the foreign exchange rate to protect the drachma, which became necessary because of the preparations for joining the single currency and the global reverberations of the Asian Financial Crisis that year (Christodoulakis 2018: 4). Greece's external debts were like a thermometer that measured the country's internal economic weaknesses as it negotiated the challenges of globalisation.

Deindustrialisation was the main reason for the decline in productivity since the 1970s. In 1975 manufacturing accounted for 20 per cent of the value of goods and services (Gross Value Added/GVA) in the economy. By 2008 it had dropped to 9.5 per cent. The productivity of the construction sector, the largest in the post-war era, fell by 70 per cent after the Olympics. In the two decades before the crisis, productivity in industries such as textiles, paper, wood products and mechanical engineering had decreased by something between 30 and 80 per cent. The new growth areas were in oil refining and construction materials like cement, but these were industries that did not require technological innovation. Industry was therefore not only becoming weaker but also more backward. Greek agriculture suffered a similar fall over the same period. As with rural sectors in other Southern European states, it fared poorly against internationally competition. Greek agriculture's contribution to GVA decreased dramatically from 19 per cent in 1975 to 3 per cent in 2008. If industry and agriculture together contributed 40 per cent to GVA and services 50 per cent, in 2008 the corresponding figures were 12.5 and 79 per cent (Vaitsos and Missos 2018: 21–66).

The increasing contribution of services to economic productivity was a feature of all developed economies, and this was particularly true for southern European economies from the mid-1980s. It contributed significantly to GDP growth during the 1990s, but information technology and the 'knowledge economy', which played a significant role in the expanding service sectors of advanced economies, played a negligible role in Greece. Rather, most of the income from services (over 20 per cent) came from rents and real estate, which produced very few jobs: it created a 'bubble' that accounted for as little as 0.5 per cent of employment. Meanwhile unemployment, which was almost non-existent in the 1970s, shot up to an average of 6.9 per cent in the 1980s and 9.5 per cent in the 1990s and up to 2008 (European Commission 2006: 34).

Declining productivity was especially problematic in a globalising world, as Greece found itself trapped between labour-intensive economies that could produce cheaper goods, and technologically advanced ones against which Greek industries could never hope to compete. One area in which Greece was world class, however, was tourism, which was covered in Chapter 7 (see pp. 242–4). The contribution of tourism to GVA between 2001 and 2008 rose from 6.9 per cent to 7.5 per cent, which was twice as much as agriculture over the same period (Hatzidakis 2015: 39). Contributing to the sector's strong performance was the steady improvement in basic services and facilities, and political troubles in the eastern Balkans and much of the Arab Mediterranean, which limited European travellers' options to Italy, Spain and Greece. And of the three, Greece offered cheaper holidays and less petty crime.

Demographic decline

The first national census of the twentieth century (1907) put the population at 2,630,381, while the 1928 census showed that the figure had almost tripled (6,184,645). In 2001 it reached 10,964,020. The same period saw a shift from one kind of demographic model to another. The first model featured large families, low life expectancy, high mortality and high fertility, which was typical of rural societies. By the 1970s, a shift had taken place as Greece became an overwhelmingly urban society. Life expectancy increased while mortality, fertility and family size fell. The first model ensured population growth regardless of poverty and war. Precisely the opposite happened with the second model. Despite increasing immigration in recent decades, population has been declining. From the end of the Civil War through to 1980, between 22 and 24 children were being produced by every ten women.

Since then, the birthrate has dropped by 14 per cent. Whereas 148,000 children were born in Greece in 1979, 102,000 were born in 1990. Meanwhile, since 1960 women have not only been producing fewer children but have been producing them at more advanced ages.

Overall, by 2000 Greece had become a country of low fertility, which from a positive perspective also meant people were living longer and enjoying rising living standards (Kotzamanis et al. 2017: 37–9). Average life expectancy, for example, increased from 45 in the early 1920s to 65 in the 1950s. In 2016 the average was 81. Meanwhile, family sizes decreased from 4.1 people in 1951 to 2.6 in 2011. Since 1988 deaths have exceeded births, but the population deficit it has created has been offset by immigration. In 2010, Greece's *annus horribilis*, the economic crisis coincided with the first year of absolute population decline. Rising unemployment and insecurity during the crisis compounded the problem. Between 2008 and 2018, the Greek population fell by 385,000, or 3.5 per cent. This was partly a function of mass emigration, with young people looking for work abroad. The trend also reflected declining fertility (Kotzamanis et al. 2017: 40).

Along with the rest of Europe and the developed world, Greece also had an ageing population. At the beginning of the twentieth century, there were 11 people over 65 for every 100 children (a ratio of 11:100); by 2001, the ratio was 110:100. In 1961, people over 65 years old constituted 8.2 per cent of the population, whereas in 2011 the figure was 20 per cent. Indeed, Greece's population is one of the oldest in Europe.[2] Inevitably, an ageing population raised demand for pensions and health services, thereby placing significant burdens on the state budget and on the social insurance sector (see next section). Among the ironies of Greece having become a developed country was that while Greeks could live longer, they were also reducing the economy's capacity for productivity and growth. Another vicious circle could be seen in the fate of the country's youth. In the 1990s and in the years leading to the Crisis, there had been a steady flow of emigration by educated youths, amounting to 10 per cent of all graduates. This loss of talent was directly linked to the fact that the economy was not seeing the rise of enterprises, such as high-tech companies, that could absorb the country's talent pool. The brain drain became much more serious during the Crisis. Between 2010 and 2015, between 280,000 and 350,000 young people, most of them highly educated and much more mobile than previous generations, were emigrating each year (Lambrianidis and Pratsinakis 2016a: 8) (see below, pp. 397–8).

An emerging crisis in social security provides a clear example of how demographic trends intersected with the productivity crisis, which together had a bearing on Greece's debt and deficit problems. Since its inception, social security was based on the principle of inter-generational responsibility. In other words, the pensions of the elderly were paid for by the contributions of employees, who in turn would be supported by the next generation's contributions, and so on. However, shrinking productivity reduced the size of pension funds, and this imbalance only became worse as productivity diminished. The state was therefore forced to provide supplementary funds. There were three reasons for the rise in the number of pensioners during the 1980s, 1990s and 2000s: (1) industry closures forced a spate of early retirements; (2) governments also tried to avoid pay rises by encouraging workers to retire on very attractive terms, which inevitably shifted an enormous burden on to the shrinking workforce; and finally (3) the state implemented its social policy through the Social Insurance Institute (IKA), which dated back to the Metaxas period, but which no longer seemed to work on the principle of inter-generational reciprocity. That meant the pension system became increasingly reliant on state subsidies. From 1950 until the middle of the 1980s, pensions were deposited interest-free at the Bank of Greece. Essentially, deposits were frozen to promote industrial development, something that depleted resources from the pension funds. Since the mid-1980s, when the banks were privatised, the pension funds could invest in high-risk bank products and financial derivatives. The stock market crisis of Athens in 1998 and the structured bonds scandal in 2007–9 contributed greatly to the impairment of the stock fund reserves and the greater dependence of pensions upon the state, which itself contributed to the ensuing debt crisis (Robolis and Betsis 2016: 38–57). The decline in stock fund reserves occurred in 2005–15, during which the largest age cohort, namely post-war 'baby boomers', entered the insurance scheme. All these developments meant that the state had to cover expanding deficits, which increased from 5.2 per cent of GDP in 2000 to a peak of 9.7 per cent in 2009. As early as 1997–8 the London-based academic Yiannis Spraos had identified the most problematic aspects of the system. However, its basic assumption was that if economic productivity increased and the employment rate remained steady despite the integration of more women and new migrants into the labour market, then the insurance scheme would go bankrupt.[3] Since at least the 1990s, leading figures within the industry and economists were aware of the problem and its dire budgetary consequences. As one CEO pointed out in 2007: 'I see ministers guessing the extent of the system's deficit and I have heard estimates that if you lump everything together it could come to €400bn.' In 2001, the then minister for social security Tasos Giannitsis proposed far-reaching reforms to the insurance scheme (Giannitsis 2016), but as Spraos noted, politicians and governments lacked the political will to see them through: 'there were huge demonstrations against reforms, Simitis was losing his grip on the party, and he just didn't [address the problem]'.[4]

Transition to a new technological world

The changes in society and politics at the end of the twentieth century were closely linked to the spread of modern technologies. This period was marked by the rapid adoption of information technologies, smartphones and the Internet, with their profound impact on day-to-day living and the critical role they played in economic life. It was a Greek Canadian, Mike Lazaridis, who founded Blackberry, one of the world's most successful smartphone companies, but this was a Canadian venture. Greece did not find any niche in the burgeoning international technology market, engaging purely as a consumer.

The history of information technology in Greece can be traced to the 1970s when the first computer, Proteus, was built at Demokritos, the National Centre of Scientific Research, and was adopted by some 200 major Greek companies, including financial services. Computer technologies were introduced systematically in 1983, when Papandreou launched the 'National Strategy for the Development of Information Technology in Greece', an ambitious programme that set up a national IT industry with the support of the nation's major academic and research centres. In 1986 Papandreou himself headed a government information council (*Kyvernitiko Symvoulio Pliroforikis/* KYSYP). These initiatives were funded mainly by EEC programmes, including the Integrated Mediterranean Programmes, which invested what at the time seemed an astronomical amount: 20 billion drachmas (Kalogirou 2016). There were also significant initiatives in the private sector, with hundreds of companies emerging, of which some became public companies, some developed software and entered the export market, and some managed programmes for extensive government services, such as the tax, health, education and police departments. The market for personal computers flourished, which had a profound impact on work and lifestyles.

However, compared to other European countries, Greek computers were less likely to be used for productive purposes and more as a consumer item, as seen with the smartphone's popularity. In 2000, nine out of ten youths aged between 16 and 24 used the Internet. Yet small companies, which formed the majority of the private sector, were slow to computerise their operations. From a user's perspective, there were two significant moments: the first was 1996–7, when the Internet became popular, and the other was 2006–7, which saw mass integration through social media. The new technologies were not merely used as a tool but became significant in terms of social practice. Thus, blogs were primarily a means of expressing individual identities and emerged in an era when, as will be discussed later, identity politics came with certain risks. The 'blogosphere' provided a space where individual expression found an audience more easily than it did in magazines or newspapers, although it was expressed without the kinds of mediation and rules imposed on the printed word. The new technologies were used in ideological battles, particularly in promoting populist nationalism (Bilalis 2015).

Telecommunications were the flagship of the new technology wave. The powerful public utility OTE had dominated telecommunications since it was founded after the Civil War. In 1973, OTE added the Satellite Communications Centre at Thermopylae, which was one of the largest in Europe. Through OTE, which kept abreast of international developments in communications technology, Greece was an early entrant into satellite communications and oversaw the transition from analog to digital technologies. OTE also followed the leading nations in the field by opening an Internet portal. Following the collapse of Communism, it then expanded into Bulgaria, North Macedonia, Romania and Armenia. In 1989 a new chapter in telecommunications began with mobile telephony. 'The mobile' (*to kinito*) took off and quickly became ubiquitous. These technologies changed daily life, providing a level of social connectivity unseen before and ready access to information sources that democratised knowledge. Within a short time, users graduated from basic phones like the Motorola to smartphones such as the iPhone, which provide users with a computer, Web access, a camera and an entertainment centre.

The social and political consequences of the mobile phone were far-reaching. Telecommunications ceased to be a state monopoly after a privatisation law was passed by the coalition government in 1989. Mobile phones and then smartphones provided new platforms for political expression, propaganda and networking. All social groups were engaged in this revolution, except the elderly, who were suspicious of credit cards and persisted with bank books. Yet those born in villages that once had only one telephone, typically at the local cafe, could appreciate the quantum leap in technology. Farmers could instantly find information about the weather and the stock market through Facebook and Instagram. Through the ether, families dispersed throughout the diaspora, in Canada, Australia and the United States, could speak face to face cheaply, instantly and at any time.

The technology that had significantly altered habits and relationships within family households was the television. Whereas the dining room was once the family's meeting place, now the television became the focus of sociability, where families watched shows and sports together. Even the layout of homes was changed to accommodate it. Sofas were placed in front of the television set, and family members engaged with it rather than each other. The TV constituted a public space that could speak to the entire nation simultaneously. Governments since the Junta had recognised its power and sought to control it with decrees and constitutional amendments (Tsimas 2014: 343–401). The medium's appeal grew in 1978, when the World Cup in Argentina was televised in colour. During the *Metapolitefsi*, governments tried to use television to educate the public, which explains the spate of serial adaptations of Greek novels, such as Stratis Myrivilis' *The School Mistress with the Golden Eyes*, Maria Iordanidou's *Loxandra*, Penelope Delta's *A Tale without a Name* and Alki Zei's *The Tiger in the Showcase*.[5]

The year 1989 marked a critical moment in television history. The ND-Synaspismos coalition passed law 1866/1989, which permitted the privatisation of the medium. Pressure to privatise television and radio stations had been building since the mid-1980s. In the meantime, municipal governments in Athens, Piraeus and Thessaloniki had allowed private television and radio stations to operate, citing freedom of expression and their opposition to monopolies. The 1989 reforms deregulated the industry, allowing new private channels to operate with minimal regulation. Programming extended to all hours, and soon there was no home or hotel room without a television. Spending endless hours before a TV, using the remote control to 'channel surf', became a feature of the family's daily life. Companies now competed for these viewers' attention, which included inventing or exaggerating 'moral panics' over matters such as national identity, immigration, crime or the contents of sixth-grade textbooks (Papailias 2017). Newspapers tried to keep up by becoming more sensationalist and tabloid-like. Such changes were driven by private television stations, which quickly marginalised the public broadcasting service ERT (Greek Radio and Television). The new private channels were owned by shipping moguls, refinery owners, large construction companies and other corporations. The new media proprietors established a more robust presence in the public sphere, given their ability to shape public opinion and given they could not be brought under the thumb of the major political parties. As in many other countries, the media giants could drive their political agenda and force the politicians to bend in their direction. Political rivals also needed media air time, which they had to buy in exchange for influence (Papathanasopoulos 1993).

New technologies, therefore, ushered in a new era of politics, helping to create a new kind of politics and new ways of governing. If television was once under the state's control, now the state was subjected to its enormous influence, as it exercised far greater power than the newspapers ever did. The reasons were its social reach and its remarkable ability to shape tastes and interests. The rulers and the ruled were forced to adapt to each other through the new media, and the new outlooks shaped by the media.

Immigration

During the 1990s, Greece became an immigrant-receiving nation. Hundreds of thousands came by land and sea, with or without passports, as immigrants with visas or as refugees. The initial responses to the newcomers were fear and panic, yet the initial wave would integrate into society over time. At the beginning of the new century, one in ten people in Greece was an immigrant.

Immigration first became a matter of public discussion in the early 1970s, when there was high employment and a labour shortage. Afterward, there would always be chronic shortages of unskilled farm labourers, particularly for seasonal work. There was also a shortage of domestic servants, and caregivers for the elderly and the infirm. Poor girls from the villages had once filled these jobs, but not anymore. Calls went out inviting immigrants, and by the late 1970s, Pakistanis were working in shipyards and carpet factories, Egyptians in fisheries, and Filipino women as domestic servants and caregivers. Having a 'Filipina' working at home became a marker of social status. In the 1980s, these newcomers from (mainly) Asia were overtaken by migrants from Eastern Europe. An initial wave came from Poland in 1981, following the Solidarity movement upheavals

and the coup by General Wojciech Jaruzelski. Most worked in construction and as skilled tradesmen (Maroufof 2009). Towards the
end of the 1980s, Perestroika relaxed Soviet emigration controls that
allowed ethnic Greeks, mostly *Rossopontioi* (Pontian Russians) to enter
the country, mainly from Georgia and Kazakhstan (see pp. 292–3).
Greece also accommodated communities of Palestinian and Kurdish
refugees.

As with Italy, Spain and Portugal, Greece had been accustomed to
exporting its people. All four had negative population growth over the
last two decades of the twentieth century, and all four had received
significant numbers of migrants since the 1990s. Traditionally, migration between the northern and southern coasts of the Mediterranean
moved in a southerly direction, but in the 1990s it changed direction
(Abulafia 2011: 629). However, the main flow into Greece was from
former communist countries. In 1991, 120,000 people from these
regions entered the country. By the end of the decade, Greece received
about a million more. When one adds the 120,000 ethnic Greeks from
Albania (Northern Epirotes) and another 143,000 'returning expatriates' from the former Soviet Union, the overall immigrant figure was
1.24 million. As a consequence, Greece conformed to the European
average when it came to the size of its immigrant population, which
was 6.8 per cent in 1990 and 10.3 per cent in 2015 (Triandafyllidou and
Maroufof 2009).

More than half of the immigrants during the 1990s were Albanians.
Young men and even entire families trekked through the steep mountain passes, following in the footsteps of earlier migrants. When they
arrived at Greek cities near the border, they were often suffering from
hunger and thirst. From there, they spread through the country in
search of jobs and lodgings. Most remember those journeys as something akin to the Exodus (Kaplani 2006). In the 1990s, about one in
five Albanians emigrated to either Italy or Greece, where they ventured
even to the remotest villages and islands, and then invited relatives
to follow once they had found work (Carletto et al. 2006: 767–85). In
Greece, Albanians formed new communities based on kinship and
local networks (Hatziprokopiou 2003), and they renegotiated their
identity boundaries vis-à-vis the related groups, namely the indigenous
Albanian-speaking Arvanites and ethnic Greeks (Northern Epirotes)
from southern Albania. A similar identity differentiation process
occurred among the Pontian communities that had arrived in the
1920s and the newcomers from the former Soviet Union during the
1990s (Voutira 1991).

In the ensuing decade, immigrants came from Asia and Africa, including refugees from war-torn Afghanistan and Iraq, or Libya, Somalia, Sudan and Syria, where conflicts were also raging. Climate change was driving desertification, and causing severe droughts, crop destruction and the disappearance of water sources. The knock-on political effects included civil wars, ethnic cleansings and inter-state conflicts. These catastrophic developments were causing upheavals not unlike those suffered in the Balkans and Anatolia in the early twentieth century. Tellingly, 90 per cent of migrants from South Asia (Pakistan, India and Bangladesh) were males seeking work to feed their families back home. In marked contrast, 80 per cent of migrants from Georgia, the Philippines, Bulgaria, Russia, Ukraine and Moldova were women. This group found work mainly in domestic service, elder care and the sex trade, or even became sex slaves (Abatzi 2008; Lazos 2011). These migrants planned to return to their homelands, whereas Albanian migrants hoped to settle and educate their children. They tended to integrate and often assimilated into the wider community, despite the obstructions presented to them by immigration authorities.

How did the Greek state manage these immigration flows? How did Greeks, well adapted to living in foreign lands, handle the influx of such large numbers of foreigners? The official policy in the 1990s and through to 2007 was to reduce immigration to zero. Immigrants were considered a threat to public safety and national identity; hence the aim was to bar entry, block newcomers at the borders and deport those who managed to slip through. An exception was extended to ethnic Greeks who, as 'expatriates', were entitled to enter the homeland, much as Jews are welcomed in Israel. Yet despite punitive legislation and thousands of arrests, nothing could stop the influx. Often driven by desperation, immigrants worldwide were resourceful when it came to crossing borders. Those from Eastern Europe and the former Soviet Union used three-month visas to enter but then disappeared into the community. Others bought fake passports from a thriving black market. There were also highly profitable but illegal trafficking networks that mainly served immigrants from Asia. An unknown number died in transit, from exposure in the freezing mountains of northern Greece, from land mines laid across the Greek–Turkish border, or by drowning while crossing to the islands in inflatable craft.

While the death toll was a regular feature on news programmes, what passed under the radar was the number of children that entered unaccompanied. According to the United Nations Human Rights Watch, in 2008 about 1,000 such children had entered the country.

In 2000 UNICEF claimed that there were as many as 5,800 children on the streets, aged between 2 and 15, most of whom had come from Albania (Human Rights Watch 2008).[6] Over the ensuing decade, however, most unaccompanied children came from war-torn Afghanistan, Somalia and Iraq, or famine-stricken parts of Africa. This group's average age was 15–17, but there were many reportedly in the 10–14 age categories. Most children were apprehended at the border, many were later deported, while others were incarcerated and treated brutally. According to a Human Rights Watch report, Greek authorities routinely violated human rights and juvenile protection legislation. In the meantime, no authority took responsibility for these children. Those lucky enough to encounter NGOs rather than state authorities were taken into care until they reached 18, after which they were left to their own devices.[7]

In 1998, under a programme disingenuously called 'Protection and social support for street children' (*Prostasia kai koinoniki frontida ton paidion tou dromou*), refugee children were collected and dumped at a facility in Agia Varvara, to the west of central Athens. In 2000 an ombudsman complained that 487 of the children had disappeared, after which it was revealed that three out of four of them had been bought by slave traffickers for 500 euros each. The scandal made international headlines, but the report merely concluded that the problem was one of lax security (Greek Ombudsman, Report no. 3094/2003). Greece continued to receive criticism from international organisations for its treatment of children and refugees generally. In 2005 the UN advocate on child trafficking, prostitution and pornography noted the lack of systematic government protections for the welfare of minors, and the near absence of shelters for children at risk.

The influx of large groups of Asian and African migrants into Italy, Greece and Spain revealed that they could be as racist as any other countries. Indeed, treatment of immigrants by authorities and the broader community could often be worse than that faced by earlier generations of Greeks and Italians in the United States, and far worse than that of *Gastarbeiter* in West Germany (Ginsborg 2001: 64). In Greece, the irony was not lost on progressive observers. One piece of graffiti in Athens put it poignantly: 'Our grandparents were refugees. Our parents were migrants. Now we are racists?'

Attempts to extend legal recognition to 'illegal immigrants' (*lathrometanastes*) in 1997 and 1998 benefited about one third of that group, but the unreasonably strict criteria, high costs and cumbersome processing procedures inhibited further progress between

2001 and 2005. National policies remained harsh but ineffective, while little was done to reduce general public hostility. Indeed, deportation remained the popular solution. Police used roadblocks and conducted operations to snare victims, which sometimes resulted in the arrest of African American tourists. Between 2003 and 2005, some 50,000 immigrants were arrested, and by 2007 the figure had reached 96,000 (Triandafyllidou and Maroufof 2009: 40). Many were forced to live in the black economy, where they had no protections and were vulnerable to unscrupulous employers. Seventy-five per cent of the labour used on the construction of the 2004 Olympic facilities were 'illegal' immigrants, who were also favoured by the merchant marine. Aside from suppressing wages, cheap migrant labour kept inflation in check and contributed to GDP growth, thereby helping Greece meet the criteria for inclusion in the eurozone. Hence, while the wealthiest two thirds of society benefited from immigration, the bottom third did not. Instead, the latter faced competition with the newcomers for low-paying jobs.

An important explanation of why so many 'illegal' migrants could settle in countries like Portugal, Spain, Greece and Italy was that each had large 'informal' economies that thrived on cheap and flexible labour. It also meant that irregular migrants were subjected to acts of mob violence. In 2008, for example, the public learned of immigrants' shocking living conditions in the village of Manolada in the northwest Peloponnese, which housed 2,000 locals and 5,000 migrants, mainly Bangladeshis. This strawberry-producing area favoured Bangladeshis because they were skilled in harvesting this delicate fruit, but their pay was often withheld on threats of deportation. When they went on strike, the landowners met them with violence that led to some strikers being sent to hospital. Similar kinds of violence were meted out to strikers on citrus farms (*Eleftherotypia*, 30 March 2008; *Kathimerini*, 15 January 2007). Another attack in 2013 in Manolada saw victims, who were incensed by the light punishments meted out to their bosses by a Greek court, plead their case successfully to the European Court of Human Rights (*Guardian*, 31 March 2017). Farmers often delivered their immigrant workers to authorities to avoid having to pay them. Such outrages became more common during the crisis-ridden 2010s, when the media continued to foment public xenophobia: the Greek media ensured that the term 'illegal immigrants' (*lathrometanastes*) became common parlance. The rising tide of xenophobia strengthened the far Right's hand, particularly in Athenian neighbourhoods with large concentrations of immigrants (see Chapter 11, pp. 421–2).

Official and social intolerance of immigrants, however, failed to stop the newcomers from finding a place in Greek society. By 2000 there were already 120,000 immigrant children enrolled in schools that taught curricula aimed at assimilating them rather than providing an intercultural education (Mavromatis and Tsitselikis 2004). By 2007 Athens was looking less monocultural, being home now to communities from Asia (Chinese, Bangladeshi, Indian, Pakistani, Afghan, Syrian, Palestinian, Kurdish), Africa (Egyptian, Ethiopian, central African, Nigerian, East African) and Eastern Europe (Albanian, Polish, Bulgarian, Romanian, Russian, Georgian, Chechen), which congregated mainly in central Athens near Omonia Square and areas along the Acharnon and Patission arteries (Iosifides and King 1998).

The new Macedonian Question

Mass immigration inevitably raised questions about citizenship and national identity, but nothing energised everyday Greeks more than the Macedonian Question, which erupted in 1991 and which would fester as a political problem until the Prespa Agreement of 2018. It began when the Republic of Macedonia within the Yugoslav federation declared its independence, kept its name and adopted symbols of the ancient Macedonian kingdom. The Greek government reacted forcefully on the international stage, while Greek society poured into the streets to conduct the largest demonstrations in living memory. Greeks in the diaspora did much the same, lobbying their parliamentary representatives and political leaders to support the Greek case (Heraclides 2020). Organisations such as the Pan-Macedonian Association of the USA, founded in 1947 to fight the 'internal enemy' within the expatriate community, orchestrated public rallies in Greek diaspora communities around the world. In Melbourne, home to a large Slav Macedonian community but to a much larger Greek one, the Victorian state premier was moved to declare that Macedonia is Greek (Danforth 1995: 172).

Yugoslavia was a country where the fall of communism had violent repercussions, but the Federated Republics of Montenegro and Macedonia, the two most impoverished Yugoslav republics, were spared the violence. Despite its sizeable Albanian community, which accounted for one third of the population and was further enlarged by a huge influx of Albanian Kosovar refugees, the Republic of Macedonia did not succumb to an ethnic civil war. Its territorial integrity was fragile, wedged between Albania and Bulgaria, each of which could potentially make territorial claims on ethnic grounds. Although Bulgaria was quick to recognise it as an independent state, primarily because it feared the territory would be partitioned by Greece and Serbia, it refused to recognise the Republic of Macedonia as a nation. For according to Bulgarian nationalist thinking, its people were ethnic Bulgarians (Crampton 2007: 398). Similarly, Serbia had historically deemed its people ethnic Serbs.

Greece preferred to have an independent state to its immediate north, but it refused to recognise it as 'Macedonia' or concede the international acceptance of its language or its culture as Macedonian. Although the problem seemed trivial to most outside observers, the EU and the US decided to withhold recognition until it was resolved. A trade embargo by Greece was compounded by UN sanctions against Serbia, which had blocked the arteries going north. With its export trade reduced by 60 per cent and growing inter-ethnic discord, the fledgling state looked close to following the other former Yugoslav republics into violence. There was also the possibility of an armed confrontation with Greece in collaboration with Serbia, a scenario favoured by nationalist extremists at the time. In 1994 the United Nations recognised the country under the compromise name of 'the Former Yugoslav Republic of Macedonia' (FYROM), which helped defuse tensions in the region. EU pressure also led Greece to drop its embargo and enter an Interim Accord in September 1995.

If perplexing to an outsider, the Macedonian Question made complete sense in Greece. The essential reason why it exercised ordinary Greeks was the neighbouring country's claim to the heritage of ancient Macedonia and more specifically to that of Alexander the Great. It was feared that international opinion would adopt Skopje's position. The typical Greek could be heard declaring that 'they are trying to steal our history', essentially because Greeks knew that the world's 'greater powers' could make that happen. Even if ordinary Greeks had but a cursory understanding of Greece's ancient history, it nevertheless informed their sense of self. For at stake was their most valuable cultural capital, Greek antiquity, which was seen as giving modern Greeks their standing in the world. The name 'Macedonia' was understood as an inheritance that a neighbouring country was trying to appropriate (Sutton 1997: 427). The dispute over the name 'Macedonia' was one that neither Greece nor FYROM was prepared to concede, if anything because public opinion in each country demanded that their politicians take a resolute stance on the matter. In February 1992, about 1 million people marched in protest in Thessaloniki, the largest protest in the city's history. In Greece, the Macedonian Question became a measure of patriotism, such that the rival parties, ND and PASOK, competed for which held the strongest position. A rising political star of ND, Antonis Samaras, split with his party in 1992 and founded a new one (*Politiki Anixi*/Political Spring) because he claimed that the Mitsotakis government was too weak on the issue. Regardless of their knowledge of ancient history, few were prepared to yield ground. Greeks referred to FYROM as 'Skopje' and its inhabitants as *Skopianoi*. Greece demanded a name change and denied FYROM's claims to the Slav Macedonian minority in northern Greece.

The name remained an intractable sticking point in inter-state discussions. Both sides rejected compromises such as 'New Macedonia' or 'Macedonia-Skopje', which led to the Greek government vetoing the Republic's entry into NATO in 2008. The new state then sued Greece in the International Court of Justice at the Hague for violating the Interim Accord after the NATO summit in Bucharest. In the struggle over international opinion, however, Greece faced a losing battle. Close to 150 countries, including China, the United States and Canada, saw the matter as trivial and gradually recognised Greece's neighbour as 'the Republic of Macedonia'. Meanwhile, academic history became a matter of political interest. The Greekness of the ancient Macedonians had undoubtedly been a long-running issue that divided serious academics, such as Ernest Badian, N. G. L. Hammond and Robin Lane Fox, whose opinions were frequently cited. None claimed a link between the ancient Macedonians and the Slavic-speaking population of FYROM. However, there was a serious school of thought which followed the Athenian orator Demosthenes in disputing the Greekness of the ancient Macedonians. Hence, when the archaeologist Manolis Andronikos conducted excavations at Vergina, near the home of the ancient Macedonian monarchy, and discovered a tomb that was quite likely that of King Philip II (reign 359–336 BCE), Alexander the Great's father (Cartledge 2004: 92), the excavation took on national importance. There were some fears in northern Greece regarding 'Skopje's' alleged claims on Thessaloniki and the province of Macedonia, which were certainly being fanned by Slav Macedonian nationalists. Although fears of losing territory to a small country seemed groundless, given the disproportionate size and military strength of Greece, such concerns had some traction among the progeny of refugees from Anatolia and other parts of the Balkans (Sjöberg 2011).

The Macedonian Question energised popular patriotic sensibilities like no other issue, but why in the 1990s? Why did crowds rally in every village and town? Why could it unite the Left and Right, and unite most Greeks at home and in the diaspora? This nationalist revival was spontaneous, but it came in the wake of the *Metapolitefsi* and the fall of Communism, and hence the demise of other related forms of collectivism. Globally, the turn to nationalism was fuelled by the growing wealth disparities caused by neoliberalism, which saw social tensions projected at the 'Other', especially foreigners and refugees. Such issues were exploited unscrupulously by political leaders, as exemplified throughout the Balkans. With its familiar symbols and stories, nationalism provided a precise sense of how Greece was placed on the broader world stage. And as in other parts of the world, it gave the Right an effective means of winning the votes of the lower classes (Liakos 1993).

Identity politics

In 2000 the Simitis government issued new police identity cards in accordance with European standards, removing the requirement to specify religion. The scale of public reaction took politicians and most observers by surprise, reminding them that Greek Orthodoxy carried as much symbolic weight in the lives of ordinary Greeks as did Greek antiquity. Massive rallies led by the populist Metropolitan of Greece, Archbishop Christodoulos, raised fears that the state was eliminating 'Orthodoxy' as a tenet of Greek identity. On television and from the pulpit, the archbishop warned against the EU-driven secularisation of identity and culture and even the removal of the cross from the Greek flag. At stake was the meaning of national identity as a combination of Hellenism and Orthodoxy. 'Without Orthodoxy', he claimed, 'there is no Hellenism'. He claimed that his warning did not just apply to Greece, as all peoples needed their traditions and to stop the state from trying to refashion them. As he said repeatedly, Greeks were being remoulded as if 'minced meat':

> You buy a piece of meat. The piece is a solid thing. However much you press it here or there, it keeps its shape. When the piece is put through a mincer, what comes out? Mince comes out! With your hands you can mould the mince, and do what you like with it, you can make souzoukakia, you can make meatballs ... What do you prefer? Being meat or mince? Don't let them make you into mince ...[8]

These extraordinary words were publicised by the new, privately owned media outlets and were heard by large audiences.

Although a pro-EU party, ND eventually sided with Christodoulos on the identity question. Several years later, in 2006, a similar kind of public reaction occurred over a sixth-grade history textbook. Around the world, the stories of persecuted or ignored minorities (e.g. racial minorities, First Nations peoples) were being heard, but their stories often challenged national narratives and heroes that ordinary people held dear. Most countries would become embroiled in so-called 'History Wars', and Greece was no exception. The textbook affair concerned allegations that Greek history was being perverted by multiculturalism, and that the nation's proudly heroic character was under threat. The book, which was withdrawn from schools the following year, was also criticised for failing to provide enough detail regarding the sufferings of the Greek people under Ottoman rule, and because it accorded too much attention to women. As with the Macedonian Question, the issue of history being 'lost' revealed the extent to which popular nationalism was based on historical narratives and symbols that every child was taught in school. Any attempt to revise or problematise these narratives or symbols was read as an attack on Greek identity itself (Repousi 2008; Liakos 2008/9; Zachos and Michailidou 2014: 3).

The identity issue came up frequently at national sporting events in this period and during the annual 28 October commemorations, when the debate was whether immigrant children should be allowed to be flag bearers. It flared up during the fracas with Turkey over ownership of a barren islet called Imia in January 1996. An important factor explaining the new prominence of identity politics in national life was the role played by new information technologies, and new information sources and networks. Together they created an environment that fostered much more public engagement, but was also conducive to more intense debates that shed more heat than light. In other words, the loudest and more hyperbolic voices were able to draw great attention, generate tension and fan people's fears. These technologies and networks created a new and more dynamic field in which identities could be debated and reformulated, but which also exposed the public to voices that fanned fears about the Other (e.g. Turks, immigrants) and encouraged the adoption of harder identities.

Immigration and the Macedonian Question posed direct questions about Greek national origins, notions of ethnic purity and Greek homogeneity. Greeks also found themselves in a liminal space. They were the target of anti-Balkan prejudices that they often applied to peoples to the north. These prejudices were reproduced and embellished in the most widely read book during the Balkan crises of the 1990s, Robert Kaplan's *Balkan Ghosts: A Journey through History* (1995), which depicted a jumble of nationalities governed by their emotions and violent predispositions. Kaplan also claimed that 'In the Balkans, history is not viewed as tracing a chronological progression, as it is in the West. Instead, history jumps around and moves in circles; and where history is perceived in such a way, myths take root' (Kaplan 1995: 58). The historian Maria Todorova coined the term 'Balkanism' for this kind of structured prejudice, which Kaplan exemplified (Todorova 2009: 8). The hyperbolic ethnocentrism attributed to Balkan peoples supposedly explained a predilection for violence, which showed why they could not follow the Western path. Greece may have belonged to the West, but the Macedonian Question suggested it was, at heart, very Balkan. It treated its northern neighbours with the same kind of contempt as Western pundits were applying to the Balkans' peoples. A slogan often heard at football matches in Athens was 'Albanian, Albanian, you will never be Greek'. It was commonplace for nationalists to distinguish 'historical peoples' (Greeks, Serbs, Romanians) from alleged bogus peoples (Bulgarians, Albanians, Macedonians). These ideas were being reintroduced to the public discourse through the new Balkan nationalisms of the 1990s, including the Greek one (Kousouris 2018: 125–32).

In the 1990s, such forms of intra-Balkan discrimination were described as 'nesting orientalisms' (Bakić-Hayden 1995), and they pointed to another conflict in the region. The Balkans had become a region where identities had been destabilised and where all groups were focusing more on their differences and the ethnic 'Other'. Yet, at the same time, some counter-movements were critiquing these ethno-nationalist trends, recognising the region's history of multi-ethnicity and coexistence. Here, nationalism was indeed a relatively recent invention. Anthropological and historical studies together with literature and film reinforced this pluralistic vision (Mackridge and Yannakakis 2004). Novels like the internationally acclaimed *The Life of Ismail Ferik Pasha: Spina nel Cuore* (1989) by Rea Galanaki, which is set in the nineteenth century, and Maro Douka's *The Innocent and the Guilty* (2004), which is set closer to the present, refer to pasts in which difference was not only familiar but an intimate fact of life. Galanaki's protagonist is an Ottoman commander and former Christian slave sent to suppress a revolt in his native Crete, where he reunites with his brother Antonis. In his novel *The Truths of Others* (2008), Nikos Themelis undermines national truths such as the heroic death of the last Byzantine emperor, Constantine XI Palaiologos.

Whereas literature projected its messages between the lines (Chatzivasiliou 2018: 625–45; Tziovas 2007: 507–50), cinema spoke to its audiences more directly. Many films at the time were about transcending borders. Among the most poignant examples were three films by the internationally renowned Theo Angelopoulos, each of which commented on the changes and challenges of the post-Cold War era. *The Suspended Step of the Stork* (*To Meteoro Vima tou Pelargou*, 1991), which featured European stars Marcello Mastroianni and Jeanne Moreau, and which is set on Greece's northern border near Florina, shows two people struggling to reconnect as the world they live in is trying to leave behind the division of the past. *Ulysses' Gaze* (*To Vlemma tou Odyssea*, 1995), starring American actor Harvey Keitel, follows an expatriate filmmaker through the Balkans as he searches for the birth-place of a particular film by the legendary Manaki Brothers. Ethnic identities are not specified, but the film's protagonist is looking for a common Balkan past. Finally, there was *Eternity and a Day* (*Mia aioni-otita kai mia mera*, 1998), a film that won the Palme d'Or and Prix du Jury at Cannes in 1998. A terminally ill poet (played by Bruno Ganz) from Thessaloniki finds renewed interest in life as he gives sanctuary to an Albanian boy hiding from traffickers and the police. Such films, which had a more immediate impact on audiences than literature, represented an explicit challenge to widespread xenophobia while also presenting different perspectives on the challenges and changes that mass immigration posed (Kartalou and Nikolaidou 2006; Karalis 2012).

The 2004 Athens Olympics

In 2004, Athens hosted the modern Olympic Games for the second time. As with the first in 1896, the games gave the nation a chance to simultaneously present its ancient and modern profile to the world. The event was used to reaffirm the unique relationship with ancient Greece and everything it symbolised, such as democracy, Classical art and the sciences. The enormous financial, technical and organisational effort to stage it was meant to signal Greece's arrival as an advanced nation. The Olympics were also a unique moment to showcase the nation before a captive global audience.

A genuinely twentieth-century phenomenon, the modern Olympics was a global ritual that combined myth and reality. Although they were accepted from an early stage as the world's premier international sporting event, Greece was accorded certain ritual privileges so that the modern games were tied more firmly to the ancient tradition.

The Greek squad would always be first to enter the stadium on opening day, while the torch, an invention of Hitler's Germany, would always be lit in ancient Olympia. In addition to 1896, Athens had hosted the 1906 Intercalated Games, and following the cancellation of the Berlin Games of 1916, there was talk of making Greece the Olympics' permanent home (Kitroeff 2004: 77–103). When the Moscow Olympics were boycotted in 1980, Constantine Karamanlis offered to make an area near the ancient site of Olympia an international zone that would serve as a permanent base for staging the games (Kitroeff 2004: 141–60). There was some support for the idea at the time, but the ensuing games in Los Angeles (1984), the first to be sponsored by the private sector, showed that the Olympics gave the host city and nation extraordinary visibility and financial opportunities. Every part of the lengthy torch relay was laden with advertising. Half of the revenues came from television rights. Therefore, the Olympic Games were no longer just a sporting event. They were also a showcase of globalisation, which advertised training and living facilities, as well as proficiency in drug testing, marketing, televising technologies, organising an impressive spectacle and much else. The games had become something akin to a public market. This most assuredly was not in keeping with the 'immortal ancient spirit' of the Olympic anthem or what Pierre de Coubertin had in mind.

Greece abandoned the idea of being the permanent home and instead competed to stage the event in time for the 1996 Olympics, which would have been the one-hundredth anniversary of the modern games. Surprisingly, Athens was beaten by Atlanta, home to Coca-Cola: many Greeks reacted by claiming 'Coca Cola defeated Greece' (Kitroeff 2004: 161–84). These games were heavily crticised because of poor organisation, largely because of excessive outsourcing of functions to the private sector, but Greek athletes broke their national Olympic records, winning four gold and four silver medals. The improvement could be explained in a broad sense by rising living standards, and more specifically to better facilities and more interest in sport, with parents encouraging children to play sports and join sporting clubs. It also reflected the significant role of immigration: all the weightlifting medals (five out of eight) were awarded to athletes who had been born and trained in former communist countries.

In 1997, an application for the 2004 games succeeded, with Athens beating Cape Town and Rome. Once it was announced, the race to prepare 'Athens 2004' began, and the initiative was led by former politician Gianna Angelopoulou-Daskalaki, who was appointed President of the Organising Committee. The three main tasks were constructing the necessary infrastructure, erecting the various sports facilities and maintaining strict security safeguards, especially in the wake of the September 11 attacks in New York. Authorities budgeted $4.9 billion, of which $3 billion would be covered by the Greek state, $700,000 by the EU and the rest from advertising revenues and donations (Kitroeff 2004: 2010). The fact that Greece was the first EU member to stage the Olympics meant that all contracts and legal arrangements had to accord with EU law; hence the authorities were forced to balance the EU's requirements with the International Olympic Committee (IOC)'s demands.

The construction works for 'Athens 2004' were among the most important in the city's history. These included the new international airport, which opened in 2001, the city's ring road (2003) and the two new metro lines, which opened in 2000. The city's numerous archaeological spaces were incorporated under a single authority. The renovation works in the city centre were the largest in the country's history, including such cultural centres as the Acropolis Museum, the Megaro Mousikis (Concert Hall), the Museum of Cycladic Art, the DESTE Foundation of Contemporary Art, the New Benaki Museum in Piraeus, the House of Letters and Arts (Onassis Foundation), the Stavros Niarchos Foundation and the Culture Centre in Phalero. These institutions were part of the city centre's gentrification and accorded with its traditional aesthetic. Most of these projects had been planned well before the Olympics, some as early as the 1960s, but now there was an urgent reason to have them completed in time. These and related projects were the locomotives of economic growth during the Simitis period (1997–2004). They remedied decades of unregulated and often reckless development in the post-war era. The new freeways and rail lines were linked by existing roads and lines that were often substandard and even dangerous. Traffic and parking congestion continued to plague everyday life. The modernisation of infrastructure was heavily concentrated on Athens, which meant that very little was spent elsewhere. Between 2000 and 2005, half of GDP was spent on Attica, which held half of the nation's population, but the effect was to exacerbate regional disparities. And despite the collapse of the construction industry after 2004, housing prices skyrocketed and would remain inflated for years to come. In the five years that followed the Olympics, real estate accounted for a third of the nation's GVA, which outpaced the decline of other sectors (Vaitsos and Missos 2018: 78, 42–7).

As these were the first Olympics since the September 11 attacks, security measures were draconian, in view of the country's proximity to the Middle East, its long coastline and the fact that members of the terrorist organisation 17 November were still at large. The English-language press pressured Greece to upgrade its security, and often claimed it to be the weak link in Western security (Tsoukala 2006). With extensive US support, including from the CIA and FBI, an organisation was set up to combat terrorism (Olympic Security Advisory Group/OSAG) and establish a surveillance network that would ultimately involve 100,000 personnel. The Greek government was pressured to sign a contract with the US security agency Science Application International Incorporated to acquire the extensive security systems it needed (Brianas 2004). Greece was now a country under intense surveillance, particularly the centre of Athens, which had cameras set up almost everywhere. The US base in Souda Bay on Crete was on standby, as were Greek, Turkish and Italian warships. Moreover, as a last resort, NATO units in Italy were ready to intervene should Greece come under attack. Given its declining relevance since the end of the Cold War, NATO welcomed the chance to provide security for the Olympics. The total costs for Greece, however, would be astronomical. According to US sources, Greece had spent $1.2 billion on security three months before the Olympics, which was four times more than Atlanta in 1996 and six times more than Sydney in 2000 (CRS 2004).

The message that Greece wanted to convey to the world was delivered in the opening ceremony. Approximately 4 billion people, more than half the world's population, watched the spectacle. The ceremony, which was staged on 13 August, and was designed by the 40-year-old choreographer and visual artist Dimitris Papaioannou, made an impression on the world press, which claimed it was the most striking opening ceremony to date (Plantzos 2008: 11–30). The Athens ceremony showcased the nation and its identity in a globalising world. It was delivered in high tech and in a high-tech language. Its narrative foregrounded myths and ancient stories that resonated with global audiences and identified Greek as a world culture. Before the procession began, a young woman holding the heavy head of a Greek statue quoted the opening lines from a section of Seferis' poetical work *Mythistorema*:

> I woke with this marble head in my hands;
> it exhausts my hands and I don't know where to put it down.

It was falling into the dream as I was coming out of the dream
So our life became one
and it will be very difficult for it to separate again.

Seferis expresses the anguish and fatigue that comes with the Greek's identification with antiquity, from which he cannot detach himself because it underpins his self-image. But with the Olympic ceremony, that burden was relieved. High tech linked myth and reality, each seeming much more tangible and hence believable (Plantzos 2008).

According to most observers and the IOC, the Athens Olympics were a success, aside from minor issues, such as the relatively poor attendances at many venues, and the melodramatic affair of Greece's fastest runner, Kostantinos Kenteris, who staged a car accident to avoid a doping test. The city functioned well, and the entire country proved equal to the challenge. Greece had passed a test, but could it bear the consequences? How much did the Olympics cost? According to reports provided by Olympic officials, the amount was somewhere between 6.5 and 8.5 billion euros (Synadinos and Houtas 2016: 48), but independent US studies show the costs more likely to be nearer 9.5 billion euros or even $11.2 billion (US Government Accounting Office 2005). Defenders of the Olympics always claimed the benefits outweighed the costs, and yet while all countries that have staged the games found doing so incredibly expensive, they were also much larger economies. The last small country to stage the Olympics, Finland, did it 1952 when the games were a comparatively small affair.

Rising tensions, December 2008

What happened after the party? Having channelled its energies into staging a global event, Greece had to deal not only with its costs but also with the deeper-seated economic and social challenges that had been building up for many years. When the geysers finally burst in 2008, it marked the beginning of a new age, and a new and more difficult relationship between state and society.

On a Saturday evening on 6 December 2008, in the gritty neighbourhood of Exarchia in central Athens, a police officer shot 18-year-old Alexandros Grigoropoulos. The teen died on the street, in his friend's arms. News of the killing spread instantly via mobile phones and the Internet. It was a Saturday night, when bars, restaurants and clubs were teeming with people, particularly the young. Upon hearing the shocking news, thousands converged on central Athens and filled the streets.

Figure 10.1 *Riot in Syntagma Square, 2008. © John Liakos*

University buildings were occupied, and mass rallies started, but matters quickly turned violent (Figure 10.1). Youths attacked the police station near the Acropolis, hurled Molotov cocktails at the phalanx of riot police assembled on the main thoroughfares and set banks (mainly commercial ones) on fire, as well as several motor vehicles, including six police patrol cars. The protests raged through the night and spread to Thessaloniki, Patras and twelve other cities with large student populations. The riots persisted over the weekend through to Monday, when students across the country conducted protests outside police stations and in public squares, where they handed out leaflets written on paper that had been torn from their school notebooks. That evening in Athens a group burned down the city's Christmas tree in Syntagma Square, giving rise to further rioting. As expected, delinquents and hooligans also joined in, hiding their identities with hoods, and using the unrest to loot and damage property. By Tuesday morning Athens looked like a city that had been bombed: more damage was done than in November 1973. Students continued to protest throughout the week by occupying schools and university buildings. Others did so by hoisting protest banners at football stadiums. Various causes found an opportunity to speak out and be noticed, including prisoners and immigrant groups. Quiet returned to the streets in the lead-up to

Christmas, but debate and recriminations continued in the press, on the airwaves and in political forums, as to the causes of this unexpected conflagration (T. Kostopoulos 2018a).

What explains the spontaneous unrest? Why was it so violent? Why did so many groups take part? Was there a connection between the students, the hooligans and the immigrant groups? Why were there not similar riots when another student (Michalis Kaletzas) was shot by the police in the same neighbourhood back in 1985?

Greece was not alone in experiencing this kind of rioting. Between 1998 and 2008, thirty such events were recorded worldwide (Mayer and Thörn 2016). In Athens protesters yelled slogans, drew graffiti and distributed leaflets. They wanted the world to hear them and so presented their case in English (Vradis and Dalakoglou 2011). The students were greatly influenced by global culture and a sense of their place in history. The Greek riots coincided with the fortieth anniversary of the May 1968 riots. In many different places, like Athens and London, one could read slogans like 'Fuck 1968, Fight Now!' The youth had developed an ambiguous relationship with the past, as conveyed by the slogan 'Delete History', which referred to removing the burdens of the past. 'V for Vendetta' was ubiquitous. 'Anonymous' served as a symbol for the anti-globalisation movements. In Athens, the slogan from the movie, 'Remember, Remember the 5th of November', inspired 'Remember, Remember the 6th of December'. Global cultural influences could also be seen in such practices as sit-ins and squatting (Kornetis 2010; Liakos 2019).

The local causes of the rioting were many. One problem was urban degeneration. Notwithstanding the significant improvements to urban infrastructure and cultural centres, Athens had also witnessed the degradation of its central residential areas, particularly in the area near Omonia and Patission, which had become a catchment for poor immigrants. This area alone contained half a million people, which made it among the most densely populated neighbourhoods in Europe. It received minimal attention from the redevelopment authorities, had minimal greenery and narrow roads, and had become progressively derelict since the 1980s. In some neighbourhoods one in five dwellings were empty; one in five was occupied by immigrants, the rest by poor Greeks. Indeed, since the end of the 1980s, much of the urban centre had become a shell, with many abandoned houses in ruins, often owned by people who could ill afford to repair them. In 2003 one in four families could not pay their electricity, telephone or heating bills. The rate of child poverty was about 20 per cent and among the highest in Europe (Maloutas et al. 2008). Many shops had closed after the original inhabitants left for the suburbs and because of the new preference for shopping malls. Immigrants took over much of the local trade. Forty-four per cent of the old working-class neighbourhood of Metaxourgeio was in immigrant hands, and much of the local trade was in cheap Chinese products. It also had a heavy presence of itinerant workers, whose numbers turned neighbourhoods like Gerani into ghettos.

Another problem was drugs. This problem only surfaced in the 1980s. Drug addiction doubled between 1984 and 2004, with a major spike in numbers in the late 1990s. Over the ensuing decade, each day, one death by drug overdose was recorded, of which 70 per cent occurred in the dilapidated inner-city neighbourhoods of Athens. Tourists straying into the backstreets of Psiri near Monastiraki Square could encounter drug addicts 'shooting up' on the sidewalk in broad daylight. Perhaps as many as two in three users contracted hepatitis B, and one in two had tuberculosis. One in three who died of HIV between 1984 and 2009 were also drug addicts. Some inner-city neighbourhoods and streets became hazardous because of drug dealers and addicts (Tsili 1995). The degradation of Athens was reflected in its broader geography, as most of the money and most of its cultural sites lay in the eastern half of the city, while urban decay was concentrated in its impoverished western half, which also lagged well behind in terms of educational opportunity and student performance (Maloutas 2000).

A less visible problem had been developing within families. For most of the twentieth century, the average family unit dealt with modern life's challenges by pooling its energies and resources. By the end of the century, it had become more of a unit of consumption and a hothouse that bred bourgeois children and a setting for bourgeois discontentment. In Yorgos Lanthimos' internationally acclaimed film *Dogtooth* (*Kinodontas*, 2009), a couple have infantilised their young adult children by rearing them in complete isolation from the outside world. This Oscar-nominated film provided a bleak parable on the suburban Greek household, where children are intensely monitored, particularly as regards their education and social lives. In a time of rising affluence, children were forced to suffer endless hours of tutoring in private crammer establishments (*frontistiria*) and had to endure closely supervised vacations with other families. The great cultural, social and economic changes of the period from the time of the *Metapolitefsi* had powerful implications for internal family dynamics, and in many ways brought the tensions of Greek modernity into sharp relief. This explains why family became the dominant theme of Greek cinema in this period. It was within the family unit that the effects of changing gender relations, sexualities, unemployment, IT and other modern technologies, and prolonged parent–child cohabitation found daily expression. Cinema considered the various forms of physical, verbal and passive aggression within the family, which refracted the tensions of the world outside. The transformations experienced by families, the changing terms of cohabitation and tensions over authority also affected the way the young related to police and immigrants (Papanikolaou 2021).

Protest movements

What were the social movements of this period? The workers' movement had been fading along with industry and the changing nature of work, and what was left of the movement was geared towards protecting vested interests rather than fighting for better conditions. Wages had fallen, working conditions worsened and job insecurity had increased. This was the predicament of some 1 million people or 22 per cent of the workforce (Mouriki 2010: 109–21). The workers' movement had flexed its muscles in 1992 following the privatisation of transport in Athens; it flexed them again in 2001 when it forced a U-turn on major insurance reforms. The unionised workforce was now made up mainly of public service employees who were essentially under the ruling party's control.

It was left to students to lead the protests. Secondary school students were at the forefront in the 1990s and tertiary students in the 2000s. The two periods where protest activism peaked were 1990–1 and 1997–8, when students left their classrooms, staged major demonstrations, occupied institutions and squatted in vacated premises. In December 1990 as many as 1,800 schools across the country were occupied by student protesters (Arsenis 2015; Skalvenitis 2016). The deeper reasons for such bold and committed activism can be found in the same issues that preoccupied people in other parts of Europe, where an increasingly better-educated generation faced a bleaker future than was promised to their parents.

Since the *Metapolitefsi*, rising living standards translated to a much greater demand for higher education. During these years, teacher and student numbers had been increasing rapidly. University places, however, were limited, forcing numerous students to study abroad, although the period 1998–2001 saw a radical expansion of the higher education sector (universities by 30 per cent, technical education colleges by 40 per cent). This expansion did not so much democratise higher education as create a hierarchy within the university system, with elite faculties (i.e. medicine, law) on the one hand, and on the other, lesser disciplines in which classes were overcrowded and students tended to be from lower-income families. More significantly, graduate output did not synergise well with the employment market, as the majority of students from lower-income families found it very difficult to get a job. Humanities degrees added to the glut of qualified teachers. Despite these conditions, the struggle for university entrance was intense, particularly for the more highly sought-after degrees, hence the high demand for private tutoring that absorbed the excess resources and energies of families (Chatzigiannis and Valasi 2008: 207–46).

Therefore, student activism was a function of deep frustration caused by the enormous demands and diminishing returns of education. It arose, on the one hand, from the inordinate sacrifices required to gain entry to degree programmes and to complete them, and the dismal employment prospects on the other. It was that sense of futility and the anger it produced that underlay the massive protests of 2006–7 against the education reforms proposed by ND education minister Marietta Giannakou. These reforms aimed to introduce private universities and to force Greek institutions to pursue and meet the objectives of the European Higher Education Area (the Bologna Process). These were seen by student groups everywhere in Europe as an attempt to make universities support the imperatives of globalisation, neoliberalism and global corporations. The students created a language and protest practices to express their despair about living in a society of diminishing opportunities and growing wealth disparities (Mouzelis 2009).

So, when the Global Financial Crisis hit the United States in October 2008, Greek society was already expressing its disappointments with the post-*Metapolitefsi* age. For decades, state and society had been transformed by a stream of silent reforms that were required by the European Union and were needed for navigating a globalising world. The two crucial moments in this journey, namely the Maastricht Treaty (1992) and the adoption of the euro in 2001, determined the agenda of Greek politics. All the while, the new rules of globalisation had been internalised by much of Greek society. But not all were convinced. Student activism suggested that the spirit of the *Metapolitefsi* and collectivist values were not dead. Indeed, it was after 2008, as the Crisis unfolded, that the conflicting values of the post-war and post-Cold War eras threw the country into turmoil. The next decade, 2010–20, would become the era of crisis.

Notes

1. Revised Program of Economic Integration 1994–9, http://repository.costas-simitis.gr/sf-repository/pdf.js/web/viewer.html?file=/sf-repository/retrieve/39203/A1S4_OikExe_F1T14.pdf.
2. European Commission, *The 2021 Ageing Report: Underlying Assumptions and Projection Methodologies*. Institutional Paper 142, 193, https://ec.europa.eu/info/publications/economic-and-financial-affairs-publications_en.
3. Spraos Report: http://repository.costas-simitis.gr/sf-repository/handle/11649/11148.
4. https://www.ipe.com/committees-grapple-with-pensions-deficit/22257.article.
5. https://book.ert.gr/archeio-ert/seires-mythoplasias/.
6. http://www.unicef.org/greece/παιδιά-στην-Ελλάδα.
7. https://www.hrw.org/report/2008/12/22/left-survive/systematic-failure-protect-unaccompanied-migrant-children-greece.
8. http://www.opaidagogos.blogspot.com/2012/01/4_20html.

CHAPTER 11

The Crisis years (2008–2021)

> Athens is a city on the edge, and not just because of the protests. It was the empty storefronts, the sleeping addicts, the beggars, and the squeegee men that caught my eye. And there was the polite conversation with working professionals about their 40 per cent pay cuts and their escalating taxes, and about moving their money out of the country while they can. The data show total output falling at a 5 per cent annual rate, but specialists are sure the final figures will be worse. The business leaders I spoke with all said there is no hope at all.

Writing in October 2011, economist James K. Galbraith depicts a nation trapped in a debt prison, serving a sentence of indeterminate length (Galbraith 2018: 31). The road map to economic recovery that was drawn up by the European Union foreshadowed at least a generation of hardship. The austerity measures international lenders forced Greece to implement in return for the record-sized loans were meant to service its record-sized debt, but were also meant to instil economic discipline and responsibility on a society widely castigated for being lazy, profligate and unwilling to pay its fair share of taxes. Yet four years after Galbraith made his sombre observations, conditions had worsened. A BBC report entitled 'How Bad Are Things for the Greek People?' described a country in 'an economic crisis on the scale of the US Great Depression of the 1930s'.[1]

Much of the Greek population was reluctant to accept its fate, as seemingly incessant protests and the occasional riot made international headlines. Most protesters simply wanted manageable loan arrangements, but some were also calling for the overthrow of the political order. For its part, the EU's greatest concern was that Greece might default. It had done so several times in its history, but this time such a move might jeopardise the EU project and especially the euro. Hence Greece was also regarded as a potential vandal. Headlined 'The End of the Euro', the 17 May cover of *Newsweek* showed a protester with a gas mask throwing stones with one hand, while holding a red flag with the other (Figure 11.1).

This chapter deals with the 2010s, a decade dominated by an interminable economic crisis. A succession of governments since the 1980s had allowed a dangerous accumulation of public debt. Despite having tried to follow prescribed programmes of economic adjustments to meet EU requirements, neither PASOK nor ND managed to achieve fiscal consolidation. Both parties allowed a dysfunctional taxation system and corrupting party-political spoils practices to fester. Neither did enough to address the problem of declining productivity. What remains in dispute is the extent to which the European Union, which was struggling with its own banking crisis after the GFC, exploited the Greek crisis to bail out its banks and at the same time impose on Greece a severe regime of economic discipline. According to global economic historian Adam Tooze, the GFC was skilfully transformed within two years from a crisis of lenders to a crisis of borrowers. To address the disasters facilitated by the delinquent behaviour of the European banks, the EU 'induced one of the worst self-inflicted economic disasters on record': 'That tiny Greece, with an economy that amounts to 1–1.5 per cent of EU GDP, should have been the pivot for this disaster twists European history into the image of bitter caricature' (Tooze 2018: 15).

At the time of writing, Greece is still grappling with the consequences of that crisis. Historians typically avoid dealing with the very recent past because it is too close: to get a sense of the mountain, as the saying goes, it must be seen from a distance. Even when covering less turbulent times, historians need a perspective that only the flow of time can provide. Therefore, the aim of this chapter is to prepare the way for a more developed historical account, as it focuses most of its attention on what was obviously the most salient issue of the decade.

One can say with some confidence that the Greek crisis marked a new stage in the unification of Europe, which had transitioned from its long foundational period of 'policies without politics' and 'permissive consensus' to one of high politicisation and even polarisation over the way European integration was unfolding. The politicisation of Europe's future did not overshadow national politics but became entangled with it. It did not split along Eurosceptic and pro-European lines, but between those who feared losing the country's place in the European Union and those who feared the loss of national sovereignty (Balampanidis et al. 2021: 1–2). This perspective connects the Greek case with Spain and Portugal. All three countries had transitioned from dictatorship to democracy, had connected with the European Community in the 1980s, and were immersed in crisis around 2010.

Despite local differences, the basic lines of public debate over national sovereignty versus European sovereignty in the three countries were strikingly similar (Cavallaro and Kornetis 2018).

The global beginnings of the Greek crisis

Following the Global Financial Crisis (GFC) of 2008, several European countries were trapped in a spiral of rising public deficits and explosive borrowing costs that drove them out of markets and into bailout agreements, which were jointly undertaken by the International Monetary Fund (IMF), the European Union (EU) and the European Central Bank (ECB). Facing the dual challenge of massive and rising debt, and the comparative loss of competitiveness, Greece was first after Ireland to fall into the trap. Greece, Spain, Portugal, Italy and Ireland had entered the eurozone in conditions of reduced interest rates, expanding credit access and an air of confidence. Growth accelerated, but it was driven by domestic services, real estate, construction and rising government spending, and all the while, exports continued to decrease as a share of GDP. Domestic demand for imported products and services escalated, which was made possible by the fact that wage growth outpaced productivity. The corollary was increasing unit labour costs, while the rigidity of internal markets further eroded external competitiveness. Meanwhile, countries on Europe's periphery were locked in an impasse between the emergence of China and Asian markets brandishing low-cost products, and the rise of Germany and other northern European countries as the major exporters of new technologies. Imports, public spending and deficits were funded by drawing credit from the European banks and the money markets. Therefore, fears regarding the repayment of the accumulating debt created a vicious cycle of increased rates of interest, more unpayable debt and renewed fears of default. The Greek liquidity problem also became a solvency problem for the European banks, with unforeseen consequences for the fragile world bank system when the GFC struck in 2008.

The economic history of Greece since the Second World War can be divided into three phases (Iordanoglou 2020). The first (c.1952–73) was the boom period that ended with the global oil crisis, and the second, which ran through to the mid-1990s, was one of stagnation and the shrinkage of the industrial and agrarian sectors. The third phase, which ended abruptly with the GFC, was one of renewed economic growth, but also of declining competitiveness and mounting deficits.

With the banking sector deregulated, consumers attained easy access to various types of loans and credit cards. These developments changed everyday habits and the traditional image of Greeks as frugal people. Demographic developments had a vital bearing on these economic patterns. The post-war economic boom was accompanied by population growth (7.7 million in 1950 to 9 million in 1975). The ensuing phases were then marked by rising living standards, low fertility and an ageing population, which meant pensions became an increasingly significant burden on the budget.

Although historically high by national standards, Greek household debt was comparatively low by international ones and not a significant issue on the eve of the GFC. Of critical importance, however, was public debt and how it was managed by successive governments.[2] Public debt in GDP terms was twice the eurozone average, and the nation's external deficit, which was near $5,000 per capita in 2008, was one of the largest worldwide (Figure 11.3). To that point, the ballooning deficit and public spending were addressed by borrowing in international capital markets, and by rolling over old debts into new debts. Lenders understood Greece was not a 'good borrower', but in the growth period questions of creditworthiness were often set aside, while the mere fact that Greece was part of the EMU gave the impression that it was solvent. The GFC interrupted this rotation. It had particularly adverse effects on small countries with fragile economies. Lenders suddenly became very cautious, and the Greek state found it exceedingly difficult to borrow to meet its debt obligations. Hence, in April 2009 Greece was compelled to join the Excessive Deficit Procedure.

The EU was reluctant, however, to pressure the Kostas Karamanlis government to implement draconian spending cuts. In October 2009 PASOK, now led by George Papandreou, the son of Andreas, resoundingly defeated ND, but like his predecessor, he could not find a politically palatable solution. In the meantime, the national debt kept ballooning. By January 2010, public debt was €300 billion and climbing. Papandreou requested a bailout but was told by German Chancellor Angela Merkel that Greece would not be bailed out, would not receive lower interest rates or be permitted to default. The message was clear: the country would have to service its loans by cutting spending and selling off public assets. Leaving the eurozone, or 'Grexit' as it came to be called, was unthinkable to most Greeks because of the prospect of capital flight, hyperinflation and the kind of societal collapse that occurred during the Occupation of 1941–4 (see pp. 156–63). In February 2010, however, it was revealed that the national deficit far exceeded all previous estimates. As a result, the nation's credit rating was downgraded precipitously by the international agencies Fitch, Moody's and Standard & Poor's: Greece's sovereign bond rating was reduced to 'junk' status (Christodoulakis 2018).

But Greece's nightmare was also Europe's nightmare. The threat was felt immediately by the European banks, which held most of Greece's debt. While part of the eurozone, it could neither devalue its currency nor default. Greece's largest creditors were German and French banks, which meant that a chaotic Greek collapse could bring down European banks and unleash a domino effect that threatened the end of the euro, with unpredictable consequences for the US dollar and world financial stability. European finance capitalism had been even more cavalier and overextended than its American counterpart (Tooze 2018: 116). As Timothy Geithner, then US Secretary of the Treasury, noted, the EU had 'also enjoyed a wild credit boom … with much of the risky borrowing in the periphery funded by risky lending by banks in the German and French "core"' (Geithner 2014: 443). The world was on the brink of a crisis far worse than 2008, and Greece was the epicentre. At the time, US President Barack Obama regarded Europe's crisis as his top priority: 'Greece's attachment to an already shaky Europe made its sovereign debt problems the equivalent of a lit stick of dynamite being tossed into a munitions factory' (Obama 2020: 528).

Greece's eurozone problem

However, whereas the Obama administration had the political will to act decisively, the European Union did not. Its complex decision-making processes delayed possible responses to a crisis that might have been contained (Tooze 2018: 14). As Geithner put it, 'Now Europe was burning again, and it did not seem to have the tools or the desire to contain the fire' (Geithner 2014: 443). But as it happened, the Greek crisis provided a handy solution to the eurozone's delinquent financial sector, which had been created during 'the greatest private credit bubble of all time' (Sandbu 2015: 24), and which had been channelling funds mainly to southern Europe. German and French banks were dangerously overexposed because of practices that were not unlike those of the US banks at the centre of the GFC (Tooze 2018: ch. 4). In 2009 the so-called PIIGS (Portugal, Italy, Ireland, Greece and Spain) owed German banks 704 billion euros. By bailing out Greece, the EU found a way of saving 84 of northern Europe's dangerously overexposed banks, which held about 60 per cent of Greece's $183 billion debt.

Indeed in May 2010 the ECB purchased Greek government bonds in order to restore market confidence and prevent further sovereign debt contagion throughout the eurozone.[3] Eurozone taxpayers were told they were rescuing the irresponsible Greeks, but the bulk of that money never went to Greece: it was simply used to transfer the toxic burden from EU banks to EU institutions and the IMF (Wyplosz and Sgherri 2016: 10–14). Regardless of the threat of contagion, France championed the view that no member state could be 'thrown under the bus' in a time of crisis, but Germany insisted that solidarity must come with radical restructuring so that good German money was not wasted (Sandbu 2015: 59). European governments were aware of the difficulties of selling any rescue package to their electorates, which had experienced austerities since before the GFC and deeply resented having to support the weaker economies, particularly Greece. Hence, politicians did their best to fan prejudices about Greeks as profligate spenders and lazy tax-dodgers. Anti-Greek sentiment was particularly strong in Germany, where cuts in government spending, wage control and a decrease in living standards made ordinary Germans resent having to bail out spendthrift and treacherous Greeks. The mainstream press fanned these resentments. Later, in April 2013, the leading German news magazine, *Der Spiegel*, produced a cover with the headline 'The Poverty Lie' ('Die Armutslüge'). It showed an old Greek shielded from the sun by an EU umbrella, riding lazily on a donkey, with baskets stashed with euros (14 April 2013; Figure 11.1). In Germany and some other eurozone member countries, politicians and the press played on the alleged moral failings of the Greek people, who were typecast as idle spendthrifts and swindlers threatening the welfare of the entire eurozone (Sternberg et al. 2018: ch. 2). Yet what was lacking in 2010 and throughout the unfolding Greek crisis was a reflection on the moral bankruptcy that underlay the eurozone system, and the fact that growth in the north had depended on the sale of cheap exports to the south, which paid for these goods with cheap loans provided by European banks.

In the teeth of widespread opposition in Germany and other member countries, the Papandreou government cut a deal at the beginning of May 2010. Greece was to receive the largest credit facility in history (110 billion euros or $146 billion). The IMF provided 30 billion euros and the EU 80 billion euros. Germany, as the largest and strongest economy participated with 22 billion euros. Greece in turn was required to (a) raise 30 billion euros through spending cuts and tax increases, and (b) implement structural reforms, the liberation of sectors of the Greek

Figure 11.1 *International media and the Greek crisis. Collage created by Antonis Liakos; Der Spiegel cover 2013 © DER SPIEGEL 14/2013*

economy from state regulations, and the deregulation of the labour market. All these requirements were described in the first Memorandum of Mutual Understanding (MoU, or *Mnimonio* in Greek). There were no illusions regarding the drastic social consequences of the MoU. The President of the Hellenic Republic, Karolos Papoulias, warned that the country was on the edge of an abyss (Tooze 2018: 340).

The most striking aspect of the GFC was the extent to which a crisis precipitated by delinquent finance sectors was used to drive neoliberal economic reforms. Germany was critical here, both as the most powerful and influential member of the EU, and as the implacable driver of public sector contraction throughout the eurozone. For decades Germany had led Europe economically because of its high productivity, insatiable external demand for its quality products, and because of the devalued deutschemark. The euro made Germany even more vital in that it now effectively controlled monetary policy for the eurozone, which no longer allowed members to devalue currencies to restore competitiveness (Blyth 2013: 77). Germany's economic power was also strengthened in 2003 following the implementation of 'Agenda 2010', which involved the radical restructuring of its labour market, lowering wages and reducing labour conditions, but which also accounted for a boom in exports and GDP. Germany's proviso for leading Europe into the future required member states to impose severe controls on their budgets and effectively roll back the welfare state. By giving Greece no quarter after 2010, the EU intentionally made clear that it would force France and other member states to exercise much greater fiscal discipline. In other words, Greece's public debt problem presented an opportunity to roll back further the welfare state and discredit Keynesian economics throughout the eurozone. Pressure for this came largely from the IMF. As economist Mark Blyth puts it: 'Austerity's moment in the sun had arrived courtesy of the Greeks.' The offensive against Keynesianism at the global level was married to the discovery of the Greek debt crisis and amplified via the threat of contagion to establish fiscal austerity and the new policy *du jour* (Blyth 2013: 77). But in doing so, cause and correlation were confused, quite deliberately, on a massive scale. According to Blyth, 'The result of all this opportunistic rebranding was the greatest bait-and-switch in modern history. What were essentially private-sector debt problems were rechristened as "the Debt" generated by out of control spending' (Blyth 2013: 77).

In Greece, of course, public debt was more critical than the private sector's weaknesses. In summary, the Greek crisis not only brought the country's structural problems into stark relief but also those of the eurozone. Both Greece and the EU attracted extensive critical attention from journalists and academics. Each was condemned as dysfunctional and intractable (e.g. Sandbu 2015; Tooze 2018). The eurozone was shown to be marred by political compromises that made it incapable of managing economic diversity, particularly that of the south, and as dangerously ill equipped for emergencies. The EU remained somewhere between a multinational state or a coalition of nation states, lacking the merits of either. As would be revealed in Britain's 'Brexit' referendum of 2016, national belonging was (and still is) far stronger than European identity, which, if anything, grew weaker in the wake of the GFC. The absence of European solidarity was demonstrated by the unconcealed contempt for the PIIGS but especially for Greece from the northern European media and in public opinion polls. US President Barack Obama and his treasury secretary Timothy Geithner sensed that contempt at a meeting of the G20 in Cannes on 2–3 November 2011. Each was struck by the fact that Germans and other northern European officials treated the Greek crisis as a moral hazard that required punitive or 'Old Testament' forms of retribution (Geithner 2014: 445). Obama commented on how delegates read the Greek problem in cultural terms, suggesting that Greece simply was not European enough to belong to the EU. While washing his hands in the lavatory, he overheard an official 'of undetermined origin' say 'They don't think like us' (Obama 2020: 531).

The weakness of the EU as a political and economic union was demonstrated by the willingness of member states to expel a weaker one during a crisis. In July 2011, Geithner was invited by Wolfgang Schäuble, German Minister of Finance and the leading figure of eurozone economic policy, to his resort on the island of Sylt in the North Sea. Schäuble was considering strategies for 'Grexit'. He confided that 'many in Europe' were thinking of 'kicking the Greeks out of the Eurozone'. This decision would satisfy the German electorate and 'would help scare the rest of Europe into giving up more sovereignty to a stronger banking and fiscal union'. According to Geithner, Schäuble's argument was that, however traumatic the circumstances might appear, 'letting Greece burn would make it easier to build a stronger Europe with a more credible firewall' (Geithner 2014: 483).

Greece under the Troika, 2010–2015

Overseeing the implementation of bailout funds to Greece, Cyprus, Ireland, Spain and Portugal was the so-called 'Troika', a body representing the lenders, namely the ECB, the European Commission and the IMF. It was headed by IMF executive and Danish national Poul M. Thomsen, who oversaw the strict implementation of austerities, and who became the most hated man in Greece. But most decisions were taken by the Eurogroup. An additional taskforce headed by the European Bank's vice president and German national Horst Reichenbach was formed to provide technical assistance for the needed reforms. Under its watchful eyes, the Greek government was also expected to balance the budget and improve competitiveness. Between 2010 and 2018, Greek governments signed three successive MoUs. The first, signed in May 2010, was meant to deal with short-term balance-of-payment issues. Two years later (February/March 2012), when the first bailout proved inadequate, a second bailout of €141.8 billion followed to cover 2012–14, which was financed by the European Financial Stability Facility (EFSF), a fund established in August 2010 to deal specifically with the Greek crisis. In addition, there was a 50 per cent 'haircut' on debt owed to private stockholders in 2011 (€100 billion). Greek investors, pension funds, welfare organisations and even universities were forced to accept a 'private sector involvement' (PSI) agreement in February 2012. The PSI cut 53.5 per cent of the value of Greek government bonds. This was a massive loss for small investors, the backbone of the Greek economy.[4] At the same time, a sizeable part of the debt-cut was immediately reissued by the state to cover the losses in the banking sector. Thus, the effective debt reduction was much smaller, to the tune of €30–40 billion.[5]

The Troika inflicted a shock to the Greek economy. There were radical cuts to pensions, salaries and welfare spending, as well as labour market deregulation that was severe by European standards. Consequently, household income shrank dramatically. During the first years (2009–13), the cumulative taxable income of all households decreased by 22.6 per cent, while total wage income decreased by 27.4 per cent (Giannitsis and Zografakis 2015: 22–4). As Greek incomes collapsed, indirect tax revenues were raised, while direct tax revenue was increased by extending the tax base. By 2016, the government had introduced twelve rounds of tax increases, mainly on property and consumption (VAT). Public services, notably in the health sector and in education, deteriorated sharply. Thousands of small enterprises and shops closed, as was patently clear to anyone visiting the half-deserted central boulevards of Athens, where countless establishments, some of which had been in operation since the early twentieth century, disappeared. Tourism suffered because of the social upheavals and because of adverse international press on Greece and the Greek people. As poverty spiked, tourists were confronted by many more beggars among the outdoor restaurants of Plaka and the cafes of Kolonaki. Greece was also forced to sell public assets, such as the Public Power Corporation and the country's airports. Difficulties in selling infrastructure caused delays that had impatient critics in the German press demanding Greece should sell its ancient monuments and islands.[6] Archaeological sites were indeed being considered for sale, although that option was removed in 2016 because it violated the constitution. In 2011 a privatisation program was initiated with a view to raising €50 billion by 2015, though it only managed to raise 3.2 billion, and 5 billion by 2018.

Overall, the bailouts met their objective of stabilising the EMU, but they decimated the Greek economy. Severe fiscal consolidation led to a deep recession. GDP between 2008 to 2015 fell by 24.7 per cent, producing social conditions that were comparable to those of the Great Depression. Greece set a series of abysmal records, including the highest unemployment rate among EU nations in September 2013 (28 per cent of the working force) and youth unemployment at a staggering 60 per cent.[7] The percentage of Greeks on the verge of poverty increased from 28.1 per cent in 2008 to 35.7 per cent in 2013, while the proportion suffering deprivation of basic goods in 2013 was almost double the figure for 2008 (from 11.2 per cent to 20.3 per cent). Three years after the outbreak of the crisis, over 44 per cent of the Greek population had incomes below the poverty level, and purchasing power levels had dropped well below those of other southern European states (Figure 11.2; Giannitsis and Zografakis 2015: 22, 83–94, 112–22).

The crisis forced a new round of mass emigration. Between 2010 and 2019, about half a million Greeks left the country, almost all of them young and in the prime of their working lives. The main destinations were Britain, Germany and other northern EU countries. Many also returned to North America and Australia: these were often the children of returned émigrés who had retained their US, Canadian or Australian passports. The size of this emigration wave was almost as large as that of the post-war era, but in most other respects, it was very different (Figure 11.4). First, whereas the post-war wave was composed of low-skilled, under-educated villagers, the new wave also consisted of young professionals and the highly skilled, most having university qualifications. Those resettling in the 'Anglosphere' also arrived with functional English. The Greek brain drain of the 1990s and 2000s, which had exceeded the 'brain gain', accelerated dramatically during the 2010s

(Lambrianidis and Pratsinakis 2016). Second, the new wave included some half a million people who had migrated to Greece from Albania and other countries since the 1990s, and who now believed they had better prospects in their homelands. Third, this mass emigration wave occurred just as Greece began receiving large numbers of refugees (of which more will be said below), and people from poor countries such as Bangladesh seeking work, many of whom were transiting to northern EU countries.

The political earthquake

The economic crisis hit the Greek political system like an earthquake. It effectively destroyed PASOK, the main governing party since 1981. More significantly, it had dramatic implications for national sovereignty: Jean-Claude Juncker, the president of the Eurogroup, told the Belgium-based magazine *EuObserver*, it 'will be massively limited' (4 July 2011).[8] The country was placed under a hybrid form of rule, as all proposals had to be approved first by the Troika before being put before the parliament. The nation's limited sovereignty was exposed in early November 2011, when the Greek prime minister's announcement of a referendum on the terms of the second bailout was effectively overruled by his German and French counterparts, Angela Merkel and Nicolas Sarkozy. As with Silvio Berlusconi in Italy, Papandreou lost the confidence of the EU and was replaced by a 'reliable' technocrat: both Mario Monti and Loukas Papademos had senior roles in the ECB. Papademos, who happened to be a former vice president of the ECB as well as governor of the Bank of Greece, stated the aim of his interim prime ministership was to facilitate the implementation of the bailout. He insisted his new government should have ministerial representation from both PASOK and ND, as well as an emergent far-Right party, LAOS (*Laikos Orthodoxos Synagermos*/Popular Orthodox Rally). Papademos retained office until the second bailout was secured. Fresh elections were called in May 2012. The result was a hung parliament and another interim prime minister, Panagiotis Pikrammenos, but a follow-up election in July saw the return of an ND-dominated coalition under Antonis Samaras. Although he had opposed the first bailout, the conservative Samaras had changed his mind in time for the second. Oscillating between nationalist populism and pro-European elitism, Samaras eventually settled on the latter. This alleged 'turn' happened following a meeting on 23 June 2011 in Berlin with Angela Merkel (Varoufakis 2017: 44).

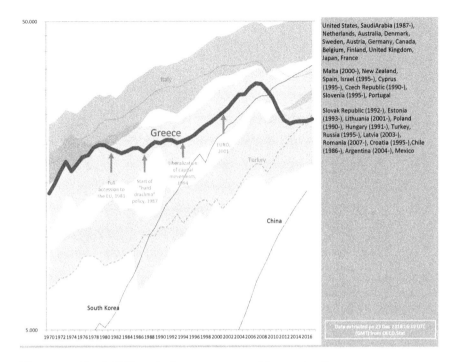

Figure 11.2 *Greek GDP purchasing power compared internationally.*

Source: Alexis Frangkiadis, https://www.academia.edu/40647962/The_Greek_crisis_and_the_
need_to_incorporate_geographical_historical_social_and_political_factors_in_economic_
models

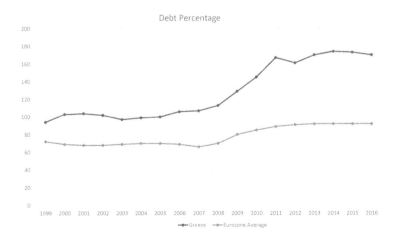

Figure 11.3 *Greek debt in comparison to the European average.*

Source: https://www.researchgate.net/figure/Greek-debt-compared-to-Eurozone-average_
fig2_276498890

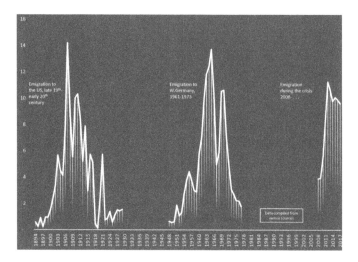

Figure 11.4 *Greek migration wave table, 1894–2017.*
Source: https://www.academia.edu/40647962/The_Greek_crisis_and_the_need_to_incorporate_
geographical_historical_social_and_political_factors_in_economic_models

The social costs of the crisis were borne unevenly. Tourists arriving by chartered flights from European cities flew directly to Santorini, Mykonos, Corfu and Rhodes, where the signs of the crisis were barely noticeable, although unbeknownst to them hotel staff were often working at severely reduced pay rates. In Athens and the larger cities, however, visitors could see the abandoned shops and the larger than usual host of beggars. Poverty was a condition that now extended to people who had previously been accustomed to a middle-class lifestyle and who suddenly had to learn how to scrounge and live on the streets. In an ethnography of the 'new poor' (*neoptochoi*), anthropologist Neni Panourgiá claimed the 'situation in Greece has shifted on all grounds – not only the economic one (which was the most obvious) but also, much more ominously, the grounds of meaning, signification and understanding' (Panourgiá 2018: 136).

Inevitably, the economic crisis greatly impacted social relations and mental health. There were significant increases in homicide and divorce rates. There was also a spike in the daily consumption of anti-depressants, in reports of suicidal thoughts and attempts, and in actual suicides.[9] Greek suicide rates were normally very low by European standards, but after 2008 the long-term unemployed and retirees facing a future with drastically cut pensions became especially vulnerable to taking their own lives (Economou et al. 2013: 57). According to hospital reports, the Greek birth rate in 2013 had dropped by 10 per cent since the beginning of the crisis, while stillbirths rose by 21.5 per cent because of women's reduced access to healthcare and employment.[10]

Throughout the period 2010–15, Greece often made international headlines. The foreign press fixated on the seemingly endless protests and riots. Greeks themselves were split into two camps: the *mnemoniakoi* ('pro-memorandum-ists') and *anti-mnemoniakoi* ('anti-memorandum-ists'). While there was general agreement that society had been living beyond its means, the two camps held very different explanations. The *mnemoniakoi* emphasised public irresponsibility, popular ill discipline and the compulsive predilection among Greeks for bending the rules, which included everything from tax avoidance to routine flouting of traffic regulations. They blamed Andreas Papandreou, PASOK and the 'cancerous' populist culture that metastasised during the *Metapolitefsi*. This viewpoint was common among the upper middle class, intellectuals, conservatives and those who were particularly anxious about expulsion from the eurozone if Greece failed to comply with the Troika's dictates. The crisis did not, however, reflect a simple Left–Right divide. Greeks of all political persuasions, and especially older age groups, had been critical of consumerism and over-spending, and deemed the unremitting protests and strikes both disturbing and embarrassing (Theodossopoulos 2013: 203). Diaspora Greeks, who overall seemed unaffected by the GFC, and who had grown accustomed to the ways and norms of the USA, Canada, Germany and Australia, also tended to believe that the motherland was too focused on leisure. Their viewpoint was often as harsh as that of northern Europeans, i.e. that homeland Greeks had been living beyond their means and were now getting their comeuppance.

Many politicians were keen to shift the blame on to society. With the support of the pro-memorandum mainstream media, they depicted the preceding decades as one long and expensive party. In September 2010, the outspoken deputy prime minister, Theodoros Pangalos, stated in the Parliament that:

> The answer to the outcry against the country's political personnel that comes from you who ask 'how did you eat-up the money?' is this ... We ate-up the money together, within a relationship based on clientelism, corruption, bribery and debasement of the very concept of politics.[11]

The Pangalos line that circulated widely was *mazi ta fagame*: 'we ate it [the money] all, together'. This claim, from someone who also happened to be obese, fuelled popular anger because the political class was widely regarded as having 'eaten' far more than the rest of society (Knight 2015: 103).

Members of the anti-memorandum camp also questioned the necessity of the measures, and suggested they were merely a ruse for imposing radical neoliberal reforms. Some were more concerned about the loss of national sovereignty, while others questioned the merits of EU membership (Stavrakakis and Katsambekis 2019). The *anti-mnemoniakoi* came from all walks of life. The strikes and protests brought together unionists, high school and university students, middle-class civil servants, small shop owners, professionals, homemakers, migrant workers, pensioners and the unemployed masses. On 6 May 2010, three people were killed during a major rally that turned violent, with rioters setting a bank on fire. Police tried to disperse them with tear gas. Starting from 25 May 2011, diverse groups of protesters gathered in front of the parliament each afternoon until well into the night, launching the *Aganaktismenoi*, or the 'Indignant Citizens Movement', which was inspired directly by the *Indignados* in Spain. The upper end of Syntagma Square was occupied by elderly protesters with Greek flags and gallows, denouncing members of parliament as 'thieves' and demanding justice, while the lower part was filled with radicalised youths, holding red flags and demanding social change (Simiti 2017). Protests were held in other major cities and continued well into the summer months, and more intermittently into autumn and winter. The significance of the *Aganaktismenoi* was that, like the *Indignados* in Spain, they were a genuinely popular movement that was organised through social media, which provided daily briefings about such things as protest locations. The mainstream media were perplexed by a movement that did not represent any particular brands of politics or have any political party behind it, but which was galvanised by democratic values and the rights of the citizenry (C. Kostopoulos 2013: 7–8).

Some Greeks were actually 'infuriated by the infuriated [protesters]' (Theodossopoulos 2013), but others responded to the protests in a spirit of social solidarity by setting up soup kitchens, food pantries and charity stalls (Papataxiarchis 2016 and 2016a). The crisis also spawned an unexpected cultural movement. The struggle of everyday life fostered creative energies that found expression in forms of art that encouraged public participation. Young poets read their works in town squares, where music bands also performed, short films were screened, festivals were held, and panels discussed and debated art, culture and politics. This cultural flowering presented a different face of Greece to the wider world, one that attracted artists and young intellectuals from all Europe. It explains why 'documenta 14', the international art exhibition in Kassel (Germany), a big cultural event held every five years, was conducted for the first time in Athens as well as Kassel in 2017, under the headline 'Learning from Athens' (Zorba 2017; Tziovas 2017).

Boiling point, 2015

Support for both major parties had plummeted by the May 2012 elections. PASOK's share of the vote plunged from 3 million in the previous election to just 833,452 votes. ND support dropped from 2.3 million to 1.19 million. ND had recovered much of its support by the June 2012 election, with 1,825,497 votes, but PASOK with 756,024 votes had lost another 77,428. The new rising star was the radical left party SYRIZA, which achieved a popular vote comparable to ND: 1,061,938 in May and 1,655,022 in June. SYRIZA (Alliance of the Radical Left) had emerged during the 1990s as a fusion of old Eurocommunists and youths from the anti-globalisation movement. This was a distinct group linked to the international protest movement against economic globalisation, which had made its mark in protests before a series of international economic forums in places like Seattle in 1999 and Genoa in 2001 (della Porta and Andretta 2006). SYRIZA had boosted its stocks by identifying with the local anti-austerity movements and the *Aganaktismenoi*, and by using patriotic language against the Troika whilst also advocating inter-European solidarity (Stavrakakis and Katsambekis 2014).

SYRIZA was led by Alexis Tsipras, a young charismatic activist with a long record in student politics and in the anti-globalisation movement. In 2008, at the age of 33, he became SYRIZA leader and in 2009 was elected to Parliament. Tsipras railed against corruption in the established parties and their subservience to the foreign creditors. He campaigned for an end to austerities and for the cancellation of the national debt. Tsipras also advocated reform of the EU itself and the implementation of a progressive agenda on the environment, social justice and immigration. To lift his international profile, he ran for the presidency of the European Commission in 2014. Under his leadership, SYRIZA's stocks rose dramatically as the crisis dragged on and as the prospect of another bailout loomed. By 25 January 2015, Tsipras was prime minister, although to form a government he had to form a coalition with the populist right-wing party ANEL (*Anexartitoi Ellines*), which also opposed the creditors' demands (Perrier 2019).

The EU now had to contend with the radical-Left government of a member state that was challenging its authority. Greece once again was perceived as a threat to the eurozone, not only to its efforts to stabilise the eurozone's finances but to the culture of discipline that was expected by member states. Tsipras affirmed that he would renegotiate the bailout terms and that he would increase public spending, for which he needed funding. The ECB refused, however, to release further loan instalments until his government affirmed the obligations committed to in the previous MoU. Over the next few months, the EU and the Greek government leadership were locked in a political standoff. A solution was proposed by the charismatic and highly articulate Finance Minister Yanis Varoufakis, an economics professor who had been a prominent critic of austerity economics, and who sought a revision of Greece's debt obligations. The Tsipras government hoped to prolong the period of repayments and use the loans for the development of the economy, the logic being that Greece would then be capable of servicing its debts. Varoufakis tried to win over other EU finance ministers, including Germany's Wolfgang Schäuble, with economic arguments regarding the futility of the current and new austerity regimes. In his personal account of the period, *Adults in the Room* (2017), Varoufakis claimed that many of his chief counterparts understood his case and had the ability to reflect on the EU's approach, but in public the same people maintained the line that Varoufakis, Tsipras and the SYRIZA government were being irresponsible (Varoufakis 2017: 2). It was IMF chief Christine Lagarde who called for 'adults in the room' after claiming the Greek proposals were all smoke and mirrors.[12] And yet, it was not just Greece that was critical of the EU approach. In January 2015 a great number of internationally renowned academics issued a statement supporting Greece and called for a compromise solution.[13] Even the IMF had described the existing agreement as unworkable (Tooze 2018: 529).

While Tsipras and Varoufakis claimed they had received a mandate from the Greek people to renegotiate the terms of the bailout, Schäuble and the president of the EU Commission, Jean-Claude Juncker, responded with the Latin maxim *pacta sunt servanda*: new governments must abide by commitments made by the old. An economic principle was set against a political one. While there was some sympathy for the Greek position within the Obama administration and within French and southern European governments, the northern European political leaders, most of them politically conservative, were reluctant to negotiate with the radical-Left government in Athens, in particular because any concessions would encourage other indebted members to renegotiate their own obligations. By May, Schäuble's plan for Grexit or a period of 'time out' was back on the table (Varoufakis 2017: 408–9). There was also another deep reason that related to the EU's governance culture. Its bailout programme and the structural reforms implemented by the Troika were conceived as a purely 'technical' enterprise and within the framework of the dominant economic orthodoxy. Policies were decided behind closed doors, with minimum, if any, political interference. The Greeks tried to reassert the rights of politics, demanding political renegotiation and not 'technical' handling of the problems. That approach was deemed as posing a threat not only to the EU leadership's authority but also to the methods it had been applying to drive European unification since Maastricht (1992) (Souliotis 2021: 192–5).

In the days leading to 30 June, the next debt payment date, it was clear that an impasse had been reached. On 27 June, Tsipras greatly incensed the EU when he announced that acceptance of the third bailout and MoU would be put to a referendum on 5 July. The EU leadership and the opposition campaigned for a Yes vote, claiming a No vote would mean Grexit. To remind Greece of its power, the EU, through the European Central Bank, cut the flow of money to Greek banks, forcing account holders to form long queues to withdraw what was left from ATMs. The government reacted by imposing capital controls. The five-year crisis had come to a head. For Europe generally, the spectre of default and questions regarding the future of the union re-emerged – on 4 July 2015 *The Economist* headlined its issue with the title 'Europe's Future in Greece's Hands'. On the contrary, Europe's future was in the ECB's hands, since Mario Draghi had created a firewall around Greece, announcing a gigantic programme of €1.1 trillion called 'quantitative easing' (QE), which involved buying up the bonds of other peripheral members in order to fight economic stagnation in the eurozone and eliminate the potential for contamination and defaults. Under QE rules, however, Greek bonds were not eligible. Quantitative easing was a sign that Europe could not persist in using Schäuble's austerity straitjacket. But the tough attitude towards Greece could be maintained.

The announcement of a referendum by the Tsipras government brought to a head the five-year long confrontation between the *mnimoniakoi* and *antimnimoniakoi*, which now formed the 'YES' and 'NO' camps. This split was presented in the media in terms of a pro-European versus anti-European group, when in fact most of the latter wished to remain in the eurozone while opposing austerities. The vast rallies held on the eve of the referendum said much about the opposing camps. The first rally held by the YES camp took place at the Panathinaikos Stadium on 2 July, while the second, much bigger, NO rally on the 3rd was held in Syntagma Square. The first consisted of middle-class and mature-aged people; the second, of people much younger and from lower socio-economic backgrounds. For the YES camp, the referendum was seen as presenting an existential dilemma for Greece: whether it was to remain in the EU or not, and hence whether it belonged to the West. To lose would invite a national catastrophe. At the second rally, participants were preoccupied by questions of national dignity, and the democratic will of the Greek people versus the EU leadership. There was no interest in withdrawal from the eurozone. Memories of the wartime resistance against the Axis and fascism were invoked, but there were also calls for European solidarity. The NO rally featured participants from the far Left through to the far Right, while the YES rally was a more homogeneous group representing liberal-leaning members of the upper social strata. Tellingly, the YES rally featured English pop music while at the NO rally people sang along to Greek protest ballads (Balampanidis et al. 2021: 6–8). The NO case was a complex one, but it was rendered simply but accurately by a banner raised on the island of Patmos: 'No to austerity, Yes to Europe' (Figure 11.5).

The referendum took place on 5 July, on a hot day. The ballot (Figure 11.6) posed the following question:

> Should the draft of agreement submitted by the European Commission, the European Central Bank and the International Monetary Fund to the Eurogroup on 25.06.2015, which consists of two parts in a single proposal, be accepted? The first document is entitled 'Reforms for the Completion of the Current Programme and Beyond', and the second 'Preliminary Debt Sustainability Analysis'.
> Not approved/NO
> Approved/YES

Few people read the two documents mentioned, but the referendum produced an emphatic NO vote in every electoral district across the country. The national vote was an decisive 61.31 per cent. It accounted for double the number of people who elected the government coalition back in January, which means the NO case was supported by most KKE and far Right voters, and a minority of PASOK and ND voters. The YES vote consisted mainly of ND, PASOK, Potami and Democratic Left (Dimar) supporters (Xezonakis and Hartmann 2020:

Figure 11.5 *Banner calling for a 'No' vote during the 2015 Referendum, Patmos.*
Source: https://commons.wikimedia.org/wiki/File:Ptmos.Non.juil15.jpg

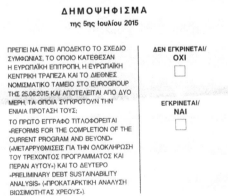

Figure 11.6 *2015 Referendum ballot paper.* © *Antonis Liakos*

367). In Athens the vote was clearly split along socio-economic lines, between the poor districts in western Athens, which voted overwhelming for NO, and the prosperous suburbs in the north and southeastern Athens, which voted YES.[14] The NO vote reached 75 per cent in some regions. The age division was also quite clear: 85 per cent of people between 18 and 24 voted NO, as did the majority of every age group below 64.[15]

The scale of the NO camp victory was unexpected. The polls had predicted a marginal victory for the NO case, while in a television interview on ERT1 on 29 June, Tsipras made it clear that he would resign in the event of YES victory. The emphatic NO vote, however, perplexed the government, and strong disagreement erupted immediately within the government regarding its meaning and consequences. Did it strengthen the government's hand? Would European public opinion understand the mandate and express solidarity with Greece, and how effective might that solidarity be? How far were Greeks prepared to go regarding their opposition to the new austerity terms? Would the referendum result risk a Grexit? Varoufakis and other hardline ministers resigned moments after the victory, as Tsipras, fearing the EU might force a Grexit, believed the matter could not be taken any further (cf. Varoufakis 2017: 467–71). There was no doubt that the Greek people did not want Grexit, which was the consistent message of polling throughout the crisis (Balampanidis et al. 2021: 5–9). As the referendum was disregarded by Brussels and Berlin, Tsipras was presented with a fait accompli. On 12 July, in a dramatic summit meeting in Brussels that went long into the night, Tsipras had to surrender but tried to mitigate the terms the EU leadership was determined to impose. Most Greeks stayed awake for the breaking news. After sixteen hours of exhaustive negotiations, which saw French prime minister François Hollande act as mediator between Greeks and Germans, Tsipras signed the new €61.8 billion bailout package that included a new set of draconian austerity measures.[16] Among the punitive measures was the fire-sale privatisations of Greek public assets, but Tsipras ensured that some of the income (€12.5 billion) from these sell-offs would be reinvested in the Greek economy.[17]

Holding the referendum was not an impromptu decision. Indeed, for SYRIZA it was unavoidable. The first attempt to give the Greek people a say on the bailouts was in 2012, but it was denied to them by the EU leadership, making Papandreou's position as prime minister untenable. However, popular demand for a vote on the matter did not go away, and if anything, it increased with the prospect of a third bailout. The referendum was conceived as the denouement of five years of Greek protests, and as the anti-austerity party, SYRIZA had to take the lead in that final part of the story. It had raised public expectations that the bailout terms could be renegotiated. Therefore, to capitulate to the EU without a show of defiance would have brought the party into disrepute. Defeat in the face of overwhelming odds was understandable, but cowardly acceptance without a show of defiance was not. The Greek people faced inevitable defeat with dignity, and managed to stay in Europe, avoiding the chaos that Grexit promised. Significantly, SYRIZA also denied the anti-austerity ground to the radical Right, which was unable to fully capitalise on the deep frustration and anger of most Greeks. These factors go some way towards explaining why SYRIZA was then given a new mandate in September. Despite the split in the party, SYRIZA won the elections with 35.46 per cent, compared to 36.34 the previous January. The ND vote picked up only marginally, rising from 27.81 to 28.09 per cent. Another reason for the return of the SYRIZA government was that Tsipras could be expected to push for debt relief and mitigate the effects of austerities on society's most vulnerable.

Perhaps the key outcome of the referendum was that the fallout removed any thought in the minds of Greek voters that they had alternatives; this was to have long-term consequences for the Greek Left and radicalism (see below, p. 412). Although the economic difficulties continued, Greek society developed a passive acceptance of 'Troikonomics'. In an important sense, the 'crisis' had come to an end, and the new social, demographic and economic realities that it created became a new 'normality'. The memorandum/anti-memorandum divide lost its meaning. As the country became resigned to its fate, demonstrations shrank in size and became less frequent. In 2017, leading correspondent for Britain's *Financial Times* Simon Kuper, after seeing a small demonstration before the parliament of only a few dozen people, wrote the Greeks had 'given up':

> 'For me, there is no crisis' shouted my friend from under his [motorcycle] helmet. 'This is how we live. And we're learning to live with our fears.' Athenians have adjusted to a forever crisis. (Kuper 2017)

Within a few years, key performance indicators had been met. On 20 August 2018, a triumphant Tsipras was able to announce that Greece had exited from the regime of controls as defined by the three memoranda (2010, 2012 and 2015). Since 2010, Greece had borrowed a total of €290 billion: €256 billion from European institutions and the rest from the IMF and eurozone countries.[18] On paper, at least, Greece was out of the woods. The loans still had to be repaid before 2060, but now under more favourable conditions. Yet the end of the bailout programmes period did not mean the end of surveillance of the Greek economy regarding its debt commitments and EU priorities. Troika staff, for example, met with their Greek counterparts on 10 September 2018 as part of a routine of 'enhanced surveillance' to ensure that Greece continued along the path of high budget surpluses and low public spending.

The reality was that the economy remained in the doldrums. Most social indices showed that by the end of the decade Greeks were poorer and less secure, as indebtedness worsened. In 2010, at the beginning of the crisis, the debt to GDP ratio was 170.1 per cent: the debt totalled almost €300 billion and threatened a national financial meltdown. Eight years later, the debt was €330 billion and the debt to GDP ratio 181.2 per cent, one of the highest in the world (Figure 11.5). In 2021, the ratio exceeded 210 per cent and was the third largest in the world. The priority of the EU and IMF was to secure the EU's financial stability and to work like a 'cordon sanitaire' around the Greek economy. The politics of internal devaluation by horizontal cuts to income only served to deepen and prolong the country's economic depression. Meanwhile, the crisis had left a deep impression on Greek mentalities and emotions, and the sense that energy expenditure on the matter seemed futile. 'I feel as if I'm running on a treadmill and, as I'm trying more and more, I end up with zero …' said a 30-year-old female health worker (Tsekeris et al. 2015: 17). That was also the conclusion of a University of Athens professor of European Studies, who claimed that austerities seemed like interminable yet meaningless punishment:

> The pain (during the crisis) has been much stronger than initially anticipated, the suffering has lasted longer, and the fairness of its distribution has left much to be desired. As income kept falling and more jobs were lost, fewer Greeks continued to believe (or hope) that the particular therapy could cure them. They tended to see themselves as guinea pigs in a nasty experiment. (Tsoukalis 2013: 36–7)

At the very beginning of the crisis graffiti appeared in Athens that encapsulated the mood of whole city in one word: *vasanizomai* ('I am being tortured'; Figure 11.7). This verb, in the passive voice, without suggestion of past or end, nor blame or guilt, where the subject is affected by an unidentified action, was a recurring expression (Boletsi 2019). Without a sense of the distress, anger, frustration and futility that

Figure 11.7 Graffiti in Athens during the Crisis: 'I am being tortured'. Courtesy of Tassos Kostopoulos

Greeks felt during the Crisis decade, it is difficult to understand Greek behaviour and why most of them voted NO during the referendum.

The European Union, however, emerged much stronger. Controls imposed on Greece and other economically 'irresponsible' member states not only helped to resolve the financial crisis precipitated by the EU's major banks, but also created new institutions like the European Stability Mechanism (created in 2012) to serve as the EU's own IMF. The European Fiscal Compact treaty (also signed in 2012), which had all but two EU member states signing an agreement to enforce fiscal discipline, required governments to keep deficits below 0.5 per cent of GDP, and imposed an 'automatic correction mechanism' for countries that missed the target. The EU also assumed control over social policy spending. All Greek public property, including land, highways, ports and airports, public facilities substructures, as well as shareholdings in banks and public companies, was detached from the state administration and was to be managed by a body appointed in Brussels and Frankfurt (Souliotis 2021: 223–4). As had been argued several years earlier by the distinguished sociologist Saskia Sassen (2006), the denationalisation of sectors of the nation state, as exemplified by the independence of the central banks, is central to the neoliberal adaptation of national states to globalisation. The EU had become an effective agent of neoliberal reform.

Greece was just one example of how national debates in member states were more Europeanised than ever. EU politics were internalised in national politics, becoming 'normal politics'. At the same time the terms 'European' and 'national' were reconceptualised. The European leadership's insistence that political problems should be approached as if they were technical problems brought it into direct conflict with proponents of national sovereignty and defenders of democracy. Soon after the 2015 Referendum, Varoufakis and other leftists across Europe formed the Democracy in Europe (DiEM25) movement, whose stated mission was the democratisation of the EU.[19]

The fate of the Tsipras government underlines this new reality. It sacrificed all it stood for so as not to jeopardise Greece's membership of the eurozone. SYRIZA would inevitably pay the price for overseeing the third bailout. After four and half years in office, Tsipras lost the July 2019 elections, winning only Crete and four electoral districts on the mainland. ND returned with an economic agenda aligned to the Troika's neoliberal reforms, promising greater foreign investment and job creation. ND was led by 51-year-old Kyriakos Mitsotakis, whose background was in corporate finance. He also happened to be the son of former prime minister Konstantinos Mitsotakis, demonstrating once again the remarkable resilience of the established political families.

The Cypriot economic crisis

The EU's principal concern with the Greek crisis, at least initially, had been the danger of contagion, yet in the end Greece's only victim was Cyprus. In 2013 the island republic was placed under the Troika's tutelage, although uniquely it was also subjected to a 'bail-in'. In other words, to meet its debt obligations, the Cypriot state had to raid the bank accounts of its citizens and foreign account holders. However, as Cyprus' problems were caused essentially by the behaviour of its financial sector and had little to do with public debt, its period in purgatory would be relatively short.

The Republic of Cyprus had formally joined the EU in May 2004. Membership had significant economic implications, including deregulation and reductions in the size of the public sector. It was also meant to address the island's reputation as a tax haven. Since 1963, its tax laws had been devised to attract shipping interests, but it was after 1990 that its low corporate tax rates and strict privacy laws began to attract major depositors, particularly from the former Soviet Union. By the time Cyprus had joined the EU in 2004, the financial services sector was the most important driver of the economy, having overtaken tourism a few years earlier (2001). The effects of financialisation could be measured by local interest in the Cypriot stock market and a phenomenal rise in stock prices (Featherstone 2000: 151). After accession, the sector expanded even more. Money flooded into the country from the EU, given that Cypriot banks were now domestic banks that also offered returns far above what depositors could expect in mainstream EU member countries. Meanwhile, the 'dirty' money of Russian plutocrats and other sources kept pouring in. According to Moody's credit rating agency, Russian banks and individuals held a combined $31 billion in Cypriot banks (Theodore and Theodore 2015: 40).

By the time Cyprus had joined the Monetary Union, the banking and financial service sector was huge compared to the others. By 2011, it held €141 billion and was almost ten times (9.5) larger than GDP (Katsourides 2020: 35). Moreover, the sector was utterly dominated by two banks (the Bank of Cyprus and Laiki Bank), both four times larger the size of GDP, which meant the fate of the Cypriot economy was effectively in their hands. As a senior banker and academic economist, Panicos Demetriades, put it, these two banks became 'too big to fail, too big to save and arguably, too big to regulate' (Demetriades 2017: xvi). The dramatic increase in liquidity since joining the eurozone also had the effect of fuelling private borrowing and consumption, and of creating an ever-expanding property bubble.

The GFC forced Cyprus into recession. In 2009 its economy shrank by 1.67 per cent, but conditions were mild compared to the rest of the eurozone. Debt to GDP ratio was 49 per cent as compared to the eurozone average of 70 per cent and that of Greece (170 per cent), while the effects of the housing boom were moderated by the fact that Cypriot banks demanded 30 per cent equity on property purchases (Theodore and Theodore 2015: 44). The election of AKEL in February 2008 was secured with promises of increased public spending. However, Cypriot analysts remained deeply divided over the extent to which the AKEL government's spending over the next two years made matters worse. GFC public debt was still 10 per cent below the EU average and lower than that of Germany (71 per cent compared to 77.8 per cent of GDP) (Demetriades 2017: 23; Katsourides 2020: 37), but critics pointed out that lenders were sufficiently alarmed that they refused to lend the Cypriot government any more money (Theodore and Theodore 2015: 48–9). Steady improvement in that period was reversed when an explosion at the Evangelos Florakis Naval Base at Mari (between Larnaca and Limassol) in May 2011 killed thirteen and injured over sixty people, while cutting the island's electricity supplies. The estimated cost of the accident, the fourth greatest non-nuclear explosion ever recorded, was $2.83 billion (Theodore and Theodore 2015: 49).

What made Cyprus' crisis more than just a recession was the insolvency of its two behemoth banks, the fact that most Cypriot households depended on them, and that most of the banks' activities were in Greece. During 2009 and 2010 the Bank of Cyprus and the Laiki had been busily acquiring stakes in banks and risky assets in Eastern Europe and Greece. When haircuts were applied to Greek government bonds in 2011 and 2012, the Cypriot banks incurred enormous losses: €1.9 billion for the Bank of Cyprus and €2.4 for the Laiki. Moreover, Cypriot banks were not afforded some of the protections given to Greek banks; hence they suffered comparatively heavier losses (Demetriades 2017: 192; Theodore and Theodore 2015: 59–60). On 13 June 2012, as incoming governor of the Central Bank of Cyprus, Panicos Demetriades asked the chairman of the Bank of Cyprus, Theodoros Aristodemou, why his bank 'had a risk concentration of over 100 per cent of their own capital in Greek Government Bonds', to which Aristodemou responded that he had been given a reassurance by a former official (Papademos) of the ECB in 2010 'that there will not be any restructuring of Greek debt':

> It was a naive, if not altogether arrogant, answer for a bank chairman to be using to justify a gamble that didn't pay off: they had 'invested' around 100 per cent of the bank's capital into a single financial instrument, which, by any definition, constituted an excessive concentration of risk. Moreover, it wasn't just any instrument. It was, according to financial markets, the riskiest sovereign bond in Europe not least because it reflected what markets saw as the necessity of Greek debt restructuring. Yet Bank of Cyprus' leaders behaved as if they knew better. (Demetriades 2017: 56)

By the time Cyprus sought assistance, the EU was suffering from 'bailout fatigue'. Merkel's Christian Democrats were preparing for federal elections in September 2013, and they were mindful that German taxpayers would resent bailing out yet another southern state. They were also aware that about one third of the deposits in Cypriot banks belonged to Russian plutocrats, and there was some reluctance on the island to relinquish its money-laundering role. A settlement was not reached until 20 March, while the Cypriot economy continued to deteriorate. Finally, on 16 March 2013, the EU offered €10 billion of the

€17 billion requested. Another €5.8 billion would have to come from a 'bail-in'. That meant Cypriot bank deposits would incur a unique, one-off tax or haircut of 60 per cent on accounts above €100,000. The measure would extend to deposits in banks that had behaved responsibly, not just the delinquents. To avoid a run on the banks, branch doors were kept shut for the next twelve days, forcing Greek Cypriots to cue at ATMs. The national parliament initially rejected the deal, but the prospect of default and expulsion from the eurozone forced Cyprus to sign up on 28 March. At the very least, continuing membership provided Greek Cypriots with some protection against Turkey. As Demetriades points out:

> It wasn't just the economy and the currency at stake. The unobstructed view of the gigantic Turkish flag on Pentadaktylos, the mountain range in the occupied part of Cyprus, from the Governor's office on the fourth floor of the modern CBC [Central Bank of Cyprus] building was a daily reminder of those risks. (Demetriades 2017: 108)

All the while, Cyprus was forced to privatise public assets, cut public service jobs, and push through extensive market deregulation. Initially, the austerity measures seemed to wreak devastation. As happened in Greece, national debt and unemployment increased sharply, as the economy suffered its most significant contraction since 1974. Employment fell by 11 per cent between 2012 and 2014, while 31,600 people emigrated in 2013 and 2014. Youth unemployment in the south in 2012 was 11.9 per cent and 16 per cent in 2015, which surpassed youth unemployment in the north (8.7 per cent and 7.4 per cent, respectively).[20] In general, income inequality and poverty increased during the crisis, with about 10,600 families obtaining food from food banks in 2015.[21]

However, in 2016 the country was able to withdraw from the Troika's oversight, and achieved restored confidence in its banking sector. The main reason was that the Cypriot government implemented nearly all of the austerity measures, partly because they were not as severe as those applied in Greece, and partly because there was much less demand for structural change. Cyprus was also able to deal with its Achilles heel. The size of the financial sector was reduced from 750 per cent of GDP to 420 per cent by 2015, bringing it closer to the EU average (Hardouvelis and Gkionis 2016: 16). The signs of a Cypriot rebound were clear by the end of 2015 when the national economy began to post growth figures.

The Greek refugee crisis: Odysseys without *nostos*

Compounding Greece's difficulties throughout the 2010s was the refugee issue, as streams of displaced people fleeing from war, oppression and poverty poured into the country. Greece had for decades served as a corridor through which people from the Middle East and further afield tried to enter Europe. The most common route was via Istanbul and the Turkish land border. But as the economic crisis was reaching a boiling point in 2015, refugees began to pour in from across the Aegean. A century after the first wave of Asia Minor refugees took to the sea, the eastern Aegean islands were once again flooded with thousands of desperate men, women and children.

Much of Europe had a refugee crisis following the failure of the Arab Spring in 2011. The initial influx came mainly from Libya and Tunisia, via the sea crossing to Sicily. From the outset, the EU and its member governments, including Greece, capitalised politically by raising fears about illegal immigration and promising more robust border protection. Samaras' ND campaigned heavily on an anti-immigrant agenda during the 2012 elections, promising to stop new arrivals and to remove or confine existing 'illegal' migrants. After assuming power, it oversaw the erection of a barbed-wire fence along the Evros/Maritza River, which had been the main entry point for migrants from Middle Eastern, Asian and African countries. Surveillance was strengthened with more border guards and armed civilian patrols, while detainees were confined in prison camps. The government also flirted with the idea of forcing refugees back across the Turkish border. Such human rights violations drew international criticism (Cabot 2014: 30), yet little was done internationally to cater to the needs of refugees fleeing across the Aegean Sea.

During that period, the presence of refugees and migrants in Greece revived debate on the long-running questions on citizenship and what constituted Greekness. For the children of migrants and refugees who had grown up in Greece, the issue was a matter of serious concern. A report published in 2012 noted that immigrants numbered 1.3 million, among whom one third (390,000)[22] were undocumented – detractors insisted on labelling them 'illegal immigrants' (*lathrometanastes*). To address their needs, a new nationalisation law had been passed in 2010 to regulate the process for the second and third generation. The children of immigrants born in Greece, whose parents had lived in the country for five years, were eligible to apply. The bill was opposed by ND and other right-wing parties and then revoked by the Supreme

Court in February 2012 because it did not account for 'natural' bonds to the nation, as required by the constitution (Figgou 2016: 153).

The civil war in Syria sparked the largest exodus since the Arab Spring. The ongoing conflict would produce 500,000 fatalities and the internal displacement of 6.7 million people. It forced 3,600,000 to cross into Turkey, 880,000 to Lebanon, 662,000 to Jordan, 242,000 to Iraq and 130,000 to Egypt. About 1 million of the refugees in Turkey made their way towards Europe via Greece. EU countries recorded more than 2,300,000 people crossed over during 2015–16.[23]

During the summer of 2015, the shores of Lesbos, Chios, Samos, Kos and other Greek islands were inundated with small boats filled with destitute and desperate people (Figure 11.8). Not all managed to arrive safely: an unknown number perished in defective vessels that sank at sea. In September 2015, the body of a 2-year-old Syrian boy, Alan Kurdi, washed up on a beach near Bodrum after his family attempted to cross the sea in a small dinghy. The photo of his lifeless body washed up on the seashore went viral and elicited a global humanitarian rallying cry. More than 880 lives were lost in the Aegean Sea over the next two years.[24] Islanders welcomed the disembarked families and children. Despite the nation's strained economic circumstances, a significant amount of fundraising took place throughout

Figure 11.8 *Syrian refugees arriving on Lesbos in 2016.* © *John Liakos*

the country in a spirit of solidarity. Schoolchildren were even running campaigns. Much of this can be explained by Greece's own experiences with refugees, and the fact that many Greeks were descended from refugees who had also arrived from Turkey's shores. The influx also presented an opportunity for many Greeks to make amends for the anti-immigrant frenzy of recent years. At the time the SYRIZA government implemented a programme to facilitate interaction between children in camps and schools. Meanwhile, networks of volunteers and international NGOs received the refugees and facilitated their relocation to camps. For the moment, Greece's image improved, as the country earned praise for its humane responses to the refugee influx. In the tiny village of Skala Sykamnias on Lesbos, which had a mere 140 permanent inhabitants at the time, Greek grandmothers were photographed by the international press, feeding the babies of refugees (Papataxiarchis 2016). Situated as the closest point between the Asia Minor coast and the islands, less than 10 km, the village became the informal gateway to Europe. Meanwhile, in April 2016, Pope Francis visited the refugee camps on the island, calling for solidarity to help the destitute.[25]

It was clear that the refugees wanted to move on to Western Europe. Given its depressed economic conditions and minimal employment opportunities, Greece was never more than a stopover. After staying for some time in overcrowded camps, some transferred to Piraeus, from where they made their way to Italy via Patras and Igoumenitsa. Others ventured northward through the Balkans to central Europe, often walking along train tracks or hiding in trucks and railway carriages. The European Union soon found that it had a new crisis on its hands. Here too, humanitarian instincts kicked in early. Chancellor Merkel described the crisis as a 'historic test' for Europe and announced that Germany would adopt 1 million of Syria's asylum seekers in 2015 and 2016.[26] Back in 1945 Germany had had a refugee crisis that was much larger in scale than the one Greece had in the 1920s (Yoder 2019: 668). Merkel's humanitarian sensibilities, however, were not necessarily shared by her government colleagues. Indeed, the EU and many member states quickly began to treat the refugee crisis as a border problem. In May 2015, it produced the 'European Agenda on Migration', followed by a ten-point plan that included a 'hotspot approach' designed to contain and control movements. The first hotspots were established in Greece and Italy, where asylum seekers were vetted to allow the possibility of returning those who did not qualify as refugees, and to limit the number of persons entering the asylum procedure (Papadopoulou 2016). These measures failed to reduce the flow. Therefore, in January 2016 several European governments urged the suspension of the Schengen Agreement, which had abolished internal EU border checks. Then, in March 2016, the EU reached an agreement with Turkey, promising €6 billion in regular and additional funding per year if it would better control the flow of refugees into Europe. The deal provided for the return to Turkey of those deemed unqualified for asylum.[27] The Common European Asylum System was subjected to further revision, but it would remain a means of consigning the issue of processing and asylum responsibility to Greece and Italy, and for restricting the rights granted to refugees in the EU.

Europe's refugee crisis in 2015–16 was the greatest since the Second World War, prompting an identity crisis that questioned the EU's moral foundations as an organisation dedicated to promoting peace and progressive values, particularly human rights. Meanwhile, it tapped latent xenophobia throughout Europe, especially among Eastern Bloc countries, which also refused to share the burden of the refugee intake. Public opinion in Europe was split between those who believed their governments should treat the crisis as a humanitarian disaster, and those who insisted that borders be strengthened. It was widely suspected that the measures were motivated by Islamophobia. Eastern European states were more ready than most to shut their borders completely to refugees. When North Macedonia did so during the winter of 2016, thousands of people were trapped in Greece, placing added stress on overcrowded facilities.[28]

Soon enough, Greece too began to draw criticism from humanitarian organisations and the international press. Much of that attention was focused on the grossly understaffed 'hotspots', where refugees were forced to wait interminable periods in unsanitary and squalid housing. Especially vulnerable were unaccompanied minors and women, who were susceptible to physical or sexual abuse.[29] Not surprisingly, tensions sometimes boiled over into violent protests (Papadopoulou 2016: 34). Tensions also developed between refugees and the locals, but as the former were keen to move on, the latter focused more of their hostility on the authorities detaining them. The establishment of new hotspots on Lesbos and Chios in February 2020 provoked riots by locals, to which the police responded by using tear gas.[30]

Indeed, the crisis prompted intense re-examinations of the function of political borders, whether national or European, land or maritime, and specifically the question of access for protection. It became readily apparent that the Schengen Agreement, which allowed free access between member states, was not devised with the needs and rights of asylum seekers in mind. New agencies, technologies and terminologies were employed with a view to erecting barriers against purported traffickers, smugglers and 'illegal' migrants. EU institutions like the EASO (European Asylum Support Office), Frontex (*Frontières extérieures*), Eurosur (European Border Surveillance System), Europol (European Union Agency for Law Enforcement Cooperation), Eurojust (European Union Agency for Criminal Justice Cooperation) and Eurodac (European Data Archive Convention) intervened to support frontline member states such as Greece and Italy so as to regulate immigration but mainly to protect EU borders. Border guards from EU member states provided expertise for border management, including sea border surveillance and biometric technologies to record identities among the teeming migrating masses. The operations, which were often named after ancient gods (e.g. 'Operation Triton' in Italy and 'Operation Poseidon' in Greece), included the deployment of private agencies, and were part of a broader aim of normalising the use of camps for Europe's new and 'unwanted'. In this period, populist politicians and media outlets played on public fears, claiming migrants and refugees posed threats to public safety. Right-wing intellectuals found ways of construing the newcomers as a threat to liberty and Western culture.[31]

The migration movements of the 2010s raised anxieties in many European societies, where there was much questioning of such basic values as pluralism and human rights. The 'invasions' gave right-wing parties an opportunity to demand restrictions on democracy and democratic institutions. It also prompted host communities to rediscover their own refugee histories, to face the fact that many Europeans were the progeny of displaced peoples who had fled death and oppression. These impulses competed with powerful official narratives that usually overlooked or hid these histories of displacement. The crisis also produced debates about European fertility and the continent's ageing population, which generated anxieties about the youthfulness and the high reproduction rates among the newcomers. Above all, the refugee crisis tested the very meaning of 'Europe' and its place in a globalising world. Was Europe a promoter of enlightenment, progressive values, liberalisation and emancipation? Or did it represent neo-colonialism, authoritarianism, exclusive nationalism and neoliberalism? In Greece, new forces emerged that resurrected some old spectres of national identity politics.

The rise and fall of Golden Dawn

In the 2010s, the economic and refugee crises provided fertile ground for a marginal neo-Nazi movement to emerge from the shadows and become the nation's third-largest political party. 'Golden Dawn' (*Chrysi Avgi*) presented itself as a patriotic movement by drawing on a selection of familiar patriotic key words and symbols. It was focused on ideas of Greeks as a chosen race, on the virtues of national exclusivity, and on the need to expunge the nation of its non-Greek impurities. Founded in 1983, this ultra-nationalistic party attracted only a tiny following during the 1990s, when Greece received its first waves of migrants and refugees, and when much of society had been galvanised by the Macedonian Question. Its members lived in poor Athenian neighbourhoods like Agios Panteleimon, which were seen as being 'swamped' by foreigners, who were blamed for such problems as robberies, street assaults, high unemployment and deteriorating public services. More specifically, their presence fanned Islamophobia and an irrational fear of terrorism and communicable diseases (Ersland 2014; A. A. Ellinas 2013: 558–9).

Such popular prejudices had been exploited by far-Right groups and parties since 1974, which included *Ethniki Politiki Enosi* (EPEN), whose nominal leader was the jailed former dictator Papadopoulos, and the more electorally successful LAOS, which had formed in 2000. What made Golden Dawn different from previous far-Right parties was its brazen identification with Nazism. Although it officially denied being a neo-Nazi party, it nevertheless drew heavily on fascist ideas, symbols and practices. It adopted a variant of the swastika as the movement's symbol, and members used the fascist salute as its official gesture (Psarras 2012: 250–1). Its founder and head, Nikolaos Michaloliakos, an outspoken anti-Semite, Holocaust denier and Islamophobe, wielded the kind of domineering influence expected of an ideology that required a charismatic and powerful leader. Initially, his party was too extreme to attract voters: in the 2009 elections it could only muster about 20,000 votes, a mere 0.29 per cent of the electorate. LAOS won 5.6 per cent of the vote, but when it became part of a coalition government and had to cooperate with the government in power, it lost credibility as a far-Right populist voice. In the May 2012 elections, LAOS lost all its 15 seats, attracting only 2.9 per cent of the vote (A. A. Ellinas 2013: 557–8), whereas Golden Dawn won 20 seats and received 7 per cent of the national vote. Some 441,000 Greeks therefore voted for a party that celebrated Nazism. It performed well in Attica and especially Piraeus, where it received just under 10 per cent of the vote in each district, and it performed well in the traditionally conservative districts of Lakonia, the Argolid and Corinth (Vasilopoulou and Halikiopoulou 2015: 18).

But whereas LAOS had moderated its behaviour and rhetoric when it had seats in Parliament, Golden Dawn refused to do so. Its foot soldiers continued to assault immigrant street vendors, critics and left-wing activists, often with the assistance of sympathetic police. In a notorious live television debate in June 2012 that attracted international attention, Golden Dawn MP Ilias Kasidiaris physically assaulted SYRIZA deputy Rena Dourou and KKE deputy Liana Kanelli, throwing a glass of water at the former and aggressively slapping the latter's face three times, after which he hastened from the studio. The panellists had tried to discuss the fact that Kasidiaris was facing charges of assault and robbery.[32] Indeed, Golden Dawn's weakness was that its criminal activities could be linked to the party leadership, which meant most of it was vulnerable to criminal prosecution (Psarras 2012). Some were implicated in the murders of Pakistani worker Shehzad Luqman in Petralona, Athens, who was stabbed to death in January 2013, and rapper musician Pavlos Fyssas in September 2013. It was the murder of Fyssas, a Greek national, that prompted the ND government to move against Golden Dawn and to treat it as a criminal organisation. The assailants and leading members of the party were arrested (Walker and Kakaounaki 2013). Despite that, the party lost very little ground in the European parliamentary elections of 2014 and in the two national elections in 2015, when Golden Dawn was still the third-largest party and when its aggregate vote fell only marginally compared to 2012.

In the 2019 elections, however, its vote plummeted to 190,000, and it failed to win any seats. Its demise can be explained by the fact that most of the leadership was on trial for serious crimes. In addition, its supporters, like most Greeks after the 2015 Referendum, ceased believing the nation's major problems could be addressed through political action. In October 2020, Golden Dawn was eliminated as a political force. In a trial touted as the largest against a Nazi organisation since Nuremberg, Golden Dawn was found to be a criminal organisation, and party leaders were convicted and handed sentences of varying length. Fyssas' murderer was sentenced to life imprisonment (Roumanias et al. 2020).

Southeastern Europe: peaceful lakes, rough seas

During the latter half of the decade, as people became accustomed to living with the economic and refugee crises, public attention focused more on regional politics. The most striking development concerned the long-awaited resolution to the Macedonian Question (Heraclides 2020; Neofotistos 2021). In June 2018, to normalise relations between the two countries, and despite fierce opposition in both Greece and the renamed Republic of North Macedonia, Tsipras and his counterpart Zoran Zaef signed an agreement at a meeting on the shores of Lake Prespa. Once again, hundreds of thousands of Greeks of all ages, including women and children, participated in massive countrywide rallies against the agreement. These mass rallies were the first of the post-Memorandum era, although their style and slogans were reminiscent of the 1990s demonstrations on the Macedonian issue. The participants included supporters of the pro-memorandum and the anti-memorandum case: about half had voted NO and 25 per cent had voted YES in the 2015 Referendum (Balampanidis et al. 2021: 9–11). In return for name recognition, Tsipras received assurances regarding North Macedonia's claims to the ancient Macedonian heritage, while the new name presupposed that 'Macedonia' designated a region to which no country had an exclusive claim (Skoulariki 2021). From a geopolitical perspective, the agreement removed the only real impediment to normal bilateral relations, and it ended what international observers and many Greeks regarded as a trivial dispute over a name. In Brussels, Tsipras and Zaef were each heralded as peacemakers and nominated for a Nobel Prize (Maatsch and Kurpiel 2021: 59). As opposition leader, Mitsotakis fiercely opposed the agreement. In an interview in June 2019, he claimed that it:

> is nationally dangerous and wounded the Greeks ... We need to protect the Macedonian products ... and naturally to safeguard the Greekness of the term Macedonia. [We need to] promote internationally the real Macedonia that is an inseparable part of Greek history and heritage. (Karakasidou 2021: 124)

Once in office, however, Mitsotakis recognised the practical benefits of normalisation and stated that he would abide by the agreement. He offered his support for North Macedonia's accession to the EU and proposed other cooperative ventures.[33]

In contrast, relations with Turkey had deteriorated markedly. Aside from the intractable disputes over Cyprus and the Aegean, the new issue of contention was access to gas deposits in the eastern Mediterranean. The discovery of up to 120 trillion cubic feet of gas deposits (equivalent to half the USA's reserves) in the eastern Mediterranean basin brought into focus the competing maritime territorial claims of five nations: Egypt, Israel, Cyprus, Greece and Turkey. The problem was exacerbated by the geographical fact that Cyprus and many Greek islands are very close to the Turkish coast, so that their maritime territorial claims overlapped with those of Turkey. The prospect of dividing the eastern Mediterranean into exclusive economic zones (EEZ) of exploitation for energy resources brought Greece and Turkey close to military confrontation. Turkey refused to acknowledge that Greece and Cyprus could impose maritime limitations on its rights to drill for gas in the Aegean or the eastern Mediterranean, and Greece insisted Turkey could be excluded from exploiting gas deposits in these seascapes. Together with Israel and Egypt, Greece sought to block Turkey from obtaining EEZ in the eastern Mediterranean, and Turkey with Libya declared unilaterally an EEZ between Libya and Bodrum, which included eastern Crete, Rhodes and other southern Dodecanese islands. Greek and Turkish warships faced off in August and September 2020, when the seismic survey vessel *Oruç Reis* explored the disputed seabed between the southern Turkish coast, Crete, Cyprus and the Greek island of Kastellorizo. A confrontation was avoided through German and US mediation. The issue then dropped from the headlines because of the COVID-19 pandemic and the collapse of natural gas prices (Roussos 2017; C. Ellinas 2020).

Relations between the two countries had already deteriorated in the 2000s, when it became clear that the EU was unwilling to welcome Turkey as a member, and as the latter began to develop a new role as a power in the Middle East. This shift was driven by the political ambitions of Recep Tayyip Erdoğan, who first became prime minister in 2003 and then president in 2014, and who ensconced himself in power through constitutional changes and the suppression of political opponents. More than any of his predecessors, Erdoğan sought a major role for Turkey in regional politics. As a right-wing populist, he formed part of a global trend that saw authoritarian leaders such as Vladimir Putin and Viktor Orbán turn to nationalism to mobilise popular support. Erdoğan also went further than any of his predecessors in tapping anti-Greek sentiment in Turkey, which in turn fuelled anti-Turkish sentiment in Greece and Cyprus. Of particular concern to Greeks, especially those living in the Eastern Sporades and the Dodecanese, were his calls for revising the Treaty of Lausanne, thus challenging Greece's possession of these islands.

Towards the bicentenary of Greece, 1821–2021

As Greece was preparing for the bicentenary of the 1821 Revolution, the outbreak of the COVID-19 pandemic in December 2019, and its rapid spread across the globe during the first half of 2020, presented a new crisis while the country was still suffering severe economic hardship. Around the world, scientists and particularly epidemiologists called for wholesale public responses that would inevitably disrupt economic activity and threaten depression levels of unemployment. All governments made political calculations as to how far they would follow scientific recommendations. Hardened by years of crisis conditions, Greece appeared more prepared than most Western countries to take the hard decisions required. Greek society was more receptive to government directives than it had been in the past, especially as this was a health crisis and given general awareness of the weaknesses of the public health system.[34]

The COVID-19 pandemic affected economic recovery and threatened to disrupt the 2021 tourist season and the sizeable income it delivered even during the worst years of the economic crisis. That year, Greece welcomed just under 8 million visitors, compared to the 34 million it hosted in 2019. It was the lowest number since the economic crisis of 2009.[35] Unemployment was still extremely high in 2020 at 17.3 per cent, but it began to climb again in 2021 with the spread of the highly infectious Delta variant of COVID-19.

Where is Greece now? In economic terms, the short answer is nowhere. Most social indices showed that by 2020, Greeks were poorer and less secure. Indebtedness had worsened. In 2022, the purchasing power of Greeks was ranked marginally above all neighbouring countries, but below Hungary, Slovenia, Slovakia, Poland and Latvia, and well below Cyprus and all of western Europe. Rising energy costs were felt internationally following the Russian invasion of Ukraine in February 2022, but it was particularly severe in Greece given its very high dependence on Russian oil, which was twice the European average. Rising inflation was also of great concern to the average consumer, many of whom were beginning to wonder if it might lead to more austerities, salary cuts and redundancies. For seven decades, since the end of the Civil War, Greek living standards had maintained an upward trend. But in the 2010s the trend was reversed, placing Greece closer to the levels of its Balkan neighbours and other former Eastern Bloc countries.

Greece has been tested by successive and overlapping crises. The 2010s were turbulent, as indeed were the 1910s, the decade in which this book started its coverage. Since then, the population had more than doubled, yet it has declined since 2010. The Greek population is ageing, and its educated youth continue to move abroad, while the country has received successive flows of poor migrants and refugees from Asia and Africa. The environmental crisis, with its catastrophic conflagrations (Peloponnese 2007, Mati 2018) and floods, constitutes an ever-present threat. In August 2021, Greece and much of the southern Mediterranean was in flames, the causes being a combination of record temperatures and strong winds.

The country seems to be in a perennial state of crisis. Urban graffiti often provides deep insights into grass-roots social ideas and collective feelings at any given time (Zaimakis 2015: 392). One Athenian example, 'Crisis … what else?' (Figure 11.9), captures the idea of 'crisis' as a permanent state of mind: as the new normality and as the keynote of the times (Boletsi 2018). It has shaped the identities of the young, who have grown up in a country beset by uncertainty and relentless crisis.

Did Greece's twentieth century end with the crisis? Or does it continue as the crisis continues? There are some suggestions that the

Figure 11.9 *Graffiti in Athens during the Crsis: 'Crisis … what else?' Courtesy of Tassos Kostopoulos*

century *has* ended. The issue came up when, on 2 September 2021, Greece's best-known composer, Mikis Theodorakis, passed away only a few years short of his own century. Like the funerals of Ritsos, Odysseas Elytis and Seferis, his was a national event that prompted public reflection on values. Theodorakis provided music that has served as the nation's soundtrack, most particularly 'Zorba's Dance', but he was also known as a political activist who fearlessly engaged in his country's politics, often at significant personal cost. His music explicitly addressed themes of solidarity, injustice and political action (Herzfeld 2020: 409). He crossed political boundaries later in life, hence his funeral drew mourners from across the political spectrum. And as he was involved in many of the nation's crises, his death stimulated considerable interest in the nation's past. In the French newspaper *Libération*, his biographer, Yorgos Archimandritis, claimed poignantly that it marked the end of Greece's twentieth century: 'Il est devenu le symbole de la Grèce. Avec la mort de Míkis Theodorákis, c'est le XXe siècle grec qui se termine.'[36]

Much depends on how we interpret the 2010s, the decade of relentless crisis. But should the focus be on crisis? Reflecting on the subject matter covered in this book, it is difficult not to read Greece's long twentieth century and the histories of Greeks in the wider world in terms of unrelenting upheavals. From this perspective, the concept of crisis becomes synonymous with historical change that dramatically affected the lives of individuals and families. In such circumstances, historical consciousness becomes the consciousness of crisis in historical time. A response to 'Crisis … what else?' would be 'No crisis, no History'.

Last thoughts

But as history is an open-ended narrative, it is not the role of the historian to propose an optimistic or pessimistic national narrative. Thus, only with time will we know if the economic crisis will alter the long-term Greek trend of rising living standards and lengthening life expectancy. Among our aims in writing this book has been to understand the multiple ways Greeks, including minorities in Greece and Greeks abroad, have navigated the kind of dramatically changing circumstances that presented themselves in the modern era. For this reason, we think that historians should keep an open research agenda, allowing the possibility for new questions, and the rereading of history in light of the new problems, national and global, and newly emerging interests and sensitivities in Greek society and throughout the Greek world. That is, after all, what we have tried to do in this book.

Notes

1. https://www.bbc.com/news/world-europe-33507802.
2. http://appsso.eurostat.ec.europa.eu/nui/show.do?dataset=tipspd22 (last accessed 12 July 2021).
3. https://www.ecb.europa.eu/press/pr/date/2010/html/pr100510.en.html; https://www.economist.com/charlemagne/2010/05/10/europes-750-billion-euro-bazooka.
4. https://ec.europa.eu/info/business-economy-euro/economic-and-fiscal-policy-coordination/financial-assistance-eu/which-eu-countries-have-received-assistance/financial-assistance-greece_en (last accessed 5 April 2021).
5. https://ec.europa.eu/info/business-economy-euro/economic-and-fiscal-policy-coordination/financial-assistance-eu/which-eu-countries-have-received-assistance/financial-assistance-greece_en (last accessed 5 April 2021).
6. https://www.theguardian.com/business/2015/jul/24/greek-debt-crisis-great-greece-fire-sale; https://www.reuters.com/article/us-eurozone-greece-privatisations-interv-idUSKCN1FZ1SU.
7. https://www.europarl.europa.eu/RegData/etudes/BRIE/2015/542220/IPOL_BRI(2015)542220_EN.pdf.
8. https://euobserver.com/news/32582.
9. https://scielo.isciii.es/scielo.php?script=sci_arttext&pid=S0213-61632014000100004.
10. https://www.theguardian.com/world/2013/sep/18/greece-birthrate-austerity-measures-healthcare.
11. http://pangalos.gr/portal/%CE%BC%CE%B1%CE%B6%CE%AF-%CF%84%CE%B1-%CF%86%CE%AC%CE%B3%CE%B1%CE%BC%CE%B5/.
12. https://www.straitstimes.com/business/economy/imfs-lagarde-says-greece-talks-need-adults-in-the-room.
13. https://inthesetimes.com/article/joseph-stiglitz-thomas-piketty-greece-syriza-austerity.
14. https://www.theguardian.com/news/datablog/ng-interactive/2015/jul/09/greek-referendum-how-athens-voted-interactive-map.
15. https://www.publicissue.gr/en/greek-referendum-2015-no-voter-demographics/.
16. https://www.consilium.europa.eu/en/infographics/financial-assistance-to-greece-2010-2018/.
17. https://www.huffpost.com/entry/thisisacoup_n_7781736.
18. https://www.esm.europa.eu/assistance/greece (last accessed 7 April 2021).

19. https://diem25.org/about/.
20. http://library.fes.de/pdf-files/id-moe/12825.pdf.
21. https://cyprus.fes.de/fileadmin/user_upload/documents/CyprusEconom icCrisis_en_v03_DIGITAL__002_.pdf.
22. https://www.files.ethz.ch/isn/144536/Briefing-Notes_21_June-2012_Tha nos-Maroukis1.pdf.
23. https://www.europarl.europa.eu/news/en/headlines/society/20170629ST O78630/asylum-and-migration-in-the-eu-facts-and-figures.
24. https://www.iom.int/news/iom-counts-3771-migrant-fatalities-mediterra nean-2015.
25. http://www.vatican.va/content/francesco/en/travels/2016/outside/docum ents/papa-francesco-lesvos-2016.html.
26. https://www.bbc.com/news/world-europe-35091960.
27. https://ec.europa.eu/commission/presscorner/detail/en/MEMO_16_963.
28. https://www.hrw.org/news/2016/03/24/greece-humanitarian-crisis-athe ns-port.
29. https://reliefweb.int/sites/reliefweb.int/files/resources/Emergency-With in-an-Emergency-FXB.pdf (last accessed 28 September 2021).
30. https://greekcitytimes.com/2020/02/25/riots-break-out-in-lesvos-and-chio s54828/.
31. https://www.migreurop.org/IMG/pdf/migrant-detention-eu-en.pdf.
32. https://www.theguardian.com/world/2012/jun/07/greek-golden-dawn-mp-assaults-females-tv.
33. https://balkaninsight.com/2019/09/25/new-greek-pm-pledges-to-respect-macedonia-deal/.
34. https://theconversation.com/greece-despite-a-decade-of-health-cuts-coro navirus-death-rates-appear-comparatively-low-136293.
35. https://www.statista.com/statistics/444847/total-number-of-inbound-visi tors-in-greece/.
36. https://www.liberation.fr/culture/musique/avec-la-mort-de-mikis-theodorakis-cest-le-xxe-siecle-grec-qui-se-termine-20210902_ XIPXNDUMVRH4VLTAP6F4WBI3FA/.

Guide to further reading

Beaton, R. (2020), *Greece: Biography of a Modern Nation*, London: Allen Lane.

Clogg, R. (ed.) (1999), *The Greek Diaspora in the Twentieth Century*, Basingstoke: Macmillan.

Clogg, R. (2021), *A Concise History of Greece*. 4th ed., Cambridge: Cambridge University Press.

Close, D. H. (2002), *Greece since 1945: Politics, Economy and Society*, London. Longman.

Dertilis G. B. (2018), *Ιστορία της Νεότερης και Σύγχρονης Ελλάδας 1750–2015*, Iraklion: Crete University Press.

Doumanis, N. (2010), *A History of Greece (Essential Histories Series)*, London: Palgrave Macmillan.

Gallant, T. W. (2015), *The Edinburgh History of the Greeks, 1768–1913: The Long Nineteenth Century*, Edinburgh: Edinburgh University Press.

Gallant, T. W. (2016), *Modern Greece; From the War of Independence to the Present*. 2nd ed. London: Bloomsbury.

Hatziiosif, C. (ed.) (1999–2009), *Ιστορία της Ελλάδας του 20ού αιώνα*, 8 vols, Athens: Bibliorama.

Hering, G. (1992), *Die politischen Parteien in Griechenland, 1821–1936*. 2 vols, Munich: Oldenbourg

Kalyvas, S. (2015), *Modern Greece: What Everyone Needs to Know*, Oxford: Oxford University Press.

Koliopoulos, J. S. and Veremis, T. (2009), *Modern Greece: A History since 1821*, Oxford: Wiley Blackwell.

Liakos, A. (2019), *Ο Ελληνικός 20ός Αιώνας*, Athens: Polis.

Panagitotoulos, V. (ed.) (2003), *Ιστορία του Νέου Ελληνισμού 1770–2000*, (Vol 1–10), Athens: Ελληνικά Γράμματα.

Woodhouse, C. M. (1999), *Modern Greece: A Short History*, New York: Faber.

Bibliography

Bank of Greece 2009. Διεύθυνση Οικονομικών Μελετών της Τράπεζας της Ελλάδος (ed.), *Η κρίση του 1929, η ελληνική οικονομία και οι εκθέσεις της Τράπεζας της Ελλάδος για τα έτη 1928–1940*. Athens.

Bank of Greece 2014. *Το χρονικό της Μεγάλης Κρίσης, 2008–2013*. Athens.

British Legal Mission to Greece 1946. *Report of the British Legal Mission to Greece (London, 17 January 1946)*. London: His Majesty's Stationery Office.

Bulletin of the European Communities 1982. 'Greek Memorandum: Position of the Greek Government on Greece's Relations with the European Communities, 22 March 1982', *Bulletin of the European Communities* 3, pp. 90–3.

Carnegie Report 1915. *Report of the International Commission to Inquire into the Causes and Conduct of the Balkan War*, Carnegie Endowment for International Peace, Washington (republication: 1993). http://www.pollitecon.com/html/ebooks/Carne gie-Report-on-the-Balkan-Wars.pdf.

CRS 2004. 'Athens Olympics 2004: U.S. Government Involvement in Security Preparations'. https://tinyurl.com/3njzm8hu.

ΕΚΤΕΠΝ 2010. 'Ετήσια Έκθεση για την Κατάσταση του Προβλήματος των Ναρκωτικών και των Οινοπνευματωδών στην Ελλάδα 2010', *Εθνικό Κέντρο Τεκμηρίωσης και Πληροφόρησης για τα Ναρκωτικά (ΕΚΤΕΠΝ)*, 2010. https://tinyurl.com/334975f2.

European Commission 2006. ECFIN, *Statistical Annex of European Economy, Autumn 2006* (ECFIN/REP/52683/2006-EN). https://ec.europa.eu/economy_finance/publica tions/pages/publication7889_en.pdf (last accessed 22 August 2019).

European Commission 2021. *The 2021 Ageing Report: Underlying Assumptions and Projection Methodologies*. Institutional Paper 142. https://ec.europa.eu/info/publicatio ns/economic-and-financial-affairs-publications_en.

European Commission 2021. 'Financial Assistance to Greece: Information of the Enhanced Surveillance Framework for Greece. Overview of the ESM Stability Support Programme and Previous Programmes'. https://ec.europa.eu/info/business-economy-euro/economic-and-fiscal-policy-coordination/eu-financial-assistance/whi ch-eu-countries-have-received-assistance/financial-assistance-greece_en.

Greek Refugee Settlement Commission 1926. *Greek Refugee Settlement*. Geneva: League of Nations.

Hellenic Parliament 1993. *Πόρισμα της Διακομματικής Κοινοβουλευτικής Επιτροπής για τη μελέτη του δημογραφικού προβλήματος της χώρας και διατύπωση προτάσεων για την αποτελεσματική αντιμετώπισή του*. Athens: Hellenic Parliament.

Hellenic Parliament 2010. *Πόρισμα της Εξεταστικής Επιτροπής για την πλήρη διερεύνηση της υπόθεσης των ομολόγων*, November 2010. Athens: Hellenic Parliament.

Hellenic Parliament 2018. *Έκθεση της διακομματικής κοινοβουλευτικής επιτροπής για το δημογραφικό*. Athens: Hellenic Parliament.

Human Rights Watch 2008. 'Greece: Left to Survive. Systematic Failure to Protect Unaccompanied Migrant Children in Greece', *Human Rights Watch*, 22 December 2008. https://www.hrw.org/report/2008/12/22/left-survive/systematic-failure-protect-unaccompanied-migrant-children-greece (last accessed 18 August 2019).

I Exodos. I Έξοδος, ed. F. D. Apostolopoulos, vols 1–5. 1980, 1982, 2013, 2015, 2016. Athens: Centre for Asia Minor Studies.

IOBE 2015. *Το αποτύπωμα της διοργάνωσης των Ολυμπιακών Αγώνων του 2004 στην ελληνική οικονομία*. Athens: Ίδρυμα Οικονομικών και Βιομηχανικών Ερευνών (IOBE).

KANEP 2010. *Τα βασικά μεγέθη της εκπαίδευσης 2010: Πρωτοβάθμια και δευτεροβάθμια εκπαίδευση*. Athens (2011): Κέντρο Ανάπτυξης Εκπαιδευτικής Πολιτικής (KANEP).

KANEP 2014. *Τα βασικά μεγέθη της εκπαίδευσης 2014: Η ελληνική τριτοβάθμια εκπαίδευση, Μέρος Β΄: Το εθνικό πλαίσιο αναφοράς (2002–2012)*. Athens: Κέντρο Ανάπτυξης Εκπαιδευτικής Πολιτικής (KANEP).

KMS: Centre for Asia Minor Studies, Oral history collection.

Marshall Plan 1953. *Το Σχέδιον Μάρσαλλ στην Ελλάδα: Ο πλήρης απολογισμός της βοήθειας του σχεδίου Μάρσαλλ προς την Ελλάδα, Ιούλιος 1948–Ιανουάριος 1952*.

Mavri Vivlos 1920. *Μαύρη Βίβλος των Μαρτυριών του εν Τουρκία Ελληνισμού από της ανακωχής μέχρι τέλους 1920*. Constantinople: Patriarchate Press. http://medusa.libv er.gr/jspui/handle/123/10802.

OECD 1988. *Historical Statistics 1960–1986*. Paris: OECD Publishing.

OECD 2005. OECD Social, Employment and Migration Working Papers, No. 22. *OECDiLibrary*, 10 May 2005. https://doi.org/10.1787/882106484586 (last accessed 1 May 2019).

OECD 2012. *Greece: Review of the Central Administration* (2011). Paris: OECD Publishing.

PRO: Public Records Office (National Archives UK).

US Government Accounting Office 2005. 'Olympic Security: US Support to Athens Games Provides Lessons for Future Olympics', Report to Congressional Requesters, United States Government Accountability Office (GAO-05-547), May 2005. http://www.documentcloud.org/documents/241853-olympic-security-u-s-support-to-athe ns-games.html (last accessed 4 September 2019).

Secondary works

Abatzi, L. 2008. *Λιόπη Αμπατζή, Προσεγγίζοντας το φαινόμενο του trafficking*. Athens: EKKE.

Abatzopoulou, F. 1998. *Ο άλλος εν διωγμώ: Η εικόνα του Εβραίου στη λογοτεχνία – Ζητήματα ιστορίας και μυθοπλασίας*. Athens: Themelio.

Abbott, G. E. 1922. *Greece and the Allies, 1914–1922*. London: Methuen.

Abulafia, D. 2011. *The Great Sea: A Human History of the Mediterranean*, Oxford: Oxford University Press.

Accornero, G. 2016. 'Preface', in *Consumption and Gender in Southern Europe since the Long 1960s*, ed. K. Kornetis and E. Kotsovili, pp. xii–xvi. London: Bloomsbury.

Acheson, D. G. 1987. *Present at the Creation: My Years in the State Department*. Athens and New York: W. W. Norton.

Adamantidou, M. 2005. *Ελληνικός αθλητισμός στο Καιρό του 20όυ αιώνα*, Athens: Elliniki Koinotita Kairou.

Adanır, F. 2017. 'Ethnonationalism, Irredentism, and Empire', in *The Balkan Wars from Contemporary Perception to Historic Memory*, ed. K. Boeckh and S. Rutar, pp. 13–55. London: Palgrave Macmillan.

Agelopoulos, G. 2010. 'Contested Territories and the Quest of Ethnology: Peoples and Places in İzmir 1919–1922', in *Spatial Conceptions of the Nation. Modernizing Geographies in Greece and Turkey*, ed. N. Diamandouros and T. Dragonas, pp. 181–299. London: I. B. Tauris.

Agtzidis, V. 1995. *Ποντιακός Ελληνισμός από τη Γενοκτονία και τον Σταλινισμό στην Περεστρόικα*. Thessaloniki: Kiriakidis.

Ailianos, M. C. 1921. *Το έργον της ελληνικής περιθάλψεως*. Athens: Ekdosis Grafeiou Typou Exoterikon.

Akın, Y. 2018. *When the War Came Home: The Ottomans' Great War and the Devastation of an Empire*. Stanford, CA: Stanford University Press.

Aksakal, M. 2008. *The Ottoman Road to War in 1914: The Ottoman Empire and the First World War*. Cambridge: Cambridge University Press.

Aktar, A. 2007. 'Debating the Armenian Massacres in the Late Ottoman Parliament, November–December 1918'. *History Workshop Journal* 64.1, pp. 240–70.

Alecou, A. 2016. *Communism and Nationalism in Postwar Cyprus, 1945–1955: Politics and Ideologies under British Rule*. Basingstoke: Palgrave Macmillan.

Alexakis, E., and L. Janiszewski. 1995. '"That Bastard Odysseus": An Insight into the Early Greek Presence, 1810s–1940', in *Minorities: Cultural Diversity in Sydney*, ed. S. Fitzgerald and G. Wootherspoon, pp. 14–34. Sydney: State Library of NSW Press.

Alexakis, E., and L. Janiszewski. 2016. *Greek Cafés and Milk Bars of Australia*. Sydney: Halstead.

Alexandris, A. 1983. *The Greek Minority in Istanbul and Greek–Turkish Relations, 1918–1974*. Athens: Centre for Asia Minor Studies.

Alexandris, A. 1999. 'The Greek Census of Anatolia and Thrace (1910–1912): A Contribution to Ottoman Historical Demography', in *Ottoman Greeks in the Age of Nationalism: Politics, Economy, and Society in the Nineteenth Century*, ed. D. Gondicas and C. Issawi, pp. 45–76. Princeton, NJ: Darwin.

Alexandrou, A. 1982. *Έξω από τα δόντια*. Athens: Ypsilon.

Alexandrou, C. 2008. *Μεραρχία Πινερόλο: Χρονικό της αντίστασης και του μαρτυρίου της*. Athens: Gruppo d'Arte.

Alivizatos, N. 1995. *Οι πολιτικοί θεσμοί σε κρίση, 1922–1974: Όψεις της ελληνικής εμπειρίας*. Athens: Themelio.

Alivizatos, N. 2011. *Το Σύνταγμα και οι εχθροί του στη νεοελληνική ιστορία, 1800–2010*. Athens: Polis.

Alivizatos, N., and N. Diamandouros. 1997. 'Politics and the Judiciary in the Greek Transition to Democracy', in *Transitional Justice and the Rule of Law in New Democracies*, ed. J. McAdams, pp. 27–60. Notre Dame, IN: University of Notre Dame Press.

Alvanos, R. 2019. *Σλαβόφωνοι και πρόσφυγες: Κοινοβουλευτισμός και πολιτικές ταυτότητες στη Μακεδονία του Μεσοπολέμου*. Thessaloniki: Epikentro.

Alvanos, S. 1998. *Το φαινόμενο Μακρόνησος: Ένα πρωτόγνωρο εγκληματικό πείραμα*. Athens: Ellinka Grammata.

Ampatzi, L. 2008. *Προσεγγίζοντας το φαινόμενο του trafficking*. Athens: EKKE.

Anagnostopoulou, S. 1997. *Μικρά Ασία, 19ος αι.–1919: Οι Ελληνορθόδοξες κοινότητες – από το Μιλλέτ των Ρωμιών στο Ελληνικό Έθνος.* Athens: Ellinika Grammata.

Anagnostopoulou, S. 2013. 'Makarios III, 1950–77: Creating the *Ethnarch* State', in *The Archbishops of Cyprus in the Modern Age: The Changing Role of the Archbishop-Ethnarch, Their Identities and Politics*, ed. A. Varnava and M. N. Michael, pp. 240–92. Newcastle upon Tyne: Cambridge Scholars.

Anagnostou, D., and A. Triandafyllidou. 2006. *Regions, Minorities and European Integration: a Case Study on Muslims in Western Thrace, Greece.* http://www.eliamep.gr/wp-content/uploads/en/2006/05/Case_study_report_Thrace.pdf.

Anagnostou, Y. 2004. 'Forgetting the Past, Remember the Ancestors! Modernity, "Whiteness", and the Politics of Memory in Early Greek America'. *Journal of Modern Greek Studies* 1.22, pp. 24–71.

Anagnostou, Y. 2009. *Contours of White Ethnicity: Popular Ethnography and the Making of Usable Pasts in Greek America.* Athens, OH: Ohio State University Press.

Anastassiadis, T. 2020. 'Eastern Orthodoxy: An *histoire croisée* and Connected History Approach', *Bulletin de Correspondance hellénique-moderne et contemporain*, 1–8.

Anderson, B. 2016. *Imagined Communities: Reflections on the Origin and Spread of Nationalism*, revised ed. London: Verso.

Anderson, P. 2008. 'The Divisions of Cyprus'. *London Review of Books* 30.8, pp. 7–16.

Andreopoulos, H. M. 2017. *Η Εκκλησία κατά τη δικτατορία 1967–1974. Ιστορική και νομοκανονική προσέγγιση.* Thessaloniki: Epikentro.

Andreou, G., and N. Maravegias. 2018. 'Η ελληνική οικονομία στο πλαίσιο της ευρωπαϊκής ολοκλήρωσης (1962–2018)', in *Ελλάδα και Ευρωπαϊκή Ενοποίηση: Η Ιστορία μιας πολυκύμαντης, 1962–2018*, ed. N. Maravegias and T. Sakellaropoulos, pp. 56–9. Athens: Dionikos.

Angold, M. 2003. *The Fourth Crusade: Event and Context.* London: Longman.

Antoniou, G., and A. D. Moses (eds). 2018. *The Holocaust in Greece.* Cambridge: Cambridge University Press.

Apoifis, N. 2017. *Anarchy in Athens: An Ethnography of Militancy, Emotions and Violence.* Manchester: Manchester University Press.

Apostolidou, V. 2003. *Λογοτεχνία και ιστορία στη μεταπολεμική αριστερά: Η παρέμβαση του Δημήτρη Χατζή, 1947–1981*, Athens: Polis.

Apostolidou, V. 2011. *Τραύμα και μνήμη: Η πεζογραφία των πολιτικών προσφύγων.* Athens: Polis.

Apostolou, A. 2018. 'Greek Collaboration in the Holocaust and the Course of the War', in *The Holocaust in Greece*, ed. G. Antoniou and D. A. Moses, pp. 89–112. Cambridge: Cambridge University Press.

Appadurai, A. 1996. *Modernity at Large: Cultural Dimensions of Globalisation.* Minneapolis: University of Minnesota Press.

Arsenis, G. 2015. *Γιατί δεν έκατσα καλά: Η εμπειρία της Εκπαιδευτικής Μεταρρύθμισης, 1996–2000.* Athens: Gutenberg.

Ascherson, N. 1995. *The Black Sea.* New York, NY: Hill and Wang.

Asdrachas, S. 1982. *Ιστορική έρευνα και ιστορική παιδεία: Πραγματικότητες και προοπτικές.* Athens: Mnimon.

Asimakopoulos, B., and C. Tassis (eds). 2018. *ΠΑΣΟΚ, 1974–2018: Πολιτική οργάνωση – Ιδεολογικές μετατοπίσεις – Κυβερνητικές πολιτικές.* Athens: Gutenberg.

Asmussen, J. 2008. *Cyprus at War: Diplomacy and Conflict during the 1974 Crisis*. London: I. B. Tauris.

Athanassopoulou, E. 1999. *Turkey–Anglo-American Security Interests, 1945–1952: The First Enlargement of Nation*. London: Frank Cass.

Avdela, E. 2002. *Διά λόγους τιμής: Βία, συναισθήματα και αξίες σε μια μετεμφυλιακή Ελλάδα*. Athens: Nefeli.

Avdela, E. 2010. 'Η ιστορία του φύλου στην Ελλάδα: Από τη διαταραχή στην ενσωμάτωση', in *Φύλο και κοινωνικές επιστήμες στη σύγχρονη Ελλάδα*, ed. V. Kantsa, V. Moutafi et al., pp. 89–117. Athens: Alexandreia.

Avdela, E. 2013. *'Νέοι εν κινδύνω': Επιτήρηση, αναμόρφωση και δικαιοσύνη ανηλίκων μετά τον πόλεμο*. Athens: Polis.

Avdela, E., and A. Psara (eds). 1985. *Ο φεμινισμός στην Ελλάδα του μεσοπολέμου: Μια ανθολογία*. Athens: Gnosi.

Avgeridis, E. 2019. *Ιστορικοποιώντας το βίωμα: Από την ελληνική Αντίσταση στην ιστορία της (1945–1967)*. Doctoral dissertation: ΕΚΠΑ.

Axioti, M., and D. Xadzis. 1960. *Antigone lebt: Neugriechische Erzählungen*. Berlin: Verlag Volk und Welt.

Aymard, M. 1998. 'La Mediterrannée: Un autre developpement'. *Bulletin d'histoire contemporaine de l'Espagne* 27, pp. 13–27.

Babac, D. M. 2016. *The Serbian Army in the Great War, 1914–1918*. Solihull, West Midlands: Helion and Co.

Baerentzen, L. 1984. 'Η Λαϊκή υποστήριξη του ΕΑΜ στο τέλος της Κατοχής'. *Mnemon* 9, pp. 157–73.

Baerentzen, L., and D. H. Close. 1993. 'The British Defeat of EAM, 1944–5', in *The Greek Civil War, 1943–1950: Studies of Polarisation*, ed. D. H. Close, pp. 72–96. London: Routledge.

Baerentzen, L., and J. O. Iatrides (eds). 1987. *Studies in the History of the Greek Civil War, 1945–1949*. Copenhagen: Museum Tusculanum Press.

Bakić-Hayden, M. 1995. 'Nesting Orientalisms: The Case of Former Yugoslavia'. *Slavic Review* 54.4, pp. 917–31.

Balambanidis, Y. 2007. *Για μια κοινωνία ισχυρή, για μια ισχυρή Ελλάδα. Κριτική ανάγνωση του εκσυγχρονιστικού εγχειρήματος (1996–2004): πολιτική και ιδεολογία*. Doctoral dissertation, Athens: Panteion University.

Balambanidis, I. (ed.). 2019. *Σύριζα, ένα κόμμα εν κινήσει*. Athens: Themelio.

Balambanidis, D., and I. Polizou. 2015. 'Αναχαιτίζοντας τάσεις εγκατάλειψης του αθηναϊκού κέντρου: Η παρουσία των μεταναστών στην κατοικία και στις επιχειρηματικές δραστηριότητες'. *Athens Social Atlas*. http://www.athenssocialatlas.gr/άρθρο/μετανάστες-κατοικία-και-επιχειρήσεις/ (last accessed 18 July 2019).

Balampanidis, L., G. KatsambekisIliadis and E. Papataxiarchis. 2021. 'Ambiguous Identities in Crisis-Ridden Greece: "Us" and/against "Europe"'. *Journal of Contemporary European Studies* 11.1, pp. 1–16.

Baltsiotis, L. 2009. 'Η ανακάλυψη των νέων Ελλήνων: Οι περιπτώσεις των Γκαγκαούζων και των "Ποντίων" της Τουρκίας', in *Μετανάστες και μειονότητες: Λόγος και πολιτικές*, ed. M. Pavlou and A. Skoulariki, pp. 141–93. Athens: Bibliorama.

Bampilis, T. 2013. *Greek Whisky: The Localization of a Global Commodity*. Oxford: Berghahn.

Barkey, K., and G. Gavrilis. 2016. 'The Ottoman *Millet* System: Non-Territorial Autonomy and Its Contemporary Legacy'. *Ethnopolitics* 15.1, pp. 24–42.

Barkey, K., and M. von Hagen (eds). 1997. *After Empire. Multiethnic Societies and Nation-Building: The Soviet Union, and the Russian, Ottoman and Habsburg Empires*. Boulder: Westview.

Bartov, O., and E. D. Weitz (eds). 2013. *Shatterzones of Empire: Coexistence and Violence in the German, Habsburg, Russian, and Ottoman Borderlands*. Bloomington: University of Indiana Press.

Bastea, E. 2000. *The Creation of Modern Athens: Planning the Myth*. New York, NY: Cambridge University Press.

Batalas, A. 2003. 'Send a Thief to Catch a Thief: State-Building and the Employment of Irregular Military Formations in Mid-Nineteenth-Century Greece', in *Irregular Armed Forces and Their Role in Politics and State Formation*, ed. D. E. Davis and A. W. Pereira, pp. 149–77. Cambridge: Cambridge University Press.

Bayly, C. A. 2004. *The Birth of the Modern World, 1780–1914: Global Connections and Comparisons*. Oxford: Blackwell.

Beevor, A. 2005. *Crete: The Battle and the Resistance*. London: Penguin.

Benveniste, H.-R. (ed.) 1998. *Οι Εβραίοι της Ελλάδος στην Κατοχή*. Thessaloniki: Vanias.

Benveniste, H.-R. 2001. 'The Coming Out of Jewish History in Greece'. *Usages publics du passé* 27.1. http://anciensiteusagespublicsdupasse.ehess.fr/index.php?id=130 (last accessed 12 August 2019).

Benveniste, R. 2014. *Αυτοί που επέζησαν: Αντίσταση, Εκτόπιση, Επιστροφή – Θεσσαλονικείς Εβραίοι στη δεκαετία του 1940*. Athens: Polis.

Berend, I. T. 2010. *Europe since 1980*. Cambridge: Cambridge University Press.

Beze, E. 2019. 'Being Leftist and Jewish in Greece during the Civil War and Its Aftermath: Constraints and Choices'. *Historein* 18.2. http://dx.doi.org/10.12681/historein.14601 (last accessed 12 August 2019).

Bika, Z. 2012. 'Entrepreneurial Sons, Patriarchy and the Colonels: Experiment in Thessaly, Rural Greece'. *Entrepreneurship and Regional Development* 24.3–4, pp. 235–57.

Bilalis, M. 2003. 'The Internet as a Cultural Object: Perception of the New and the Technological in Greece during the '90s', in *New Media in South East Europe*, ed. O. Spassov and C. Todorov, pp. 185–207. Sophia: Südosteuropäisches Medienzentrum.

Bilalis, M. 2015. *Το παρελθόν στο Δίκτυο: Εικόνα, τεχνολογία και ιστορική κουλτούρα στη σύγχρονη Ελλάδα (1994–2005)*. *Historein* e-book. http://ebooks.epublishing.ekt.gr/index.php/historein/catalog/book/5.

Biondich, M. 2011. *The Balkans: Revolution, War and Political Violence since 1878*. Oxford: Oxford University Press.

Bithimitris, G. 2018. 'Μια ιδιότυπη σοσιαλδημοκρατική συνδικαλιστική ταυτότητα: ΠΑΣΟΚ και συνδικάτα από τη Μεταπολίτευση στην κρίση', in *ΠΑΣΟΚ, 1974–2018: Πολιτική οργάνωση – Ιδεολογικές μετατοπίσεις – Κυβερνητικές πολιτικές*, ed. B. Asimakopoulos and C. Tassis, pp. 134–61. Athens: Gutenberg.

Bloch, S. 1990. 'Athens and Beyond: Soviet Psychiatric Abuse and the World Psychiatric Association'. *Psychiatric Bulletin* 14.3, pp. 129–33.

Bloomfield, J. (ed.). 1989. *The Soviet Revolution: Perestroika and the Remaking of Socialism*. London: Lawrence and Wishart.

Bloxham, D. 2005. *The Great Game of Genocide: Imperialism, Nationalism, and the Destruction of the Ottoman Armenians*. Oxford: Oxford University Press.

Bloxham, D. 2009. 'The Great Unweaving: Forced Population Movement in Europe, 1875–1949', in *Removing Peoples: Forced Removal in the Modern World*, ed. R. Bessel and C. Haake, pp. 167–208. Oxford: Oxford University Press.

Blyth, M. 2013. *Austerity: The History of a Dangerous Idea*. Oxford: Oxford University Press.

Bohotis, T. N. 1999. 'Εσωτερική Πολιτική', in *Ιστορία της Ελλάδος του 20ού αιώνα*, vol. 1: *1900–1922, Οι Απαρχές*, ed. C. Hatziiosif, pp. 37–105. Athens: Bibliorama.

Boletsi, M. 2018. 'The Futurity of Things Past: Thinking Greece beyond Crisis'. Inaugural lecture, published by the University of Amsterdam, 21 September 2018, pp. 1–35.

Boletsi, M. 2019. 'Recasting the Indebted Subject in the Middle Voice'. *Social Science Information* 50.3, pp. 1–24.

Boswell, L. 2016. 'Rural Society in Crisis', in *The Oxford Handbook of European History 1914–1945*, ed. N. Doumanis, pp. 243–60. Oxford: Oxford University Press.

Bosworth, R. J. B. 2002. *Mussolini*. London: Arnold.

Bowman, S. 2012. *Η αντίσταση των Εβραίων στην κατοχική Ελλάδα*, trans. I. Benmagior. Athens: Kentriko Israelitiko Symboulio Elladas.

Boyiatzis, B. 2012. *Μετέωρος μοντερνισμός: Τεχνολογία, ιδεολογία της επιστήμης και πολιτική στην Ελλάδα του Μεσοπολέμου (1922–1940)*. Athens: Evrasia.

Bratu, R., and D. Sotiropoulos. 2017. 'Through the Lens of Social Constructionism: The Development of Innovative Anti-Corruption Policies and Practices in Bulgaria, Greece and Romania, 2000–2015'. *Slavonic and East European Review* 95.1, pp. 117–50.

Brianas, J. J. 2004. *NATO, Greece and the 2004 Summer Olympics*. Doctoral dissertation, Monterey, CA: Naval Postgraduate School.

Broersma, F., and D. Lazarescu. 2009. 'Pakistani and Bangladeshi Migration to Greece: "Chasing the Dream"'. IDEA Project, Hellenic Foundation for European and Foreign Policy (ELIAMEP). https://www.eliamep.gr/wp-content/uploads/2009/06/policy_brief_pakistani_bangladeshi.pdf (last accessed 13 August 2019).

Brouskou, A. 2015. '*Λόγω της κρίσεως σας χαρίζω το παιδί μου': Η διακίνηση των παιδιών στην ελληνική κοινωνία του 20ού αιώνα – Το παράδειγμα του Δημοτικού Βρεφοκομείου Θεσσαλονίκης 'Άγιος Στυλιανός'*. Thessaloniki: Epistimonikos Syllogos Merimnas Paidiou kai Efivou.

Brown, C. L. 2004. *Diplomacy in the Middle East*. London: I. B. Tauris.

Browning, C. 2001. *Ordinary Men: Reserve Battalion 101 and the Final Solution in Poland*, 2nd ed. New York, NY: Harper.

Brummett, P. 2000. *Image and Imperialism in the Ottoman Revolutionary Press, 1908–1911*. Albany, NY: State University of New York Press.

Brunnermeier, M., H. James and J.-P. Landau. 2016. *The Euro and the Battle of Ideas*. Princeton, NJ: Princeton University Press.

Bryant, R., and Y. Papadakis (eds). 2012. *Cyprus and the Politics of Memory: History, Community and Conflict*. London: I. B. Tauris.

Bryer, A. 1991. 'The Pontian Greeks before the Diaspora'. *Journal of Refugee Studies* 4.4, pp. 315–34.

Bulled, N. L., and R. Sosis. 2010. 'Examining the Relationship between Life Expectancy, Reproduction, and Educational Attainment'. *Human Nature* 21.3, pp. 269–89.

Cabot, H. 2014. *On the Doorstep of Europe: Asylum and Citizenship in Greece*. Philadelphia: University of Pennsylvania Press.

Cajani, L., and S. Lässig (eds). 2019. *The Palgrave Handbook of Conflict and History Education in the Post-Cold War Era*. Basingstoke: Palgrave Macmillan.

Calic, M.-L. 2019. *A History of Yugoslavia*. Lafayette, IN: Purdue University Press.

Calogero, C., and D. Benjamin. 2006. 'A Country on the Move: International Migration in Post-Communist Albania'. *International Migration Review* 40.4, pp. 767–85.

Calotychos, V. 2013. *The Balkan Prospect: Identity, Culture, and Politics in Greece after 1989*. Basingstoke: Palgrave Macmillan.

Campbell, J. 1964. *Honour, Family and Patronage: A Study of Institutions and Moral Values in a Greek Mountain Community*. Oxford: Clarendon Press.

Carabott, P. J. 1993. 'The Temporary Italian Occupation of the Dodecanese: a Prelude to Permanency'. *Diplomacy and Statecraft* 4.2, pp. 285–312.

Carletto, C., B. Davis, M. Stampini and A. Zezza. 2006. 'Country on the Move: International Migration in Post-Communist Albania'. *International Migration Review* 40.4, pp. 767–85.

Cartledge, P. 2004. *Alexander the Great: The Hunt for a New Past*. New York, NY: Overlook.

Cavallaro, M. E., and K. Kornetis (eds). 2018. *Rethinking Democratization in Spain, Greece and Portugal*. Basingstoke: Palgrave Macmillan.

Çetinkaya, Y. D. 2014. 'Atrocity Propaganda and the Nationalisation of the Masses in the Ottoman Empire during the Balkan Wars (1912–13)'. *International Journal of Middle East Studies* 46, pp. 759–78.

Chakrabarty, D. 2000. *Provincializing Europe: Postcolonial Thought and Historical Difference*. Princeton, NJ: Princeton University Press.

Chaldeos, A. 2016. 'The French Colonial Policy in Tunisia between 1920 and 1930 and its Influence on the Greek Community'. *Journal of North African Studies* 21, pp. 3, 379–91.

Chandler, G. 1959. *The Divided Land: An Anglo-Greek Tragedy*. London: Macmillan.

Chandrinos, I. 2012. *Το τιμωρό χέρι του λαού: Η δράση του ΕΛΑΣ και της ΟΠΛΑ στην κατεχόμενη πρωτεύουσα, 1942–1944*. Athens: Themelio.

Chandrinos, I. 2020. *Συναγωνιστές: Το ΕΑΜ και οι Εβραίοι της Ελλάδας*. Thessaloniki: Psifides.

Chandrinos, I. G., and A. M. Droumpouki. 2018. 'The German Occupation and the Holocaust in Greece: A Survey', in *The Holocaust in Greece*, ed. G. Antoniou and A. D. Moses, pp. 15–35. Cambridge: Cambridge University Press.

Chaplin, T. and J. E. Pieper Mooney (eds). 2018. *The Global 1960s: Convention, Contest and Counterculture*. New York and London: Routledge.

Chapoutot, J. 2016. *Greeks, Romans, Germans: How the Nazis Usurped Europe's Classical Past*, trans. R. R. Nybakken. Berkeley, CA: University of California Press.

Charalambidis, M. 2012. *Η εμπειρία της Κατοχής και της Αντίστασης στην Αθήνα*. Athens: Alexandreia.

Charalambidis, M. 2014. *Δεκεμβριανά 1944: Η μάχη της Αθήνας*. Athens: Alexandreia.

Chardouvelis, G. 2007. 'Μακροοικονομική διαχείριση και η ανάγκη διαρθρωτικών μεταρρυθμίσεων μετά την είσοδο στη νομισματική ένωση'. *Eurobank Research: Οικονομία και Αγορές* 2.8, pp. 1–27.

Chasiotis, L. 2013. *Τα παιδιά του Εμφυλίου: Από την 'κοινωνική πρόνοια' του Φράνκο στον 'έρανο' της Φρειδερίκης (1936–1950)*. Athens: Estia.

Chasiotis, L. 2019. *Λουκιανός Χασιώτης, 'Γεια σας, εγγλεζάκια!' Βρετανοί στρατιώτες στην Ελλάδα (1941–1945)*. Athens: Metaichmio.

Chatzidakis, A. 2015. *Τάσεις της τουριστικής κίνησης 2008–2015*. Athens: EOT.

Chatzigeorgiou, T. 2006. Έλληνες Πόντιοι από την (πρώην) Σοβιετική Ένωση: Εκφράσεις της ταυτότητας και της κοινωνικοποίησης στην Ελλάδα. Doctoral dissertation, University of Crete.

Chatzigiannis, A., and D. Valasi. 2008. 'Ανώτατη εκπαίδευση και αναπαραγωγή των διακρίσεων: Η "μικρή και η μεγάλη πόρτα" στην ελληνική τριτοβάθμια εκπαίδευση', in *Κοινωνικοί και Χωρικοί Μετασχηματισμοί στην Αθήνα του 21ου αιώνα*, ed. T. Maloutas et al. Athens: EKKE, pp. 207–46.

Chatzivasiliou, E. 2010. *Ελληνικός φιλελευθερισμός: Το ριζοσπαστικό ρεύμα, 1932–1979.* Athens: Patakis.

Chatzivasiliou, E. 2014. *Βιώματα του Μακεδονικού Ζητήματος: Δοξάτο Δράμας, 1912–1946.* Athens: Patakis.

Chatzivasiliou, V. 2018. *Η κίνηση του εκκρεμούς: Άτομα και κοινωνία στη νεότερη ελληνική πεζογραφία, 1974–2017.* Athens: Polis.

Chatzis, T. 1983. *Η νικηφόρα επανάσταση που χάθηκε: Εθνικοαπελευθερωτικός αγώνας 41–45.* Athens: Dorikos.

Chimbos, P. D. 1999. 'The Greeks in Canada: an Historical and Sociological Perspective', in *The Greek Diaspora in the Twentieth Century*, ed. R. Clogg, pp. 87–102. Basingstoke: Macmillan.

Christian, D. 2018. *A History of Russia, Central Asia and Mongolia*, vol. 2: *Inner Eurasia from the Mongol Empire to Today, 1260–2000.* Oxford: Wiley Blackwell.

Christidis, C. 2016. 'Οι κυβερνήσεις των αποστατών'. *Καθημερινή*, 31 December 2016. https://www.kathimerini.gr/society/889980/oi-kyverniseis-ton-apostaton/.

Christodoulakis, N. 2014. *Germany's War Debt to Greece: A Burden Unsettled.* Basingstoke: Palgrave Macmillan.

Christodoulakis, N. 2018. *Greek Crisis in Perspective: Origins, Effects and Ways-Out.* Basingstoke: Palgrave Macmillan.

Christodoulou, D. 1992. *Inside the Cyprus Miracle: The Labours of an Embattled Mini-Economy.* Minneapolis: University of Minnesota Press.

Christopoulos, D. 2012. *Ποιος είναι Έλληνας πολίτης; Το καθεστώς ιθαγένειας από την ίδρυση του ελληνικού κράτους ως τις αρχές του 21ου αιώνα.* Athens: Bibliorama.

Christopoulos, D. (ed.). 2014. *Το 'βαθύ κράτος' στη σημερινή Ελλάδα και η Ακροδεξιά: Αστυνομία, Δικαιοσύνη, Στρατός, Εκκλησία.* Athens: Nisos.

Christou, A., and R. King. 2010. 'Imagining "Home": Diasporic Landscapes of the Greek-German Second Generation'. *Geoforum* 41.4, pp. 638–46.

Clark, B. 2007. *Twice a Stranger: How Expulsions Forged Modern Greece and Turkey.* London: Granta.

Clark, C. 2012. *The Sleepwalkers: How Europe Went to War in 1914.* London: Allen Lane.

Clay, D. 1977. 'The Silence of Hermippos: Greece in the Poetry of Cavafy'. *Byzantine and Modern Greek Studies* 3.1, pp. 95–116.

Clay Large, D. 2007. *Nazi Games: The Olympics of 1936.* New York, NY: W. W. Norton.

Clogg, R. 1979. 'The Greek Government in Exile 1941–4'. *International History Review* 1.3, pp. 376–98.

Clogg, R. 1986. *Politics and the Academy: Arnold Toynbee and the Koraes Chair.* London: Frank Cass.

Clogg, R. 1997. 'The Greek Government-in-Exile, 1941–44'. *International Review of History* 1.3, pp. 376–98.

Clogg, R. 2000. *Anglo-Greek Attitudes: Studies in History.* Basingstoke: Palgrave Macmillan.

Clogg, R. 2002. *Greece 1940–1949: Occupation, Resistance, Civil War: a Documentary History*. New York and Basingstoke: Palgrave Macmillan.

Clogg, R. (ed.). 2008. *Bearing Gifts to Greeks: Humanitarian Aid to Greece in the 1940s*. Basingstoke: Palgrave Macmillan.

Clogg, R. (ed.). 2017. *Greece 1940–1949: Occupation, Resistance, Civil War*. Basingstoke: Palgrave Macmillan.

Close, D. H. 1993. 'The Reconstruction of a Right-Wing State', in *The Greek Civil War Studies in Polarization*, ed. D. H. Close, pp. 156–89. London and New York: Routledge.

Close, D. H. 1995. *The Origins of the Greek Civil War: Politics, Economy and Society*. London: Longman.

Close, D. H. 1995a. 'The Changing Structure of the Right', in *Greece at the Crossroads: The Civil War and Its Legacy*, ed. J. O. Iatrides and L. Wigley, pp. 122–56. University Park: Pennsylvania State University Press.

Close, D. H. 2002. *Greece since 1945: Politics, Economy and Society*. London: Longman.

Close, D. H. and T. Veremis. 1993. 'The Military Struggle, 1945–9', in *The Greek Civil War*, ed. D. H. Close, pp. 97–128. London and New York: Routledge.

Conrad, S., and J. Osterhammel (ed.). 2018. *An Emerging Modern World 1750–1870*. Cambridge, MA: Harvard University Press.

Conway, M. 2020. *Western Europe's Democratic Age, 1945–1968*. Princeton, NJ: Princeton University Press.

Cooper, F. 2005. *Colonialism in Question: Theory, Knowledge and History*. Berkeley, CA: University of California Press.

Costa Pinto, A., and N. Severiano Teixeira (eds). 2002. *Southern Europe and the Making of the European Union*. Boulder and New York: Columbia University Press.

Crampton, R. 2007. *Bulgaria*. Oxford: Oxford University Press.

Dafnis, G. 1997. *Η Ελλάς μεταξύ δύο πολέμων, 1923–1940*, 2 vols. Athes: Kaktos.

Dalachanis, A. 2015. *Ακυβέρνητη παροικία: Οι Έλληνες στην Αίγυπτο από την κατάργηση των προνομίων στην έξοδο, 1937–1962*. Iraklion: PEK.

Dalachanis, A. 2017. *The Greek Exodus from Egypt: Diaspora Politics and Emigration, 1937–1962*. New York, NY: Berghahn.

Dalègre, J. 2012. 'Félix Sartiaux et Phocée, Eski Foça, Παλαιά Φώκια', *Cahiers Balkaniques*, pp. 1–11. https://journals.openedition.org/ceb/874 (last accessed 16 November 2022).

Daliani-Karampatsaki, M. 2009. *Παιδιά στη δίνη του ελληνικού εμφυλίου πολέμου 1946–1949, σημερινοί ενήλικες: Διαχρονική μελέτη για τα παιδιά που έμειναν στη φυλακή με τις κρατούμενες μητέρες τους*, trans. K. A. Zervos. Athens: Benaki Museum.

Damaskos, D., and D. Plantzos (ed.). 2008. *A Singular Antiquity: Archaeology and Hellenic Identity in Twentieth Century Greece*. Athens: Benaki Museum.

Damilakou, M. 2006. 'Κεντρική και Νότια Αμερική', in *Οι Έλληνες στη Διασπορά, 15ος–21ος αι.*, ed. I. Hasiotis, O. Katsiardi-Hering and E. Abatzi, pp. 291–300. Athens: Hellenic Parliament.

Damousi, J. 2015. *Memory and Migration in the Shadow of War: Australia's Greek Immigrants after World War II and the Greek Civil War*. Cambridge: Cambridge University Press.

Danforth, L. 1995. *The Macedonian Conflict: Ethnic Nationalism in a Transnational World*. Princeton, NJ: Princeton University Press.

Danforth, L. M. 2000. 'How Can a Woman Give Birth to One Greek and One Macedonian? The Construction of National Identity among Immigrants to Australia from Northern Greece', in *Macedonia: The Politics of Identity and Difference*, ed. J. K. Cowan, pp. 85–103. London: Pluto Press, London.

Danforth, L. M., and R. van Boeschoten. 2012. *Children of the Greek Civil War: Refugees and the Politics of Memory*. Chicago and London: University of Chicago Press.

Danova, N., and R. Avramov (ed.). 2013. *The Deportation of the Jews from Western Thrace, Vardar's Macedonia and Pirot, March 1943: Documents from the Bulgarian Archives*, 2 vols. Sofia: Obedineni Izdateli.

Darwin, J. 2009. *The Empire Project: The Rise and Fall of the British World System, 1830–1970*. Cambridge: Cambridge University Press.

Davis, D. E., and A. W. Pereira (ed.). 2003. *Irregular Armed Forces and Their Role in Politics and State Formation*. Cambridge: Cambridge University Press.

Dawkins, R. M. 1916. *Modern Greek in Asia Minor: A Study of the Dialects of Sílli, Cappadocia and Phárasa with Grammar Texts, Translations and Glossary*. Cambridge: Cambridge University Press.

De Felice, R. 1996. *Mussolini l'alleato*, vol. 1: *L'italia in Guerra (1940–1943): Dalla guerra 'breve' alla guerra lunga*. Turin: Einaudi.

De Grazia, V. 2005. *Irresistible Empire: America's Advance through Twentieth-Century Europe*. Cambridge, MA: Belknap Press of Harvard University Press.

Delis, P. 2018. 'The Treatment of Prisoners of War Captured by the Greek Army during the Balkan Wars of 1912–13'. *Journal of Military History* 82.4, pp. 1123–47.

Delis, P. 2018a. 'Violence and Civilians during the Balkan Wars (1912–1913)'. *Journal of Balkan and Near Eastern Studies* 20.6, pp. 547–63.

della Porta, D., and A. Vannucci. 1999. *Corrupt Exchanges: Actors, Resources and Mechanisms of Political Corruption*. New York, NY: Taylor and Francis.

della Porta, D., and M. Andretta (eds). 2006. *Globalisation from Below: Transnational Activists and Protest Networks*. Minneapolis: University of Minnesota Press.

Delta, P. S. 1988. *Ελευθέριος Κ. Βενιζέλος: Ημερολόγιο – Αναμνήσεις – Μαρτυρίες – Αλληλογραφία*. Athens: Ermis.

Demas, L. 2004–5. 'Immigrant Entrepreneurs and the Formation of Chicago's Greektown, 1890–1921'. *Journal of Modern Hellenism* 21–2, pp. 105–55.

Demetriades, P. 2017. *A Diary of the Euro Crisis in Cyprus: Lessons for Bank Recovery and Resolutions*. Cham, Switzerland: Springer.

Dertilis, G. B. 1984. *Ελληνική οικονομία (1830–1910) και βιομηχανική επανάσταση*. Athens: Sakkoulas.

Dertilis, G. B. 1992, 1993. 'Terre, paysans et pouvoir économique (Grèce XVIIIᵉ–XXᵉ siècle)'. *Annales* 47.2, pp. 273–91 and 48.1, pp. 85–107.

Dertilis, G. B. 1993. *Ατελέσφοροι ή τελεσφόροι; Φόροι και εξουσία στο νεοελληνικό κράτος*. Athens: Alexandreia.

Dertilis, G. B. 2016. *Επτά πόλεμοι, τέσσερις εμφύλιοι, επτά πτωχεύσεις, 1821–2016*. Athens: Polis.

Dertilis, G. B. 2018. *Ιστορία της νεότερης και σύγχρονης Ελλάδας, 1750–2015*. Iraklion: PEK.

Diamandouros, P. N. 1984. 'Transition to, and Consolidation of, Democratic Politics in Greece, 1974–1983: A Tentative Assessment'. *West European Politics* 7.2, pp. 50–71.

Diamandouros, N. 2000. *Cultural Dualism and Political Change in Post Authoritarian Greece*. Madrid: Instituto Juan March de Estudios e Investigaciones.

Dickinson, E. R. 2018. *The World in the Long Twentieth Century: An Interpretive History.* Berkeley, CA: University of California Press.

Didi-Huberman, G. 2008. *Images in Spite of All: Four Photographs from Auschwitz.* Chicago: University of Chicago Press.

Dodd, C. 2010. *The History and Politics of the Cyprus Conflict.* Basingstoke: Palgrave Macmillan.

Dordanas, S. N. 2006. *Έλληνες εναντίον Ελλήνων: Ο κόσμος των Ταγμάτων Ασφαλείας στην κατοχική Θεσσαλονίκη, 1941–1944.* Thessaloniki: Epikentro.

Dordanas, S. N. 2007. *Το αίμα των αθώων: Αντίποινα των γερμανικών αρχών Κατοχής στη Μακεδονία, 1941–1944.* Athens: Estia.

Dordanas, S. N. 2011. *Η γερμανική στολή στη ναφθαλίνη: Επιβιώσεις του δοσιλογισμού στη Μακεδονία, 1945–1974.* Athens: Estia.

Dordanas, S. N. 2018. 'The Jewish Community of Thessaloniki and the Christian Collaborators: "Those That Are Leaving and What They Are Leaving Behind"', in *The Holocaust in Greece*, ed. G. Antoniou and D. A. Moses, pp. 208–27. Cambridge: Cambridge University Press.

Doukas, Y. 2018. 'Η Κοινή Αγροτική Πολιτική και ο Ελληνικός Αγροτικός Τομέας', in *Ελλάδα και Ευρωπαϊκή Ενοποίηση: Η Ιστορία μιας πολυκύμαντης, 1962–2018*, ed. N. Maravegias and T. Sakellaropoulos, pp. 209–44. Athens: Dionikos.

Doumanis, N. 1992. 'Eastern Orthodoxy and Migrant Conflict: The Greek Church Schism in Australia, 1959–74'. *Journal of Religious History* 17.1, pp. 60–77.

Doumanis, N. 1993. 'Ecclesiastical Expansion and the Greek Diaspora: The Formative Years of the Greek Church in Australia'. *St. Vladimir's Theological Quarterly* 1.37, pp. 59–72.

Doumanis, N. 1997. *Myth and Memory in the Mediterranean: Remembering Fascism's Empire.* Basingstoke and New York: Macmillan and St. Martin's.

Doumanis, N. 1999. 'The Greeks in Australia', in *The Greek Diaspora in the Twentieth Century*, ed. R. Clogg, pp. 58–86. Basingstoke: Macmillan.

Doumanis, N. 2013. *Before the Nation: Christian–Muslim Coexistence and Its Destruction in Late Ottoman Anatolia.* Oxford: Oxford University Press.

Doumanis, N. 2013a. 'The Ottoman Roman Empire, c. 1680–1900: How Empires Shaped a Modern Nation', in *The Routledge History of Western Empires*, ed. R. Aldrich and K. MacKenzie, pp. 208–20. London and New York: Routledge.

Doumanis, N. 2013b. 'Peasants into Nationals: Violence, War, and the Making of Turks and Greeks, 1912–1922', in *Totalitarian Dictatorship: New Histories*, ed. D. Baratieri, G. Finaldi and M. Edele, pp. 172–89. London and New York: Routledge.

Doumanis, N. 2016. 'Europe's Age of Catastrophe in Context', in *Oxford Handbook for European History 1914–1945*, ed. N. Doumanis, pp. 1–19. Oxford: Oxford University Press.

Doxiades, K. 1946. *Αι θυσίαι της Ελλάδος στο Δεύτερο Παγκόσμιο Πόλεμο.* Athens: no stated publisher.

Dragostinova, T. 2011. *Between Two Motherlands: Nationality and Emigration among the Greeks of Bulgaria, 1900–1949.* Ithaca, NY: Cornell University Press.

Drapac, V., and G. Pritchard. 2017. *Resistance and Collaboration in Hitler's Empire.* London: Palgrave.

Dritsa, K., and D. Mitropoulos (eds). 2018. 'Aspects of the History of Computing in Modern Greece'. *IEEE Annals of the History of Computing* 40.1. https://ieeexplore.ieee.org/document/8356170 (last accessed 24 August 2019).

Dritsa, M. 1990. *Βιομηχανία και τράπεζες στην Ελλάδα του Μεσοπολέμου*. Athens: MIET.

Du Boulay, J. 2009. *Cosmos, Life, and Liturgy in a Greek Orthodox Village*. Limni, Evvia: Dennis Harvey.

Duara, P. 1995. *Rescuing History from the Nation: Questioning Narratives of Modern China*. Chicago: University of Chicago Press.

Eberhard, E. 2007. 'Γερμανοί αντιφασιστές στις τάξεις του ΕΛΑΣ', in *Ιστορία της Ελλάδας του 20ού αιώνα*, ed. C. Hatziiosif, vol. 3, part 2. Athens: Bibliorama.

Economou, M., M. Madianos, L. E. Peppou, C. Theleritis, A. Patelakis and C. Stefanis. 2013. 'Suicidal Ideation and Reported Suicide Attempts in Greece during the Economic Crisis'. *World Psychiatry* 12.1, pp. 53–9.

Edwards, L., and E. E. Spalding. 2016. *A Brief History of the Cold War*. Washington, DC: Regnery.

Elefantis, A. 1991. *Στον αστερισμό του λαϊκισμού*. Athens: Politis.

Elefantis, A. 2002. 'Προσλήψεις του εμφυλίου μετά τον εμφύλιο', *Μας πήραν την Αθήνα … Ξαναδιαβάζοντας την ιστορία, 1941–1950*, Athens: Bibliorama.

Eleftheriou, M. 1986. '"Το μαύρο ταξίδι": Η μαρτυρία ενός αγνώστου στρατιώτη από τον πόλεμο της Μικράς Ασίας'. *To Tetarto* 16, pp. 42–55.

Ellinas, A. A. 2013. 'The Rise of Golden Dawn: The New Face of the Far Right in Greece'. *South European Society and Politics* 18.4, pp. 543–65.

Ellinas, C. 2020. *Settling East Med EEZ Disputes: A Path Ahead*. Athens: ELIAMEP.

Ellwood, D. W. 2012. *The Shock of America: Europe and the Challenge of the Century*. Oxford: Oxford University Press.

Elytis, O. 2000. *Ανοιχτά Χαρτιά*. Athens: Ikaros.

Embirikos, L., and L. Baltsiotis. 2019. 'Έλληνες και Αλβανοί στον 19ο και 20ό αιώνα: Διαδοχικές και αντεστραμμένες αναγνώσεις'. *Σύγχρονα Θέματα* 143–4 (Mar.), pp. 100–5.

Emke-Poulopoulou, I. 1986. *Προβλήματα μετανάστευσης – παλιννόστησης*. Athens: Instituto Meletis tis Ellinikis Ikonomias kai Elliniki Etaireia Dimografikon Meleton.

Emke-Poulopoulou, I. 2018. *Ο πληθυσμός της Ελλάδας υπό διωγμόν*. Athens: Bogiatzi – ErmisGraphics.

Emmanouil, D. 2008. *Πολεοδομικός χώρος, κατοικία και τιμές στην Αθήνα (1984–2004)*. Athens: EKKE.

Erickson, E. J. 2003. *Defeat in Detail: The Ottoman Army in the Balkans, 1912–1913*. Westport, CT, and London: Praeger.

Erol, E. 2016. *The Ottoman Crisis in Western Anatolia: Turkey's Belle Époque and the Transition to a Modern Nation State*. London: I. B. Tauris.

Ersland, B. H. L. L. 2014. *One Step Further to the Right: Right-Wing Extremism in Greece and the Rise of Golden Dawn*. Master's thesis, University of Oslo.

Espagne, M. 1999. *Les transferts culturels franco-allemands*. Paris: PUF.

Eudes, D. 1972. *The Kapetanios: Partisans and Civil War in Greece, 1943–1949*. London: Verso.

Evelpidis, C. 1953. 'Το Γεωργικόν Εισόδημα'. https://spoudai.unipi.gr/index.php/spoudai/article/view/178 (last accessed 16 November 2022).

Exertzoglou, H. 1996. *Εθνική Ταυτότητα στην Κωνσταντινούπολη τον 19ο Αι.: Ο Ελληνικός Σύλλογος Κωνσταντινουπόλεως 1861–1912*. Athens: Nefeli.

Fakiolas, R. 2000. 'Migration and Unregistered Labour in the Greek Economy', in *Eldorado or Fortress? Migration in Southern Europe*, ed. R. King and G. Lazaridis, pp. 57–78. London: Palgrave Macmillan.

Fakiolas, R., and R. King. 1996. 'Emigration, Return, Immigration: A Review and Evaluation of Greece's Postwar Experience of International Migration'. *International Journal of Population Geography* 2.2, pp. 171–90.

Fann, P. 1991. 'The Pontian Myth of Homeland: Cultural Expressions of Nationalism and Ethnicism in Pontos and Greece, 1870–1990'. *Journal of Refugee Studies* 4.4, pp. 340–56.

Farakos, G. (ed.). 2000. *Δεκέμβρης του '44: Νεότερη έρευνα, νέες προσεγγίσεις. Πρακτικά επιστημονικής συνάντησης.* Athens: Filistor.

Fauri, F. 2015. 'European Migrants after the Second World War', in *The History of Migration in Europe: Perspectives from Economics, Politics and Sociology*, ed. F. Fauri, pp. 103–25. Abingdon and New York: Routledge.

Featherstone, K. 2000. 'Cyprus and the Onset of Europeanization: Strategic Usage, Structural Transformation and Institutional Adaptation'. *South European Society and Politics* 5.2, pp. 141–64.

Featherstone, K. (ed.). 2014. *Europe in Modern Greek History*. London: Hurst.

Featherstone, K., and D. Papadimitriou (eds). 2011. *The Last Ottomans: The Muslim Minority of Greece, 1940–1949*. New York, NY: Palgrave Macmillan.

Featherstone, K., and D. Papadimitriou. 2015. *Prime Ministers in Greece: The Paradox of Power*. Oxford: Oxford University Press.

Ferati-Sachsenmaier, F. 2019. 'Postwar Kosovo: Global and Local Dimensions of Interethnic Reconciliation Processes'. *International Journal of Transitional Justice* 13.2, pp. 310–27.

Ferrera, M. 1996. 'The "Southern Model" of Welfare State in Social Europe'. *Journal of European Social Policy* 6.1 (Feb.), pp. 17–37.

Fifis, C. N. 2015. *Από τους καθ' ημάς Αντίποδες: Όψεις της ιστορίας της ελληνοαυστραλιανής παροικίας.* Athens: Zacharopoulos.

Figgou, L. 2016. 'Constructions of "Illegal" Immigration and Entitlement to Citizenship: Debating an Immigration Law in Greece'. *Journal of Community and Applied Social Psychology* 26, pp. 150–63.

Fischer, B. J. 2016. 'The Balkan Wars and the Creation of Albanian Independence', in *War in the Balkans: Conflict and Diplomacy before World War I*, ed. J. Pettifer and T. Buchanan, pp. 102–14. London: I. B. Tauris.

Fitzpatrick, S., and R. Gellately (eds). 1997. *Accusatory Practices: Denunciation in Modern European History 1789–1989*. Chicago: University of Chicago Press.

Fleischer, H. 1984. 'Επαφές μεταξύ των γερμανικών αρχών κατοχής και των κυριοτέρων οργανώσεων της ελληνικής αντίστασης', in *Η Ελλάδα στη δεκαετία 1940–1950: Ένα Έθνος σε Κρίση*, ed. J. O. Iatrides, pp. 91–116. Athens: Themelio.

Fleischer, H. 1988, 1995. *Στέμμα και σβάστικα: Η Ελλάδα της Κατοχής και της Αντίστασης, 1941–1944*, 2 vols. Athens: Papazisis.

Fleischer, H. 1994. 'Kollaboration und deutsche Politik im besetzten Griechenland', in *Europa unterm Hakenkreuz: Okkupation und Kollaboration (1938–1945)*, ed. W. Röhr, pp. 17–30. Berlin: Hüthig.

Fleischer, H. 1995. 'EAM 1941–1947: A Reassessment', in *Greece at the Crossroads: The Civil War and Its Legacy*, ed. J. O. Iatrides and L. Wrigley, pp. 48–89. University Park, PA: Penn State University Press.

Fleischer, H. (ed.). 2005. *Η Ελλάδα '36–'49: Από τη Δικτατορία στον Εμφύλιο – Τομές και συνέχειες.* Athens: Kastaniotis.

Fleischer, H. 2010. 'Το κατοχικό δάνειο και η γερμανική οφειλή προς την Ελλάδα', in *Κατοχή – Αντίσταση, 1941–1944*, ed. H. Fleischer, pp. 73–7. Athens: Ta Nea.

Fleischer, H., and S. Aristides (eds). 1984. 'Ημερολόγιο Φαίδωνα Μαηδώνη (24.6–10.9.1944)'. *Μνήμων 9*, pp. 33–156.

Fleming, K. E. 1999. *The Muslim Bonaparte: Diplomacy and Orientalism in Ali Pasha's Greece*. Princeton, NJ: Princeton University Press.

Fleming, K. E. 2008. *Greece: A Jewish History*. Princeton, NJ: Princeton University Press.

Flyvbjerg, B., A. Stewart and A. Budzier (eds). 2016. 'The Oxford Olympics Study 2016: Cost and Cost Overrun at the Games', Saïd Business School Working Papers, pp. 1–27. Oxford: Oxford University Press.

Förster, M., and M. M. d'Ercole. 2005. 'Income Distribution and Poverty in Selected OECD Countries in the Second Half of the 1990s', OECD Social, Employment and Migration Working Papers, No. 22, *OECDiLibrary*, pp. 1–78. https://www.oecd.org/els/soc/34483698.pdf.

Foster, Z. J. 2015. 'The 1915 Locust Attack in Syria and Palestine and Its Role in the Famine during the First World War'. *Middle Eastern Studies* 51.3, pp. 370–94.

Fotakis, A. 2016. *Η δημιουργία της Αστυνομίας Πόλεων και η Βρετανική Αποστολή (1918–1932)*. Doctoral dissertation, ΕΚΠΑ.

Fountanopoulos, K. 2005. *Εργασία και εργατικό κίνημα στη Θεσσαλονίκη, 1908–1936: Ηθική οικονομία και συλλογική δράση στο Μεσοπόλεμο*. Athens: Nefeli.

Frangiadis, A. 2007. *Ελληνική Οικονομία, 19ος–20ός αιώνας: Από τον αγώνα της ανεξαρτησίας στην Οικονομική και Νομισματική Ένωση της Ευρώπης*. Athens: Nefeli.

Frangiadis, A. 2019. *1932: Η χρεοκοπία και το τέλος του Βενιζελισμού*. Athens: Kathimerini.

Frank, M. 2017. *Making Minorities History: Population Transfer in Twentieth Century Europe*. Oxford: Oxford University Press.

French, D. 2015. *Fighting EOKA: The British Counter-Insurgency Campaign on Cyprus, 1955–1959*. Oxford: Oxford University Press.

Frieser, K. H. (ed.) 2017. *Germany and the Second World War*, vol. 8: *The Eastern Front 1943–1944: The War in the East and on the Neighbouring Fronts*. Oxford: Oxford University Press.

Fukuyama, F. 1992. *The End of History and the Last Man*. New York, NY: Free Press.

Furat, M. 2010. 'Relation with Greece', in *Turkish Foreign Policy, 1919–2006: Facts and Analyses with Documents*, ed. B. Oran, pp. 344–9. Salt Lake City: University of Utah Press.

Gabaccia, D. 2000. *Italy's Many Diasporas*. London: UCL Press.

Galanis, G. 2018. 'Το ΕΑΜ και τα Τάγματα Ασφαλείας κατά την Απελευθέρωση της Πελοποννήσου: Η περίπτωση του Άργους', in *Από την Απελευθέρωση στα Δεκεμβριανά: Μια τομή στην πολιτική ιστορία της Ελλάδας*, ed. P. Papastratis, M. Limperatos and L. Sarafi, pp. 113–23. Athens: Panteion University.

Galbraith, J. K. 2018. *Welcome to the Poison Chalice: The Destruction of Greece and the Future of Europe*. New Haven, CT: Yale University Press.

Gallant, T. W. 2015. *The Edinburgh History of the Greeks, 1768–1913: The Long Nineteenth Century*. Edinburgh: Edinburgh University Press.

Gallant, T. W. 2016. *Modern Greece: From the War of Independence to the Present*, 2nd ed. London: Bloomsbury.

Gallant, T. W., G. Treheles and M. Vitopoulos. 2005. *The 1918 Anti-Greek Riot in Toronto*. Toronto: Thessalonikeans Society of Metro Toronto Inc. and the Canadian Hellenic Historical Society.

Ganser, D. 2005. *NATO's Secret Armies: Operation GLADIO and Terrorism in Western Europe*. London: Frank Cass.

Gardikas, K. 2008. 'Relief Work and Malaria in Greece, 1943–1947'. *Journal of Contemporary History* 43.3, pp. 493–508.

Gardikas, K. 2018. *Landscapes of Disease: Malaria in Modern Greece*. Budapest: Central European University Press.

Gatrell, P. 2006. 'Economic and Demographic Change: Russia's Age of Economic Extremes', in *The Cambridge History of Russia*, vol. 3: *The Twentieth Century*, ed. R. Suny, pp. 383–410. Cambridge: Cambridge University Press.

Gatrell, P. 2008. 'Refugees and Forced Migrants during the First World War'. *Immigrants and Minorities* 26.1–2, pp. 82–110.

Gatrell, P. 2013. *The Making of the Modern Refugee*. Oxford: Oxford University Press.

Gatrell, P. 2019. *The Unsettling of Europe: The Great Migration, 1945 to the Present*. London: Allen Lane.

Gazi, E. 2000. *'Scientific' National History: The Greek Case in Comparative Perspective (1850–1920)*. Frankfurt: Peter Lang.

Gazi, E. 2011. *Πατρίς, θρησκεία, οικογένεια: Ιστορία ενός συνθήματος, 1880–1930*. Athens: Polis.

Gazi, E. 2017. 'Άγγλοι, Γάλλοι και Σενεγαλέζοι: Αντιλήψεις για το ελληνικό έθνος, τη φυλή και τις αυτοκρατορίες κατά τον Α΄ Παγκόσμιο Πόλεμο', in *Φυλετικές θεωρίες στην Ελλάδα: Προσλήψεις και χρήσεις στις επιστήμες, την πολιτική, τη λογοτεχνία και την ιστορία της τέχνης κατά τον 19ο και 20ό αιώνα*, ed. E. Avdela and D. Arvanitakis, pp. 245–72. Iraklion: PEK.

Geithner, T. F. 2014. *Stress Test: Reflections on Financial Crises*. New York, NY: Penguin Random House.

Gekas, S. 2020. 'From the Nation to Emancipation: Greek Women Warriors from the Revolution (1820s) to the Civil War (1940s)', in *Women Warriors and National Heroes: Global Histories*, ed. B. Cothran, J. Judge and A. Shubert, pp. 113–28. London: Bloomsbury.

Genoni, P., and T. Dalzeill. 2018. *Half the Perfect World: Writers, Drifters and Dreamers on Hydra, 1955–1964*. Melbourne: Monash University Press.

Georgakas, D. 1996. 'Greek American Radicalism: The Twentieth Century', in *The Immigrant Left in the United States*, ed. P. Buhle and D. Georgakas, pp. 207–27. Albany, NY: State University of New York Press.

George, V., and G. Millerson. 1967. 'The Cypriot Community in London'. *Race* 8.3, pp. 277–92.

Georgelin, H. 2005. *La fin de Smyrne: Du cosmopolitisme aux nationalisme*. Paris: CNRS.

Georgiadis-Arnakis, G. 1963. 'Byzantium and Greece'. *Balkan Studies* 4, pp. 133–78.

Georgiadou, V. 2019. *Η Άκρα Δεξιά στην Ελλάδα, 1965–2018*. Athens: Kastaniotis.

Geppert, D., and W. Mulligan (eds). 2015. *The Wars before the Great War: Conflict and International Politics before the Outbreak of the First World War*. Cambridge: Cambridge University Press.

Gerolymatos, A. 2016. *An International Civil War: Greece 1943–1949*. New Haven, CT: Yale University Press.

Gerwarth, R. 2016. *The Vanquished: Why the First World War Failed to End, 1917–1923*. London: Allen Lane.

Giakoumakatos, A. 1987. 'Η σχολική αρχιτεκτονική και η εμπειρία του μοντέρνου στην Ελλάδα του μεσοπολέμου'. *Θέματα Χρόνου και Τεχνών* 18, pp. 50–61.

Gialourakis, M. 1967. *Η Αίγυπτος των Ελλήνων: Συνοπτική ιστορία του ελληνισμού της Αιγύπτου*. Athens: Metropolis.

Giannitsis, A. 2011. 'Διεθνείς κεφαλαιακές ροές', in *Οικονομική Ιστορία του Ελληνικού Κράτους: Συγκρότηση εθνικής οικονομίας*, vol. 2: *Οικονομικές λειτουργίες και επιδόσεις*, ed. S. Asdrachas, pp. 525–97. Athens: Politistiko Idrima Omilou Pireaos.

Giannitsis, A. 2016. *Το ασφαλιστικό και η κρίση*. Athens: Polis.

Giannitsis, T. 1994. 'Trade Effects, the Balance of Payments and Implications for the Productive System', in *Greece and EU Membership Evaluated*, ed. P. Kazakos and P. Ioakeimidis, pp. 36–55. London: Pinter.

Giannitsis, T., A. Dialla and I. Hasiotis. 2006. 'Ουκρανία – Λευκορωσία – Ρωσική Ομοσπονδία Κεντροασιατικές Δημοκρατίες', in *Οι Έλληνες στη Διασπορά, 15ος–21ος αι.*, ed. I. Hasiotis, O. Katsiardi-Hering and E. Abatzi, pp. 191–202. Athens: Hellenic Parliament.

Giannitsis, T., and S. Zografakis. 2015. 'Greece: Solidarity and Adjustment in Times of Crisis', IMK Institut für Makroökonomie und Konjunkturforschung, Hans-Boeckler-Foundation, Paper 38, March 2015.

Giddens, A. 1998. *The Third Way: The Renewal of Social Democracy*. Cambridge: Polity.

Gildea, R. 2019. *Empires of the Mind: The Colonial Past and the Politics of the Present*. Oxford: Oxford University Press.

Gildea, R., O. Wieviorka and A. Warring (eds). 2006. *Surviving Hitler and Mussolini: Daily Life in Occupied Europe*. Oxford and New York: Berg.

Gingeras, R. 2009. *Sorrowful Shores: Violence, Ethnicity and the End of the Ottoman Empire, 1912–1923*. Oxford: Oxford University Press.

Gingeras, R. 2016. *Fall of the Sultanate: The Great War and the End of the Ottoman Empire, 1912–1922*. Oxford: Oxford University Press.

Ginsborg, P. 1990. *A History of Contemporary Italy: Society and Politics 1943–1988*. London: Penguin.

Ginsborg, P. 2001. *Italy and Its Discontents: Family, Society, the State, 1980–2001*. London: Penguin.

Giourgou, O. K. 2014. 'Οι ενώσεις παλαιών πολεμιστών και το ΣΕΚΕ (1922–1925): Κοινωνικές αναφορές, ιδεολογικές και πολιτικές επιρροές'. Doctoral dissertation, Panteion University.

Gkotzaridis, E. 2016. *A Pacifist's Life and Death: Grigorios Lambrakis and Greece in the Long Shadow of Civil War*. Cambridge: Cambridge Scholars Press.

Gkotzaridis, E. 2017. '"Who Rules This Country?": Collusion between State and Deep State in Post-Civil War Greece and the Murder of Independent MP Grigorios Lambrakis 1958–1963'. *Diplomacy and Statecraft* 28.4, pp. 646–73.

Glavinas, Y. 2013. *Οι μουσουλμανικοί πληθυσμοί στην Ελλάδα (1912–1923): Από την ενσωμάτωση στην ανταλλαγή*. Thessaloniki: Stamoulis.

Glinos, D. 1944. *Τι είναι και τι θέλει το Εθνικό Απελευθερωτικό Μέτωπο*. Athens: Ο Ρήγας.

Goldstein, E. 1989. 'Great Britain and Greater Greece'. *Historical Journal* 32.2, pp. 339–56.

Gooch, J. 2020. *Mussolini's War: Fascist Italy from Triumph to Collapse, 1935–1943*. London: Allen Lane.

Gorman, A. 2005. 'Egypt's Forgotten Communists: The Postwar Greek Left'. *Journal of Modern Greek Studies* 20.1, pp. 1–27.

Gorman, A. 2009. 'Repatriation or Readjustment: Egyptian Greek Dilemmas of the 1950s', in *Greek Diaspora and Migration since 1700: Society, Politics and Culture*, ed. D. Tziovas, pp. 6–72. London: Ashgate.

Gorman, A. 2009a. 'The Failure of Readjustment (Anaprosarmoge): The Post-War Egyptian Greek Experience'. *Journal of the Hellenic Diaspora* 35.2, pp. 45–61.

Gorman, A. 2013. 'Radical Internationalists on the Nile and across the Mediterranean', in *Social Transformation and Mass Mobilisation in the Balkan and Eastern Mediterranean Cities, 1900–1923*, ed. A. Lyberatos, pp. 307–21. Iraklion: Crete University Press.

Gounaris, V. K. 2002. *Εγνωσμένων κοινωνικών φρονημάτων: Κοινωνικές και άλλες όψεις του αντικομμουνισμού στη Μακεδονία του εμφυλίου πολέμου.* Thessaloniki: Paratiritis.

Gourgouris, S. 1996. *Dream Nation: Enlightenment, Colonization and the Institution of Modern Greece*. Stanford, CA: Stanford University Press.

Graham, H. and A. Quiroga. 2012. 'After the Fear Was Over? What Came after the Dictatorships of Spain, Greece and Portugal', in *The Oxford Handbook of Postwar European History*, ed. D. Stone, pp. 502–25. Oxford: Oxford University Press.

Gramsci, A. 1977. *Quaderni del carcere*, vol. 1. Turin: Einaudi.

Grandits, H., and N. Clayer (ed.). 2011. *Conflicting Loyalties in the Balkans: The Great Powers, the Ottoman Empire and Nation-Building*. London: I. B. Tauris.

Greene, M. 2015. *The Edinburgh History of the Greece 1453–1768: The Ottoman Empire*. Edinburgh: Edinburgh University Press.

Greif, G. 2005. *We Wept without Tears: Testimonies of the Jewish Sonderkommando from Auschwitz*. New Haven, CT: Yale University Press.

Gunther, R., and N. Diamandouros (eds). 1995. *The Politics of Democratic Consolidation: Southern Europe in Comparative Perspective*. Baltimore: John Hopkins University Press.

Hall, R. C. 2000. *The Balkan Wars 1912–1913: Prelude to the First World War*, London and New York: Routledge.

Halstead, P. 2014. *Two Oxen Ahead: Pre-Mechanized Farming in the Mediterranean*. Oxford: Wiley Blackwell.

Hamilakis, Y. 2007. *The Nation and Its Ruins: Antiquity, Archaeology and National Imagination in Greece*. Oxford: Oxford University Press.

Hanioğlu, M. S. 2008. *A Brief History of the Late Ottoman Empire*. Princeton, NJ: Princeton University Press.

Hannes, G., and N. Clayer (eds). 2011. *Conflicting Loyalties in the Balkans: The Great Powers, the Ottoman Empire and Nation-Building*. London: I. B. Tauris.

Hantzaroula, P. 2021. *Child Survivors of the Holocaust in Greece: Memory, Testimony and Subjectivity*. London and New York: Routledge.

Hardouvelis, G. A., and I. Gkionis. 2016. 'A Decade Long Economic Crisis: Cyprus versus Greece'. *Cyprus Economic Policy Review* 10.2, pp. 3–40.

Harlaftis, G. 1995. *A History of Greek-Owned Shipping: The Making of an International Tramp Fleet, 1830 to the Present Day*. London and New York: Routledge.

Harlaftis, G. 2001. *Ιστορία της Ελληνόκτητης Ναυτιλίας, 19ος–20ός αιώνας*. Athens: Nefeli.

Hart, J. 1996. *New Voices in the Nation: Women in the Greek Resistance, 1941–1964*. Ithaca, NY: Cornell University Press.

Hasiotis, I. 1993. *Επισκόπηση της ιστορίας της νεοελληνικής διασποράς*. Athens: Vanias.

Hasiotis, I. 2006. 'Εἰσαγωγή', in *Οι Έλληνες στη Διασπορά, 15ος–21ος αι.*, ed. I. Hasiotis, O. Katsiardi-Hering and E. Abatzi, pp. 13–31. Athens: Hellenic Parliament.

Hasiotis, L. 2013. *Τα παιδιά του Εμφυλίου: Από την 'κοινωνική πρόνοια' του Φράνκο στον 'έρανο' της Φρειδερίκης (1936–1950)*. Athens: Estia.

Hatzidakis, A. 2015. *Τάσεις της τουριστικής κίνησης 2008–2015*. Athens: EOT.

Hatziiossif, C. 1997. 'Class Structure and Class Antagonism in Late Nineteenth-Century Greece', in *Greek Society in the Making, 1863–1913: Reality, Symbols and Vision*, ed. Philip Carabott, pp. 3–17. London and New York: Routledge.

Hatziiosif, C. (ed.) 1999–2009, *Ιστορία της Ελλάδας του 20ού αιώνα*, 8 vols, Athens: Bibliorama.

Hatziprokopiou, P. 2003. 'Albanian Immigrants in Thessaloniki, Greece: Processes of Economic and Social Incorporation'. *Journal of Ethnic and Migration Studies* 29.6, pp. 1033–57.

Helmreich, P. C. 1974. *From Paris to Sèvres: The Partition of the Ottoman Empire at the Peace Conference*. Columbus: Ohio State University Press.

Hendrickx, B., E. Thanou and S. Pavlis. 2006. 'Νοτιοαφρικανική Ένωση', in *I Ellines sti Diaspora, 15os–20os ai*, ed. I. H. Hassiótis, O. Katsiardí-Hering and E. A. Ampatzí, pp. 249–53. Athens: Hellenic Parliament.

Heraclides, A. 2007. *Άσπονδοι Γείτονες. Ελλάδα–Τουρκία: Η διένεξη του Αιγαίου*. Athens: Sideris.

Heraclides, A. 2010. *The Greek–Turkish Conflict in the Aegean: Imagined Enemies*. Basingstoke: Palgrave Macmillan.

Heraclides, A. 2011. *Imagined Enemies: The Aegean Conflict*. London and New York: Routledge.

Heraclides, A. 2018. *Το Μακεδονικό Ζήτημα, 1978–2018: Από τις εθνικές διεκδικήσεις στις συγκρουσιακές εθνικές ταυτότητες*. Athens: Themelio.

Heraclides, A. 2020. *The Macedonian Question and the Macedonians: A History*. Basingstoke: Palgrave.

Heraclides, A. and G. A. Çakmak (eds). 2019. *Greece and Turkey in Conflict and Cooperation: From Europeanization to de-Europeanisation*. London and New York: Routledge.

Herbert, U. 2019. *A History of Twentieth Century Germany*, trans. by B. Fowkes. Oxford: Oxford University Press.

Hering, G. 1992. *Die politischen Parteien in Griechenland 1821–1936*. Berlin: De Gruyter.

Hering, G. 2006. *Τα πολιτικά κόμματα στην Ελλάδα, 1821–1936*, trans. by T. Paraskevopoulos. Athens: Morfotiko Idrima Ethnikis Trapezis.

Herzfeld, M. 1982. *Ours Once More: Folklore, Ideology and the Making of Modern Greece*. New York, NY: Pella.

Herzfeld, M. 1987. *Anthropology through the Looking-Glass: Critical Ethnography in the Margins of Europe*. Cambridge: Cambridge University Press.

Herzfeld, M. 1996. *Cultural Intimacy: Social Poetics in the Nation-State*. London: Routledge.

Herzfeld, M. 2002. 'The Absent Presence: Discourses of Crypto-Colonialism'. *South Atlantic Quarterly* 101.4, pp. 899–926.

Herzfeld, M. 2020. 'Seductions of the Bouzouki and the Brass Band: Transgressive Reflections on Mikis Theodorakis and Giuseppe Verdi'. *Annual of the British School at Athens* 115, pp. 403–17.

Hionidou, V. 2006. *Famine and Death in Occupied Greece, 1941–1944*. Cambridge: Cambridge University Press.

Hirschon, R. 1998. *Heirs of the Greek Catastrophe: The Social Life of Asia Minor Refugees in Piraeus*, 2nd ed. New York, NY: Berghahn.

Hobsbawm, E. J. 1987. *The Age of Empire, 1875–1914*. London: Weidenfeld and Nicolson.

Hobsbawm, E. J. 1992. *Nations and Nationalism since 1780: Programme, Myth, Reality*, 2nd ed. Cambridge: Cambridge University Press.

Hobsbawm, E. J. 1994. *The Age of Extremes, 1914–1990*. London: Vintage.

Holland, R. 1999. *Holland–Britain and the Revolt in Cyprus, 1954–1959*. New York, NY: Oxford University Press.

Holmes, L. 2006. *Rotten States? Corruption, Post-Communism, and Neoliberalism*. Durham, NC: Duke University Press.

Hondros, J. 1983. *Occupation and Resistance: The Greek Agony, 1941–1944*. New York, NY: Pella.

Hroch, M. 1985. *The Social Preconditions of National Revival in Europe: A Comparative Analysis of the Social Composition of Patriotic Groups among Smaller European Nations*. Cambridge: Cambridge University Press.

Huntington, S. 1968. *Political Order in Changing Societies*. New Haven, CT: Yale University Press.

Iatrides, J. O. 1997. 'Lincoln MacVeagh', in *Notable U.S. Ambassadors since 1775: A Biographical Dictionary*, ed. C. J. Nolan, pp. 242–3. Westport, CT: Greenwood Press.

Iatrides, J. O. 2004. *Greece at the Crossroads: The Greek Civil War and Its Legacy*. University Park: Pennsylvania State University Press.

Iliou, P. 2002. 'Η πορεία προς τον εμφύλιο: Από την ένοπλη εμπλοκή στην ένοπλη ρήξη', in *Ο Εμφύλιος Πόλεμος: Από τη Βάρκιζα στο Γράμμο*, ed. I. Nikolakopoulos, and A. Rigos, pp. 25–30. Athens: Themelio.

Ioannidis, S. 2019. 'Το κίνημα των εργοστασιακών επιτροπών (1974–1981)'. Doctoral dissertation, EKPA.

Ioannou, G. 2020. *Ο Ντεκτάς στον Νότο: Η κανονικοποίηση της διχοτόμησης στην ελληνοκυπριακή πλευρά*. Thessaloniki: Psifides.

Iordanoglou, C. 2020. *Η ελληνική οικονομία μετα το 1950*, vol. 1: *Περίοδος 1950–1973: Ανάπτυξη, νομισματική σταθερότητα και κρατικός παρεμβατισμός*. Athens: Bank of Greece.

Iosifides, T., and R. King. 1998. 'Socio-Spatial Dynamics and Exclusion of Three Immigrant Groups in the Athens Conurbation'. *South European Society and Politics* 3.3, pp. 205–29.

Iriye, A. (ed.). 2014. *Global Interdependence: The World after 1945*. Cambridge, MA: Harvard University Press.

Isabella, M., and K. Zanou. 2015. 'The Sea, Its People and Their Ideas in the Long Nineteenth Century', in *Mediterranean Diasporas: Politics and Ideas in the Long 19th Century*, ed. M. Isabella and K. Zanou, pp. 1–23. London: Bloomsbury.

Jackson, J. 2001. *France: The Dark Years, 1940–1944*. Oxford: Oxford University Press.

Janiszewski, L., and E. Alexakis. 2003. 'California Dreaming: the "Greek Café" and Its Role in the Americanisation of Australian Eating and Social Habits'. *Modern Greek Studies* 2, pp. 177–97.

Judt, T. 2005. *Postwar: A History of Europe since 1945*. London: Penguin.

Kafaoglou, I. 2018. *Η δημοκρατία στην παραλία: Μικρό δοκίμιο για το μπικίνι*. Athens: Portes.

Kahl, T. 2009. *Για την ταυτότητα των Βλάχων: Εθνοπολιτισμικές προσεγγίσεις μιας βαλκανικής πραγματικότητας*, trans. S. Boulasikis. Athens: Bibliorama.

Kakridis, A. 2021. *Bearing Gifts to Greeks: American Aid in Greece's Post War Recovery, 1947–1953*. https://economichistorygreece.files.wordpress.com/2021/01/kakridis-short-paper.pdf.

Kalantzis, G. 2016. *Το ελληνικό κράτος και οι μουσουλμάνοι της Δυτικής Θράκης, 1903–1928: Από τη στρατηγική συμμαχία στην εγκατάλειψη*. Athens: Themelio.

Kaldellis, A. 2007. *Hellenism in Byzantium: The Transformations of Greek Identity and the Reception of the Classical Tradition*. Cambridge: Cambridge University Press.

Kalfa, K. 2019. *Αυτοστέγαση, τώρα! Η αθέατη πλευρά της αμερικανικής βοήθειας στην Ελλάδα*. Athens: Futura.

Kallis, A. 2021. 'The Transnational Co-production of Interwar "Fascism": On the Dynamics of Ideational Mobility and Localization'. *European History Quarterly* 51.2, pp. 189–213.

Kallivretakis, L. 2017. *Δικτατορία και Μεταπολίτευση*. Athens: Themelio.

Kalogirou, Y. 2016. 'Η Κοινωνία της Πληροφορίας στην Ελλάδα (1997–2012): Ο δύσβατος δρόμος. Μια πρώτη απόπειρα απολογισμού', in *Αγορές και Πολιτική: Ιδιωτικά συμφέροντα και Δημόσια εξουσία, 18ος–20ός αιώνας. 2ο Διεθνές Συνέδριο Οικονομικής και Κοινωνικής Ιστορίας*, ed. C. Agriantoni, L. Papastefanaki, pp. 175–94. Volos: University of Thessaly Press.

Kaloudis, G. 2018. *Modern Greece and the Diaspora Greeks in the United States*. Lanham, MD: Lexington.

Kalyvas, S. 2006. *The Logic of Violence in Civil War*. New York, NY: Cambridge University Press.

Kalyvas, S. 2008. 'Η κουλτούρα της Μεταπολίτευσης'. *Η Καθημερινή*, 14 December 2008.

Kalyvas, S. 2015. *Modern Greece: What Everyone Needs to Know*. Oxford: Oxford University Press.

Kammas, M. 1992. 'Smallness, Economic Development and Cyprus'. *Cyprus Review* 4.1, pp. 65–76.

Kamouzis, D. 2012. 'Elites and the Formation of National Identity: the Case of the Greek Orthodox *Millet* (Mid-nineteenth Century to 1922)', in *State-Nationalisms in the Ottoman Empire, Greece and Turkey: Orthodox and Muslims, 1830–1945*, ed. B. C. Fortna and S. Katsikas, pp. 13–46. London and New York: Routledge.

Kaplan, R. 1995. *Balkan Ghosts: A Journey through History*. New York, NY: St. Martin's Press.

Kaplani, G. 2006. *Μικρό ημερολόγιο συνόρων*. Athens: Livanis.

Kapoli, P. 2014. 'Η εσωτερική μετανάστευση στην Αθήνα 1950–1970'. Doctoral dissertation, University of Athens.

Karabıçak, Y. Z. 2020. 'Ottoman Attempts to Define the Rebels during the Greek War of Independence'. *Studia Islamica* 114, pp. 316–54.

Karadimou-Gerolympou, A. 2014. *Η ανάδυση της σύγχρονης Θεσσαλονίκης*. Thessaloniki: University Studio Press.

Karadimou-Gerolympou, A. 2017. *Καταστροφή και αναμόρφωση της Θεσσαλονίκης μετά την πυρκαγιά του 1917*. Thessaloniki: University Studio Press.

Karakasidou, A. 1997. *Fields of Wheat, Hills of Blood: Passages to Nationhood in Greek Macedonia, 1870–1990*. Chicago: University of Chicago.

Karakasidou, A. 2002. 'Cultural Illegitimacy in Greece: the Slavo-Macedonian "Non-minority"', in *Minorities in Greece: Aspects of a Plural Society*, ed. R. Clogg, pp. 122–64. London: Hurst.

Karakasidou, A. 2021. 'Voters and Clients: Elections in Florina before and after the Prespa Accord', in *Macedonia and Identity Politics after the Prespa Agreement*, ed. V. P. Neofotistos, pp. 121–46. London and New York: Routledge.

Karakatsanis, N. M., and J. Swarts. 2007. *American Policy towards the Colonel's Greece: Uncertain Allies and the 1967 Coup d'État*. London: Palgrave.

Karalis, V. 2012. *A History of Greek Cinema*. New York, NY: Continuum.

Karamanolakis, V. (ed.). 2010. *Η στρατιωτική δικτατορία 1967–1974*. Athens: Ta Nea.

Karamanolakis, V. 2019. *Ανεπιθύμητο παρελθόν: Οι φάκελοι κοινωνικών φρονημάτων στην Ελλάδα στον 20ό αιώνα και η καταστροφή τους*. Athens: Themelio.

Karamouzi, E. 2014. *Greece, the EEC and the Cold War, 1974–1979: The Second Enlargement*. Basingstoke: Palgrave Macmillan.

Karampetsos, E. D. 1998. 'Nativism in Nevada: Greek Immigrants in White Pine County'. *Journal of the Hellenic Diaspora* 21.4, pp. 61–96.

Karanasou, F. 1999. 'The Greeks of Egypt: from Mohammed Ali to Nasser', in *The Greek Diaspora in the Twentieth Century*, ed. R. Clogg, pp. 24–57. Basingstoke: Macmillan.

Karatas, E. 2011. 'The Politics of Accession', in *An Island in Europe: The EU and the Transformation of Cyprus*, ed. J. Ker-Lindsay, H. Faustmann and F. Mullen, pp. 13–41. London: I. B. Tauris.

Karavidas, K. 1931. *Αγροτικά: Έρευνα επί της οικονομικής και κοινωνικής μορφολογίας εν Ελλάδι και εν ταις γειτονικαίς σλαϋικαίς χώραις*. Athens.

Karavidas, K. 2015. 'Αναζητήσεις της λαϊκότητας: Ιδεολογικές διασταυρώσεις και απομακρύνσεις στο *Αντί* και τον *Πολίτη*', in *Μεταπολίτευση: Η Ελλάδα στο μεταίχμιο δύο αιώνων*, ed. M. Avgeridis, E. Gazi and K. Kornetis, pp. 302–16. Athens: Themelio.

Karpozilos, A. 1999. 'The Greeks in Russia', in *The Greek Diaspora in the Twentieth Century*, ed. R. Clogg, pp. 137–57. Basingstoke: Macmillan.

Karpozilos, K. 2014. 'The Defeated of the Greek Civil War: From Fighters to Political Refugees in the Cold War'. *Journal of Cold War Studies* 16.3, pp. 62–87.

Karpozilos, K. 2017. *Κόκκινη Αμερική: Έλληνες μετανάστες και το όραμα ενός Νέου Κόσμου 1900–1950*. Iraklion: University of Crete.

Kartalou, A., and A. Nikolaidou (eds). 2006. *Σε ξένο τόπο: Η μετανάστευση στον ελληνικό κινηματογράφο, 1956–2006*. Thessaloniki and Athens: Aigokeros and Festival Kinimatografou.

Kassimeris, G. 2005. 'Junta by Another Name? The 1974 *Metapolitefsi* and the Greek Extra-Parliamentary Left'. *Journal of Contemporary History* 40.4, pp. 745–62.

Kassimeris, G. (ed.). 2006. *The Barbarisation of War*. New York, NY: New York University Press.

Kassimeris, G. 2013. *Inside Greek Terrorism*. Oxford: Oxford University Press.

Katsambekis, G. 2016. '"The People" and Political Opposition in Post-democracy: Reflections on the Hollowing of Democracy in Greece and Europe', in *The State We're In: Reflecting on Democracy's Troubles*, ed. J. Cook and N. J. Long, pp. 144–66. New York, NY: Berghahn.

Katsambekis, G. 2018. 'Ο πολιτικός λόγος του "εκσυγχρονισμού" (1989–2004)', in *ΠΑΣΟΚ, 1974–2018: Πολιτική οργάνωση – Ιδεολογικές μετατοπίσεις – Κυβερνητικές πολιτικές*, ed. B. Asimakopoulos and C. Tassis, pp. 424–66. Athens: Gutenberg.

Katsambekis, G. 2019. 'Αριστερός λαϊκισμός στην αντιπολίτευση και στην εξουσία: Η περίπτωση Σύριζα', in *Σύριζα, ένα κόμμα εν κινήσει*, ed. I. Balambanidis, pp. 97–120. Athens: Themelio.

Katsapis, K. 2003. 'Αντιπαραθέσεις ανάμεσα σε γηγενείς και πρόσφυγες στην Ελλάδα του Μεσοπολέμου', in *Πέρα από την καταστροφή. Μικρασιάτες πρόσφυγες στην Ελλάδα του Μεσοπολέμου*, ed. G. Tzedopoulos, pp. 104–26. Athens: IME.

Katsapis, K. 2007. *Ήχοι και απόηχοι: Κοινωνική ιστορία του Rock en Roll φαινομένου στην Ελλάδα*. Athens: Insitituto Neoellinikon Erevnon.

Katsapis, K. 2011. 'Το Προσφυγικό Ζήτημα', in *Το 1922 και οι πρόσφυγες: Μια νέα ματιά*, ed. A. Liakos, pp. 125–69. Athens: Nefeli.

Katsapis, K. 2013. *Το 'πρόβλημα νεολαία': Μοντέρνοι νέοι, παράδοση και αμφισβήτηση στη μεταπολεμική Ελλάδα, 1964–1974*. Athens: Aprovleptes.

Katsiaounis, R. 1996. *Labour, Society and Politics in Cyprus during the Second Half of the Nineteenth Century*. Nicosia: Cyprus Research Centre.

Katsikas, I., and L. Lambrianidis. 1994. 'Πληθυσμιακές μετακινήσεις στο εσωτερικό της υπαίθρου και η τάση για τη δημιουργία μεσαίου μεγέθους αστικών κέντρων', in *Η ελληνική κοινωνία κατά την πρώτη μεταπολεμική περίοδο (1945–1967)*, ed. Idrima Saki Karagiorga, pp. 490–501. Athens: Idrima Saki Karagiorga.

Katsikostas, D. 2010. 'Ο Ελληνικός Στρατός στην Εξορία, 1941–1944: Οργάνωση, συγκρότηση, πολεμικές αποστολές και κινήματα στη Μέση Ανατολή'. Athens: Alfeios.

Katsourides, Y. 2014. *The History of the Communist Party in Cyprus: Colonialism, Class and the Cypriot Left*. London: I. B. Tauris.

Katsourides, Y. 2020. 'Institutional Inertia, Ignorance and Short Circuit: Cyprus', in *The Politics of the Eurozone Crisis in Southern Europe: A Comparative Reappraisal*, ed. L. Morlino and C. E. Sottiliotta, pp. 27–56. Cham, Switzerland: Springer.

Kaurinkoski, K. 2003. 'Les Grecs de Mariupol (Ukraine): Réflexions sur une identité en diaspora', *Revue européenne des migrations internationales* 19.1, pp. 125–46.

Kavala, M. 2009. *Η Θεσσαλονίκη στη Γερμανική κατοχή (1941–1944), Κοινωνία, Οικονομία, Διωγμός των Εβραίων*. Doctoral dissertation, University of Crete.

Kavala, M. 2015. 'Η Καταστροφή των Εβραίων της Ελλάδας (1941–1944): Μια ιστορία με πολλές πτυχές'. *Κάλλιπος*. https://repository.kallipos.gr/handle/11419/4437 (last accessed 5 July 2019).

Kavala, M. 2018. 'The Scale of Jewish Property Theft in Nazi-occupied Thessaloniki', in *The Holocaust in Greece*, ed. G. Antoniou and D. A. Moses, pp. 183–207. Cambridge: Cambridge University Press.

Kavoulakos, K. I. 2008. 'Προστασία και διεκδίκηση δημόσιων χώρων: Ένα κίνημα της πόλης στην Αθήνα του 21ου αιώνα', in *Κοινωνικοί και Χωρικοί Μετασχηματισμοί στην Αθήνα του 21ου αιώνα*, ed. T. Maloutas et al., pp. 387–426. Athens: EKKE.

Kaya, S. Y. 2014. *Land Use, Peasants and the Republic: Debates on Land Reform in Turkey, 1923–1945*. Doctoral dissertation, Middle East Technical University Istanbul.

Kazakos, P. 2001. *Ανάμεσα σε κράτος και αγορά: Οικονομία και οικονομική πολιτική στη μεταπολεμική Ελλάδα, 1944–2000*. Athens: Patakis.

Kazakos, P., and P. Liargovas. 2016. *Το δημόσιο χρέος της Ελλάδας*. Athens: Papazisis.

Kazamias, A. 2014. *Greece and the Cold War: Diplomacy, Rivalry and Colonialism in Post-Civil War Greece*. London: I. B. Tauris.

Kechriotis, V. 2005. *The Greeks of Izmir at the End of the Empire: a Non-Muslim Ottoman Community between Autonomy and Patriotism*. Doctoral dissertation, Leiden University.

Keeley, E. 1976. *Cavafy's Alexandria*. Cambridge, MA: Harvard University Press.

Ker-Lindsay, J. 2011. *The Cyprus Problem: What Everyone Needs to Know*. Oxford: Oxford University Press.

Klemann, H., and S. Kudryashov. 2012. *Occupied Economies: An Economic History of Nazi-Occupied Europe, 1939–1945*. London: Berg.

Khrushchev, N. 2007. *Memoirs of Nikita Khrushchev*, vol. 3: *Statesman, 1953–1964*, trans. S. Khrushchev. University Park, PA: The Pennsylvania State University Press.

Kieser, H. L. 2018. *Talaat Pasha: Father of Modern Turkey, Architect of Genocide*. Princeton, NJ: Princeton University Press.

Kiesling, J. B. 2014. *Greek Urban Warriors: Resistance and Terrorism, 1967–2014*. Athens: Lycabettus Press.

King, R. 2000. 'Southern Europe in the Changing Global Map of Migration', in *Eldorado or Fortress? Migration in Southern Europe*, ed. R. King and G. Lazaridis, pp. 1–26. London: Palgrave MacMillan.

Kiramargiou, E. 2019. *Δραπετσώνα 1922–1967: Ένας κόσμος στην άκρη του κόσμου*. Athens: Ethniko Idrima Erevnon.

Kırlı, B. K. 2005. 'Forgetting the Smyrna Fire'. *History Workshop Journal* 60, pp. 25–44.

Kitis, D. 2015. 'The Anti-Authoritarian Chóros: a Space for Youth Socialization and Radicalization in Greece (1974–2010)'. *Journal for the Study of Radicalism* 9.1, pp. 1–36.

Kitroeff, A. 1989. *Greeks in Egypt, 1919–1937*. London: Ithaca Press.

Kitroeff, A. 2004. *Wrestling with the Ancients: Modern Greek Identity and the Olympics*. New York, NY: Greekworks.

Kitroeff, A. 2019. *The Greeks and the Making of Modern Egypt*. Cairo: American University of Cairo Press.

Kitroeff, A. 2020. *The Greek Orthodox Church in America: a Modern History*, NIU Series in Orthodox Christian Studies. Ithaca, NY: Cornell University Press.

Kitromilides, P. M. 1998. 'On the Intellectual Content of Greek Nationalism: Paparrigopoulos, Byzantium and the Great Idea', in *Byzantium and the Modern Greek Identity*, ed. D. Ricks and P. Magdalino, pp. 25–34. London: Ashgate.

Kitromilides, P. M., and A. Alexandris. 1984–5. 'Ethnic Survival, Nationalism and Forced Migration: the Historical Demography of the Greek Community of Asia Minor at the Close of the Ottoman Era'. *Δελτίο Κέντρου Μικρασιατικών Σπουδών 5*, pp. 9–44.

Kızılyürek, N. 2019. *Μια ιστορία βίας και μνησικακίας: Η γένεση και εξέλιξη της εθνοτικής διένεξης στην Κύπρο*, trans. M. Theodorou. Lefkosia: Heterotopia.

Klarevas, L. 2004. 'Were the Eagle and the Phoenix Birds of a Feather? The United States and the Greek Coup of 1967', Discussion Paper No. 15. London: Hellenic Observatory–European Institute.

Knight, D. M. 2015. *History, Time, and Economic Crisis in Central Greece*. New York, NY: Palgrave Macmillan.

Knox, M. 1982. *Mussolini Unleashed, 1939–1941: Politics and Strategy in Fascist Italy's Last War*. Cambridge: Cambridge University Press.

Knox, M. 2000. *Hitler's Italian Allies: Royal Armed Forces, Fascist Regime and the War of 1940–43*. Cambridge: Cambridge University Press.

Kofos, E. 1964. *Nationalism and Communism in Macedonia*. Thessaloniki: Institute of Balkan Studies.

Koliopoulos, J. S. 1987. *Brigands with a Cause: Brigandage and Irredentism in Modern Greece, 1821–1912*. Oxford: Oxford University Press.

Koliopoulos, J. S. 1995. *Ληλασία φρονημάτων: Το μακεδονικό ζήτημα στην περίοδο του εμφυλίου πολέμου 1945–1949 στη δυτική Μακεδονία*. Thessaloniki: Vanias.

Koliopoulos, J. S. 2005. *Η ληστεία στην Ελλάδα (19ος αι.): Περί λύχνων αφάς*. Thessaloniki: Epikentro.

Koliopoulos, J. S., and T. M. Veremis. 2010. *Modern Greece: A History since 1821*. London: Wiley Blackwell.

Kolovos, Y. 2015. *'Κοινωνικά απόβλητα'; Η ιστορία της πανκ σκηνής στην Αθήνα, 1979–2015*. Athens: Aprovleptes Ekdoseis.

Komninou, M. 2001. *Από την αγορά στο θέαμα: Μελέτη για τη συγκρότηση της δημόσιας σφαίρας και του κινηματογράφου στη σύγχρονη Ελλάδα, 1950–2000*. Athens: Papazisis.

Kontente, L. 2005. *Smyrne et l'Occident, d'Antiquité au XXIᵉ siècle*. Montigny-le-Bretonneux: Yvelinédition.

Kontogiannopoulos, V. 1991. *Παιδεία: Εκσυγχρονισμός υπό αναστολή*. Athens: Gutenberg.

Kontogiorgi, E. 2006. *Population Exchange in Greek Macedonia: The Rural Settlement of Refugees 1922–1930*. Oxford: Oxford University Press.

Kontos, M. 2009. 'Greek Migrant Women in Germany: Strategies of Autonomy in Diaspora', in *Women, Gender and Diasporic Lives: Labor, Community, and Identity in Greek Migrations*, ed. E. Tastsoglou. Lanham, MD: Lexington.

Kordatos, G. 1924. *Η κοινωνική σημασία της ελληνικής επαναστάσεως του 1821*. Athens.

Korma, L. 2017. 'The Historiography of the Greek Diaspora and Migration in the Twentieth Century'. *Historein* 16.1–2, pp. 47–73.

Kornetis, K. 2010. 'No More Heroes? Rejection and Reverberation of the Past in the 2008 Events in Greece'. *Journal of Modern Greek Studies* 28.2, pp. 173–97.

Kornetis, K. 2013. *Children of the Dictatorship: Student Resistance, Cultural Politics, and the 'Long 1960s' in Greece*. New York, NY: Berghahn.

Kornetis, K. 2015. '"Let's Get Laid because It's the End of the World!": Sexuality, Gender and the Spanish Left in Late Francoism and the Transicio'. *European Review of History/Revue européenne d'histoire* 22.1, pp. 176–98.

Kornetis, K. 2016. 'Expropriating the Space of the Other: Property Spoliations of Thessalonican Jews in the 1940s', in *The Holocaust in Greece*, ed. G. Antoniou and D. A. Moses, pp. 228–52. Cambridge: Cambridge University Press.

Kornetis, K. 2019. 'Ο Σύριζα και το αμφίσημο παρελθόν: Από το '40 στη Μεταπολίτευση', in *Σύριζα, ένα κόμμα εν κινήσει*, ed. Y. Balambanidis, pp. 202–24. Athens: Themelio.

Kornetis, K., E. Kotsovili and N. Papadogiannis (eds). 2016. *Consumption and Gender in Southern Europe since the Long 1960s*. London: Bloomsbury.

Kornetis, K., and M. E. Cavallaro. 2019. 'Introduction: Lost in Transition?', in *Rethinking Democratization in Spain, Portugal and Greece*, ed. M. E. Cavallaro and K. Kornetis, pp. 1–17. Cham, Switzerland: Palgrave Macmillan.

Koselleck, R. 1985. *Futures Past: On the Semantics of Historical Time*. Cambridge, MA: MIT Press.

Kostantinakou, D.-G. 2015. *Πολεμικές οφειλές και εγκληματίες πολέμου στην Ελλάδα: Ψάχνοντας την ηθική και υλική δικαίωση μετά τον Β΄ Παγκόσμιο Πόλεμο*. Athens: Alexandreia.

Kostis, A. 2008. *Νοσολογία των παιδικών ηλικιών και της νεολαίας (20ό αι.)*. Athens: Istoriko Archeio Ellinikis Neolaias.

Kostis, K. 1990. *Αγροτική οικονομία και Γεωργική Τράπεζα: Όψεις της ελληνικής οικονομίας στο Μεσοπόλεμο (1919–1928)*. Athens: MIET.

Kostis, K. 2018. *History's Spoiled Children: The Story of Modern Greece*. London and Oxford: Hurst and Oxford University Press.

Kostis, K. 2019. *Ο Πλούτος της Ελλάδας: Η ελληνική οικονομία από τους Βαλκανικούς Πολέμους μέχρι σήμερα*. Athens: Patakis.

Kostopoulos, C. 2013. *Making Democracy Work in Greece: the Indignant Citizen Movement, Media, and Political Engagement*. MA thesis, Lund University.

Kostopoulos, T. 2000. *Η απαγορευμένη γλώσσα: Κρατική καταστολή των σλαβικών διαλέκτων στην ελληνική Μακεδονία*. Athens: Mavri Lista.

Kostopoulos, T. 2007. *Πόλεμος και εθνοκάθαρση: Η ξεχασμένη πλευρά μιας δεκαετούς εθνικής εξόρμησης, 1912–1922*. Athens: Bibliorama.

Kostopoulos, T. 2018. 'Καταγράφοντας το ανομολόγητο: Το πολεμικό ημερολόγιο ενός βιαστή στρατιώτη (1912–13)', in *Ιστορίες πολέμου στη νοτιοανατολική Ευρώπη: Μια προσέγγιση στη διαχρονία*, ed. A. Kolia-Dermitzaki and B. Seirinidou, pp. 471–89. Athens: Hirodotos.

Kostopoulos, T. (ed.). 2018a. *Ο Δεκέμβρης της Οργής: Αφιέρωμα στη νεανική εξέγερση του 2008*. Athens: Efimerida ton Syntakton.

Kostopoulos, T., and D. Psarra (eds). 2018. *Μακεδονικό: Τα ντοκουμέντα – επίσημα έγγραφα από τα ελληνικά αρχεία (1904–1998)*. Athens: Efimerida ton Syntakton.

Kotzamanis, B. 2019. 'Ελλάδα, δημογραφικές εξελίξεις και δημογραφικές προκλήσεις'. *Δημογραφικά Νέα* 35. http://www.e-demography.gr/news/docs/eDemography_News _Doc_00015_gr.pdf (last accessed 1 July 2019).

Kotzamanis, B., P. Baltas and A. Kostaki. 2017. 'The Trend of Period Fertility in Greece and Its Changes during the Current Economic Recession'. *Population Review* 56.2, pp. 30–48.

Kouki, H., and A. Liakos. 2015. 'Narrating the Story of a Failed National Transition: Discourses on the Greek Crisis, 2010–2014'. *Historein* 15.1, pp. 49–61.

Koumoulides, J. 1974. *Cyprus and the Greek War of Independence*. Athens: National Centre of Social Research.

Koun, K. 2008. *Οι παραστάσεις*, ed. P. Mavromoustakos. Athens: Benaki Museum.

Kounio-Amarilo, E., and A. Nar. 2015. *Προφορικές Μαρτυρίες Εβραίων της Θεσσαλονίκης για το Ολοκαύτωμα*, ed. F. Abatzopoulou. Athens: Evrasia.

Kouroundis, H. 2018. *Το Σύνταγμα και η Αριστερά: Από τη 'βαθεία τομή' του 1963 στο Σύνταγμα του 1975*. Athens: Nisos.

Kousoulidis, P. 2016. *Η Χωροφυλακή, η Εθνοφυλακή και η Εθνοφρουρά στην μετακατοχική Ελλάδα, 1944–1949*. Doctoral dissertation, University of Thessaloniki.

Kousouris, D. 2014. 'Ο φασισμός στην Ελλάδα: Συνέχειες και ασυνέχειες κατά τον ευρωπαϊκό 20ού αιώνα', in *Το 'βαθύ κράτος' στη σημερινή Ελλάδα και η Ακροδεξιά*, ed. D. Christopoulos, pp. 33–82. Athens: Nisos.

Kousouris, D. 2014a. *Οι Δίκες των δοσίλογων 1944–1949: Δικαιοσύνη, συνέχεια του κράτους και εθνική μνήμη*. Athens: Polis.

Kousouris, D. 2018. 'From the Roaring 1990s to the Global 2000s: Interpretations of Race, Nation, Class in Greece', in *Balibar/Wallerstein's Race, Nation, Class: Rereading a Dialogue for Our Times*, ed. M. Bojadzijev and K. Klingan, pp. 120–32. Hamburg: Argument Verlag.

Koutrouvidis, S. 2018. 'Πολιτική Πασόκ και αγροτική πολιτική (1974–1990): Δύο ασύμβατες πορείες;', in *ΠΑΣΟΚ 1974–2018: Ιδεολογικές μετατοπίσεις – Κυβερνητικές πολιτικές*, ed. B. Asimakopoulos and C. Tassis, pp. 695–720. Athens: Gutenberg.

Koutsoukas, K. S., and I. D. Sakkas (eds). 2000. *Πτυχές του εμφυλίου πολέμου, 1946–1949*. Athens: Filistor.

Kouzinopoulos, S. 2011. *Δράμα 1941: Μια παρεξηγημένη εξέγερση*. Athens: Kastaniotis.

Kramer, M. 2014. 'Stalin, the Split with Yugoslavia, and Soviet-East European Efforts to Reassert Control, 1948–1953', in *Stalin and Europe: Imitation and Domination, 1928–1953*, ed. T. Snyder and R. Brandon, pp. 295–315. Oxford: Oxford University Press.

Kremmydas, T. G. 1984. *Οι άνθρωποι της χούντας μετά τη Δικτατορία*. Athens: Exantas.

Kreuter, P. M. 2015. 'The Flâneur of Salonica: The First Balkan War in the Private Correspondence of George I, King of the Hellenes with Fritz Peter Uldall (1847–1931)', in *Romanica et Balcanica*, ed. T. Kahl and J. Krammer, pp. 761–78. Munich: Akademische Verlagsgemeinschaft München.

Kulischer, E. M. 1948. *Europe on the Move: War and Population Changes, 1917–1947*. New York, NY: Columbia University Press.

Kuniholm, B. R. 1980. *The Origins of the Cold War in the Near East: Great Power Conflict and Diplomacy in Iran, Turkey and Greece*. Princeton, NJ: Princeton University Press.

Kuper, S. 2017. 'How Greeks Adjusted Forever to the Crisis'. *Financial Times*, 6 July 2017.

Kuromiya, H., and A. Peplonski. 2014. 'Stalin, Espionage, and Counterespionage', in *Stalin and Europe: Imitation and Domination, 1928–1953*, ed. T. Snyder and R. Brandon, pp. 73–91. Oxford: Oxford University Press.

Kyriopoulos, Y. (ed.). 2008. *Δημόσια υγεία και κοινωνική πολιτική: Ο Ελευθέριος Βενιζέλος και η εποχή του*. Athens: Papazisis.

Kyriopoulos, Y., and A. Karela. 2011. *Από την Υγειονομική Σχολή Αθηνών στην Εθνική Σχολή Δημόσιας Υγείας. Σύντομη Ιστορική Αναδρομή (1929–1994)*. Athens: Kastaniotis.

Laiou, A. E. 1987. 'Population Movements in the Greek Countryside during the Civil War', in *Studies in the History of the Greek Civil War, 1945–1949*, ed. L. Baerentzen, J. O. Iatrides and O. Smith, pp. 55–104. Copenhagen: Museum Tusculanum Press.

Laliotou, I. 2004. *Transatlantic Subjects: Acts of Migration and Cultures of Transnationalism between Greece and America*. Chicago: Chicago University Press.

Laliotou, I. 2005. 'The Greek Diaspora', in *Encyclopedia of Diasporas: Immigrant and Refugee Cultures around the World*, ed. C. R. Ember, M. Ember and I. Skoggard (eds), pp. 85–92. Dordrecht: Kluwer Academic Publishers.

Lambrianidis, L. 2011. *Επενδύοντας στη φυγή: Διαρροή Επιστημόνων από την Ελλάδα την Εποχή της Παγκοσμιοποίησης*. Athens: KritikiH.

Lambrianidis, L. 2014. 'Investing in Leaving: The Greek Case of International Migration of Professionals'. *Mobilities* 9.2, pp. 314–35.

Lambrianidis, L., and M. Pratsinakis. 2016. 'Greece's New Emigration at Times of Crisis', Hellenic Observatory Papers on Greece and Southeast Europe, GreeSE Paper No. 99, May 2016.

Lambrianidis, L., and M. Pratsinakis. 2016a. 'Outward Migration from Greece during the Crisis', Hellenic Observatory and London School of Economics. http://www.lse.ac.uk/europeanInstitute/research/hellenicObservatory/pubs/GreeSE.aspx (last accessed 6 July 2019).

Lambrinou, K. 2017. *ΕΔΑ, 1956–1967: Πολιτική και ιδεολογία*. Athens: Polis.

Lambropoulou, D. 1999. *Γράφοντας από τη φυλακή: Όψεις της υποκειμενικότητας των πολιτικών κρατουμένων, 1947–1960*. Athens: Nefeli.

Lambropoulou, D. 2009. *Οικοδόμοι: Οι άνθρωποι που έχτισαν την Αθήνα, 1950–1967*. Athens: Bibliorama.

Lampatos, G. 2001. *Έλληνες πολιτικοί πρόσφυγες στην Τασκένδη (1940–1957)*. Athens: Courier.

Lampsa, K., and I. Simbi. 2012. *Η Διάσωση: Η σιωπή του κόσμου, η αντίσταση στα γκέτο και τα στρατόπεδα, οι Έλληνες Εβραίοι στα χρόνια της Κατοχής*. Athens: Kapon.

Lappas, K. (ed.). 1999. *Η τελευταία ημέρα του έτους 1999: Ο φανταστικός κόσμος του 20ού αιώνα όπως περιγράφεται σε ένα κείμενο του τέλους του 19ου αιώνα*. Athens: Paraskinio.

Larrabee, F. S. 2005. 'Greece's Balkan Policy in a New Strategic Era'. *Journal of Southeast European and Black Sea Studies* 5.3 (Sept.), pp. 405–25.

Lawlor, S. 1994. *Churchill and the Politics of War, 1940–1941*. Cambridge: Cambridge University Press.

Lax, V. M. 2008. 'Must EU Borders Have Doors for Refugees? On the Compatibility of Schengen Visas and Carriers' Sanctions with EU Member States' Obligations to Provide International Protection to Refugees'. *European Journal of Migration and Law* 10, pp. 315–64.

Lazos, G. 2011. *Πορνεία και διεθνική σωματεμπορία στη σύγχρονη Ελλάδα: Η εκδιδόμενη*. Athens: Kastaniotis.

Lazou, V. 2016. *Η επιβολή του κράτους: Ο εμφύλιος πόλεμος στη Λαμία, 1945–1949*. Athens: Taxideftis.

Le Goff, J., and R. Chartier (ed.). 1978. *La nouvelle histoire*. Paris: Retz.

Le Goff, J., and P. Nora (eds). 1974. *Faire de l'histoire*. Paris: Gallimard.

Lecoeur, S. 2009. *Mussolini's Greek Island: Fascism and the Italian Occupation of Syros in World War II*. London: I. B. Tauris.

Leeper, R. 1950. *When Greek Meets Greek*. London: Chatto and Windus.

Leffler, M. P., and D. S. Painter (eds). 2005. *Origins of the Cold War: An International History*. New York, NY: Routledge.

Lehrman, H. 1946. 'Greece: "Unused Cakes of Soap": the Pattern of Jewish Fate Repeats Itself'. *Commentary* 1, pp. 48–52.

Leon, G. B. 1974. *Greece and the Great Powers, 1914–17*. Thessaloniki: IMXA.

Leontaritis, G. B. 1979. *Το ελληνικό σοσιαλιστικό κίνημα κατά τον πρώτο παγκόσμιο πόλεμο*, trans. S. Antiochos. Athens: Exantas.

Leontaritis, G. B. 2000. *Η Ελλάδα στον Πρώτο Παγκόσμιο Πόλεμο, 1917–1918*, trans. V. Oikonomidis. Athens: MIET.

Leontidou, L. 1990. *The Mediterranean City in Transition: Social Change and Urban Development*. Cambridge: Cambridge University Press.

Leontidou, L. 2001. *Πόλεις της σιωπής: Εργατικός εποικισμός της Αθήνας και του Πειραιά, 1909–1940*. Athens: Politistiki Idrima Omilou Peiraios.

Leontis, A. 1995. *Topographies of Hellenism: Mapping the Homeland*. Ithaca, NY: Cornell University Press.

Leontis, A. 2019. 'Street History: Coming to Terms with the Past in Occupy Movements', in *The Engaged Historian: Perspectives on the Intersections of Politics, Activism and the Historical Profession*, ed. S. Berger, pp. 261–77. New York, NY: Berghahn.

Leustean, L. 2010. 'Eastern Christianity and the Cold War: An Overview', in *Eastern Christianity and the Cold War, 1945–1991*, ed. L. Leustean, pp. 1–16. London and New York: Routledge.

Levene, M. 2013. *The Crisis of Genocide*, vol. 1: *Devastation: the European Rimlands, 1912–1938*. Oxford: Oxford University Press.

Liakos, A. 1985. *Η Σοσιαλιστική Εργατική Ομοσπονδία Θεσσαλονίκης (Φεντερασιόν) και η σοσιαλιστική νεολαία: Τα καταστατικά τους*. Thessaloniki: Paratiritis.

Liakos, A. 1993. 'Βαλκανική κρίση και εθνικισμός', in *Ο Ιανός του εθνικισμού και η ελληνική βαλκανική πολιτική*, ed. A. Elefantis and A. Liakos, pp. 9–30. Athens: Ο Πολίτης.

Liakos, A. 2004. 'Modern Greek Historiography (1974–2000): the Era of Transition from Dictatorship to Democracy', in *Writing History: Historiography in Southeastern Europe after Socialism*, ed. U. Brunbauer, pp. 351–78. Munster: LIT Verlag.

Liakos, A. 2005. 'Αντάρτες και συμμορίτες στα ακαδημαϊκά αμφιθέατρα', in *Η Ελλάδα '36–'49: Από τη Δικτατορία στον Εμφύλιο – Τομές και συνέχειες*, ed. H. Fleischer, pp. 25–36. Athens: Kastaniotis.

Liakos, A. 2008/9. 'History Wars: Notes from the Field'. *Yearbook of the International Society for the Didactics of History*, pp. 57–74.

Liakos, A. (ed.) 2011. *Το 1922 και οι πρόσφυγες: Μια νέα ματιά*. Athens: Nefeli.

Liakos, A. 2016. *Εργασία και πολιτική στην Ελλάδα του Μεσοπολέμου*. Athens: Nefeli.

Liakos, A. 2019. *Ο ελληνικός 20ος αιώνας*. Athens: Polis.

Lianos, T. P., and T. Kavounidi. 2012. *Μεταναστευτικά ρεύματα στην Ελλάδα κατά τον 20ό αιώνα*. Athens: Kentro Programmatismou kai Oikonomikou Erevnon.

Likos, M. 2018. 'Η ανάπτυξη των ελληνικών περιφερειών στο πλαίσιο της ευρωπαϊκής ολοκλήρωσης', in *Ελλάδα και Ευρωπαϊκή Ενοποίηση: Η Ιστορία μιας Πολυκύμαντης σχέσεις*, ed. N. Maravegias and T. Sakellaropoulos, pp. 191–208. Athens: Dionikos.

Lim, P. J. 2018. *The Evolution of British Counter-Insurgency during the Cyprus Revolt, 1955–1959*. Cham, Switzerland: Springer.

Limnios-Sekeris, I. 2015. 'Stakeholders and Competition in the Transportation of Migrants: Moving Greeks to Australia in the Post-War Era'. *Journal of Transport History* 36.1, pp. 97–115.

Linz, J. J., and A. Stepan. 1996. *Problems of Democratic Transition and Consolidation: Southern Europe, South America, and Post-Communist Europe*. Baltimore: Johns Hopkins University Press.

Llewellyn Smith, M. 1998. *Ionian Vision: Greece in Asia Minor 1919–1922*, 2nd ed. Ann Arbor: University of Michigan Press.

Loizos, P., and C. Constantinou. 2007. 'Hearts, as Well as Minds: Wellbeing and Illness among Greek Cypriot Refugees'. *Journal of Refugee Studies* 20.1, pp. 86–107.

López, M. A. M. (ed.). 2018. *The Urban Politics of Squatters' Movements*. New York, NY: Palgrave Macmillan.

Louis, W. R. 1984. *The British Empire in the Middle East, 1945–1951: Arab Nationalism, the United States and Postwar Imperialism*. Oxford: Oxford University Press.

Loukakos, P. 2013. *Η αθέατη όψη: Τύπος και πολιτική στη Μεταπολίτευση*. Athens: Estia. https://ec.europa.eu/regional_policy/archive/policy/future/pdf/8_manzella_final-for matted.pdf (last accessed 5 July 2019).

Lykogiannis, A. 2001. 'Why Did the "Varvaressos Experiment" Fail?'. *Journal of Modern Greek Studies* 19.1, pp. 117–42.

Maatsch, A., and A. Kurpiel. 2021. 'Between Collective and Particularistic Interests: Ratification of the Prespa Agreement by National Parliaments in Greece and North Macedonia'. *Southeast European and Black Sea Studies* 21.1, pp. 53–75.

Macar, O. D. 2013. 'Epidemic Diseases on the Thracian Front of the Ottoman Empire during the Balkan Wars', in *War and Nationalism: The Balkan Wars, 1912–1913, and Their Sociopolitical Implications*, ed. H. Yavuz and I. Blumi, pp. 272–97. Salt Lake City: University of Utah Press.

McCarthy, J. 1995. *Death and Exile: The Ethnic Cleansing of Ottoman Muslims, 1821–1922*. Princeton, NJ: Darwin.

Machado, B. F. 2007. *In Search of a Usable Past: The Marshall Plan and Postwar Reconstruction Today*. Lexington, VA: George C. Marshall Foundation.

Macherá, A. 2002. 'Ή Θεσσαλονίκη του Μεσοπολέμου', in *Ιστορία της Ελλάδας του 20ου αιώνα: 1922–1940 – Ο Μεσοπόλεμος*, ed. C. Hatziiosif, pp. 106–31. Athens: Bibliorama.

Mackridge, P. 2009. *Language and Identity in Greece, 1766–1976*. Oxford: Oxford University Press.

Mackridge, P., and E. Yannakakis (eds). 2004. *Contemporary Greek Fiction in a United Europe: From Local History to the Global Individual*. Oxford: Legenda.

McMeekin, S. 2015. *The Ottoman Endgame: War, Revolution, and the Making of the Modern Middle East, 1908–1923*. New York, NY: Penguin.

MacMillan, M. 2001. *The Peacemakers: the Paris Peace Conference of 1919 and Its Attempt to End War*. London: John Murray.

McNeill, W. H. 1947. *The Greek Dilemma: War and Aftermath*. Philadelphia and New York: J. B. Lippincott.

McNeill, W. H. 1957. *Greece: American Aid in Action, 1947–56*. New York, NY: Twentieth Century Fund.

McNeill, W. H. 1977. 'Greek Metamorphosis, 1945–1975'. *Bulletin of the American Academy of Arts and Sciences* 30.7 (April), pp. 11–20.

McNeill, W. H. 1978. *The Metamorphosis of Greece since World War II*. Chicago: Chicago University Press.

Maier, C. S. 1987. *In Search of Stability: Explorations in Historical Political Economy*. Cambridge: Cambridge University Press.

Maier, C. S. 2016. *Once within Borders: Territories of Power, Wealth and Belonging since 1500*. Cambridge, MA: Harvard University Press.

Mallinson, W. 2009. *Cyprus: A Modern History*. London: I. B. Tauris.

Maloutas, T. (ed.). 2000. *Κοινωνικός και Οικονομικός Άτλας της Ελλάδας*, vol. 1: *Οι πόλεις*, Athens: EKKE.

Maloutas, T., D. Emmanouil and M. Pantelidou-Malouta. 2006. *Αθήνα – Κοινωνικές δομές, πρακτικές και αντιλήψεις: Νέες παράμετροι και τάσεις μεταβολής 1980–2000. Ερευνητικό πρόγραμμα 'Κοινωνικές προϋποθέσεις για την αειφόρο ανάπτυξη της Αθήνας – Αττικής'*. Athens: EKKE.

Maloutas, T., D. Emmanouil, E. Zakopoulou and P. Kaftantzoglou (eds). 2008. *Κοινωνικοί και Χωρικοί Μετασχηματισμοί στην Αθήνα του 21ου αιώνα*. Athens: EKKE.

Manitakis, N., and S. Jollivet (ed.). 2018. *Ματαρόα, 1945: Από τον μύθο στην ιστορία*. Athens: Asini.

Mann, M. 2005. *The Dark Side of Democracy: Explaining Ethnic Cleansing*. Cambridge: Cambridge University Press.

Manomi, K., and L. Istikopoulou. 2006. *Σωματειακή οργάνωση του ελληνισμού στη Μικρά Ασία (1861–1922)*. Athens: Estia.

Manousakis, B. 2014. *Οικονομία και Πολιτική στην Ελλάδα του Β΄ Παγκοσμίου πολέμου*. Doctoral dissertation, ΑΠΘ.

Manousakis, B., and M. Chronakis. 2019. *Στο νότιο προπύργιο του Ράιχ': Ο απολογιστικός φάκελος του γερμανικού οικονομικού επιτελείου για την Ελλάδα της Κατοχής*. Iraklion: PEK.

Mansel, P. 2010. *Levant: Splendor and Catastrophe in the Mediterranean*. New Haven, CT: Yale University Press.

Manta, E. 2004. *Οι μουσουλμάνοι τσάμηδες της Ηπείρου (1923–2000)*. Thessaloniki: IMXA.

Mantzaris, E. A. 1999. 'The Greeks in South Africa', in *The Greek Diaspora in the Twentieth Century*, ed. R. Clogg, pp. 120–36. Basingstoke: Macmillan.

Manzella, G. P., and C. Mendez. 2009. *The Turning Points of EU Cohesion Policy: Working Paper Report to Barca Report*. Brussels: European Policies Research Centre and University of Strathclyde.

Marantzidis, N. 2001. *Γιασασίν Μιλλέτ: Ζήτω το Έθνος. Προσφυγιά, κατοχή και εμφύλιος – Εθνοτική ταυτότητα και πολιτική συμπεριφορά στους τουρκόφωνους ελληνορθόδοξους του Δυτικού Πόντου*. Iraklion: PEK.

Marantzidis, N. (ed.). 2006. *Οι άλλοι καπετάνιοι: Αντικομμουνιστές ένοπλοι στα χρόνια της Κατοχής και του Εμφυλίου*. Athens: Estia.

Margaritis, G. 1999. 'Οι Πόλεμοι', in *Ιστορία της Ελλάδος του 20ού αιώνα*, vol. 1: *1900–1922, Οι Απαρχές*, ed. C. Hatziiosif, pp. 149–87. Athens: Bibliorama.

Margaritis, G. 2001. *Ιστορία του ελληνικού εμφυλίου πολέμου 1946–1949*, vol. 1. Athens: Bibliorama.

Margaritis, G. 2005. *Ανεπιθύμητοι συμπατριώτες: Στοιχεία για την καταστροφή των μειονοτήτων της Ελλάδας – Εβραίοι, Τσάμηδες*. Athens: Bibliorama.

Margaritis, G. 2009. *Προαγγελία θυελλωδών ανέμων … Ο πόλεμος στην Αλβανία και η πρώτη περίοδος της Κατοχής*. Athens: Bibliorama.

Marketos, S. 2000. *Ο Αλέξανδρος Παπαναστασίου και η εποχή του: Αντινομίες του μεταρρυθμιστικού σοσιαλισμού*. Doctoral dissertation, EKPA.

Marketos, S. 2006. *Πώς φίλησα τον Μουσολίνι, τα πρώτα βήματα του ελληνικού φασισμού*. Athens: Bibliorama.

Markides, D., and G. S. Georghallides. 1995. 'British Attitudes to Constitution-Making in Post-1931 Cyprus'. *Journal of Modern Greek Studies* 13.1, pp. 63–81.

Markopoulos, I., K. C. Miris and N. Xilouris. 1972. *Ithageneia*. Athens: Columbia.

Markwick, R., and N. Doumanis. 2016. 'The Nationalisation of the Masses', in *The Oxford Handbook for European History 1914–1945*, ed. N. Doumanis, pp. 365–87. Oxford: Oxford University Press.

Maroufof, M. A. 2009. 'Polish Immigrants in Greece'. *Hellenic Foundation for European and Foreign Policy (ELIAMEP)*, July. https://www.eliamep.gr/wp-content/uploads/en/2009/10/michaela_maroufof_polish-migration_en_july091.pdf (last accessed 13 August 2019).

Marsot, A. L. A.-S. 2007. *A History of Egypt: from the Arab Conquest to the Present*, 2nd ed. Cambridge: Cambridge University Press.

Martin, T. D. 2001. *Affirmative Action Empire: Nations and Nationalism in the Soviet Union, 1923–1939*. Ithaca, NY: Cornell University Press.

Marwick, A. 1998. *The Sixties: Cultural Revolution in Britain, France, Italy, and the United States, c. 1958–c. 1974*. Oxford: Oxford University Press.

Marwick, A. 2005. 'The Cultural Revolution of the Long Sixties: Voices of Reaction, Protest, and Permeation'. *International History Review* 27.4 (Dec.), pp. 780–806.

Matthaiou, A., and P. Polemi. 2003. *Η εκδοτική περιπέτεια των ελλήνων κομμουνιστών: Από το βουνό στην υπερορία, 1947–1968*. Athens: Bibliorama and ASKI.

Matthiopoulos, E. 2003. 'Η ιστορία της τέχνης στα όρια του έθνους', in *Η ιστορία της τέχνης στην Ελλάδα: Πρακτικά Α΄ Συνεδρίου Ιστορίας της Τέχνης, Πανεπιστήμιο Κρήτης, Ρέθυμνο, 6–8 Οκτωβρίου 2000*, ed. E. Matthiopoulos and N. Chatzinikolaou, pp. 419–75. Iraklion: PEK.

Matthiopoulos, E. 2003a. 'Οι εικαστικές τέχνες κατά την περίοδο 1922–1940', in *Ιστορία της Ελλάδος του 20ού αιώνα*, vol. 1: *1900–1922, Οι Απαρχές*, ed. C. Hatziiosif, pp. 400–59. Athens: Bibliorama.

Mavrogordatos, G. T. 1983. *Stillborn Republic: Social Coalitions and Party Strategies in Greece, 1922–1936*. Berkeley: University of California Press.

Mavrogordatos, G. T. 1996. *Εθνικός διχασμός και μαζική οργάνωση: Οι Επίστρατοι του 1916*. Athens: Alexandreia.

Mavrogordatos, G. T. 2015, 1915. *Ο εθνικός διχασμός*. Athens: Pataki.

Mavrogordatos, M., and A. Chamoudopoulos. 1931. *Η Μακεδονία: Μελέτη δημογραφική και οικονομική*. Thessaloniki: Papadopoulou-Marinelii.

Mavromatis, G., and K. Tsitselikis. 2004. 'Η εκπαίδευση των μεταναστών στην Ελλάδα (1990–2003): Πολιτικές και πρακτικές', in *Η Ελλάδα της Μετανάστευσης: Κοινωνική συμμετοχή, δικαιώματα και ιδιότητα του πολίτη*, ed. M. Pavlou and D. Christopoulou, pp. 121–40. Athens: Kritiki.

Mayer, A. J. 1981. *The Persistence of the Old Regime: Europe to the Great War*. New York, NY: Pantheon.

Mayer, M., and C. Thörn (eds). 2016. *Urban Uprisings: Challenging Neoliberal Urbanism in Europe*. Basingstoke: Palgrave Macmillan.

Maynard, A. 1989. 'Misery of Lost Souls on Holiday Island'. *Health Service Journal* 99, p. 1213.

Mazower, M. 1991. *Greece and the Inter-War Economic Crisis*. Oxford: Oxford University Press.

Mazower, M. 1993. *Inside Hitler's Greece: the Experience of Occupation, 1941–1944*. New Haven, CT: Yale University Press.

Mazower, M. 1998. *Dark Continent: Europe's Twentieth Century*. London: Penguin.

Mazower, M. 1999. 'Structures of Authority in the Greek Resistance, 1941–1944', in *Opposing Fascism: Community, Authority and Resistance in Europe*, ed. T. Kirk and A. McElligott (eds), pp. 120–3. Cambridge: Cambridge University Press.

Mazower, M. 2000. *After the War Was Over: Reconstructing the State, Family and the Law in Greece, 1943–1960*. Princeton, NJ: Princeton University Press.

Mazower, M. 2000a. *The Balkans*. London: Weidenfeld and Nicolson.

Mazower, M. 2000b. 'The Cold War and the Appropriation of Memory: Greece after the Liberation', in *The Politics of Retribution in Europe: World War II and Its Aftermath*, ed. I. Deak, J. T. Gross and T. Judt, pp. 212–32. Princeton, NJ: Princeton University Press.

Mazower, M. 2004. *Salonica, City of Ghosts: Christians, Muslims and Jews, 1430–1950*. New York, NY: Knopf.

Mazower, M. 2008. *Hitler's Empire: Nazi Rule in Occupied Europe*. London: Allen Lane.

Meinardus, R. 2002. 'Muslims', in *Minorities in Greece: Aspects of a Plural Society*, ed. R. Clogg, pp. 81–93. London: Hurst.

Merkouris, G. S. 1933. *Η ανεργία*. Athens.

Merritt, J. 1989. 'Europe's Guilty Secret'. *The Observer*, 10 September 1989.

Meyer, F. H. 2002. *From Vienna to Kalavryta: the Bloody Trail of the 117th Jäger Division through Serbia and Greece*. Mannheim: Bibliopolis.

Meyer, F. M. 1999. *Kommeno: Narrative Reconstruction of a Wehrmacht Crime in Greece*. Cologne: Romiosini.

Meynaud, J. 1974. *Πολιτικές δυνάμεις στην Ελλάδα*, in collaboration with P. Merlopoulos and G. Notaras, trans. P. Merlopoulos. Athens: Bavron.

Meynaud, J. 2002. *Οι πολιτικές δυνάμεις στην Ελλάδα: Βασιλική εκτροπή και στρατιωτική δικτατορία*, vol. 2, trans. P. Merlopoulos. Athens: Savvalas.

Michailidis, I. D. 2003. *Μετακινήσεις σλαβόφωνων πληθυσμών (1912–1930): Ο πόλεμος των στατιστικών*. Athens: Kritiki.

Michailidis, I. D. 2017. *Παιδιά του Οδυσσέα: Έλληνες πρόσφυγες στη Μέση Ανατολή και στην Αφρική (1941–1946)*. Athens: Metaichmio.

Middle East Journal 1966. 'President Johnson and Prime Minister Inonu: Correspondence between President Johnson and Prime Minister Inonu, June 1964, as Released by the White House, January 15, 1966'. *Middle East Journal* 20.3, pp. 386–93.

Middleton, R. 2016. 'The Great Depression in Europe', in *The Oxford Handbook of Europe 1914–1945*, ed. N. Doumanis, pp. 179–206. Oxford: Oxford University Press.

Migdal, J. S. 1988. *Strong Societies and Weak States: State–Society Relations and State Capabilities in the Third World*. Princeton, NJ: Princeton University Press.

Mikanowski, J. 2012. 'Dr Hirszfeld's War: Tropical Medicine and the Invention of Sero-Anthropology on the Macedonian Front'. *Social History of Medicine* 25.1 (Feb.), pp. 103–21.

Miller, J. E. 2009. *The United States and the Making of Modern Greece: History and Power 1950–1974*. Chapel Hill: University of North Carolina Press.

Milton, G. 2008. *Paradise Lost: Smyrna 1922*. London: Hodder and Stoughton.

Mina, N. 2015. *Homeland Activism, Public Performance, and the Construction of Identity: an Examination of Greek Canadian Transnationalism, 1900s–1990s*. Doctoral dissertation, University of Toronto.

Mitsopoulos, T. 1987. *Το 30ό Σύνταγμα του ΕΛΑΣ*. Athens: Odysseas.

Moisis, A. P. 2011. *Κληροδότημα: Επιλογή από μελετήματα του Έλληνα-Εβραίου ηγέτη και συγγραφέα με εισαγωγή και σχόλια από το γιο του*. Athens: Rafail Mouisis.

Molho, R. 2001. *Οι Εβραίοι της Θεσσαλονίκης, 1856–1919: Μια ιδιαίτερη κοινότητα*. Athens: Themelio.

Morack, E. 2017. *The Dowry of the State? The Politics of Abandoned Property and the Population Exchange in Turkey, 1921–1945*. Bamberg: University of Bamberg Press.

Morack, E. 2017a. 'Fear and Loathing in "Gavur" Izmir: Emotions in Early Republican Memories of the Greek Occupation (1919–22)'. *International Journal of Middle East Studies* 49, pp. 71–89.

Morgan, T. 2010. *Sweet and Bitter Island: a History of the British in Cyprus*. London: I. B. Tauris.

Moses, J. 2016. 'Social Policy, Welfare, and Social Identities, 1900–1950', in *The Oxford Handbook of European History 1914–1945*, ed. N. Doumanis, pp. 323–42. Oxford: Oxford University Press.

Moskos, C. 1990. *Greek Americans: Struggle and Success*, 2nd ed. New Brunswick, NJ: Transaction Publishers.

Moskos, C. 2000. 'The Greeks in the United States', in *The Greek Diaspora in the Twentieth Century*, ed. R. Clogg, pp. 103–19. Basingstoke: Palgrave Macmillan.

Mourelos, G. G. 1990. 'Πληθυσμιακές ανακατατάξεις την επομένη των Βαλκανικών Πολέμων: Η πρώτη απόπειρα Ανταλλαγής των Πληθυσμών ανάμεσα στην Ελλάδα και την Τουρκία', in *Πρακτικά Συμποσίου: Η Συνθήκη του Βουκουρεστίου και η Ελλάδα. 75 χρόνια από την απελευθέρωση της Μακεδονίας, Θεσσαλονίκη, 16–18 Νοεμβρίου 1988*, pp. 175–90. Thessaloniki: IMXA.

Mouriki, A. 2010. 'Το "νέο προλεταριάτο": Οι επισφαλώς εργαζόμενοι – οι παρίες της σύγχρονης αγοράς εργασίας', in *Το κοινωνικό πορτραίτο της Ελλάδας 2010*, ed. M. Naoumi and G. Papapetrou, pp. 109–21. Athens: EKKE.

Mouzelis, N. 1978. *Νεοελληνική κοινωνία, όψεις υπανάπτυξης*. Athens: Exantas.

Mouzelis, N. 1987. *Κοινοβουλευτισμός και εκβιομηχάνιση στην ημι-περιφέρεια: Ελλάδα, Βαλκάνια, Λατινική Αμερική*. Athens: Themelio.

Mouzelis, N. 2009. 'On the December Events', in *The Return of Street Politics? Essays on the December Riots in Greece*, ed. S. Economides and V. Monastiriotis, pp. 41–4. London: LSE, The Hellenic Observatory.

Moysis, A. 2011. *Κληροδότημα*. Athens: Rafael Moysis.

Müller, J.-W. 2011. *Contesting Democracy: Political Ideas in the Twentieth Century*. New Haven, CT: Yale University Press.

Myers, E. C. W. 1955. *Greek Entanglement*. London: Hart-Davis.

Mylonas, H. 2012. *The Politics of Nation-Building: Making Co-Nationals, Refugees, and Minorities*. New York, NY: Cambridge University Press.

Naar, D. E. 2016. *Jewish Salonica: Between the Ottoman Empire and Modern Greece*. Stanford, CA: Stanford University Press.

Naar, D. E. 2020. 'The Boundaries of Hellenism: Language and Loyalty among Salonican Jewry, 1917–1933', in *Thessaloniki: A City in Transition, 1912–2012*, ed. D. Keridis and J. B. Kiesling, pp. 154–68. Abingdon and New York: Routledge.

Nachmani, A. 1990. *International Intervention in the Greek Civil War: the United Nations Special Committee on the Balkans, 1947–1952*. New York, NY: Praeger Publishers.

Nachmani, A. 1993. 'Mirror Images: the Civil Wars in China and Greece'. *Journal of the Hellenic Diaspora* 19.1, pp. 71–112.

Natzari, M. 2018. *Χειρόγραφα 1944–1977: Από τη Θεσσαλονίκη στο Ζόντερκομάντο του Άουσβιτς*. Athens: Alexandreia.

Neocleous, G. 2019. *Social Insurance and Older People in Cyprus*. Cham, Switzerland: Springer.

Neofotistos, V. P. (ed.). 2021. *Macedonia and Identity Politics after the Prespa Agreement*. London and New York: Routledge.

Neuwirth, R. 2012. *Stealth of Nations: the Global Rise of the Informal Economy*. New York, NY: Anchor Books.

Nikolaidis, L. 1954. 'Το ελληνικόν πρόγραμμα ανασυγκροτήσεως και η προβολή του εις το εξωτερικόν'. *Σπουδαί* 4.4, pp. 257–68.

Nikolakakis, M. 2017. *'Μοντέρνα Κίρκη': Τουρισμός και ελληνική κοινωνία την περίοδο 1950–1974*. Athens: Alexandreia.

Nikolakopoulos, I. 1990. 'Η εκλογική επιρροή των πολιτικών δυνάμεων', in *Εκλογές και Κόμματα στη Δεκαετία του '80: Εξελίξεις και προοπτικές του πολιτικού συστήματος*, ed. C. Linintzis and I. Nikolakopoulos, pp. 203–37. Athens: Themelio.

Nikolakopoulos, I. 2001. *Η καχεκτική δημοκρατία: Κόμματα και εκλογές, 1946–1967*. Athens: Patakis.

Nikolakopoulos, I. 2003. 'Ελεγχόμενη Δημοκρατία: από το τέλος του Εμφυλίου έως τη

Δικτατορία', in *Ιστορία του Νέου Ελληνισμού 1770–2000*, vol. 9, ed. V. Panagiotopoulos, pp. 9–47. Athens: Ellinika Grammata.

Nikolakopoulos, I. 2005. 'Η εκλογική επιρροή της κομμουνιστικής Αριστεράς, 1936–1951: Συνέχειες και ασυνέχειες', in *Η Ελλάδα '36–'49: Από τη Δικτατορία στον Εμφύλιο – Τομές και συνέχειες*, ed. H. Fleischer, pp. 223–34. Athens: Kastaniotis.

Nikolakopoulos, I. 2017. *Ηλίας Ηλιού: Πολιτική Βιογραφία*. Athens: Hellenic Parliament.

Nikolakopoulos, I., and A. Rigos (eds). 2002. *Ο Εμφύλιος Πόλεμος: Από τη Βάρκιζα στο Γράμμο, Φεβρουάριος 1945–Αύγουστος 1949, Συνέδριο του Πανεπιστημίου Αθηνών, του Παντείου Πανεπιστημίου του Ιόνιου Πανεπιστημίου και της ΕΔΙΑ, Πάντειο Πανεπιστήμιο, 20–23 Οκτωβρίου 1999*. Athens: Themelio.

Oakley, R. 1987. *Changing Patterns of Distribution of Greek Cypriot Settlement*. Coventry: Centre for Research in Ethnic Relations, University of Warwick.

Obama, B. 2020. *A Promised Land*. London: Allen Lane.

Ogle, V. 2017. 'Archipelago Capitalism: Tax Havens, Offshore Money, and the State, 1950s–1970s'. *American Historical Review* 122.5 (Dec.), pp. 1431–58.

Oikonomou, G. 2018. 'Ευρωπαϊκή ολοκλήρωση και θεσμοί διακυβέρνησης στην Ελλάδα', in *Ελλάδα και Ευρωπαϊκή Ενοποίηση: Η Ιστορία μιας Πολυκύμαντης σχέσης*, ed. N. Maravegias and T. Sakellaropoulos, pp. 101–28. Athens: Dionikos.

Oikonomou, G., and K. Kalantzis. 2018. 'Ο προϋπολογισμός της Ευρωπαϊκής Ένωσης και οι χρηματικές ροές Ελλάδας–Ευρωπαϊκής Ένωσης', in *Ελλάδα και Ευρωπαϊκή Ενοποίηση: Η Ιστορία μιας Πολυκύμαντης σχέσης*, ed. N. Maravegias and T. Sakellaropoulos, pp. 128–58. Athens: Dionikos.

Orzoff, A. 2016. 'Interwar Democracy and the League of Nationals', in *The Oxford Handbook of European History 1914–1945*, ed. N. Doumanis, pp. 261–81. Oxford: Oxford University Press.

Ozil, A. 2013. *Orthodox Christians in the Late Ottoman Empire: a History of Communal Relations in Anatolia*. London and New York: Routledge.

Pachet, P. 1973. 'World War One and the Interpretation of Freud's Concept of the Event'. *Comparative Literature* 88.6, pp. 1316–25.

Pagoulatos, G. 2006. *Η Εθνική Τράπεζα της Ελλάδος, 1940–2000*. Athens: Historical Archive of the National Bank of Greece.

Panayi, P. 2008. *Spicing Up Britain: the Multicultural History of British Food*. London: Reaktion.

Panikos P. 2014. 'Minorities', in *The Cambridge History of the First World War*, vol. 3: *Civil Society*, ed. J. Winter, pp. 216–41. Cambridge: Cambridge University Press.

Panourgiá, N. 2009. *Dangerous Citizens: the Greek Left and the Terror of the State*. New York, NY: Fordham University Press.

Panourgiá, N. 2018. 'New-Poor: the Being, the Phenomenon, and the Becoming in "Greek Crisis"', in *Critical Times in Greece: Anthropological Engagements with the Crisis*, ed. D. Dalakoglou and G. Agelopoulos, pp. 132–47. London and New York: Routledge.

Panourgiá, N. 2019. *Λέρος: Η γραμματική του εγκλεισμού*. Athens: Nefeli.

Pantelakis, N. 1991. *Ο εξηλεκτρισμός της Ελλάδας (1889–1956)*. Athens: MIET.

Papachelas, A. 1998. *Ο βιασμός της ελληνικής δημοκρατίας: Ο αμερικανικός παράγων, 1947–1967*. Athens: Estia.

Papadakis, Y. 1998. 'Greek Cypriot Narratives of History and Collective Identity: Nationalism as a Contested Process'. *American Ethnologist* 25.2, pp. 149–65.

Papadatos-Anagnostopoulos, D. 2018. *Ο Μαυροκόκκινος Δεκέμβρης: Άκρα και Κέντρο στην εξέγερση του 2008 [πλήθος, ηγεμονία, στρατηγική]*. Athens: Topos.

Papadimitriou, D. I., and S. I. Seferiadis (eds). 2012. *Αθέατες όψεις της ιστορίας: Κείμενα αφιερωμένα στον Γιάνη Γιανουλόπουλο*. Athens: Asini.

Papadogiannis, N. 2015. *Militant around the Clock? Left-Wing Youth Politics, Leisure, and Sexuality in Post-dictatorship Greece, 1974–1981*. Oxford: Berghahn.

Papadopoulos, G. 1968. *Το πιστεύω μας*, vol. 1. Athens: Ekdosis Genikis Diefthinseos Typou.

Papadopoulou, A. 2004. 'Smuggling into Europe: Transit Migrants in Greece'. *Journal of Refugee Studies* 17.2, pp. 167–84.

Papadopoulou, A. 2016. 'The Implementation of the Hotspots in Italy and Greece'. https://www.ecre.org/wp-content/uploads/2016/12/HOTSPOTS-Report-5.12.2016.

Papailias, P. 2005. *Genres of Recollection: Archival Poetics and Modern Greece*. New York, NY: Palgrave Macmillan.

Papailias, P. 2017. '(Re)sounding Histories: On the Temporalities of the Media Event'. *Social Analysis* 61.1, pp. 86–101.

Papaioannou, G. 1976. *From Mars Hill to Manhattan: the Greek Orthodox in America under Athenagoras I*. Minneapolis, MN: Light and Life.

Papaioannou, S. S. 2012. *Balkan Wars between the Lines: Violence and Civilians in Macedonia, 1912–1918*. Doctoral dissertation, University of Maryland.

Papanikolaou, D. 2007. *Singing Poets: Literature and Popular Music in France and Greece*. Oxford: Legenda.

Papanikolaou, D. 2018. *Κάτι τρέχει με την οικογένεια: Έθνος, πόθος και συγγένεια την εποχή της κρίσης*. Athens: Patakis.

Papanikolaou, D. 2021. *Greek Weird Wave: a Cinema of Biopolitics*. Edinburgh: Edinburgh University Press.

Papanikolas, H. 1974. *Toll and Rage in a New Land: the Greek Immigrants in Utah*. Salt Lake City, UT: Utah State Historical Society.

Papanikolas, H. 1979. 'Greek Workers in the Intermountain West: the Early Twentieth Century'. *Byzantine and Modern Greek Studies* 5.1, pp. 187–215.

Papanikolas, Z. 1991. *Buried Unsung: Louis Tikas and the Ludlow Massacre*. Lincoln, NE: Nebraska University Press.

Papanikolopoulos, D. 2013. *Συλλογική δράση και δημοκρατία στην προδικτατορική Ελλάδα: Ο κύκλος διαμαρτυρίας του '60, Αθήνα*. Doctoral dissertation, Panteion University.

Papanikolopoulos, D. 2019. 'Σύριζα και κοινωνικά κινήματα: Η σχέση, ο γάμος, η διάσταση', in *Σύριζα, ένα κόμμα εν κινήσει*, ed. Y. Balambanidis, pp. 121–41. Athens: Themelio.

Papari, K. 2017. *Ελληνικότητα και αστική διανόηση στον Μεσοπόλεμο: Το πολιτικό πρόγραμμα των Π. Κανελλόπουλου, Ι. Θεοδωρακόπουλου και Κ. Τσάτσου*. Athens: Asini.

Paparrigopoulos, C. 1878. *Histoire de la civilisation hellénique*. Paris: Librairie Hachette.

Papastratis, P. 2000. 'Purging the University after Liberation', in *After the War Was Over: Reconstructing the Family, Nation and State in Greece 1943–1960*, ed. M. Mazower, pp. 62–72. Princeton, NJ: Princeton University Press.

Papastratis, P., M. Limperatos and L. I. Sarafi (eds). 2018. *Από την Απελευθέρωση στα Δεκεμβριανά: Μια τομή στην πολιτική ιστορία της Ελλάδας*. Athens: Sygchroni Elliniki Istoria.

Papataxiarchis, E. 2016. 'Being "There": at the Front Line of the "European Refugee Crisis" – Part 1'. *Anthropology Today* 32.2, pp. 5–9.

Papataxiarchis, E. 2016a. 'Unwrapping Solidarity? Society Reborn in Austerity'. *Social Anthropology* 24, pp. 205–10.

Papathanasopoulos, S. 1993. *Απελευθερώνοντας την τηλεόραση*. Athens: Kastaniotis.

Papathanasopoulos, S. 1997. *Η Δύναμη της τηλεόρασης: Η λογική του μέσου και η αγορά*. Athens: Kastaniotis.

Papathanasopoulos, S. 2000. *Η τηλεόραση και το κοινό της*. Athens: Kastaniotis.

Papatheodorou, Y. 2010. 'Μαρτυρίες για την πολιτιστική ζωή στα χρόνια της Κατοχής και της Αντίστασης', in *Κατοχή – Αντίσταση, 1941–1944*, ed. H. Fleischer, pp. 181–97. Athens: Ta Nea.

Pappas, N. G. 1994. *Castellorizo: an Illustrated History of the Island and Its Conquerors*. Sydney: Halstead.

Parsanoglou, D. 2009. *Grèce, pays d'immigration: Perspectives historiques et sociologiques*. Doctoral dissertation, École des hautes études en sciences sociales.

Paschalidis, G. 2018. 'Το χαμένο παράδειγμα της ελληνικής τηλεόρασης', in *50 Χρόνια Ελληνικής Τηλεόρασης*, ed. V. Vamvakas and G. Paschalidis, pp. 9–41. Thessaloniki: Epikentro.

Patrikiou, A. 2012. 'Να φύγουν: Οι Εβραίοι ως εχθροί της Νέας Ευρώπης στον κατοχικό Τύπο της Θεσσαλονίκης, 1941–43', in *Αθέατες όψεις της ιστορίας: Κείμενα αφιερωμένα στον Γιάνη Γιανουλόπουλο*, ed. D. I. Papadimitriou and S. I. Seferiadis, pp. 245–58. Athens: Asini.

Pekesen, B. 2012. 'Expulsion and Emigration of the Muslims from the Balkans'. *European History Online (EGO)*, 3 July 2012. http://www.ieg-ego.eu/pekesenb-2011-en (last accessed 16 June 2019).

Pelagidis, T. (ed.). 2005. *Η εμπλοκή των μεταρρυθμίσεων στην Ελλάδα: Μια αποτίμηση του εκσυγχρονισμού*. Athens: Papazisis.

Peloni, A. 2010. *Ιδεολογία κατά ρεαλισμού: Η αμερικανική πολιτική απέναντι στην Ελλάδα, 1963–1976*. Athens: Polis.

Peri, M., M. Herzfeld and S. Barberani (eds). 2009. *La politica culturale del fascismo nel Dodecaneso*. Padua. Esedra Editrice.

Perrier, F. 2019. *Alexis Tsipras: Une histoire grecque*. Paris: Les Pérégrines.

Peterson, P. 2009. *The Education of an American Dreamer: How a Son of Greek Immigrants Learned His Way from a Nebraska Diner to Washington, Wall Street, and Beyond*. New York and Boston: Twelve.

Petmezas, S. D. 1999. 'Αγροτική Οικονομία', in *Ιστορία της Ελλάδος του 20ού αιώνα*, vol. 1: *1900–1922, Οι Απαρχές*, ed. C. Hatziiosif, pp. 52–85. Athens: Bibliorama.

Petmezas, S. D. 2002. 'Αγροτική Οικονομία', in *Ιστορία της Ελλάδος του 20ού αιώνα*, vol. 2: *1922–1940, Ο Μεσοπόλεμος*, ed. C. Hatziiosif, pp. 189–249. Athens: Bibliorama.

Petmezas, S. D. 2012. *Προλεγόμενα στην ιστορία της ελληνικής αγροτικής οικονομίας του Μεσοπολέμου*. Athens: Alexandreia.

Petrakis, M. 2006. *The Metaxas Myth: Dictatorship and Propaganda in Greece*. London: I. B. Tauris.

Petropulos, J. A. 1978. 'The Modern Greek State and the Greek Past', in *Byzantina kai Metabyzantina*, vol. 1, ed. S. Vryonis, pp. 163–76. Malibou, CA: Undena Publications.

Petrov, B. 2007. 'Η πολιτική της Βουλγαρίας έναντι της Ελλάδας', in *Ιστορία της Ελλάδας του 20ου αιώνα*, vol. 3, ed. C. Hatziiosif, pp. 151–73. Athens: Bibliorama.

Philliou, C. 2010. *Biography of an Empire: Governing Ottomans in an Age of Revolution*. Berkeley, CA: University of California Press.

Piketty, T. 2014. *Capital in the 21st Century*, trans. A. Goldhammer. Cambridge, MA: Harvard University Press.

Piperoglou, A. 2018. '"Border Barbarisms", Albury 1902: Greeks and the Ambiguity of Whiteness'. *Australian Journal of Politics and History* 64.4, pp. 529–43.

Pipyrou, S. 2016. *The Grecanici of Southern Italy: Governance, Violence, and Memory Politics*. Philadelphia: University of Pennsylvania Press.

Plantzos, D. 2008. 'Archaeology and Hellenic Identity, 1896–2004: the Frustrated Vision'. https://ejournals.epublishing.ekt.gr/index.php/benaki/article/viewFile/179 69/16065.

Pleios, G., and C. A. Frangonikolopoulos. 2010. *Τα 'εθνικά θέματα' στη δίνη των ΜΜΕ: Το Μακεδονικό, οι Ελληνοτουρκικές Σχέσεις και το Κυπριακό στην τηλεόραση και τον Τύπο*. Athens: Sideris.

Ploumidis, S. 2011. *Έδαφος και μνήμη στα Βαλκάνια. Ο 'γεωργικός εθνικισμός' στην Ελλάδα και στη Βουλγαρία (1927–46)*. Athens: Patakis.

Ploumidis, S. 2016. *Τα μυστήρια της Αιγηίδος. Το μικρασιατικό ζήτημα στην ελληνική πολιτική (1891–1922)*. Athens: Estia.

Pohl, O. J. 1996. 'The Dispersal of the Crimean and Black Sea Greeks'. *Journal of the Hellenic Diaspora* 22.2, pp. 101–10.

Pohl, O. J. 2000. 'Stalin's Genocide against the "Repressed Peoples"'. *Journal of Genocide Research* 2.2, pp. 267–93.

Polian, P. 2004. *Against Their Will: the History and Geography of Forced Migration in the USSR*, trans A. Yastrzhembaska. Budapest: Central European Press.

Politakis, G. 2018. *The Post-war Reconstruction of Greece: a History of Economic Stabilisation and Development, 1944–1952*. New York, NY: Palgrave Macmillan.

Pophiades, I. 2013. 'Kyrillos III, 1916–33: Between Sophronios III and Kyrillos II', in *The Archbishops of Cyprus in the Modern Age: the Changing Role of the Archbishop-Ethnarch, Their Identities and Politics*, ed. A. Varnava and M. N. Michael, pp. 177–210. Newcastle upon Tyne: Cambridge Scholars.

Popov, A. 2010. 'Making Sense of Home and Homeland: Former Soviet Greeks' Motivations and Strategies for a Transnational Migrant Circuit'. *Journal of Ethnic and Migration Studies* 36.1, pp. 67–85.

Porter, P. 2008. *Ζητείται: Ένα θαύμα για την Ελλάδα. Ημερολόγιο ενός προεδρικού απεσταλμένου (1947)*, trans. N. Kioseglou. Athens: Metamesonikties Ekdoseis.

Potamianos, N. 2016. *Οι νοικοκυραίοι: Μαγαζάτορες και βιοτέχνες στην Αθήνα, 1880–1925*. Iraklion: PEK.

Poulis, K. 2019. *Απ' το αλέτρι στο smartphone: Συζητήσεις με τον πατέρα μου*. Athens: Melani.

Poulos, M. 2009. *Arms and the Woman: Just Warriors and Greek Feminist Identity*. New York, NY: Columbia University Press.

Pratsinakis, E. 2013. *Contesting National Belonging: an Established-Outsider Figuration on the Margins of Thessaloniki, Greece*. Doctoral dissertation, University of Amsterdam.

Prineas, P. 2006. *Katsehamos and the Great Idea: a True Story of Greeks and Australians in the Early Twentieth Century*. Sydney: Plateia.

Priovolos, Y. 2018. *Εθνικιστική 'αντίδραση' και Τάγματα Ασφαλείας: Εμφύλιος και αντικατοχικός πόλεμος, 1943–1944*. Athens: Patakis.

Pritchard, G. 2016. 'Power Relations during the Transition from Nazi to Non-Nazi Rule', in *The Oxford Handbook of European History 1914–1945*, ed. N. Doumanis, pp. 593–612. Oxford: Oxford University Press.

Prott, V. 2016. *The Politics of Self-Determination: Remaking Territories and National Identities in Europe, 1917–1923*. Oxford: Oxford University Press.

Psalidopoulos, M. 2014. *Ιστορία της Τράπεζας της Ελλάδος, 1928–2008: Από τράπεζα του κράτους εγγυήτρια της χρηματοπιστωτικής σταθερότητας.* Athens: Bank of Greece.

Psarras, D. 2012. *Η Μαύρη Βίβλος της Χρυσής Αυγής.* Athens: Polis.

Rajak, S. 2010. 'The Cold War in the Balkans, 1945–1956', in *The Cambridge History of the Cold War*, vol. 1: *Origins*, ed. M. P. Leffler and O. A. Westad, pp. 198–220. Cambridge: Cambridge University Press.

Ramsay, R. 1990. 'Banished to a Greek Island'. *Psychiatric Bulletin* 141, pp. 34–135.

Raptis, P. 1997. *Οι εκπαιδευτικές μεταρρυθμίσεις του μεσοπολέμου στην Ελλάδα (1917–1940).* Doctoral dissertation, Panteion University.

Reinhart, C. M., and C. Trebesch. 2015. 'The Pitfalls of External Dependence: Greece, 1829–2015', NBER Working Paper No. 21664. *The National Bureau of Economic Research.* https://www.nber.org/papers/w21664.pdf (1 October 2019).

Repousi, M. 2008. 'New History Textbooks in Greece: the Chronicle of an Ideological War on the National Past'. http://users.auth.gr/~marrep/html/intro/articles/Newper cent20Historyper cent20Booksper cent20inper cent20Greece.pdf.

Repousi, M. 2012. *Τα Μαρασλειακά, 1925–1927.* Athens: Polis.

Repousi, M., and A. Psara. 2017. *Ο φεμινισμός στα χρόνια της Μεταπολίτευσης, 1974–1990: Ιδέες, συλλογικότητες, διεκδικήσεις.* Athens: Hellenic Parliament.

Reynolds, D., and V. Petchatnov. 2018. *The Kremlin Letters: Stalin's Wartime Correspondence with Churchill and Roosevelt.* New Haven, CT: Yale University Press.

Ritsos, Y. 2001. *Δεκαοχτώ λιανοτράγουδα της πικρής πατρίδας (1968–1970).* Athens: Kedros.

Rittersporn, G. T. 2013. 'Terror and Soviet Legality, Police vs Judiciary, 1933–1940', in *The Anatomy of Terror: Political Violence under Stalin*, ed. J. Harris, pp. 176–90. Oxford: Oxford University Press.

Rizas, S. 2002. *Οι Ηνωμένες Πολιτείες, η δικτατορία των συνταγματαρχών και το Κυπριακό ζήτημα, 1967–1974.* Athens: Patakis.

Rizas, S. 2011. *Απ' την απελευθέρωση στον εμφύλιο.* Athens: Kastaniotis.

Rizas, S. 2015. *Το τέλος της Μεγάλης Ιδέας: Ο Βενιζέλος, ο αντιβενιζελισμός και η Μικρά Ασία.* Athens: Kastaniotis.

Rizas, S. 2016. *Παρατάξεις και κόμματα στη μεταπολεμική Ελλάδα.* Athens: Estia.

Robolis, S., and B. Betsis. 2016. *Η Οδύσσεια του Ασφαλιστικού.* Athens: Livanis.

Robson, L. 2020. *The Politics of Mass Violence in the Middle East.* Oxford: Oxford University Press.

Rodogno, D. 2006. *Fascism's European Empire: Italian Occupation during the Second World War.* Cambridge: Cambridge University Press.

Roshwald, A. 2016. 'Europe's Civil Wars, 1941–1949', in *The Oxford Handbook of European History 1914–1945*, ed. N. Doumanis, pp. 537–54. Oxford: Oxford University Press.

Rossi, E. A. 2016. *Cefalonia: La resistenza, l'eccidio, il mito.* Bologna: Il Mulino.

Rossos, A. 1997. 'Incompatible Allies: Greek Communism and Macedonian Nationalism in the Civil War in Greece, 1943–1949'. *Journal of Modern History* 69.3 (Mar.), pp. 42–76.

Rostow, W. W. 1960. *The Stages of Economic Growth: a Non-Communist Manifesto*. Cambridge: Cambridge University Press.

Roumanias, C., S. Skouras and N. Christodoulakis. 2020. 'Crisis and Extremism: How Does an Extreme Far Right Emerge in a Modern Democracy? Evidence from Greece's Golden Dawn'. *Journal of Elections, Public Opinion and Parties* 15.2, pp. 1–22.

Roussos, S. 2017. 'Greece and Regional Dynamics in the Eastern Mediterranean', in *Foreign Policy under Austerity*, ed. S. N. Litsas and A. Tziampiris, pp. 95–115. London: Palgrave Macmillan.

Rugaru, N. 2017. 'Contrasting Destinies: the Plight of Bulgarian Jews and the Jews in Bulgarian-Occupied Greek and Yugoslav Territories during World War Two'. Mass Violence and Resistance Network. https://www.sciencespo.fr/mass-violence-war-ma ssacre-resistance/en/document/contrasting-destinies-plight-bulgarian-jews-and-jews bulgarian-occupied-greek-and-yugoslav-.html.

St. Martin, K. 1984. *Λαμπράκηδες. Ιστορία μιας γενιάς*, trans. C. Dali. Athens: Polytipo.

Sajjad, T. 2018. 'What's in a Name? "Refugees", "Migrants" and the Politics of Labeling'. *Race and Class* 60.2 (Oct.), pp. 40–62.

Sakkas, J. 2000. 'The Civil War in Evrytania', in *After the War Was Over: Reconstructing the Family, Nation and State in Greece 1943–1960*, ed. M. Mazower, pp. 184–209. Princeton, NJ: Princeton University Press.

Saloutos, T. 1964. *The Greeks in the United States*. Cambridge, MA: Harvard University Press.

Saltiel, L. 2020. *The Holocaust in Thessaloniki: Reactions to the Anti-Jewish Persecution, 1942–1943*. New York and London: Routledge.

Salvanou, A. (ed.). 2016. *Από τα 3 σημεία του ορίζοντα: Ιστορίες ζωής προσφύγων και μεταναστών*. Athens: Fairead.

Salvanou, A. 2018. *Η συγκρότηση της προσφυγικής μνήμης: Το παρελθόν ως ιστορία και πρακτική*. Athens: Nefeli.

Samatas, M. 2015. 'Η πανοπτική ασφάλεια των Ολυμπιακών αγώνων μετά την 11η Σεπτεμβρίου 2001 και οι επιπτώσεις στις ατομικές και δημοκρατικές ελευθερίες', in *Κοινωνία και αθλητισμός στην Ελλάδα: Κοινωνιολογικές και ιστορικές προσεγγίσεις*, ed. Y. Zaimakis and E. Fournaraki, pp. 153–78. Athens: Alexandreia.

Samson, P. 2020. *A Theatre of Dreamers*. London: Bloomsbury.

Sánchez, A. C. 2010. *Fear and Progress: Ordinary Lives in Franco's Spain, 1939–1975*. Oxford: Wiley.

Sandbu, M. 2015. *Europe's Orphan: the Future of the Euro and the Politics of Debt*. Princeton, NJ: Princeton University Press.

Santarelli, L. 2004. 'Muted Violence: Italian War Crimes in Occupied Greece'. *Journal of Modern Italian Studies* 9.3, pp. 280–99.

Santarelli, L. 2005. *Guerra e occupazione italiana in Grecia 1940–1943*. Doctoral dissertation, Florence: European University Institute.

Sapir, A., P. Aghion, G. Bertola, M. Hellwig, J. Pisani-Ferry, D. Rosati, J. Viñals, H. Wallace, M. Buti, M. Nava and P. M. Smith (eds). 2004. *An Agenda for Growing Europe: the Sapir Report*. Oxford: Oxford University Press.

Sarantakos, D. (ed.). 2004. *Αιγαίο: Αρχιπέλαγος μαρτυρίων*. Athens: Etaireia Diasosis Istorikon Archeion kai Ypourgeion Aigaiou.

Sassen, S. 2006. *Territory, Authority, Rights: from Medieval to Global Assemblages*. Princeton, NJ: Princeton University Press.

Sassoon, D. 1996. *One Hundred Years of Socialism: the West European Left in the Twentieth Century*. London. I. B. Tauris.

Scheidel, W. 2017. *The Great Leveler: Violence and the History of Inequality from the Stone Age to the Twenty-First Century*. Princeton, NJ: Princeton University Press.

Schminck-Gustavus, C. U. 2008. *Μνήμες κατοχής*, vol. 2: *Ιταλοί και Γερμανοί στα Γιάννενα και η καταστροφή της εβραϊκής κοινότητας*, trans. A. Nettas and S. Georgallidi. Ioannina: Isnafi.

Schmitt, C. 1962. *Theory of a Partisan: an Interjection to the Concept of the Political*, trans. C. J. Miller. Albuquerque, NM: Antelope Hill.

Schmitt, K. 2007. *Theory of the Partisan: Intermediate Commentary on the Concept of the Political*, trans. G. L. Ulmen. London: Telos.

Schmitz, D. 2006. *The United States and Right-Wing Dictatorships, 1965–1989*. Cambridge: Cambridge University Press.

Schneider, V. 2019–21. Database of German Military and Paramilitary Units in Greece 1941–1944/45. http://www.eie.gr/nhrf/institutes/ihr/projects/GermanOccupationDatabase/GermanOccupationDatabase_en.html.

Schumpeter, J. A. 1943. *Capitalism, Socialism, and Democracy*, 6th ed. London and New York: George Allen and Unwin.

Seferis, G. 1992. *Dokimes*, vol. 1: *1936–1947*. Athens: Ikaros.

Seferis, G. 2014. *Ποιήματα*. Athens: Ikaros.

Sfikas, T. 1991. '"The People at the Top Can Do These Things, Which Others Can't Do": Winston Churchill and the Greeks, 1940–45'. *Journal of Contemporary History* 26.2, pp. 307–32.

Sfikas, T. 1997. *Οι Άγγλοι Εργατικοί και ο εμφύλιος πόλεμος στην Ελλάδα: Ο ιμπεριαλισμός της μη-επέμβασης*. Athens: Filistor.

Shepherd, B., and J. Pattinson (ed.). 2010. *War in a Twilight World: Partisan and Anti-Partisan Warfare in Eastern Europe, 1939–45*. London: Palgrave Macmillan.

Shubert, A. 1990. *A Social History of Modern Spain*. London and New York: Routledge.

Simiti, M. 2017. 'Civil Society and the Economy: Greek Civil Society during the Economic Crisis'. *Journal of Civil Society* 13.4, pp. 357–73.

Simitis, K. 2005. *Πολιτική για μια δημιουργική Ελλάδα, 1996–2004*. Athens: Polis.

Simitis, K. 2012. *Ο εκτροχιασμός*. Athens: Polis.

Sinadinos, P., and N. Choutas. 2016. *Ολυμπιακοί αγώνες 'Αθήνα 2004'. Αποτίμηση των επιπτώσεων των Αγώνων στην κοινωνία και την οικονομία μέσω κριτικής προσέγγισης: Αλήθειες και μύθοι*. Athens: Diethnis Olympiaki Akadimia.

Sissouras, A. 2012. *Τα μετέωρα βήματα του ΕΣΥ. Τριάντα χρόνια Εθνικού Συστήματος Υγείας: Ανάλυση της υλοποίησης και μαθήματα πολιτικής υγείας*. Athens: Kastaniotis.

Sjöberg, E. 2011. *Battlefields of Memory: the Macedonian Conflict and Greek Historical Culture*. Umeå: Department of Historical, Philosophical and Religious Studies, Umeå University.

Sjöberg, E. 2016. *The Making of the Greek Genocide: Contested Memories of the Ottoman Greek Catastrophe*. Oxford: Berghahn.

Skalidakis, Y. 2014. *Η ελεύθερη Ελλάδα: Η εξουσία του ΕΑΜ στα χρόνια της Κατοχής (1943–1944)*. Athens: Asini.

Skalieris, G. K. 1922. *Λαοί και φυλαί της Μικράς Ασίας: Μετά πινάκων και χαρτών*. Athens: Typografeion 'Typos'.

Sked, A. 2016. 'Belle Époque: Europe before 1914', in *The Oxford Handbook of European History 1914–1945*, ed. N. Doumanis, pp. 23–40. Oxford: Oxford University Press.

Sklavenitis, D. 2016. 'Κάτσε καλά, Γεράσιμε...': Μαθητικό κίνημα και καταλήψεις, 1974–2000. Athens: Asini.

Skliros, G. 1908. Το κοινωνικόν μας ζήτημα. Athens.

Skopetea, E. 1988. Το 'Πρότυπο Βασίλειο' και η Μεγάλη Ιδέα: Όψεις του εθνικού προβλήματος στην Ελλάδα (1830–1880). Athens: Polytypo.

Skopeteas, S. 2015. 'Caucasian Urums and Urum Language'. https://xn–uni-gttingen-8ib.academia.edu/StavrosSkopeteas?from_navbar=true.

Skoulariki, A. 2021. 'Political Polarisation in Greece: the Prespa Agreement, Left/Right Antagonism and the Nationalism/Populism Nexus'. *South European Society and Politics* 26.1, pp. 1–29.

Skouras, F., and A. Chatzidimos (eds). 1947, 1991. Η ψυχοπαθολογία της πείνας, του φόβου και του άγχους: Νευρώσεις και ψυχονευρώσεις. Athens: Καραβίας.

Smith, H. K. 1949. *The State of Europe*. New York, NY: Knopf.

Smith, O. 1993. '"The First Round": the Civil War during the Occupation', in *The Greek Civil War, 1943–1950*, ed. D. Close, pp. 58–72. London: Routledge.

Sotiropoulos, D. A. 2014. 'Civil Society in Greece in the Wake of Economic Crisis'. *Hellenic Foundation for European and Foreign Policy*. http://www.eliamep.gr/wp-content/uploads/2014/05/kas.pdf.

Souliotis, N. 2021. Οικονομολόγοι τεχνοκράτες στην ελληνική πολιτική σκηνή 1974–2019. Athens: Alexandreia.

Spiegel, P. 2014. 'Inside Europe's Plan Z: Financial Times Plan Z for Grexit'. *Financial Times*. https://www.ft.com/content/0ac1306e-d508-11e3-9187-00144feabdc0.

Spilioti, S.-S. 2000. '"An Affair, Not Justice": the Merten Trial (1957–59) and Greek–German Relations', in *After the War Was Over: Reconstructing the Family, Nation and State in Greece 1943–1960*, ed. M. Mazower, pp. 293–302. Princeton, NJ: Princeton University Press.

Stamatopoulos, D. 2006. 'From Millets to Minorities in the 19th-Century Ottoman Empire: an Ambiguous Modernization', in *Citizenship in Historical Perspective*, ed. S. G. Ellis, G. Hálfadanarson and A. K. Isaacs, pp. 253–73. Pisa: Pisa University Press.

Stamatopoulos, D. 2011. 'Η Μικρασιατική εκστρατεία: Η ανθρωπογεωγραφία της καταστροφής', in Το 1922 και οι πρόσφυγες, ed. A. Liakos, pp. 55–99. Athens: Nefeli.

Stanard, M. G. 2016. 'Interwar Crises and Europe's Unfinished Empire', in *The Oxford Handbook of European History, 1914–1945*, ed. N. Doumanis, pp. 223–40. Oxford: Oxford University Press.

Stathakis, G. 2004. Το δόγμα Τρούμαν και το σχέδιο Μάρσαλ: Η ιστορία της αμερικανικής βοήθειας στην Ελλάδα. Athens: Bibliorama.

Stavrakakis, Y., and G. Katsambekis. 2014. 'Left-Wing Populism in the European Periphery: the Case of SYRIZA'. *Journal of Political Ideologies* 19.2, pp. 119–42.

Stavrakakis, Y., and G. Katsambekis. 2019. 'The Populism/Anti-populism Frontier and Its Mediation in Crisis-Ridden Greece: from Discursive Divide to Emerging Cleavage?'. *European Political Science* 18.1, pp. 37–52.

Stavrakis, P. J. 1989. *Moscow and Greek Communism, 1944–1949*. Ithaca, NY: Cornell University Press.

Stavrianos, L. S. 1952. *Greece: American Dilemma and Opportunity*. Chicago: H. Regnery.

Stavrianos, L. S. 2000. *Balkans since 1453*. London: Hurst.

Stavridi-Patrikiou, R. (ed.). 1976. Δημοτικισμός και κοινωνικό πρόβλημα. Athens: Ermis.

Stavrou, M. 2009. *Resolving the Cyprus Conflict: Negotiating History*. New York, NY: Palgrave Macmillan.

Stefanidis, I. 2011. 'Δημοκρατία δυσχερής; Η ανάπτυξη των μηχανισμών του "αντικομμουνιστικού αγώνος" 1958–1961'. Μνήμων 29, pp. 199–241.

Stefanidis, I. D. 1999. *Isle of Discord: Nationalism, Imperialism and the Making of the Cyprus Problem*. New York, NY: New York University Press.

Steil, B. 2018. *The Marshal Plan: Dawn of the Cold War*. Oxford: Oxford University Press.

Stephenson, P. 2003. *The Legend of Basil the Bulgar-Slayer*. New York, NY: Cambridge University Press.

Sternberg, C., K. Gartzou-Katsouyanni and K. Nicolaidis. 2018. *The Greco-German Affair in the Euro Crisis: Mutual Recognition Lost?* Basingstoke: Palgrave Macmillan.

Stevenson, D. 2011. *With Our Backs to the Wall: Victory and Defeat in 1918*. Cambridge, MA: Belknap Press of Harvard University Press.

Stockings, C., and E. Hancock. 2013. *Swastika over the Acropolis: Re-interpreting the Nazi Invasion of Greece in World War II*. Leiden and Boston: Brill.

Storrs, R. 1937. *Orientations*. London: Nicholson and Watson.

Sutton, D. E. 1997. 'Local Names, Foreign Claims: Family Inheritance and National Heritage on a Greek Island'. *American Ethnologist* 24.2, pp. 415–37.

Sulzberger, C. L. 1970. *Foreign Affairs*, January 1970. https://www.foreignaffairs.com/ar ticles/europe/1970-01-01/greece-under-colonels (last accessed 1 May 2019).

Svoronos, N. 1975. *Επισκόπηση της νεοελληνικής ιστορίας*. Athens: Themelio.

Swain, G. 2011. *Tito: A Biography*. London: I. B. Tauris.

Syggelakis, A. I. 2018. 'Ενάντια στην παλίρροια του μονεταρισμού: Η τομή του ΕΣΥ ως ορόσημο του ανολοκλήρωτου εγχειρήματος οικοδόμησης κράτους πρόνοιας στην Ελλάδα', in *ΠΑΣΟΚ, 1974–2018: Πολιτική οργάνωση – Ιδεολογικές μετατοπίσεις – Κυβερνητικές πολιτικές*, ed. B. Asimakopoulos and C. Tassis, pp. 774–815. Athens: Gutenberg.

Synadinos, P., and N. Houtas. 2016. *Ολυμπιακοί αγώνες 'Αθήνα 2004'. Αποτίμηση των επιπτώσεων των Αγώνων στην κοινωνία και την οικονομία μέσω κριτικής προσέγγισης: Αλήθειες και Μύθοι*. Athens: International Olympics Academy.

Synarelli, M. 1989. *Δρόμοι και λιμάνια στην Ελλάδα 1830–1880, Αθήνα*. Piraeus: Bank Cultural Foundation.

Tata-Arsel, L. 2014. *Με το Διωγμό στην ψυχή: Το τραύμα της Μικρασιατικής Καταστροφής σε τρεις γενιές*. Athens: Kedros.

Telloglou, T. 2009. *Το Δίκτυο: Φάκελος Siemens*. Athens: SKAI Biblio.

Theodore, J., and J. Theodore. 2015. *Cyprus and the Financial Crisis: the Controversial Bailout and What It Means for the Eurozone*. New York and Basingstoke: Palgrave Macmillan.

Theodorou, V., and D. Karakatsani. 2010. *'Υγιεινής παραγγέλματα': Ιατρική επίβλεψη και κοινωνική πρόνοια για το παιδί τις πρώτες δεκαετίες του 20ού αιώνα*. Athens: Dionikos.

Theodossopoulos, D. 2013. 'Infuriated with the Infuriated? Blaming Tactics and Discontent about the Greek Financial Crisis'. *Current Anthropology* 54.2, pp. 200–10.

Theotokas, G. 1996. *Στοχασμοί και Θέσεις: Πολιτικά κείμενα 1925–1949*, vol. 1: *1925–1949*, ed. N. Alivizatos and M. Tsapogas. Athens: Estia.

Theotokas, G. 2005. *Τετράδια Ημερολογίου 1905–66*. Athens: Estia.

Therianos, K. 2018. 'Η εκπαιδευτική πολιτική του ΠΑΣΟΚ στη δευτεροβάθμια εκπαίδευση από το 1976 μέχρι το 2004', in *ΠΑΣΟΚ, 1974–2018: Πολιτική οργάνωση – Ιδεολογικές μετατοπίσεις – Κυβερνητικές πολιτικές*, ed. B. Asimakopoulos and C. Tassis, pp. 600–17. Athens: Gutenberg.

Thomas, E. 1918. *L'oeuvre civilisatrice de l'armée française en Macédoine*. Thessaloniki: L'Indépendant.

Todorova, M. 2009. *Imagining the Balkans*, 2nd ed. New York: Oxford University Press.

Tomara-Sideris, M. 2009. 'Women's Status in the Greek Colonies of Egypt', in *Women, Gender, and Diasporic Lives: Labor, Community and Identity in Greek Migrations*, ed. E. Tastsoglou, pp. 153–80. Lanham, MD: Lexington.

Tomka, A. 2013. *Social History of Europe in the Twentieth Century*. London and New York: Routledge.

Tontsef, P. (ed.). 2007. 'Ασιάτες Μετανάστες στην Ελλάδα: Προέλευση, Παρόν, Προοπτικές', *ΙΔΟΣ και Τμήμα Ασιατικών Σπουδών*, January 2007. http://idos.gr/wp-content/uploads/2015/12/Greek-Report-on-Asian-Migrants-13-2-07.pdf (last accessed 13 August 19).

Tooze, A. 2018. *Crashed: How a Decade of Financial Crises Changed the World*. New York, NY: Viking.

Topali, P. 2004. *Η έμμισθη οικιακή εργασία ως διαπολιτισμική σχέση: Η περίπτωση των Φιλιππινέζων οικιακών βοηθών στην Αθήνα*. Doctoral dissertation, University of the Aegean.

Tounta-Fergadi, A. 1986. *Το προσφυγικό δάνειο του 1924*. Thessaloniki: Paratiritis.

Toynbee, A. J. 1922. *The Western Question in Greece and Turkey: a Study in the Contact of Civilizations*. London, Boston and New York: Constable and Co. and Houghton Mifflin.

Trasokopoulou-Tzimou, K. 2020. 'The Care of Monuments in Modern Thessaloniki: Perceptions and Practices', in *Thessaloniki: a City in Transition, 1912–2012*, ed. D. Keridis and J. B. Kiesling, pp. 352–74. Abingdon and New York: Routledge.

Traverso, E. 2016. *Fire and Blood: the European Civil War, 1914–1945*, trans. D. Fernbach. London: Verso.

Tremopoulos, M. 2018. *Τα τρία Ε (ΕΕΕ) και ο εμπρησμός του Κάμπελ: Το πογκρόμ του 1931 στη Θεσσαλονίκη*. Thessaloniki: Antigone.

Triandafyllidou, A., and M. Maroufof (eds). 2009. 'Immigration towards Greece at the Eve of the 21st Century: a Critical Assessment', IDEA Working Papers, No. 9. *Hellenic Foundation for European and Foreign Policy (ELIAMEP)*, March 2009. http://www.eliamep.gr/wp-content/uploads/en/2009/10/idea_wp4_greece8.pdf (13 August 2019).

Triantopoulos, C. 2018. 'Οι εμπορικές σχέσεις της Ελλάδας με την Ευρωπαϊκή Ένωση', in *Ελλάδα και Ευρωπαϊκή Ενοποίηση: Η Ιστορία μιας Πολυκύμαντης σχέσης*, ed. N. Maravegias and T. Sakellaropoulos, pp. 179–80. Athens: Dionikos.

Tronti, M. 2010. 'Workerism and Politics'. *Historical Materialism* 18, pp. 186–9.

Trubeta, S. 2001. *Κατασκευάζοντας ταυτότητες για τους μουσουλμάνους της Θράκης: Το παράδειγμα των Πομάκων και των Τσιγγάνων*. Athens: Kritiki.

Trubeta, S. 2013. *Physical Anthropology, Race and Eugenics in Greece (1870s–1970s)*. Leiden: Brill.

Tsakas, C. 2018. 'Europeanisation under Authoritarian Rule: Greek Business and the Hoped-for Transition to Electoral Politics, 1967–1974'. *Business History* 62.4, pp. 686–709.

Tsarapatsanis, D. 2018. 'ΠΑΣΟΚ και φιλελευθερισμός (1974–1986): "Αντιφιλελεύθερος δημοκρατισμός" ή "φιλελεύθερος πλειοψηφισμός";', in *ΠΑΣΟΚ, 1974–2018: Πολιτική οργάνωση – Ιδεολογικές μετατοπίσεις – Κυβερνητικές πολιτικές*, ed. B. Asimakopoulos and C. Tassis, pp. 367–88. Athens: Gutenberg.

Tsaroucha-Szabo, E. 2006. 'Ουγγαρία' ['Hungary'], in *Οι Έλληνες στη Διασπορά, 15ος–21ος αι.*, ed. I. Hasiotis, O. Katsiardi-Hering and E. Abatzi, pp. 175–81. Athens: Hellenic Parliament.

Tsekeris, C., N. Kaberis and M. Pinguli. 2015. 'The Self in Crisis: the Experience of Personal and Social Suffering in Contemporary Greece', Hellenic Observatory Papers on Greece and Southeast Europe, June 2015, Paper No. 92.

Tsekou, K. 2013. *Έλληνες πολιτικοί πρόσφυγες στην Ανατολική Ευρώπη, 1945–1989.* Athens: Alexandreia.

Tsetlaka, A.-M., and T. Athanasiou-Marina. 2011. 'Η αντίστροφη πορεία: Οι μουσουλμάνοι πρόσφυγες', in *Το 1922 και οι πρόσφυγες: Μια νέα ματιά*, ed. A. Liakos, pp. 171–90. Athens: Nefeli.

Tsilaga, F. 2007. *The UNRRA Mission to Greece: the Politics of International Relief, October 1944–June 1947.* Doctoral dissertation, King's College London.

Tsili, S. 1995. *Η τοξικομανία ως ιδεολογικό διακύβευμα: Η περίπτωση της Ελλάδας.* Athens: EKKE.

Tsimas, P. 2014. *Ο φερετζές και το πηλήκιο: Το πολιτικό μυθιστόρημα της ελληνικής τηλεόρασης.* Athens: Metaichmio.

Tsirimokou, L. 2002. 'Αντιγόνη μασκοφόρος'. *Επτά Ημέρες της Καθημερινής*, 11 July 2002, pp. 8–9.

Tsitselikis, K. 2012. *Old and New Islam in Greece: from Traditional Minorities to Immigrant Newcomers.* Leiden and Boston: Martinus Nijhoff.

Tsotsoros, S. 1995. *Ενέργεια και ανάπτυξη στη μεταπολεμική περίοδο: Η Δημόσια Επιχείρηση Ηλεκτρισμού, 1950–1992.* Athens: Ethniko Idrima Erevnon.

Tsoucalas, K. 1977. *Εξάρτηση και αναπαραγωγή: Ο κοινωνικός ρόλος των εκπαιδευτικών μηχανισμών στην Ελλάδα (1830–1922).* Athens: Themelio.

Tsoucalas, K. 1981. *Η ελληνική τραγωδία.* Athens: Nea Sinora.

Tsoucalas, K. 1981a. *Κοινωνική ανάπτυξη και κράτος: Η συγκρότηση του δημόσιου χώρου στην Ελλάδα.* Athens: Themelio.

Tsoucalas, K. 1987. *Κράτος, κοινωνία, εργασία στη μεταπολεμική Ελλάδα.* Athens: Themelio.

Tsoukala, A. 2006. 'The Security Issue at the 2004 Olympics'. *European Journal for Sport and Society* 3.1, pp. 43–54.

Tsoukalis, L. 2013. 'International Bubbles, European Currency Union, and National Failures: the Case of Greece and the Euro-Crisis', in *The Greek Crisis and European Modernity*, ed. A. Triantafyllidou, R. Gropas and H. Kouki, pp. 25–43. London: Palgrave Macmillan.

Tsounis, M. 1971. *Greek Communities in Australia.* Doctoral dissertation, University of Adelaide.

Tsoutsoumpis, S. 2012. *Irregular Warfare in Occupied Greece 1941–1944: Masculinity and Morale in the British Special Operations Executive and the Greek Resistance.* Doctoral dissertation, University of Manchester.

Tsoutsoumpis, S. 2016. *A History of the Greek Resistance in the Second World War.* Manchester: Manchester University Press.

Türköz, M. 2018. *Naming and Nation-Building in Turkey: the 1934 Surname Law.* New York, NY: Palgrave Macmillan.

Tziovas, D. 1989. *Οι μεταμορφώσεις του εθνισμού και το ιδεολόγημα της ελληνικότητας στο μεσοπόλεμο.* Athens: Odysseas.

Tziovas, D. 2007. *Ο άλλος εαυτός: Ταυτότητα και κοινωνία στη νεοελληνική πεζογραφία.* Athens: Polis.

Tziovas, D. (ed.). 2017. *Greece in Crisis: the Cultural Politics of Austerity.* London and New York: I. B. Tauris.

Tzortzis, I. 2020. *Greek Democracy and the Junta: Regime Crisis and the Failed Transition of 1973.* London: I. B. Tauris.

Tzoukas, V. 2013. *Οι οπλαρχηγοί του ΕΔΕΣ στην Ήπειρο, 1942–44: Τοπικότητα και πολιτική ένταξη.* Athens: Estia.

Üngör, U. U. 2015. 'Mass Violence against Civilians during the Balkan Wars', in *The Wars before the Great War*, ed. D. Geppert, W. Mulligan and A. Rose, pp. 76–91. Cambridge: Cambridge University Press.

Vaiou, N., and A. Psarra (eds). 2017. *Εννοιολογήσεις και πρακτικές του φεμινισμού: Μεταπολίτευση και 'μετά'.* Athens: Hellenic Parliament.

Vaitsos, K., and V. Missos. 2018. *Πραγματική οικονομία: Εμπειρίες ανάπτυξης, κρίσης και φτωχοποίησης στην Ελλάδα.* Athens: Kritiki.

Valaoras, B. 1980. *Ο πληθυσμός της Ελλάδος κατά το δεύτερο ήμισυ του ΧΧ αιώνος.* Athens: Ethniki Statistiki Ipiresia Elladas.

Valden, S. (ed.). 2017. *Η ανθρωπιστική βοήθεια στην κατοχική Ελλάδα: Η σουηδική αποστολή του Ερυθρού Σταυρού, 1942–1945.* Athens: Themelio.

Valden, S. 2018. *Δικτατορία και αντίσταση, 1967–1974: Προσωπική μαρτυρία.* Athens: Themelio.

Vamvakas, V., and P. Panagiotopoulos (eds). 2010. *Η Ελλάδα στη Δεκαετία του '80: Κοινωνικό, πολιτικό και πολιτισμικό λεξικό.* Athens: To Perasma.

Van Boeschoten, R. 1997. *Ανάποδα χρόνια: Συλλογική μνήμη και ιστορία στο Ζιάκα Γρεβενών (1900–1950).* Athens: Plethron.

Van Steen, G. 2015. *Stage of Emergency: Theater and Public Performance under the Greek Military Dictatorship of 1967–1974.* Oxford: Oxford University Press.

Van Steen, G. 2019. *Adoption, Memory, and Cold War Greece: Kid pro quo?* Ann Arbor, MI: University of Michigan Press.

Varnava, A. 2009. *British Imperialism in Cyprus, 1878–1915: the Inconsequential Possession.* Manchester: Manchester University Press.

Varnava, A. 2012. 'British Military Intelligence in Cyprus during the Great War'. *War in History* 19.3, pp. 353–78.

Varnava, A. 2017. *Serving the Empire in the Great War: the Cypriot Mule Corps, Imperial Identity and Silenced Memory.* Manchester: Manchester University Press.

Varnava, A. 2017a. 'The Impact of the Cypriot Contribution to the Great War on Colonial Society and Loyalties/Disloyalties to the British Empire'. *First World War Studies* 8.1, pp. 17–36.

Varnava, A. 2019. *British Cyprus and the Long Great War, 1914–1925. Empire: Loyalties and Democratic Deficit.* London: Routledge.

Varnava, M. 2020. *Cyprus before 1974: the Prelude to Crisis*, ebook ed. London: I. B. Tauris.

Varon-Vassar, O. 2009. *Η ενηλικίωση μιας γενιάς: Νέοι και νέες στην Κατοχή και στην Αντίσταση.* Athens: Estias.

Varon-Vassar, O. 2019. 'The Emergence and Construction of the Memory of the Shoah in Greece (1945–2015): from Oblivion to Memory'. *Historein* 18.1. https:// ejournals.epublishing.ekt.gr/index.php/historein/article/view/14399 (last accessed 12 August 2019).

Varoufakis, Y. 2017. *Adults in the Room: My Battle with the European and American Deep Establishment*. London: Vintage.

Varvaressos, K. 1952, 2002. Έκθεσις επί του οικονομικού προβλήματος της Ελλάδος. Athens: Savvalas.

Vasilopoulou, S., and D. Halikiopoulou. 2015. *The Golden Dawn's 'Nationalist Solution'*. New York, NY: Palgrave.

Venturas, L. 1999. Έλληνες μετανάστες στο Βέλγιο. Athens: Nefeli.

Venturas, L. 2002. 'Greek Immigrants in Postwar Belgium: Community and Identity Formation Processes'. *Journal of the Hellenic Diaspora* 28.1, pp. 33–72.

Venturas, L. 2006. 'Ομοσπονδιακή Γερμανία', in *Οι Έλληνες στη Διασπορά, 15ος–21ος αι.*, ed. I. Hasiotis, O. Katsiardi-Hering and E. Abatzi, pp. 135–46. Athens: Hellenic Parliament.

Veremis, T. 1995. *Greece's Balkan Entanglement*, Hellenic Foundation for European and Foreign Policy. Athens: ELIAMEP.

Veremis, T. 1997. *The Military in Greek Politics: from Independence to Democracy*. London: Black Rose.

Veremis, T. 2018. *Οι επεμβάσεις του στρατού στην ελληνική πολιτική, 1916–1936*. Athens: Alexandreia.

Vermeulen, H. 1993. 'Το βάρος του παρελθόντος: Η εξουσία των καπετάνιων στο χωριό του Κάιν και του Άβελ', in *Ανθρωπολογία και Παρελθόν*, ed. E. Papataxiarchis and T. Paradellis, pp. 42–53. Athens: Alexandreia.

Vervenioti, T. 1994. *Η γυναίκα της αντίστασης: Η είσοδος των γυναικών στην πολιτική*. Athens: Odysseas.

Vincent, M. 2008. *Spain 1833–2002: People and State*. Oxford: Oxford University Press.

Vincent, M. 2016. 'Political Violence and Mass Society: a European Civil War?' in *The Oxford Handbook of European History 1914–1945*, ed. N. Doumanis, pp. 388–406. Oxford: Oxford University Press.

Vlahopoulos, S. 2012. *Η κρίση του κοινοβουλευτισμού στον μεσοπόλεμο και το τέλος της Β΄ ελληνικής δημοκρατίας το 1935: Οι θεσμικές όψεις μιας οικονομικής κρίσης*. Athens: Evrasia.

Vlahos, A. F. 2016. *Τουρισμός και δημόσιες πολιτικές στη σύγχρονη Ελλάδα (1914–1950): Η ανάδυση ενός νεοτερικού φαινομένου*. Athens: Ekdoseis Kerkyra.

Vlavianos, H. 1992. *Greece, 1941–49: from Resistance to Civil War. The Strategy of the Greek Communist Party*. New York: St. Martin's Press.

Voglis, P. 2002. *Becoming a Subject: Political Prisoners during the Greek Civil War*. New York, NY: Berghahn.

Voglis, P. 2006. 'Surviving Hunger: Life in the Cities and the Countryside during the Occupation', in *Surviving Hitler and Mussolini: Daily Life in Occupied Europe*, ed. R. Gildea, O. Wieviorka and A. Warring, pp. 16–41. Oxford and New York: Berg.

Voglis, P. 2007. 'Κομμένα κεφάλια'. *Αρχειοτάξιο* 9 (May), pp. 80–3.

Voglis, P. 2014. *Η αδύνατη επανάσταση: Η κοινωνική δυναμική του εμφυλίου πολέμου*. Athens: Alexandreia.

Voulgaris, Y. 2013. *Η μεταπολιτευτική Ελλάδα 1974–2009*. Athens: Polis.

Voulgaris, Y., K. Kostis and S. Rizas (eds). 2021. *Ο Μεγάλος Μετασχηματισμός: Κράτος και Πολιτική στην Ελλάδα του 20ου αιώνα*. Athens: Patakis.

Voutira, E. A. 1991. 'Pontian Greeks Today: Migrants or Refugees?' *Journal of Refugee Studies* 4.4, pp. 400–20.

Voutira, E. A. 2003. 'Refugees: Whose Term Is It Anyway? Emic and Etic Constructions of "Refugees" in Modern Greek', in *The Refugee Convention at Fifty: a View from Forced Migration Studies*, ed. J. van Selm and K. Kamanga, pp. 65–80. Lanham, MD: Lexington.

Voutira, E. A. 2006. 'Post-Soviet Diaspora Politics: the Case of the Soviet Greeks'. *Journal of Modern Greek Studies* 24.2, pp. 379–414.

Vradis, A., and D. Dalakoglou (eds). 2011. *Revolt and Crisis in Greece: between a Present Yet to Pass and a Future Still to Come*. Chico, CA: AK Press/Occupied London.

Vryonis, S. 2005. *The Mechanism of Catastrophe: the Turkish Pogrom of September 6–7, 1955, and the Destruction of the Greek Community of Istanbul*. New York: Greekworks.

Wakefield, A., and S. Moody. 2011. *Under the Devil's Eye: the British Military Experience in Macedonia 1915–1918*. London: Sutton Publishing.

Walker, M., and M. Kakaounaki. 2013. 'Greece Struggles to Outlaw Its Golden Dawn Fascist Party: Conservative Government Mounts Risky Effort to Declare Group a Criminal Organization'. *Wall Street Journal*, 4 December.

Warner, J., S. Akis and N. Peristianis. 1997. 'The Impact of Tourism on Local Residents: Environmental and Socioeconomic Effects'. *Cyprus Review* 9.2, pp. 82–99.

Weber, M. 1919, 2004. *The Vocation Lectures: 'Science as Vocation'; 'Politics as Vocation'*, trans. R. Livingstone. Indianapolis and Cambridge: Hackett.

Weitz, E. D. 2013. 'Germany and the Ottoman Borderlands: the Entwining of Imperial Aspirations, Revolution, and Ethnic Violence', in *Shatterzone of Empires: Coexistence and Violence in the German, Habsburg, Russian, and Ottoman Borderlands*, ed. O. Bartov and E. D. Weitz, pp. 152–71. Bloomington, IN: Indiana University Press.

Williams, B. G. 2000. 'Hijra and Forced Migration from Nineteenth-Century Russia to the Ottoman Empire: a Critical Analysis of the Great Tatar Emigration of 1860–1861'. *Cahiers du monde russe* 41.1, pp. 79–108.

Wittner, L. S. 1982. *American Intervention in Greece, 1943–1949: a Study in Counterrevolution*. New York, NY: Columbia University Press.

Woodhouse, C. M. 1948. *Apple of Discord: a Survey of Recent Greek Politics in their International Setting*. London: Hutchinson.

Woodhouse, C. M. 1985. *The Rise and Fall of the Greek Colonels*. London: Granada.

Wouters, N., and L. van Ypersele (ed.). 2018. *Nations, Identities and the First World War: Shifting Loyalties to the Fatherland*. London: Bloomsbury.

Wyplosz, C., and S. Sgherri. 2016. 'The IMF's Role in Greece in the Context of the 2010 Stand-By Arrangement', Background Paper, Independent Evaluation Office of the International Monetary Fund.

Xezonakis, G., and F. Hartmann. 2020. 'Economic Downturns and the Greek Referendum of 2015: Evidence Using Night-Time Light Data'. *European Union Politics* 21.3, pp. 361–82.

Yannakopoulos, K. 2016. '"Naked Piazza": Male (Homo)Sexualities, Masculinities and Consumer Cultures in Greece since the 1960s', in *Consumption and Gender in Southern Europe since the Long 1960s*, ed. K. Kornetis and E. Kotsovili, pp. 173–89. London: Bloomsbury.

Yiakoumis, H., A. Hermary, M. Tsalikidis and N. Chrobos. 2008. *Phocée (1913–1920): Le témoignage de Félix Sartiaux*. Paris: Editions Kallimages.

Yiannakis, J. 1996. 'Kalgoorlie Alchemy: Xenophobia, Patriotism and the 1916 Anti-Greek Riots'. *Journal of the Royal Western Australian Historical Society* 11.1, pp. 199–211.

Yildirim, O. 2006. *Diplomacy and Displacement: Reconsidering the Turco-Greek Exchange of Populations 1922–1934*. London: Routledge.

Yoder, J. A. 2019. 'Angela Merkel's Discourse about the Past: Implications for the Construction of Collective Memory in Germany'. *Memory Studies* 12.6, pp. 660–76.

Yosmaolğlu, I. 2014. *Blood Ties: Religion, Violence, and the Politics of Nationhood in Ottoman Macedonia, 1878–1908*. Ithaca, NY: Cornell University Press.

Zabala, J. C. 2018. *State Expansion and Economic Integration: a Transnational History of Oriental Tobacco in Greece and Germany (1880–1941)*. Doctoral dissertation, University of California, San Diego.

Zachos, D., and A. Michailidou. 2014. '"Others" in Textbooks: the Case of Greek Sixth Grade's History Textbook'. *Theory in Action* 7.3, pp. 1–25.

Zagaras, K. 2019. *Η κατάρρευση του 'Υπαρκτού' και η διάσπαση του ΚΚΕ: Η κομβική στιγμή του 1991*. Athens: Themelio.

Zahra, T. 2011. *The Lost Children: Reconstructing European Families after World War II*. Ithaca, NY: Cornell University Press.

Zaimakis, Y. 2015. '"Welcome to the Civilization of Fear": on Political Graffiti Heterotopias in Greece in Times of Crisis'. *Visual Culture* 14.4, pp. 373–96.

Zanou, K. 2019. *Transnational Patriotism in the Mediterranean, 1800–1850: Stammering the Nation*. Oxford: Oxford University Press.

Zeiler, T. W. 2014. 'Opening Doors in the World Economy', in *Global Interdependence: the World after 1945*, ed. A. Iriye, pp. 201–361. Cambridge, MA: Harvard University Press.

Zetter, R. 1992. 'Refugees and Forced Migrants as Development Resources: the Greek Cypriot Refugees'. *Cyprus Review* 4.1, pp. 7–39.

Zigou, Y. G., and N. Leandros. 1994. 'Ορισμένα βασικά χαρακτηριστικά του "Κράτους Πρόνοιας" στην Ελλάδα κατά την πρώτη μεταπολεμική περίοδο', in *Η ελληνική κοινωνία κατά την πρώτη μεταπολεμική περίοδο (1945–1967)*, ed. Idrima Saki Karagiorga. Athens: Idrima Saki Karagiorga.

Zolotas, X. 1936. *Κατευθύνσεις της οικονομικής πολιτικής*. Athens.

Zorba, M. 2014. *Πολιτική του πολιτισμού: Ευρώπη και Ελλάδα στο δεύτερο μισό του 20ού αιώνα*. Athens: Patakis.

Zorba, M. 2017. 'Culture as a Mirror of Crisis: Representations, Solidarity, Resilience and Paradigm Shift', in *Culturescapes Greece/Griechenland Archaeology of Future*, ed. K. Botanova et al., pp. 194–215. Basel: Christoph Merian.

Zorba, M. 2019. *Ανδρέας Παπανδρέου: Πολιτισμικό πορτρέτο*. Athens: Pedio.

Zürcher, E. J. 2003. 'Greek and Turkish Refugees and Deportees, 1912–1924'. *Turkology Update Leiden Project Working Papers Archive*, Department of Turkish Studies, Universiteit Leiden. http://www.transanatolie.com/english/turkey/turks/ottomans/ejz18.pdf.

Index

CPSIA information can be obtained
at www.ICGtesting.com
Printed in the USA
JSHW052344010523
41136JS00001B/1